Global
Economic
Prospects

A World Bank Group
Flagship Report

JANUARY 2016

Global Economic Prospects

Spillovers amid Weak Growth

🌐 **WORLD BANK GROUP**

Table of contents

Foreword xv

Acknowledgments xvii

Executive Summary xix

Abbreviations xxi

Chapter 1   **Global Outlook: Disappointments, Risks, and Spillovers** 1

      Summary and key messages 3

      Major economies 6

      Global trends and spillovers 12

      Developing countries 17

      Risks to the outlook 24

      Policy challenges 31

      References 39

Special Focus **From Commodity Discovery to Production: Vulnerabilities and Policies in LICs** ..45

      Introduction...47

      Lead times between discovery and production 48

      Evolution from commodity discovery to production..49

      Determinants of the lead time 51

      Policy implications 52

      Recent developments and near-term outlook in low-income countries 53

      Annex SF.1 57

      References 59

Chapter 2   **Regional Outlooks** 61

      East Asia and Pacific 63

          Recent developments 63

          Outlook..65

          Risks 67

          Policy challenges...69

          Box 2.1.1 Regional integration and spillovers: East Asia and Pacific.....................73

Europe and Central Asia 83

    Recent developments...83

    Outlook 87

    Risks 88

    Policy challenges 89

    Box 2.2.1 Regional integration and spillovers: Europe and Central Asia 93

Latin America and the Caribbean..101

    Recent developments..101

    Outlook 106

    Risks 107

    Policy challenges 108

    Box 2.3.1 Regional integration and spillovers: Latin America and the Caribbean .. 112

Middle East and North Africa 123

    Recent developments..123

    Outlook 126

    Risks 127

    Policy challenges 128

    Box 2.4.1 Regional integration and spillovers: Middle East and North Africa 132

South Asia..139

    Recent developments..139

    Outlook 141

    Risks 143

    Policy challenges 143

    Box 2.5.1 Regional integration and spillovers: South Asia 147

Sub-Saharan Africa..153

    Recent developments..153

    Outlook 156

    Risks 157

    Policy challenges 158

    Box 2.6.1 Regional integration and spillovers: Sub-Saharan Africa 162

References..169

Chapter 3   **Who Catches a Cold When Emerging Markets Sneeze?**............................... 177

Introduction.. 179

What are the key channels of spillovers from the major emerging markets?............. 184

Do business cycles in BRICS move in tandem with those in other emerging markets and frontier markets?.. 187

How large are the spillovers from the major emerging markets? 190

What are the policy implications? 195

Conclusion.. 202

Box 3.1 Sources of the growth slowdown in BRICS... 182

Box 3.2 Understanding cross-border growth spillovers 188

Box 3.3 Within-region spillovers 198

Annex 3.1 Data 204

Annex 3.2 Methodology... 205

Annex 3.3 Empirical estimates of spillovers from emerging markets..................... 210

References 212

Chapter 4   **Two Topical Issues.** 217

Potential Macroeconomic Implications of the Trans-Pacific Partnership........................219

Introduction 219

How do new generation trade agreements differ from traditional FTAs?...............220

What are the main features of the Trans-Pacific Partnership? 222

What are the potential macroeconomic implications of the TPP?........................225

Conclusion 229

Box 4.1.1 Regulatory convergence in mega-regional trade agreements 230

Annex 4.1 Methodology 234

Peg and Control? The Links between Exchange Rate Regimes and Capital Account Policies...237

Introduction 237

What does economic theory say about the choice of ERRs and CFMs?...............238

What do the data say about ERRs and CFMs?...240

What are the main empirical linkages between the choices of ERR and CFM?......243

Conclusion 244

Annex 4.2 Data and methodology..245

References 249

Statistical Appendix 257

Figures   1.1   Global and developing-country growth prospects...5
           1.2   Global trade, finance, and risks..6
           1.3   United States..7
           1.4   Euro Area...8
           1.5   Japan..10
           1.6   China..11
           1.7   Financial volatility and asset valuations..12
           1.8   Capital flows...13
           1.9   Commodity markets 15
           1.10   Global trade slowdown 16
           1.11   Growth in emerging and developing economies...17
           1.12   Domestic demand conditions in developing countries...19
           1.13   Macro-financial vulnerabilities...20
           1.14   Monetary and fiscal policy space 21
           1.15   Developing-country outlook..21
           1.16   Regional outlook..22
           1.17   Slowdown in China 24
           1.18   Spillovers from slowing growth in BRICS 26
           1.19   Rising borrowing costs and balance sheet pressures 27
           1.20   Deteriorating capital flows and sudden stops 28
           1.21   Growth slowdown in BRICS combined with financial stress.....................................29
           1.22   Weakening potential growth..29
           1.23   Terrorism and geopolitical tensions...30
           1.24   Unrealized gains due to low oil prices..31
           1.25   Policy challenges in the United States..32
           1.26   Policy challenges in Euro Area and Japan 33
           1.27   Policy challenges in China..34
           1.28   Monetary policy challenges in developing countries 35
           1.29   Fiscal frameworks and financial stability...36
           1.30   Fiscal policy challenges in developing countries..37
           1.31   Structural reform needs 38

SF.1   Prospects and risks from resource investment 48

SF.2   The mining project cycle 49

SF.3   Developments during lead times between resource discovery and extraction . 50

SF.4   Lead times between resource discovery and extraction 51

SF.5   Growth prospects in LICs 53

2.1.1   Activity in East Asia and Pacific 64

2.1.2   Internal rebalancing in China 65

2.1.3   External rebalancing in China 66

2.1.4   Trade 67

2.1.5   Financial markets 68

2.1.6   Policy rates, credit growth, inflation, and fiscal balances 69

2.1.7   Regional vulnerabilities 70

2.1.8   Policy issues 71

2.1.1.1   Cross-region comparisons 73

2.1.1.2   Regional integration 74

2.1.1.3   Main spillover channels 75

2.1.1.4   Trade and finance with China and Japan 76

2.1.1.5   Portfolio liabilities and capital account restrictions 78

2.1.1.6   Intra-regional spillovers 78

2.1.1.7   Spillovers from G7 excluding Japan 79

2.2.1   Key indicators 84

2.2.2   Inflation and exchange rates for selected countries 85

2.2.3   Monetary and fiscal policy 85

2.2.4   Remittances 86

2.2.5   Exposure to spillovers through trade and foreign direct investment 86

2.2.6   Recent developments at the country level 87

2.2.7   External financing 89

2.2.1.1   Cross-region comparison 93

2.2.1.2   Main features of the ECA region 94

2.2.1.3   Trade, remittances, and foreign direct investment 95

2.2.1.4   Main export markets 96

2.2.1.5   Tourism and remittances 97

2.2.1.6   Regional spillovers 98

2.2.1.7 Spillovers from G7 99

2.3.1   GDP growth, 2014-2015 102

2.3.2   Commodity prices...102

2.3.3   Exchange rates 103

2.3.4   Exports...103

2.3.5   Inflation rates...103

2.3.6   Central bank policy rates, 2014-2015 104

2.3.7   Fiscal indicators 104

2.3.8   Current account balances...105

2.3.9   Gross capital flows..105

2.3.10   Regional outlook...106

2.3.11   Remittance flows...106

2.3.1.1 International linkages: Cross-region comparison 113

2.3.1.2 Evolution of openness 114

2.3.1.3 Sources of trade and financial flows...115

2.3.1.4 LAC exports 116

2.3.1.5 LAC commodity exports 117

2.3.1.6 Within-region trade and FDI..118

2.3.1.7 The role of the largest economies in LAC 119

2.3.1.8 Correlations with Brazil and Mexico 119

2.3.1.9 Spillovers from Brazil, Mexico, G7 and China 120

2.3.1.10 Ease of trading across borders...121

2.4.1   Oil production and fiscal balance 125

2.4.2   Exchange rates, inflation, and current account balances 125

2.4.3   Trade 128

2.4.4   Labor market conditions..128

2.4.5   Perception of standard of living...129

2.4.1.1 Cross-region comparison 132

2.4.1.2 Trade, FDI, and remittances..133

2.4.1.3 Openness inside and outside the region 134

2.4.1.4 Spillovers from Egypt and Turkey..137

2.5.1   Recent developments..140

2.5.2   Risks and challenges...141

2.5.3   Demographic challenges...144

2.5.1.1 Cross-region comparison...147

2.5.1.2 Regional and global integration in South Asian countries...........148

2.5.1.3 Financial flows to SAR...150

2.5.1.4 Global and regional growth spillovers.......................................151

2.6.1   Commodity market developments 154

2.6.2   Capital market developments 155

2.6.3   Domestic constraints..156

2.6.4   Fiscal deficits and government debt...157

2.6.5   Exchange rates and inflation 158

2.6.6   Outlook 159

2.6.1.1 Cross-region comparison...163

2.6.1.2 Linkages between Sub-Saharan Africa and the rest of the world 164

2.6.1.3 Intra-regional linkages..165

2.6.1.4 Linkages between South Africa and the rest of Sub-Saharan Africa..166

2.6.1.5 Linkages between Nigeria and the rest of Sub-Saharan Africa 167

2.6.1.6 Regional spillovers in SSA 168

3.1   Emerging market growth slowdown...180

3.2   Rising economic significance of emerging markets 181

3.1.1   Sources of the growth slowdown in BRICS 183

3.3   BRICS in EM and FM trade 185

3.4   Commodity demand and supply..186

3.5   BRICS in regional trade and remittances...................................187

3.6   Emergence of emerging and frontier market business cycle............191

3.7   Role of BRICS in business cycle synchronization........................191

3.8   Growth slowdown in BRICS..192

3.9   Spillovers from BRICS..193

3.10   Spillovers from BRICS and advanced markets 194

3.11   Spillovers from individual BRICS 195

3.12   Channels of spillovers 196

3.13   Spillovers from a synchronous slowdown in BRICS 196

3.14   Growth slowdown in BRICS combined with financial stress 197

3.3.1   Openness 198

3.3.2   Within-region integration... 199

3.3.3   Spillovers from large emerging markets in each region............................ 200

3.15   Fiscal policy and fiscal space... 201

3.16   Monetary policy room.. 202

3.17   Growth slowdown and structural reforms 202

4.1.1   Growth in world trade.. 220

4.1.2   Importance of regional trade agreements... 221

4.1.3   RTAs: Tariffs and membership 221

4.1.4   The main features of the TPP 223

4.1.5   Aggregate impact of TPP: GDP and trade by 2030 226

4.1.6   Country specific impact of TPP: GDP and trade by 2030 227

4.1.7   Impact of TPP on sectoral output by 2030 228

4.1.8   Comparing TPP to other trade agreements 228

4.1.1.1 Implications of a common regulatory approach.. 233

A.4.1.1 Modeling assumptions 236

4.2.1   Exchange rate regime categories by country grouping 239

4.2.2   Capital control categories by country grouping 240

4.2.3   Trade and exchange rate regimes: Frequency distributions 241

4.2.4   Trade and capital controls: Frequency distributions................................ 241

4.2.5   Financial development and capital controls: Frequency distributions.......... 242

4.2.6   Pegged regimes and capital controls.. 242

4.2.7   Pegged regimes and capital controls across per capita income levels 243

Tables   1.1   Global growth 4

SF.1   Low Income country forecasts 56

Annex SF.1 Duration regression of lead times.. 58

2.1.1   East Asia and Pacific forecast summary 72

2.1.2   East Asia and Pacific country forecasts 72

2.1.1.1 Membership of major actual and potential free trade agreements 80

2.1.1.2 Literature review... 81

2.2.1   Europe and Central Asia forecast summary 91

2.2.2   Europe and Central Asia country forecasts 92

2.2.1.1 Summary of the literature 100

2.3.1   Latin America and the Caribbean forecast summary 110

2.3.2   Latin America and the Caribbean country forecasts 111

2.4.1   Middle East and North Africa forecast summary 130

2.4.2   Middle East and North Africa country forecasts 131

2.5.1   South Asia forecast summary 145

2.5.2   South Asia country forecasts 146

2.6.1   Sub-Saharan Africa forecast summary 160

2.6.2   Sub-Saharan Africa country forecasts 161

Foreword

Emerging market economies have been an engine of global growth during the 2000s, especially after the 2007-08 global financial crisis. However, times are changing. Growth rates in several emerging market economies have been declining since 2010. The global economy will need to adapt to a new period of more modest growth in large emerging markets, characterized by lower commodity prices and diminished flows of trade and capital. This is the message that underlies this issue of the World Bank Group's *Global Economic Prospects*.

The report offers a detailed outlook for the global economy and each of the world's emerging market regions. It analyzes themes vital to policy makers in emerging markets and elsewhere. These include how the slowdown in major emerging markets affects the rest of the world, including their regions and their neighbors; the potentially far-ranging macro-economic implications of the Trans-Pacific Partnership trade accord; and risks and opportunities offered by low commodity prices for low-income countries with recent discoveries of natural gas, oil, metals, and other natural resources. The report also examines capital controls and other strategies that countries with different exchange rate regimes can use to better shield themselves from financial turmoil.

Looking ahead, global growth is poised to recover modestly, by 2.9 percent in 2016, after (once again) falling short of expectations at 2.4 percent in 2015, held back by weak capital flows to emerging and developing countries, weak trade and low commodity prices. Under the baseline scenario, it is expected that China will steer its economy to a more consumption- and services-led growth and the monetary policy tightening cycle in the United States will proceed without undue turbulence; as a consequence, global growth will see a modest upturn.

This outlook is expected to be buttressed by recovery in major high-income economies, stabilizing commodity prices, and a continuation of low interest rates. All this does not rule out the fact that there is a low-probability risk of disorderly slowdown in major emerging markets, as U.S. interest rates rise after a long break and the US dollar strengthens, and as a result of geopolitical concerns.

The simultaneous slowing of four of the largest emerging markets—Brazil, Russia, China, and South Africa—poses the risk of spillover effects for the rest of the world economy. Global ripples from China's slowdown are expected to be greatest but weak growth in Russia sets back activity in other countries in the region. Disappointing growth again in the largest emerging markets, if combined with new financial stress, could sharply reduce global growth in 2016.

Meanwhile, the Trans-Pacific Partnership could potentially provide a boost to growth and trade in its member countries. The detrimental effects on non-members as trade is diverted could be mitigated by beneficial effects from greater regulatory harmonization, streamlining and transparency.

In the current environment, developing countries need to brace for possible shocks by building resilience to risks to growth. Where they are able to boost government spending or lower interest rates, they can provide support to economic activity. They can further encourage investor confidence with reforms to governance, labor market functioning, and business environments. Measures to absorb young workers or to increase workforce participation will relieve demographic pressures in many countries.

Kaushik Basu
Chief Economist and Senior Vice President
The World Bank

Acknowledgments

This World Bank Group Flagship Report is a product of the Prospects Group in the Development Economics Vice Presidency. The project was managed by Ayhan Kose and Franziska Ohnsorge, under the general guidance of Kaushik Basu.

Many people contributed substantively to the report. Chapter 1 (Global Outlook) was prepared Carlos Arteta and Marc Stocker with contributions from John Baffes, Tehmina Khan, Eung Ju Kim, Ekaterine Vashakmadze and Dana Vorisek. The Special Focus was prepared by Tehmina Khan, Trang Nguyen, Franziska Ohnsorge and Richard Schodde.

Chapter 2 (Regional Outlooks) was coordinated by Carlos Arteta and Franziska Ohnsorge. The authors were Ekaterine Vashakmadze (East Asia and Pacific), Christian Eigen-Zucchi and Ekaterine Vashakmadze (Europe and Central Asia), Derek Chen (Latin America and the Caribbean), Dana Vorisek (Middle East and North Africa), Tehmina Khan (South Asia), and Gerard Kambou (Sub-Saharan Africa). Box 2.1 (Regional integration and spillovers: East Asia and Pacific) was prepared by Ekaterine Vashakmadze, Nikola Spatafora, and Duygu Guven; modeling work was done by Raju Huidrom and Jesper Hanson. Box 2.2 (Regional integration and spillovers: Europe and Central Asia) was prepared by Ekaterine Vashakmadze and Duygu Guven with contributions from Raju Huidrom and Jesper Hanson. Box 2.3 (Regional integration and spillovers: Latin America and the Caribbean) was prepared by Derek Chen with contributions from Raju Huidrom, Duygu Guven, Jesper Hanson, and Mai Anh Bui. Box 2.4 (Regional integration and spillovers: Middle East and North Africa) was prepared by Ergys Islamaj and Jesper Hanson. Box 2.5 (Regional integration and spillovers: South Asia) was prepared by Tehmina Khan, Jesper Hanson and Raju Huidrom. Box 2.6 (Regional integration and spillovers: Sub-Saharan Africa) was prepared by Gerard Kambou and Jesper Hanson with contributions from Raju Huidrom.

Chapter 3 (Who Catches a Cold When Emerging Markets Sneeze) was prepared by Raju Huidrom, Ayhan Kose and Franziska Ohnsorge with contributions from Jose Luis Diaz Sanchez, Lei Sandy Ye, Jaime de Jesus Filho, Xiaodan Ding, Sergio Kurlat, and Qian Li. Box 3.1 (Sources of the growth slowdown in BRICS) was prepared by Lei Sandy Ye; Box 3.2 (Understanding cross-border growth spillovers) was prepared by Raju Huidrom; and Box 3.3 (Within-region spillovers) was prepared by Jesper Hanson, Raju Huidrom, and Franziska Ohnsorge.

Chapter 4 (Two Topical Issues) has two essays. The first essay (Potential Macroeconomic Implications of the Trans-Pacific Partnership) was prepared by Csilla Lakatos, Maryla Maliszewska, Franziska Ohnsorge, Peter Petri, and Michael Plummer. The second essay (Peg and Control? The Links between Exchange Rate Regimes and Capital Account Policies) was prepared by Carlos Arteta, Michael Klein, and Jay Shambaugh. Aaditya Mattoo was the author of Box 4.1.1 (Regulatory convergence in mega-regional trade agreements).

Modeling and data work were produced by Jungjin Lee, assisted by Mai Anh Bui, Xinghao Gong, Xiaodan Ding, Qian Li, and Trang Thi Thuy Nguyen.

The online publication was produced by a team including Graeme Littler, Praveen Penmetsa, Mikael Reventar, and Katherine Rollins, with technical support from Marjorie Patricia Bennington. Phillip Hay and Mark Felsenthal managed media relations and the dissemination. The print publication was produced by Jose Maria Lopez Martin-Duarte, Maria Hazel Macadangdang, Adriana Maximiliano, and Quinn Sutton.

Many reviewers offered extensive advice and comments. These included: Ahmad Ahsan, Ibrahim Al-Ghelaiqah, Enrique Aldaz-Carroll, Kassia Antoine, Enrique Blanco Arma, Marina Bakanova, Ulrich Bartsch, Davaadalai Batsuuri, William Battaile, Hans Anand Beck, Fabio

Sola Bittar, Rogier J. E. Van Den Brink, César Calderón, Jose R. Lopez Calix, Jasmin Chakeri, Shubham Chaudhury, Jean-Pierre Chauffour, Rodrigo A. Chaves, Menzie Chinn, Marcel Chistruga, Ajai Chopra, Karl Kendrick Tiu Chua, Punam Chuhan-Pole, Roland Clarke, Kevin Clinton, Andrea Coppola, Tito Cordella, Barbara Cunha, Stefano Curto, Somneuk Davading, Simon Davies, Agim Demukaj, Shantayanan Devarajan, Tatiana Didier, Viet Tuan Dinh, Ndiame Diop, Calvin Zebaze Djiofack, Doerte Doemeland, Mariam Dolidze, Ralph van Doorn, Jozef Draaisma, Franz R. Drees-Gross, Bakyt Dubashov, Sebastian Eckardt, Nur Nasser Eddin, Kim Alan Edwards, Olga Emelyanova, Wilfried Engelke, Michael Ferrantino, Erik Feyen, Fitria Fitrani, Cornelius Fleischhaker, Caroline Freund, Laura Sofia Olivera Garrido, Michael Geiger, Anastasia Golovach, Anabel Gonzalez, David Gould, Poonam Gupta, Gohar Gyulumyah, Faris H. Hadad-Zervos, Kiryl Haiduk, Lea Hakim, Birgit Hansl, Marek Hanusch, Wissam Harake, Leonardo F. Hernandez, Marco Hernandez, Yumeka Hirano, Sandra Hlivnjak, Bert Hofman, Paulina Ewa Holda, Shantae Holland, Zahid Hussain, Stella Illieva, Fernando Gabriel Im, Alain Ize, Ivailo V. Izvorski, Evans Jadotte, Steen Jorgensen, Satu Kristiina Kahkonen, Leszek Pawel Kasek, Michelle Keane, Mizuho Kida, Markus Kitzmuller, David Knight, Fritzi Koehler-Geib, Naoko C. Kojo, Ewa Joanna Korczyc, Tigran Kostanyan, Christos Kostopoulos, Auguste Tano Kouame, Ahmed Kouchouk, Aart Kraay, Aurelien Kruse, Megumi Kubota, Sibel Kulaksiz, Chandana Kularatne, Matija Laco, Daniel Lederman,

Tae Hyun Lee, Joseph Louie C. Limkin, Julio Ricardo Loayza, Rohan Longmore, Sodeth Ly, Dorsati Madani, Sanja Madzarevic-Sujster, Sandeep Mahajan, Paul Mariano, Miguel Eduardo Sanchez Martin, Martin Melecky, Elitza Mileva, Shabih Ali Mohib, Rafael Munoz Moreno, Lili Mottaghi, Ranjana Mukherjee, Zafer Mustafaoglu, Pierre Nadji, Evgenij Najdov, Raj Nallari, Khwima Nthara, Antonio Nucifora, Rei Odawara, Lucy Pan, John Panzer, Marcelo Echague Pastore, Catalin Pauna, Suzana Petrovic, Keomanivone Phimmahasay, Samuel Pienknagura, Miria Pigato, Ruslan Piontkivsky, Juan Pradelli, Catriona Mary Purfield, Rong Qian, Habib Rab, Martin Raiser, Martin Rama, Nadir Ramazanov, Elliot Joseph Riordan, David Robinson, Daniel Francisco Barco Rondan, David Rosenblatt, Michele Ruta, Pablo Saavedra, Seynabou Sakho, Ilyas Sarsenov, Cristina Savescu, Marc Tobias Schiffbauer, Sergio Schmukler, Luis Servén, Lazar Sestovic, Radwan Shaban, Rashmi Shankar, Sudhir Shetty, Altantsetseg Shiilegmaa, Bojan Shimbov, Maryna Sidarenka, Alex Sienaert, Emilia Skrok, Gregory Smith, Karlis Smits, Ravshan Sobirzoda, Nikola Spatafora, Abdoulaye Sy, Ashley Taylor, Theo David Thomas, Hans Timmer, Augusto de la Torre, Eskender Trushin, Sergei Ulatov, Ekaterina Ushakova, Boris Enrique Utria, Robert Utz, Sona Varma, Julio Velasco, Mathew Verghis, Gallina Andronova Vincelette, Jan Walliser, Ayberk Yilmaz, Pui Shen Yoong, Albert Zeufack, and Luan Zhao. Regional Projections and write-ups were produced in coordination with country teams, country directors, and the offices of the regional chief economists.

Executive Summary

Global growth again fell short of expectations in 2015. Growth is projected to edge up in 2016-18 but the forecast is subject to substantial downside risks. In addition to discussing global and regional economic developments and outlook, this edition of the Global Economic Prospects also includes analysis of key challenges and opportunities currently confronting emerging and developing countries: spillovers from a slowdown in major emerging markets; the potential macroeconomic implications of the Trans-Pacific Partnership; and the links between exchange rate regimes and capital controls in emerging and developing countries. It also includes a study on vulnerabilities accumulating between commodity discovery and production in low-income countries.

Global Outlook: Disappointments, Risks, and Spillovers. Global growth again fell short of expectations in 2015, decelerating to 2.4 percent from 2.6 percent in 2014 (Chapter 1). The disappointing performance mainly reflected a continued growth deceleration in emerging and developing economies amid post-crisis lows in commodity prices, weaker capital flows and subdued global trade. Global growth is projected to edge up in the coming years, but at a slower pace than envisioned in June 2015, reaching 2.9 percent in 2016 and 3.1 percent in 2017-18. This pickup is predicated on continued gains in major high-income countries, a gradual tightening of financing conditions, a stabilization of commodity prices, and a gradual rebalancing in China. The forecast is subject to substantial downside risks, including a disorderly slowdown in major emerging market economies, financial market turmoil arising from sudden shifts in borrowing costs amid deteriorating fundamentals, lingering vulnerabilities in some countries, and heightened geopolitical tensions. Weakening growth and sharply lower commodity prices have narrowed the room for policy makers to respond, especially in commodity-exporting countries, should risks materialize.

Who Catches a Cold When Emerging Markets Sneeze? Given the size and global economic integration of the largest emerging markets—Brazil, the Russian Federation, India, China, and South Africa (BRICS)—the simultaneous slowdown underway in all but one of them could have significant spillovers to the rest of the world (Chapter 3). Specifically, a 1 percentage point decline in growth in BRICS is associated with a reduction in growth over the following two years by 0.8 percentage points in other emerging markets, 1.5 percentage points in frontier markets, and 0.4 percentage points in the global economy. Spillovers could be considerably larger if the growth slowdown in BRICS were combined with financial market turbulence.

Within-Region Spillovers. Within-region spillovers from BRICS and other major emerging markets are discussed in Boxes 2.1-2.6 of Chapter 2. Since most BRICS are the largest and most integrated economies in their respective regions, they tend to generate larger spillovers than other major emerging markets. Strong within-region trade and remittance links are reflected in sizeable spillovers in Europe and Central Asia from a growth decline in Russia, and in East Asia and Pacific from a growth decline in China (Boxes 2.1 and 2.2). In other regions, measured within-region spillovers are typically small (Boxes 2.3-2.6), partly reflecting the lesser openness of major regional emerging markets or the prevalence of integration with major advanced economies. Many emerging market and developing countries are still most susceptible to growth spillovers from major advanced markets.

Potential Macroeconomic Implications of the Trans-Pacific Partnership. On October 4, 12 Pacific Rim countries concluded negotiations on the Trans-Pacific Partnership. The first essay in Chapter 4 shows that, if ratified by all, the agreement could raise GDP in member countries by an average of 1.1 percent by 2030. It could also increase member countries' trade by 11 percent by 2030. A common regulatory approach could buoy trade provided it is not associated with excessively restrictive requirements on rules of origin and standards. As long as regulatory reforms benefit non-members, the detrimental effects of the agreement due to trade diversion and preference erosion on non-members would be limited.

Peg and Control? The Links between Exchange Rate Regimes and Capital Account Policies. As emerging and developing countries prepare to shield themselves from risks to the global outlook, they need to consider policy responses to adjust to external shocks. Among these, some countries might rely on exchange rate flexibility as a buffer, some might aim to minimize currency fluctuations, and some might consider measures to limit capital flows as they seek to keep some

degree of monetary policy control. The second essay in Chapter 4 explores how emerging markets and developing countries manage these competing pressures. The results suggest that developing countries with fixed exchange rate regimes appear to be more likely to have capital flow restrictions. This effect is particularly pronounced for lower-income countries.

From Commodity Discovery to Production: Vulnerabilities and Policies in Low-Income Countries. Major natural resource discoveries have transformed growth prospects for many low-income countries (LICs), though the sharp post-crisis downturn in commodity prices may delay development of these discoveries into production. During the pre-production period, macroeconomic vulnerabilities in these economies may rise as a result of large-scale investment needs. This heightens the importance of reducing lead times between discovery and production. The Special Focus finds that such lead times can be shortened by several years through improvements in business environments that benefit resource and non-resource sectors alike. Separately, while growth in LICs eased in 2015, it continued to be robust at about 5 percent, sustained by investment (both public and private, including in mining) and rising farm output. For 2016-17, strengthening import demand in advanced economies should help support activity in these countries.

Abbreviations

ASEAN	Association of Southeast Asian Nations
bbl	barrel
BRICS	Brazil, Russian Federation, India, China, and South Africa
BVAR	Bayesian Vector Autoregression
CFM	capital flow measures
DEV	developing countries
EAP	East Asia and Pacific
ECA	Europe and Central Asia
ECB	European Central Bank
EM	emerging market economies
EMBI	Emerging Markets Bond Index
ERR	exchange rate regime
EU	European Union
FDI	foreign direct investment
FM	frontier markets
FTA	free trade agreements
FY	fiscal year
GCC	Gulf Cooperation Council
GDP	gross domestic product
GEP	Global Economic Prospects
HIC	high-income country
HIY	high-income country
IMF	International Monetary Fund
LAC	Latin America and Caribbean
LDC	least developed country
LIC	low-income country
MNA	Middle East and North Africa
MIMT	Mexico, Indonesia, Malaysia, and Turkey
MRTA	mega-regional trade agreements
NAFTA	North America Free Trade Agreement
NTM	non-tariff measures
ODA	official development assistance
OECD	Organisation for Economic Co-operation and Development
OPEC	Organization of the Petroleum Exporting Countries
PPP	purchasing power parity
REER	real effective exchange rate
RHS	right-hand side (in figures)

RTA	Regional Trade Agreements
SAR	South Asia region
SSA	Sub-Saharan Africa
TFP	total factor productivity
TPP	Trans-Pacific Partnership
T-TIP	Transatlantic Trade and Investment Partnership
VAR	vector autoregression
VAT	value-added tax
WDI	World Development Indicators
WEO	World Economic Outlook
WTO	World Trade Organization

CHAPTER 1

GLOBAL OUTLOOK

Disappointments, Risks, and Spillovers

Global growth again fell short of expectations in 2015, slowing to 2.4 percent from 2.6 percent in 2014. The disappointing performance was mainly due to a continued deceleration of economic activity in emerging and developing economies amid weakening commodity prices, global trade, and capital flows. Going forward, global growth is projected to edge up, but at a slower pace than envisioned in the June 2015 forecast, reaching 2.9 percent in 2016 and 3.1 percent in 2017-18. The forecast is subject to substantial downside risks, including a sharper-than-expected slowdown in major emerging and developing economies or financial market turmoil arising from a sudden increase in borrowing costs that could combine with deteriorating fundamentals and lingering vulnerabilities in some countries.

Summary and key messages

A further deceleration of activity in key emerging and developing economies overshadowed a modest recovery in major high-income countries in 2015. This deceleration was accompanied by further declines in commodity prices, subdued global trade, bouts of financial market volatility, and weakening capital flows. Global growth continued to disappoint, and is now estimated at a slower-than-expected 2.4 percent in 2015, 0.4 percentage point below June 2015 *Global Economic Prospects* projections.

In developing countries, growth in 2015 is estimated at a post-crisis low of 4.3 percent, down from 4.9 percent in 2014 and 0.4 percentage point lower than projected in June (Figure 1.1). In a development unprecedented since the 1980s, most of the largest emerging economies in each region have been slowing simultaneously for three consecutive years. The economic rebalancing in China is continuing and accompanied by slowing growth. Brazil and Russia have been going through severe adjustments in the face of external and domestic challenges. On average, activity in emerging and developing commodity exporters stagnated in 2015, as they continued to be hard hit by declining commodity prices. As a result, the contribution to global growth from these economies has declined substantially. More generally, 2015 growth estimates for more than half of developing countries were further downgraded. Disappointments are concentrated in Latin America and, to a lesser degree, Sub-Saharan Africa, where a number of commodity exporters are struggling to maintain growth.

Notable exceptions in an otherwise gloomy outlook for developing countries include South Asia (reflecting reduced macroeconomic vulnerabilities and domestic policy reforms in India), as well as some commodity-importing countries in East Asia. Growth in low-income countries generally remained robust in 2015, albeit slowing to 5.1 percent from 6.1 percent in 2014. Some low-income economies showed continued strength (Ethiopia, Rwanda, Tanzania), supported by large-scale infrastructure investment, ongoing mine development, and consumer spending. However, fiscal risks have increased in several countries in East Africa because of sharp increases in public debt and contingent liabilities.

These scattered bright spots aside, the widespread slowdown across emerging and developing economies is a source of concern for the global economy and poses a threat to hard-won achievements in poverty reduction: more than 40 percent of the world's poor live in the developing countries where growth slowed in 2015.

Worsening prospects for developing countries have coincided with a sharp slowdown in global trade, a rise in financial market volatility, and a substantial decrease in capital inflows (Figure 1.2). In anticipation of tighter U.S. monetary policy, currency pressures have intensified and borrowing costs have increased, particularly for a number of commodity exporters. Significant nominal currency depreciations against the U.S. dollar are straining balance sheets in countries with elevated dollar-denominated liabilities. In an environment of weak global trade, exports are likely to languish. On the domestic front, a trend deceleration in productivity growth, rising private sector leverage, depleted fiscal buffers, and heightened policy uncertainty are major headwinds.

TABLE 1.1 Global real GDP growth[1]

(Percent)

(Percentage point difference from June 2015 projections)

	2013	2014	2015e	2016f	2017f	2018f	2015e	2016f	2017f
World	2.4	2.6	2.4	2.9	3.1	3.1	-0.4	-0.4	-0.1
High income[2]	1.2	1.7	1.6	2.1	2.1	2.1	-0.3	-0.2	-0.1
United States	1.5	2.4	2.5	2.7	2.4	2.2	-0.2	-0.1	0.0
Euro Area	-0.2	0.9	1.5	1.7	1.7	1.6	0.0	-0.1	0.1
Japan	1.6	-0.1	0.8	1.3	0.9	1.3	-0.3	-0.4	-0.3
United Kingdom	2.2	2.9	2.4	2.4	2.2	2.1	-0.2	-0.2	0.0
Russia	1.3	0.6	-3.8	-0.7	1.3	1.5	-1.1	-1.4	-1.2
Developing countries[2]	5.3	4.9	4.3	4.8	5.3	5.3	-0.4	-0.6	-0.2
East Asia and Pacific	7.1	6.8	6.4	6.3	6.2	6.2	-0.3	-0.4	-0.4
China	7.7	7.3	6.9	6.7	6.5	6.5	-0.2	-0.3	-0.4
Indonesia	5.6	5.0	4.7	5.3	5.5	5.5	0.0	-0.2	0.0
Thailand	2.8	0.9	2.5	2.0	2.4	2.7	-1.0	-2.0	-1.6
Europe and Central Asia[2]	3.9	2.3	2.1	3.0	3.5	3.5	0.3	-0.4	-0.2
Kazakhstan	6.0	4.4	0.9	1.1	3.3	3.4	-0.8	-1.8	-0.8
Turkey	4.2	2.9	4.2	3.5	3.5	3.4	1.2	-0.4	-0.2
Romania	3.5	2.8	3.6	3.9	4.1	4.0	0.6	0.7	0.6
Latin America and the Caribbean[2]	3.0	1.5	-0.7	0.1	2.3	2.5	-1.5	-2.3	-0.6
Brazil	3.0	0.1	-3.7	-2.5	1.4	1.5	-2.4	-3.6	-0.6
Mexico	1.4	2.3	2.5	2.8	3.0	3.2	-0.1	-0.4	-0.5
Colombia	4.9	4.6	3.1	3.0	3.3	3.5	-0.4	-0.9	-0.9
Middle East and North Africa	0.6	2.5	2.5	5.1	5.8	5.1	0.1	1.4	2.0
Egypt, Arab Rep.[3]	2.1	2.2	4.2	3.8	4.4	4.8	0.0	-0.7	-0.4
Iran, Islamic Rep.	-1.9	4.3	1.9	5.8	6.7	6.0	0.9	3.8	4.7
Algeria	2.8	3.8	2.8	3.9	4.0	3.8	0.2	0.0	0.0
South Asia	6.2	6.8	7.0	7.3	7.5	7.5	-0.1	0.0	0.0
India[3]	6.9	7.3	7.3	7.8	7.9	7.9	-0.2	-0.1	-0.1
Pakistan[3 4]	4.4	4.7	5.5	5.5	5.4	5.4	-0.5	1.8	0.9
Bangladesh[3]	6.1	6.5	6.5	6.7	6.8	6.8	0.2	0.0	0.1
Sub-Saharan Africa[2]	4.9	4.6	3.4	4.2	4.7	4.7	-0.8	-0.3	-0.3
South Africa	2.2	1.5	1.3	1.4	1.6	1.6	-0.7	-0.7	-0.8
Nigeria	5.4	6.3	3.3	4.6	5.3	5.3	-1.2	-0.4	-0.2
Angola	6.8	3.9	3.0	3.3	3.8	3.8	-1.5	-0.6	-1.3
MEMORANDUM ITEMS									
Real GDP growth									
World (2010 PPP weights)	3.2	3.4	3.1	3.6	3.8	3.9	-0.3	-0.4	-0.2
BRICS	5.7	5.1	3.9	4.6	5.3	5.4	-0.6	-0.8	-0.5
Low-income countries	6.4	6.1	5.1	6.2	6.6	6.6	-0.7	-0.1	0.1
Emerging markets (EME)[5]	4.9	4.5	3.7	4.2	4.8	4.9	-0.5	-0.7	-0.4
Frontier markets (FME)[6]	3.7	2.2	1.1	2.3	3.4	3.8	-0.7	-0.9	-0.6
Commodity-exporting EME & FME[7]	3.3	1.9	-0.4	0.9	2.6	2.9	-1.3	-1.7	-0.8
Other EME & FME	5.6	5.7	5.7	5.7	5.7	5.8	-0.1	-0.2	-0.3
World trade volume growth[8]	3.3	3.6	3.6	3.8	4.3	4.5	-0.8	-1.1	-0.6
Oil price growth[9]	-0.9	-7.5	-46.5	-8.5	7.2	7.2	-6.8	-18.1	1.6
Non-energy commodity price growth	-7.2	-4.6	-14.8	-1.8	1.9	1.9	-3.8	-3.0	0.6
International capital flows to developing countries (percent of GDP)[10]									
Developing countries	5.9	5.3	3.1	3.7	4.2	4.5	-2.0	-1.3	-0.6
East Asia and Pacific	6.2	5.3	2.0	3.0	3.8	4.3	-3.1	-1.9	-0.8
Europe and Central Asia	6.8	4.6	2.7	3.1	3.6	4.1	-2.3	-2.7	-2.9
Latin America and the Caribbean	6.9	6.7	5.5	5.4	5.3	5.3	0.1	-0.1	0.1
Middle East and North Africa	2.4	2.3	3.1	3.2	3.3	3.5	0.9	1.1	1.1
South Asia	4.3	4.9	5.0	5.1	5.2	5.2	-0.8	-0.5	-0.3
Sub-Saharan Africa	5.0	5.1	4.0	4.0	4.1	4.3	-0.2	0.0	0.2

Source: World Bank.

Notes: PPP = purchasing power parity; e = estimate; f = forecast.

World Bank forecasts are frequently updated based on new information and changing (global) circumstances. Consequently, projections presented here may differ from those contained in other Bank documents, even if basic assessments of countries' prospects do not differ at any given moment in time.

1. Aggregate growth rates calculated using constant 2010 U.S. dollars GDP weights.

2. Since July 2015, Argentina, Hungary, Seychelles, and Venezuela, RB have been classified as high income, and have been removed from respective developing regions. Percentage differences from previous Global Economic Prospects projections are calculated after modifying previous numbers to this new classification.

3. In keeping with national practice, data for Bangladesh, Arab Republic of Egypt, India, and Pakistan are reported on a fiscal year basis in Table 1.1. Aggregates that depend on these countries are calculated using data compiled on a calendar year basis.

4. GDP data for Pakistan are based on market prices.

5. Includes Brazil, Chile, China, Colombia, Czech Republic, Egypt, Hungary, India, Indonesia, Korea, Rep., Malaysia, Mexico, Morocco, Pakistan, Peru, Philippines, Poland, Qatar, Russian Federation, Saudi Arabia, South Africa, Thailand, Turkey, and United Arab Emirates.

6. Includes Argentina, Azerbaijan, Bahrain, Bangladesh, Bolivia, Botswana, Bulgaria, Costa Rica, Côte d'Ivoire, Croatia, Ecuador, El Salvador, Gabon, Georgia, Ghana, Guatemala, Honduras, Jamaica, Jordan, Kazakhstan, Kenya, Kuwait, Lebanon, Mauritius, Mongolia, Namibia, Nigeria, Oman, Panama, Paraguay, Romania, Senegal, Serbia, Sri Lanka, Tunisia, Ukraine, Uruguay, Venezuela, RB, Vietnam, and Zambia.

7. Includes Argentina, Azerbaijan, Bahrain, Bolivia, Botswana, Brazil, Chile, Colombia, Costa Rica, Côte d'Ivoire, Ecuador, Gabon, Ghana, Guatemala, Honduras, Indonesia, Jamaica, Kazakhstan, Kenya, Kuwait, Malaysia, Mongolia, Namibia, Nigeria, Oman, Panama, Paraguay, Peru, Qatar, Russian Federation, Saudi Arabia, Senegal, South Africa, Sri Lanka, Ukraine, United Arab Emirates, Uruguay, Venezuela, RB, and Zambia.

8. World trade volume for goods and non-factor services.

9. Simple average of Dubai, Brent, and West Texas Intermediate.

10. Balance of payments data for capital inflows of foreign direct investment, portfolio investment, and other investment (BPM6).

In contrast to developing countries, the recovery in major high-income countries gained traction in 2015 and has been increasingly driven by stronger domestic demand as labor markets heal and credit conditions improve. However, 2016 growth forecasts for high-income countries have been marked down in light of the effect on the United States of dollar appreciation and the impact on Japan of slowing trade in Asia. Conditions for a continued but fragile upturn in the Euro Area still appear in place, despite soft external demand and rising geopolitical concerns. Albeit gradually dissipating, legacies from the global financial crisis continue to be felt across high-income countries, limiting both aggregate demand and the underlying growth potential of these economies.

Going forward, global growth should pick up, albeit at an appreciably slower pace than previously projected, reaching 2.9 percent in 2016 and 3.1 percent in 2017-18. Global inflation is expected to increase moderately in 2016 as commodity prices level off, but will remain low by historical standards. A modest upturn in global activity in 2016 and beyond is predicated on a continued recovery in major high-income countries, a gradual slowdown and rebalancing in China, a stabilization of commodity prices, and an increase in global interest rates that is gradual and stays well contained. All of these projections, however, are subject to substantial downside risks.

Although it is still a low-probability scenario, a faster-than-expected slowdown in China combined with a more protracted deceleration in other large emerging markets is a risk. Empirical estimates suggest that a sustained 1 percentage point decline in growth in the BRICS (Brazil, the Russian Federation, India, China, and South Africa) would reduce growth in other emerging and developing economies by around 0.8 percentage point and global growth by 0.4 percentage point. This suggests a substantial risk of contagion through other emerging markets, with potential adverse effects for some advanced economies as well. Compounding this risk is the possibility of a protracted decline in potential growth throughout emerging and developing economies, persistently subdued growth in major high-income countries, and an escalation of

FIGURE 1.1 Global and developing-country growth prospects

Despite a modest recovery in high-income countries, global growth slowed in 2015, as developing-country growth dipped to a post-crisis low. The upturn in 2016 and 2017 is projected to be shallower than previously anticipated. Weakening prospects are most visible among key commodity exporters, pointing to a significantly lower contribution to global growth than in the past. China's gradual slowdown and rebalancing continued. Low-income countries continued to show some resilience, but a rising share of the world's extreme poor live in countries with slowing growth.

A. GDP growth, actual and projected

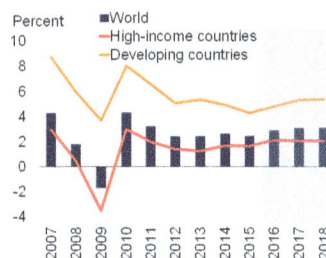

B. Global GDP growth forecasts over time

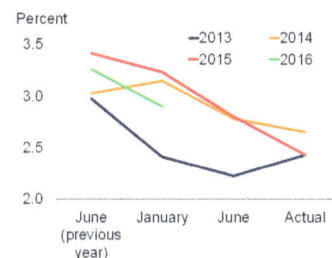

C. Contribution to global growth revisions

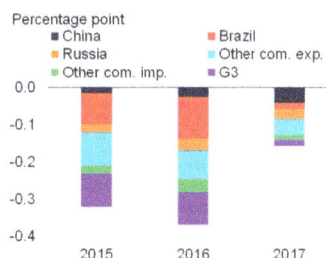

D. Contribution to global growth

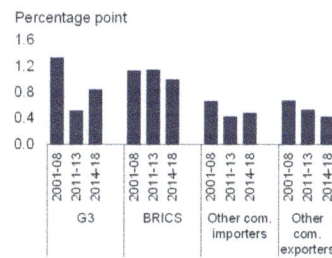

E. Share of developing countries with slower growth than 1990-2008 average

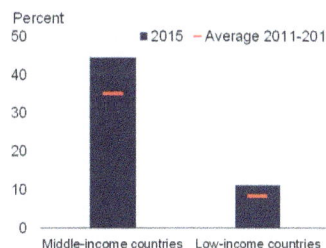

F. Share of world's poor living in countries with slowing growth

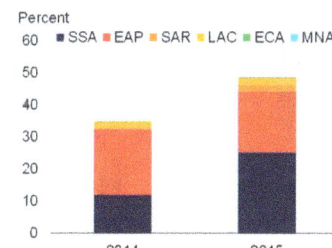

Sources: Haver Analytics; CPB Netherlands Bureau for Economic Policy Analysis; World Bank.
A. Shaded areas indicate forecasts.
B. Global GDP growth forecasts for a given year over subsequent Global Economic Prospects projection exercises.
C. Contribution to global growth revisions measured in constant 2010 U.S. dollars. "Other Com. Exp." stands for other commodity exporters, and excludes Russia and Brazil; "Other Com. Imp." stands for other commodity importers, and excludes China and G3 (Euro Area, Japan, and United States). Cumulative contributions from individual country growth revisions can differ from global growth revisions reported in Table 1.1 due to decimal rounding.
D. Contributions to global growth measured in constant 2010 U.S. dollars. "Other Com. Exp." stands for other commodity exporters, and excludes Russia, Brazil and South Africa; "Other Com. Imp." stands for other commodity importers, and excludes China, India and G3 (Euro Area, Japan, and United States).
E. For each year, the fraction of middle- and low-income countries in which growth is slower than its historical average for 1990-2008.
F. Share of extreme poor ($1.90/day) living in developing countries that grew more slowly in the current year than in the previous year. EAP= East Asia and Pacific, ECA = Europe and Central Asia, LAC = Latin America and the Caribbean, MNA = Middle East and North Africa, SAR = South Asia, SSA = Sub-Saharan Africa.

FIGURE 1.2 Global trade, finance, and risks

Deteriorating growth prospects for developing countries have been accompanied by weakening global trade, capital flows, and commodity prices. Currency pressures have increased, particularly for some commodity exporters. Domestic challenges have intensified as well, with elevated private sector debt, slowing credit, and weaker productivity growth. Prospects of rising borrowing costs combined with lingering vulnerabilities in some countries could heighten the risk of financial market turbulence. Further growth disappointments in major emerging economies could disproportionately affect other developing countries.

A. Global merchandise trade growth

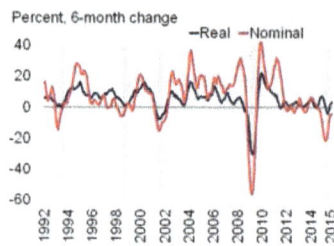

B. Capital flows in emerging and developing countries

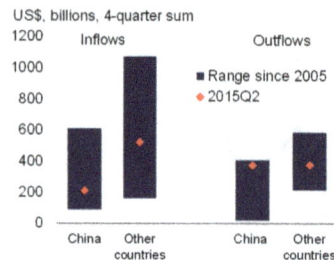

C. Exchange rates

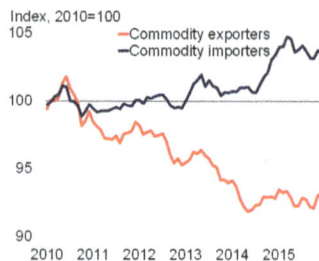

D. Credit growth and private debt

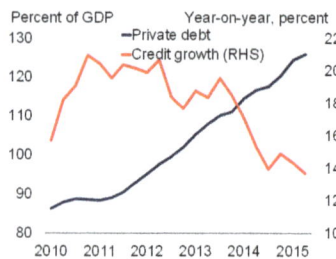

E. Productivity growth in BRICS

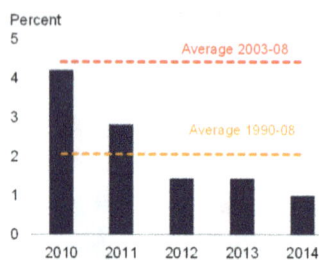

F. Impact of a 1 percentage point decline in BRICS on growth

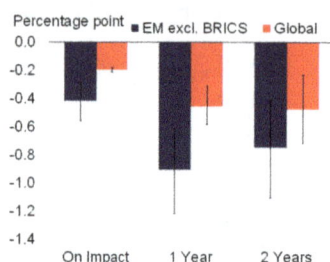

Sources: Haver Analytics; World Bank; CPB Netherlands Bureau for Economic Policy Analysis; Bank for International Settlements.
A. Global merchandise trade is the average of global imports and exports. Volumes are computed by deflating nominal trade flows by unit value indexes. Latest observation is October, 2015.
B. Based on quarterly balance of payment data for the largest 23 emerging and developing economies. Includes foreign direct investment, portfolio, short-term debt, and other investment flows. Countries are classified as either emerging or frontier markets when they have either full or partial access to international financial markets.
C. Median effective exchange range of developing countries classified as either commodity exporters or commodity importers. An increase denotes appreciation. Latest observation is November 2015.
D. GDP-weighted average of credit growth to and debt-to-GDP ratios of households and non-financial corporations in BRICS and MIMT (BRICS are Brazil, Russia, India, China, and South Africa; MIMTs are Mexico, Indonesia, Malaysia, and Turkey). Latest observation is 2015 Q2.
E. Unweighted average of total factor productivity growth in BRICS using 2010 USD GDP weights.
F. Weighted average of the responses of other emerging market and global GDP to a 1 percentage point decline in growth of BRICS countries' GDP, according to a vector-autoregression models presented in Chapter 3. Confidence bands span the 16th-84th percentiles. EM (excluding BRICS) comprises Chile, Colombia, Czech Republic, Egypt, Hungary, Indonesia, Korea, Morocco, Mexico, Malaysia, Pakistan, Peru, Philippines, Poland, Qatar, Saudi Arabia, Thailand, Turkey, United Arab Emirates.

geopolitical tensions. In addition, baseline forecasts of a smooth monetary policy tightening cycle in the United States are subject to considerable uncertainty. A sudden readjustment of expectations about the future trajectory of U.S. interest rates could combine with domestic fragilities and policy uncertainties in some developing countries to generate financial stress. Given the weak outlook and lingering vulnerabilities in many developing countries, these risks have the potential to be a source of damaging sudden stops in capital flows in the most fragile economies.

Policies can play an important role in mitigating risks and supporting growth. A combination of cyclical and structural policies could be mutually reinforcing. In the near term, policy actions need to be focused on building the ability to withstand financial market turbulence. Cyclical policies need to be supplemented with structural reform measures that boost investors' confidence in the short term and enhance growth prospects in the long term.

Major economies

The recovery in major high-income countries gained traction last year. This has been increasingly driven by stronger domestic demand, particularly in the United States, where employment conditions are robust. In the Euro Area, credit growth is picking up and unemployment is declining. The recovery remains fragile in Japan despite substantial policy stimulus. With external demand negatively affected by a slowdown in large emerging market economies, growth forecasts across major high-income economies in 2016 have been shaded down, but growth should still show some improvement from 2015. The tightening cycle of the U.S. Federal Reserve is projected to be very gradual, while policy accommodation will likely continue in the Euro Area and Japan. China's gradual slowdown and rebalancing continued in 2015, as further deceleration in sectors with excess capacity was partially offset by robust growth in services.

United States

Domestic demand in 2015 was supported by robust consumption and dynamic investment outside the oil sector. In contrast, net exports remained a drag on growth and industrial activity continued to be subdued in the second half of 2015 (Figure 1.3). For 2015 as a whole, growth is estimated at 2.5 percent—the highest annual rate in the post-crisis period. Solid labor market conditions continued to support a consumption-led recovery, with job creation averaging more than 200,000 per month in 2015 and the unemployment rate falling to 5 percent in the final quarter of 2015. However, labor participation has continued to trend down, and is unlikely to recover much as the number of baby-boomers approaching retirement age increases. Labor productivity has moved downward in recent years, constraining potential output growth (Gordon 2014, Hall 2014, Fernald and Wang 2015). Household real disposable income has been boosted by employment gains, declining oil prices and moderate wage growth. This led to rising personal consumption growth in 2015, despite an increase in the savings ratio. A recovery in housing markets and prospects of strengthening wage growth amid tight labor market conditions support a positive outlook in 2016.

The decline in net exports is a principal factor dampening growth at present. This is the result of the strength of the dollar and the softness in external demand, particularly from large emerging markets. Reflecting in part asynchronous monetary policy stances among major central banks, the dollar has appreciated more than 20 percent in nominal effective terms—and 18 percent in real effective terms—since mid-2014. Empirical studies suggest that an appreciation around this size may reduce GDP growth by one percentage point after two years (Laporte and Roberts 2014; Brayton, Laubach, and Reifschneider 2014).

Headline inflation continued to hover around zero in the second half of 2015, with the renewed fall in oil prices during the summer of 2015 and the strengthening dollar exerting downward pressures. Excluding food and energy, inflation stayed below 2 percent and is projected to rise only gradually in

FIGURE 1.3 United States

Robust consumer spending and investment in the non-oil private sector supported above-trend growth in 2015, and should continue to be the main drivers of growth in 2016. The unemployment rate has dropped to lows seen during previous recoveries, but labor participation and growth in productivity have been declining, constraining potential output. A strengthening U.S. dollar and weakening external demand are weighing on exports and manufacturing activity. This points to a very gradual tightening cycle by the U.S. Federal Reserve.

A. GDP and demand components

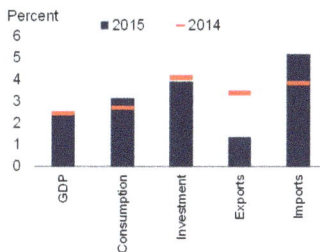

B. Growth and inflation

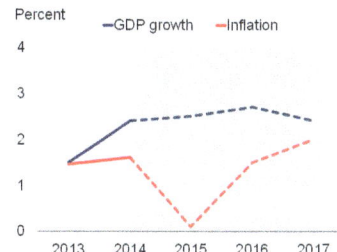

C. Unemployment rate from cyclical troughs

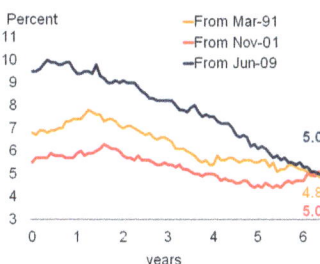

D. Labor participation and productivity growth

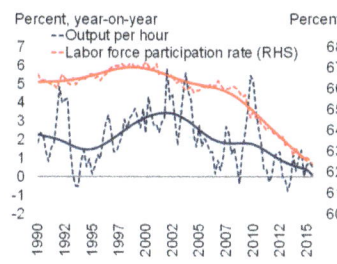

E. U.S. dollar exchange rate and real exports

F. U.S. policy interest rate expectations

Sources: Haver Analytics; World Bank; Federal Reserve Economic Data (FRED).
B. Inflation is the year-on-year percent change of the overall Consumer Price Index.
C. Based on the last three cyclical troughs identified by the NBER's Business Cycle Dating Committee: March 1991, November 2001, and June 2009.
D. Productivity growth is measured as annual change in real output per hour worked of all persons in the non-farm business sector. The civilian labor force participation rate is the ratio of people either employed or actively looking for work to the active age population. The thick lines show the trend measured by a Hodrick-Prescott filter. Latest observation is 2015 Q3.
E. REER: real effective exchange rate based on relative CPI inflation. An increase denotes appreciation. Latest observation is October 2015 for real exports and November, 2015 for exchange rates.
F. Past tightening cycles refer to average of Fed fund rate hikes during previous tightening cycles (December 1986, March 1988, February 1994, March 1997, June 1999, and June 2004).

FIGURE 1.4 Euro Area

The recovery in the Euro Area in 2015 has been supported by both strengthening domestic demand and exports. Pickups in credit and intra-European trade growth point to a broadening recovery. Deflation concerns have receded, but core inflation and wage growth remain subdued among economies with high long-term unemployment rates.

A. GDP and demand components

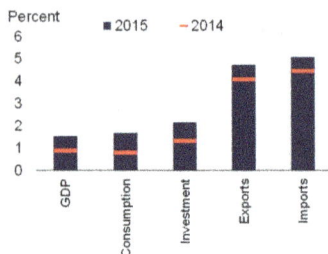

B. Growth and inflation

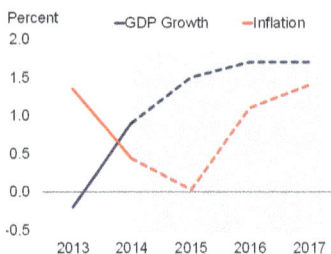

C. Private loan growth and credit standards

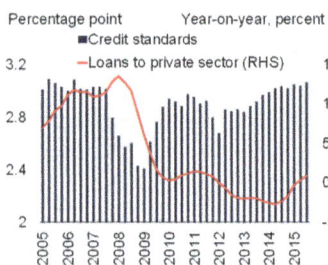

D. Extra and intra-EU export growth (nominal)

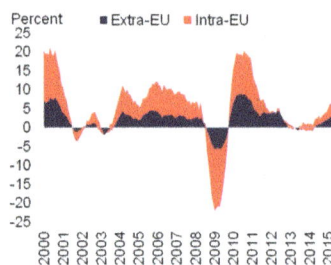

E. Wage growth and core inflation

F. Long-term unemployment and core inflation, 2015

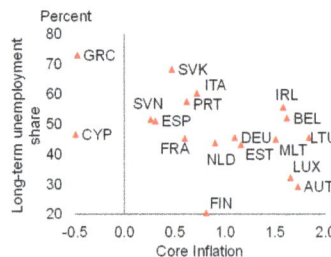

Sources: Haver Analytics; World Bank; Eurostat; European Central Bank, Bank Lending Survey.
B. Inflation is the year-on-year percent change of the Harmonized Index of Consumer Prices.
C. Credit standard is calculated as the difference (net percentage) between the share of banks reporting that credit standards have been easing and the share of banks reporting that they have been tightened. A positive net percentage indicates that a larger proportion of banks have eased credit standards. Latest observation is 2015 Q3.
D. Six month moving average. Latest observation is September, 2015.
E. Wage growth is measured as percentage change, year-over-year, in negotiated wage rates. Latest observation is 2015 Q3 for wage growth and November, 2015 for core inflation.
F. Standard ISO country codes. Long-term unemployment rate refers to people who are actively seeking for employment for at least a year in percent of total unemployment. Long-term unemployment is 2015 Q3 for most countries. Core inflation is the average of January to November 2015. Core Inflation is Harmonized Consumer Price Index excluding energy, foods, and tobacco.

2016. Market-based inflation expectations remained somewhat below the Federal Reserve's 2 percent inflation target in the second half of 2015, pointing towards a gradual normalization of policy rates. The fiscal deficit is estimated to have fallen

further to 2.8 percent of GDP in 2015, the result of stronger growth and consolidation efforts. Fiscal policy has eased to a broadly growth-neutral stance in 2014-15, having weighed on activity in previous years.

Robust employment growth, still-accommodative financing conditions, and low oil prices should continue to support domestic demand in the period ahead. Growth is projected to average 2.7 percent in 2016, above potential but somewhat lower than predicted in June, reflecting a larger drag from net exports. Growth is expected to stabilize around 2.3 percent in 2017-18, with the output gap closing in 2017. Monetary policy tightening is likely to be very gradual throughout the forecast period.

Euro Area

Growth picked up in 2015, as domestic demand strengthened and exports accelerated, partly due to the lagged effect of a euro depreciation (Figure 1.4). For the year as a whole, Euro Area growth is estimated at 1.5 percent, in line with previous expectations, with activity firming in Spain, somewhat disappointing in Germany, and still lagging (albeit gradually recovering) in France and Italy. Low oil prices and favorable financing conditions are supporting consumer spending and investment. In the absence of further escalation, security concerns following the terrorist attacks in Paris are not expected to have lasting effects on confidence and activity.

Diminishing fiscal consolidation and healing labor markets are underpinning domestic demand, although conditions vary across countries. Since the start of the European Central Bank's (ECB) quantitative easing program, credit conditions have improved and credit growth has resumed following several years of contraction. However, credit remains tight in some countries because of elevated non-performing loans and impaired bank balance sheets. Despite the monetary policy easing, the euro appreciated about 7 percent in trade-weighted terms since reaching a low in April 2015, mainly reflecting the broad-based depreciation of emerging-market currencies. This may reduce somewhat the momentum of export growth and delay a pick-up in inflation. Although the impact may vary depending on the underlying factors driving currency movements, results from a number of macroeconomic models indicate that a 7 percent euro appreciation reduces Euro Area GDP growth by between 0.2-0.4 percentage point, and inflation by 0.1-0.5 percentage point (ECB 2015a, European Commission 2015a).

Peripheral economies have been little affected by contagion from the Greece crisis. A third bailout program was agreed to with European partners in August 2015, amounting to €86 billion ($95 billion), in exchange for pension, tax, and other reforms. The weakening of the Greek economy following the implementation of capital controls in June 2015 will make program implementation challenging, but the disbursement of bailout funds and the agreed bank recapitalization plan have reduced immediate funding pressures.

Deflation concerns have receded since the start of 2015 but have not disappeared, with core inflation and wage growth remaining subdued, particularly among economies with high long-term unemployment rates. Headline inflation remained close to zero in 2015. Market-based inflation expectations have bottomed out but remain below the 2 percent target. This situation led the ECB to ease monetary policy further in December 2015.

Conditions should continue to improve in 2016, with growth reaching 1.7 percent, a bit slower than expected in June, reflecting a weakening external environment. Growth should average 1.6 percent in 2017-18, slightly above potential. However, concerns persist about low potential growth, high unemployment, and large public debt. While population ageing limits growth potential (Jimeno 2015), labor mobility and migration can help alleviate some of these constraints (World Bank 2015b) and help adjustments to country-specific shocks in monetary union (Beyer and Smets 2015).

The recent acceleration in the number of asylum seekers is creating important absorption and policy challenges that could strain public services and government finances in exposed countries, but is expected to provide some marginal support to Euro Area-wide growth in the short-term through rising public expenditure and private

consumption.[1] Over the medium term, the influx may also help to meet labor shortages in the face of an ageing population. However, the ultimate effect on growth and public finances remains highly uncertain, depending on the performance of migrants in the labor market (Münz et al. 2006, OECD 2014) as well as the coherence of national and EU policy responses.

Japan

Japan experienced a soft growth patch in mid-2015, confirming a weak underlying trend despite rising corporate profits and continued policy stimulus. Private consumption contracted in 2015 and investment was stagnant, which was only partially offset by positive but relatively subdued export growth (Figure 1.5). Overall, GDP growth is estimated at 0.8 percent for 2015, 0.3 percentage point lower than projected in June.

Despite the low value of the yen since 2013, the export response has been modest. This disappointment partly owes to past offshoring of production to the rest of Asia, which helped develop regional value chains and shifted sales to overseas subsidiaries. The transition to foreign plants was led by the more productive enterprises (Wakasugi et al. 2014). This offshoring trend appears to have lowered Japan's gross export elasticity. Weakening external demand from the rest of Asia also played a dampening role on exports, as value-added trade between Japan and other Asian countries intensified during the 2000s (Ito and Wakasugi 2015).

The Bank of Japan maintained its commitment to quantitative easing, and a further expansion of asset purchases is likely as inflation is not expected to reach the central bank's target before 2017. Tax revenues have increased following the rise in the consumption tax in April 2014 and the growth in corporate profits, but achieving primary balance by 2020-21 will be challenging, as spending pressures on social security and defense remain significant. Skill shortages in key services sectors

---

[1]The European Commission predicts that the influx of 3 million migrants over the next three years would provide a net gain of up to ¼ of percentage point to EU growth by 2017 (European Commission 2015b).

FIGURE 1.5 Japan

Growth in Japan remains fragile, with private consumption and investment failing to pick up in 2015. Growth is expected to recover moderately to 1.3 percent in 2016, from 0.8 percent in 2015. Past offshore investments have helped raise sales and profit by overseas subsidiaries, but restrained exports. Skill shortages continued to increase, raising prospects of a gradual acceleration in wage growth. Rising female participation has boosted employment rates and is helping to offset demographic pressures. Long-term inflation expectations remain below the 2 percent inflation target, despite further policy easing by the Bank of Japan.

A. GDP and demand components

B. Growth and inflation

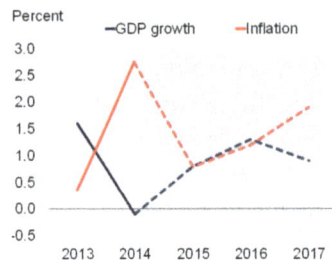

C. Exports and sales of overseas subsidiaries

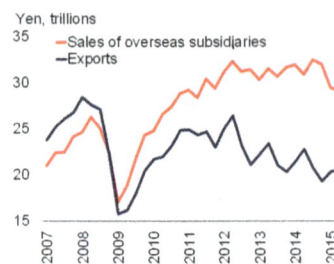

D. Employment shortages by industry

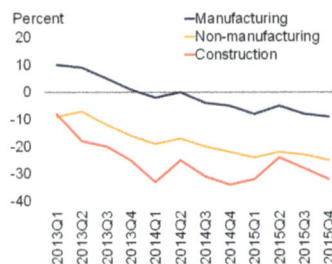

E. Female and overall employment rate

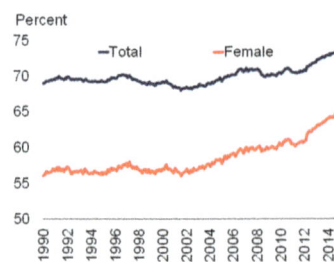

F. Inflation expectations and central bank balance sheet

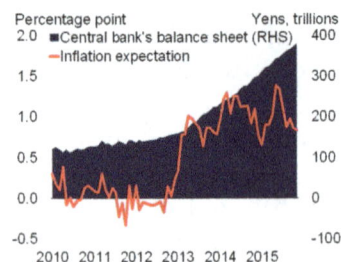

Sources: Haver Analytics; World Bank; Bank of Japan.
B. Inflation is the year-on-year percent change of the Consumer Price Index.
C. Latest observation is 2015 Q2.
D. Percent of reporting companies based on the Bank of Japan's Tankan survey data on labor market shortages is a diffusion index taking a negative value when companies report perceived labor shortages (as factor hampering production). Latest observation is 2015 Q3.
E. Percent of the active age population. Latest observation is October, 2015.
F. Inflation expectations extracted from 5-year swap rates. Central Bank's balance sheet is total assets held. Latest observation is November, 2015.

continued to increase, as reforms that have encouraged female labor force participation have only partially offset demographic pressures on labor supply. The tight labor market in the services sector raises the prospect of a gradual acceleration in wage growth.

Sustained policy accommodation, and the prospect of higher earnings and record low unemployment, are positives for the outlook. Going forward, growth is expected to recover to 1.3 percent in 2016, less than expected in June due to a downward revision to both domestic demand and exports. The recovery remains fragile and dominated by downside risks.

China

Sectoral rebalancing in China became more pronounced in 2015. It was accompanied by bouts of volatility in financial markets and additional government stimulus measures. Growth in 2015 is estimated at 6.9 percent, down from 7.3 percent the previous year. The deceleration reflects an ongoing correction in the property sector, weakness in industrial activity, and slower growth in non-traditional credit. The robust expansion of consumer spending and services has helped boost the economy, and is in line with the rebalancing sought by policymakers. Even so, forecasts for 2016-17 have been downgraded, with growth expected to reach 6.5 percent by 2017.

In line with rebalancing efforts, the deceleration in activity during 2015 has been most visible in industry and real estate—sectors with considerable overcapacity and, in the case of industry, a high presence of state-owned enterprises (Figure 1.6). These sectors saw the sharpest increase in investment and leverage in 2009-13, resulting in a significant concentration of debt among a small number of large firms (Chivakul and Lam 2015). Balance sheets and credit quality have deteriorated in sectors with excess capacity. Policy efforts to reduce supply mismatches in the real estate sector, and to tighten nonbank credit flows, continued to weigh on non-traditional credit growth, which slowed notably during 2015. Weaker activity in manufacturing and construction have significantly impacted import demand, which contracted in the first half of 2015.

The service sector has seen its share of employment increasing in recent years, and accounted for the majority of new urban jobs created in 2015 (World Bank 2015a). This helped offset stagnant hiring in shrinking industrial sectors, and kept urban labor markets tight. Wages and real incomes have continued to increase, albeit at lower rates, contributing to sustained growth of private consumption. A continued rebalancing from industry to services should support the shift from investment to consumption, whose share in GDP is gradually recovering from a post-crisis dip.

Policies became more supportive throughout the course of 2015, in order to counter slowing activity. The People's Bank of China (PBOC) continued to lower benchmark interest rates and required reserve ratios, while implementing new collateral policies to facilitate refinancing for commercial banks. The central bank also continued to inject liquidity into the financial system, especially during the June stock market correction. The fiscal deficit widened to a six-year high of 2.3 percent of GDP in 2015, reflecting accelerated infrastructure investment by the central government in the second half of the year. The increase in central government spending more than offset cutbacks at the local government level resulting from lower revenues due to falling land sales, restrictions imposed on borrowing through Local Government Financing Vehicles (LGFV), and other off-budget transactions.

To foster greater exchange rate flexibility, the PBOC introduced a change in the calculation of the renminbi reference rate on August 10. This led to an almost 3 percent depreciation against the U.S. dollar, the largest three-day drop since the mid-1990s. The change was implemented against a backdrop of accelerated capital outflows and slowing growth. While it sparked some market volatility in the short term, the decision was fully aligned with the objective of allowing market forces to play a greater role in the economy. With this exception, the renminbi has been stable throughout 2015, and has continued to appreciate in real effective terms despite strong capital outflows.

Private capital outflows have increased as capital controls have been loosened. The net outflow reflects corporate efforts to reduce net foreign currency exposures and foreign short-term debt. Currency interventions to reduce the resulting downward pressure on the renminbi contributed to an estimated US$443 billion decline in foreign currency reserves since September 2014 (11.5

FIGURE 1.6 China

The growth slowdown in China has been most noticeable among enterprises operating in the manufacturing and real estate sectors. Growth forecasts have been revised down to 6.9 percent in 2015 and 6.7 percent in 2016. In evidence of the rebalancing of China's economy, the share of services employment has increased, supporting real incomes and contributing to robust private consumption. A drop in equity prices and a change in exchange rate policy led to market turbulence, but foreign reserves remain plentiful and the current account is in surplus, reducing risks associated with capital outflows.

A. Value-added by type of companies

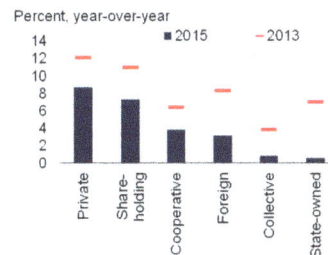

B. Growth and inflation

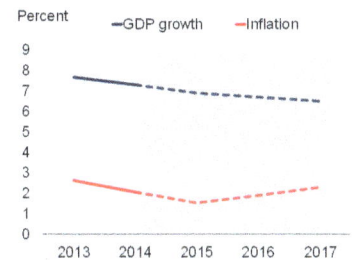

C. GDP share of services and industry

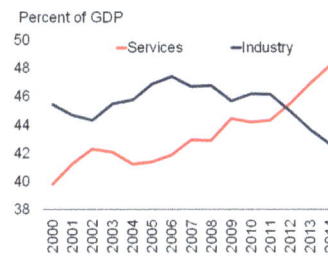

D. Employment by sector

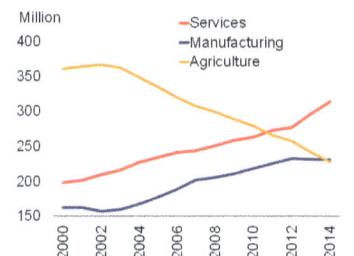

E. Stock market index and exchange rate

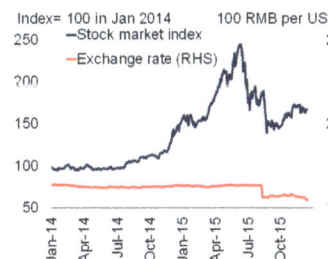

F. Current account balance and reserves

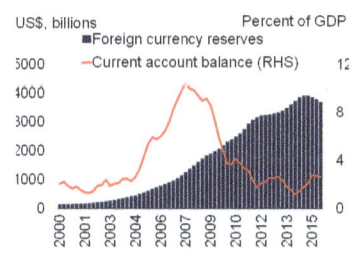

Sources: Haver Analytics; World Bank.
A. 2015 is the average of January to October.
B. Inflation is the year-on-year percent change of the Consumer Price Index.
E. Stock market index is the Shanghai Stock Exchange Composite Index (SHCOMP). Latest observation is December 16, 2015.
F. Foreign currency reserves is the foreign exchange holdings of the People's Bank of China. Latest observation is 2015Q3.

percent off their peak level). The drop in reserves in August 2015, US$94 billion, was the sharpest drop on record, and partly reflected valuation effects, as well as an effort to diversify foreign

FIGURE 1.7 Financial volatility and asset valuations

Concerns about prospects in emerging markets, combined with China's stock-market correction in the summer of 2015 and uncertainty about the impact of a normalization in U.S. monetary policy, contributed to greater financial market volatility. Equity and currency markets were particularly affected, with the most significant currency depreciations among key commodity exporters and in countries with lingering vulnerabilities. Borrowing costs also rose in line with heightened risk-aversion.

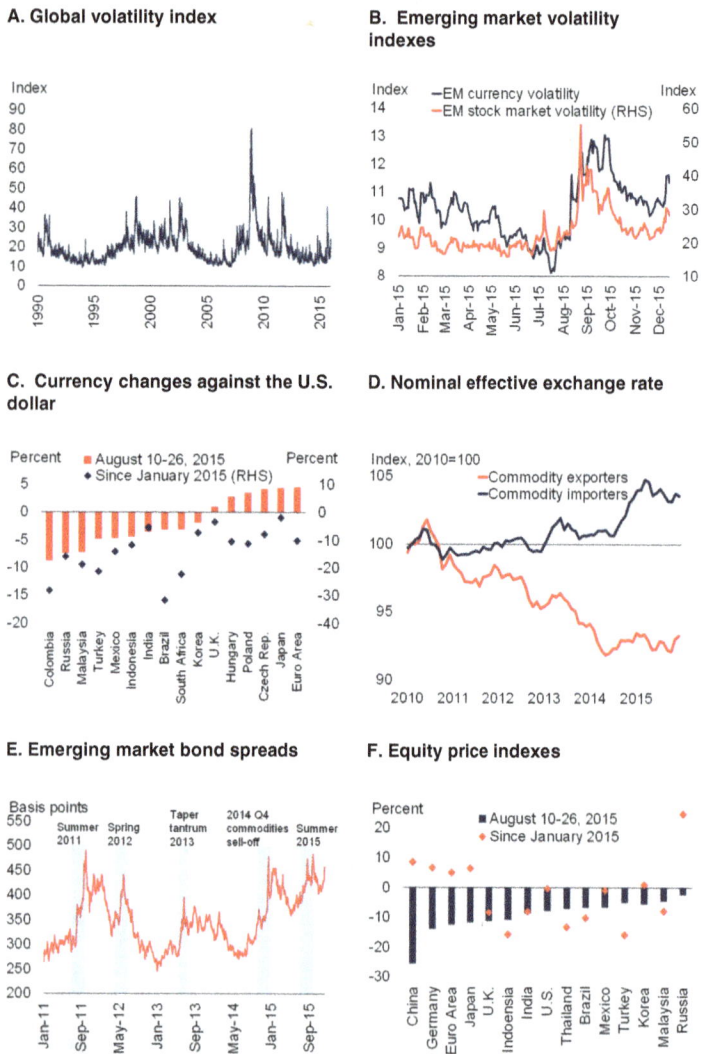

A. Global volatility index

B. Emerging market volatility indexes

C. Currency changes against the U.S. dollar

D. Nominal effective exchange rate

E. Emerging market bond spreads

F. Equity price indexes

Sources: World Bank; Haver Analytics; Bloomberg.
A. Implied stock-market volatility derived from option pricing on the U.S. S&P 500 Index (VIX index). Latest observation is December 15, 2015.
B. EM currency and stock market volatility computed by Bloomberg. Latest observation is December 15, 2015.
C. An increase denotes appreciation. Latest observation is December 15, 2015.
D. Median effective exchange range of developing countries classified as either commodity exporters or commodity importers. A decline denotes depreciation. Latest observation is November 2015.
E. EMBI Global bond spreads measured from emerging market U.S.dollar-denominated Brady bonds, loans, and Eurobonds with an outstanding face value of at least $500 million. Latest observation is December 15, 2015.
F. Latest observation is December, 2015.

assets through the purchase of gold. Notwithstanding this decline, China's foreign exchange reserves remain substantial, at about US$3.5 trillion (or 32.8 percent of GDP).

Global trends and spillovers

Concerns about the growth outlook and prospects of rising U.S. interest rates led to a tightening in financing conditions for many developing countries and contributed to a significant slowdown in capital inflows in 2015. Commodity exporters, and countries with heightened domestic challenges, are especially affected. The widespread slowdown in emerging market economies contributed to a contraction in global trade in the first half of the year, adding headwinds to the global recovery. The broad weakness in commodity prices in 2015 is expected to persist in 2016, maintaining pressure on commodity exporters while supporting real income gains among importers.

Increasingly difficult financial conditions

Global financial market volatility rose noticeably in 2015 against the backdrop of slowing activity in large emerging economies, diverging monetary policies of major central banks, continued declines in commodity prices, and fragile liquidity conditions. In this context, market adjustments to adverse or unexpected news have been abrupt. Following a correction from overvalued equity prices in China and an unforeseen change in its exchange rate regime during the summer of 2015, the VIX index of stock-market volatility, often considered a proxy of global risk aversion, briefly surged to levels last seen during the 2011-12 Euro Area crisis (Figure 1.7)[2]. While there was no unusual stress in short-term funding markets, nor a credit crunch in any large emerging markets, the summer market turmoil led to a sharp sell-off in developing country assets and a drop in capital inflows to those economies.

Half of the 20 largest developing-country stock markets saw plunges of 20 percent or more from their 2015 peaks. Currencies of key commodity exporters (including Brazil, Indonesia, Malaysia, the Russian Federation, and South Africa), and developing countries subject to heightened political risk (including Brazil and Turkey) fell to multi-year lows both against the U.S. dollar as

---

[2] In contrast, currencies in high-income Eastern European countries appreciated in nominal effective terms, alongside the euro, which strengthened during the turmoil on safe-haven flows.

well as in trade-weighted terms (Figure 1.7). Since July 2015, sovereign debt spreads have widened by 45 basis points and emerging market corporate debt spreads by 80 basis points, with the largest increases occurring among commodity exporters in Africa, Latin America, and East Asia. Since October, equity markets have rebounded, and sovereign bond spreads have narrowed, although remaining elevated in many countries. Several emerging market currencies also retraced some of their losses against the U.S. dollar, led by the Malaysian ringgit and the Indonesian rupiah.

Global investors pulled about $52 billion from emerging market equity and bond funds in the third quarter of 2015, the largest quarterly outflow on record (Figure 1.8). This was mostly driven by institutional investors reducing their exposure in a sign of deteriorating confidence about long-term prospects. Net short-term debt and bank outflows from China, combined with a broad-based retrenchment in the Russian Federation, accounted for the bulk of the outflow from emerging markets, but portfolio and short-term capital inflows also dried up elsewhere in the third quarter of 2015. Meanwhile, FDI inflows remained generally steady, although they decelerated in some economies.

International bond issuance by emerging market corporates slowed significantly, particularly in the oil and gas sector. This has partially reversed the post-crisis doubling of bond issuance by developing country corporates, especially in commodities-related sectors. Since 2010, bonds have been issued more often to refinance debt than for investment purposes (Rodrigues Bastos, Kamil, and Sutton 2015). In consequence, some commodity firms have become highly leveraged, and are now vulnerable to a combination of rising borrowing costs and declining commodity prices.

Looking ahead, the diverging monetary policy stances of major economies will continue to be a key determinant of financial conditions in developing countries.

- *United States.* Following a first hike in December 2015, the pace of interest rate increases in the United States is expected to be

FIGURE 1.8 Capital flows

Capital flows decelerated to their weakest level since the global financial crisis, particularly in China. Foreign direct investment has shown greater resilience, while short-term debt and portfolio inflows have decelerated significantly. Weakening capital flows have exacerbated currency and equity market pressures in many countries, particularly among commodity exporters. Borrowing costs also rose in line with heightened risk-aversion, and corporate bond issuance slowed significantly, particularly from construction, oil and financial companies.

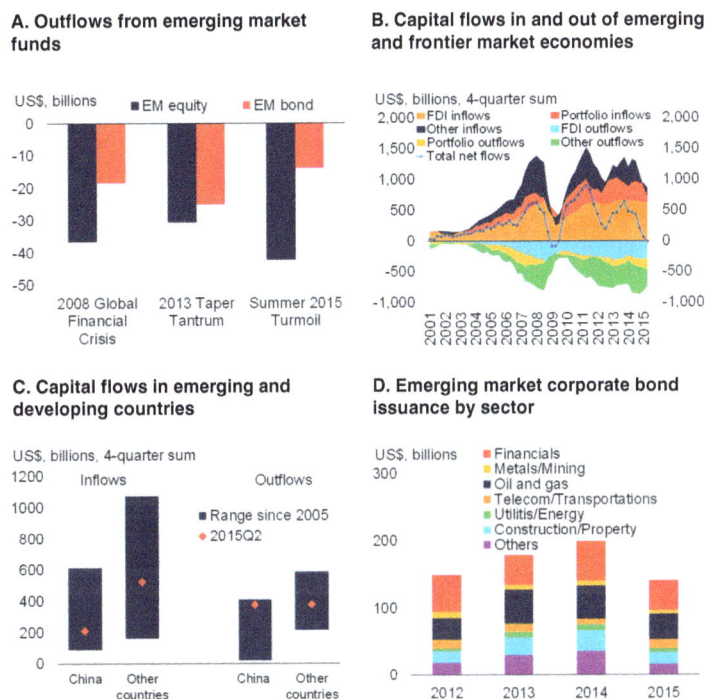

A. Outflows from emerging market funds

B. Capital flows in and out of emerging and frontier market economies

C. Capital flows in emerging and developing countries

D. Emerging market corporate bond issuance by sector

Sources: World Bank; EPFR Global; Bloomberg; Dealogic; JP Morgan; U.S. Federal Open Market Committee.
A. Figure shows cumulative EPFR weekly flows. "Global Financial Crisis " refers to June 11, 2008 to October 28, 2009. "Taper Tantrum" refers to May 29 to September 4, 2013. "Summer 2015 Turmoil" refers to July 17 to September 16, 2015.
B. C. Based on quarterly balance of payment data for the largest 23 emerging and developing economies. Includes foreign direct investment, portfolio, short-term debt, and other investment flows. Last observation is 2015Q2. Four-quarter moving sum.
D. Last observation is December, 2015.

gradual and notably slower than in previous tightening cycles, reflecting in part low inflation expectations and U.S. dollar appreciation. Legacies from the crisis, such as elevated household debt and weak productivity growth, also point towards a protracted period of low interest rates. Since the tightening cycle has been widely anticipated, baseline projections assume a benign impact on capital inflows to emerging and developing economies. However, as financial market expectations are susceptible to scares, risks of volatility during the Fed tightening cycle remain significant (Arteta et al. 2015).

- *Euro Area and Japan.* Continued quantitative easing by the ECB and the Bank of Japan should help shore up global liquidity. Negative interest rates in Europe and increasing yield differentials with the United States could contribute to a further appreciation of the U.S. dollar and have mixed effects for developing countries. On the one hand, the increase in cross-border lending from European banks and Eurobond issuance during 2015 is likely to continue as the Euro Area recovery becomes more firmly entrenched and as bank balance sheets improve. On the other hand, continued strengthening of the dollar could contribute to refinancing pressures in countries with significant dollar-denominated liabilities.

Capital inflows to developing countries dipped to a post-crisis low relative to GDP in 2015 (Table 1.1). They are expected to recover slowly in 2016-17 as developing-country growth stabilizes. A gradual shift from portfolio to cross-border bank lending flows is likely to continue, supported in particular by a healing European banking sector and ongoing policy accommodation by the ECB. A gradual rise in global interest rates and continued weakness in commodity prices could affect FDI decisions, particularly in mining and exploration, while the cost of infrastructure financing is expected to rise. Renewed bouts of volatility, or heightened concerns about developing country growth prospects, represent downside risks to this benign scenario.

Renewed decline in commodity prices

Commodity prices fell further in the second half of 2015. By November, the three industrial commodity price indexes—energy, metals, and agricultural raw materials—were down, on average, 45 percent from their 2011 peaks (Figure 1.9). Abundant supplies, due in part to investment during the decade-long price boom, and softening demand are the main factors behind the continued weakness. The appreciation of the U.S. dollar, the currency in which most commodities are traded, has also contributed to the price weakness.

- *Oil.* The price of oil (simple average of Brent, Dubai, and West Texas Intermediate)

dropped below $40 per barrel towards the end of 2015. Prices have been driven lower by high stocks in OECD economies, ample global supplies, and expectations of slower global demand (particularly from large emerging markets). U.S. crude oil production has begun to decline due to lower investment and drilling but was resilient for most of 2015. OPEC production increased further, reaching a three year high, with much of the increase coming from Saudi Arabia and Iraq. A removal of sanctions following the implementation of the Iran nuclear agreement could increase Iranian oil exports by 0.5-0.7 million barrels per day by 2016, nearing the pre-sanctions level of 4 percent of global consumption. Since other energy prices are at least partially linked to oil prices, prices for other energy products, including natural gas, have also fallen.

- *Metals.* The slump in metal prices, which reached their lowest levels in more than 6 years in November, reflects well-supplied markets as well as weaker growth in major emerging markets. New mining capacity came into operation in several countries, especially Australia, adding to already abundant supplies.

- *Agricultural commodities.* Grain and oilseed prices dipped in 2015, mostly in response to well-supplied markets, with the agricultural price index standing 33 percent below its early -2011 high as of November. The stocks-to-use ratio (a measure of how well supplied markets are) for key grains remains well above its 5- and 10-year average levels. Ample supplies and the weak influence of global food prices on most local prices, suggest that the El Niño weather pattern, which some forecasts say may be the strongest since 1997-98, is unlikely to raise global food commodity prices in a significant way (World Bank 2015c).

Conditions remain in place for a protracted period of low commodity prices in coming years. Oil prices are projected to average $49 per barrel in 2016, and then rise only gradually. Metal and agricultural prices are likely to edge up in the range of 1-2 percent. While geopolitical risks and adverse weather conditions could lead to a more rapid recovery in prices, risks are on the downside. In the case of oil, prices may come under renewed downward pressure if weakness in emerging and developing economies persists or if the Islamic Republic of Iran receives substantial foreign investment to expand capacity quickly (Iran has the world's largest proven natural gas reserves, and fourth largest oil reserves). These developments suggest continued significant headwinds for the outlook for growth, fiscal positions, and trade of commodity-exporting countries, emphasizing the need to accelerate the diversification of their economies.

Global trade weakness

Global merchandise trade contracted in the first half of 2015, for the first time since 2009 (Figure 1.10). This was largely driven by a drop in import demand from emerging and developing economies, including in East Asia and the Pacific, Europe and Central Asia, and Latin America and the Caribbean. Growing import demand from the United States and the Euro Area did not offset the drop in developing countries' import demand, which now accounts for half of global trade.

The contraction in import demand from emerging and developing economies reflected four trends:

- *GDP contractions in Brazil and the Russian Federation.* Recessions in these two countries sharply reduced import demand. Sanctions against the Russian Federation further restricted trade. More generally, sharp declines in commodity prices reduced export revenues and demand across commodity exporters, leading to a significant slowdown in imports from these countries.

- *Rebalancing in China.* As a result of an increasingly pronounced shift in sources of growth from trade-intensive investment and exports toward less trade-intensive consumption and services, import growth has slowed.

- *Currency depreciations.* Real effective exchange rate depreciations have been accompanied by a decline in imports in several countries, but

FIGURE 1.9 Commodity markets

By end-2015, the three World Bank industrial commodity price indexes—energy, metals, and agricultural raw materials—were down, on average, 45 percent from their 2011 peaks. Oil prices declined further in the second half of 2015, despite large reductions in investment and drilling in U.S. shale oil. The agreement with the Islamic Republic of Iran over its nuclear program could provide a boost to its oil exports. Metal prices continued to reflect well-supplied markets and weaker demand from major emerging markets. The strong El Niño weather pattern may affect numerous local markets but it is unlikely to have major effects on global food prices given well-supplied markets.

A. Commodity prices

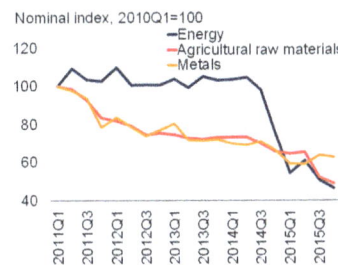

B. Islamic Republic of Iran's oil production

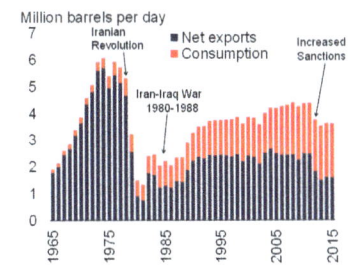

C. Oil consumption growth

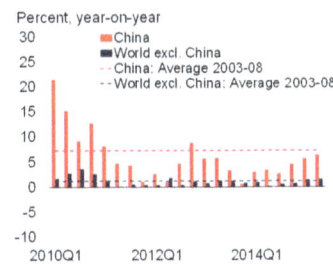

D. Refined metal consumption growth

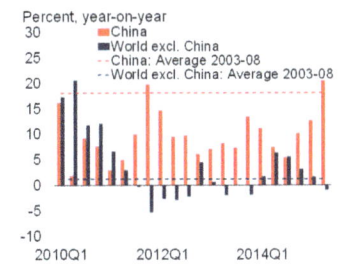

E. El Niño index

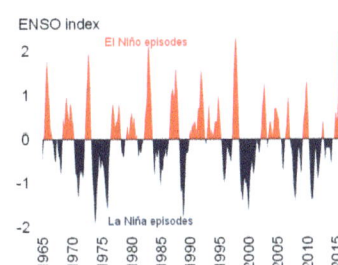

F. Stock-to-use ratios

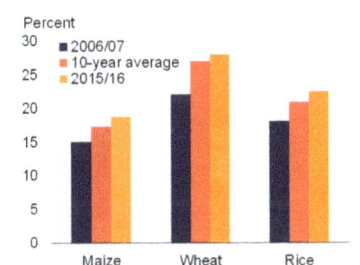

Sources: Baker Hughes; BP Statistical Review of World Energy; World Bank; World Bureau of Metal Statistics.
A. Last observation is 2015Q4.
B. Last observation is 2015.
C. D. Last observation is 2015Q2.
E. The ENSO (El Niño Southern Oscillation) index represents a centered three-month mean SST (Sea Surface Temperature) anomaly for the Niño 3.4 region. Latest historical observation is October 2015. November 2015 through June 2016 are forecasts.
F. The stocks-to-use ratio indicates the level of stocks for any given commodity as a percentage of consumption. Latest observation is November 2015.

have thus far shown limited benefits for exports. This may partly reflect changes in global value chains that may be reducing the elasticity of exports to real effective appreciation (Ahmed, Appendino, and Ruta 2015).

FIGURE 1.10 Global trade slowdown

Global merchandise trade slowed considerably in 2015, driven by a deceleration in import demand from large emerging markets. China's rebalancing away from import- and commodity-intensive sectors and economic contraction in Brazil and Russia appear to have played a particularly significant role. Given the rising importance of "south-south" trade flows, developing-country exports have been negatively affected. Currency depreciations have thus far shown limited benefits for exports, which could partly reflect a reduced exchange rate elasticity. Slower value chain integration could also be factor capping trade opportunities for developing countries.

A. Global merchandise trade growth

B. Merchandise import growth

C. Contribution to global import growth

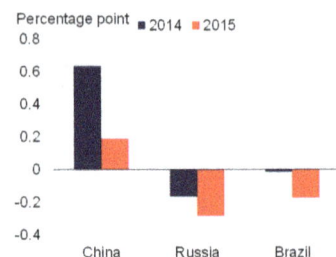

D. Composition of global import demand

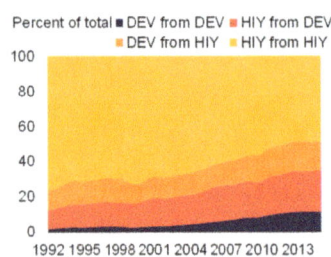

E. Elasticity of exports to change in real effective exchange rate

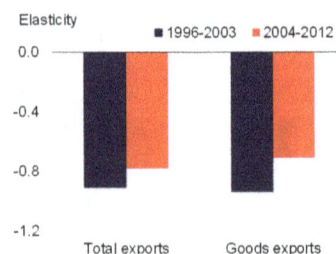

F. Export growth and value chain integration

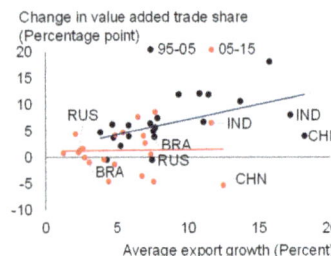

Sources: World Bank, IMF Direction of Trade Statistics (DOTS); CPB Netherlands Bureau for Economic Policy Analysis; Organization for Economic Co-operation and Development, TiVA; Ahmed, Appendino, and Ruta (2015).
A. Global merchandise trade measured in real term (deflated by unit value indexes); average of global imports and exports. Grey areas indicate period of global trade contraction. Last observation is October, 2015.
B. Merchandise import volumes. Recently-graduated high-income countries (Argentina, Chile, Hungary, and the Russian Federation) are included in the developing country aggregate. Last observation is October, 2015.
C. Import volumes for goods and non-factor services. 2015 are estimates.
D. HIY are high-income countries, DEV are developing countries. Based on bilateral trade flows between G20 economies. Recently-graduated high-income countries (Argentina, Chile, Hungary, the Russian Federation and República Bolivariana de Venezuela) are included in the developing-country aggregate.
E. Elasticities derived from a panel model regressing annual real export growth over annual real exchange rate growth across 46 countries and over the period 1996-2012 as in Ahmed, Appendino, and Ruta (2015).
F. Value chain integration measured as share of foreign value added in gross exports. Change in value added trade share is computed from 2005 to 2011 (latest available data).

However, conventional trade, which still represents roughly half of global trade flows, shows greater responsiveness to exchange rate developments (IMF 2015a).

- *Stabilization of value chains.* During 1990-2008, countries that were integrating faster into global value chains also saw more rapid export growth than others (Escaith and Miroudot 2015). Since then, value chains appear to have stabilized such that manufacturing sub-sectors with a higher degree of vertical specialization witnessed the largest deceleration in trade growth (Constantinescu, Mattoo, and Ruta 2015, World Bank 2015d).

Estimates for trade flows in 2015 and forecasts for 2016-17 have been revised down, in line with the weakened post-crisis relationship between trade and activity.[3] Persistent weakness in global trade diminishes export opportunities but also the scope for productivity gains through increasing specialization and diffusion of technologies. This could continue to put a cap on growth prospects, particularly among smaller and more open developing economies. Renewed liberalization efforts could help reinvigorate trade.[4] The Trans-Pacific Partnership (TPP), agreed at the technical level between Australia, Brunei, Canada, Chile, Japan, Malaysia, Mexico, New Zealand, Peru, Singapore, the United States, and Vietnam, could provide a new impetus to trade, and lift activity, by helping to reduce tariffs and other trade barriers (Chapter 4). By 2030, the TPP could lift member country GDP by an average of 1.1 percent, with much larger benefits in countries with currently high trade barriers like Vietnam and Malaysia. The spillover effects for non-members remain uncertain. Losses due to preference erosion and trade diversion could be partially offset by positive spillovers from regulatory convergence.

[3]The post-crisis slowdown in global trade has been attributed to a number of factors including (i) anemic growth in advanced economies, (ii) the changing composition of global demand and persistent weakness in investment, (iii) the maturation of global value chains, (iv) weak trade finance and (v) slow trade liberalization momentum (World Bank 2015a).

[4]According to some estimates, removing all tariffs, state aid, export subsidies and other trade restrictions affecting LDCs could boost their exports by up to 30 percent (Evenett and Fritz 2015).

Developing countries

Growth in developing countries slowed to 4.3 percent in 2015, reflecting domestic and external challenges. Domestic difficulties included slowing productivity growth, policy uncertainty, and eroding policy buffers that have led to contractionary monetary and fiscal policies in some countries. External headwinds include persistently low commodity prices, subdued global trade, spillovers from weakness in major emerging markets, decelerating capital flows and rising borrowing costs. The slowdown reflects both cyclical and structural components. Commodity exporters have continued to adjust to steep declines in oil and other commodity prices. In low-income countries, however, growth has remained robust, as solid infrastructure investment and consumer spending has partly offset weakening external demand. The modest pickup in activity in developing countries expected in 2016 and 2017 is predicated on continued growth momentum in high-income countries, stabilization of commodity prices, still-accommodative monetary policy in major economies, and a steady process of rebalancing in China.

Recent developments

Developing-country growth slowed in 2015 to 4.3 percent, its weakest showing since 2009, and a pace well below its pre-crisis average (Figure 1.11). China's economy continued to slow in an orderly fashion, and its rebalancing away from import and commodity-intensive activities has had repercussions for global trade and commodity prices. Brazil and the Russian Federation have taken a turn for the worse as a result of global and domestic headwinds, with both countries experiencing deepening contractions, above-target inflation, and deteriorating public finances. In South Africa, chronic power supply bottlenecks are a major factor behind weak growth. In contrast to other major developing countries, growth in India remained robust, buoyed by strong investor sentiment and the positive effect on real incomes of the recent fall in oil prices.

The fact that four of the five BRICS are experiencing slowing or contracting activity, as are a substantial fraction of other developing countries, highlights the synchronous nature of

FIGURE 1.11 Growth in emerging and developing economies

Growth in emerging and developing economies slowed to post-crisis low in 2015. The deceleration was driven by external and domestic factors and was highly synchronous. Investor confidence and credit ratings have been adversely affected by deteriorating growth prospects, particularly among commodity-exporting countries. The recent slowdown partly results from the unwinding of cyclically strong post-crisis growth but also has a structural component across many developing regions.

A. GDP Growth

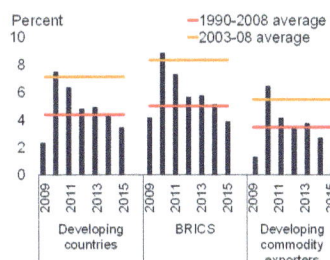

B. Share of countries experiencing three consecutive years of declining growth

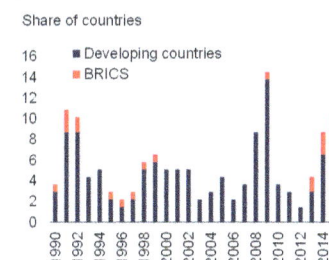

C. Sovereign credit ratings

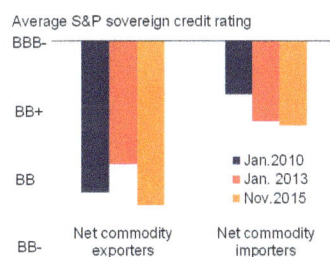

D. Cyclical and structural growth slowdown in developing countries

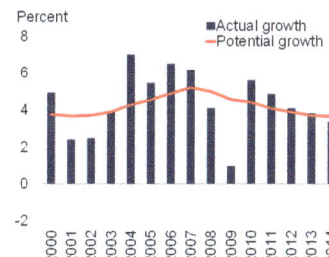

Sources: World Bank; Standard & Poor's; Haver Analytics; Didier et al. (2015).
A. B. Recently-graduated high-income countries (Argentina, Chile, Hungary, the Russian Federation, and República Bolivariana de Venezuela) are included in the developing country aggregate.
B. Figure shows share of emerging and developing countries slowing for three consecutive years out of a sample of 138 countries.
C. Latest observation is November, 2015.
D. Unweighted average of emerging market economies. Potential growth defined as in Didier et al. (2015).

the ongoing deceleration in developing countries—more so than in any episode over the past 25 years, with the exception of the Great Recession of 2009.[5]

In about half of developing countries, growth in 2015 is likely to fall short of expectations, with the largest disappointments among energy exporters (Angola, Colombia, Ecuador, Kazakhstan, Nigeria, the Russian Federation, the República Bolivariana de Venezuela) and countries experiencing conflicts (Ukraine) or policy

---

[5]The impact of the BRICS on other emerging and developing economies is discussed in more detail in Chapter 3.

uncertainty (Brazil). In contrast, the continued recovery in the Euro Area has lifted growth more than expected in some of its developing country trading partners, including those in Europe and Central Asia and North Africa.

Both external factors—including weak global trade, financial market volatility, and persistently low commodity prices—and domestic factors have contributed to the slowdown. Adverse external developments have continued to hit commodity-exporting developing economies particularly hard. Growth in several of the largest ones (Brazil, Colombia, Nigeria, Peru, South Africa) weakened considerably in 2015, as the impact of deteriorating terms of trade on exports was compounded by tightening macroeconomic policy and softening investor confidence. Governments responded to falling fiscal revenues from the resource sector with spending cuts. Central banks raised interest rates to help moderate pressures on exchange or inflation rates. Investor confidence weakened on deteriorating growth prospects and credit ratings, resulting in declining capital inflows and currency depreciations.

The recent slowdown in developing-country growth partly reflects an unwinding of cyclically strong, policy-supported, post-crisis growth, especially in East Asia and Pacific and in Latin America and the Caribbean. However, it also has a considerable structural component, which is most pronounced in Europe and Central Asia and the Middle East and North Africa. On average, among the 24 largest emerging and developing economies, about one-third of the slowdown between 2010 and 2014 was structural in nature (Didier et al. 2015). In particular, demographic trends have passed a turning point since the global crisis—with potentially profound implications for growth (World Bank 2015b). Since 2010, working-age population growth has slowed, particularly in Europe and Central Asia and the Middle East and North Africa. As a result, the share of the working-age population has risen only marginally or fallen in most regions other than Sub-Saharan Africa, where many countries are still in a phase of pre- or early demographic dividends. Other domestic sources of the slowdown include

slowing productivity growth, continued domestic policy uncertainty, and—as discussed in detail later—eroding policy buffers that narrowed policy options.

- *Slowing productivity growth.* Total factor productivity (TFP) growth in emerging markets has declined steadily since 2010. By 2014, TFP growth had returned to its long-term average of around 0.5 percent, well below the 2.3 percent gain recorded in 2010 (Didier et al. 2015). The TFP slowdown was pronounced in the Middle East and North Africa, where TFP has been contracting since 2007. In Latin America and the Caribbean, and Eastern Europe and Central Asia TFP growth has ground to a virtual halt.

- *Policy uncertainty.* Domestic policy uncertainty increased in 2015 (including in Latin America, East Asia and the Pacific, and Europe and Central Asia), as a result of elections, or political unrest. Among low-income countries, a flare-up of violence (Afghanistan), political tensions (Burkina Faso, Burundi, Guinea Bissau, Nepal), and uncertainty surrounding elections and labor disputes (Benin, Democratic Republic of Congo) drove up political risk in 2015. Concerns about policy direction can hold back domestic and foreign investors, reduce capital flows and dampen investment and consumption growth (Gourio, Siemer, and Verdelhan 2014; Julio and Yook 2013).

Policy uncertainty and the removal of policy stimulus have weighed on investment and consumption growth rates, which have fallen well below pre-crisis levels. Growth of credit to the private sector has slowed sharply in several countries (Figure 1.12). In some places, credit retrenchment reflects monetary policy tightening to mitigate inflation concerns (Brazil, South Africa) and slowing capital inflows, weighing further on domestic liquidity and credit conditions. Other reasons behind the slowdown in credit growth include weak domestic demand, heightened uncertainty, and the government's decision to reduce the use of public credit as a counter-cyclical tool. In several countries, consumption growth has been further dampened by rising unemployment rates (including Brazil and South Africa), and moderating employment growth.

Partly reflecting uncertainty about the outlook, consumption growth remains below its pre-crisis and long-term averages, despite increased real incomes due to declines in food inflation and oil prices. In several countries, these developments have sharply reduced headline inflation, especially in countries with a large share of food in their consumption baskets (India, Pakistan, the Philippines). In some regions and countries (Europe and Central Asia, Thailand), falling food and oil prices have coincided with persistent economic slack and played a role in lowering inflation below target rates.

Low-income countries have generally remained resilient, growing by 5.1 percent in 2015. Large-scale infrastructure investment and sustained consumer spending helped offset weakening external demand and low commodity prices. Even so, commodity-exporting low-income countries faced currency pressures, which contributed to a sharp increase in interest rates in Uganda and a decline in reserves in many countries (Burundi, Democratic Republic of Congo, Mozambique, Tanzania, Zimbabwe).

Eroding buffers and lingering vulnerabilities

Weakening activity in developing countries has been accompanied by eroding policy space and lingering vulnerabilities (Figure 1.13). Slowing growth, rising debt, and, for commodity exporters, weakening export and fiscal revenues, have eroded credit ratings. Some large emerging and developing economies lost, or risked losing, investment grade status in 2015 (Brazil, the Russian Federation), and some others appeared to be struggling to maintain it.

Eroding policy space. As growth has slowed and as authorities have supported economic activity with fiscal stimulus and monetary policy loosening, policy buffers have eroded. Fiscal

FIGURE 1.12 Domestic demand conditions in developing countries

Credit growth has slowed, but private sector debt remains high in many countries. Investment and private consumption growth in emerging and developing economies has been below pre-crisis rates. Rising unemployment has weighed on consumer confidence and spending in some countries, despite the increase in real incomes resulting from falling food and energy inflation.

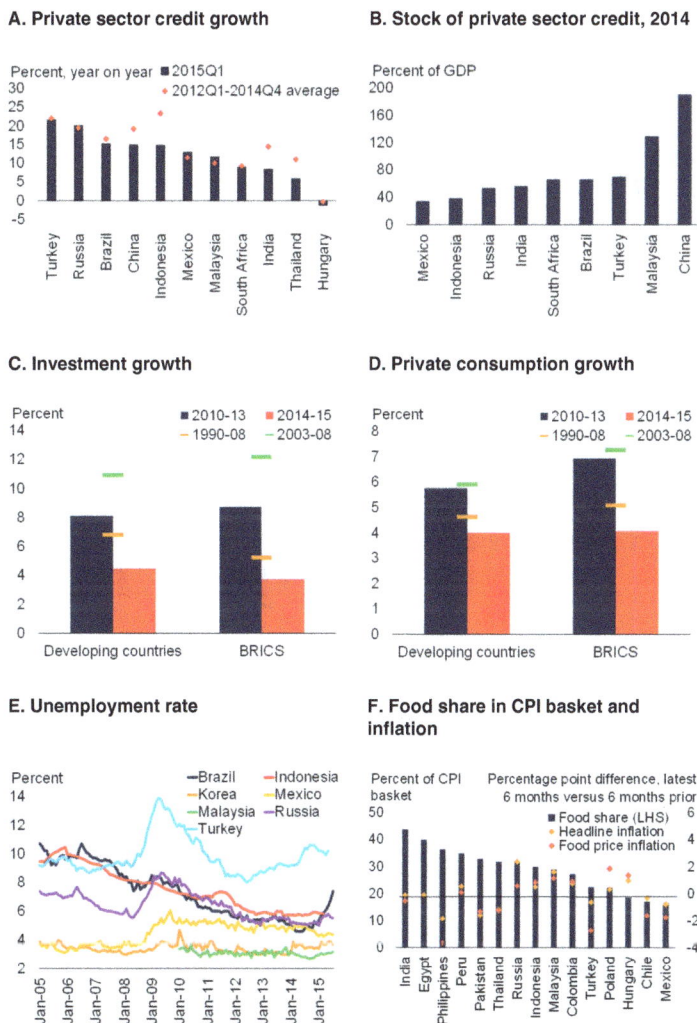

A. Private sector credit growth

B. Stock of private sector credit, 2014

C. Investment growth

D. Private consumption growth

E. Unemployment rate

F. Food share in CPI basket and inflation

Sources: World Bank; Bank for International Settlements; International Labor Organization; Haver Analytics.
C. D. Recently-graduated high-income countries (Argentina, Chile, Hungary, the Russian Federation, and República Bolivariana de Venezuela) are included in the developing country aggregate.
E. Unemployment rate data is seasonally adjusted. Latest observation November, 2015.
F. Right vertical axis shows percentage point difference in average year-over-year inflation from April to October 2015 versus October 2014 to April 2015.

deficits have widened from pre-crisis levels in commodity exporters and importers alike (World Bank 2015d,e). Inflation, especially in commodity exporters, has risen outside target bands and external and foreign currency debt has increased. With shrinking policy room, domestic policy stimulus has been gradually withdrawn.

FIGURE 1.13 Macro-financial vulnerabilities

Current account balances have improved modestly among oil importers, but deteriorated among exporters. Countries with elevated external debt or with a high share of short-term external debt have made only limited progress in reducing these exposures. More countries have seen government debt and the sustainability gap deteriorate from pre-crisis levels. Fiscal balances have worsened rapidly among oil and other commodity exporters in 2015 .

A. Current account balance

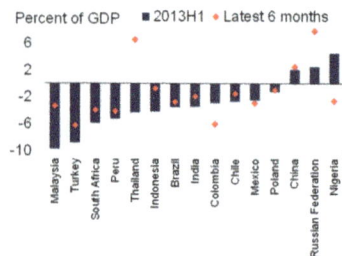

B. External debt denominated in foreign currency

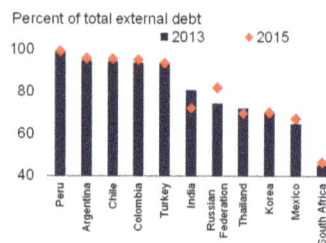

C. Short-term share of external debt

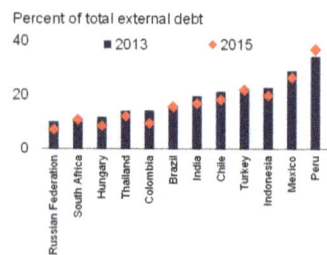

D. Foreign reserve coverage

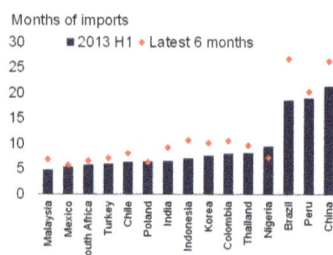

E. General government sustainability gaps

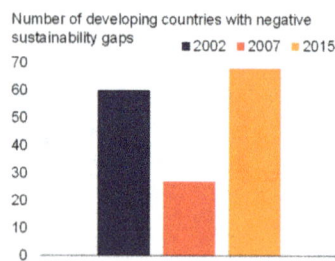

F. Projected fiscal balances, 2015

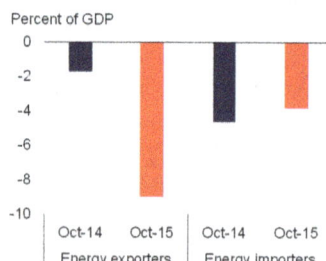

Source: World Bank, World Bank QEDS database; IMF World Economic Outlook October 2014 and October 2015.
A. Latest observation is 2015 Q3 for most countries.
D. Latest observation is October, 2015 for most countries.
E. Sustainability gap is defined as the difference between the actual primary balance and the debt-stabilizing primary balance at current interest rates and growth rates. A negative sustainability gaps indicates an unsustainable stock of debt and deficit. Figure reflects data for the 123 developing countries with available data for all three years shown.
F. Structural fiscal balance projections from October 2014 and October 2015 IMF World Economic Outlook reports.

Weakening corporate balance sheets. Corporate leverage has grown significantly since 2009. It has become increasingly concentrated in sectors more exposed to business cycle swings, such as

construction and mining, and among firms with weakening balance sheets (IMF 2015b). Corporate debt has been increasingly financed through international bond issuance rather than bank lending. In some cases this has meant rising currency exposures, with debt service costs more sensitive to changing global financing conditions. Past experience suggests that rising corporate leverage increases the probability of capital flow reversals (Mendoza 2010; Mendoza and Terrones 2008; Elekdag and Wu 2011). Finally, many developing-country banking sectors with high non-performing loan ratios have not seen much improvement in asset quality.

Large external debt. Some developing countries with elevated total external debt, or with a high share of short-term external debt, have made little progress in reducing such burdens (the Czech Republic, Malaysia, Mongolia, South Africa, Turkey). India, Mexico, and South Africa have reduced the share of their external debt denominated in foreign currency but still carry sizable stocks. As monetary policy tightens in the United States, some of these countries may be vulnerable to rollover, exchange rate, and interest rate risks (Borio 2014, IMF 2015b). Foreign reserves have come under pressure in many commodity exporters (Indonesia, Malaysia), and in countries which are prone to capital flow reversals (Turkey). Current account balances have improved among a number of oil-importing economies, although deficits remain elevated for several of them.

Deteriorating public sector balance sheets. General government debt has increased in many developing countries. Fiscal deficits have deteriorated considerably more than expected in commodity exporters, while remaining broadly steady in other developing countries. As a result, the number of countries in which debt is rising has surged from pre-crisis levels. In a number of developing countries (Indonesia, Peru, Poland, South Africa, Turkey), foreign participation in government debt markets remains elevated, making them potentially vulnerable to global shifts in investor sentiment (Arslanalp and Tsuda 2014).

These vulnerabilities are further constraining policy room to support weakening activity (see Section on developing country policies). Large fiscal deficits and high government debt dampen the effectiveness of fiscal stimulus (World Bank 2015d, Figure 1.14). Rising foreign currency-denominated debts, or rollover requirements generate risks from sharp depreciations or from spikes in interest rates (Chow et al. 2015). This requires central banks to take financial stability into greater account than otherwise when considering monetary stimulus to support activity, even when inflation expectations are anchored.

Outlook

Baseline projections assume that 2015 marked a low point for developing country growth (Figure 1.15). Growth is expected to rise to 4.8 percent in 2016, similar to the pace in 2014, and to 5.3 percent in 2017 and 2018. This modest improvement is predicated on continued momentum in high-income countries, a stabilization of commodity prices, still-accommodative monetary policy in major economies with no bouts of financial market turbulence, and a continued gradual slowdown in China. With stabilizing commodity prices, growth in commodity exporters is expected to resume.

Among low-income countries, growth is mostly steady or rising. However, forecasts for 2016 have been downgraded for some countries from previous projections, reflecting lower commodity prices and rising security and political tensions in some countries.

The persistent growth slowdown in emerging and developing economies has led to repeated forecast downgrades. The largest emerging markets are among the countries subject to significant downward revisions to their long-term forecasts in recent years. Many of the factors underpinning the slowdowns – low commodity prices, weak global trade, and slow productivity growth – are expected to persist (World Bank 2015e, World Trade Organization 2015). Also, developing countries will likely face rising borrowing costs. In particular, countries with large borrowing needs and high levels of dollar-denominated debt could be adversely impacted by rising U.S. interest rates.

FIGURE 1.14 Monetary and fiscal policy space

Fiscal stimulus becomes less effective as fiscal deficits widen. Real policy rates in many commodity exporting countries may still be below levels implied by Taylor rules. This constrains central banks' ability to respond to weakening growth with policy accommodation.

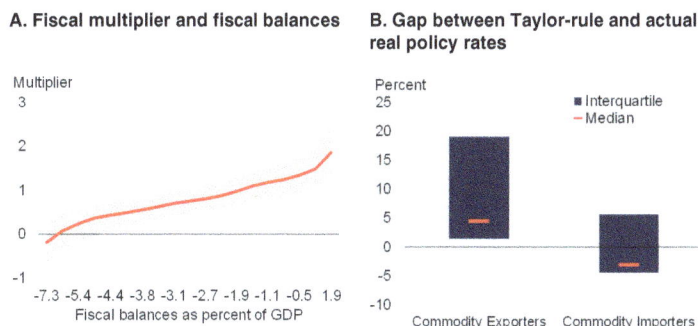

A. Fiscal multiplier and fiscal balances

B. Gap between Taylor-rule and actual real policy rates

Source: World Bank.
A. Fiscal multipliers for different levels of fiscal balance (in percent of GDP) after two years, estimated from an IPVAR model using a sample of 15 emerging and frontier markets. Values on the x-axis correspond to percentiles of the fiscal balance; shaded area is the 16-84 percent confidence band. Fiscal multipliers are larger (fiscal stimulus is more effective), when fiscal deficits are lower.
B. Real policy rate and inflation target data are for October 2015, expected inflation as of September 2015. Taylor rules stipulate how much central banks should change interest rates in response to deviations from policy objectives (inflation target or others). The real Taylor rule interest rate is calculated as 1.353*(expected inflation - inflation target) + 2.233 (Ostry, Ghosh, and Chamon 2012). A positive gap denotes current policy rates below those implied by the Taylor rule.

FIGURE 1.15 Developing-country outlook

Developing-country and emerging-market growth is expected to recover somewhat in 2016. However, Brazil and Russia are expected to see further contractions, which will exert a drag on trading partners' activity. Among low-income countries, the pace of growth is expected to be steady or increasing. Persistent slowdown in emerging and developing economies have resulted in a significant downgrade of their underlying growth potential in recent years.

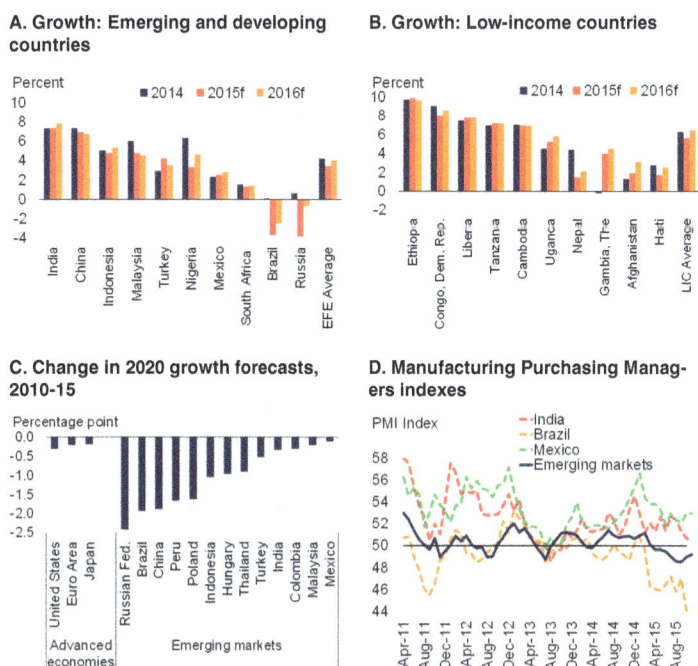

A. Growth: Emerging and developing countries

B. Growth: Low-income countries

C. Change in 2020 growth forecasts, 2010-15

D. Manufacturing Purchasing Managers indexes

Sources: World Bank; Haver Analytics; Consensus Economics.
C. Figure shows percentage-point revision to 2020 forecast between October 2010 and October 2015.
D. Latest data as of November 2015.

FIGURE 1.16 Regional outlook

There is considerable heterogeneity in regional developments and outlooks. In the East Asia and Pacific region, growth remains sustained and inflation generally subdued. In Europe and Central Asia, the eastern part is negatively affected by developments in Russia while the western part is benefits from the recovery in the Euro Area. Low commodity prices and domestic challenges will continue to weigh on growth in Latin America and the Caribbean, the Middle East and North Africa, and Sub-Saharan Africa. Currency and fiscal pressures are building in 2015 in commodity-exporting regions.

A. Developing regions: Growth

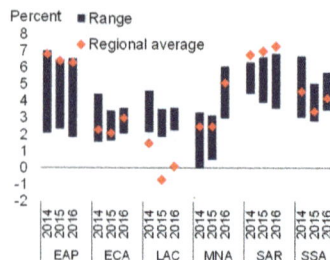

B. Developing regions: Inflation in 2015

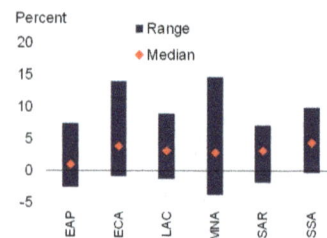

C. Developing regions: Commodity exports

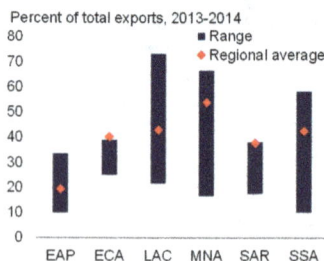

D. Developing regions: Fiscal deficits

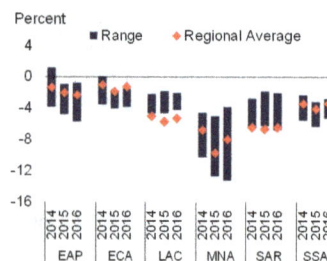

Sources: World Bank; Haver Analytics; IMF World Economic Outlook October 2015.
A.D. "Range" denotes range from lowest quartile to highest quartile among countries in each region. Regional averages are GDP-weighted.

Underneath these broad trends, there is considerable heterogeneity in regional growth outlooks (Figure 1.16). In the East Asia and Pacific region, a gradual slowdown is underway. In Europe and Central Asia, weakness in the eastern part, mainly due to developments in Ukraine and spillovers from Russia, is offsetting improvements in the western part resulting from recovery in the Euro Area. In Latin America and the Caribbean, persistently weak commodity prices and domestic challenges will continue to weigh on regional growth. In the Middle East and North Africa, an international agreement expected to lift international sanctions on the Islamic Republic of Iran is pushing up regional growth. South Asia

will be a bright spot, reflecting improved conditions in India. And growth in Sub-Saharan Africa will continue to be negatively impacted by low commodity prices and infrastructure constraints, although low-income countries are expected to remain resilient.

- *East Asia and Pacific.* Growth is estimated to have slowed to 6.4 percent in 2015, and is expected to decelerate to 6.3 on average in 2016-18, reflecting the gradual slowdown in China and a sluggish recovery in the rest of the region. Growth is expected to rise modestly in Indonesia and Malaysia in 2016-18, as political tensions subside in Malaysia, and reforms are implemented to spur investment growth in Indonesia. In Thailand, growth is expected to remain weak, at 2-2.7 percent in 2016-18, as political uncertainty continues to weigh on private investment, and high household debt constrains private consumption. Among the large developing ASEAN economies, growth in the Philippines and Vietnam will benefit from rising household incomes caused by low commodity prices, a diversified and competitive export base (Vietnam), and investment driven by robust FDI flows. Risks to the outlook remain tilted to the downside, stemming from a larger-than-expected slowdown in China and tightening global financing conditions.

- *Europe and Central Asia.* Growth is estimated to have dipped to 2.1 percent in 2015—the slowest rate since 2009. This reflects the combination of an unexpectedly sharp output contraction in Ukraine, slowdown in all major energy-exporting economies of the region, and negative regional spillovers from Russia. Growth in Ukraine may start rebounding, helped by easing tensions and the IMF-supported stabilization program. Economic activity in Turkey will benefit from low fuel prices, but will face headwinds from tepid export demand (including negative effects from Russian sanctions) and tighter external financing conditions. Regional growth is projected to strengthen to an average of 3.0 percent in 2016 and 3.5 per cent in 2017-18, helped in part by the ongoing Euro Area recovery, though there are several downside risks to the outlook, including possible escalation of geopolitical tensions and continued recession in Russia and Ukraine.

- *Latin America and the Caribbean.* After three years of slowing growth, activity in the broader region is estimated to have contracted by 0.9 percent in 2015, as it grappled with the protracted decline of commodity prices and domestic challenges weighing on the region's largest economies. Declining demand and wage rigidities have led to deteriorating labor market conditions and rising unemployment (World Bank 2015f). However, there are substantial differences among the sub-regions. Bearing the brunt of the slump in commodity prices, along with domestic headwinds, developing South America's output is estimated to have declined 2.1 percent in 2015, including a contraction of 3.7 percent in Brazil. In contrast, estimated growth rates for developing Central and North America and the Caribbean were significantly more favorable, at 2.7 and 3.3 percent, respectively. For the region as a whole, stagnation is still predicted in 2016, followed by a modest recovery of about 2.2 percent in 2017-18, as commodity prices stabilize and some of the policy challenges in large economies subside. The current recession in Brazil is expected to extend into 2016 reflecting tight macroeconomic policy and, particularly, a loss of consumer and investor confidence partly due to political uncertainty. Although weighed down by low oil prices and associated fiscal pressures, growth is expected to pick up in Colombia and Mexico thanks to robust demand from the U.S. market, dividends from implementation of structural reforms (Mexico), and a peace agreement with insurgents (Colombia).

- *Middle East and North Africa.* Growth is estimated at 2.5 percent in 2015, unchanged from 2014. Among oil exporters, growth mostly slowed or was negative in 2015. The one exception was Iraq, where oil production has risen despite security problems. Oil

exporters are grappling with the economic consequences of low oil prices; most oil importers are seeing benefits. Despite low oil prices, growth in the region will accelerate to above 5 percent in 2016-18. The improvement is predicated on a strong recovery in the Islamic Republic of Iran, the region's largest developing economy. The international agreement to suspend or remove sanctions on international trade and financial transactions, beginning in 2016, is an important supporting factor for the Iranian economy (Devarajan and Mottaghi 2015). The agreement stands to have positive spillover effects for oil-importing neighboring countries, but might have negative effects on developing oil exporters in the region if additional oil production and exports put downward pressure on international oil prices (Ianchovichina, Devarajan, and Lakatos forthcoming). Risks to the regional outlook are tilted to the downside and arise from both low oil prices and protracted domestic security challenges.

- *South Asia.* Growth is projected to accelerate to 7.5 percent in 2016-18, from 7.0 percent in 2015—the fastest pace among all developing regions. Falling oil prices have improved investor and consumer confidence, and domestic policy reforms in India and Pakistan have reduced vulnerabilities. Domestic risks include a stalling of the reform process and political tensions in some countries. High levels of problem loans on bank balance sheets remain a challenge to financial stability and to the supply of credit for productive investment (World Bank 2015g). External risks stem from potential volatility amid tightening global financial conditions and weak remittances from Gulf Cooperation Council (GCC) countries.

- *Sub-Saharan Africa.* Growth slowed to an estimated 3.4 percent in 2015, the lowest rate since 2009, due to low commodity prices and infrastructure constraints. A rebound is expected in 2016-18, as these headwinds wane, providing some support for government spending and private investment. A modest

FIGURE 1.17 Slowdown in China

Downside risks to Chinese growth have risen, debt levels are elevated and continued to increase despite decelerating credit growth. Total debt as a percent of GDP is now significantly larger that in most other emerging and developing economies. However, ample policy buffers, large international reserves and current account surpluses limit the risk of sharp adjustment. Should the slowdown be more abrupt than currently predicted, other emerging and developing economies and, in particular, commodity exporters would be most affected.

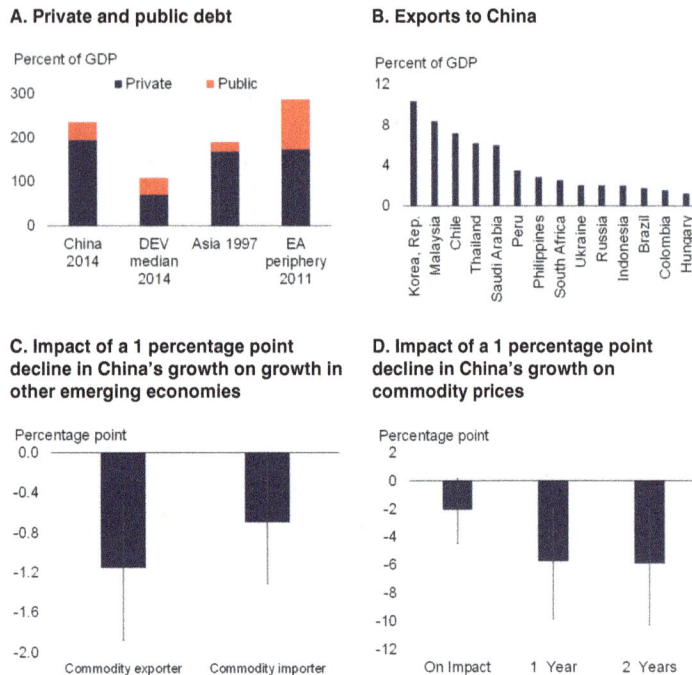

A. Private and public debt

B. Exports to China

C. Impact of a 1 percentage point decline in China's growth on growth in other emerging economies

D. Impact of a 1 percentage point decline in China's growth on commodity prices

Sources: Haver Analytics; IMF Direction of Trade Statistics (DOTS); Bank for International Settlements; World Bank.
A. "DEV median" refers to the median value across developing countries in 2014. EA is Euro Area.
C. D. Cumulated impulse responses for different horizons due to a one-off (but persistent) unexpected 1 percentage-point decline in Chinese growth. Commodity exporters are defined as those countries for which commodity exports exceed 30 percent of total exports during the estimation period, 1998-2014. Confidence bands span the 16th-84th percentiles.
D. Cumulated impulse responses of trade-weighted commodity prices at different horizons due to a 1 percentage point decline in China growth. Confidence bands span the 16th-84th percentiles.

recovery is projected in Nigeria and South Africa, the region's two largest economies. For Nigeria, the forecast assumes that uncertainty around government policy is lessened; that fuel and power shortages become less severe; that fiscal consolidation tapers off; and that import costs decline. In South Africa, labor and social tensions, high unemployment, and constraints associated with electricity supply will continue to weigh on activity. However, low-income countries may register relatively high growth, supported by large-scale infrastructure investment and resilient consumer spending. Overall, growth in the region is projected to accelerate to 4.2 percent in 2016, strengthening further to 4.7 percent

in 2017-18. Overvalued currencies and larger fiscal and current account deficits over the period 2011-14 have eroded policy buffers, thus limiting policy options should shocks arise (World Bank 2015h).

Risks to the outlook

Downside risks dominate and have become increasingly centered on emerging and developing countries, as a gradual recovery in major high-income countries takes hold. A slowdown in China, and widespread weakness across other BRICS, could have substantial spillovers on other emerging and developing economies. Financial market turbulence—triggered, for instance, by spikes in borrowing costs during the U.S. tightening cycle or by rising risk aversion—could significantly impact capital flows to the more vulnerable emerging and developing economies and intensify balance-sheet vulnerabilities. Commodity exporters and countries with large imbalances and policy uncertainty are particularly exposed to these risks. While past experience suggests that isolated terrorism-related events amid heightened global geopolitical risks do not appear to have lasting economic consequences, escalation could have uncertain regional and global repercussions. As yet, unrealized gains from declining oil prices for importers pose an upside risk.

Global growth prospects have become more uncertain, and risks are more skewed to the downside, than in the June 2015 forecasts. Rising uncertainty is evidenced by heightened volatility in global financial markets and a greater dispersion of private sector forecasts for global growth, interest rates, and inflation. While the balance of risks to global growth remains tilted to the downside, the likelihood of a global recession in 2016 appears to be low, as world GDP per capita (measured in 2010 US$) was still growing by an estimated 1.5 percent in 2015.[6] The downside

---

[6]A global recession corresponds to a contraction in world real output per capita accompanied by a broad, simultaneous decline in various other measures of global economic activity, including industrial production, trade, capital flows, employment, and energy consumption. This has happened four times over the past half century: in 1975, 1982, 1991, and 2009. The world economy also experienced two periods—in 1998 and 2001—when growth slowed significantly without tipping into an outright recession (Kose and Terroes 2015).

risks do though have the potential to exert a significant drag on global growth.

Slowdown in China

Although the growth slowdown in China continues to be gradual, downside risks to growth may have increased. Baseline growth forecasts are predicated on the assumption that reforms will continue, and that the authorities will maintain sufficient buffers to ensure an orderly rebalancing.

Domestically, the main short-term risk is the unwinding of high leverage in sectors with excess capacity. This may cause a sharper-than-expected slowdown in investment, especially in residential estate, and hence in aggregate demand (Figure 1.17). Debt levels are high and continue to rise despite decelerating credit growth. Total (public and private) debt relative to GDP is larger than in most other developing countries, and is also above levels observed in economies affected by the Asian crisis in 1997. However, public debt is estimated at less than 40 percent of GDP—or 60 percent if off-budget liabilities are included—and is predominantly held domestically. This provides the government with the fiscal space to deploy stimulus in the event of a sharper-than-expected slowdown (IMF 2015c).

Capital controls on portfolio investment and bank lending, as well as a largely state-owned financial system, limit the risk of financial instability and disorderly capital outflows. If reduced confidence in the financial system leads to attempts to convert local currency deposits into foreign currency, the resulting spike in demand for foreign currency could be met, for instance, with the ample central bank international reserves, estimated at over $3 trillion.

Over the last decade, China has become a major driver of demand for developing-country exports and a key source of investment and, most recently, finance (Eichengreen, Park, and Shin 2012). Trade linkages with China are significant for the East Asia region, and for commodity exporters globally; hence, the transmission of any growth fluctuation through trade should be larger for those countries. This effect would be amplified

through the impact on international commodity prices. Countries with impaired macroeconomic policy buffers could be particularly affected. Financial stress in one or several commodity exporters could outweigh potential real income gains for importers in the short term, hence adding downward pressure on global growth.

Widespread weakness across the BRICS

A growth slowdown in BRICS could have global repercussions, dampening growth across emerging and developing economies. A 1 percentage point growth slowdown in the BRICS as a whole could result in a 0.8 percentage point decline in growth in other emerging market countries over a span of two years (Figure 1.18, Chapter 3). Growth shocks in Russia would reverberate across the ECA region, reducing ECA growth almost one-for-one. In contrast, the international spillovers from growth shocks in Brazil, India, and South Africa are not likely to be widespread. In the event of acute stress in any of the BRICS, confidence in emerging market assets more broadly could suffer from contagion effects, in which case spillovers could be considerably larger.

Such spillovers would transmit through a number of channels (Chapters 2 and 3). China is deeply integrated into supply chains in East Asia and the Pacific, and constitutes a large export market for commodity-exporting countries in Sub-Saharan Africa and Latin America. Brazil trades significantly with neighboring Latin American countries, partly as a result of regional free trade agreements. Remittances from Russia account for more than 10 percent of GDP in several countries in the Caucasus and Central Asia (Armenia, Kyrgyz Republic, Tajikistan). India is an important source of foreign direct investment and official development assistance for neighboring countries (Bhutan, Nepal).[7]

---

[7]Spillover risks also emanate from large advanced and emerging markets other than BRICS. For example, commodity-exporting countries are an important export market for several commodity-importing countries, accounting for 25 percent or more of exports from the latter group (Hungary, Korea, Poland, Thailand, Turkey).

FIGURE 1.18 Spillovers from slowing growth in BRICS

Spillovers from the slowdown in BRICS are primarily impacting other emerging and developing economies. This reflects strengthening trade, financial, and commodity market linkages. China constitutes a significant export destination for commodity-exporting countries, which in turn are important export markets for many commodity importers. The Russian Federation has particularly tight interconnections with neighboring economies though trade and remittance flows.

A. Impact of a 1 percentage point decline in BRICS growth on global and EM growth

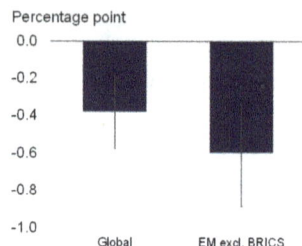

B. Impact of a 1 percentage point decline in each of the BRICS on global and EM growth

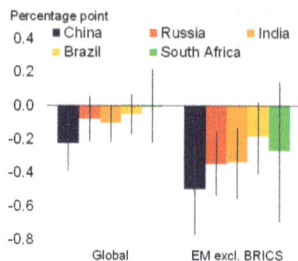

C. Value of exports from emerging markets

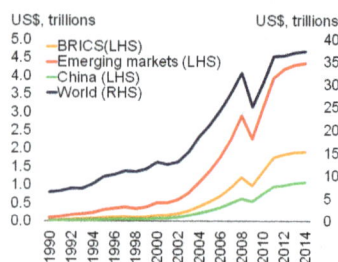

D. Share of goods exports from commodity-importing EMs to commodity exporters, 2014

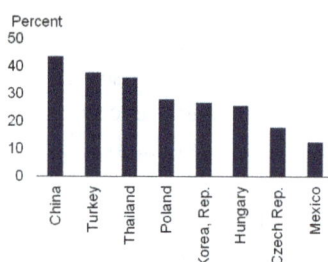

E. Countries with largest share of exports to BRICS, 2014

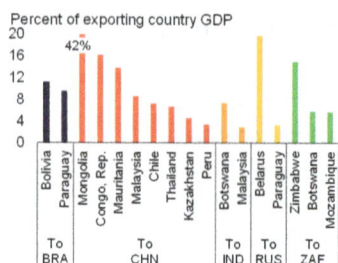

F. FDI and remittances from Russia to neighboring developing countries

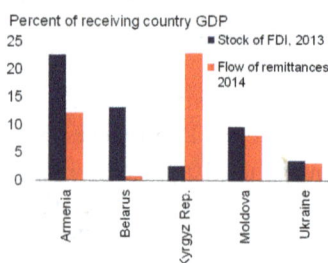

Sources: World Bank; United Nations Comtrade; IMF Direction of Trade Statistics (DOTS), IMF Coordinated Direct Investment Survey (CDIS).
A. B. Cumulated impulse responses at the two year horizon due to a 1 percentage point decline in growth in each of the BRICS economies. "EM" is emerging markets excluding BRICS. "Global" is GDP weighted average of BRICS, EM, and G7. Confidence bands span the 16th-84th percentiles.
E. BRA, CHN, IND, RUS and ZAF are respectively Brazil, China, India, Russia and South Africa.

Financial market turbulence

Amid lingering developing-country vulnerabilities, the risk of financial turbulence in some emerging and developing economies has increased. This risk is exacerbated by an expected tightening in global borrowing costs and financial conditions, the potential for further U.S. dollar appreciation, the possibility of heightened risk aversion, and worsening creditworthiness in emerging and developing economies.

U.S. monetary policy tightening. Tighter U.S. monetary policy may affect the outlook for global borrowing costs. The adjustment may be smooth, as rising U.S. policy rates have long been anticipated by markets in the context of a robust recovery in the United States. At the same time, other major central banks will continue their very accommodative policies, likely dampening the global impact of higher U.S. interest rates. However, this baseline of a modest and smooth U.S. tightening is subject to substantial risks (Figure 1.19). First, the U.S. term premium is unusually low and well below its historical average, and could rebound abruptly. Second, market expectations of future policy rates remain well below those of Fed policymakers following a first hike in December, 2015. A sudden closing in this gap could be disruptive. Third, fragile market liquidity conditions, even in deep sovereign bond markets, could amplify the impact of the initial shock and facilitate its propagation to other market segments. This context increases the risks of spikes in U.S. long-term yields and of financial market and exchange rate volatility.

U.S. dollar strength, currency exposures, and corporate debt. A further appreciation of the U.S. dollar could add pressure on emerging and developing country currencies. This could contribute to a rising cost of debt refinancing and expose vulnerabilities in domestic corporate and banking sectors. Considering the negative correlation between commodity prices and the dollar, this effect could be reinforced by a negative income effect for some exporters (Druck, Magud, and Mariscal 2015). In the past, periods of rapid dollar appreciations were sometimes associated with a greater incidence of financial crisis in emerging markets, such as during the first half of 1980s in Latin America and second half of the 1990s in Asia. In the latter episode, countries with currencies tightly connected to the dollar experienced a greater proportion of sudden stops and sharper economic downturns (IMF 2015b). High and rising levels of private indebtedness increase the risk of corporate defaults. Banking sectors generally remain well capitalized, but corporate debt represents a significant share of their assets, despite rising intermediation through bond markets in recent years. Widespread corporate distress could impair capital and reduce collateral values, constraining the supply of bank finance for the rest of the economy.

Risk aversion and contagion effects. An abrupt increase in risk aversion—triggered, for instance, by a sudden increase in global interest rates, by heightened concerns about debt in key developing countries, by a credit event in a major emerging market, or by rising geopolitical tensions—could lead to contagion affecting other economies, even if they have limited vulnerabilities. In particular, further credit downgrades in large emerging market economies could cause a general reappraisal of risk. Market-implied ratings, based on credit default swap prices, indicate heightened investor concerns about exposures to weak commodity prices, soft growth, and political risks. In a financial stress situation, pro-cyclical behavior of asset managers could amplify asset price movements and contagion effects.

Capital flow reversals and the cost of sudden stops. The materialization of the aforementioned risks could have significant effects on borrowing conditions and have a sizable adverse impact on developing-country capital flows (Arteta et al. 2015). A 50 basis point (two standard deviations) jump in global long-term interest rates could temporarily reduce aggregate capital flows to developing countries by 0.9 percentage points of their combined GDP, with the effect peaking after one year (Figure 1.20). Analogously, a 10 point (two standard deviations) shock in the VIX index of implied stock-market volatility (a proxy for risk aversion) could reduce aggregate developing-country capital flows on impact by up to 2.2 percent of GDP, with the effect dissipating

FIGURE 1.19 Rising borrowing costs and balance sheet pressures

The U.S. tightening cycle is expected to have a benign impact, but there are risks of sudden adjustments in long-term yields and a further strengthening of the U.S. dollar. High levels of private indebtedness could increase the risk of corporate defaults, while further credit downgrades and rising political uncertainty could lead to a broad-based repricing of risk.

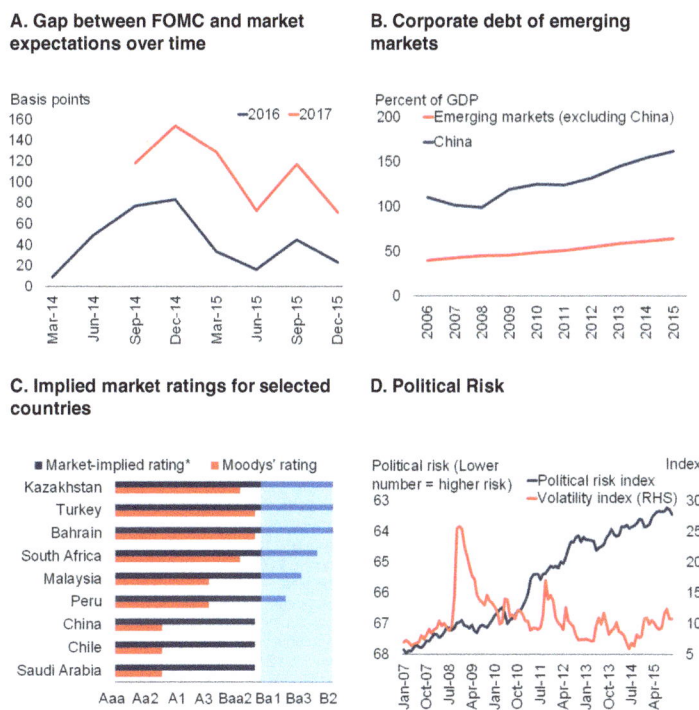

A. Gap between FOMC and market expectations over time

B. Corporate debt of emerging markets

C. Implied market ratings for selected countries

D. Political Risk

Source: World Bank; U.S. Federal Open Market Committee; Bloomberg; International Country Risk Guide (ICRG); World Bank; Escolano, Kolerus, and Ngouana (2014).
B. GDP-weighted average. List of emerging markets includes China, Czech Republic, Hungary, India, Indonesia, Mexico, Poland, South Africa, Thailand, and Turkey.
C. Latest observation December, 2015.
D. Unweighted averages of Political Risk Rating for emerging markets according to the International Country Risk Guide. A higher Political Risk Rating indicates lower political risk. Political Risk Ratings are a weighted average of ratings of government stability, socioeconomic conditions, investment profile, corruption, the role of the military in politics, law and order, external and internal conflict, religious and ethnic tensions, democratic accountability, and bureaucratic quality. Volatility index is calculated by JPMorgan and tracks implied volatility from 13 emerging-market currencies against the U.S. dollar. Latest observation is November, 2015.

rapidly. Financial stress associated with these events could combine with domestic fragilities and increase the risks of multiple sudden stops across more vulnerable developing countries. The short-run costs of these events could be substantial. In the two years following a sudden stop, developing countries could experience an average decline in GDP of almost 7 percentage points, a drop in investment of more than 21 percentage points, and currency depreciation vis-á-vis the U.S. dollar of about 14 percentage points more than before the event.

FIGURE 1.20 Deteriorating capital flows and sudden stops

Rising borrowing costs and risk aversion could lead to an abrupt decline in developing-country capital flows. Financial stress could combine with domestic fragilities, increasing the risks of damaging sudden stops in more vulnerable developing countries. The short-run costs of sudden stops in terms of lost activity and investment can be substantial.

A. Impact of U.S. interest rate and volatility shock on capital flows to developing and emerging markets

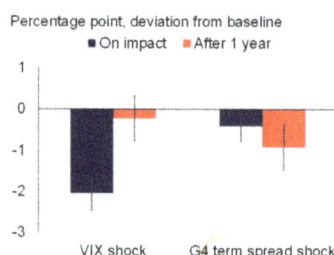

C. Sudden stops and investment growth in developing and emerging markets

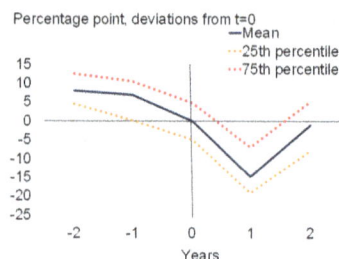

Sources: World Bank; Arteta et al. (2015).
A. VIX and G4 (Euro Area, Japan, the United Kingdom, and the United States) term spread shocks are two-standard deviation shocks, amounting respectively to a 10 index-point increase in VIX and 45 basis-point increase G4 term spreads. Impulse response are derived from VAR model linking capital inflows to emerging and frontier markets to quarterly real GDP growth in emerging and frontier markets as well as G4 countries, real G4 short-term interest rates (three-month money market rates minus annual inflation measured as changes in GDP deflator), G4 term spread (10-year government bond yields minus three month money market rates), and the VIX index of implied volatility of S&P 500 options. Confidence bands span the 16th-84th percentiles.
B. Blue line denotes averages for EFEs that experienced systemic sudden stops. Grey shades denote 75th and 25th percentiles. A systemic sudden stop is a period when capital flows fall one standard deviation below their historical mean and, at the same time, the VIX index surpasses by one standard deviation its historical mean. The calculations include 21 nonconsecutive systemic sudden stop episodes for 58 EFEs in 1995-2014.

Combined risk of BRICS weakness and financial stress

The spillover effects from a synchronous BRICS slowdown could be much more pronounced if it is combined with a tightening of risk spreads that could result from developing-country financial stress. The BRICS slowdown scenario discussed earlier, when combined with tightening financial conditions—for instance, the EMBI spread increasing by 100 basis points from the current level in 2015—could cut growth in emerging and frontier markets by about 1.3-1.5 percentage points in 2015 (Figure 1.21). The effects of such a financial market turbulence would be more muted on the advanced economies. Global growth would decline about 0.9-1.2 percentage point in 2015 from the baseline forecast. Financial tightening would reduce growth particularly sharply in frontier markets, with their less liquid, more volatile, and fragile financial markets.

Weak commodity prices and other risks for low-income countries

Although all commodity prices have declined sharply from their 2011 peaks, they are still higher in real terms than their 1985 to 2004 average. While geopolitical risks and adverse weather conditions could lead to a more rapid recovery in commodity prices than currently predicted, most of the risks are on the downside. Since nearly two-thirds of current LICs are commodity exporters, the fall in commodity prices in recent years has dealt a major terms of trade shock and led to a substantial widening of fiscal and current account deficits. Further weakness in global commodity prices could result in even sharper fiscal and currency adjustments. It could also lead to delays in investments in energy and mining, particularly in East African countries. Fiscal risks are elevated in several countries in East Africa, relating to sharp increases in public debt due to large infrastructure projects, public-private partnerships, contingent liabilities, and devolution processes (Mauro et al. 2015). Other risks involve political tensions and security issues (Afghanistan, Burkina Faso, Burundi, Chad, Nepal, Niger), upcoming elections (Benin), and labor disputes (Niger, Sierra Leone).

Slower potential output growth

Slowing actual and potential growth amid lingering vulnerabilities has left developing countries more susceptible to external and domestic shocks. Potential growth in developing countries has declined steadily since the global financial crisis, mainly reflecting the trend slowdown in total factor productivity growth (Figure 1.22). The slowdown in potential output and productivity growth reflects slowing efficiency gains as well as demographic trends, which have passed a turning point since the global crisis with potentially profound implications (World Bank 2015b). Looking ahead, falling fertility rates and rising life expectancy will intensify these trends in countries with ageing populations, which may put additional pressures on productivity growth and, more broadly, on GDP growth. In particular, by 2025, outright declines in working age populations are expected in Europe and Central

Asia—partly as a result of emigration—and in East Asia and the Pacific. South Asia and Sub-Saharan Africa are exceptions, since still-high population growth will lead to an increase in the share of the working-age population. Although these trends should support stronger growth in pre- and early-dividend regions, these also face the highest poverty rates. Without improvements in poverty headcount rates, these regions could experience even greater concentrations of global poverty in the future.

Terrorism and geopolitical tensions

Recent terrorism-related violence in France and elsewhere has raised security concerns and highlighted rising geopolitical risks. Experience from past terrorist attacks in major economies suggests that isolated events are unlikely to have lasting economic consequences. Direct costs and the fiscal impact of security and emergency measures were generally limited, while effects on confidence and activity were generally short-lived. Even in the case of the September 11, 2001 attacks in the United States, financial markets and business confidence recovered within a few months (Figure 1.23).[8] Other terrorist attacks in Europe, such as the Madrid and London bombings in 2004 and 2005, had similarly small effects on their respective economies and no perceptible global impacts (Kollias et al. 2011). The negative effect of terrorism on economic activity is generally estimated to be considerably smaller and less persistent than that related to external wars or internal conflict (Blomberg, Hess, and Orphanides 2004). It is also viewed as less pronounced in high income countries, with negative short-term effects offset by rising government spending.

However, repeated threats or escalating geopolitical risks could potentially have more significant adverse effects. These include a more protracted impact on consumer and investor confidence, disruption to travel and tourism, heightened risk aversion, and higher transaction and insurance costs (IMF 2001, Johnston and

---

[8] The overall cost of the September 11 attacks for the U.S. economy has been estimated at less than ½ percentage point of GDP (Roberts 2009).

FIGURE 1.21 Growth slowdown in BRICS combined with financial stress

A combination of continued weak BRICS growth and rising emerging market bond spreads could considerably reduce growth in other emerging and developing countries.

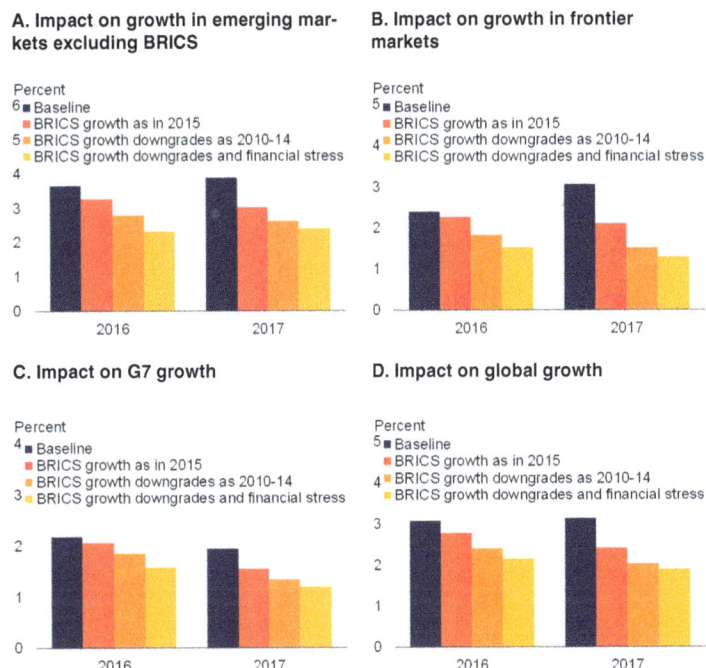

A. Impact on growth in emerging markets excluding BRICS

B. Impact on growth in frontier markets

C. Impact on G7 growth

D. Impact on global growth

Source: World Bank staff estimates.
Note: EMBI = Emerging Markets Bond Index. Conditional forecasts of emerging markets excluding BRICS, frontier markets, G7, and global growth, with conditions imposed on future BRICS growth and EMBI. The conditions are: (i) BRICS growing at the curent rate in 2015: BRICS continue to grow at its current 2015 level (annualized rate of 3.2 percent) during the forecast horizon; (ii) BRICS growth with forecast downgrades as during 2010-14: BRICS continue to grow during the forecast horizon at its current 2015 level minus the average forecast downgrades it saw during 2010-14. The forecast downgrades are based on the World Bank forecasts. In these two scenarios, EMBI is restricted to equal the unconditional forecasts from the aggregate VAR model during the forecast horizon; (iii) BRICS growth with forecast downgrades and financial stress: The second scenario is combined with EMBI rising by 100bp during the forecast horizon. Global growth is the GDP-weighted average of BRICS, emerging markets excl. BRICS, frontier markets, and G7 growth. The baseline forecasts are constructed from the forecasts presented in Chapter 1 by aggregating across countries in a given group. Conditional forecasts are based on the aggregate VAR model.

FIGURE 1.22 Weakening potential growth

Potential growth in emerging and developing countries has declined steadily since the global financial crisis, mainly because of the trend slowdown in total factor productivity (TFP) growth.

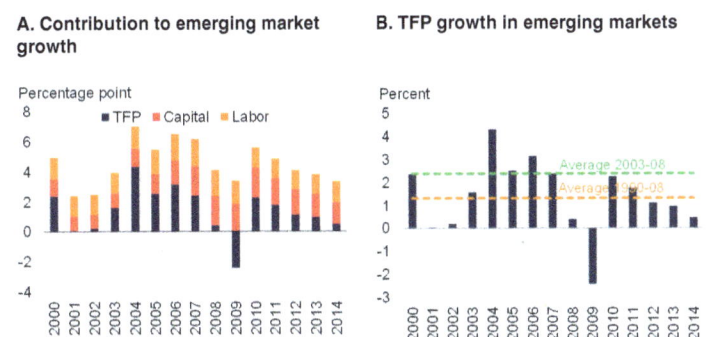

A. Contribution to emerging market growth

B. TFP growth in emerging markets

Source: World Bank.
A. Unweighted averages of key emerging and developing countries. GDP is decomposed into total factor productivity (TFP) and factors of production using a Cobb-Douglas production function. Labor is proxied by employment, and the capital stock derived using the perpetual inventory method (assuming a labor share of national income of 0.7). Total factor productivity is derived as the residual.

FIGURE 1.23 Terrorism and geopolitical tensions

Terrorist attacks in the United States in 2001, Spain in 2004, the United Kingdom in 2005 and France in January 2015 did not lead to lasting effects on confidence and activity. Recurring terrorist-induced violence has been highly concentrated in a small number of developing countries, with significant regional implications.

A. Purchasing Managers Index around significant terrorist attacks in major high-income countries

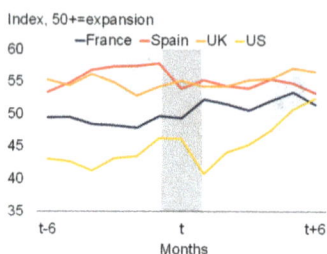

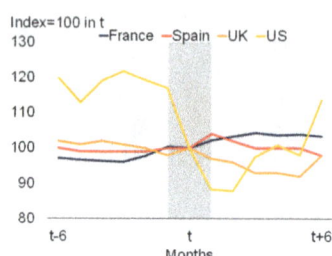

B. Consumer confidence around significant terrorist attacks in major high-income countries

C. Number of terrorist attacks across regions

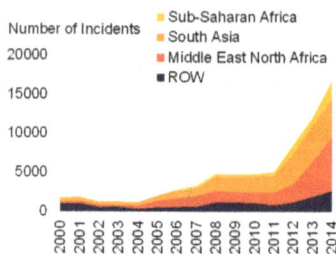

D. Stock markets around major terrorist attacks in developing countries in 2015

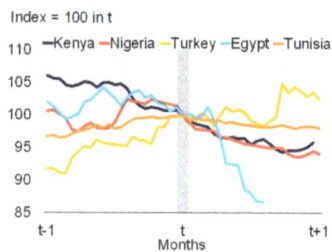

Source: World Bank; Global Terrorism Database; Haver Analytics.
A. Date of significant attacks incorporated are: France (1/7/2015), UK (7/7/2005), Spain (3/11/2004) and United States (9/11/2001). Confidence measures are composite PMI indexes for France, Spain and the United Kingdom, and manufacturing ISM for the United States.
B. Data was originally collected by Pinkerton Global Intelligence Service (PGIS), Center for Terrorism and Intelligence Studies (CETIS), and Institute for the Study of Violent Groups (ISVG). Original GTD1 (1970-1997) employed the definition of terrorism utilized by PGIS, and based on the original GTD1 definition, each incident included in the GTD2 (1998-2007) had to be an intentional act of violence or threat of violence by a non-state actor. In addition, two of the following three criteria also had to be met for inclusion in GTD2:
1. The violent act was aimed at attaining a political, economic, religious, or social goal;
2. The violent act included evidence of an intention to coerce, intimidate, or convey some other message to a larger audience (or audiences) other than the immediate victims; and
3. The violent act was outside the precepts of International Humanitarian Law.
C. Date of significant attacks incorporated are: Kenya (4/1/2015), Nigeria (1/3/2015, 7/1/2015, 9/20/2015), Turkey (10/10/2015) and Egypt (10/31/2015).

Nedelescu 2005). In developing countries, the rising number of terrorist incidents and related conflict have already inflicted significant economic, social and humanitarian costs for the affected countries. In 2014 alone, roughly 80 percent of the people killed in terrorist activities were in just five countries (Afghanistan, Iraq, Nigeria, Pakistan, and Syria), with significant cross-border repercussions.[9] The global cost of

[9]Since 1989, 88 percent of all terrorist attacks occurred in countries experiencing or involved in violent conflict (START 2015).

terrorist attacks in 2014 was estimated at US$ 52 billion, a 10-fold increase from 2000 (Institute for Economics and Peace 2015).

A flaring up of geopolitical risks in the Middle East remains a significant risk, as tensions have increased and non-conflict countries have been affected by terrorist activity in 2015 (including Egypt, Tunisia and Turkey).[10] Security concerns also remain prominent in some Sub-Saharan countries (Cameroon, Chad, Kenya, Mali, Niger, Nigeria) as well as in South Asia, with Afghanistan beset by domestic security and insurgency challenges. Taken together, a significant rise in geopolitical risks could potentially affect regional prospects and might, in a scenario of escalating tensions, disrupt an already fragile global recovery.

Upside risk: Unrealized gains from the oil supply shock

The expected positive effect of falling oil prices on large oil importers and hence on global activity has been surprisingly muted. The increase in retail trade and private consumption across major high-income countries has fallen short of the real income gains conferred by lower energy prices since mid-2014 (Figure 1.24). There are several reasons for the muted response. First, the speed of the decline in oil prices has put severe strains on both private and public sector balance sheets among major oil exporters, with significant cross-border spillovers for regional trading partners. Second, oil importers are reacting with caution. High indebtedness, limited room for additional monetary policy accommodation, and slowing long-term growth prospects have encouraged debt reduction and precautionary savings, rather than consumption and investment. Empirically, there is evidence that increased oil price volatility may have a depressing effect, particularly on consumer durables and investment outlays (Kilian 2011; Plante and Traum 2012; Guo and Kliesen 2005; Elder and Serletis 2010; Kilian 2014). Should this uncertainty decline, the positive effects in

[10]Global repercussions could include a further intensification of migration flows and rising volatility on international oil markets. In the medium and long term, the negative economic impacts in the region, along with already weak indicators of living conditions, may contribute to further violence.

importing economies represent an upside risk to baseline forecasts. Stable lower oil prices could eventually release pent-up demand. Such delayed reaction to lower oil prices was observed in the 1980s and 1990s, especially in the United States, where consumption initially slowed as consumers were unsure whether lower prices would persist (IMF 2015d). As prices stabilized at lower levels, savings dropped and spending accelerated.

Policy challenges

Challenges in major economies

In major high-income countries, monetary policy is expected to tighten very gradually in the United States, and to remain highly accommodative elsewhere. Fiscal consolidation is also expected to ease, but most major economies have yet to put in place plans for medium-term fiscal sustainability. China faces the policy challenge of supporting a gradual slowdown and rebalancing while limiting financial vulnerabilities. However, the authorities retain significant policy buffers, and the government is proceeding with its comprehensive reform agenda.

United States. U.S. labor market conditions have made significant headway over the last year, but there is still considerable uncertainty about the underlying strength of the economy, and the amount of remaining slack. This has led to a debate about where policy interest rates are heading over the medium term. According to U.S. Fed policy makers, short-term interest rates should stabilize around 3 percent over the long-run, reflecting a gradual increase in the natural rate of interest from current low levels (Figure 1.25). However, uncertainty around estimates of this natural rate could imply a more gradual increase in policy rates than suggested by simple policy rules (Hamilton et al. 2015). Conditions at present therefore warrant a very gradual normalization of policy rates, balancing the risk of raising too quickly and potentially derailing the recovery, against that of raising too slowly and seeing accelerated inflation. Very low interest rates carry the additional risk of potentially excessive risk taking amid a search for yield (IMF 2015d). Signs of rising credit risks are already present, with weakening underwriting standards and an

FIGURE 1.24 Unrealized gains due to low oil prices

Given the income boost from lower energy prices, the observed pickup in private consumption generally fell short of expectations across oil importing countries. Stronger domestic demand might yet emerge, representing an upside risks to projections. For instance, following the 1985-86 and 1997-98 oil price declines, the household saving rate in the United States initially increased but subsequently decline. Debt deleveraging pressures and policy uncertainty could limit the potential for lower household savings this time.

A. Income gain from lower energy prices and retail sales volume since June 2014

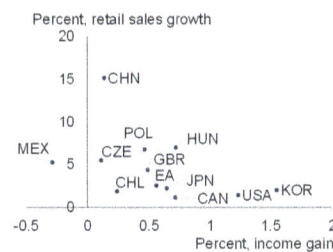

B. U.S. personal savings rate around previous oil price declines

C. Debt

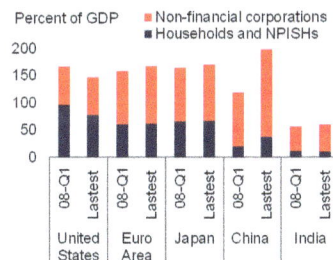

D. Policy uncertainty

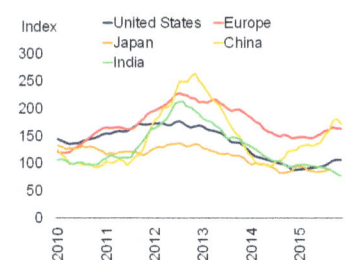

Sources: World Bank; Baker, Bloom and Davis (2015).
A. Standard ISO country codes. Income gain measured as changes in the energy component of consumer prices times the weight of energy consumption in the CPI basket.
B. Latest observation 2015 Q3.
D. The Economic Policy Uncertainty Index is derived from the weighted average of newspaper coverage of policy-related economic uncertainty and, depending on the country, disagreement among forecasters. A higher value indicates more uncertainty about economic policy. Latest observation November, 2015.

increasing volume of funds flowing to lower-rated U.S. companies (OCC 2015). The U.S. banking sector has strengthened its capital base since the crisis, but some risks have migrated to non-bank intermediaries which are subject to fewer regulatory and supervisory rules (FSOC 2015).

Fiscal deficits have been declining thanks to spending restrictions and stronger growth, but a there is still a need for a comprehensive plan for long-term fiscal sustainability. This will require tax reform, and improved quality of public spending, including infrastructure investment (CBO 2015). Brinkmanship around budget negotiations,

FIGURE 1.25 Policy challenges in the United States

According to U.S. Federal Reserve policy makers, short-term interest rates should stabilize slightly above 3 percent over the long-run, reflecting a gradual increase in the natural rate of interest from current low levels. U.S. fiscal deficits have been declining thanks to stronger growth, but there is still a need for a comprehensive plan to ensure fiscal sustainability over the medium-term.

A. United States: Contribution to policy interest rate projections

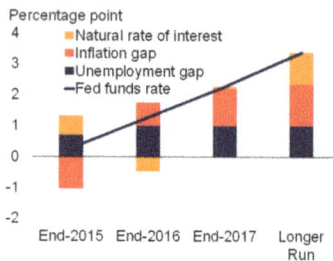

B. United States: Government deficit projections

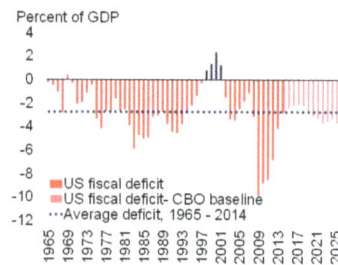

Sources: World Bank; International Monetary Fund; U.S. Congressional Budget Office.
A. Using the Taylor rule described in Yellen (2015) and the central tendency of FOMC forecasts for unemployment and inflation, FOMC projections for the federal funds rate path can be decomposed into the expected contribution from future labor market improvements, rising inflation, and the natural rate of interest. More specifically, the Taylor Rule is defined as $R = RR^* + p + 0.5(p - 2) - (U - U^*)$, where R denotes the Taylor Rule federal funds rate, RR* is the estimated value of the natural rate of interest, p is the current inflation rate (measured as PCE inflation), U is the unemployment rate, and U* is the natural rate of unemployment (considered to be the long-run FOMC forecast for the unemployment rate).
B. Baseline assumes current laws do not change.

spending, and debt caps remain an important source of uncertainty, sporadically affecting investor confidence and global financial markets. Structural reforms to facilitate re-entry into the labor market and boost labor productivity are needed. Longer-term challenges include stagnating wages for lower-income families, and deteriorating public infrastructure (OECD 2015).

Euro Area. The ECB's asset purchase program has helped ease financial conditions in the Euro Area. It has reduced bond yields, weakened the euro, and improved the supply of credit (Georgiadis and Grab 2015). It has also mitigated the possible fall-out from the Greek debt crisis (European Commission 2015b). Ongoing bank balance sheet repair, and high levels of non-performing loans, may nevertheless continue to constrain the supply of credit in parts of the Euro Area (Figure 1.26). Speeding up the resolution of distressed assets is needed to support bank lending. Further efforts to accelerate capital markets integration could help improve the allocation of credit and support private sector investment.

Reflecting a pickup in growth and low borrowing costs, the aggregate Euro Area fiscal deficit is expected to narrow to 2.0 percent of GDP in 2015. Fiscal policy appears to have been broadly neutral to growth in 2015, a trend that may continue in 2016, although several countries require additional consolidation measures (European Commission 2015b). Countries with available fiscal space could use it flexibly to support the recovery, generating positive cross-border spillovers, especially when cyclical conditions are weak (Auerbach and Gorodnichenko 2013), especially as monetary policy is constrained by the zero lower bound (Goujard 2013 and in't Veld 2013). Effective implementation of the European Investment Plan (catalyzing up to €315 billion in private investment through public funds and guarantees) could also help support growth in countries with limited fiscal space and more fragile banking sectors.

Efforts to implement structural reforms are moving forward, but greater emphasis is needed to address rigidities and fragmentations of labor, product, and services markets, which are hampering productivity, innovation, and growth. Reforms in core countries could generate significant cross-border spillovers, particularly in the area of innovation policies (Coe, Helpman, and Hoffmaister 2009). Peripheral economies have urgent needs for reform to deal with domestic structural issues (Varga, Roeger, and in't Veld 2014). In response to the unprecedented flow of refugees and migrants along the Eastern Mediterranean-Western Balkans, European policymakers have agreed on a series of short-term actions to rescue and support refugees, while coordinating border policies. Establishing equitable sharing of responsibility for resettlement of refugees and associated financial costs is key, along with upholding EU's law regarding the free movement of people, and addressing the root causes of displacement through development efforts.

Japan. Amid record-low interest rates, continued vigilance regarding financial stability risks is warranted, in particular through monitoring of balance sheets and the use of stress tests to assess banks' resilience to lower market liquidity and higher volatility of asset prices, exchange rates, and interest rates.

Fiscal consolidation has been delayed, and public debt is expected to continue edging up (Figure 1.26). The structural reform agenda is making progress, with important new legislation passed or under consideration by parliament, including in the areas of energy, agriculture, and tax policies. Removing tax-induced disincentives to work, broadening the availability of child-care facilities, increasing the participation of older workers and relaxing immigration restrictions in sectors with labor shortages would help counteract demographic pressures (IMF 2015e). Further reforms to reduce labor market duality, improve corporate governance, deregulate agriculture and domestic services, and eliminate barriers to investment in Japan remain key policy priorities.

China. Progress continues to be made in several of the reform areas announced in late 2013.[11] According to the preliminary information following the fifth plenum, the 13th Five-Year Plan (FYP) indicative target for GDP growth is likely to be lowered to 6.5 percent (vs. 7 percent in the 12th FYP). By lowering growth targets, Chinese authorities are in a better position to address key short-term risks while promoting the reforms needed for sustained medium-term growth.[12] A key policy challenge is to achieve an orderly shift to a more sustainable economic path. The transition will encompass an expanding role for the market and a shift from excessive investment in real estate and manufacturing towards greater domestic consumption and services (Figure 1.27). Achieving this will require policies that facilitate the reallocation of resources

---

[11] In particular, there has been progress in financial reforms (e.g., interest rate liberalization, deposit insurance), external sector reforms (e.g., steps toward capital account liberalization and exchange-rate flexibility), fiscal reforms (i.e., changes in fiscal framework of local government debt), and pension reform (e.g., unification of civil servants' pensions with the urban pension system).

[12] The new Five-Year Plan covers a broad range of reform areas to be implemented by 2020. It pledges to accelerate reforms to: (i) reduce government intervention in the pricing of goods and services; (ii) relax restrictions on foreign investment; (iii) adjust fiscal responsibilities between central and local governments; and (iv) reform state-owned enterprises as mixed ownership. It also relaxed the one-child policy.

FIGURE 1.26 Policy challenges in Euro Area and Japan

Elevated levels of non-performing loans in the Euro Area continue to constrain the supply of credit. Faster resolution of distressed assets would help support bank lending. The recent acceleration of migrant flows to Europe creates absorption challenges in the short term, but could have benefits over time. In Japan, fiscal consolidation has been delayed and public debt is expected to edge further up. Relaxing immigration restrictions in sectors with labor shortages could help counteract demographic pressures.

A. Euro Area: Non-performing loans across member states

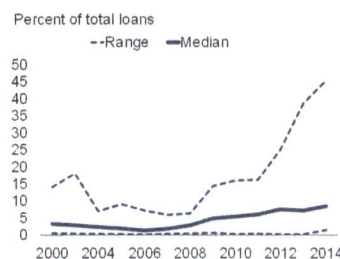

B. Euro Area: Migrant flows

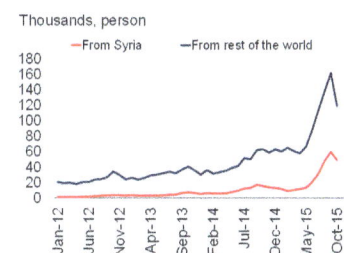

C. Japan: Public deficit and debt projections

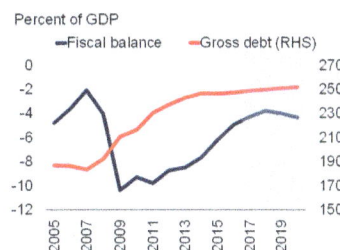

D. Share of migrants in the labor force

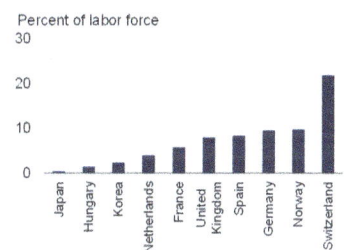

Sources: World Bank; European Central Bank; International Monetary Fund; Organization for Economic Co-operation and Development.
A. Bank nonperforming loans to total gross loans are the value of nonperforming loans divided by the total value of the loan portfolio (including nonperforming loans before the deduction of specific loan-loss provisions). The loan amount recorded as nonperforming should be the gross value of the loan as recorded on the balance sheet, not just the amount that is overdue.
B. Last observation is October, 2015.

from sectors that have accumulated excess capacity to those with higher growth potential. Examples of such policy steps include a gradual removal of implicit state guarantees for loans (e.g. through implementing an integrated budget law and unified fiscal accounting), and allowing the orderly exit of inefficient firms, including state-owned enterprises. In the short term, market discipline in the financial sector should be strengthened to mitigate risks associated with a concentration of leverage among slowing sectors (IMF 2015c). At the same time, ad hoc administrative measures should be gradually replaced by market-based mechanisms so that

FIGURE 1.27 Policy challenges in China

China's key policy priorities include calibrating stimulus measures, providing a greater role to market forces, and ensuring a smooth transition from manufacturing and real estate to services and consumption.

A. China: Lending rates

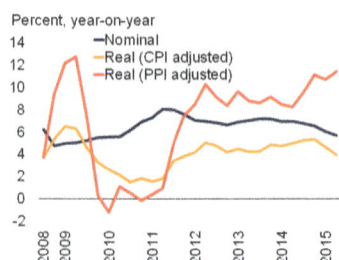

B. China: Nominal GDP growth by sector

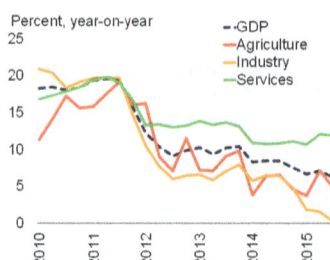

Sources: World Bank; International Monetary Fund; U.S. Congressional Budget Office.
A. Lending rates are the interest rates applied to private sector companies and households. Latest observation is September 2015.
B. Latest observation is 2015Q3.

credit is more efficiently allocated (World Bank 2015i). The recent inclusion of the renminbi in the Special Drawing Right (SDR) basket of the International Monetary Fund is an important milestone in the integration of the Chinese economy into the global financial system.

Structural reforms will help support growth. For instance, removing entry barriers and reducing regulatory and administrative burdens will enhance incentives for private investment. Likewise, implementation of fiscal reforms, such as consolidating the business tax with the VAT, will lower the tax burden and promote investment, particularly in the transportation and financial services sectors. Making more land available for commercial activities will also improve the prospects for service-sector investment and growth. Furthermore, efforts to gradually increase the retirement age could contribute to an increase in labor force participation. Reform efforts to accelerate unification of the urban-rural hukou system would also support more efficient labor markets. Removing barriers to a structural shift towards services could help moderate the trend decline in productivity growth, while an increase in the labor share of GDP is critical to rebalance growth on the demand side from investment to consumption.

Challenges in developing economies

In the short term, policy actions need to focus on building resilience against downside risks to growth. As noted above, these risks include a slowdown in major emerging and developing economies, financial sector turmoil amid tighter global borrowing conditions, and persistently low commodity prices. Where cyclical slowdowns are underway, and where there is sufficient policy space, countercyclical fiscal and monetary stimulus can be employed to support activity. Cyclical policies need to be reinforced with longer-term structural measures. These should focus on easing supply side constraints, and offsetting demographic headwinds in the relatively higher-income developing regions, where the working-age share of the population is shrinking. Global poverty will increasingly be concentrated in regions with the highest working-age population growth rates. Policy makers in such regions will face pronounced challenges to ensure productive employment for their expanding labor force.

Monetary and exchange rate policies

Monetary policies continue to diverge between oil-exporting and oil-importing countries. The deceleration of inflation in oil-importing countries has allowed some easing in monetary policy. In oil-exporting countries, depreciation pressures have increased inflation and financial stability risks. Several central banks have responded with foreign exchange market intervention (Azerbaijan, Kazakhstan, Mexico, Nigeria), and policy interest rate increases (Angola, Colombia, Kazakhstan) in the second half of 2015. Nevertheless, in several countries, policy rates may still be lower than required to meet inflation targets, particularly among commodity-exporting countries (Figure 1.28).[13] In the event of a further slowdown in these countries, central banks may not be able to lower rates further without raising risks to financial stability or inflation.

---

[13]Such a relationship between monetary policy rates, cyclical conditions, and inflation targets is estimated in a Taylor rule (e.g., as estimated in Ostry, Ghosh, and Chamon 2012) for a sample of emerging markets. The calculation assumes that monetary policy is in practice geared towards meeting the announced inflation target, that the monetary policy rate is the main policy instrument, and that the coefficient estimates from a cross-country regression is an adequate representation of the country-specific relationships.

Greater exchange rate flexibility may help absorb shocks, while conserving foreign exchange reserves. However, this benefit has to be balanced against domestic financial stability and inflation risks, which may be significant in some countries. In Kazakhstan, the shift to a floating exchange rate regime over the past year has raised concerns about the balance sheet risks associated with large foreign currency exposures. In contrast, in Qatar, Saudi Arabia, and the United Arab Emirates, large fiscal and reserve buffers have allowed fiscal policy to be loosened and currency pegs to remain supported (IMF 2015a).

Financial globalization, and the rising influence of global interest rates in determining domestic financing conditions, will likely make domestic monetary policy objectives more difficult to achieve (Obstfeld 2015; Sobrun and Turner 2015). This places a premium on credible monetary policy that maintains price stability over the medium term, and institutional reforms that limit the risk of pro-cyclical policies associated with capital flows.

Policies concerning the joint choice of exchange-rate regimes and the use of capital controls are of key importance for emerging and developing economies. Developing countries with fixed exchange rates may choose to use capital controls to give monetary policy a degree of autonomy to achieve domestic macroeconomic objectives. Developing countries appear to be more likely to have controls on capital flows if they also have fixed exchange rates, and that the presence of this effect depends upon the level of income per capita (Chapter 4). In particular, lower-income countries appear to set their policy with respect to capital account measures with less independence relative to their exchange rate policies.[14]

---

[14]In principle, countries that choose to control both the exchange rate and the capital account may still exercise monetary policy autonomy to stabilize economic conditions (Cordella and Gupta 2015). This is only possible, however, if they have the necessary monetary policy space—which has generally been narrowing recently, amid inflation and foreign reserve pressures.

FIGURE 1.28 Monetary policy challenges in developing countries

Commodity-exporting countries have tightened monetary policy to ease currency depreciation pressures and contain inflation and financial stability risks. Inflation was still above targets in several commodity-exporting countries in the second half of 2015.

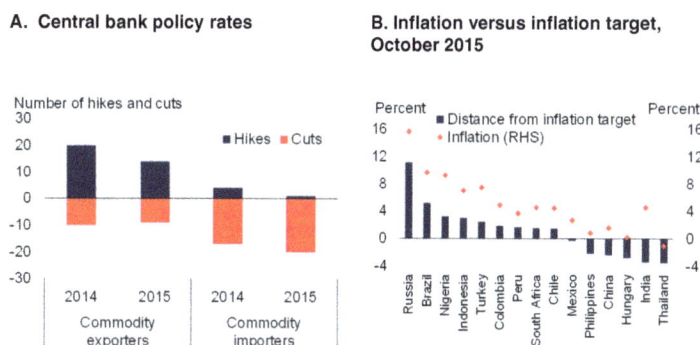

A. Central bank policy rates

B. Inflation versus inflation target, October 2015

Sources: World Bank; International Monetary Fund; Haver Analytics; Federal Reserve Board.
A. Data includes 11 commodity exporters and 13 commodity importers. Hikes and cuts refer to central bank rate decisions, including base rate, policy rate, repo rate, Selic rate, discount rate, reference rate, lending rate, refinancing rate, and benchmark rate. Latest data as of December, 2015.

Financial sector policies

The pro-cyclicality of capital flows has been reflected in domestic credit conditions. Credit cycles have also turned in developing countries, and high stock levels, which are the result of past rapid expansions in credit, remain a source of concern where growth is slowing or economies are already in recession. This highlights the need to reinforce macro-prudential policies aimed at mitigating systemic risk and reducing the pro-cyclicality in domestic financial sectors (World Bank 2015b). Beyond the implementation of counter-cyclical capital buffers under Basel III requirements, macro-prudential frameworks can be strengthened through a range of instruments, including caps on loan-to-value or debt-to-income ratios, dynamic provisioning, and credible stress tests.

Banking sector vigilance and prudential monitoring also need to be stepped up where credit and solvency risks are high due to dollarized banking systems and currency depreciations (Central Asia and South Caucasus). In Europe and Central Asia and, to a lesser extent, the Middle East and North Africa, South Asia, and Sub-Saharan Africa, banking sectors are weighed down

FIGURE 1.29 Fiscal frameworks and financial stability

A growing number of developing countries have adopted fiscal rules but many still need to strengthen fiscal management, including of commodity revenues for exporting countries. Banking sectors have elevated nonperforming loans in ECA, MNA, and South Asia. This warrants close supervision and monitoring.

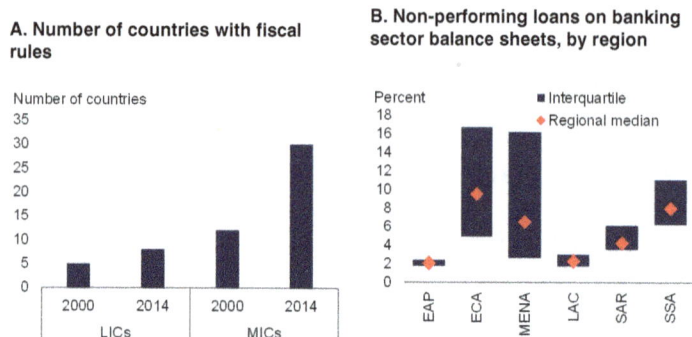

A. Number of countries with fiscal rules

B. Non-performing loans on banking sector balance sheets, by region

Sources: World Bank; International Monetary Fund; Haver Analytics.
Note: A. Number of national and supranational fiscal rules in 89 LIC, MIC and HIC countries, covering four types: budget balance rules, debt rules, expenditure rules, and revenue rules, applying to the central or general government or the public sector.
B. Bank nonperforming loans to total gross loans are the value of nonperforming loans divided by the total value of the loan portfolio (including nonperforming loans before the deduction of specific loan-loss provisions). The loan amount recorded as nonperforming should be the gross value of the loan as recorded on the balance sheet, not just the amount that is overdue.

by high levels of non-performing loans, and rising concerns about asset quality and bank solvency (Figure 1.29). This necessitates measures to recapitalize banks and address problem loans and longer-term reforms to improve governance, particularly in countries with a high share of state-owned banks.

Fiscal policy

Like monetary policy, fiscal policies have diverged among oil-importing and oil-exporting countries (Figure 1.30). For oil importers, the fall in oil prices has been fortuitous. Coupled with domestic policy efforts, which include reducing energy subsidies, fiscal deficits have shrunk, especially in South Asia, East Asia and the Pacific, and Europe and Central Asia. In many countries (including Egypt and Lebanon) windfalls were typically saved to rebuild fiscal buffers. This fiscal consolidation amounted to about 0.5 percent of GDP, on average. In some countries, they were used to support investment spending (including India and Peru). Commodity exporters have seen a widening in fiscal deficits due to revenue losses from the resource sector.

Fiscal consolidation is expected to weigh increasingly on growth in commodity-exporting

countries. For commodity exporters in Sub-Saharan Africa, developing Middle East and North Africa, and (to a lesser extent) Latin America and the Caribbean, fiscal spending sustained by high commodity prices has been an important driver of growth in the non-tradable sector (IMF 2015g). With revenues under pressure, and relatively small non-oil sectors, major fiscal adjustments have begun in several countries (Angola, Ecuador, Iraq, Nigeria). However, there has been considerable heterogeneity, with some oil-exporters with ample reserves implementing fiscal stimulus to support growth (Kazakhstan, Peru). Breakeven oil prices are particularly high in several Middle East and North African countries (Libya, the Republic of Yemen), and non-oil fiscal deficits exceed 50 percent of non-oil GDP in some GCC countries. In Bolivia, Colombia, and Ecuador, fiscal revenues over 2015-19 are expected to fall well below peak levels of 2011-14 (IMF 2015).

Fiscal policy as a countercyclical tool becomes particularly important to address cyclical weakness when monetary policy is constrained by inflation, exchange rate movements, or financial stability risks. However, in order for fiscal policy to be implemented and be effective, economies need to have the necessary fiscal space to employ countercyclical measures (World Bank 2015a). Yet buffers have been significantly depleted since 2009, partly due to stimulus deployed during the Great Recession. Rebuilding fiscal space therefore remains a priority in order to expand buffers and reduce sovereign funding risks in case of an adverse shock. In addition, rebuilding buffers will enhance policy credibility and anchor investor confidence in major developing countries where external and domestic imbalances remain large.

Fiscal consolidation could also represent an opportunity for major public expenditure and revenue reforms, for instance through better targeted social welfare spending, subsidy reforms, and more productive public investment spending to alleviate supply side constraints. Governments need to look more closely at the composition and efficiency of public spending and address fiscal risks that may be emerging from the way public infrastructure investments are financed. Better information on sources of fiscal risks from contingent liabilities (e.g., from subnational borrowings, special purpose financial vehicles, and public-private partnerships) and improved public debt management will be of critical importance. Although many commodity exporting developing countries have made progress in enhancing transparency in the extractive sector—11 are compliant with the Extractive Industries Transparency Initiative—only nine have fiscal rules or stabilization funds to act as buffers. Moreover, fiscal policy appears to have become more pro-cyclical in the years following the Great Recession, suggesting the need to further strengthen fiscal management of commodity revenues (World Bank 2015b).

Structural reforms

The deceleration of growth in emerging and developing economies is partly due to slower productivity growth. Structural reforms are therefore essential to support long-term growth. In the short run, a credible reform agenda could help lift investor confidence. In the longer run, reforms that improve economic governance, labor market functioning, and the efficient allocation of capital will help boost productivity, and may also help offset demographic headwinds facing many countries.

The benefits from governance and business environment reforms are potentially large. Past governance reform episodes in emerging markets have been associated with increased growth rates (Didier et al. 2015). Similarly, large improvements in business environments are associated with a significant increase in annual per capita growth (Divanbeigi and Ramalho 2015). Banking, trade, and agricultural liberalization can have particularly large economic benefits, while lower startup costs, easier registration requirements, improved management practices, and better access to finance, have been linked to more firm entry and employment creation in a range of countries.[15]

---

[15]The positive effects of market liberalization are highlighted in Beck and Demirguc-Kunt (2006); IMF (2008); Klapper and Love (2004); Topoleva and Khandelwal (2011), while factors supporting market entry are described in Desai, Gompers, and Lerner (2003); Klapper and Love (forthcoming); Klapper, Laeven, and Rajan (2006); McKenzie and Woodruff (2015).

FIGURE 1.30 Fiscal policy challenges in developing countries

Fiscal buffers in developing countries have been significantly depleted post-crisis, partly due to stimulus deployed to support growth, and more recently due to the impact of falling global commodity prices. Although commodity exporters on average have provided fiscal stimulus in 2015, several are implementing or planning to implement fiscal consolidation.

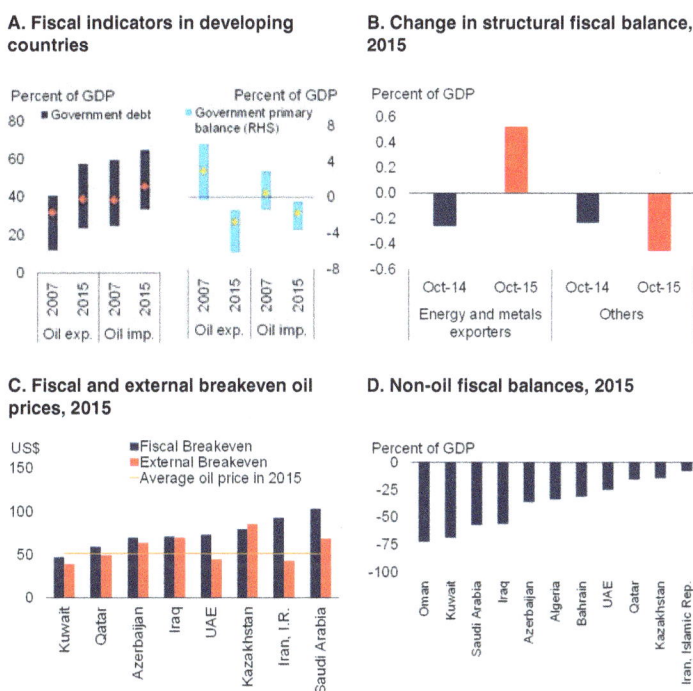

A. Fiscal indicators in developing countries

B. Change in structural fiscal balance, 2015

C. Fiscal and external breakeven oil prices, 2015

D. Non-oil fiscal balances, 2015

Sources: World Bank; International Monetary Fund; Haver Analytics, Federal Reserve Board.
A. Data includes 23 oil exporting and 112 oil importing developing countries. Bars show interquartile range, dots show median across countries.
B. Structural balances are available for five energy-exporting developing countries (Colombia, Ecuador, Indonesia, Kazakhstan, Malaysia, Peru, and South Africa) and 25 non-energy exporting developing countries (Bosnia and Herzegovina, Brazil, Bulgaria, China, Dominican Republic, Egypt, Georgia, Guyana, India, Lebanon, Mauritius, Mexico, Morocco, Panama, Paraguay, the Philippines, Romania, Serbia, Suriname, Thailand, Tunisia, Turkey, and Ukraine).
C. Fiscal break-even prices are oil prices associated with a balanced budget, while external breakeven prices are those that balance the current account.
D. Non-oil fiscal balances are fiscal balances that excludes revenues from the oil sector.

However, reform payoffs may take some time to be realized. It is therefore important to tailor policies to the stage of development and the technology level of the country (Dabla-Norris et al. 2013a-b).

Structural reforms combined with infrastructure investment can have especially potent growth effects. In China, for example, the long-term increase in real incomes from eliminating hukou restrictions allied to large-scale infrastructure investment is larger than that from infrastructure investment alone (Bosker, Deichmann and Roberts 2015).

Major changes in the size of working-age populations have taken place (Figure 1.31). More

FIGURE 1.31 Structural reform needs

Commodity-boom years have left many exporters with small or shrinking manufacturing sectors. The quality of infrastructure and access to electricity remain key bottlenecks for many developing countries. Structural reforms are generally associated with higher growth and will become increasingly necessary in the face of significant demographic shifts and to prevent a reversal of hard-won achievements in poverty reduction.

A. Size of manufacturing sectors in commodity exporters, 2000 and 2014

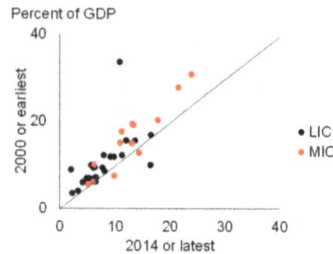

B. Infrastructure quality index

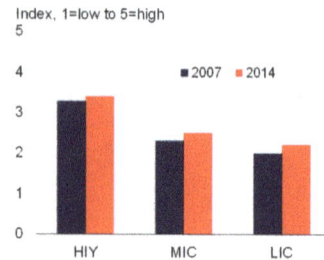

C. Access to electricity

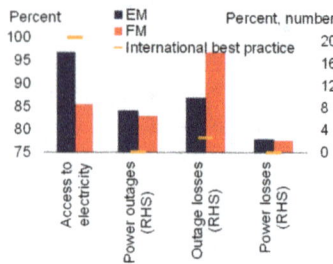

D. Growth differential during episodes of reforms and setbacks in governance quality since 1996

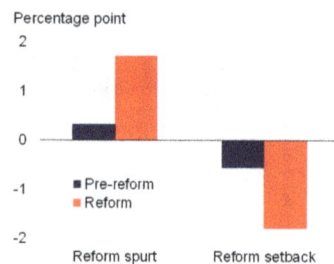

E. Working-age population growth

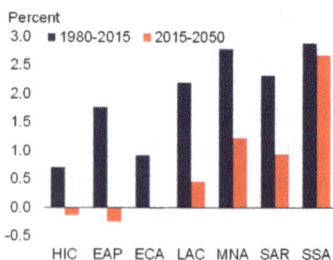

F. Extreme poverty in low-income countries

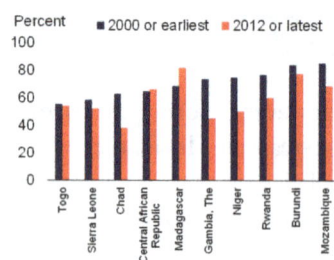

Sources: World Bank; International Monetary Fund; Haver Analytics; World Bank Doing Business database; Didier et al. (2015).
C. Shows access to electricity as a percent of population; number of power outages; value lost due to power outages in percent of sales; and electricity transmission and distribution losses in percent of total output. International best practice is the average of values for the top 5th percentile for access to electricity and the average of the bottom 5th percentile for power outages, value lost to power outages, and power losses.
D. Based on an event study of episodes of significant reform spurts and setbacks (two standard-error change in at least one of four WGI ratings) for 64 EM and FM countries for 1996-2014 (Didier et al. 2015). Growth differential from baseline without significant reform spurts or setbacks.
E. Working-age population is population aged 15-64 years.
F. Measured as poverty headcount ratio (% of population) at $1.25 a day (purchasing power parity).

than 90 percent of poverty is concentrated in pre- and early-dividend countries with young populations that lag in key human development indicators, register rapid population growth, and are seeing their working-age populations swell.[16] In these countries, the demographic transition to lower fertility should help raise living standards and should be supported by policies investing in better education, health, and women empowerment. In late- and post-dividend countries, which exhibit much lower fertility rates and more pronounced population ageing, it will be especially important to mobilize savings for productive investment and reforming welfare systems to ensure fiscal sustainability, while supporting the elderly and more vulnerable (World Bank 2015b). Most countries in East Asia and the Pacific and Europe and Central Asia already have shrinking working-age populations. Incentives for greater or longer labor force participation may offset these demographic pressures. The associated reduction in benefits and increased social contributions could also help increase fiscal space. In many countries in Europe and Central Asia, however, policies need to go beyond reforming transfer and pension systems, and must encompass improvements in health and education that increase productive lifetimes, and labor market reforms that encourage greater participation by older people and women (World Bank 2015l).

Where the working-age population is expanding, structural reforms are vital for other reasons. In South Asia, for instance, an estimated 300 million-plus working-age adults are expected to enter the labor force by 2040, more than half of them in a handful of historically slow-growing and less-developed sub-regions. Reforms that equip new cohorts of workers entering the labor force with the right skills will accordingly remain key to absorbing the growing workforce. Important areas of policy intervention for South Asian governments include improving access and quality of education, as well as strengthening accountability mechanisms, particularly in public schools (Dundar et al. 2014).

---

[16]See World Bank 2015c for a description of typologies.

Poverty-related policy challenges

There are growing concerns that poverty will become increasingly concentrated in natural-resource-based economies, and in fragile and conflict states. Many of these are in Sub-Saharan Africa (World Bank 2015c). This region, which has very high poverty rates, will account for more than half of working age population growth through 2050. For low-income commodity

exporters in the region, where extreme poverty rates average 43 percent in the region, even the limited gains in poverty reduction made over the past decade could rapidly reverse. Poor households in these countries have been hit by higher import prices from sharp currency declines, the disappearance of jobs in construction and other non-tradable sectors, and cutbacks in relief programs because of fiscal pressures (World Bank 2015a-b).

References

Ahmed, S., M. Appendino, and M. Ruta. 2015. Global Value Chains and the Exchange Rate Elasticity of Exports." IMF Working Paper, International Monetary Fund, Washington, DC.

Arslanalp, S., and T. Tsuda. 2014. "Tracking Global Demand for Emerging Market Sovereign Debt." IMF Working Paper, International Monetary Fund, Washington, DC.

Arteta, C., A. Kose, F. Ohnsorge, and M. Stocker. 2015. "The Coming U.S. Interest Rate Tightening Cycle: Smooth Sailing or Stormy Waters?" Policy Research Note No. 2, World Bank, Washington, DC.

Auerbach A., and Y. Gorodnichenko. 2013. "Output Spillovers from Fiscal Policy." *American Economic Review* 103 (3): 141-146.

Beyer, R., and F. Smets. 2015. "Labour Market Adjustments in Europe and the U.S.: How Different?" ECB Working Papers Series no. 1767. European Central Bank, Frankfurt.

Blomberg, S, G. Hess, and A. Orphanides. 2004. "The Macroeconomic Consequences of Terrorism." *Journal of Monetary Economics*, 51 (5): 1007-1032.

Brayton, F., T. Laubach, and D. Reifschneider. 2014. "The FRB/U.S. Model: A Tool for Macroeconomic Policy Analysis," FEDS Notes.

Board of Governors of the Federal Reserve System, Washington, DC.

Borio, C. 2014. "The International Monetary and Financial System: Its Achilles Heel and What to Do about It." BIS Working Paper 456, Bank for International Settlements, Basel.

Ceriani, L., and R. Laderchi, C. 2011. "Poverty and Social Exclusion in Bosnia and Herzegovina: Insights from the 2011 Extended Household Budget Survey." World Bank, Washington, DC.

Chow, J. T. S., F. Jaumotte, S. G. Park, and Y. S. Zhang. 2015. "Spillovers from Dollar Appreciation." Policy Discussion Paper 15/2. International Monetary Fund, Washington, DC.

Coe D., E. Helpman, and A. Hoffmaister. 2009. "International R&D Spillovers and Institutions." *European Economic Review* 53 (7): 723-741.

Congressional Budget Office. 2015. "The 2015 Long-term Budget Outlook." Washington, June.

Cordella, T., and P. Gupta. 2015. "What Makes a Currency Procyclical? An Empirical Investigation." *Journal of International Money and Finance* 55 (July): 240-259.

Dabla-Norris, E., G. Ho, K. Kochhar, A. Kyobe, and R. Tchaidze. 2013. "Anchoring Growth: The Importance of Productivity-Enhancing Reforms in Emerging Market and Developing Economies." IMF Staff Discussion Note 13/08 (December). International Monetary Fund, Washington, DC.

Dabla-Norris, E., G. Ho, and A. Kyobe. 2013. "Reforms and Distance to Frontier." IMF Technical Note to Staff Discussion Note 13/08. International Monetary Fund, Washington, DC.

De La Torre, A., T. Didier, and M. Pinat. 2014. "Can Latin America Tap the Globalization Upside?" Policy Research Working Paper No. 6837, World Bank, Washington.

Devarajan, S., and Mottaghi, L. 2015. "Economic Implications of Lifting Sanctions on Iran." MENA Quarterly Economic Brief, World Bank, July.

Didier, T., A. Kose, F. Ohnsorge, and L. S. Ye. 2015. "Slowdown in Emerging Markets: A Rough Patch or Hard Landing?" Policy Research Note No. 4, World Bank, Washington, DC.

Dundar, H., T. Beteille, M. Riboud, and A. Deolalikar. 2014. *Student Learning in South Asia: Challenges, Opportunities, and Policy Priorities.* Washington, DC: World Bank.

Eichengreen, B., D. Park, and K. Shin. 2012. "When Fast-growing Economies Slow Down: International Evidence and Implications for China." *Asian Economic Papers* 11 (1): 42–87.

Elekdag, S., and Y. Wu. 2011. "Rapid Credit Growth: Boon or Boom-Bust?" Working Paper 11/241, International Monetary Fund, Washington, DC.

European Commission. 2015a. "Spring 2015 Economic Forecast: Tailwinds Support the Recovery." Directorate-General for Economic and Financial Affairs, European Economy, 2/2015.

_____. 2015b. "Autumn 2015 Economic Forecast." Directorate-General for Economic and Financial Affairs, European Economy, Institutional Paper 011.

European Central Bank. 2015a. "September 2015 ECB Staff Macroeconomic Projections for the Euro Area." European Central Bank, Eurosystem, September.

_____. 2015b. "October 2015 Euro Area

Bank Lending Survey." European Central Bank, Eurosystem, October.

Fernald, J., and B. Wang. 2015. "The Recent Rise and Fall of Rapid Productivity Growth." Economic Letter 2015-04, Federal Reserve Bank of San Francisco.

Financial Stability Oversight Council. 2015. "Annual Report." Washington, DC, May.

Gauvinyand, L., and C. Rebillard. 2013. "Towards Recoupling? Assessing the Impact of a Chinese Hard Landing on Commodity Exporters: Results from Conditional Forecast in a GVAR Model." Banque de France.

Georgiadis, G., and F. Gräb. 2015. "Global Financial Market Impact of the Announcement of the ECB's Extended Asset Purchase Programme." Federal Reserve Bank of Dallas Globalization and Monetary Policy Institute, Working Paper No. 232, March 2015.

Gill, I., I. Izvorski, W. van Eeghen, and D. De Rosa. 2014. *Diversified Development: Making the Most of Natural Resources in Eurasia.* Washington, DC: World Bank.

Gordon, R. J. 2014. "The Demise of U.S. Economic Growth: Restatement, Rebuttal, and Reflections." NBER Working Paper No. 19895. National Bureau of Economic Research, Cambridge, MA.

Goujard, A. 2013. "Cross-country Spillovers from Fiscal Consolidations." OECD Economics Department Working Papers, No 1099.

Gourio, F., M. Siemer, and A. Verdelhan. 2014. "Uncertainty and International Capital Flows." Unpublished manuscript, Massachusetts Institute of Technology.

Hall, R. E. 2014. "Quantifying the Lasting Harm to the U.S. Economy from the Financial Crisis." In J. Parker and M. Woodford (eds.) *NBER Macroeconomics Annual 2014*, Volume. 29.

Hamilton, J., E. Harris, J. Hatzius, and K. West.

2015. "The Equilibrium Real Funds Rate: Past, Present and Future." Brookings Working Paper No. 16, Washington, DC.

Hooley, J. 2013. "Bringing Down the Great Wall? Global Implications of Capital Account Liberalisation in China." Quarterly Bulletin 2013 Q4. Bank of England.

Huang, H., 2015. "The Development of the RMB Offshore Market and the Liberalization of China's Capital Account." International Economics Department. Project summary. Chatham House. The Royal Institute of International Affairs.

Ianchovichina, E., S. Devarajan, and C. Lakatos. Forthcoming. "The Lifting of Sanctions on Iran: Global Effects and Strategic Responses." World Bank, Washington, DC.

Institute for Economics and Peace. 2015. "Global Terrorism Index 2015: Measuring and Understanding the Impact of Terrorism." IEP report 36, November.

in't Veld, J. 2013. "Fiscal Consolidations and Spillovers in the Euro Area Periphery and Core." European Economy Economics Paper No. 506. Brussels.

International Monetary Fund. 2001. "The Global Economy After the September 11 Attacks." IMF World Economic Outlook, Washington, DC, December 2001.

International Monetary Fund. 2008. "Structural Reforms and Economic Performance in Advanced and Developing Countries." Research Department, International Monetary Fund, Washington, DC.

_____. 2012. *Brazil: Consumer Credit Growth and Household Financial Stress.* Technical Note. Washington D.C.: International Monetary Fund.

_____. 2014. "Sustaining Long-run Growth and Macroeconomic Stability in Low-income Countries: The Role of Structural Transformation and Diversification." IMF Policy Paper, Washington, DC.

_____. 2015a. "Exchange Rates and Trade Flows: Disconnected?" IMF World Economic Outlook, Chapter 3, Washington, October 2015.

_____. 2015b. *Global Financial Stability Report—Vulnerabilities, Legacies, and Policy Challenges: Risks Rotating to Emerging Markets.* Washington, DC: International Monetary Fund. October.

_____. 2015c. China, Staff Report for the 2015 Article IV Consultation. International Monetary Fund, Washington, DC.

_____. 2015d. "United States: 2015 IMF Article IV Consultation – Staff Report." IMF Country Report No. 15/168, International Monetary Fund, Washington, DC.

_____. 2015e. "Japan: 2015 IMF Article IV Consultation – Staff Report." IMF Country Report No. 15/168, Washington, DC.

_____. 2015f. "Northern Spring, Southern Chills." IMF Regional Economic Outlook: Western Hemisphere, Washington, DC.

_____. 2015g. "Middle East and Central Asia." Regional Economic Outlook series. October. International Monetary Fund, Washington, DC.

Ito, K., and R. Wakasugi. 2015. "Growth and Structural Change in Trade: Evidence from Japan." In VoxEU.org eBook *The Global Trade Slowdown: A New Normal?* January 2015.

Jimeno, J. F. 2015. "Long-lasting Consequences of the European Crisis." ECB Working Paper Series No. 1832, July 2015.

Julio, B., and Y. Yook. 2013. "Policy Uncertainty, Irreversibility, and Cross-border Flows of Capital." Finance and Economics Discussion Series Working Paper No. 2013-64, Board of Governors of the Federal Reserve System, Washington, DC.

Kollias, C., Papadamou, S. and A. Stagiannis. 2011. "Terrorism and capital markets: The effects of the Madrid and London bomb attacks."

International Review of Economics and Finance, 20 (4): 532-541.

Kose, M. A., and M. E. Terrones, 2015. *Collapse and Revival: Understanding Global Recessions and Recoveries.* Washington, DC: International Monetary Fund.

Laforte, J-P. and J. Roberts. 2014. "November 2014 Update of the FRB/U.S. Model", FEDS Notes, April 2014.

Mauro P., H. Joly, A. Aisen, C. Emre Alper, F. Boutin-Dufresne, J. Dridi, N. Gigineishvili, et al. 2015. "Monitoring and Managing Fiscal Risks in the East African Community" African Departmental Paper No. 15/7. International Monetary Fund, Washington, DC.

Mendoza, E. G. 2010. "Sudden Stops, Financial Crises and Leverage." *American Economic Review* 100 (5): 1941–1966.

Mendoza, E. G., and M. E. Terrones. 2008. "An Anatomy of Credit Booms: Evidence from Macro Aggregates and Micro Data." Working Paper No. 14049, National Bureau of Economic Research, Cambridge, MA

Münz, R., T. Straubhaar, F. Vadean, and N. Vadean. 2006. "The Costs and Benefits of European Immigration," Hamburg Institute of International Economics Report No. 3, Migration Research Group.

National Consortium for the Study of Terrorism and Responses to Terrorism (START). 2015. "Global Terrorism Database." Retrieved from http://www.start.umd.edu/gtd

Nedelescu, O and R. Johnston. 2005. "The Impact of Terrorism on Financial Markets." IMF Working Paper No. 05/60, Washington, DC.

Obstfeld, M. 2015. "Trilemmas and Tradeoffs: Living with Financial Globalization." BIS Working Papers No 480. Bank for International Settlements, Basel.

Office of the Comptroller of the Currency. 2015.

"Semiannual Risk Perspective from the National Risk Committee." U.S. Treasury Department, Washington, June 2015.

Organisation for Economic Co-operation and Development. 2014. "Is migration good for the economy?" OECD Migration Policy Debates, May 2014.

_____. 2015. "2015 Going for Growth: Breaking the Vicious Circle." OECD, Paris, February 2015.

Ostry, J., A. Ghoshand M. Chamon. 2012. "Two Targets, Two Instruments: Monetary and Exchange Rate Policies in Emerging Market Economies." IMF Staff Discussion Notes No 12/01, International Monetary Fund, Washington.

Roberts, B. 2009. "The Macroeconomic Impacts of the 9/11 Attack: Evidence from Real-Time Forecasting." Working Paper Series, Department of Homeland Security, Washington, DC.

Sobrun, J., and P. Turner. 2015. "Bond Markets and Monetary Policy Dilemmas for the Emerging Markets." BIS Working Papers No 508. Bank for International Settlements, Basel.

Verikios, G. 2015. "The Implications for Trade and FDI Flows from Liberalisation of China's Capital Account." Centre of Policy Studies Working Paper No. G-251. January 2015. Victoria University, Melbourne, Australia.

Wakasugi, R., B. Ito, T. Matsuura, H. Sato, A. Tanaka, and Y. Todo. 2014. "Features of Japanese Internationalized Firms: Findings Based on Firm-Level Data", in R Wakasugi (ed.) *Internationalization of Japanese Firms: Evidence from Firm-level Data*. Tokyo: Springer.

World Bank. 2012. *Skills, Not Just Diplomas: Managing Education for Results in Eastern Europe and Central Asia*. Edited by L. Sondergaard, M. Murthi, D. Abu-Ghaida, C. Bodewig, and J. Rutkowski. Washington, DC: World Bank.

World Bank. 2015a. China Economic Update,

June. World Bank, Washington, DC.

—————————. 2015b. *Global Monitoring Report.* Washington, DC: World Bank

—————————. 2015c. *Commodity Markets Outlook October 2015.* Washington, DC: World Bank.

—————————. 2015d. *Having Space and Using It. Global Economic Prospects January 2015.* Washington, DC: World Bank.

—————————. 2015e. *The Global Economy in Transition. Global Economic Prospects June 2015.* Washington, DC: World Bank.

—————————. 2015f. "Jobs, Wages and the Latin American Slowdown." LAC Semiannual Report, October 2015. World Bank, Washington DC.

—————————. 2015g. "Getting Prices Right— The Recent Disinflation and Its Implications." South Asia Economic Focus, Fall 2015. World Bank, Washington, DC.

—————————. 2015h. Africa Pulse, Volume 12. Washington DC: World Bank.

—————————. 2015i. "Doing Business 2016. Measuring Regulatory Quality and Efficiency: Economy Profile 2016 China." Available at http:// www.doingbusiness.org/data/exploreeconomies/ china. World Bank, Washington, DC

—————————. 2015j. East Asia and Pacific Economic Update, October. World Bank, Washington, DC.

—————————. 2015k. Europe and Central Asia: Regional Brief. Available at http:// www.worldbank.org/content/dam/Worldbank/ document/eca/eca-regional-brief-sm2015.pdf. World Bank, Washington, DC.

—————————. 2015l. *Golden Aging: Prospects for Healthy, Active and Prosperous Aging in Europe and Central Asia.* Washington, DC: World Bank.

World Bank and Development Research Center of the State Council, the People's Republic of China. 2014. *Urban China: Toward Efficient, Inclusive, and Sustainable Urbanization.* Washington, DC: World Bank.

World Trade Organization. 2015. "Falling Import Demand, Lower Commodity Prices Push Down Trade Growth Prospects." Press Release No. 752. World Trade Organization, Geneva.

Yellen, J. 2015. "Normalizing Monetary Policy: Prospects and Perspectives." Speech at "The New Normal Monetary Policy," Research Conference Sponsored by the Federal Reserve Bank of San Francisco, March 27.

SPECIAL FOCUS

From Commodity Discovery to Production: Vulnerabilities and Policies in LICs

Special Focus
From Commodity Discovery to Production:
Vulnerabilities and Policies in LICs

Major resource discoveries have transformed growth prospects for many LICs. The sharp downturn in commodity prices may delay the development of these discoveries into production. During the pre-production development process, macroeconomic vulnerabilities in these economies may widen as a result of large scale investment needs. This heightens the importance of reducing lead times between discovery and production. Over the medium term, lead times may be reduced by improved quality of governance. Growth has eased in LICs but continued to be robust at about 5 percent in 2015, sustained by public investment, rising farm output and continued mining investments. For 2016-17, strengthening import demand in major advanced economies should help support activity in these countries.

Introduction

The surge in commodity prices over the past decade has played a pivotal role in spurring faster growth in low-income countries (LICs). As industry exploration and investment spending climbed to record highs, a spate of commodity discoveries—notably "giant" oil and gas discoveries in East and West Africa—has transformed the long-term growth outlook in several countries (World Bank, 2015a and b).[1] Mining has expanded rapidly in many LICs in Sub-Saharan Africa over the past decade. For example, the number of active industrial gold mines reached historic highs by 2011 across Sub-Saharan Africa after half a decade of soaring gold prices (Tolonen 2015).

However, with the turn in the commodity supercycle, industry spending on investment has dropped sharply.[2] In Africa the number of oil rigs for on-land drilling has already fallen by 40 percent from their peak in Q1 2014 (Figure SF.1), and mining production has been disrupted in Sierra Leone and Democratic Republic of Congo (DRC). There are risks of delays in major mining and energy projects under development in East

African LICs that could affect growth prospects. In Uganda, for instance, slower-than-anticipated infrastructure development has already delayed oil production start dates, from 2016 to as late as 2020. In Tanzania and Mozambique, final investment decisions on major LNG projects have yet to be made (Bennot, 2015).[3] In Afghanistan, investment plans for the development of copper and iron ore mines leased for development in 2008 and 2012 have been significantly scaled back.

Project delays are detrimental for several reasons. They prolong the period of heightened vulnerabilities associated with the pre-production investment and delay the boost to growth that is typically associated with production. Additional concerns arise in hydrocarbon projects where delays may increase the risk of "stranded assets" as global efforts to tackle climate change induce a shift towards less carbon-intensive technologies and greater energy efficiency (Stevens et. al. 2015, Carbon Tracker Initiative 2004, McGlade and Ekins 2015).[4] Such stranded assets pose financial and growth risks to the companies that own or operate them and the governments that back them.

Note: This Special Focus was prepared by Tehmina Khan, Trang Nguyen, Franziska Ohnsorge and Richard Schodde.

[1] "Giant" fields are conventional fields with recoverable reserves of 500 million barrels of oil equivalent or more. Despite the increasing importance of unconventional shale oil and gas fields, current and future oil and gas supply is dominated by conventional giant fields (Bai and Xu 2014).

[2] The drop in industry investment has partly reflected growing concerns about misallocation of capital expenditures into exploration over the past decade (McIntosh, 2015).

[3] Coal projects in Mozambique are reportedly losing money, because of the slump in coal prices, and inadequate infrastructure (Almeida Santos, Roffarello, and Filipe 2015).

[4] "Stranded assets" refer to resource capacity, specifically for hydrocarbons (coal, oil, gas), that remains unused as the world reduces its hydrocarbon consumption in order to reduce risks arising from climate change (Carbon Tracker Initiative, 2004, McGlade and Ekins, 2015).

FIGURE SF.1 Prospects and risks from resource investment

Following a decade of major resource discoveries, the drop in oil prices raises concerns that long-planned investment to develop discoveries into production is delayed in low-income countries. This would set back growth.

A. Rig counts in Africa and North America

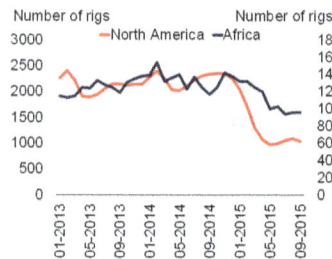

B. Resource discoveries eventually converted into production

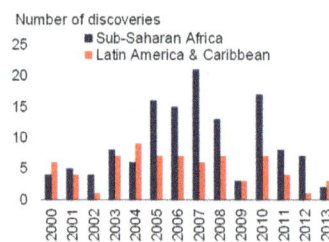

C. Contribution of investment to real GDP growth, 2010-14

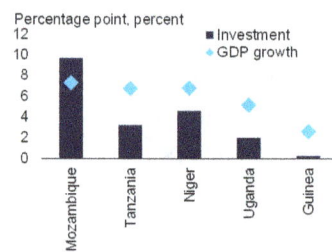

D. Growth in low- and middle-income countries with resource discoveries

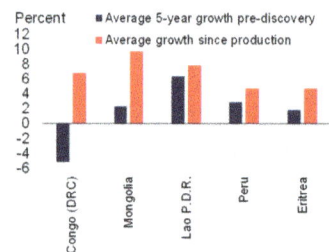

Source: World Bank staff estimates, World Development Indicators, MinEx Consulting.
A. The rig count is the number of oil rigs in operation.
C. Contribution of investment in percentage point, GDP growth in percent.

This Special Focus discusses the evolution of macroeconomic vulnerabilities during the development of major resource discoveries, the impact of slowing commodity prices on development times, and policies to shorten these times. The analysis rests on a dataset for gold and copper discoveries worldwide since 1950 (proprietary to MinEx Consulting). Over this period, gold and copper discoveries have accounted for two-thirds of non-ferrous discoveries worldwide. The results shown here therefore are illustrative of the impact of policies and commodity prices on project development.

This Focus addresses the following issues:

- What are typical lead times between discovery and production?

- How do economies evolve between commodity discovery and production?

- What factors determine the lead time between discovery and production?

- What are growth prospects for LICs?

Lead times between discovery and production

Typically, developing a resource discovery requires large upfront investments, over a considerable period. During this time, there may be high uncertainty about prices and macroeconomic and policy environments (IMF, 2012a).

Broadly, the process of development of most mines undergoes five major stages. Since cross-country data is not publicly available, four of these stages are illustrated in Figure SF.2 for two copper mines, one in the United States and another in Mongolia. The process begins with exploration to establish the existence of a *potentially* commercially viable deposit (4-5 years in the two illustrative examples).[5] Once such a deposit is confirmed, feasibility, environmental and other impact studies are conducted and financing plans developed to establish commercial viability. Once commercial viability has been confirmed, a mining license is obtained, a process that can take several years in some countries (2-3 years, on average, in Africa; Gajigo et al. 2012). Finally, the duration of construction of the physical facility (3 years in the two illustrative examples) depends on the accessibility of the deposit.

All steps depend on the quality of governance, the reliability of institutions, and macroeconomic stability that facilitates predictable policies. Investment risks tend to be high in the exploration, pre-feasibility and feasibility stages, and decline as a deposit gets closer to production. Stylized facts on lead times by type of commodity and size of deposit are as follows:

- *Oil and gas.* Conventional discoveries can take 30-40 years to develop (Clo 2000), but lead times for giant oil and gas discoveries can be shorter (Arezki et al. 2015). For oil deposits,

---
[5]In African LICs, the average duration of an exploration license is for three years (Gajigo et al. 2012).

such as shale, short lead times of 2-3 years reflect technological improvements since the 1980s, and reduced entry barriers for small, agile firms (Wang and Xue, 2014, World Bank 2015a). Monetizing gas discoveries is harder than oil discoveries: final markets are typically far away, so that simultaneous investments in drilling and transport infrastructure are required, and long-term price contracts need to be agreed with end-users (Huurdeman 2014)

- *Mining.* Lead times can range from a few years to decades, depending on the type of mineral, size and grade of the deposit, financing conditions, country factors and commodity prices (UNECA 2011, Schodde 2014).

- *Copper mining versus other mining.* Average lead times for gold discoveries are ten years, but more than 15 years for zinc, lead, copper and nickel discoveries (Schodde 2014). Development of most gold deposits tends to begin immediately, whereas a significant share of copper discoveries takes several decades (Figure SF.4). For instance, one-third of copper discoveries since 1950 have had lead times to eventual production of 30 or more years, compared with only 4.5 percent of gold discoveries. Similarly, industry estimates place the period from early exploration to final production of copper mines at close to 25 years (McIntosh 2015). Longer lead times for copper mines reflect greater complexity and greater infrastructure investment to transport the ore to export markets.[6] Average lead times to production have fallen sharply in recent decades.

Evolution from commodity discovery to production

Resource discoveries matter to the economy only insofar as they can be developed into production. However, since 1950, less than 60 percent of gold, zinc and lead discoveries have made it to eventual

FIGURE SF.2 The mining project cycle

Most mining projects are characterized by several key stages that include exploration, discovery, feasibility assessments and regulatory compliance (including obtaining licenses), project construction, production and eventually closure.

A. Time lines for mine development

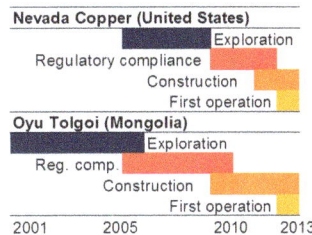

B. Duration of mining leases and exploration licenses in selected LICs

C. Investment risk over a mining project lifecycle

D. Number of years from gold and copper discovery to production

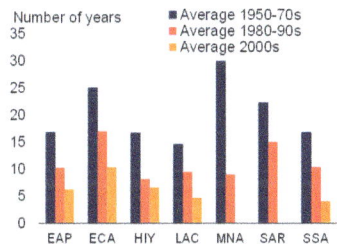

Source: World Bank, Perott-Humphrey (2011); Gajigo et. al. (2012); http://ot.mn/history, http://pumpkinhollowcopper.com/project-timeline/, both accessed November 4, 2015.
A. Illustrative example of timeline from two copper mines, in the United States and Mongolia. Exploration is not included in lead times discussed in the text.
D. Based on a sample of 46 countries with copper discoveries and 73 countries with gold discoveries. SST denotes Sub-Saharan Africa. EAP = East Asia and Pacific; ECA = Europe and Central Asia; HIY = High-income countries; LAC = Latin America and the Caribbean; MNA = Middle East and Africa; SAR = South Asia; SSA = Sub-Saharan Africa.

production, and less than 40 percent of copper and nickel discoveries (Schodde, 2014). Once developed, the market value of discoveries can be large compared to the size of LIC and MIC economies. For copper mines, for example, production in 2014 alone accounted for 6 percent of LIC GDP and 2 percent of MIC GDP, on average (Figure SF.3).

Depending on the commodity and the size of discovery, during the lead time between commodity recovery and extraction, countries can accumulate sizeable vulnerabilities as investment rises and external liabilities grow.[7] In the dataset used here, investment growth increased sharply in

---

[6]For instance, the location of Chile's copper mines close to the sea has made it easier to profitably ship concentrates, whereas copper mines in central Africa have had to rely on local smelting and refining to reduce the volumes transported to ports (Crowson, 2011).

[7]An event study of macroeconomic developments between discovery and production of copper deposits illustrates the domestic demand pressures that can prevail during these lead times. In a panel regression, inflation, import growth and the current account deficit were regressed on a dummy variable that takes the value of 1 during

FIGURE SF.3 Developments during lead times between resource discovery and extraction

Gold and copper discoveries have been sizeable compared to the size of LIC and MIC economies. However, a significant portion of discoveries never get developed. Between resource discovery and production, investment growth rises sharply and vulnerabilities can increase. Growth can become vulnerable to setbacks in mining sectors.

A. Share of non-ferrous discoveries converted into production

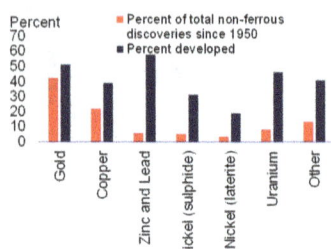

B. Average value of copper production, 2014

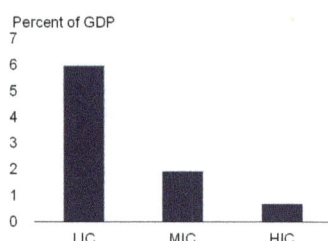

C. Investment growth during lead times

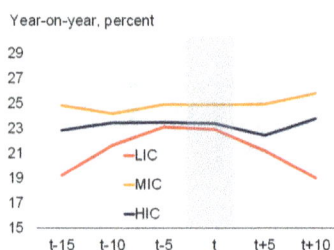

D. GDP growth in Sierra Leone

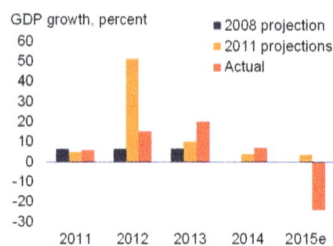

E. Public debt ratios in selected East African LICs

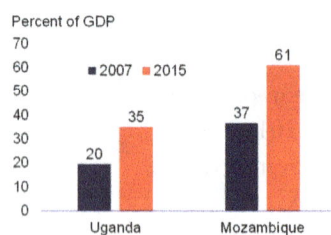

F. Current account deficits in selected East African LICs

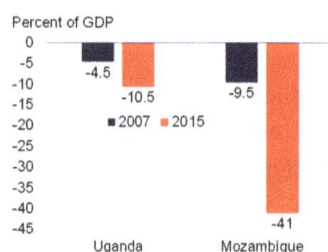

Source: World Development Indicators, World Economic Outlook, MINEX Consulting, World Bank staff estimates., World Bank Commodity Markets Outlook World Bank (2015d).
A. C. LIC stands for low-income countries, MIC for middle-income countries, and HIC for high-income countries.
B. Annual copper production evaluated at average 2014 price in percent of GDP (World Bank 2015a).
C. Based on a sample of 46 countries with copper discoveries and 73 countries with gold discoveries.
D. IMF projections for GDP growth in Sierra Leone, which discovered major iron-ore deposits in 2009.

the five years that precede the beginning of production. Time and country dummies control for global and country-specific factors. The sample period is 1980-2014. The estimates suggest that on average, lead-time investment associated with resource development contributed to an increase in inflation of 9 percentage points, and of import growth by 1 percentage point. The estimates were somewhat larger for copper than other mineral discoveries. Current account deficits were 3.6 percentage points of GDP wider. These estimated effects were particularly pronounced in LICs: inflation was 14.5 percentage points higher during these episodes and current account deficits 4.3 percentage point of GDP wider.

the five to ten years before actual extraction of the resource began (Figure SF.3). This effect was only apparent in low-income countries. Since they tend to be smaller and less diversified than middle- and high-income countries, the development of a large mine can create significant domestic demand pressures. Using a global database on giant oil discoveries (those exceeding ultimately recoverable reserves of 500 million barrels), including in Africa, Arezki et. al. (2015a) find that investment growth rises immediately upon discovery and current account deficits widen. GDP growth and private consumption growth respond only once extraction begins. The full increase in GDP growth materializes with commercial production, when vulnerabilities unwind as exports expand.

The size of vulnerabilities depends on two factors: how mine construction is financed, whether governments borrow in anticipation of rising commodity revenues in the future, and whether private consumption and investment rises in anticipation of rising incomes. If rising imports and current account deficits are financed by FDI, which tends to be less prone to sudden stops than debt financing, short-term vulnerabilities are more limited (Levchenko and Mauro 2008). Nevertheless, a sudden stop in FDI projects could also disrupt foreign exchange markets and sharply dampen activity. In particular, expectations of greater FDI (including as a result of recent natural resource discoveries) can encourage long-maturity non-resource investment projects. If these expectations are not validated, a sudden stop could follow and trigger fire sales of long-term assets and a collapse in activity (Calvo 2014). Additional, fiscal risks arise if governments expand spending and borrow against future commodity revenues.

The following examples illustrate the heightened vulnerabilities associated with lead times in a number of LICs.

• *Sierra Leone:* The discovery of major iron-ore deposits in 2009 led to a substantial upward revision in growth forecasts to over 50 percent in 2012 as mining production came onstream. However, work stoppages and a breakdown in the railway system delayed the start of the mine, so that actual growth results were much lower than initial projections. Since then, a collapse in global iron ore prices by 50 percent in 2014 has led to severe financial difficulties at the country's two foreign-owned and highly indebted mining operators, with one declaring bankruptcy and the other halting operations (World Bank 2015e, IMF 2012b and 2015a). This and the outbreak of the Ebola epidemic set back activity, with the economy estimated to have contracted by 20 percent in 2015.

- *Uganda:* Oil was discovered in 2006. Although production has yet to start, the government has borrowed in anticipation of future oil revenues. The public debt ratio has nearly doubled since 2007, reflecting loans from Chinese state banks and other lenders to finance large hydropower and other infrastructure projects. With production dates being postponed, infrastructure projects affected by cost overruns, and the current account deficit reaching over 10 percent of GDP in 2015, fiscal risks and external financing risks have increased (World Bank 2015f).

- *Mozambique.* The discovery of massive gas deposits in 2012 has lifted medium to long-term growth prospects. However, the sharp fall in oil and gas prices since 2014, delays in mining infrastructure projects and highly expansionary fiscal policies are generating major short-term challenges. Public debt ratios have risen sharply from 2007, to finance government infrastructure spending. But with finances under pressure, the country has turned to the IMF for a potential loan program (IMF 2015b).

Determinants of the lead time

Lead times to production depend on a wide range of technical, economic, social, and political factors. They include the accessibility and quality of the discovery, commodity prices, and policy environments. Larger discoveries closer to the surface in more predictable policy environments appear to see faster development (World Bank 2015a). Higher commodity prices increase the feasibility of marginal projects, and could

FIGURE SF.4 Lead times between resource discovery and extraction

Lead times between discovery and production are considerably longer for copper deposits than gold deposits, especially when commodity prices are low. However, they can be shortened by improving business environments.

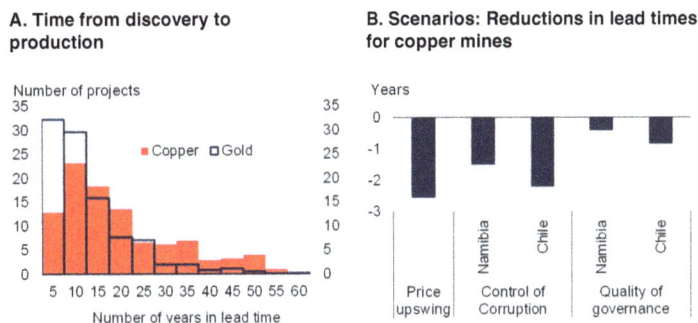

A. Time from discovery to production

B. Scenarios: Reductions in lead times for copper mines

Source: World Bank staff calculations, MinEx Consulting.
A. Number of discoveries for each number of years.
B. Reduction in average lead times for average LIC mine if price downturn shifts to price upswing, if control of corruption is improved to the level of Chile or Namibia, or if quality of governance was improved to the level of Chile or Namibia. Derived from differences in predicted values predicted by a duration model described in Annex SF.1. "Price upswings" denotes reductions in lead times for the largest quartile of copper discoveries in LIC since 2000 as a result of switching from a commodity price downturn to an upswing. Reductions in other variables for the same mines as a result of raising control of corruption and quality of governance to average levels prevailing in Namibia and Chile.

accelerate the start of development after discovery (Schodde 2014). Once started, however, sunk costs may make mining companies reluctant to disrupt ongoing projects, particularly if development is already well advanced (McIntosh 2015, Crowson 2011).[8]

A duration analysis helps assess the relative importance of these factors, using a proprietary dataset for the years 1950-2015 provided by MinEx Consulting. It comprises 273 copper discoveries in 46 countries, and 687 gold discoveries in 73 countries. The methodology is a standard survival analysis (Jenkins 2006, Annex SF.1) to estimate the probability of a particular mine reaching production in any given year. Explanatory variables are global gold and copper prices (World Bank 2015d), and the policy environment at the time of discovery, controlling for the physical characteristics of the deposit.

A "good" policy environment conducive for

---

[8]In general, the option value of delaying project completion may be lower in the resource sector than in non-resource sectors, due to a limited number of alternative feasible projects, and heavy involvement of the state, which provides some insulation from political shocks (Crowson, 2011).

resource investment—as well as non-resource investment—has many dimensions. It includes sound macroeconomic policies that ensure sustainable fiscal positions (as measured by government debt in percent of GDP at the time of discovery), and domestic demand pressures (as proxied by inflation at the time of discovery). A more stable macroeconomic environment can be associated with more predictable tax and expenditure decisions. A conducive policy environment also includes high quality of institutions, at the time of the discovery, that affect mining operations. This is proxied by the World Bank Governance Indicators for Control of Corruption and by the QOG Institute's Index of the Quality of Government.[9] These are some of the same conditions that would help avoid the macroeconomic volatility and stunted growth in resource-based economies that has been labelled the "resource curse" (Sachs and Warner 2001; Mehlum, Moene and Torvik 2002; Humphreys, Sachs and Stiglitz 2007).

The results suggest an important role for the commodity price cycle, sound macroeconomic management and the quality of governance. Higher commodity prices, on average, are not significant determinants of lead times, probably because of the significant sunk costs involved. However, for copper deposits, an upswing in copper prices at the time of discovery—the crucial period when licenses are obtained and exploration and extraction rights negotiated—accelerates development. For example, in LICs since 2000, rising copper prices at the time of discovery may have shaved off about two to three years from lead times. For the largest quartile of copper discoveries in LICs since 2000, the price boom may have reduced lead times by 2½ years (Figure SF.4). Sound macroeconomic policies also appear to be important: lowering government debt below 40 percent of GDP, or reducing inflation below 10 percent, accelerates development times by about 10 percent. These variables may proxy for

---

[9]The importance of the policy environment is also borne out in anecdotal evidence. For instance, the Oyu Tolgoi mine in Mongolia—despite being one of the largest copper deposits in the world—took nearly a decade to become operational in 2013, following initial exploration in the early 2000s, lengthy feasibility studies and negotiations between the government and Rio Tinto over the financing of the mine's construction.

generally sounder and more predictable macroeconomic policies.

While lower commodity prices could lengthen lead times for copper mines, their effects can be mitigated by strengthened policies. Had the average LIC had the same quality of government index or the same control of corruption index as Chile or Namibia, the lead times for the development of copper discoveries since 2000 might have been shortened by as much as two years (Figure SF.4).

Policy Implications

Many low-income countries remain at the frontier of resource exploration and they are expected to be a major source of commodity supplies over the long-term (ICMM, 2012). Under the right conditions, new resource production should boost their exports and growth. With fiscal institutions in place to manage the volatility of resource revenues (World Bank 2015a), new resource production could provide a major opportunity for development over the medium to long term.

However, the sharp drop in commodity prices since 2014 is already affecting resource sector investments and could further delay the development of discoveries in several LICs. This, in turn, could prolong vulnerabilities—inflation, fiscal and balance of payments pressures—often associated with resource development as governments and private sectors borrow and invest in anticipation of future income growth. For the largest deposits, a price downturn in the early stages of development, when licenses and extraction rights are negotiated, could potentially delay development by a few years, which could be critical for some LICs with growing fiscal and current account pressures.

Countries, in which resource development is still in initial stages, could consider accepting further delays to contain vulnerabilities and reduce the long-term risk of stranded assets (Steven et. al. 2015). Where development is already far advanced, this option may be unattractive. In these countries, especially, improvements in business environments could offset some of the price pressures on resource development. At the same time, they would benefit non-resource investment and help reduce macroeconomic vulnerabilities (Loayza and Raddatz 2007). Other means of expediting resource developments are likely to be less helpful in the long-run, including increased tax incentives for mining companies. Mining companies have reportedly often negotiated tax exemptions that go above provisions specified in enacted legislation and are higher than warranted by mine profits (Curtis et al. 2009; Gajigo et al. 2012).

Recent developments and near-term outlook in low-income countries

Growth in low-income economies (LICs) eased during 2015, reflecting headwinds from falling commodity prices and security and political tensions (Figure SF.5, Table SF.1). Nevertheless, on average, growth has remained solid at 5.1 percent.

Growth was particularly strong in several of the largest LICs, sustained by public investment, rising farm output and continued mining investments.[10] In oil-importers, including Ethiopia and Rwanda, low commodity prices supported activity. In Ethiopia, the largest LIC economy, growth of 10.2 percent in 2015 was also lifted by good harvests, rising public investment and booming manufacturing and construction. Even in several metal and mineral resource-rich LICs, activity has thus far been resilient despite the commodity price decline, as development of major mining and gas projects has continued (Tanzania, Mozambique, Uganda). Growth in these countries ranged between 5-7 percent during 2015.

In other commodity-exporting countries, in contrast, the fall in commodity prices led to outright disruptions in production. Sierra Leone's economy, already hit hard by Ebola in 2014, is estimated to have contracted by a fifth during 2015 due to the closure of mining operations at

---

[10]Strong growth over the past few years has lifted four LIC countries (Bangladesh, Kenya, Myanmar and Tajikistan) to middle income status.

FIGURE SF.5 Growth prospects in LICs

Growth remains supported by strong outturns in the largest LICs. However the fall in commodity prices is taking a toll on commodity exporters. Risks lie on the downside.

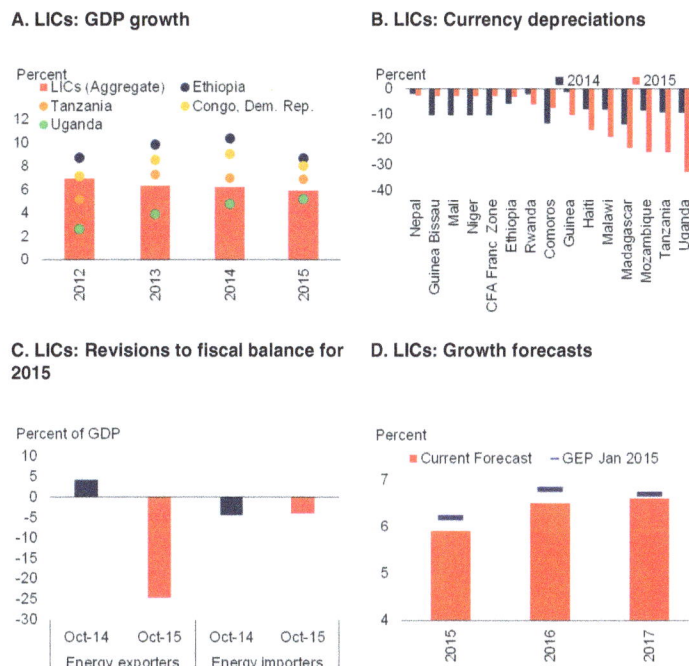

A. LICs: GDP growth

B. LICs: Currency depreciations

C. LICs: Revisions to fiscal balance for 2015

D. LICs: Growth forecasts

Source: World Bank World Development Indicators, IMF, World Economic Outlook.
B. A negative value indicates depreciation.
D. "GEP Jan 2015" indicated forecasts published in the January 2015 Global Economic Prospects (World Bank 2015a).

Tonkolili (the second largest iron ore mine in Africa) after its operator when bankrupt. Copper production in the Democratic Republic of Congo has been hit hard, following the suspension of copper and cobalt production at the Katanga Mining unit by Glencore, its mining operator, amid declining profitability and a slump in copper prices to a six-year low. In Afghanistan, large investments associated with the award of copper and iron-ore mining projects have failed to materialize – partly due to unsettled domestic security and political conditions, but also due to the fall in global commodity prices – weighing on sentiment and outlook, and resulting in a downward revision in medium term growth prospects. Monetary tightening has further weighed on growth as policy makers responded to sharp depreciations by lifting interest rates (Uganda) or drawing down reserves (Burundi, Tanzania, Dem. Rep. of Congo, Zimbabwe and Mozambique).

In several LICs, political and social tensions are

taking a toll on economic activity. In Afghanistan, growth has slowed as a result of continued political uncertainty and increase in violence, amidst a drawdown in NATO troops. In Nepal, the estimated value of damage from the earthquakes in April-May 2015 amounts to a third of GDP. Since the earthquakes, domestic tensions due to a new constitution, and severe fuel shortages resulting from the closure of land trading routes through India have further weighed on activity. Political tensions remain elevated in several LICs in Sub-Saharan Africa, as a result of insurgencies or unsettled political conditions (Burkina Faso, Burundi, Chad, Niger), upcoming elections (Benin), or labor disputes (Sierra Leone, Niger). This has increased uncertainty and weighed on activity.

Fiscal and current account deficits have widened in most countries. Falling commodity prices (commodity exporters), political tensions (Burundi), or uneven policy direction (The Gambia) have weakened export and fiscal revenues. In several countries, however, large current account and/or public sector deficits reflect rising infrastructure spending or the construction of mining projects that should support potential growth over the medium term. In Ethiopia for instance, the current account deficit has remained relatively well funded by FDI, as is also the case in Mozambique and Tanzania, while aid inflows have been important in Rwanda.

While lower global oil prices have kept inflation pressures muted in some oil importers (Afghanistan, Benin, Rwanda), inflation has remained high in several other countries due to limited spare capacity (Ethiopia); large currency depreciations over the past year (commodity exporting LICs) and those where political and social tensions remain high. Nepal has also seen a sharp acceleration in essential food and fuel prices, due to the severe disruption in trade through India.

For 2016-18, growth in LICs is expected to remain resilient at above 6 percent, on aggregate. Strengthening import demand in the U.S. and Euro Area, which are key trading partners for West African countries, should help support

activity in these countries. Large-scale investment projects in mining, energy and transport, consumer spending, and public investment should help keep growth upwards of 7 percent in Ethiopia, Mozambique, Rwanda, and Tanzania. Improvements in electricity supply in Ethiopia and Rwanda but particularly in Guinea—where supply has doubled with the start of production from the Kaleta dam in 2015—will also support activity, but a shortage of power is expected to remain a drag in Benin and Madagascar. The growth outlook remains weak, and only a gradual recovery is projected due to persistent political tensions in Haiti, Burundi, Benin, Guinea Bissau, Burkina Faso, Nepal and Afghanistan.

Risks to the outlook are mainly tilted on the downside. These include:

- *Further weakness in global commodity prices* could require sharper fiscal adjustments in commodity exporters. Several countries have limited reserve buffers to stem depreciation pressures to contain financial stability risks and inflation. Lower commodity prices and high expected investment costs also increase the risk of a delay of investments in energy and mining in East African countries that would weigh on medium-term prospects.

- *Fiscal risks* are elevated in some countries, relating to large infrastructure projects, Public-Private Partnerships, and contingent liabilities (Mauro et. al. 2015). Countries where government debt has risen rapidly in recent years, such as Uganda, to finance mining infrastructure, may find it harder to service debt if production start dates for oil projects are delayed further. Inconsistent and poor macroeconomic management has been accompanied by sizeable fiscal slippages in The Gambia. As a result of growing fiscal pressures from the drop in commodity prices and contingent liabilities in state-owned enterprises, which required government support in 2015, considerable risks remain in Mozambique and have led it into negotiations with the IMF for a fiscal support program (IMF, 2015b).

- *Political risks* could deter domestic and foreign investment in some countries, weigh on tourism, and add to fiscal pressures. Fragmented political situations could also undermine the ability of governments to undertake and implement needed policies.

One-third of the world's poor are located in LIC countries (World Bank 2015c).[11] Their growth prospects are therefore key to reducing global poverty. A robust policy environment can strengthen growth to levels that can make a clear dent in poverty. For commodity-exporting LICs, this includes policies that ensure that the growth potential from natural resources is used effectively: reducing regulatory hurdles, clarifying legislation and strengthening infrastructure.

---

[11]There remain bright spots among LICs, notably Rwanda: the country is on track to meet all of its Millennium Development Goals, and some 650,000 Rwandans have been lifted out of poverty since 2011.

Table SF.1 Low Income country forecasts[a]
(Annual percent change unless indicated otherwise)

(percentage point difference from June 2015 projections)

	2013	2014	2015e	2016f	2017f	2018f	2015e	2016f	2017f
Low Income Country, GDP[b]	6.4	6.1	5.1	6.2	6.6	6.6	-0.7	-0.1	0.1
Afghanistan	2.0	1.3	1.9	3.1	3.9	5.0	-0.6	-1.9	-1.2
Benin	5.6	5.4	5.7	5.3	5.1	5.1	1.1	0.7	0.4
Burkina Faso	6.7	4.0	4.4	6.0	7.0	7.0	-0.6	-0.2	0.5
Burundi	4.6	4.7	-2.3	3.5	4.8	4.8	-7.1	-1.5	-0.4
Cambodia	7.4	7.0	6.9	6.9	6.8	6.8	0.0	0.0	0.0
Chad	5.7	7.3	4.1	4.9	6.1	6.5	-4.9	0.2	0.5
Comoros	3.5	3.0	2.3	2.5	3.1	3.1	-1.1	-1.2	-0.7
Congo, Dem. Rep.	8.5	9.0	8.0	8.6	9.0	9.0	0.0	0.1	0.0
Eritrea	1.3	1.7	0.9	2.0	2.2	2.2	-0.6	0.0	0.0
Ethiopia[c]	10.5	9.9	10.2	10.2	9.0	9.0	0.7	-0.3	0.5
Gambia, The	4.8	-0.2	4.0	4.5	5.3	5.3	1.0	-0.6	-0.8
Guinea	2.3	-0.3	0.4	3.5	4.0	4.2	0.7	1.2	1.5
Guinea-Bissau	0.3	2.5	4.4	4.9	5.3	5.3	0.2	1.0	1.3
Haiti[c]	4.2	2.7	1.7	2.5	2.8	3.0	0.0	-0.7	-0.3
Liberia	8.7	1.0	3.0	5.7	6.8	6.8	..	..	..
Madagascar	2.4	3.0	3.2	3.4	3.6	3.6	-1.4	-1.4	-1.4
Malawi	5.2	5.7	2.8	5.0	5.8	5.8	-2.3	-0.6	-0.1
Mali	1.7	7.2	5.0	5.0	5.0	5.0	-0.6	-0.1	-0.2
Mozambique	7.3	7.4	6.3	6.5	7.2	7.2	-0.9	-0.8	-0.1
Nepal[c]	4.1	5.4	3.4	1.7	5.8	4.5	-0.8	-2.8	0.3
Niger	4.6	6.9	4.4	5.3	9.3	5.7	-0.1	-0.2	1.6
Rwanda	4.7	7.0	7.4	7.6	7.6	7.6	0.4	0.6	0.1
Sierra Leone	20.1	7.0	-20.0	6.6	5.3	5.3	-7.2	-1.8	-3.6
South Sudan	13.1	3.4	-5.3	3.5	7.0	7.0	..	..	..
Tanzania	7.3	7.0	7.2	7.2	7.1	7.1	0.0	0.1	0.0
Togo	5.1	5.7	5.1	4.9	4.7	4.7	0.0	0.0	0.0
Uganda[c]	3.6	4.0	5.0	5.0	5.8	5.8	-0.5	-0.7	0.0
Zimbabwe	4.5	3.2	1.0	2.8	3.0	3.0	0.0	0.3	-0.5

Source: World Bank.
World Bank forecasts are frequently updated based on new information and changing (global) circumstances. Consequently, projections presented here may differ from those contained in other Bank documents, even if basic assessments of countries' prospects do not significantly differ at any given moment in time.
a. Central African Rep., Democratic People's Republic of Korea, and Somalia are not forecast due to data limitations.
b. GDP at market prices and expenditure components are measured in constant 2010 U.S. dollars.
c. GDP growth based on fiscal year data.

Annex SF.1

The duration model used in the multivariate analysis is a standard accelerated-failure-time (AFT) model (Jenkins, 2006), based on the gamma distribution. In AFT models, the natural logarithm of the survival time, log t, is expressed as a linear function of the covariates, yielding the linear model:

$$\log t_j = x_j \beta + z_j$$

where x_j is a vector of covariates and β is a vector of regression coefficients. The choice of z_j determines the regression method. Here, and based on the Akaike Information Criterion to evaluate the best fit across types of distributions, the standard generalized Gamma distribution appears to be most appropriate.

The effects of the explanatory variables on the baseline are given by time ratios (the exponentiated coefficients). These are reported below for each explanatory variable. The magnitude of these time ratios denotes the factor by which the expected lead time to production would be shortened or lengthened by a one-unit change in a variable. A one-unit change in the variable changes the time scale by a factor of $\exp(x_j \beta)$. Depending on whether this factor is greater or less than 1, time is either accelerated or decelerated. That is, if a subject at baseline experiences a probability of survival past time t equal to $S(t)$, then a subject with covariates x_j would have probability of survival past time t equal to $S(t)$ evaluated at the point $\exp(x_j \beta)t$, instead.[12]

The main explanatory variables x_j are measures for commodity prices (an indicator if prices are rising at time of discovery and the price change between discovery and production); indicators of macro policy environment (dummies if public debt ratios are greater than 40 percent and inflation rates higher than 10 percent); and measures for governance, including the QOG Institute's ICRG Index of Quality of Governance, and the World

Bank Governance Indicator for control of corruption (Dahlberg et al 2015).[13] By choosing all these explanatory variables at the time of discovery, i.e. before the lead time begins, concerns about reverse causality are attenuated.[14] Given that data on some of these variables (in particular, the governance variables) is not available for much of the 1980s (QOG) or the mid-1990s (governance indicator), the earliest values are taken to indicate the quality of governance for discoveries that occurred prior to those dates. Control variables are the logarithm of the size of the discoveries, a dummy variable for copper deposits, and dummy variables for middle-income and low-income countries. In the absence of mine specific information on the depth of the deposit and in light of the changing depth over time as deposits get depleted, it is not possible to control for this factor directly. Country dummies proxy for unobserved characteristics like the landlocked nature of the country. In addition, regression results are robust to the use of decadal dummies which could help control for the decelerating time to production since the 1950s (See Annex Table SF.1).

The regression in Column (1) shows that expected times to production are nearly twice as long for copper deposits, and similarly 30-40 percent higher in MIC and LIC countries. High levels of debt and inflation expand the lead times to production. Column (2) shows that high levels of debt and inflation lengthen the lead time to production by 16 and 8 percent respectively. The commodity price cycle measure is not statistically significant, but interacted with copper mine size, shows that copper mines tend to get developed faster when commodity prices are rising.[15] Governance variables indicate that when governance improves (indicated by higher values

---

[12]Ideally, the regression would have taken into account the selection bias of mines that have been discovered but are not being developed. However, such data is not available.

[13]The QOG Institute's ICRG Index of Quality of Governance is the mean of the ICRG indices of corruption, bureaucracy quality, and law and order.

[14]Prices are evaluated relative to peaks and trough, defined as in Harding and Pagan (2002). Higher values of the quality of governance and control of corruption reflect better governance.

[15]A similar interaction for the price change between discovery and production is not significant.

of the corruption index), expected times to production fall by nearly 10 percent. The quality of government index is not statistically significant on its own, but when interacted with the variable indicating a copper deposit, shows that times to production fall by nearly 30 percent when governance improves.

ANNEX TABLE SF.1 Duration regression of lead times

	Column (1)	Column (2)	Column (3)	Column (4)
Log(size of deposit, mt cu)	1.000	1.000	1.010	1.010
	0.770	0.900	0.660	0.610
Copper	1.74***	1.72***	1.74***	2.29***
	0.000	0.000	0.000	0.000
Comm. price upswing at discovery	0.940	0.950	0.950	0.990
	0.160	0.270	0.290	0.860
Comm. price upswing x Copper mine Size	0.91**	0.92*	0.930 †	0.910 †
	0.040	0.070	0.130	0.100
Comm. price change during lead time to production	1.00***	1.00***	1.00***	
	0.000	0.000	0.000	
LIC	1.33***	1.25***	1.020	1.260 †
	0.000	0.000	0.850	0.120
MIC	1.42***	1.33***	1.11	1.55***
	0.000	0.000	0.290	0.000
Debt>40%		1.16***	1.16***	1.38***
		0.000	0.000	0.000
Inflation>10%		1.080	1.080 †	1.010
		0.160	0.150	0.920
Corruption			0.92**	
			-0.020	
Quality of government				1.120
				0.630
Copper x Quality of government				0.710 †
				0.140
Non-linear interaction terms				
Comm. price upswing x Copper mine size + Comm. price upswing	0.85**	0.87**	0.89**	0.9 $\dagger$
Copper x Quality of government + Quality of government				0.79
Kappa	0.92	0.88	0.86	0.49
N	948	948	943	921
Log Likelihood	-1080.04	-1072.31	-1059.94	-1166.18
Akaike Information Criterion	2180.09	2168.61	2145.88	2358.36

Note: P-values are given below coefficient estimates. † indicates statistical significance at 15%, * at 10%, ** at 5%, *** at 1%. The Pagan-Harding measure of commodity prices is based on the Pagan-Harding algorithm (2002) which identifies turning points in a times series as local minima and maxima. These are used to identify up-cycles (when gold and copper prices are rising). Higher values of the Corruption indicator correspond to better outcomes (i.e. lower corruption) as do higher values of the ICRG Quality of Government indicator. As interaction terms are non-linear, the combined impact of these is shown separately.

References

Almeida Santos, A., L. M. Roffarello, and M. Filipe. 2015. "African Economic Outlook: Mozambique." www.africaneconomicoutlook.org, Issy les Moulineaux, France.

Arezki, R., V. A. Ramey, and L. Sheng. 2015. "News Shocks in Open Economies: Evidence from Giant Oil Discoveries." NBER Working Paper 20857, National Bureau of Economic Research, Cambridge, Massachusetts.

Bai, G, and Y. Xu. 2014. "Giant Fields Retain Dominance in the Reserves Growth." *Oil and Gas Journal* 122(2): 44-51.

Bennot, A. 2015. "Is East Africa's Gas Asset Boom About to Go Bust?" Mineweb. http://www.mineweb.com/articles-by-type/independent-viewpoint/is-east-africas-gas-asset-boom-about-to-go-bust/. Accessed November 30, 2015.

Calvo, Guillermo A. (2014) "Sudden Stop and Sudden Flood of Foreign Direct Investment: Inverse Bank Run, Output, and Welfare Distribution." *Scandinavian Journal of Economics* 116(1): 5-19

Carbon Tracker Initiative. 2014. *Unburnable Carbon: Are the World's Financial Markets Carrying a Carbon Bubble?* London: Carbon Tracker Initiative.

Clo, A. 2000. *Oil Economics and Policy.* New York: Springer Science and Business Media.

Crowson, P. 2011. "Economics of the Minerals Industry." In *SME Mining Engineering Handbook,* edited by Peter Darling. Englewood, CO: Society for Mining, Metallurgy and Exploration.

Curtis, M., T. Lissu, T. Akabzaa, J. Lungu, A. Fraser, L. Okitonemba, D. Kampata, and P. Kamweba. 2009. *Breaking the Curse: How Transparent Taxation and Fair Taxes can Turn Africa's Mineral Wealth into Development.* Jointly published by Open Society Institute of Southern Africa, Third World Network Africa, Tax Justice Network Africa, Action Aid International, Christian Aid.

Dahlberg, S., S. Holmberg, B. Rothstein, F. Hartmann and R. Svensson. 2015. The Quality of Government Basic Dataset, version January 2015. University of Gothenburg: The Quality of Government Institute. Available at http://www.qog.pol.gu.se.

Gajigo, O., E. Mutambatsere, and G. Ndiaye . 2012. "Gold Mining in Africa: Maximizing Economic Returns for Countries." Working Paper 147, African Development Bank, Tunis, Tunisia.

Harding, D., and A. Pagan. 2002. "Dissecting the Cycle: A Methodological Investigation." *Journal of Monetary Economics* 49 (2): 365-381.

Humphreys, M., J. Sachs, and J. E. Stiglitz, eds. 2007. *Escaping the Resource Curse.* New York: Columbia University Press.

Huurdeman, W. 2014. "Natural Gas: Fiscal Regime Challenges." Presentation for workshop on "Fiscal Management of Oil and Natural Gas in East Africa." East African Community and IMF Workshop, Jan.15-17, 2014, Arusha, Tanzania.

ICMM. 2012. "Trends in the Mining and Metals Industry." InBrief Publication.

International Monetary Fund. 2012a. "Macroeconomic Policy Frameworks for Resource-Rich Developing Countries." IMF Policy Paper. Washington, D.C.: IMF.

International Monetary Fund. 2012b. "Sierra Leone: Fourth Review under the Three-Year Arrangement under the Extended Credit Facility, and Financing Assurances Review." Country Report 12/285. International Monetary Fund, Washington, DC.

_____. 2015a. "Sierra Leone: Second Review Under the Extended Credit Facility Arrangement and Financing Assurances Review, and Requests for Augmentation of Access Under the Extended Credit Facility and Debt Relief Under the Catastrophe Containment and Relief

Trust." Country Report 15/76. International Monetary Fund, Washington, DC.

_____. 2015b. "IMF Holds Discussions on the 5th Review under the PSI, on a New SCF Arrangement, and on the 2015 Article IV Consultation with Mozambique." IMF Press Release 15/488, October 29, 2015, Washington, DC.

Jenkins, S. 2006. "Introduction to the Empirical Analysis of Spell Duration Data." Institute for Social and Economic Research, University of Essex.

Levchenko, A. A., and P. Mauro. 2007. "Do Some Forms of Financial Flows Help Protect Against 'Sudden Stops'?" *The World Bank Economic Review* 21 (3): 389-411.

Loayza, N. V., and C. Raddatz. 2007. "The Structural Determinants of External Vulnerability." *The World Bank Economic Review* 21 (3): 359-387.

Mauro P., H. Joly, A. Aisen, E. Alper, F. Boutin-Dufresne, J. Dridi, N. Gigineishvili, T. Josephs, C. Mira, V. Thakoor, A. Thomas, and F. Yang. 2015. "Monitoring and Managing Fiscal Risks in the East African Community." African Departmental Paper 15/7, International Monetary Fund, Washington, DC.

McGlade, C., and P. Ekins. 2015. "The Geographical Distribution of Fossil Fuels Unused when Limiting Global Warming to 2 Degrees." *Nature* 517 (7533): 187–90.

McIntosh, S. 2015. "Mining Exploration in Emerging Markets – A Major's Perspective." Presentation at Global Mining Finance, Autumn 2015 conference, London.

Mehlum, H., K. Moene, and R. Torvik. 2006. "Institutions and the Resource Curse." *The Economic Journal* 116 (508): 1-20.

Perott-Humphrey, F. 2011. "Market Capitalization." In *SME Mining Engineering Handbook,* edited by Peter Darling. Englewood, CO: Society for Mining, Metallurgy and Exploration.

Sachs, J. D., and A. M. Warner. 2001. "The Curse of Natural Resources." *European Economic Review* 45 (4): 827-838.

Schodde, R. 2014. "Key Issues Affecting the Time Delay Between Discovery and Development." MinEx Consulting presentation, March 3, 2014, Toronto.

Stevens, P. G. Lahn, and J. Kooroshy. 2015. "The Resource Curse Revisited." Chatham House Research Paper, London.

Tolonen, A. 2015. "Local Industrial Shocks, Female Empowerment and Infant Health: Evidence from Africa's Gold Mining Industry." Draft paper presented at the World Bank, Nov. 5, 2014.

UNECA. 2011. *Minerals and Africa's Development: The International Study Group Report on Africa's Mineral Regimes.* Addis Abbaba, Ethiopia: Economic Commission for Africa.

Wang, Z., and Q. Xue. 2014. "The Market Structure of Shale Gas Drilling in the United States." Discussion Paper 14-31, Resources for the Future, Washington, DC.

World Bank. 2015a. *Global Economic Prospects January 2015: Having Fiscal Space and Using It.* Washington, DC: World Bank.

_____. 2015b. *Global Economic Prospects June 2015: Global Economy in Transition.* Washington, DC: World Bank.

_____. 2015c. *Global Monitoring Report 2015.* Washington, DC: World Bank. World Bank. 2015f. *The Growth Challenge: Can Ugandan Cities get to Work?* Washington, D.C.: World Bank.

CHAPTER 2

REGIONAL OUTLOOKS

EAST ASIA and PACIFIC

Growth in the East Asia and Pacific (EAP) slowed from 6.8 percent in 2014 to 6.4 percent in 2015, and is expected to ease further through 2018. This projection assumes that a gradual slowdown in China offsets a modest pickup in ASEAN countries. Risks to the forecast remain tilted to the downside. They include a faster-than-expected slowdown in China, which would have sizable spillovers on the rest of the region. Highly leveraged economies, in particular, face risks. Divergent monetary policies among high-income countries and an overall tightening of global financing conditions could lead to financial market volatility and interruptions in lending to countries with lower credit ratings. Key policy challenges include ensuring a gradual rebalancing of economic activity in China from investment to consumption and services, and strengthening medium-term fiscal and macroprudential frameworks. Structural reforms to improve the functioning of labor markets could play a vital role in mitigating the impact of aging populations and supporting long-term growth.

Recent developments

Growth in the EAP region slowed to an estimated 6.4 percent in 2015, down from 6.8 percent the previous year (Table 2.1.1, Figure 2.1.1). This estimate represents a 0.3 percentage point downward revision from June 2015 (World Bank 2015a). Decelerating growth in China and a weaker-than-expected recovery in Thailand account for much of the decline. Growth in the region excluding China was 4.6 percent, about the same as in 2014. The weak growth in commodity-exporting economies (Indonesia, Malaysia) was expected, while Vietnam surprised with a stronger-than-expected performance.

In China, policies are aimed at putting growth on a more sustainable footing and reducing leverage in heavily indebted sectors (World Bank 2015b). In 2015, growth eased slightly more than expected to below 7 percent, reflecting soft exports and a slowdown in investment. The deceleration was especially pronounced in the real estate and manufacturing sectors during the first half of the year. Policy support, including an easing of financial regulations, helped stabilize the property

sector in the second half.[1] But excess capacity has been a drag on investment across a wide range of goods-producing industries. The producer price index declined further, reflecting lower commodity prices and considerable industrial overcapacity. Robust service sector growth is supporting consumption and helping to rebalance the economy (Figure 2.1.2). Core inflation has been broadly stable, but consumer price inflation has remained below the 3 percent target of the People's Bank of China (PBOC) since mid-2014 as a result of low food and energy prices.

Slowing growth and rebalancing in China have been accompanied by bouts of financial market volatility. Following a 90 percent run-up in equity prices between November 2014 and early-June 2015, valuations unwound sharply. Policy measures helped restore order to markets, and by September, equity prices had returned to January 2015 levels. This correction was accompanied by sizeable capital outflows, reflecting steps to ease capital account restrictions, and efforts to reduce

---

Note: The author of this section is Ekaterine Vashakmadze. Research assistance was provided by Trang Nguyen.

[1] The PBOC progressively cut benchmark one-year lending rate (to 4.35 percent) and reserve requirements (to 17.5 percent). The government implemented fiscal support measures through infrastructure investment, which led to widening of the fiscal deficit to a six-year high (around 2.3 percent of GDP) and eased regulations (such as cutting the down payment requirements for home buyers).

FIGURE 2.1.1 Activity in East Asia and Pacific

Growth in EAP eased to 6.4 percent in 2015, largely because of a continued slowdown in China. EAP's slowdown has been driven by weak exports, and slower domestic demand in the case of Malaysia. Sharply deteriorating terms of trade and a decline in investment growth from previous high rates are also important factors. Consumption has remained resilient.

A. Growth, year

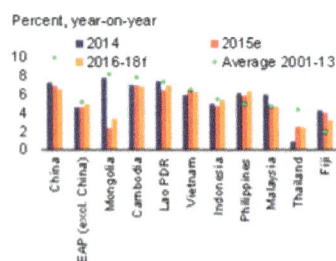

B. Growth, quarter

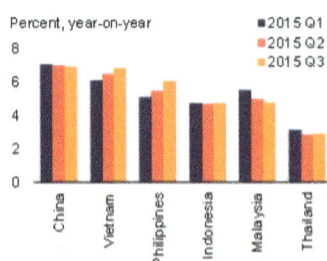

C. Components of growth

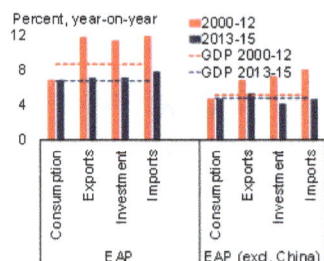

D. Contribution to GDP growth for selected economies

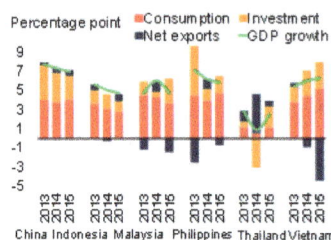

Sources: World Bank; Haver; China Economic and Industry database (CEIC).
C. Weighted averages.

foreign currency exposures and foreign short-term debt among corporations, as well as concerns about growth prospects.

International reserves remain large, equivalent to 32.8 percent of GDP in 2015, despite sales in support of the Chinese currency (Figure 2.1.3). As a result, the renminbi remained broadly stable against the U.S. dollar throughout 2015, with the exception of a 3 percent depreciation in August that was triggered by an unexpected change in the calculation of the renminbi reference rate. On a trade-weighted basis, the renminbi continued to rise in 2015 to new highs, in spite of the decline against the U.S. dollar. The implied loss of cost competitiveness contributed to weaker exports. This was offset by stronger import compression, reflecting weaker domestic demand and lower commodity prices, resulting in a widening current account surplus.

Relatively slow growth in the rest of the region since 2014 reflects weak global trade, slow investment growth, and, to a lesser degree, continued fiscal consolidation. Export growth slowed across the region (Cambodia and Vietnam were exceptions) as global trade contracted (World Bank 2015c).[2] Several countries made efforts to reduce fiscal deficits in 2015—by reforming fuel subsidies (Indonesia, Malaysia) and sales tax regimes (Malaysia)—despite revenue losses from lower commodity prices (World Bank 2015c, d, e).

Weak external demand was partially offset by strong private consumption growth, which was supported by tight labor markets, a dynamic services sector, low domestic fuel prices, robust inflows of remittances, and broadly accommodative monetary policies. In Thailand, fragile confidence in the aftermath of political tensions in 2014 continued to weigh on consumption growth. Declining commodity prices have helped improve current account balances in commodity-importing countries. The Philippines and Thailand, both net oil importers, recorded larger current account surpluses. In Indonesia, also a net oil importer, the current account deficit dropped below 2 percent of GDP through 2015Q3 for the first time since 2011Q4, also reflecting falling imports (Figure 2.1.4).

Despite an accommodative monetary policy in advanced economies, external financing conditions tightened across EAP in 2015, particularly for commodity exporters and countries with significant financing needs.[3] Capital outflows have accelerated, and corporate and sovereign spreads have risen (Figure 2.1.5). Currencies, including the Indonesian rupiah and the Malaysian ringgit, experienced sharp drops in the second half of the year. Credit default swap (CDS) spreads widened,

---

[2]Vietnam, in particular, appears to benefit from China's rebalancing. Factors include its competitive and diversified export base, and China's move from low-skill, labor-intensive exports toward more sophisticated products. Appreciation of the renminbi has accelerated the shift of labor-intensive production from China to lower-income countries, including Cambodia and Vietnam.

[3]Although regional economies have increasingly relied on domestic credit markets for finance, external debt exceeds 60 percent of GDP in Malaysia and Lao PDR, 100 percent in Papua New Guinea, and is close to 200 percent in Mongolia.

as did spreads over U.S. Treasury yields for U.S. dollar bonds of the major EAP issuers (Indonesia, Malaysia, and Thailand). Prices on regional stock markets fell sharply amid volatility.

In contrast to volatile portfolio flows, foreign direct investment (FDI) remains robust and has helped to mitigate external pressures. In particular, China became the world's largest single recipient of FDI in 2014, while Indonesia saw its highest FDI inflows since 1990, both in dollar terms ($23 billion) and relative to GDP (3 percent). FDI inflows to other large EAP economies remained generally robust in the first half of the year, rising in all large countries except the Philippines in year-on-year terms. In Thailand, FDI inflows rose above pre-global crisis levels. In the Philippines, FDI has lagged, partly owing to regulatory restrictions. Inflows to Vietnam remained buoyant, and were mostly directed at labor-intensive manufacturing (UNCTAD 2015; World Bank 2015c).

Exchange-rate depreciation served as a shock absorber, but some countries have also responded to balance of payments pressures by using reserves. Commodity exporters Indonesia and Malaysia tapped reserves when their currencies came under strong pressure in the second half of the year. This helped contain depreciation to 25 percent. Commodity importers Thailand and Philippines experienced less pressure on their currencies, with exchange rates depreciating 5-10 percent, and reserves even rising. Despite the declines in foreign exchange reserves and depreciations of several major currencies, reserves to imports ratios remain adequate and consumer price inflation held steady across the region (Figure 2.1.6).

Tightening external financial conditions contributed to a gradual stabilization of domestic debt-to-GDP ratios. Credit-fueled investment growth has slowed across most of the region from double-digit rates in 2011-12, to about 4 percent in 2014-15. Credit growth slowed across the region, reflecting tighter monetary policy in Indonesia (since 2013), proactive use of macroprudential policies in Malaysia, and firmer non-bank lending conditions in China. Nevertheless, private sector debt remains

FIGURE 2.1.2 Internal rebalancing in China

Rebalancing from investment to consumption has been slow, but rebalancing from industry to services activity has proceeded rapidly.

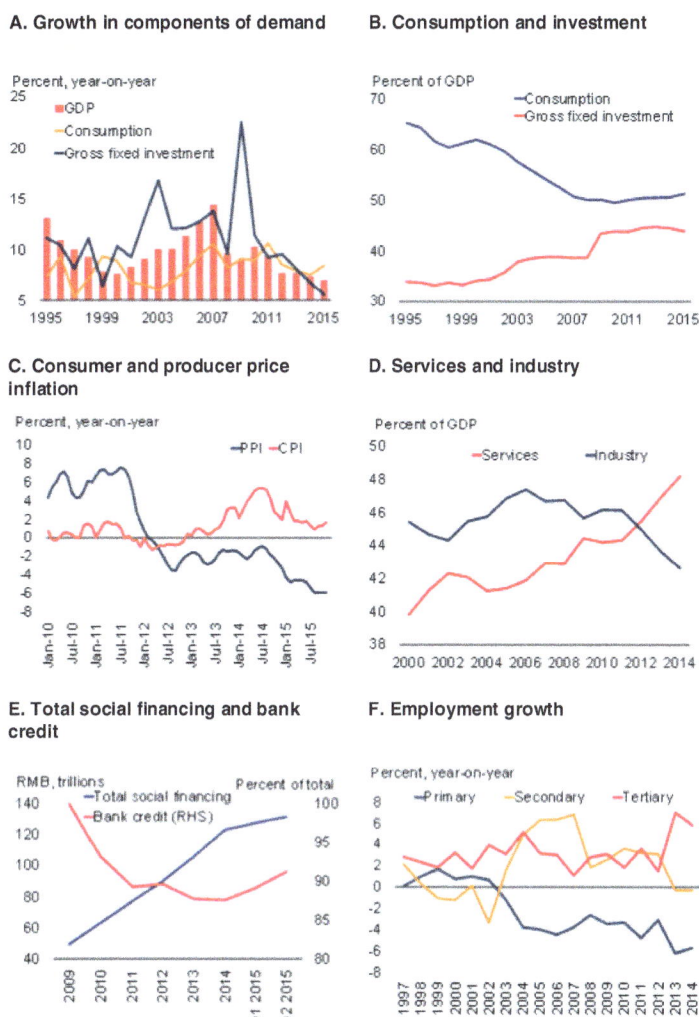

Sources: World Bank; Haver Analytics; China Economic and Industry database (CEIC).
C. Latest observation is November 2015.
E. Total social financing is the sum of total fundraising by Chinese non-state entities, including individuals and non-financial corporations.
F. The secondary sector is predominantly industry, while the tertiary sector is predominantly services.

substantial, especially for the non-financial corporate sector. Domestic debt-to-GDP ratios exceed pre-crisis levels in several countries, and are above 150 percent in China, Malaysia, and Thailand (Figure 2.1.7).

Outlook

The global economic environment is expected to remain challenging. Although there are signs of a modest pickup in growth, global trade and commodity prices remain weak (Chapter 1).

FIGURE 2.1.3 External rebalancing in China

Although China's export market share continues to rise, its current account surplus declined to 2 percent of GDP in 2014 from a peak of 10 percent of GDP in 2007. In 2015, the renminbi appreciated in real, trade-weighted terms, while it depreciated against the U.S. dollar, for a cumulative increase of 55 percent since the exchange rate reform in 2005. Rapid capital outflows in 2015 have been met with foreign exchange market intervention, but reserves remain ample.

A. Exports to selected major economies

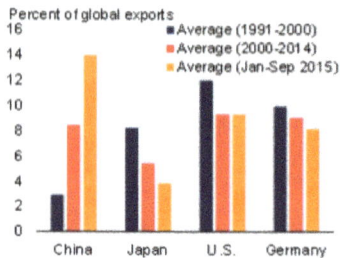

B. Current account balance and real effective exchange rate (REER)

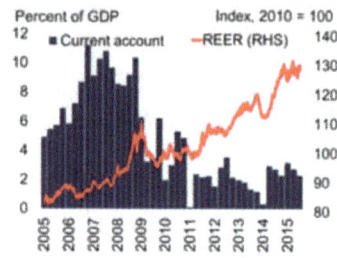

C. Balance of payments

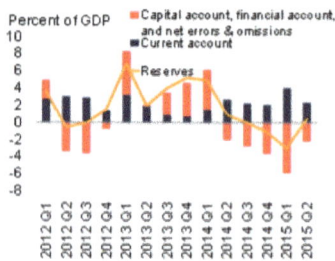

D. Foreign currency reserves

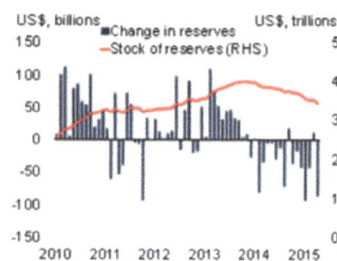

Sources: Haver Analytics; China Economic and Industry database (CEIC); World Bank.
B. CPI deflated real exchange rate (REER). An increase denotes appreciation. Latest observation is December 17, 2015 for the REER and 2015 Q3 for the current account.

Gradually strengthening output growth in high-income countries is expected to provide opportunities for competitive and diversified economies in the EAP region. Global financial conditions are expected to tighten further, albeit only gradually. Combined with low commodity prices, tighter conditions are expected to weigh on capital flows to the region, particularly portfolio flows and FDI into commodity sectors. Tighter financing conditions and slowing growth in major emerging markets may also be associated with bouts of financial market volatility. EAP countries mostly benefit from low fuel prices, but their impact varies across countries, depending on the magnitude of net fuel imports, the energy intensity of production, and the share of oil and gas in energy consumption.

Against this backdrop, regional growth is expected to ease from 6.4 percent in 2015 to 6.2 percent on average in 2016-18. The continued slowdown in China should be partly offset by a modest pickup in the rest of the region, which is expected to benefit from recovery in advanced countries, low energy prices, improved political stability, and still ample liquidity in global financial markets (despite an expected gradual tightening in the United States). In the rest of the region, growth is expected to pick up to 5 percent on average in 2016-18, driven by the large ASEAN economies (Table 2.1.2).

- In China, growth is projected to moderate to 6.7 percent in 2016 and 6.5 percent in 2017 and 2018, reflecting policy efforts to promote sustainable and balanced growth. Continued measures to contain local government debt, curb the shadow banking industry, and tackle excess capacity will weigh on investment and industrial output. Low oil prices will soften adverse impacts, and targeted policy measures are expected to be applied as needed to ensure that the growth slowdown is gradual.

- The slowdown of GDP growth in Indonesia is expected to have bottomed out at 4.7 percent in 2015, and accelerate to 5.4 percent on average in 2016-18. This assumes implementation of a reform package announced by the government in September-October 2015 to unlock investment and boost productivity growth.[4]

- In Malaysia, adjustment to lower energy prices is expected to keep growth at 4.7 percent in 2015, lower than in recent years. The slowdown in domestic demand is expected to reduce GDP growth to 4.5 percent in 2016 and 2017, before it accelerates to 5 percent in 2018, helped by gradually strengthening global growth.

- In Thailand, growth will remain weak, at 2.4 percent on average over 2016–18. Policy

---

[4]The reforms aim to cut regulatory red tape, lowering costs and uncertainty for private investment, and reducing bottlenecks holding back public investments.

uncertainty is likely to weigh on private investment, high levels of household debt may dampen private consumption, and export growth could remain subdued. The central bank cut its interest rate three times in 2015, but inflation remains well below the policy target of 2.5 percent.

- The Philippines and Vietnam are among the countries with the strongest growth prospects. In the Philippines, growth is projected to firm to 6.4 percent in 2016, reflecting accelerated implementation of public-private partnership projects and spending related to the May 2016 presidential election. In 2017-18, growth is forecast to ease to 6.2 percent. In Vietnam, growth is expected to expand at an average of 6.3 percent in 2016-18. Contributing to the gains are rapid investment growth buoyed by robust confidence and FDI, consumption growth fueled by solid labor markets, and export growth as Chinese FDI projects in export industries come onstream.

In several of the small economies in the region, growth will decelerate due to low commodity prices and measures to unwind financial vulnerabilities. Mongolia continues to adjust to the end of a mining boom, with economic activity held back by weakening mineral exports and efforts by the government to control its debt. In Cambodia, growth will remain slightly below 7 percent in 2016–18, reflecting weaker prices for agricultural commodities, constrained garment exports amid real currency appreciation and competition from market entrants in other countries, and moderating growth in tourism after a period of strong gains.

Growth is expected to pick up to average about 7 percent in Lao PDR in 2016-18 as a result of higher electricity exports, and accelerate to 8.5 percent in Myanmar in 2017-18 as a result of commodity-related investment. Growth in the small Pacific Island countries will be supported by rising tourism and remittances, but the commodity exporters will face significant headwinds. In Papua New Guinea, in particular, growth will decline sharply after a 2015 peak,

FIGURE 2.1.4 Trade

The terms of trade have deteriorated sharply in commodity-exporting EAP countries. Slowing or contracting export volumes have further weakened current account balances. This has been accompanied by sharp, real effective exchange rate depreciations.

A. Terms of trade

B. Current account balance

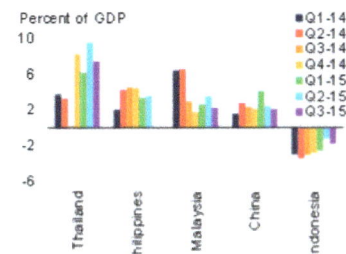

C. Real effective exchange rates

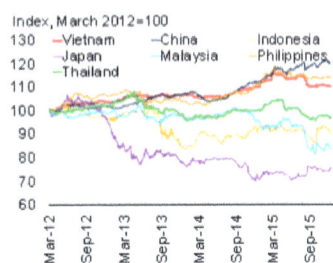

D. Merchandise export growth, Sep 2014-Sep 2015

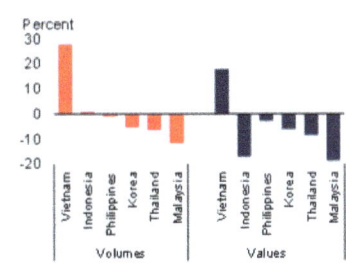

Sources: Haver Analytics; International Monetary Fund; International Financial Statistics; Bank for International Settlements; World Bank, World Development Indicators; Dealogic.
A. Terms of trade refers to the relative price of exports in terms of imports and is defined as the ratio of export prices to import prices. Latest observation is 2015 Q3.
B. Rolling four-quarter sums in percent of annual GDP. Latest observation is 2015 Q3.
C. Latest observation is December 16, 2015. CPI-deflated real effective exchange rates. An increase denotes an appreciation.

reflecting the completion of liquefied natural gas-related construction work. In Timor-Leste, where government spending is expected to help the non-energy sector, growth should gradually recover to 7 percent in 2017-18 (World Bank 2015c).

Risks

Risks to this outlook remain tilted to the downside. Key downside risks include a faster slowdown in China than expected, which would have spillovers to the rest of the region. Heightened market volatility and tightened global financing conditions are also potential risks, especially given high domestic debt and fiscal consolidation challenges in a number of countries. Other risks include a sharp U.S. dollar appreciation, which would exacerbate financial

FIGURE 2.1.5 Financial markets

Capital outflows have accelerated, and corporate and sovereign spreads have risen. Stock prices dropped sharply between July–September 2015. Currencies of oil exporters depreciated substantially. Cumulatively, the portfolio outflows during this period have surpassed those during the "taper tantrum" episode in May–June 2013.

A. Interest rate spreads

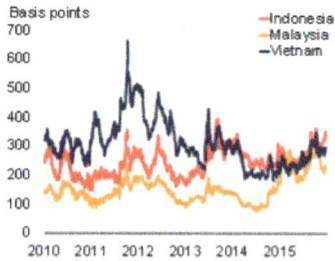

B. Stock prices

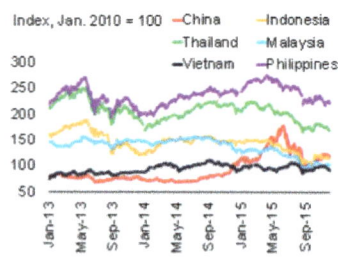

C. Commodity prices and nominal effective exchange rates

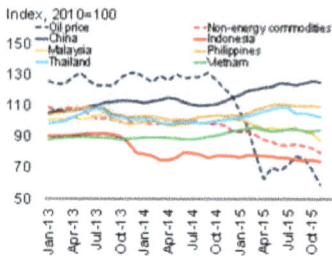

D. International bond and equity issuance

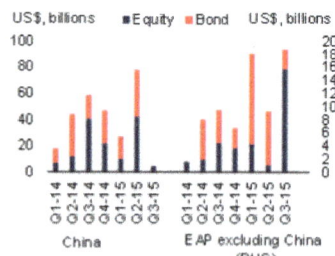

Sources: Haver Analytics; International Monetary Fund; International Financial Statistics; Bank for International Settlements; World Bank, World Development Indicators; Dialogic.
A. Interest rate spreads refer to the credit risk premium over US 10-year Treasury bonds which is measured as the difference between the Yield to Maturity Bond and the Yield to Maturity of the corresponding point on the US Treasury spot curve. Latest observation is December 14, 2015.
B. Latest observation is December 7, 2015.
C. An increase denotes an appreciation. Non-energy commodities include agriculture products, fertilizers, raw materials, metals and minerals, precious metals. Latest observation is November 2015.

vulnerabilities stemming from foreign-currency denominated external debt, and a weaker-than-expected pickup in high-income country growth and trade, especially in high-income Asia (Japan, Republic of Korea).[5] Further weakening of commodity prices, if sustained, are an upside risk to the overall regional forecast, although a major downside risk for commodity exporters.

In China, key risks are internal. A reversal or inconsistent implementation of reforms present a downside risk to the medium-term forecast. Growth stabilization measures may prove less effective. Excess capacity could combine with producer price deflation to steepen debt overhangs and precipitate corporate financial distress. Failure

to contain domestic financial contagion in the event of an abrupt unwinding of financial leverage could pose short-term risks. These could result in a major correction in property and stock markets, and a sharper-than-expected slowdown in investment. Policy levers, however, are available to reduce these risks (World Bank 2015a, b, c).

A slowdown in major emerging markets would dampen regional growth through strong trade linkages and increasingly through financial market integration. Econometric estimates indicate that spillovers could be sizable, with a one-off (but persistent) unexpected 1 percentage point decline in China's growth lowering growth in the rest of Asia by 0.5-1.4 percentage points after two years (see Box 2.1, Chapter 3). Weaker commodity prices would exacerbate the impact on commodity exporters (Indonesia, Malaysia, Mongolia).

A rapid tightening of global financial conditions presents an important external risk to several countries. A sharper-than-expected rise in long-term U.S. rates during the policy tightening cycle could lead to spikes in global risk aversion and trigger sharp capital outflows from the region. This would weaken regional currencies and raise domestic borrowing costs, posing potential balance sheet risks for corporations with significant foreign exchange exposure or high indebtedness (IMF 2015a; Acharya et al. 2015). Financial stability and creditworthiness could be compromised as asset quality deteriorates (IMF 2015b). Total debt as a share of GDP in major regional economies at above 200 percent on average, is now comparable to that in some advanced economies (averaging 280 percent of GDP, compared with 121 percent for developing countries, Dobbs et al. 2015). Although debt in major economies remains predominantly local-currency denominated, a high share of non-resident holdings of local-currency debt poses risks of a debt selloff.[6]

Although falling commodity prices are an upside risk for the region as a whole, they would negatively affect commodity exporters. The steep decline in oil prices since mid-2014 has so far

---

[5]Exports to China and high-income countries account for about 60 percent of Thailand's exports and 90 percent of Malaysia's exports.

[6]Nonresident investors remain key players in the local currency bond markets of Indonesia and Malaysia, holding around 40 percent of domestic government bonds.

provided limited impetus to growth in the region. Windfalls are estimated to have been mostly saved, either by the public sector (through reformed subsidy regimes in some countries) or the private sector (for precautionary purposes). If the declines prove to be persistent, consumers may start saving less and businesses investing more, providing a boost to aggregate demand, especially in commodity importing economies, and a larger upside impetus to growth than currently envisaged. On the other hand, lower oil prices could hurt investment in the broader oil and gas sector (see IMF 2015a), which accounts for around 12 percent of corporate investment in Asia (even in oil-importing economies).

Policy challenges

Key policy challenges in the EAP region include ensuring a gradual slowdown and rebalancing in China, strengthening medium-term fiscal and macroprudential frameworks, and implementing structural reforms to support long-term growth and mitigate the impact of aging populations. The continued slowdown and rebalancing may require diversification in some highly exposed trading partners.

In China, reforms continue to focus on lowering leverage in the economy, while shifting growth away from credit-fueled investment in housing and industry towards consumption and services. In this process, the key short-term challenge is to prevent a sharp drop in overall demand and avoid the risk of broad-based deflation that exacerbates debt burdens (Blanchard 2014). Going forward, setting appropriate growth targets will allow Chinese policymakers to strike a balance between addressing key short-term risks, while reducing financial vulnerabilities and promoting the reforms needed for sustained medium-term growth. Preliminary information about the fifth plenum indicates that the 13th Five Year Plan targets growth of about 6.5 percent over 2016-20, compared with 7 percent during 2011-15. This would still allow a doubling of GDP and household income by 2020 from 2010.

Progress is being made in implementing reforms in China. Ongoing reforms are expected to have

FIGURE 2.1.6 Policy rates, credit growth, inflation, and fiscal balances

Policy tightening has helped ease credit growth in some EAP countries. Lower oil prices have reduced headline inflation, but core inflation has remained stable and, in Indonesia it is elevated. Several countries are implementing fiscal consolidation to stabilize debt.

A. Policy rates

B. Real credit growth

C. Fiscal balances

D. Consumer price inflation

Sources: Haver Analytics; International Monetary Fund, International Financial Statistics; Bank for International Settlements; World Bank, World Development Indicators; Dialogic.
B. Year-on-year credit growth as of June for 2012-14. Year-on-year credit growth as of July for 2015.
C. CHN = China, IDN = Indonesia, KHM = Cambodia, LAO = Lao PDR., MMR = Myanmar, MYS = Malaysia, PHL = Philippines, VNM = Vietnam.
D. Malaysia does not have an inflation-targeting regime.

positive impacts on the financial sector (introducing of deposit insurance, liberalizing de jure of deposit and lending rates, and enabling the establishment of private banks), the external sector (liberalizing the capital account and adopting more exchange rate flexibility), the fiscal framework (implementing measures to contain risks on local government debt), and the pension system (unifying pension systems for civil servants with the urban pension system, World Bank 2015b, c). Some progress has also been made in simplifying administrative barriers and implementing reforms of prices, state-owned enterprises, and labor markets (World Bank 2015f). Key policy steps include strengthening financial market discipline to improve credit allocation to high-productivity sectors.

FIGURE 2.1.7 Regional vulnerabilities

Despite a recent slowdown, gross domestic debt-to-GDP ratios remain significantly above 2007 levels—more than 150 percent of GDP in China, Malaysia, and Thailand. Although debt in major economies is largely local-currency denominated, a significant share is held by non-residents.

A. Nonresident and foreign-currency sovereign bond holdings, 2014

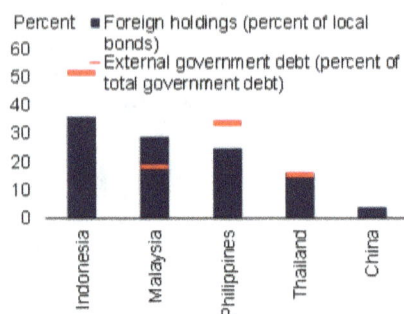

B. Public and private debt

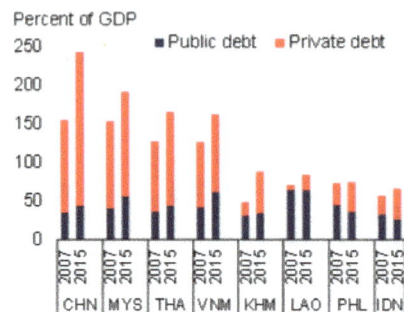

C. Household debt in selected countries

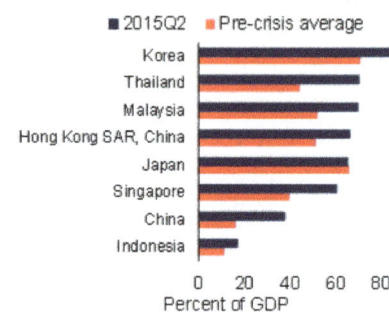

D. Non-financial corporate debt in selected countries

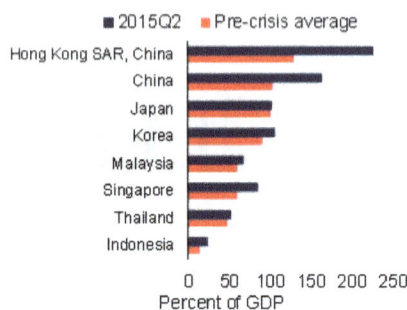

E. External financing needs, 2014

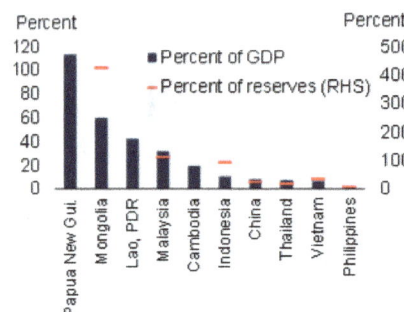

F. External and short-term debt, 2014

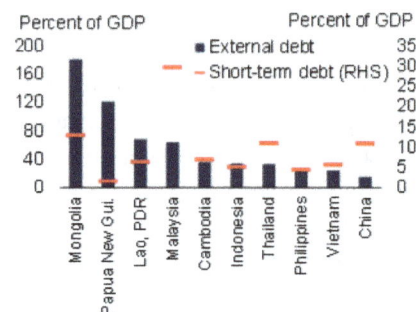

Sources: Moody's Statistical Handbook; Haver Analytics; International Monetary Fund, International Financial Statistics; Bank for International Settlements; World Bank, World Development Indicators; Debt database; McKinsey.
A. Local debt is locally issued debt, including local-currency-denominated debt held by foreigners (a large part of external debt in Malaysia). In Mongolia, intra-company debt makes up a large share of external debt.
B. For private debt, 2015 data is the average of 2015 Q1 and 2015 Q2. CHN = China, IDN = Indonesia, KHM = Cambodia, LAO = Lao PDR., MYS = Malaysia, PHL = Philippines, THA=Thailand, VNM = Vietnam.
C. D. Pre-crisis indicates average of 2006Q1 to 2008Q4.
E. Reserve data not available for Papua New Guinea.

Strengthened fiscal frameworks could provide a buffer if risks materialize. Fiscal deficits remain elevated in several countries (Mongolia, Papua New Guinea, Vietnam) where fiscal reform is needed to stabilize government debt (World Bank 2015c, g, h). Tax revenues are low by high-income country standards and expenditure efficiency is weak (World Bank 2015c) (Figure 2.1.8). Fiscal policy measures should be framed within a medium-term outlook to strengthen revenue, increase investment, and bolster fiscal institutions. On the revenue side, there is a need to broaden tax bases (Indonesia, Malaysia, Philippines), reduce reliance on commodity-related revenues (Indonesia, Malaysia, Mongolia), raise energy taxes (Indonesia), and strengthen public revenue administration (Lao PDR, Philippines) (World Bank 2015c).[7] Expenditure reforms should improve the efficiency and transparency of public spending, and focus on productivity enhancements (investment in human capital and infrastructure), basic service delivery, and poverty-reduction programs. State-owned enterprise reforms, including measures to enhance transparency and governance, could reduce drains on fiscal resources (Thailand, Vietnam) (World Bank 2015 b, c, h).

---

[7]Malaysia remains heavily dependent on fiscal revenues from the oil and gas sectors, although the introduction of a general sales tax in April has helped diversify the revenue mix.

Strengthened financial sector (macro- and micro-prudential) policies could help buttress financial stability in the event of market turmoil. Such measures include risk-informed pricing, rigorous borrower affordability assessments, supervisory vigilance over underwriting practices and adequacy of capital requirements, elevated reserve requirements, higher liquidity ratios or loan-loss provisions, and appropriate loan-to-value limits (IMF 2015d). Exchange rate policies should remain a key shock absorber, but reserve interventions may be necessary to smooth large fluctuations (World Bank 2015c). The use of reserve interventions may be particularly constrained where growth prospects and/or terms of trade have deteriorated sharply (Indonesia, Lao PDR, Malaysia, Mongolia).

Structural reforms should focus on supporting long-term growth and mitigating the impact of aging populations. Raising the mandatory retirement age for civil servants and increasing female participation will help mitigate the impact of aging (ADB 2015, World Bank 2015j). The appropriate reform agenda differs considerably across specific countries. In Thailand, key priorities include reducing price distortions by reforming rice and rubber price-support schemes, and improving public infrastructure (World Bank 2015a). Banking sector reforms rank high for improving efficiency and the allocation of capital in Vietnam and Mongolia (World Bank 2015 g-h).

For commodity producers like Indonesia and Malaysia, the decline in commodity prices underscores the need to enhance fiscal institutions to improve the management of fluctuations in

natural-resource prices (World Bank 2015 d, e). Other measures to promote economic diversification include ensuring high-quality education, increasing the integration and depth of domestic financial markets, ensuring adequate infrastructure to remove bottlenecks, and improving competitiveness by removing special privileges for established sectors or enterprises. Finally, deepening regional trade and investment integration could lift economic activity and stimulate job creation (World Bank 2015c). The Trans-Pacific Partnership agreement, signed in 2015, for example, provides a good basis for energizing trade and economic growth in the region (Chapter 4).

FIGURE 2.1.8 Policy issues

Across the region, tax revenue collection remains low, by high-income country standards, and business environments are weak in several countries.

A. Tax revenue, 2014

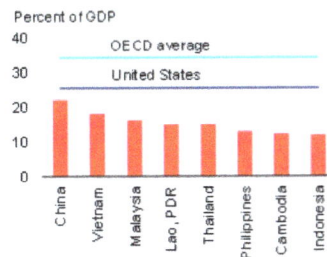

B. Ease of Doing Business: The distance to frontier score, 2016

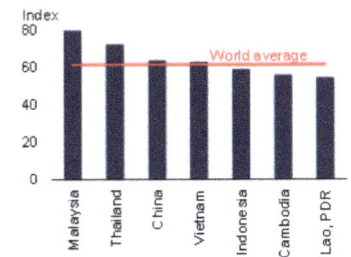

Sources: World Bank, World Development Indicators; Organization for Economic Co-operation and Development; IMF Fiscal Monitor; IMF World Economic Outlook; World Bank, Doing Business indicators.
B. The distance to frontier score aids in assessing the absolute level of regulatory performance and how it improves over time. This measure shows the distance of each economy to the "frontier," which represents the best performance observed on each of the indicators across all economies in the Doing Business sample since 2005. An economy's distance to frontier is reflected on a scale from 0 to 100, where 0 represents the lowest performance and 100 represents the frontier. For example, a score of 75 in Doing Business 2016 means an economy was 25 percentage points away from the frontier constructed from the best performances across all economies and across time.

TABLE 2.1.1 East Asia and Pacific forecast summary

(Annual percent change unless indicated otherwise)

(Percentage point difference from June 2015 projections)

	2013	2014	2015e	2016f	2017f	2018f	2015e	2016f	2017f
Developing EAP, GDP[a]	7.1	6.8	6.4	6.3	6.2	6.2	-0.3	-0.4	-0.4
(Average including countries with full national accounts and balance of payments data only)[b]									
Developing EAP, GDP[b]	7.1	6.8	6.4	6.3	6.2	6.2	-0.3	-0.4	-0.4
GDP per capita (U.S. dollars)	6.4	6.0	5.7	5.6	5.5	5.6	-0.4	-0.5	-0.6
PPP GDP	7.1	6.7	6.4	6.3	6.1	6.2	-0.2	-0.3	-0.4
Private consumption	6.8	6.9	6.9	6.9	7.0	7.0	-0.5	-0.7	-0.6
Public consumption	7.8	6.2	6.3	6.1	5.9	5.7	-1.1	-1.4	-1.5
Fixed investment	8.8	6.5	6.4	6.3	6.1	5.9	-0.3	-0.5	-0.6
Exports, GNFS[c]	7.2	6.5	3.7	4.3	4.8	5.2	-4.0	-3.0	-2.2
Imports, GNFS[c]	8.5	5.7	3.2	4.7	5.1	5.6	-5.1	-3.4	-3.2
Net exports, contribution to growth	-0.2	0.4	0.2	0.0	0.0	0.0	0.2	0.1	0.3
Memo items: GDP									
East Asia excluding China	5.2	4.7	4.6	4.8	5.0	5.1	-0.3	-0.6	-0.4
China	7.7	7.3	6.9	6.7	6.5	6.5	-0.2	-0.3	-0.4
Indonesia	5.6	5.0	4.7	5.3	5.5	5.5	0.0	-0.2	0.0
Thailand	2.8	0.9	2.5	2.0	2.4	2.7	-1.0	-2.0	-1.6

Source: World Bank.
World Bank forecasts are frequently updated based on new information and changing (global) circumstances. Consequently, projections presented here may differ from those contained in other Bank documents, even if basic assessments of countries' prospects do not differ at any given moment in time.
a. GDP at market prices and expenditure components are measured in constant 2010 U.S. dollars. Excludes American Samoa and Democratic People's Republic of Korea.
b. Sub-region aggregate excludes American Samoa, Democratic People's Republic of Korea, Fiji, Kiribati, Marshall Islands, Micronesia, Federated States, Myanmar, Palau, Papua New Guinea, Samoa, Timor-Leste, Tonga, and Tuvalu, for which data limitations prevent the forecasting of GDP components.
c. Exports and imports of goods and non-factor services (GNFS).

TABLE 2.1.2 East Asia and Pacific country forecasts[a]

(Real GDP growth at market prices in percent, unless indicated otherwise)

(Percentage point difference from June 2015 projections)

	2013	2014	2015e	2016f	2017f	2018f	2015e	2016f	2017f
Cambodia	7.4	7.0	6.9	6.9	6.8	6.8	0.0	0.0	0.0
China	7.7	7.3	6.9	6.7	6.5	6.5	-0.2	-0.3	-0.4
Fiji	4.6	4.3	4.0	3.5	3.1	3.0	1.5	1.1	0.5
Indonesia	5.6	5.0	4.7	5.3	5.5	5.5	0.0	-0.2	0.0
Lao PDR	8.5	7.5	6.4	7.0	6.9	6.9	0.0	0.0	-0.1
Malaysia	4.7	6.0	4.7	4.5	4.5	5.0	0.0	-0.5	-0.6
Mongolia	11.7	7.8	2.3	0.8	3.0	6.4	-2.1	-3.4	-0.9
Myanmar	8.5	8.5	6.5	7.8	8.5	8.5	-2.0	-0.4	0.5
Papua New Guinea	5.5	8.5	8.7	3.3	4.0	3.8	-7.3	-1.7	1.6
Philippines	7.1	6.1	5.8	6.4	6.2	6.2	-0.7	-0.1	-0.1
Solomon Islands	3.0	1.5	3.3	3.0	3.5	3.4	-0.2	-0.5	0.0
Thailand	2.8	0.9	2.5	2.0	2.4	2.7	-1.0	-2.0	-1.6
Timor-Leste[b]	2.8	7.0	6.8	6.9	7.0	7.0	0.0	0.0	0.0
Vietnam	5.4	6.0	6.5	6.6	6.3	6.0	0.5	0.4	-0.2

Source: World Bank.
World Bank forecasts are frequently updated based on new information and changing (global) circumstances. Consequently, projections presented here may differ from those contained in other Bank documents, even if basic assessments of countries' prospects do not significantly differ at any given moment in time.
a. American Samoa, Democratic People's Republic of Korea, Kiribati, Marshall Islands, Micronesia, Federated States, Palau, Samoa, and Tuvalu are not forecast due to data limitations.
b. Non-oil GDP. Timor-Leste's total GDP, including the oil economy, is roughly four times the non-oil economy, and highly volatile, sensitive to changes in global oil prices and local production levels.

BOX 2.1.1 Regional integration and spillovers: East Asia and Pacific

Countries in East Asia and Pacific (EAP) are deeply integrated with the global economy and with each other. China has become the largest trading partner and source of FDI for the region, although Japan remains one of the largest sources of FDI for several economies. Reflecting this integration, a growth slowdown in China could result in sizeable spillovers to a large number of countries, while a slowdown in Japan would primarily affect Malaysia, Thailand, and Indonesia. Slowdowns in major advanced economies outside the region could also have sizeable spillovers.

FIGURE 2.1.1.1 Cross-region comparisons

The region is open to global trade and finance.

A. EAP: Share of global activity, trade and finance, 2014

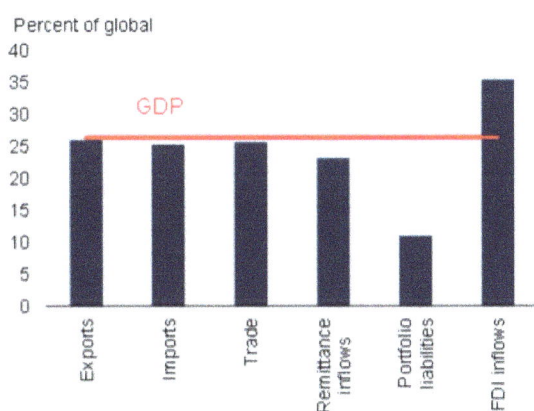

B. EAP: Trade and finance in regional comparison, 2014

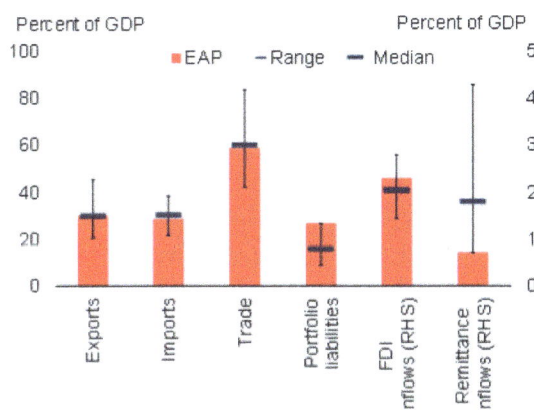

Sources: IMF October 2015 World Economic Outlook, IMF International Financial Statistics, IMF Direction of Trade Statistics, UNCTAD FDI/TNC database, IMF Coordinated Portfolio Investment Survey, World Bank Remittance and Migration Database, World Bank World Development Indicators.
B. The red bars denote exports, imports, trade, remittance inflows, portfolio liabilities and FDI inflows in percent of GDP on average across EAP countries. The vertical line denotes the range of averages for all six developing regions.

Note: This box was prepared by Ekaterine Vashakmadze, Nikola Spatafora, and Duygu Guven. Modeling work was done by Raju Huidrom and Jesper Hanson. Research assistance was provided by Trang Nguyen and Qian Li.

Introduction

EAP is characterized by deep regional and global integration through trade and investment flows.[1] The region accounts for about 25 percent of global trade (Figure 2.1.1.1), and its economies are among the most integrated into global value chains. Intra-regional trade and foreign direct investment (FDI) are substantial: in 2014, countries within the region accounted for 51 percent of the region's trade and 44.1 percent of its FDI inflows.

Deep intra-regional trade and financial integration has fostered growth. These ties are also conduits for the transmission of growth fluctuations, in particular from China and Japan. Such transmission can arise both through direct economic links and through common shifts of investor sentiment across the region. China's gradual slowdown over the past year has been accompanied market volatility and real-sector headwinds. Looking ahead, spillovers are a key concern, given the risk of a faster-than-expected slowdown in China, and the still-fragile recovery in Japan.

This box discusses two key issues:

● How open is EAP to global and regional trade and financial flows?

● How large are the potential intra-regional spillovers from the region's two largest economies, China and Japan?

The findings suggest that spillovers from growth fluctuations in China are sizeable, and affect a wide range of countries. For now, spillovers arise primarily through trade channels, given the region's deeply integrated supply chains, and more limited intra-regional non-FDI financial flows. Spillovers from growth shocks in Japan are modest in general, but pronounced in Thailand, which relies heavily on FDI from Japan.

---

[1]Throughout this box, EAP is defined as consisting of developing EAP and high-income EAP. In turn, developing EAP comprises: American Samoa, Cambodia, China, Fiji, Indonesia, Korea, Kiribati, Lao PDR, Malaysia, the Marshall Islands, Micronesia, Mongolia, Myanmar, Palau, Papua New Guinea, the Philippines, Samoa, the Solomon Islands, Taiwan, China, Thailand, Timor-Leste, Tonga, Tuvalu, Vanuatu, and Vietnam. High-income EAP comprises: Australia; Hong Kong SAR, China; Japan; New Zealand; and Singapore.

BOX 2.1.1 Regional integration and spillovers: East Asia and Pacific *(continued)*

FIGURE 2.1.1.2 Regional integration

Countries in the region are deeply integrated with each other. China is a major export destination and source of FDI for EAP countries. Japan remains one of the largest sources of FDI and portfolio inflows for several economies in EAP.

A. Within-region integration, 2014

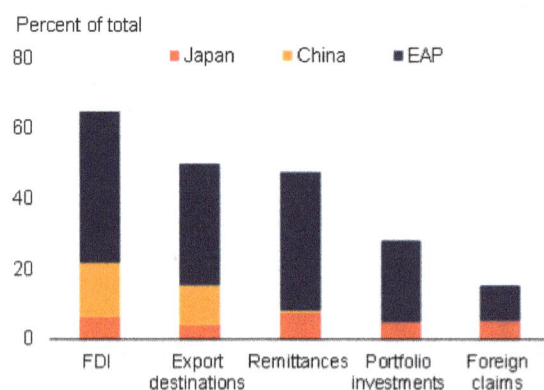

B. Major actual and potential free trade agreements

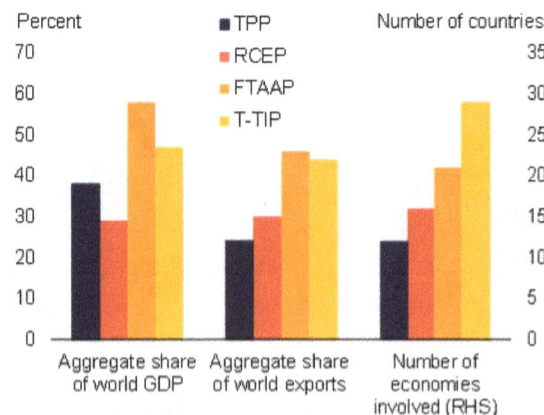

Sources: International Monetary Fund (IMF), World Economic Outlook (WEO), International Finance Statistics (IMF), Direction of Trade Statistics (DOTS), Coordinated Direct Investment Survey (CDIS); World Bank; Schott (2014), United Nations Economic and Social Commission for Asia and the Pacific (UN ESCAP).
A. EAP includes American Samoa, Cambodia, China, Fiji, Indonesia, Japan, Kiribati, Lao PDR, Malaysia, Marshall Islands, Micronesia, Mongolia, Myanmar, Palau, Papua New Guinea, Philippines, Samoa, Solomon Islands, Thailand, Timor Leste, Tonga, Tuvalu, Vanuatu, Vietnam, Australia; Hong Kong SAR, China; Japan, New Zealand, and Singapore. Portfolio liabilities data include: Australia; Hong Kong SAR, China; Indonesia, Japan, Korea, Malaysia, Mongolia, New Zealand, Philippines, Singapore, and Thailand. FDI inflow data include: Australia; Hong Kong SAR, China; Indonesia, China, Japan, Korea, Malaysia, Mongolia, New Zealand, Philippines, Samoa, Singapore, and Thailand. Portfolio investment denotes stocks of portfolio investment liabilities.
B. FTAAP=Free Trade Area of the Asia-Pacific, RCEP=Regional Comprehensive Economic Partnership, TPP=Trans-Pacific Partnership Agreement, TTIP=Transatlantic Trade and Investment Partnership.

How open is the region to global and regional trade and financial flows?

EAP is characterized by large trade flows, including intra-regional flows (Figure 2.1.1.2). The region includes two of the world's largest trading economies (China and Japan). It also hosts two global trading hubs (Hong Kong SAR, China and Singapore). As a result, trade exceeds 45 percent of GDP in three-quarters of the region's economies, and 150 percent of GDP in Cambodia, Malaysia, Thailand, and Vietnam. Intra-regional exports account for more than 60 percent of total exports in China; Hong Kong SAR, China; Malaysia; Singapore; and Thailand.

The region contains several large commodity importers and exporters. Demand from China for metals and energy has grown rapidly since 2000, reflecting the sharp expansion of the industrial sector. China now accounts for more than half of the global demand for metals, and 23 percent of the global demand for primary energy (Figure 3.5, Chapter 3).[2] Several EAP countries, including Indonesia, Malaysia, and Mongolia, are globally important commodity producers.[3]

Since 2000, intra-regional trade has gradually tilted from Japan to China, for commodity importers and exporters alike (Figure 2.1.1.4). The share of trade with China has doubled since 2000 for Australia, Japan, and the Republic of Korea, and tripled for Malaysia and New Zealand. China is now the largest trading partner for Australia; Hong Kong SAR, China; Malaysia; Myanmar; New Zealand; and Thailand. It represents the second-largest trading partner for Indonesia and Lao PDR, and the third-largest for the Philippines. That said, Japan remains an important trading partner for Australia, Indonesia, Malaysia, the Philippines, and Thailand.

China is an increasingly important source of final demand for the rest of the region, for both commodities and manufactures. A large and rapidly growing share of the rest

---

[2]In contrast, China's consumption of most agricultural commodities (except edible oils) has grown broadly in line with global consumption since 2000. Underlying this, consumption of industrial commodities, including metals and energy, tends to respond to economic activity. Consumption of food commodities (especially grains) is mainly associated with population growth (Baffes et al. 2015).

[3]Commodity exports in these countries account for 6–30 percent of their GDP. Indonesia's share of global exports is 20 percent or more for aluminum, coal, natural rubber, nickel, palm oil and rubber. Malaysia's share of global exports is 35 percent for palm oil, and 5 percent for petroleum gas. Thailand's share of global exports is 20 percent or more for natural rubber and rice (World Bank 2015b).

BOX 2.1.1 Regional integration and spillovers: East Asia and Pacific (continued)

FIGURE 2.1.1.3 Main spillover channels

Each of these charts shows trade and financial links as a percent of the region's GDP—red for outside the region, blue for inside the region. All regional economies are deeply integrated within the region through trade, FDI, and remittances.

A. Export destinations, 2014

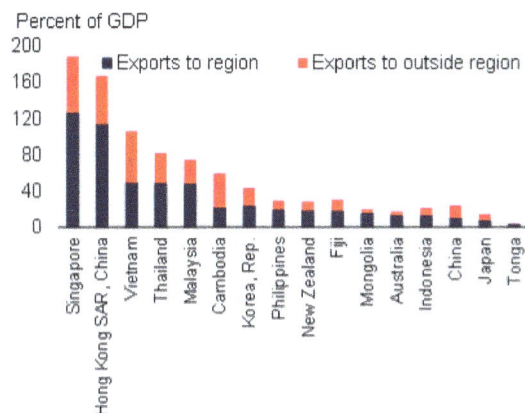

B. FDI inflows, 2008-12

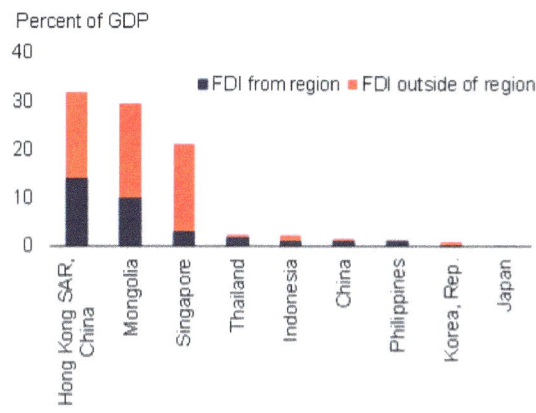

C. Remittance inflows, 2014

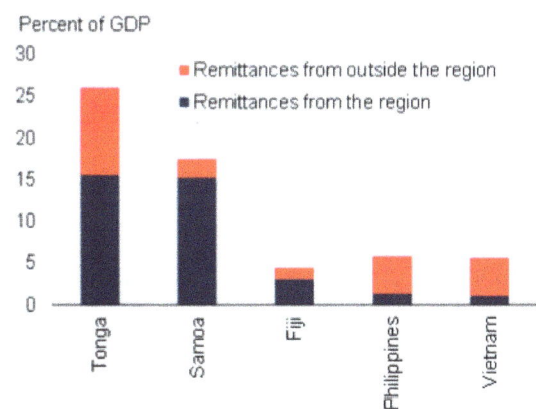

D. Foreign value added share of gross exports

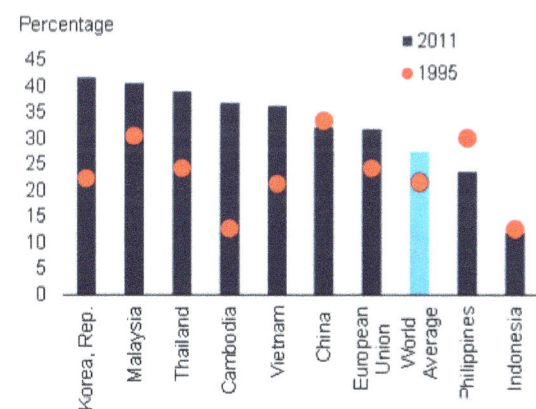

Sources: International Monetary Fund (IMF), WB, UN Comtrade, Organization for Economic Co-operation and Development (OECD).
D. This indicator reflects the share of total gross exports contributed by foreign value added in an industry's exports. The sum over all industries is the total foreign value added share of gross exports. (OECD 2015).

of the region's value added is accounted for by exports used to meet final demand from Chinese consumers (World Bank 2015c). This applies to both the commodity- and non-commodity trade. Malaysia, Thailand, and Vietnam are among the countries most dependent on final demand from China for non-commodity merchandise.

Trade liberalization has encouraged, and will continue to boost, trade and supply-chain integration. China joined the World Trade Organization in 2001; it has implemented free trade agreements (FTAs) with a wide range of countries, and is in discussions on many others,

including three comprehensive Free Trade Agreements that are currently under negotiation (Chapter 4.1, and Figure 2.1.3 and Table 2.1.1.1).[4] Partly as a result of trade liberalization, regional economies, especially the Republic of Korea and the ASEAN countries, are highly integrated

[4]China has implemented FTAs with ASEAN, other countries in Asia (Korea and Pakistan), Latin America (Chile, Costa Rica, and Peru), the Pacific (New Zealand), and Europe (Iceland and Switzerland). Negotiations are advanced for FTAs with Australia, the Gulf Cooperation Council (Bahrain, Kuwait, Qatar, Saudi Arabia, and the United Arab Emirates), Japan, Norway, and Sri Lanka. FTAs with Columbia, Georgia, India, and Moldova are under consideration.

BOX 2.1.1 Regional integration and spillovers: East Asia and Pacific *(continued)*

FIGURE 2.1.1.4 Trade and finance with China and Japan

There has been a shift in within-region trade from Japan to China since 2000. For most countries (except the Philippines), the share of exports to China has grown steeply and that to Japan has declined. For FDI, however, Japan remains one of the largest sources. Outbound tourism from China has also increased significantly.

A. Exports to China

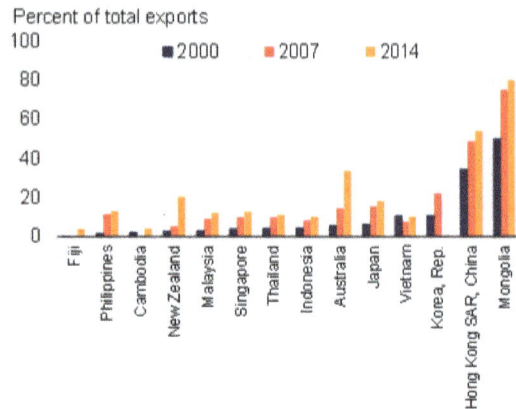

B. Exports to Japan

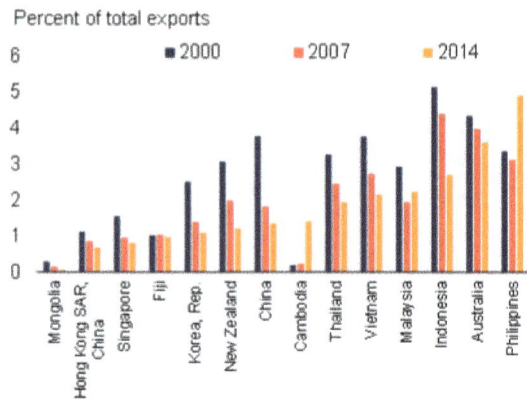

C. FDI flows to the region, 2014

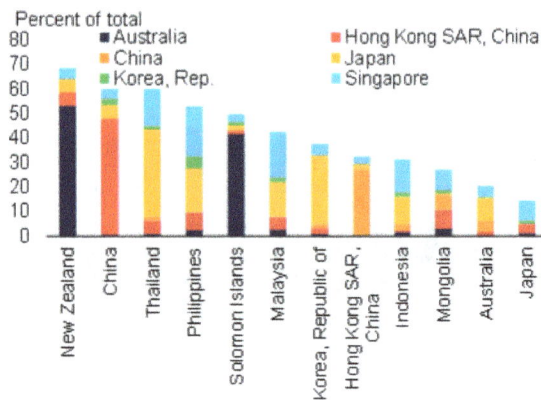

D. Total outbound tourism, 2013

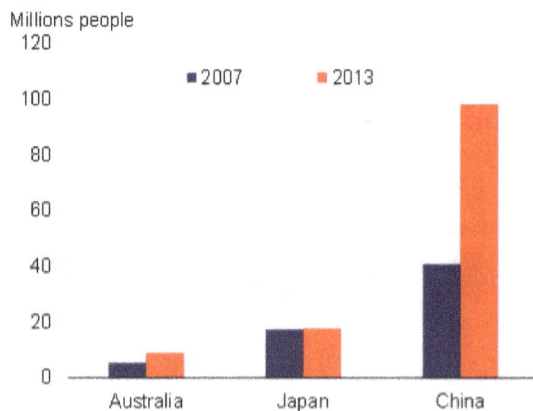

Sources: UN Comtrade.

into regional and global value chains (Figure 2.1.1.3).[5]

Intra-regional tourism has also grown robustly, with China accounting for a rapidly rising share. China has become the world's largest source of tourists (UNWTO 2015). There were 62 million outbound Chinese tourists in the first half of 2015, compared with 41 million in the whole of 2007 (China Tourism Research Institute 2015).

Chinese tourists are particularly important for Cambodia, Lao, PDR, Malaysia, Thailand, Vietnam, and some Pacific Islands (Fiji and, especially, Palau). For instance, in Thailand, they account for 18 percent of all tourists and over 2 percent of GDP in tourism revenues.

The region is also characterized by large FDI inflows and outflows. Developing EAP accounts for more than half of all FDI inflows to developing regions. FDI has typically gone into a wide variety of sectors, including manufacturing (Cambodia, Indonesia, Vietnam), construction (Cambodia and Lao PDR), tourism

[5]As measured by the Global Value Chain Participation Index. This measures the share of imported inputs used to produce a country's exports, and the share of a country's exports that serve as intermediate inputs into other countries' exports (OECD 2009).

BOX 2.1.1 Regional integration and spillovers: East Asia and Pacific *(continued)*

(Cambodia, Indonesia, Thailand), and resource extraction (Lao PDR, Mongolia, Myanmar). China was the world's largest recipient of FDI in 2014, and the second-largest source of FDI after the United States.[6] Chinese investors have been heavily involved in power projects in Lao PDR, garment manufacturing projects in Cambodia, and mining in Mongolia. Japan remains an important source of FDI flows to Thailand (accounting for 40 percent of total inflows), Korea, Malaysia, and the Philippines (Figure 2.1.1.4).

The EAP region attracts substantial portfolio investment, most of which goes to Australia, Korea, Malaysia and Singapore (Figure 2.1.1.5). Modest portfolio flows to China relative to its size reflect remaining restrictions on such flows.[7] Several regional economies have deep capital markets, including Australia; Hong Kong SAR, China; Japan; Korea; Malaysia; New Zealand; and Singapore. However, economies in EAP are more financially integrated with the major global financial centers than with each other (Park and Shin 2015; Kim et al. 2014).

How large are the potential intra-regional spillovers from the region's two largest economies, China and Japan?

Growth fluctuations in the two largest countries in the region, China and Japan, would generate spillovers on other countries in the region. The transmission channels include bilateral trade, including trade in intermediate goods within regional supply chains; FDI; and (especially for the Pacific Islands) tourism. A growth decline in China would also affect global commodity markets, further reducing demand and prices. Lower export volumes and weaker terms of trade would reduce growth prospects in commodity-exporting countries. In addition to the trade and financial channels for the transmission of growth fluctuations within the region, there may be significant spillovers through the confidence channel even though those are hard to estimate econometrically (Box 3.2).

To capture direct as well as indirect effects, we used a Bayesian structural VAR to estimate spillover effects, using quarterly data from 1998Q1 – 2015Q2. For each country, the variables included are as follows, in order they are used in the model: growth in the G7 excluding Japan; the JPMorgan Emerging Market Bond Index; growth in Japan, China, and Korea; trade-weighted average commodity prices; growth in the affected country; and the real effective exchange rate of the affected country. Explicit trade linkages (perhaps overestimated in the case of Hong Kong SAR, China because of large share of re-exports to China) should not affect estimation results, since the VAR model does not explicitly include variables for direct trade links, it is rather estimating direct growth on growth impact.

The model has a recursive structure, with earlier variables assumed to be contemporaneously unaffected by later variables. Spillovers are measured as the cumulative response of growth to a 1 percentage point decline in growth in China or Japan, upon impact, after one year, and after two years.

The estimated magnitude of these spillovers varies across countries, particularly with respect to growth fluctuations in China (Figure 2.1.1.6):

- *Spillovers from China.* A one-off, 1-percentage-point decline in China's growth reduces growth particularly sharply in the trading hub of Singapore; and in Hong Kong SAR, China.[8] After two years, their growth rates also decrease by around 1 percentage point.[9] Growth in Indonesia, Malaysia, and Thailand decreases by around 0.4 percentage point. Japan and Korea are affected to a much smaller degree. The magnitude of spillovers from China could be more pronounced if growth fluctuations are amplified via the confidence channel. In a historical decomposition, pre-crisis, China's growth appears to have contributed significantly to growth in the rest of the region. Since 2011, the slowdown in China weighed on activity in the rest of the region. These estimates are based on a sample period during which China's integration into global and regional trade was rapidly increasing.

---

[6]In 2000, China established a sovereign wealth fund to encourage companies to invest abroad. It also began easing restrictions on FDI flows. These actions resulted in sizeable FDI into foreign natural resources, including oil and minerals.

[7]The Chinese government actively encourages the use of the renminbi (RMB) in international trade. As a result, transactions volume has grown rapidly, to make the RMB the seventh most traded currency globally, with 1.72 percent of world payments settlements as of September 2014. The RMB is now the second most used currency in international trade finance.

---

[8]Explicit trade linkages (perhaps overestimated in the case of Hong Kong SAR, China because of large share of re-exports to China) should not affect estimation results, since the VAR model does not explicitly include variables for direct trade links.

[9]The impulse is quite persistent. After two years, the cumulative decline in China's output amounts to 2 percent of the baseline.

BOX 2.1.1 Regional integration and spillovers: East Asia and Pacific *(continued)*

FIGURE 2.1.1.5 Portfolio liabilities and capital account restrictions

Portfolio investment inflows are largest into Japan and Korea. They are modest in China, partly as a result of capital account restrictions.

A. Portfolio liabilities, 2011-2014

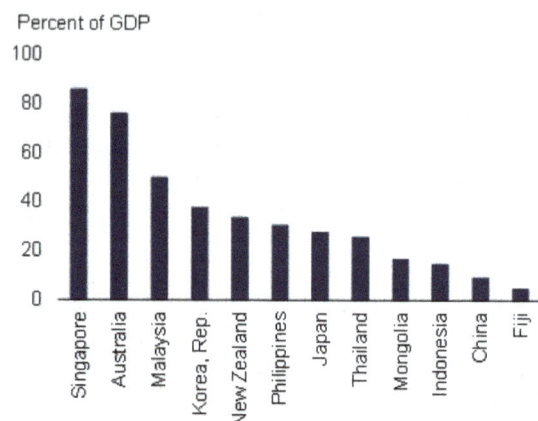

B. Capital account restrictions

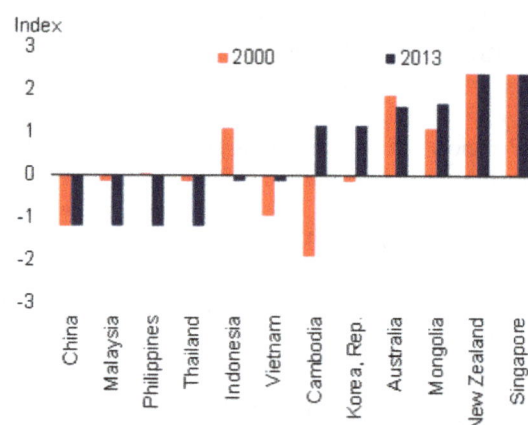

Source: Coordinated Portfolio Investment Survey (CPIS), IMF, Chinn and Ito (2006).
A. Stock of portfolio liabilities, average for 2011-14.
B. Chinn-Ito index is defined as an index measuring a country's degree of capital account openness.
The index by Chinn and Ito (2006) is based on binary dummy variables that codify the tabulation of restrictions on cross-border financial transactions reported in the IMF's Annual Report on Exchange Arrangements and Exchange Restrictions (AREAER). Negative values indicate less-than-average financial openness.

FIGURE 2.1.1.6 Intra-regional spillovers

Spillovers from a growth slowdown in China would be sizeable for Hong Kong SAR, China; Thailand; Malaysia; Singapore; and Indonesia. Spillovers from a growth slowdown in Japan mainly affect Thailand, reflecting deep FDI and trade links.

A. Response of growth to 1 percentage point decline in growth in China

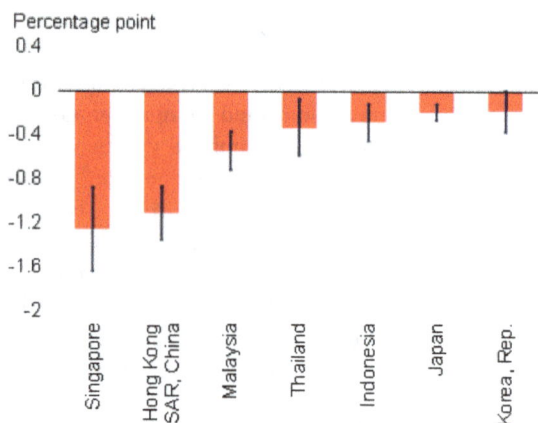

B. Response of growth to 1 percentage point decline in growth in Japan

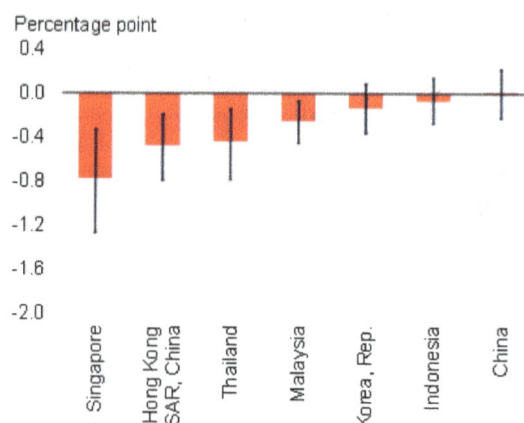

Source: World Bank.
Note: Based on a Bayesian structural VAR model. The maximum data coverage is 1998Q1-2015Q2; time series coverage for some countries is shorter. The model is estimated for each spillover destination country. For instance, when Thailand is the spillover destination country, the variables are included, in the following Cholesky ordering: G-7 growth, EMBI, Japan's growth, China's growth, Korea's growth, Thailand's trade-weighted commodity prices, Thailand's growth, and Thailand's real effective exchange rates. Global spillovers refer to spillovers from the G7 countries. The model includes a dummy that captures the global financial crisis of 2008-09. Further details of the model, including the construction of the trade weighted commodity prices, are provided in Annex 3.2 of Chapter 3. Solid bars represent the median responses and the errors bars represent the 33-66 percent confidence bands.

BOX 2.1.1 Regional integration and spillovers: East Asia and Pacific *(continued)*

FIGURE 2.1.1.7 Spillovers from G7 excluding Japan

Spillovers from the G7 (excluding Japan) are larger than spillovers from China and Japan, especially for the highly open economies of Hong Kong SAR, China; Korea; Malaysia; Singapore; and Thailand. China's growth bolstered EAP growth during the pre-crisis years, but has since weighed on regional growth. Since 2010. The slowdown in China and Japan growth has accounted for a significant portion of the slowdown in the rest of EAP region, especially in 2014 and 2015.

A. Spillovers from G7 excluding Japan

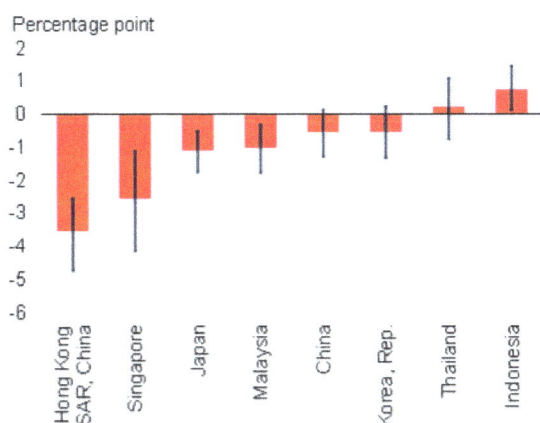

B. Contributions to EAP growth

Source: World Bank.
A. B. Based on a Bayesian structural VAR model. The maximum data coverage is 1998Q1-2015Q2; time series coverage for some countries is shorter. The model is estimated for each spillover destination country. For instance, when Thailand is the spillover destination country, the variables are included in the following Cholesky ordering: G-7 growth (excluding Japan), EMBI, Japan's growth, China's growth, Korea's growth, Thailand's trade-weighted commodity prices, Thailand growth, and Thailand's real effective exchange rates. Global spillovers refer to spillovers from G7 excluding Japan. The model includes a dummy that captures the global financial crisis of 2008-09. Further details of the model, including the construction of the trade-weighted commodity prices, are provided in Annex 3.2 of Chapter 3.
B. Demeaned growth rates. Actual is the simple average growth of Hong Kong SAR, China, Indonesia, Malaysia, Singapore, and Thailand. External variables include G7 growth (excluding Japan), EMBI, trade-weighted commodity prices, real effective exchange rate. Domestic variable is growth of the spillover destination country.

- *Spillovers from Japan.* Spillovers from Japan are considerably smaller. A 1-percentage-point decline in Japan's growth reduces growth by 0.8 percentage point in Singapore, 0.5 percentage point in Thailand (which has deep FDI links with Japan) and Hong Kong SAR, China, 0.3 percentage point in Malaysia, and smaller amounts elsewhere.

Other studies find similar results (Table 2.1.1.2). For instance, Duval et al. (2014) report that a 1 percentage point decline in China's growth would lower growth in the median Asian economy by about 0.3 percentage point after a year, as compared with 0.1 percentage point for the median non-Asian economy. The IMF (2011) estimates that a 1-percentage-point growth decline in Japan would reduce growth in China by 0.18 percentage point, and by less than this in Indonesia and Korea.[10]

Shocks to growth in major advanced countries outside the region, such as the G7 (excluding Japan), also have a material impact. The most open and diversified regional economies—including Hong Kong SAR, China; Singapore; Japan; and Malaysia—are particularly vulnerable to growth fluctuations in the G7 (excluding Japan) (Figure 2.1.1.7). Quantitatively, the spillovers on EAP countries from a 1-percentage-point decline in growth in G7 countries (excluding Japan) are in several cases more than twice as large as the spillovers from an equivalent slowdown in China, and seven times as large as the spillovers from Japan.[11] The sizeable implications of G7 (excluding Japan) growth shocks reflect both the globally diversified nature of the region's exports, and the amplification of these shocks through their impact on China and Japan.

Conclusion

Countries in EAP are highly exposed to external shocks, including those originating from developing countries within the region, advanced economies outside the region, and to a lesser degree, Japan. China has experienced a

---

[10]Since Japan's financial sector is largely domestically oriented, financial spillovers from Japan are smaller than those from other systemically important economies.

[11]Since the volatilities of growth for G7 (excluding Japan), China and Japan are historically different we also estimated impulse defined in terms of a 1-standard-deviation decline in growth. In this case, for Thailand and Indonesia, the spillovers from growth in China are larger than the spillovers from G7 growth (excluding Japan); for Singapore, the spillovers from G7 growth (excluding Japan) are slightly larger; and for most other countries, the two spillovers are comparable in magnitude.

BOX 2.1.1 Regional integration and spillovers: East Asia and Pacific *(continued)*

gradual growth slowdown since 2010. Meanwhile, Japan has struggled to emerge from recession, and a series of deflationary shocks. Slowing or weak activity in the two largest economies in the region has already weighed on growth in EAP countries. In addition, EAP countries, with their highly diversified export markets, have also been held back by the anemic recovery in high-income countries outside the region.

The magnitude of spillovers, and financial spillovers in particular, is likely to increase. So far, regional links are mainly based on trade, foreign direct investment, and tourism. Going forward, financial integration could accelerate. For example, if China were to liberalize more fully its capital account, it could generate large capital flows to other emerging markets, as Chinese investors diversify their assets (Bayoumi and Ohnsorge 2013, Hooley 2013). This would yield benefits, including through greater investment, but would at the same time raise the potential for the transmission of shocks.

TABLE 2.1.1.1 Membership of major actual and potential free trade agreements

	ASEAN	APEC	RCEP	TPP	FTAAP	T-TIP
Brunei Darussalam	X	X	X	X	X	
Malaysia	X	X	X	X	X	
Singapore	X	X	X	X	X	
Vietnam	X	X	X	X	X	
Indonesia	X	X	X		X	
Philippines	X	X	X		X	
Thailand	X	X	X		X	
Cambodia	X		X			
Lao PDR	X		X			
Myanmar	X		X			
Australia		X	X	X	X	
Japan		X	X	X	X	
New Zealand		X	X	X	X	
Korea, Rep.		X	X		X	
China		X	X		X	
Canada		X		X	X	
United States		X		X	X	X
Mexico		X		X	X	
Chile		X		X	X	
Peru		X		X	X	
Taiwan, China		X			X	
Hong Kong SAR, China		X			X	
Papua New Guinea		X			X	
Russian Federation		X			X	
India			X			
European Union						X

Source: World Bank.
Notes: ASEAN (Association of Southeast Asian Nations), APEC=Asia-Pacific Economic Cooperation, FTAAP=Free Trade Area of the Asia-Pacific, RCEP=Regional Comprehensive Economic Partnership, TPP=Trans-Pacific Partnership Agreement, TTIP=Transatlantic Trade and Investment Partnership.

BOX 2.1.1 Regional integration and spillovers: East Asia and Pacific *(continued)*

TABLE 2.1.1.2 Literature review

Author	Methodology	Results
World Bank (2016)	Bayesian SVAR (structural vector autoregression)	A 1 percentage point growth slowdown in China and Japan reduces growth in Malaysia and Thailand between -0.2 and -0.5 percentage point after two years, respectively.
Ahuja and Nabar (2012)	Panel regression	Growth slowdown in China would affect major commodity exporters with less diversified economies, such as Indonesia. Economies that lie within the Asian regional supply chain—Republic of Korea; Taiwan, China; and Malaysia—would also be adversely affected.
Duval et al. (2014)	Panel regression based on new value-added trade data for 63 advanced and emerging economies during 1995–2012	A 1 percentage point decline in China's growth may lower GDP growth in the median Asian economy by about 0.3 percentage point after a year.
Inoue, Kaya, and Ohshige (2015)	GVAR (global vector autoregressive)	A slowdown in China's real GDP growth has a significant impact on neighboring countries, especially commodity exporters (e.g., Indonesia). Export-dependent countries on the EAP production cycle (Japan, Malaysia, Singapore, and Thailand) are also severely affected.

EUROPE and CENTRAL ASIA

GDP growth in the Europe and Central Asia (ECA) region is estimated to have eased to 2.1 percent in 2015 from 2.3 percent in 2014. The eastern part of the region was hit hard by sharply lower oil prices, geopolitical tensions (resulting, inter alia, in an output collapse in Ukraine), and intra-regional spillovers, especially from the Russian Federation. The western part of the region is benefiting from lower fuel import costs and a moderate recovery in the Euro Area. Growth is projected to accelerate to 3 percent in 2016, helped by a steadying of oil prices, a smaller contraction in Russia, and a recovery in Ukraine that is being underpinned by an IMF-supported stabilization program. The projection assumes a reduction in geopolitical tensions. Risks remain biased to the downside. A deterioration in the geopolitical environment, further falls in oil prices, or financial market turbulence associated with the U.S. interest rate tightening cycle, among other factors, could darken the outlook. Key policy challenges include addressing high domestic and external imbalances, adjusting to low commodity prices, implementing structural reforms to support investment and strengthen market mechanisms, and reducing elevated levels of non-performing loans in banking systems.

Recent developments

Regional growth has slowed in recent years, decelerating from 3.9 percent in 2013 to 2.3 percent in 2014, and to an estimated 2.1 percent in 2015 (Table 2.2.1, Figure 2.2.1). Geopolitical tensions associated with Russia-Ukraine relations led to the imposition of international sanctions on Russia, and contributed to a weakening of confidence and investment. The combination of sanctions and lower oil prices have strongly affected Russia, generating adverse spillovers for the region as a whole (Box 2.2.1). Sustained low oil prices continue to dampen activity and expose vulnerabilities. The impact varies considerably within the region. The eastern part has been hit more heavily than the western part, and commodity exporters more than importers.[1] The trajectories of current account balances, foreign reserves, and exchange rates reflect these differences.

The region continues to grapple with a substantial debt overhang from the global financial crisis of 2008, as reflected in high levels of non-performing loans. Both monetary and fiscal policy are constrained by the weakness of output and employment. High inflation and downward pressure on exchange rates, including in the largest economies, limit the scope for more accommodative monetary policy (Figure 2.2.2). Central banks in the eastern part have even had to raise interest rates (Figure 2.2.3). Eroding fiscal buffers and the recognition that part of the slowdown may be structural in nature are increasing the need for consolidation. Uncertainty associated with the tightening cycle by the U.S. Federal Reserve, among other factors, are making external financing conditions more difficult, as evidenced by elevated sovereign spreads.

The eastern part of the region (Central Asia, Eastern Europe, and South Caucasus) has suffered acutely from low commodity prices (Kazakhstan), spillovers from Russia (Belarus, Georgia, Moldova), and conflict (Ukraine). Commodity exporters, especially of oil, are under pressure as persistent low prices move current accounts into

---

Note: The authors of this section are Christian Eigen-Zucchi and Ekaterine Vashakmadze. Research assistance was provided by Trang Nguyen.

[1] The eastern part of the region comprises Eastern Europe (Belarus, Moldova, and Ukraine), South Caucasus (Armenia, Azerbaijan, and Georgia), and Central Asia (Kazakhstan, Kyrgyz Republic, Tajikistan, Turkmenistan, and Uzbekistan). The western part includes Bulgaria, Romania, and Turkey, as well as the Western Balkans (Albania, Bosnia and Herzegovina, Kosovo, the Former Yugoslav Republic of Macedonia, Montenegro, and Serbia).

FIGURE 2.2.1 **Key indicators**

Growth has decelerated since 2013. While a pickup is anticipated in the forecast period, prospects have weakened, leading to downward forecast revisions. There are significant differences across the region. Eastern commodity exporters have seen more slippage in current account balances and reserves (but from a stronger starting position), and have faced greater pressure on their currencies. Elevated non-performing loans are a concern mainly among western non-commodity exporters and eastern commodity exporters.

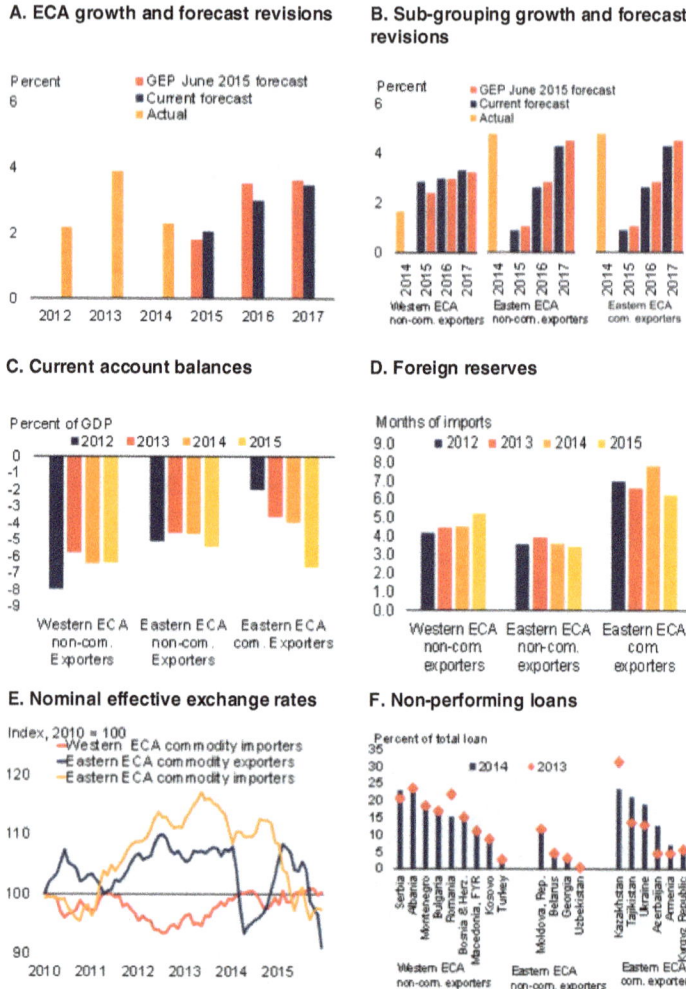

A. ECA growth and forecast revisions

B. Sub-grouping growth and forecast revisions

C. Current account balances

D. Foreign reserves

E. Nominal effective exchange rates

F. Non-performing loans

Sources: World Bank; Haver Analytics; IMF World Economic Outlook, October 2015.
B. C. D. Data for groupings are simple averages for all countries where data is available.
E. The nominal effective exchange rate (NEER) of the grouping is calculated as the median of all countries data.

deficit, push down high levels of reserves, and weaken currencies. Although currency depreciation and exchange rate flexibility may help economies adjust, it can result in accelerating inflation, necessitating tighter monetary policy. As regards fiscal policy, while several commodity exporters had built substantial buffers during the commodity boom years, these are being eroded as budgets swing into deficit, narrowing the space for significant further stimulus.

The economic contraction in Russia is generating negative spillovers to neighboring countries, through trade, investment, and remittances (ADB 2015). Eastern countries, including Armenia, Kyrgyz Republic, Moldova, Tajikistan, and Ukraine, receive substantial remittances from Russia, and these are a consumption-sustaining source of income for many households (World Bank 2015k, Figure 2.2.4). Because of the downturn in Russia and exchange rate effects, remittance flows to the ECA region (expressed in U.S. dollars) contracted in 2014, and are projected to fall sharply again in 2015: more than 15 percent in Ukraine, 30 percent in Tajikistan, and 59 percent in Uzbekistan (World Bank 2015l).

Several countries in the eastern part of the region are especially exposed to weakening external demand, with a large share of exports destined to contracting Russia and Ukraine, or to slowing China and Kazakhstan (Figure 2.2.5). Commodity exporters are exposed to the economic slowdown in China directly through lower export volumes and indirectly through weakened commodity prices in all export markets. Only Turkmenistan and Uzbekistan have been able to sustain robust expansion in 2015 (deploying substantial fiscal buffers to boost spending), though even in these countries growth is slowing as the low price of commodities and steep falls in remittances from Russia reverberate through their economies. Russia is also a key source of foreign direct investment to eastern countries, which may be slowing as Russia grapples with recession.

Economies in the western part of the region are more diversified, have closer economic links with the Euro Area, and tend to be oil importers. With a consumption-led pickup of growth in their largest trading partners in the Euro Area (World Bank 2015m), and the persistence of low fuel prices, the western part has seen strengthening external accounts, firming exchange rates, and easing inflation. These positive factors have helped to maintain a modest rate of growth. Although progress has been made in some countries, elevated levels of non-performing bank loans remain a financial stability concern (Albania, Bulgaria, Romania, and Serbia). Turkey, accounting for about half of developing ECA

GDP, is posting solid growth, despite headwinds from political uncertainty and escalating tensions, especially in the southeast of the country.

Russia has experienced an intensifying recession since late 2014, with GDP off an estimated 3.8 percent in 2015 (Figure 2.2.6). Plunging oil export revenues precipitated a deterioration of the external trade balance and a depreciation of the ruble. This has stoked inflation and undermined consumer confidence. International sanctions imposed in connection with the conflict in Ukraine are restricting access to external finance, which combined with uncertainty around U.S. interest rate tightening has led to elevated sovereign risk spreads. Russian domestic demand, especially investment, has fallen precipitously because of policy uncertainty, lack of confidence, and the high cost of capital. At the same time, the room for policy maneuver has steadily declined. Since an emergency hike of the policy interest rate to 17 percent in December 2014, it was cut by 6 percentage points to 11 percent during 2015. But the scope for further reductions is limited by high inflation. On the fiscal side, the surplus has swung into deficit mainly due to falling oil and gas revenues, which account for over 40 percent of government receipts. The 2015 budget has been revised to reflect more realistic oil prices and macroeconomic assumptions. Budgetary resources in the Reserve Fund were used aggressively to support activity at the beginning of 2015, and continue to be eroded.

Growth in Turkey is estimated to have accelerated to 4.2 percent in 2015 from 2.9 percent in 2014. Activity has been substantially above expectations, despite geopolitical tensions (violence in the Southeast and the refugee crisis emanating from Syria), as well as continuing policy uncertainty that was amplified by the inconclusive June elections. The November elections gave the ruling Law and Justice Party a majority in Parliament, enabling the formation of a government without coalition partners, but policy uncertainty remains, as key economic policy decisions of the new government are awaited. Growth in the third quarter was led by higher government and private consumption. Lower fuel import costs have provided support to the current account balance

FIGURE 2.2.2 Inflation and exchange rates for selected countries

Inflation remains elevated in the largest ECA economies, as exchange rates have come under pressure against the U.S. dollar.

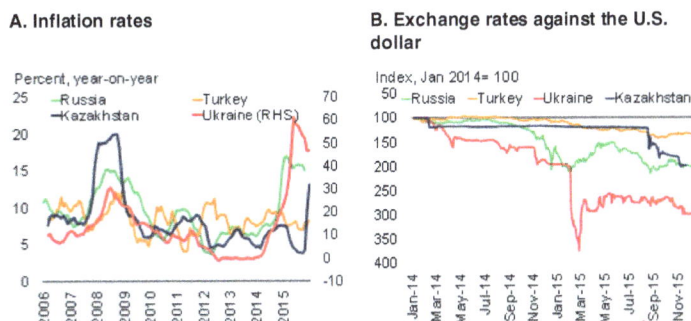

A. Inflation rates

B. Exchange rates against the U.S. dollar

Sources: World Bank; Haver Analytics.
A. Latest observation is November 2015.
B. Latest observation is December 01, 2015. An increase denotes an appreciation.

FIGURE 2.2.3 Monetary and fiscal policy

The scope for countercyclical monetary policy has declined in eastern ECA commodity exporters, as the authorities seek to stem currency depreciation and address elevated inflation. Low energy costs are easing inflationary pressures in western ECA, enabling the maintenance of low policy interest rates. Fiscal buffers have eroded, constraining potential stimulus initiatives.

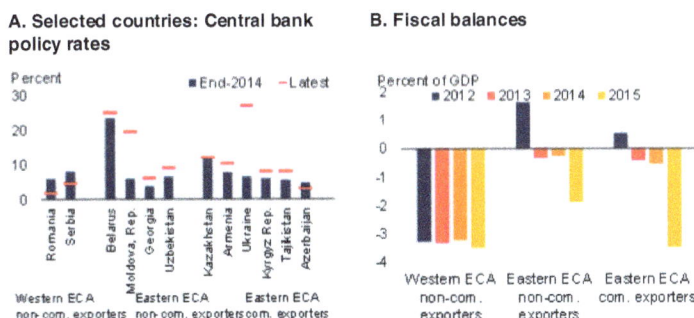

A. Selected countries: Central bank policy rates

B. Fiscal balances

Sources: World Bank; Haver Analytics; IMF World Economic Outlook, October 2015.
B. The data on sub-groupings is a simple average of all countries in each grouping.

and to output, but the lira has depreciated substantially so far this year, stoking inflation. Weak exports (especially to Russia, which will fall further with the Russian imposition of sanctions on Turkey) kept the current account deficit at around 5.0 percent of GDP in 2015, despite a substantially lower fuel import bill. Confidence-sensitive portfolio flows play an important role in the external financing picture.

Growth in Kazakhstan is estimated to have slowed to about 0.9 percent in 2015 from the high rates since the 2008 global financial crisis, largely due to weakening external and domestic demand. The fall in oil revenues (crude oil accounts for about

FIGURE 2.2.4 Remittances

Remittance flows to ECA are large. In many countries they are equivalent to a substantial share of GDP and sustain consumption spending. The combination of recession or weak growth in key remittance sending countries (like Russia) and exchange rate depreciations against the U.S. dollar has translated into declines in remittance flows expressed in U.S. dollars.

A. Remittance inflows

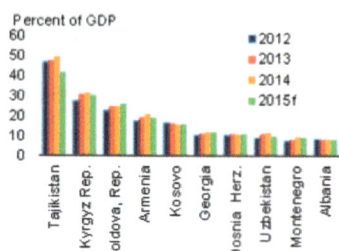

B. Remittance inflows

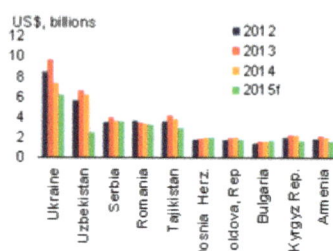

Source: World Bank 2015l.

FIGURE 2.2.5 Exposure to spillovers through trade and foreign direct investment

Several countries are exposed to weak external demand, both from the largest economies within the region and from China, and rely on Russia and Turkey for much of their foreign direct investment.

A. Export destinations, 2014

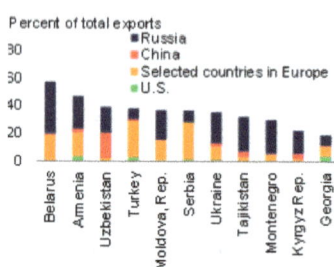

B. FDI inflows for selected countries, 2014

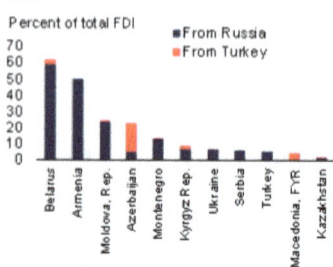

Sources: World Bank; Haver Analytics.
A. Selected countries in Europe are the 10 largest importers: Austria, Belgium, Germany, France, Italy, Netherlands, Spain, Sweden, Switzerland, and United Kingdom.

70 percent of exports) have combined with spillovers from the deepening recession and currency depreciation in Russia, and the slowdown of growth in China, to reduce export receipts. Domestic demand was slowed by tighter credit, as the authorities raised policy interest rates in defense of the exchange rate. As a result, industrial production stagnated during 2015. The Kazakh tenge has been under severe pressure in exchange markets. The central bank intervened aggressively, spending about 23 percent of official reserves in 2014 and 2015 in order to maintain the rate. In August 2015, the authorities moved to a floating exchange rate, but continued to intervene to steady the market. The tenge depreciated by more than 40 percent against the

U.S. dollar in the last 4 months of 2015. Buffers remain large, with reserves still equivalent to more than 15 months of imports (goods and services). Spending from the oil fund helped provide a cushion in 2014, but was reined in during 2015 in recognition that with persistent low oil prices, a large part of the slowdown of growth may be structural rather than just cyclical. Like other oil exporters in the region, Kazakhstan is in the midst of a challenging adjustment period. Progress has been made to bolster the stability of the banking system, with a restructuring that lowered non-performing loans from 23.5 percent at the beginning of 2015 to below 10 percent in August.

With the conflict in the east and the challenging external economic environment, output in Ukraine is estimated to have contracted by 12 percent in 2015, after falling by 6.8 percent in 2014. Industrial activity fell by even more. With the continued depreciation of the exchange rate and a utility tariff adjustment, the inflation rate stood over 50 percent (y/y) for much of 2015. Amid the economic contraction, banks have become increasingly stressed, and their capacity to lend sharply constrained. Exports are down due to disruptions in trade with Russia (which accounted for one-quarter of Ukraine's exports on average in 2010-14), conflict in the east (which damaged metals and mining production), and low commodity prices for metals and agricultural goods (which comprised more than 30 percent of exports in 2012-14). While the current account has been broadly in balance since April, helped by lower fuel costs, the capital account has seen net outflows, as external debt payments have exceeded financing assistance from abroad. Ukraine reached agreement on an $18 billion private debt restructuring deal in September (including a 20 percent write-down for creditors), but remains in a debt dispute with Russia. The authorities announced a moratorium on $3 billion in bond repayments due to Russia in December; negotiations are ongoing. Low investor confidence is reflected in sovereign spreads that are an order of magnitude larger than the wide spreads faced by Kazakhstan and Russia. Through these challenges, the authorities are endeavoring to implement a stabilization program, and fiscal consolidation was ahead of targets noted in the four-year IMF program agreed in March 2015.

Outlook

In light of the weaker-than-expected expansion in 2015, the forecast strengthening of growth for 2016-17 has been scaled back and is now expected to average about 3.3 percent in 2016-17, compared with a projection of 3.8 percent made in January 2015. The moderate growth improvement in the forecast period over 2015 depends on the management and mitigation of several key vulnerabilities, including persistent geopolitical tensions, sustained low oil prices, continuing policy uncertainty, and challenging external financing conditions. Prospects vary substantially across the eastern and western parts of the region, and between commodity exporters and importers.

After the sharp fall in 2014 and 2015, commodity prices may decline modestly in 2016 and stabilize in 2017 and 2018, helping support a modest growth pickup in the eastern part of the ECA region in 2016-18. Much depends on Russia, where the forecast assumes that a bottoming out of the ongoing recession in 2016 and the beginning of a recovery in 2017 will help support growth in the rest of the sub-region, including through the provision of FDI. Ukraine's contribution to the regional growth aggregate is likely to swing significantly, as it rebounds from the large 2015 contraction. Still, growth will be subdued compared to the average rates of the previous decade, and vulnerabilities remain.

The western part of ECA should grow moderately in 2016-18—with GDP increases ranging from an average of 2.5 percent in Serbia to 4 percent in Romania. Economic activity and trade balances of the sub-region will benefit from the recovery in the Euro Area, where output is projected to expand by an average of 1.7 percent in 2016-17 with the support of accommodative ECB policies. Some countries also receive direct support for capital spending from European Structural and Investment Funds.[2] Private consumption growth

FIGURE 2.2.6 Recent developments at the country level

Weakening or contracting activity in Kazakhstan, Russia and Ukraine may have bottomed out. Pressures on Turkey have eased despite policy uncertainty.

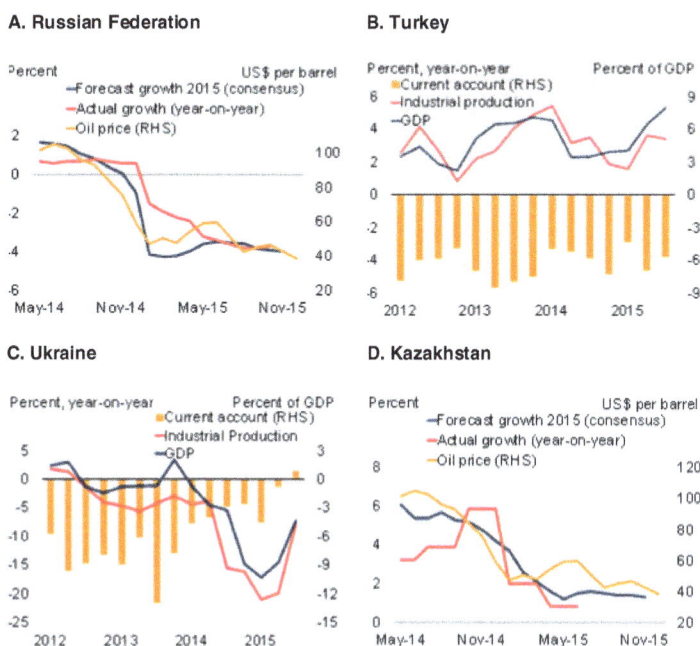

A. Russian Federation

B. Turkey

C. Ukraine

D. Kazakhstan

Sources: World Bank; Haver Analytics; IMF Regional Economic Outlook Update.
A: Latest observations are December 2015 for oil prices, November 2015 for forecast growth (consensus), and Oct 2015 for actual growth.
B: Latest observations are Q3 2015.
C: Latest observations are November 2015.
D: Latest observations are December 2015 for oil prices, November 2015 for forecast growth (consensus), and June 2015 for actual growth.

will be helped by easing unemployment, lower borrowing costs, and cheaper fuel. However, high reliance on bank finance and weak alignment of legal, tax, and regulatory regimes (both prudential and corporate), have contributed to delays in resolving the debt overhang. These need to be addressed in order to sustain credit growth and boost investment to pre-crisis levels.

In Russia, a fall in economic activity by 3.8 percent this year is expected to be followed by a further 0.7 percent contraction in 2016, before growth turns positive in 2017. Prospects are weighed down by sustained low oil prices and international sanctions. Weakening investor confidence and elevated interest rates are hampering investment, and the steep fall in consumer purchasing power is undermining consumption. Fiscal buffers are strained and the Reserve Fund may be drawn down by about two-thirds by the end of 2016 if, as planned, it is used as the main source of financing for the federal budget deficit in 2016 (projected at about 3

---

[2]European Structural and Investment Funds comprise five funds aiming "to support economic development across all European Union countries, in line with the objectives of the Europe 2020 strategy." See the European Commission website at http://ec.europa.eu/regional_policy/en/funding/.

percent of GDP). Recovery would be helped by structural reforms that diversify the economy, improve resource allocation, and strengthen corporate governance, as well as by an easing of geopolitical tensions.

In Turkey, growth could remain at about 3.5 percent in 2016-18. Vulnerabilities center on currency depreciation and elevated inflation, which are weakening private consumption. In addition, the continuing need for large capital inflows is a concern, especially since net reserves are modest. While the November elections have returned the ruling party to power with a majority adequate to form a government without coalition partners, policy uncertainty persists. Moreover, lira depreciation raises the debt service burden of the corporate sector, which has large foreign currency exposures. This dampens investment and impinges on growth. Low oil prices and a firming of activity in the Euro Area are helping stabilize the current account deficit at below 5 percent of GDP. An acceleration of growth hinges on de-escalating tensions in the southeast and managing the refugee crisis emanating from Syria.

Growth in Kazakhstan is projected to remain flat in 2016 and pickup in 2017-2018, with the Kashagan off-shore oil field coming online and Russia's economy improving. Weak domestic demand may limit industrial and services growth, however, as households seek to restore savings, firms endeavor to strengthen balance sheets, and the government moves to consolidate fiscal accounts. External demand may also remain weak, as non-commodity trade volumes are subdued. Hence, growth is likely to be less than half the average seen in 2011-14, and far below the 8.3 percent rate averaged between 2000 and 2010.

After a 12 percent contraction in 2015, Ukraine's economy may rebound modestly in 2016-18, supported by an easing of the conflict in the east and continued progress on its IMF-backed reform program. Fiscal consolidation measures have been introduced aiming to lower the deficit from 4.2 percent of GDP in 2015 to 3.2 percent of GDP in 2017. These include cuts in pension benefits, reductions in the government workforce, and an increase in utility tariffs combined with more targeted social assistance. This fiscal tightening

may weaken private consumption. Lower fuel costs are helping narrow the current account deficit, but external financing needs remain substantial. While the bulk of Ukraine's debt has been restructured, the moratorium on payments to Russia raises uncertainty around the resolution of the debt dispute. The costs of restructuring banks and reforming state-owned enterprises may pose further challenges to fiscal consolidation.

Risks

The ECA region faces numerous risks, including possible intensification of geopolitical tensions, persistent low commodity prices, and weakening remittance flows. A new shock associated with the U.S. interest rate tightening cycle could lead to less favorable external financing conditions. Overall, risks appear to be weighted on the downside, and could undermine expectations of continuing moderate growth, improving public finances, and firming external accounts.

Several countries in the region face significant geopolitical risks. An escalation or failure to resolve the conflict in eastern Ukraine would harm the prospects of one of the largest economies in the region and undermine confidence. It might also lead to sustained or sharpened sanctions on Russia, with additional negative spillovers. Similarly, intensified violence and instability in Syria, with the attendant refugee crisis, would have direct impacts on Turkey, the Western Balkans, and other parts of ECA. The economic effects of the refugee crisis over the next 1-2 years may be predominantly fiscal. Over time, as refugees integrate into host countries and find productive employment, the overall economic effects need not be negative (EC 2015, World Bank 2015l).

The structural adjustment to lower commodity prices, especially for oil, has been challenging for the region. With global markets well supplied and demand subdued, commodity prices could remain soft for some time, with a risk of further declines if the slowdown in major emerging markets sharpens and the agreement with the Islamic Republic of Iran leads to a significant rise in oil supplies on world markets over the medium term. This could increase pressure on commodity exporters and generate spillovers on economic partners. Low commodity prices are already complicating the efforts of commodity exporters to sustain buffers and pursue diversification strategies, and a further softening of prices would make this more difficult.

Modest growth and weak exchange rates of remittance sending countries, especially Russia, may delay any rebound in remittances (now at comparatively low levels). This would increase vulnerabilities in countries like Tajikistan that are highly dependent on remittance inflows. The weakness in flows is being compounded by political factors, such as the repatriation of Tajik migrants from Russia after Tajikistan chose not to join the Eurasian Economic Union.

Many ECA countries have substantial external financing needs (Figure 2.2.7), and external credit conditions may become more difficult in part as a result of the U.S. interest rate tightening cycle. An instructive example is the "taper tantrum" in mid-2013, when market participants reassessed the timeframe of the tapering of quantitative easing in the United States, and developing countries quickly felt the impact. At that time, the "Fragile Five" countries came under severe currency pressure as a result of a loss of investor confidence.[3] Today, Kazakhstan, Russia, and Ukraine face similar macroeconomic vulnerabilities, and spreads remain elevated. While a U.S. tightening cycle has been widely anticipated for some time, the first increases in U.S. policy interest rates since 2006 could bring bouts of financial market volatility, uncertainty, and shifts in risk aversion, which could combine with differences in near-term growth expectations to raise financing costs and curtail external financial flows in some countries. Elevated funding costs may also complicate efforts to repair balance sheets and address high non-performing loan levels (EBRD 2015a). In the western part of ECA, challenges in Greece may generate spillovers (especially through financial sector channels) and weaken investor confidence.

---

[3]The "Fragile Five" comprised Brazil, India, Indonesia, Turkey, and South Africa. Turkey's position is now somewhat improved, but remains vulnerable (Arteta et al. 2015).

FIGURE 2.2.7 **External financing**

In a context of elevated risk spreads and lift-off of U.S. interest rates, meeting external financing needs may become significantly more costly.

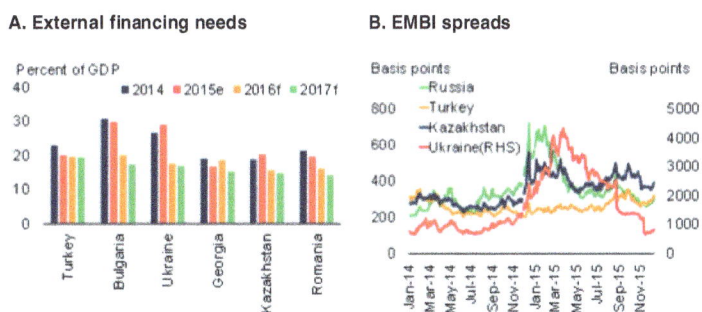

A. External financing needs

B. EMBI spreads

Sources: World Bank; Haver Analytics; IMF Regional Economic Outlook Update.
B. Latest observation is December 01, 2015.

Policy challenges

Policy needs to be aimed squarely at mitigating risks and addressing vulnerabilities, while boosting growth trajectories. Helped by stabilizing commodity prices and a more favorable economic impetus from Russia, the authorities will need to rebuild buffers, including the scope for implementing countercyclical monetary and fiscal policy (IMF 2015f). Structural reforms will also be essential to boosting long-term growth potential.

The scope for countercyclical monetary policy is mixed across the region, as the authorities seek to balance growth and stabilization goals (Figure 2.2.3). In many instances, this depends on whether or not the country is a commodity exporter, and how the vulnerabilities associated with low prices have been managed.

Some oil exporters (Kazakhstan and Russia) have had to implement pro-cyclical policy tightening to contain accelerating inflation and bolster weakening currencies. Allowing further currency depreciation could raise financial stability issues to the extent that debt is denominated in foreign currencies and debt service becomes more difficult. Countries with sizable reserves have intervened aggressively in foreign exchange markets in order to support their currencies and smooth the adjustment process (Kazakhstan in 2014 and 2015, Russia in 2014). In countries where reserves may be insufficient for credible and sustained foreign exchange market intervention, and foreign currency exposures threaten financial stability in the event of depreciation, capital outflow restrictions could be considered—as long as they are accompanied by credible macroeconomic, financial, and structural policies to restore long-term growth and reduce vulnerabilities.

In the western part of ECA, composed mainly of oil-importing countries, sustained low oil prices are easing pressure on exchange rates and helping dampen inflation. This has provided room to maintain low interest rates or reduce them further to support growth (Romania and Serbia).

Monetary policy going forward may be complicated by the U.S. interest rate tightening cycle. Higher U.S. rates could limit the scope for accommodative monetary policy in some ECA countries, which has been helping reduce borrowing costs and support efforts to repair bank balance sheets. Distressed assets held by banks are a cause for concern, calling for measures to recapitalize banks and address problem loans, as well as longer-term reforms to improve governance, particularly in state-owned banks. Enhanced supervision and prudential monitoring are needed where credit and solvency risks are exacerbated by dollarization of the banking system, as in several countries of the South Caucasus and Central Asia.

Fiscal policy has varied considerably across the region. Many countries that were negatively affected by the oil price declines (and spillovers from Russia) implemented expansionary fiscal policy to cushion their slowdowns. Those less affected (or benefiting from smaller fuel import bills) used the opportunity to build fiscal buffers and lower fuel subsidies. Hence, there is substantial heterogeneity across the region, with eastern commodity exporters and others seeing a significant erosion of fiscal buffers from positions of surplus in 2012, while western countries strengthened public accounts but with deficits still averaging between 3 and 4 percent of GDP (Figure 2.2.3).

Many oil exporters have had to tap into their reserve funds. But with buffers falling and the recognition that the growth slowdown may be in large part structural rather than cyclical, these

countries are entering a period of fiscal consolidation that may further dampen growth. They face particular challenges in seeking to rebuild fiscal space, as the fiscal break-even oil prices in many instances are far above the 2015 average of under $51/bbl.

Much of western ECA has benefitted from easing fiscal pressures in 2014 and 2015, helped by lower fuel costs. Still, several countries (Albania, Bosnia and Herzegovina, Kosovo, Former Yugoslav Republic of Macedonia, and Serbia) have had substantial budget deficits for much of the post-2008 period, and will need to accelerate fiscal consolidation in order to build fiscal space and strengthen buffers. These will be important not only to enable counter-cyclical fiscal policies going forward, but also to enhance the effectiveness of fiscal stimulus, should it be needed in the future.

In a context of slowing growth, structural reforms aimed at addressing supply side bottlenecks and boosting potential growth become all the more important. Developing and articulating a clear program of reforms can help differentiate investor sentiment and support growth. While implementation remains challenging, with benefits typically felt only in the medium and long term, they are essential and can play an important role in addressing vulnerabilities.

In the eastern part of ECA, there is substantial scope to enhance competition and ease administrative burdens (Belarus, Moldova and Ukraine), reduce energy subsidies (Azerbaijan, Tajikistan and Uzbekistan), and facilitate regional integration (as through the Eurasian Economic Union). Governance reforms will also be important to improving medium-term prospects, especially restructuring state-owned enterprises (Belarus) and implementing legal changes aimed at combating corruption and strengthening the rule of law (Turkmenistan and Ukraine).

More rapid growth in the western part of the region will hinge on supporting a rebound of investment, which remains subdued compared to pre-crisis levels. Public investment in several countries is constrained by limited fiscal space. Private investment faces headwinds from firms still working off their debt overhangs, and would be helped by improving the business environment and easing regulatory burdens (Albania, Bosnia and Herzegovina, Serbia, and Turkey). In European Union member states (Bulgaria and Romania), investment is being supported by European Structural and Investment Funds, though absorptive capacity remains a challenge. In

view of the heavy reliance on the banking sector to fund investment in the region, financial sector reforms can also play an important role in strengthening the capacity to intermediate credit, thereby boosting investment and job creation (Bulgaria, Romania, and Serbia).

TABLE 2.2.1 Europe and Central Asia forecast summary
(Annual percent change unless indicated otherwise)

(Percentage point difference from June 2015 projections)

	2013	2014	2015e	2016f	2017f	2018f	2015e	2016f	2017f
Developing ECA, GDP[a]	3.9	2.3	2.1	3.0	3.5	3.5	0.3	-0.4	-0.2
Developing ECA, GDP excl. Ukraine	4.3	3.1	3.3	3.1	3.6	3.6	0.7	-0.4	-0.2
(Average including countries with full national accounts and balance of payments data only)[b]									
Developing ECA, GDP[b]	3.9	2.3	2.1	2.9	3.4	3.4	0.4	-0.5	-0.3
GDP per capita (U.S. dollars)	3.0	1.5	1.4	2.3	2.9	3.0	0.3	-0.4	-0.2
PPP GDP	3.8	2.1	1.5	2.8	3.4	3.4	0.1	-0.5	-0.3
Private consumption	5.1	0.5	1.8	3.3	3.6	3.6	-0.7	-0.3	-0.3
Public consumption	5.0	4.8	4.6	3.9	4.3	4.3	0.2	0.1	0.3
Fixed investment	2.1	-2.2	1.1	1.7	3.4	3.5	1.2	-0.9	0.2
Exports, GNFS[c]	0.6	1.2	-0.3	4.7	4.8	4.9	-4.1	0.0	-0.1
Imports, GNFS[c]	4.2	-3.6	-1.2	4.2	5.0	5.1	-5.4	-1.4	-1.7
Net exports, contribution to growth	-1.4	1.7	0.3	0.1	-0.2	-0.2	0.6	0.6	0.7
Memo items: GDP									
Broader geographic region[d]	2.2	1.8	0.2	1.7	2.7	2.8	-0.1	-0.6	-0.4
Central Europe, Western Balkans, and Turkey	2.4	2.8	3.6	3.3	3.4	3.4	0.8	0.0	0.0
Central Europe[e]	1.3	2.8	3.3	3.2	3.4	3.4	0.5	0.2	0.2
Western Balkans[f]	2.5	0.4	1.9	2.6	3.0	3.5	0.4	0.1	0.1
Eastern Europe[g]	0.6	-4.0	-9.1	0.5	1.7	1.7	-3.0	-0.6	-0.7
South Caucasus[h]	5.0	3.2	2.1	1.3	2.0	3.1	0.6	-1.4	-1.1
Central Asia[i]	6.8	5.6	2.8	3.2	4.8	4.9	-0.6	-1.2	-0.6
Russian Federation	1.3	0.6	-3.8	-0.7	1.3	1.5	-1.1	-1.4	-1.2
Turkey	4.2	2.9	4.2	3.5	3.5	3.4	1.2	-0.4	-0.2
Ukraine	0.0	-6.8	-12.0	1.0	2.0	2.0	-4.5	-1.0	-1.0

Source: World Bank.
World Bank forecasts are frequently updated based on new information and changing (global) circumstances. Consequently, projections presented here may differ from those contained in other Bank documents, even if basic assessments of countries' prospects do not differ at any given moment in time.
a. GDP at market prices and expenditure components are measured in constant 2010 U.S. dollars.
b. Sub-region aggregate excludes Bosnia and Herzegovina, Kosovo, Montenegro, Serbia, Tajikistan, and Turkmenistan, for which data limitations prevent the forecasting of GDP components.
c. Exports and imports of goods and non-factor services (GNFS).
d. Includes developing ECA and the following high-income countries: Croatia, Czech Republic, Hungary, Poland, Russian Federation, Slovak Republic, and Slovenia.
e. Includes Bulgaria, Croatia, Czech Republic, Hungary, Poland, Romania, Slovak Republic, and Slovenia.
f. Includes Albania, Bosnia and Herzegovina, Kosovo, FYR Macedonia, Montenegro, and Serbia.
g. Includes Belarus, Moldova, and Ukraine.
h. Includes Armenia, Azerbaijan, and Georgia.
i. Includes Kazakhstan, Kyrgyz Republic, Tajikistan, Turkmenistan, and Uzbekistan.

TABLE 2.2.2 Europe and Central Asia country forecasts

(Real GDP growth at market prices in percent, unless indicated otherwise)

(Percentage point difference from June 2015 projections)

	2013	2014	2015e	2016f	2017f	2018f	2015e	2016f	2017f
Albania	1.4	2.0	2.7	3.4	3.5	3.5	-0.3	-0.1	0.0
Armenia	3.3	3.5	2.5	2.2	2.8	3.0	1.7	-0.5	-0.2
Azerbaijan	5.8	2.8	2.0	0.8	1.2	2.7	0.5	-1.8	-1.5
Belarus	1.1	1.6	-3.5	-0.5	1.0	1.0	0.0	0.5	0.0
Bosnia and Herzegovina	2.5	0.8	1.9	2.3	3.1	3.5	-0.1	0.0	0.2
Bulgaria	1.3	1.5	2.9	2.2	2.7	2.7	1.8	0.2	0.0
Georgia	3.3	4.8	2.5	3.0	4.5	5.0	0.5	0.0	-0.5
Kazakhstan	6.0	4.4	0.9	1.1	3.3	3.4	-0.8	-1.8	-0.8
Kosovo	3.4	1.2	3.0	3.5	3.7	4.0	0.0	0.0	0.0
Kyrgyz Republic	10.9	3.6	2.0	4.2	3.4	4.3	0.3	1.0	-0.6
Macedonia, FYR	2.7	3.5	3.2	3.4	3.7	3.7	-0.3	-0.4	-0.3
Moldova	9.4	4.6	-2.0	0.5	4.0	4.0	0.0	-1.0	0.0
Montenegro	3.5	1.8	3.4	2.9	3.0	2.9	0.0	0.0	0.1
Romania	3.5	2.8	3.6	3.9	4.1	4.0	0.6	0.7	0.6
Serbia	2.6	-1.8	0.8	1.8	2.2	3.5	1.3	0.3	0.2
Tajikistan	7.4	6.7	4.2	4.8	5.5	5.5	1.0	0.4	0.3
Turkey	4.2	2.9	4.2	3.5	3.5	3.4	1.2	-0.4	-0.2
Turkmenistan	10.2	10.3	8.5	8.9	8.9	8.9	0.5	-0.1	-0.1
Ukraine	0.0	-6.8	-12.0	1.0	2.0	2.0	-4.5	-1.0	-1.0
Uzbekistan	8.0	8.1	7.0	7.5	7.7	7.7	-0.6	-0.3	-0.3

	2013	2014	2015e	2016f	2017f	2018f	2015e	2016f	2017f
Recently transitioned to high income countries[a]									
Croatia	-1.1	-0.4	1.0	1.4	1.7	2.0	0.5	0.2	0.2
Czech Republic	-0.5	2.0	4.0	2.5	2.9	2.9	1.6	0.0	0.1
Hungary	1.9	3.7	2.8	2.5	2.7	3.0	0.4	0.0	0.0
Poland	1.7	3.4	3.5	3.7	3.9	3.9	-0.1	0.1	0.3
Russian Federation	1.3	0.6	-3.8	-0.7	1.3	1.5	-1.1	-1.4	-1.2
Slovak Republic	1.4	2.5	3.1	3.3	3.5	3.5	0.7	0.6	0.3
Slovenia	-1.1	3.0	2.4	2.1	2.0	2.0	0.7	-0.4	0.0

Source: World Bank.

World Bank forecasts are frequently updated based on new information and changing (global) circumstances. Consequently, projections presented here may differ from those contained in other Bank documents, even if basic assessments of countries' prospects do not significantly differ at any given moment in time.

a. Based on the World Bank's reclassification from 2004 to 2015.

BOX 2.2.1 Regional integration and spillovers: Europe and Central Asia

As a region with a generally high degree of openness, Europe and Central Asia (ECA) is vulnerable to spillovers from major advanced economies and emerging markets. Although there is wide heterogeneity, spillovers reflect the region's increasing integration with the European Union and dependence of several large economies in ECA on commodity exports. China is gaining prominence as a trading partner especially for energy exporting economies. Within-ECA ties are pronounced with the Russian Federation, particularly in the eastern part of the region. Estimates suggest that a 1 percentage point growth slowdown in Russia could set back growth in other ECA countries by an average of 0.3 percentage point over two years. Spillover effects from Turkey, the second largest emerging market economy in the region, are small and limited to a few neighboring countries. Encouraging investment into internationally competitive sectors and increasing geographic diversification could lessen vulnerabilities to growth shocks.

FIGURE 2.2.1.1 Cross-region comparison

The ECA is generally very open, despite wide within-region heterogeneity. The region accounts for about 8 percent of world trade flows and 12 percent of international remittances. Exposures to global financial investment tend to be lower, with the exception of Turkey.

A. ECA: Share of global activity, trade and finance, 2014

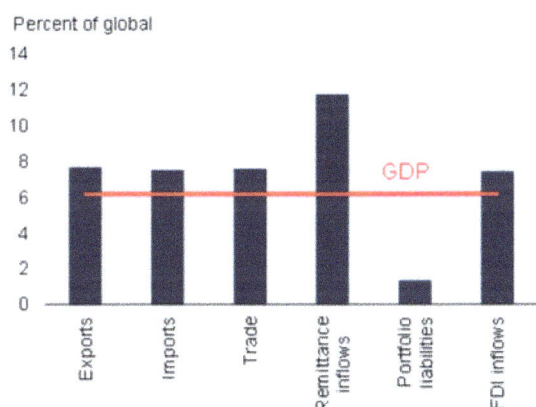

B. ECA: Trade and finance in regional comparison, 2014

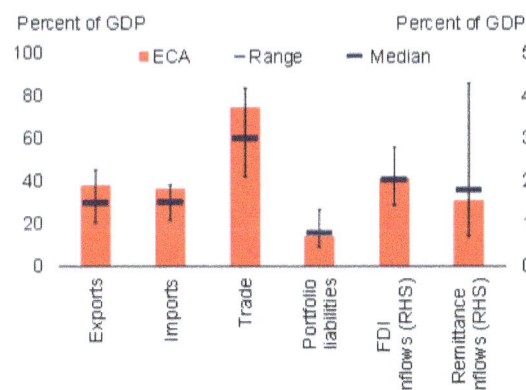

Sources: IMF October 2015 World Economic Outlook; IMF International Financial Statistics; IMF Direction of Trade Statistics; IMF Coordinated Portfolio Investment Survey; UNCTAD FDI/TNC database; World Bank Remittance and Migration Database; World Bank World Development Indicators.
B. The red bar denotes exports, imports, trade, remittance inflows, portfolio liabilities and FDI inflows in percent of GDP on average across ECA countries. The vertical line denotes the range of averages for all six developing country regions.

Introduction

The Europe and Central Asia region is generally very open, despite wide within-region heterogeneity. Its economy represents about 6 percent of global GDP, broadly similar to that of the Latin America and Caribbean region, but about a third less than that of the East Asia and Pacific region. The region accounts for about 8 percent of world trade flows, and 12 percent of international remittances (Figure 2.2.1.1). Trade is equivalent to 74 percent of GDP and remittance inflows about 1.5 percent of GDP. Exposures to global financial investment tend to be lower, with the exception of Turkey.

The region's openness reflects increasing integration with the European Union (EU) and the presence of several large commodity-exporting economies. The latter makes ECA vulnerable to global commodity price fluctuations. Goods and factor market integration with the rest of the world stems from extensive trade and economic agreements, as well as well-linked transportation networks. The Western part of the region includes several members of the EU and is integrated with EU supply chains and labor markets (Figure 2.2.1.2). In the eastern part, notwithstanding trade and economic agreements with Russia, trade and investment from China are gaining prominence (Chapter 3). Meanwhile, the share of the U.S. in regional trade has gradually diminished.

Russia is a prominent source of within-region trade and remittance flows and, to a lesser extent, foreign direct investment. These linkages are tighter in the Eastern part of the region. Integration with Turkey—the second largest regional economy—is limited, and associated spillovers are correspondingly modest.

This box discusses the main spillovers from outside the region, as well as from the two largest economies inside the region, Russia and Turkey. Specifically, it discusses the following questions:

Note: Prepared by Ekaterine Vashakmadze and Duygu Guven, with contributions from Raju Huidrom and Jesper Hanson. Research assistance was provided by Trang Nguyen and Qian Li.

BOX 2.2.1 Regional integration and spillovers: Europe and Central Asia *(continued)*

- How open is the ECA region to global and regional trade and financial flows?

- How large are the potential intra-regional spillovers from the region's two largest economies, Russia and Turkey?

How open is the ECA region to global and regional trade and financial flows?

Despite wide regional variation, the majority of ECA countries are highly open to global trade (Figure 2.2.1.3). They also receive substantial FDI and remittance inflows, especially from the Euro Area. Most countries in the region, with the exception of Turkey, receive limited portfolio inflows.

Integration with the Euro Area. ECA countries, like those in other developing regions, are predominantly linked to the major advanced countries in their proximity: the Euro Area is the single largest trading partner and source of financial flows to ECA. In addition to geographical proximity, interlinkages with the Euro Area also reflect that most countries in the western part of the region are members of the EU or have European Association Agreements in place. This has deepened supply-chain integration and encouraged labor mobility. ECA's trade with the Euro Area rose from negligible levels in the 1990s to over 50 percent of total trade in 2014, including for the eastern part of the region (over 40 percent in Azerbaijan, Kazakhstan, and Russia, and over 25 percent in Armenia, Belarus, Georgia, and Ukraine). The EU is the primary source of remittances for the Western Balkans (Albania, Bosnia and Herzegovina, Kosovo, FYR Macedonia, Montenegro, Serbia) and to a lesser extent, for Armenia, Georgia, and Moldova. They amount to around 10 percent of GDP in Kosovo and Moldova, 7 percent of GDP in Albania, and about 2 percent of GDP in Armenia and Georgia.

A tilt towards China. Trade with China has increased sharply since 2009, especially for energy-exporting economies like Azerbaijan, Kazakhstan, Russia, and Turkmenistan, where exports to China surpassed 10 percent of total exports in 2014 (Figure 2.2.1.4). Over the medium term, trade with China should continue to grow as new pipelines between the major energy exporters (Kazakhstan, Uzbekistan, Russia) and China are constructed, and the on-going negotiations of free trade agreements between China, Georgia, and Moldova are approved and implemented.

FIGURE 2.2.1.2 Main features of the ECA region

There are deep trade and remittance networks within the region and with the Euro Area. Intra-region flows of remittances are large. Russia and Turkey together account for more than 50 percent of the region's GDP and exports.

A. Regional Integration, 2014

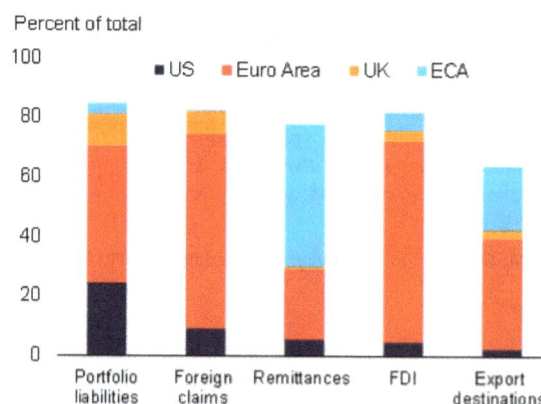

B. Six largest economies of the region (average 2011-14)

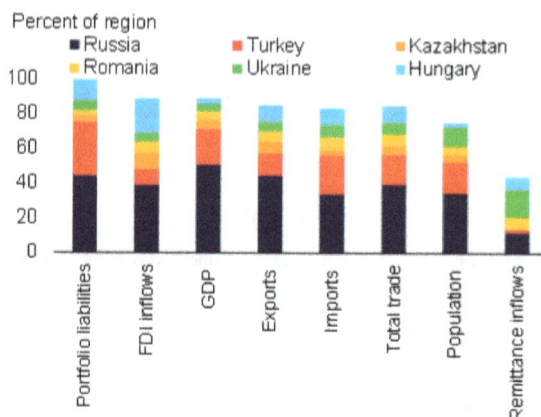

Sources. IMF World Economic Outlook; IMF International Financial Statistics; IMF Direction of Trade Statistics; IMF Coordinated Direct Investment Survey; World Bank; International Investment Position.
A. ECA countries include: Albania, Armenia, Azerbaijan, Belarus, Bosnia and Herzegovina, Bulgaria, Czech Republic, Georgia, Hungary, Kazakhstan, Former Yugoslav Republic of Macedonia, Moldova, Montenegro, Poland, Romania, Serbia, Tajikistan, Turkey, Turkmenistan, Ukraine, Uzbekistan, and Russia.
A. B. Portfolio liabilities denote stock of portfolio investment liabilities.

Within-region ties. Within-region ties to Russia are particularly strong regarding trade and remittance flows. Direct economic ties with other large economies in the region, which are predominantly trade-based, have grown rapidly from a low base. Thus, the share of exports to Turkey increased substantially in the 2000s, reaching 20

BOX 2.2.1 Regional integration and spillovers: Europe and Central Asia (continued)

FIGURE 2.2.1.3 Trade, remittances, and foreign direct investment

Intra-regional trade integration is divided between east and west. The eastern part of the ECA region is integrated with the rest of the region—especially Russia—through trade and remittances. The western part of the region is integrated with the Euro Area through trade, portfolio flows, FDI, and remittances.

A. Trade linkages, 2014

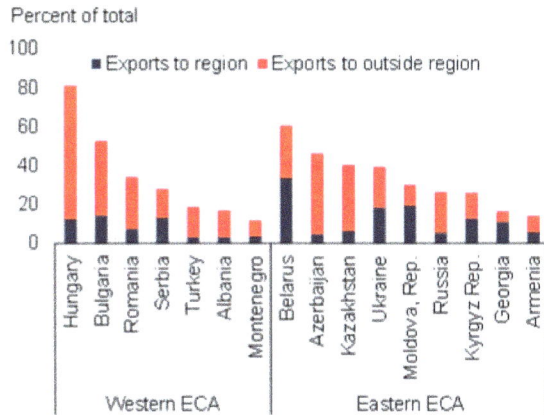

B. Remittances, 2014

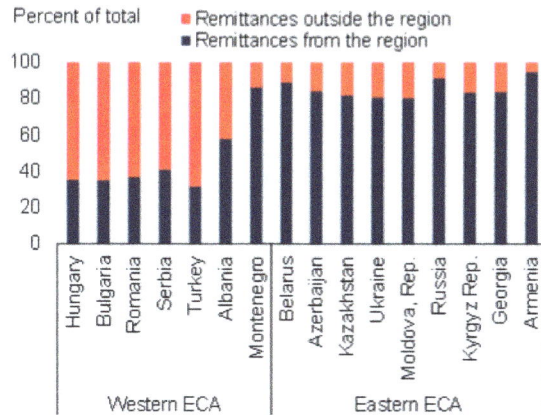

C. FDI inflows, 2008-12

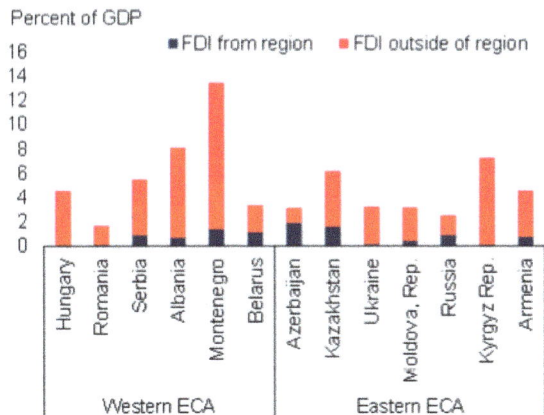

D. FDI inflows from to Russia, Euro Area, and United States, 2013

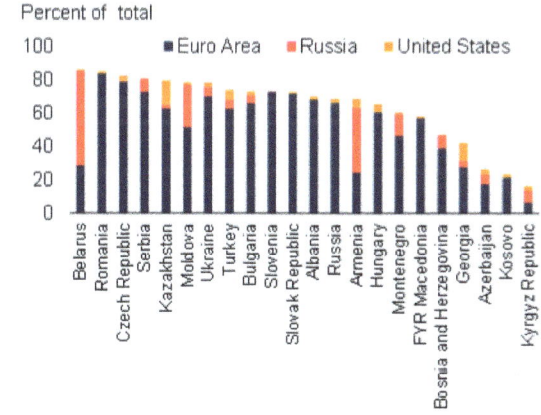

Sources: IMF; World Bank; UN Comtrade.
Note: Region includes Russia. Euro Area is considered outside the region.

percent of total trade for Georgia and is around 7 percent for Bulgaria, Tajikistan, and Uzbekistan.

Ties with Russia. Intra-regional ties are deepest in the Eastern part of the region, mainly reflecting the close links between Russia and its Eurasian Economic Union trade partners (Armenia, Belarus, Kazakhstan, and the Kyrgyz Republic), despite a declining share of Russia in the region's trade.

• *Trade.* Russia remains a major trading partner for regional economies, accounting for 8 percent of

ECA's trade and 30 percent of trade in some Central Asian countries (Figure 2.2.1.4).[1] This reflects the large size of the Russian economy and the legacy of

[1]In Central Asia, the share of exports to Russia was 15.4 percent of total exports in 2014. Exports to Russia account for about half of Azerbaijan's non-oil exports, while for Armenia, exports to Russia, mostly food and brandy, constitute about 20 percent. Turkmenistan and Uzbekistan export gas to Russia, though they have been increasingly diversifying toward other markets, primarily China. Imports from Russia, especially energy, are also relatively large. For Armenia and Tajikistan, energy imports from Russia amount to about 30 percent of their total energy consumption (IMF 2015g).

BOX 2.2.1 Regional integration and spillovers: Europe and Central Asia *(continued)*

FIGURE 2.2.1.4 Main export markets

Russia is an important export market for the eastern part of the region, whereas the Euro Area is the main export destination for the western parts of the region. Over the 2000s, there has been a gradual shift towards exports to China and, for countries in the South Caucasus, exports to Turkey.

A. Exports to major economies, 2014

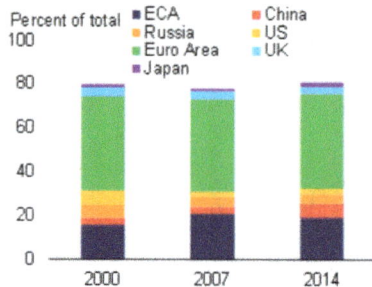

B. Exports to China, Euro Area and Russia, 2014

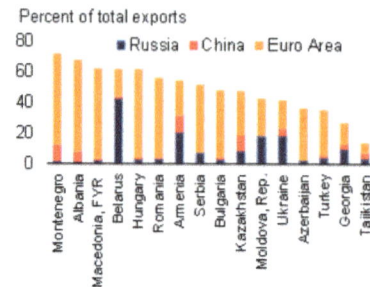

C. Exports to Russia

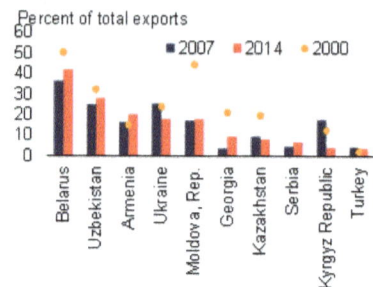

D. Exports to China

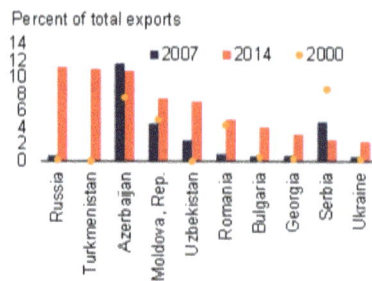

E. Share of within-region trade over time

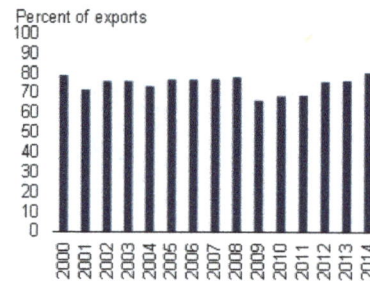

F. Exports to countries within the region, 2014

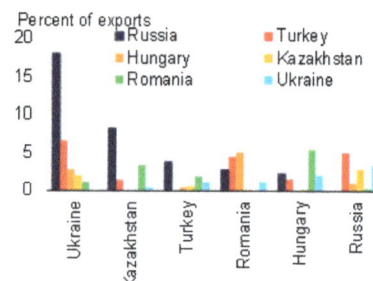

Sources: IMF; World Bank; UN Comtrade.
Note: Region includes Russia. Euro Area is considered outside the region.

trade integration and economic agreements within the region. The Eurasia Economic Union (EEU) among Armenia, Belarus, Kazakhstan, the Kyrgyz Republic, and Russia, came into force in 2015, aiming to promote closer economic integration. Still, Russia's share in the region's trade has diminished steadily over the past two decades, following trade liberalization and expansion with Europe and more recently with China.

- *Tourism.* Russia's rapidly growing tourism industry has created economic opportunities for the region. Providing tourism-related services to Russia has become an important source of external earnings for several countries in Southeastern Europe (Bulgaria, Croatia, Romania, and the Western Balkans) and the South Caucasus (Azerbaijan, Belarus, Bulgaria, Kazakhstan, Montenegro, Turkey) (World Economic Forum 2015; Figure 2.2.1.5).

- *Migration and remittances.* Remittances from Russia account for about 62 percent of remittance inflows to the eastern part of the region. Large migration movements have been fostered by free or liberal visa regimes, strong historic ties, and a common language. Opportunities created by a shrinking Russian working-age population in contrast to a growing Central Asian one have also encouraged migration of workers to Russia. Remittances from Russia represent an important source of income for several regional economies in Central Asia (the Kyrgyz Republic, Tajikistan, Uzbekistan), South Caucasus (Armenia, Georgia), and Eastern Europe (Moldova, Ukraine).[2] In 2015, these remittance flows and their real value dropped sharply with the steep recession in Russia and

---

[2]In 2014, remittances from Russia accounted for about 43 percent of GDP in Tajikistan, 30 percent in the Kyrgyz Republic, and 20 percent in Armenia.

BOX 2.2.1 Regional integration and spillovers: Europe and Central Asia *(continued)*

FIGURE 2.2.1.5 Tourism and remittances

Central Asia relies heavily on remittances from Russia, whereas countries in the South Caucasus receive large remittances from the Euro Area. Outbound tourism from Russia is an important source of income for several countries in the region, including Bulgaria, Georgia, Montenegro, and Turkey.

A. Inbound tourism

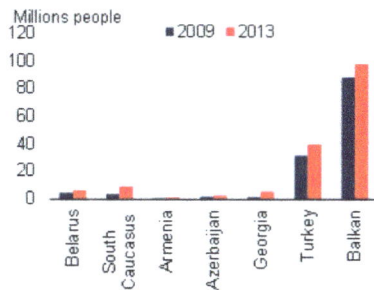

B. Outbound tourism

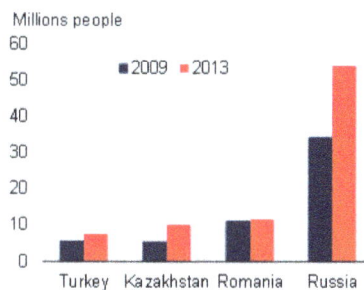

C. Remittance inflows by source economy, 2014

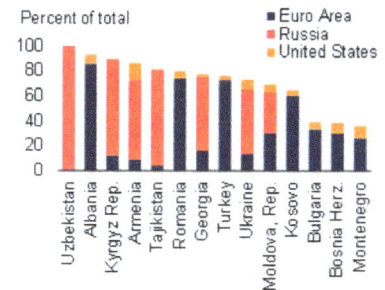

Source: World Bank; World Tourism Organization.
A. Inbound tourism denotes non-resident visitors within the economic territory of the country of reference.
B. Outbound tourism denotes resident visitors outside the economic territory of the country of reference.

the large ruble depreciation (World Bank 2015l). In addition, new Russian regulations, which took effect in January 2015, bar immigrants who overstay their one year visas from re-entering Russia for the next ten years, as well as raising fees for migrant laborers and migrants from non-EEU countries. These regulations may encourage many, especially for non-EEU countries, to leave earlier than they had planned.[3] Absorbing returning workers into domestic economies could pose challenges.

- *Bank lending.* Direct cross-border lending by Russian banks is limited, but Russian-owned banks account for about 10 percent of banking system assets in several countries (Belarus, Kazakhstan, Ukraine) (Stepanyan et al. 2015). Some Azerbaijani and Kazakh banks have subsidiaries in Russia, but their assets are small (about 2 percent of the home country's GDP). Latvia is the recipient of large non-resident deposits, equivalent to about 50 percent of total deposits, much of which is presumed of Russian origin (Stepanyan et al. 2015).

- *Foreign direct investment.* Russian foreign direct investment accounts for a sizeable share of foreign direct investment in Armenia, Belarus, and the Kyrgyz Republic (all members of the EEU), as well as in Tajikistan.

How large are the potential intra-regional spillovers from the region's two largest economies, Russia and Turkey?

Reflecting openness and substantial commodity exports, the ECA region is more vulnerable to growth shocks originating outside the region than within (Chapter 3). Nevertheless, strong within-region trade, finance and remittance links are reflected in sizeable spillovers, especially from Russia.

In addition to the trade and financial channels for the transmission of growth shocks within the region, there may be significant spillovers through less measurable channels, including through policy and confidence (Clinton et al. 2010). To capture direct as well as indirect effects, a Bayesian structural vector autoregression model is estimated for 1998Q1-2015Q2. For each country, the variables included are as follows, in order they are used in the model: growth in the rest of the world; the JPMorgan Emerging Market Bond Index; growth in Russia and Turkey; trade-weighted average commodity

---

[3]Hundreds of thousands of migrant workers are reported to have returned to Tajikistan, Uzbekistan and, to a lesser extent, the Kyrgyz Republic (EBRD 2015b).

BOX 2.2.1 Regional integration and spillovers: Europe and Central Asia *(continued)*

prices; growth in the affected country; and the real effective exchange rate of the affected country. Explicit trade linkages should not affect estimation results, since the VAR model does not explicitly include variables for direct trade links, it is rather estimating direct growth on growth impact. The exercise focuses on estimating the impact of growth shocks in the two largest economies—Russia and Turkey—on other countries in the region. Spillovers are estimated as the response of growth in a country to a 1 percentage point decline in growth in the source country of the shock (Russia or Turkey).[4]

Russian growth shocks have sizeable effects across the region. The estimates suggest that a 1 percentage point decline in Russian growth reduces growth in other ECA countries by an average of 0.3 percentage point over two years (Figure 2.2.1.6). The estimated impact is larger in countries in the South Caucasus (0.6 percentage point in Armenia). The estimated impact for Kazakhstan (0.3 percentage point)—the only central Asian economy where data was available for the estimation—was in line with the average impact for the region. In other countries, the impact is more modest.

Other authors report similar findings (see summary table below). The remittances channel is particularly important for oil importers in the eastern part of the region; the trade channel has weakened over time; the FDI channel is significant for Armenia and Tajikistan; and the financial sector channel is limited, because of the modest presence of Russian banks (Ilahi et al. 2009, IMF 2015g). Overall, the study finds that Russian growth shocks are associated with sizable effects on growth in Belarus, Kazakhstan, and Tajikistan.[5] These authors find that a severe simulated shock, involving a 4 percent decline in Russian GDP, a deterioration in confidence, an increase in capital cost, and a slowdown in the productivity growth of the Russian tradable goods sector, could reduce GDP in CIS countries by 2.5-3 percent below the baseline over one year (IMF, 2015f). This is broadly proportional to the results presented above and the magnitude of spillovers is broadly

---

[4]To facilitate comparisons across models, responses are scaled by the cumulative change in the source country in the same quarter (1 percentage point, by definition), after one year and after two years. The estimations require quarterly data .

[5]The estimated spillover effects of a one standard deviation shock to the Russian GDP (about 2 percent) peak after two quarters to reach 0.6 percent in Belarus, 1.7 percent in Kazakhstan, and 2 percent in Tajikistan. The impact would last between 3 and 6 quarters. The estimated effects are less significant in Georgia and the Kyrgyz Republic and not significant in Moldova and Uzbekistan.

FIGURE 2.2.1.6 Regional spillovers

Spillovers from Russia are sizeable, particularly in the eastern part of the region, which is deeply integrated with Russia through trade and remittances. Spillovers from Turkey are smaller, and mostly local, but may be gaining importance.

A. Impact on growth of a 1 percentage point decline in Russia's growth

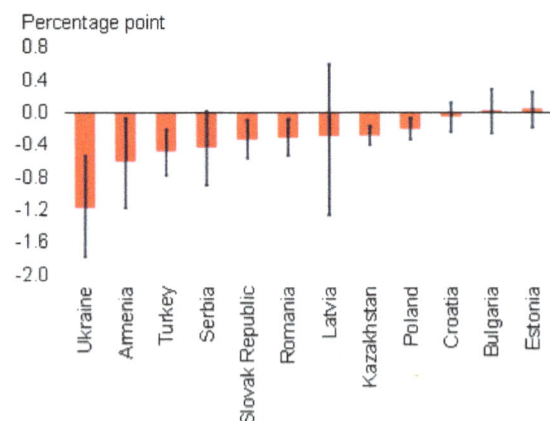

B. Impact on growth of 1 percentage point decline in Turkey's growth

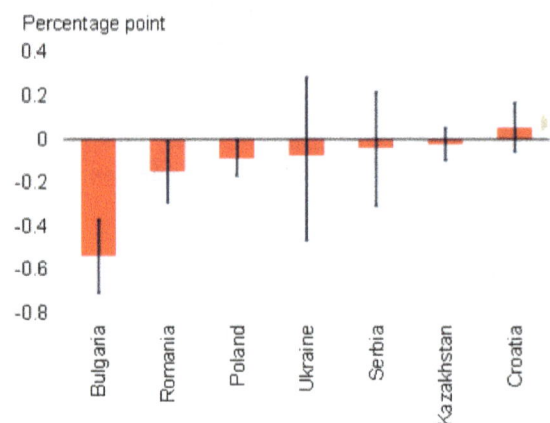

Source: World Bank.
Note: Cumulative impact response after two years of each country's real GDP growth to a 1 percentage point decline in Russia's or Turkey's growth. Based on estimates of a structural VAR using data from 1998Q2-2015Q2.

in line with trade links (Stepanyan et al. 2015). Effects are amplified by remittances from Russia (for Armenia, Moldova and other oil importers in Caucasus and Central Asia) and the impact of depreciations on banking sectors (Kazakhstan). The ongoing crisis in Russia and Ukraine has had limited spillovers on Europe (Husabø 2014). The

BOX 2.2.1 Regional integration and spillovers: Europe and Central Asia *(continued)*

FIGURE 2.2.1.7 Spillovers from the rest of the world

Global spillovers are larger than within-region spillovers, reflecting the openness of the region, especially to the Euro Area and to world commodity markets.

Impact on growth of 1 percentage point decline in the rest of the world growth

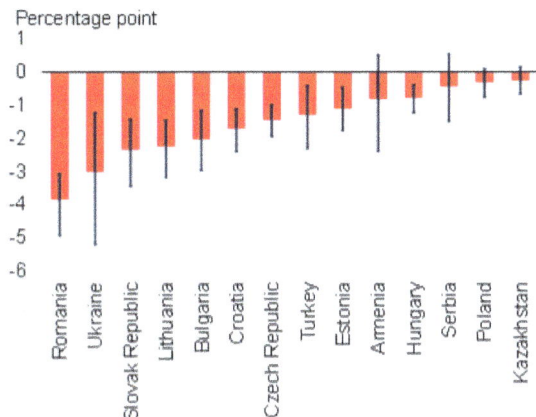

Source: World Bank.
Note: Cumulative impulse response after two years, scaled by cumulative impulse response of growth in source country of shock.
Solid bars represent the median responses and the errors bars represent the 33-66 percent confidence bands.

largest estimates are for countries with sizeable export exposures to Russia (Finland, Latvia, Lithuania, Slovakia, and Slovenia), but even in these cases there is less than 0.5 percentage point decline in growth in response to a negative 1 percent shock in Russia. Others have also found that the effects of shocks from Russian GDP on activity in Baltic countries are not large (Obiora 2009). At most, a 1 percent decline in Russia's GDP reduces Lithuania's GDP by about 0.5 percentage point. These spillovers are relatively weak because of increasing trade and financial integration with the EU and declining trade with Russia (Shiells et al. 2005).

Our estimates suggest that growth shocks in Turkey have smaller, and mostly local, repercussions for countries in the neighborhood. A 1 percentage point decline in growth in Turkey reduces growth in other ECA countries by an average of 0.1 percentage point over two years. The estimated impact is larger in Bulgaria and Romania where a 1 percentage point decline in growth in Turkey reduces

growth by 0.5 and 0.2 percentage point, respectively, over two years. Spillovers to other ECA countries are smaller.

Estimated spillovers from the rest of the world are larger than those from either Russia or Turkey. A 1 percentage point decline in the rest of the world growth would reduce growth in ECA countries by 1.7 percentage points over two years (Figure 2.2.1.7). This broadly reflects the deep integration of the western part of the region with the Euro Area, and of the eastern part of the region with global commodity markets.

Conclusion

ECA is one of the most open developing regions to trade, remittances, and FDI. For historical reasons, it has vibrant intra-regional trade and financial networks, especially in the East of the region, which retains strong ties to Russia despite a gradual shift towards China. The West of the region is deeply integrated into supply chains and, to some extent, labor markets in the EU. Because of this openness, and the presence of several large commodity exporters, the ECA region is more vulnerable to global growth shocks than to shocks originating from within the region. The rapid expansion of economic links with China is shifting the potential source of external disturbances. The eastern part of the region remains vulnerable to a growth slowdown in Russia, through trade and remittances links.

Planned infrastructure investment into regional road and rail corridors, combined with continued trade liberalization and improved business environments, could help diversify the region's trade partners and sources of finance. Barriers to open markets are particularly significant in Central Asia (World Bank 2015f). Reducing these barriers would spur productivity and increase resilience to external shocks. Tariffs remain high in Uzbekistan and Turkmenistan; non-tariff barriers require streamlining in Kazakhstan and Russia; and trade facilitation can be further improved across the region. Current low commodity prices heighten the importance of diversification in commodity-exporting countries, by initiatives to build institutions that reduce economic volatility, change incentives away from non-tradables, penetrate new and dynamic export markets, encourage FDI in new industries, and build human capital (Gill et al. 2014).

TABLE 2.2.1.1 Summary of the literature

Author	Methodology	Results
World Bank (2016)	Bayesian structural vector autoregression	A 1-percentage-point growth decline in Russia reduces GDP in Armenia and Kazakhstan by 0.6 and 0.3 percentage point, respectively, after two years. Growth shocks in Turkey have a smaller effect on growth in other countries in the region. A 1-percentage-point decline in growth in Turkey reduced growth in the region by 0.1 percentage point on average after two years.
Ilahi et al. (2009)	Panel regression; Vector autoregression (VAR). 1997-2008 Panel: annual data. VAR: quarterly data.	Russian growth shocks have strong effects on Belarus, Kazakhstan, Tajikistan, and, to some extent, Georgia and the Kyrgyz Republic. In Belarus, Kazakhstan, and Tajikistan the spillover effects on GDP growth are 0.6 percent to 2 percent, respectively. The effects are less significant in Georgia and the Kyrgyz Republic, and not significant in Moldova and Uzbekistan.
Obiora (2009)	VAR	There are significant cross-country spillovers to the Baltics with those from the EU outweighing spillovers from Russia. Lithuania's GDP response to a one percent shock from Russia occurs contemporaneously with growth of about ½ percent.
Husabø (2014)	VAR	Spillovers from Russian GDP growth are largest for Finland, Latvia, Lithuania, Slovakia, and Slovenia (i.e., countries with the largest export exposures to Russia).

LATIN AMERICA and THE CARIBBEAN

Economic activity in the broader Latin America and the Caribbean contracted in 2015, amid lower commodity prices, decelerations in major trading partners, and persistent domestic challenges among the region's largest economies. With commodity prices expected to stabilize, coupled with the continued recovery in the United States and Euro Area, regional growth is expected to improve over the medium term. Major downside risks include further declines in commodity prices, bouts of financial volatility, sharp falls in capital flows, and protracted economic downturns among the region's largest economies.

Recent developments

Economic activity in the broader Latin America and the Caribbean (LAC) region contracted in 2015. Following three consecutive years of slowing growth, output in the region fell 0.9 percent in 2015, partly reflecting sharp declines in economic activity of large regional economies, such as Brazil and the República Bolivariana de Venezuela (Table 2.3.1, Figure 2.3.1). This reduction in output stemmed from a combination of global and domestic factors, particularly the continued slump in commodity prices. Lower crude oil prices – down around 45 percent from 2014 levels – have reduced export earnings and fiscal revenues of regional oil exporters, such as Belize, Colombia, Ecuador, Mexico, and the República Bolivariana de Venezuela. Depressed prices of copper, iron ore, gold, and soy beans have worsened the terms-of-trade for commodity exporters, such as Brazil, Chile, the Dominican Republic, and Peru. A number of governments had to undertake pro-cyclical fiscal tightening, aggravating the economic slowdown. Several large South American economies have also been grappling with severe domestic macroeconomic challenges that have eroded consumer and investor confidence, further contributing to the regional output decline in 2015.

Output in the South American sub-region experienced a particularly marked reduction in 2015.[1] With GDP falling in Brazil, Ecuador and the República Bolivariana de Venezuela, South America saw overall economic growth turn negative, to an estimated -2.1 percent in 2015, after tepid growth in 2014. Investment in Brazil has been dropping since 2013 due to investors' loss of confidence, which was exacerbated in 2015 by the widening investigations into the Petrobras scandal. Monetary and fiscal tightening, accelerating inflation, and concerns about growing fiscal deficits also weighed on investment. The República Bolivariana de Venezuela too is in recession, with very high rates of inflation. Controls that restrict imports of vital consumer goods and intermediate inputs have curtailed private consumption and impeded manufacturing. The appreciation of the U.S. dollar has meant a loss of competitiveness for the fully dollarized Ecuadorean economy. This, together with lower oil prices, has pushed Ecuador into a recession in 2015. In contrast, Argentina saw activity rebound in 2015.[2] However, the increase in activity might not be sustainable as it was partly due to a surge in pre-election public spending, while net exports have been falling and inflation has been high. Other large economies, particularly commodity exporters, are continuing to grow at tepid rates.

Note: The author of this section is Derek H. C. Chen. Research assistance was provided by Mai Anh Bui. The discussion in this section includes both developing and high-income economies in the Latin America and the Caribbean region.

[1]The South American sub-region includes: Argentina, Bolivia, Brazil, Chile, Colombia, Ecuador, Guyana, Paraguay, Peru, Uruguay, and the República Bolivariana de Venezuela.

[2]Based on official national accounts data.

FIGURE 2.3.1 GDP growth, 2014-2015

Regional GDP contracted in 2015, because of recessions in large South American economies. Output continued to grow in developing Central and North America and the Caribbean.

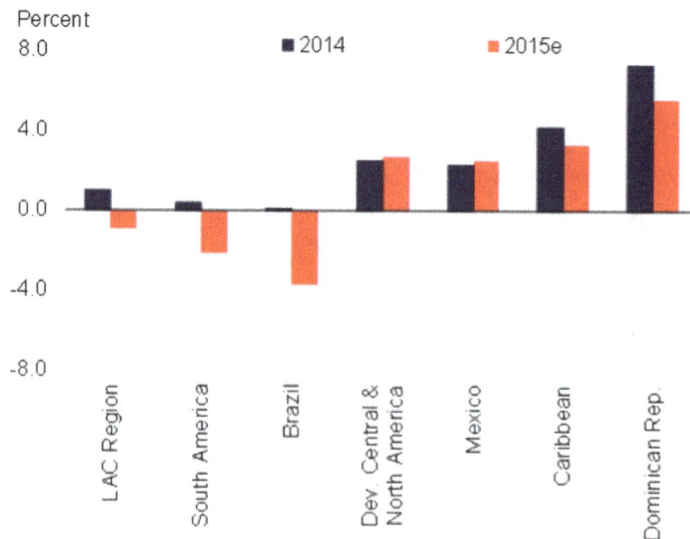

Source: World Bank.
Note: e= estimated. GDP weighted averages.

FIGURE 2.3.2 Commodity prices

Commodity prices continued to soften across the board in 2015, amidst well-supplied markets.

A. Commodity prices

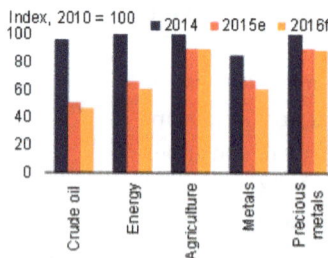

B. Prices of key commodity exports

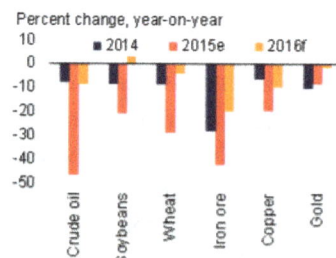

Source: World Bank.
Note: e = estimated; f = forecast.

Despite strong economic ties to a strengthening United States, developing Central and North America saw growth rates in 2015 rise modestly from 2014.[3] The sub-region's largest economy, Mexico, saw a small pickup in growth in 2015 on the back of expanding exports to the United States. However, the Mexican economy has been weighed down by low oil prices and reduced oil production. Lower oil prices have severely

curtailed government revenues, and compelled fiscal tightening.

Economic growth in the Caribbean moderated in 2015, with output expanding by 3.3 percent.[4] The Dominican Republic, the largest economy in the sub-region, experienced a contraction in mining exports, as prices fell. A surge in investment, including the construction of new public schools and two new coal-fired power plants, provided some support to output. In contrast, Jamaica saw growth pick up, amid increased business and consumer confidence, a successful IMF Extended Fund Facility program review, and stronger mining output.[5]

The sharp fall in commodity prices, predominantly due to well-supplied markets, adversely affected commodity exporters in LAC. In 2015, prices of agricultural products declined by about 13 percent, metals by 21 percent, and precious metals by 11 percent from 2014 (Figure 2.3.2). Oil prices towards the end of the year were about 45 percent below 2014 prices. This hurt tax and export revenues, and exerted pressures on fiscal balances of oil exporters (Belize, Colombia, Ecuador, Mexico, Venezuela). Similarly, the slump in copper prices, along with the continued slowdown in major trading partners, dampened investment into the mining sector, weighing on growth in Chile and Peru.

Regional currencies continued to depreciate in 2015. Commodity exporters in the region saw large depreciations on account of the continued slump in commodity prices (Figure 2.3.3). At end-October 2015, the currencies of Chile, Colombia, Mexico and Uruguay depreciated by an average of 13 percent in nominal terms and around 9 percent in real effective terms with respect to their levels at the beginning of the year. The Brazilian real saw an exceptionally large depreciation, due to investor concerns about macroeconomic imbalances and political uncertainty. The Argentine peso depreciated 27 percent on December 17, 2015 when capital controls were lifted.

---

[3]The developing Central and North America sub-region includes: Costa Rica, Guatemala, Honduras, Mexico, Nicaragua, Panama, and El Salvador.

[4]The Caribbean sub-region includes: Antigua and Barbuda, The Bahamas, Barbados, Belize, Dominica, Dominican Republic, Haiti, Jamaica, St. Lucia, St. Vincent and the Grenadines, and Trinidad and Tobago.

[5]Higher mining output was led by increased production of alumina, boosted by higher global demand.

Regional export performance improved in 2015, boosted by weak exchange rates and continued recoveries in the United States and the Euro Area. Regional export volumes of goods and services climbed around 5 percent in 2015 after remaining broadly unchanged in 2014 (Figure 2.3.4). Exports in South America expanded by about 4 percent, led by Brazil with a substantially depreciated real. Similarly, with its close ties with the United States, developing Central and North America experienced export growth of more than 8 percent. Led by strong tourism demand, the Caribbean's exports of goods and services rose almost 5 percent in 2015.

There was a large divergence in inflation performance across the region. Reduced oil prices led to lower inflation in developing Central America, North America, and the Caribbean. For example, despite seeing a 12 percent depreciation of the peso against the U.S. dollar and being an oil exporter, Mexico's consumer price inflation reached historic lows in 2015 (Figure 2.3.5). The mild inflation rates enabled the Banco de México to maintain a record low interest rate of 3 percent for most of 2015 (Figure 2.3.6).[6] Inflation pressures in Nicaragua also eased sharply following a cut in electricity prices in April. El Salvador, which imports almost all of its oil, saw annual inflation turn negative for most of 2015. Similarly, consumer prices in Costa Rica fell in the latter half of 2015, and the central bank further lowered its policy rate to 2.25 percent in October. Also with low inflation, the Dominican Republic reduced interest rates and lowered commercial bank reserve requirements in the first half of 2015.

In contrast, consumer price inflation ran at very high rates in Argentina, Brazil, and especially the República Bolivariana de Venezuela. In Brazil, inflation reached a 12-year high in the second half of 2015. This was in part due to the one-off effect of a reduction in subsidies and an increase in administered prices, but the main reason was higher underlying inflation, as the core inflation accelerated to above 9 percent. In a series of upward adjustments, the Banco do Brasil raised policy interest rates to 14.25 percent, a nine-year

---

FIGURE 2.3.3 Exchange rates

LAC currencies continued to depreciate against the U.S. dollar in 2015. The depreciation of the Brazilian real was particularly steep. Because of high inflation, the real effective exchange rates of Argentina and the Republica Bolivariana de Venezuela rose, indicating a loss of cost competitiveness.

A. Exchange rates against U.S. dollar

B. Real effective exchange rates

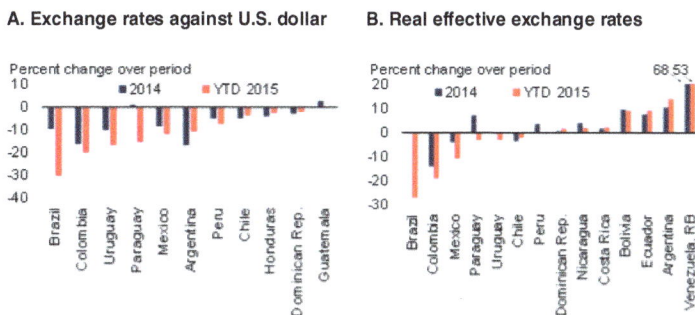

Source: Haver Analytics.
A. Last observation is November 2015.
B. Last observation is September 2015. An increase denotes real appreciation.

FIGURE 2.3.4 Exports

Regional export performance improved in 2015, boosted by weak exchange rates and continued recoveries in the United States and Euro Area.

A. . Regional export growth

B. Export growth in selected countries

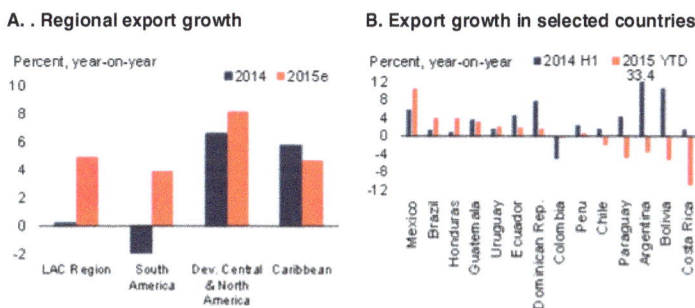

Source: IMF 2015i; Haver Analytics.
Note: e = estimated.
A. GDP weighted averages.
B. Last observation is Q2 2015, except for Brazil, Chile, Paraguay and Peru, for which the last observation is Q3 2015.

FIGURE 2.3.5 Inflation rates

Inflation rates are diverging across countries.

A. Regional consumer price inflation

B. Headline and core inflation, selected countries, 2015

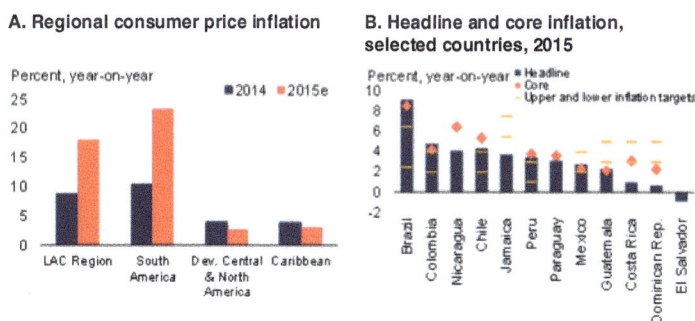

Source: IMF 2015i; Haver Analytics.
Note: e = estimated.
A. GDP weighted averages.
B. Year to date, last observation is November 2015, except for Jamaica, which is October 2015.

---

[6]The central bank of Mexico raised its benchmark interest rate by 25 bps to 3.25 percent at its December 17th, 2015 meeting.

FIGURE 2.3.6 Central bank policy rates, 2014-2015

Reflecting different inflation pressures, monetary policies are diverging among countries.

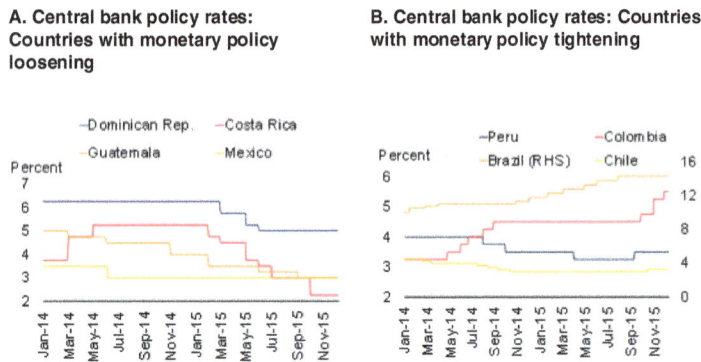

A. Central bank policy rates: Countries with monetary policy loosening

B. Central bank policy rates: Countries with monetary policy tightening

Source: Haver Analytics.
Note: The central bank of Mexico raised its benchmark interest rate by 25bps to 3.25 percent at its December 17th, 2015 meeting.

FIGURE 2.3.7 Fiscal indicators

Fiscal balances are diverging, with balances deteriorating in South America and improving in the rest of the region.

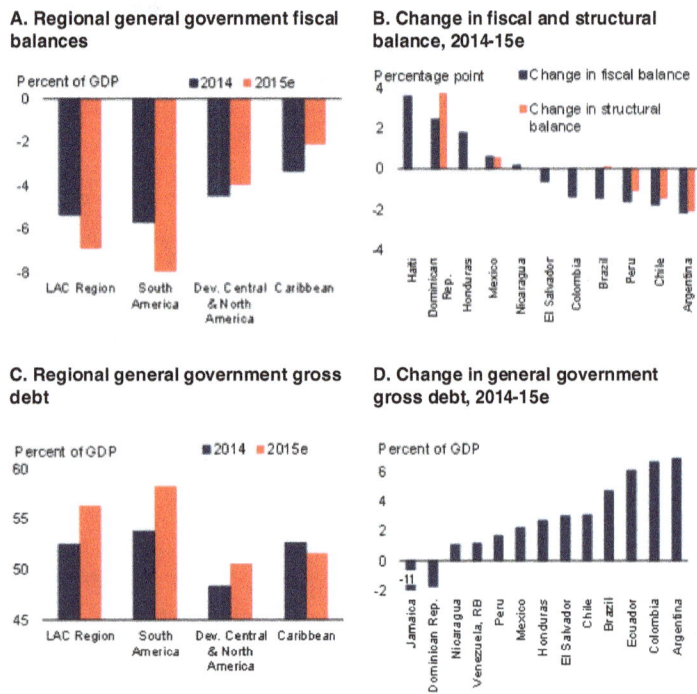

A. Regional general government fiscal balances

B. Change in fiscal and structural balance, 2014-15e

C. Regional general government gross debt

D. Change in general government gross debt, 2014-15e

Source: IMF 2015i; World Bank.
Note: e = estimated.
A. and C. GDP weighted averages.

high. Consumer price inflation in the República Bolivariana de Venezuela reached well over 100 percent in 2015, as policy has failed to establish an anchor for inflation expectations.[7] Argentina's

inflation also remains elevated, at over 14 percent in the second half of 2015.[8]

Inflation in Colombia is under better control, but has been above the central bank's 2-4 percent target band since mid-2015. Continued weakness in the peso, along with a poor harvest of staple crops, contributed to the increase. To guide inflation back to target, the central bank raised its policy rate in a number of successive adjustments in the latter half of 2015. Similarly, headline and core inflation in Peru have been steadily rising and have remained above the Peruvian central bank's upper bound target of 3 percent since 2014. This prompted the central bank to lift the policy rate in September and December.

Fiscal balances are also on differing paths across LAC. Due to lower commodity and export revenues, coupled with the slowdown in growth, regional fiscal balances deteriorated, and the debt/GDP ratio increased in 2015 (Figure 2.3.7). Given the large proportion of major commodity exporters in the sub-region, fiscal balances in South America as a share of sub-regional GDP are projected to deteriorate by more than 2 percentage points in 2015. The deficit to GDP ratio for Brazil widened further, after doubling in 2014. Weak revenues, swelling interest payments, and losses on central bank dollar swaps, were responsible for the slide. The Chilean fiscal deficit doubled in 2015. Government revenues have been depressed by low copper prices. At the same time, the government has boosted public spending in line with the fiscal stimulus program launched in 2014 to counter slowing growth. In contrast, Ecuador is projected to see a narrowing of the fiscal balance in 2015, due to a series of fiscal consolidation measures. Weaker oil export earnings have led the Ecuadorian government to decrease expenditures by $2.2 billion in 2015, with cuts almost entirely on capital expenditures.

Central and North America, and the Caribbean too saw a narrowing of fiscal deficits in 2015, predominantly due to fiscal consolidation. In Mexico, lower oil prices and production were offset by a sharp increase in non-oil revenues in the wake of the tax reform in 2014 and the

---

[7]As estimated in IMF 2015i.

[8]Based on official data.

increase in excise taxes on domestic fuels in 2015. In addition, the government enacted spending cuts equivalent to 0.7 percent of GDP. Supported by the 48-month IMF-supported Extended Fund Facility, Jamaica introduced new consumption taxes and reduced the public sector wage bill, as well as sharply lowering gross debt as a share of GDP. After settling a debt due to the República Bolivariana de Venezuela at a sharp discount, the Dominican Republic saw a large drop in its debt service costs and registered a substantial narrowing of its fiscal deficit.

Current account balances deteriorated throughout most of the region. Despite rising volumes of total exports, the LAC's current account deficit as a share of GDP widened to 3.4 percent in 2015 from 2.8 percent in 2014, partly due to reduced export revenues associated with lower commodity prices (Figure 2.3.8). South America's current account deficit is estimated to have widened 0.8 percentage point in 2015 to 3.6 percent of GDP. Developing Central and North America saw a smaller current account deterioration of 0.2 percentage point. As the exception to the trend, the Caribbean's deficit narrowed due to elevated tourism receipts. Colombia saw a current account deficit in the first half of 2015 of more than 6 percent of GDP, due to a plunge in oil export revenues. Similarly, Mexico's current account balance suffered from lower oil revenues, owing both to weaker prices and declining production. However, this was offset by strengthening export performance of manufactures, which represent a far larger share of Mexico's trade and benefited from the weak peso.

Gross capital flows contracted in 2015. Following the sharp slowdown in flows in 2014, gross capital flows to the region are estimated to have contracted by another 40 percent in 2015 (Figure 2.3.9). Brazil and Mexico accounted for around 80 percent of the decline. Weaker-than-expected growth prospects and increased political uncertainty, especially in Brazil, discouraged investors.

All three components of gross capital flows declined in 2015, with equity issuance contracting the most, falling more than 60 percent. Bond

FIGURE 2.3.8 Current account balances

Current account balances have deteriorated in a number of countries.

A. Regional current account balance

B. Current account balance in selected countries

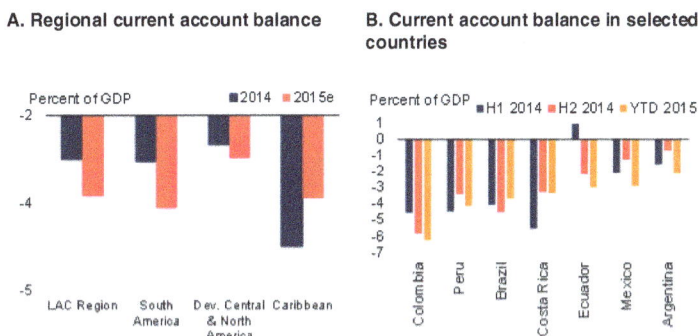

Source: IMF 2015i; Haver Analytics.
Note: e = estimated.
A. GDP weighted averages.
B. Last observation is for Q2 2015, except for Peru, Brazil and Mexico, which is for Q3 2015.

FIGURE 2.3.9 Gross capital flows

Gross capital flows declined in 2015.

A. Gross capital inflows

B. Bond issue by currency and issuer

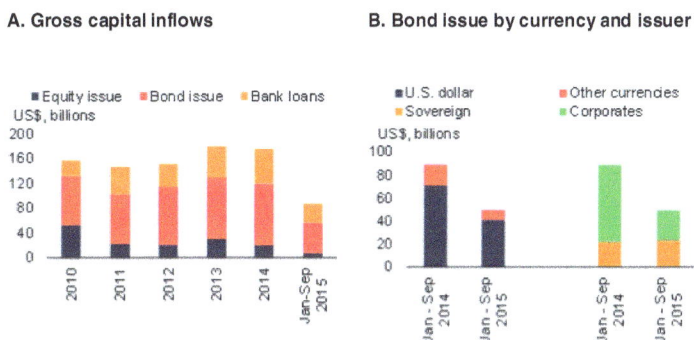

Source: Dealogic, World Bank.

issuance slumped more than 40 percent from 2014 levels, mainly on account of a $35 billion decline in new Brazilian bonds. Other economies took advantage of the still favorable global monetary conditions to put in place refinancing and pre-financing arrangements. In April, Mexico sold the world's first 100-year government notes in euros, as it locked in lower borrowing costs. Colombia issued $4 billion worth of bonds. Syndicated bank lending dove by 20 percent, reflecting local banks' lower funding needs as regional economies cooled.

The large decline in bond issuance mostly occurred among corporate issuers, particularly Brazilian corporate deals. Despite its significant appreciation, the U.S. dollar is still by far the currency of choice for debt issuance in Latin

FIGURE 2.3.10 Regional outlook

Regional growth is projected to recover in 2016-18.

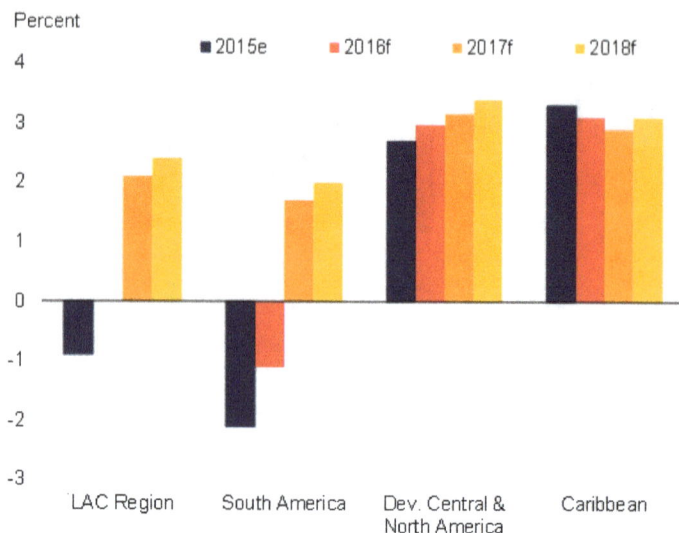

Source: World Bank.
Note: e = estimated; f = forecast.

FIGURE 2.3.11 Remittance flows

Remittance inflows to developing Central and North America surged in 2014, as incomes in the United States grew, and the U.S. dollar appreciated.

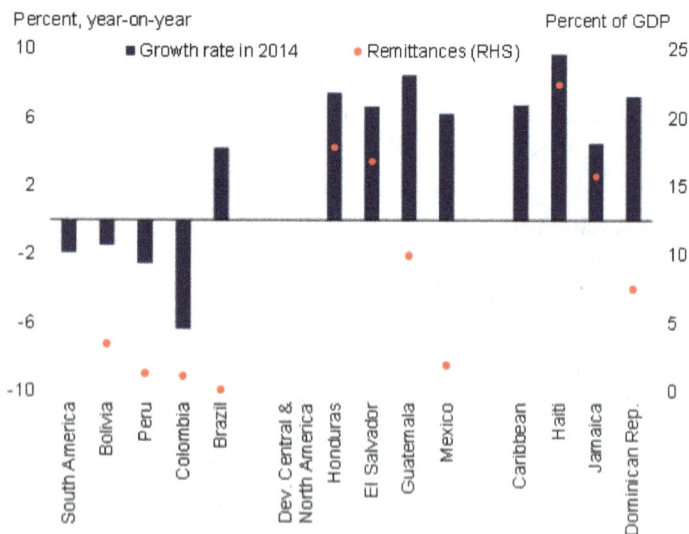

Source: World Bank Migration and Remittances Database, Central Bank of Honduras.

America. From January to September 2015, over 80 percent of bonds issued were denominated in U.S. dollars, slightly higher than the same period a year ago.

Outlook

A gradual return to growth is anticipated over the medium term, as commodity prices stabilize and economic growth firms in the United States and the Euro Area. Activity at the broader regional level is projected to be flat in 2016. Growth will then recover and strengthen to an average of 2.2 percent for 2017-18 (Figure 2.3.10).

South America is not expected to resume growth until 2017. This baseline projection assumes that the sub-region's largest economies gradually adopt policies to reduce macroeconomic imbalances and restore business and consumer confidence. Output is expected to continue contracting in 2016, before increasing by 1.8 percent in 2017-18, on a rebound in investment and exports. Depreciated LAC exchange rates and the ongoing recovery in the Euro Area underpin this projection. Domestic constraints among the regions' largest economies are also expected to gradually ease in the medium term. Brazil continues to grapple with political uncertainty, as the government faces obstacles to fiscal austerity measures in Congress. The forecast nevertheless assumes that an eventual re-anchoring of inflation expectations and narrowing of the fiscal deficit, will lessen the need for further monetary and fiscal tightening. The baseline projection for the República Bolivariana de Venezuela, with its new National Assembly, assumes a very gradual shift towards a stronger macroeconomic and business-friendly environment. The new government in Argentina is expected to implement monetary and fiscal tightening in 2016, pushing a rebound in growth to 2017, as investment slowly strengthens on renewed investor confidence and leads the recovery.

Prospects are brighter for developing Central and North America. The sub-region will benefit from close economic ties to the firming U.S. economy and is projected to see a gradual acceleration in economic activity. Growth is expected to reach 3.0 percent in 2016, and to 3.2 percent by 2017. Output in Mexico, although weighed down by fiscal austerity through 2016, will benefit from a weak peso. This will provide a competitive boost to its export-based manufacturing sector. In addition, the opening of the energy sector to foreign investment has begun to perk investors' interests, resulting in a successful auction of oil sector licenses. Implementation of other planned reforms should unclog various growth bottlenecks, providing growth dividends in the medium term.

Developing Central and North America account for about 60 percent of total remittances flows to LAC, and benefited from an 8 percent surge in remittances in 2014 (Figure 2.3.11).[9] Remittances are projected to stay robust over the next few years, in line with stronger U.S. labor market conditions and improving employment opportunities for migrants in the United States. On the other hand, remittance growth to South America has been sluggish, and even declined in Peru in 2014, partly due weak economic activity in Spain. Some 30 percent of immigrants in Spain are from South America.[10]

Prospects are also favorable for the Caribbean economies. The Caribbean is projected to expand at an average of 3.0 percent in 2016-18, in light of some positive spillovers with the continued U.S. expansion. Similar to Central America, remittance flows to the Caribbean have been robust and stable. Moreover, Caribbean economies have been buttressed by increasing tourism. For example, tourist arrivals to the Dominican Republic between January and September 2015 rose 8.4 percent relative to the same period in 2014, with visitors from the United States jumping nearly 10 percent over the same period. In the years ahead, the ongoing normalization of ties between Cuba and the United States is expected to boost travel to Cuba.[11]

Risks

The balance of risks in the regional forecasts leans heavily towards the downside. The risks are both external and internal, and include potential bouts of financial volatility, protracted slowdown in the region's largest economies, a sharper slowdown in major trading partners and further commodity price weakness, and adverse effects from El Niño weather patterns.

Financial volatility. Higher borrowing costs, amid tighter U.S. monetary policy, and heightened risk aversion could be accompanied by bouts of financial stress. Downgrades to sovereign credit ratings, such as those by Standard and Poor's and Fitch for Brazil recently, could heighten the risk of large capital outflows. Financial market volatility could also be associated with China's efforts to stabilize its economy (IMF 2015j). Should financial stresses ensue, capital flows to the region could stagnate or even reverse, hampering growth. Risks will be most pronounced among developing economies with large levels of short-term or external debt (versus long-term domestic debt), or where credit has been expanding rapidly in recent years.

Protracted slowdown in the region's largest economies. Two of the region's largest economies, Brazil and the República Bolivariana de Venezuela, are grappling with high inflation rates and output contractions, coupled with macroeconomic imbalances and political uncertainty. In Brazil, the baseline projection is predicated on a reduction in the fiscal deficit and an anchoring of inflation expectations without considerable further policy tightening, which may not prove feasible. A protracted slowdown in one or both of these economies could have sustained negative spillovers across the region. Econometric analysis presented in Box 2.3.1 shows that decreases in Brazil's GDP growth lead to statistically significant declines in output growth for Argentina, Chile, Colombia, Ecuador, Paraguay and Peru.[12] Specifically, a one percentage point decline in Brazil's growth tends to reduce growth in Argentina, after 2 years, by 0.7

---

[9]Fajnzylber and Lopez (2008) found that remittance flows lead to higher rates of economic growth throughout the developing world.

[10]Compared to 5 percent of immigrants from Central America and the Caribbean. Calculated from World Bank Bilateral Migration Matrix 2013.

[11]While U.S. citizens are still not allowed to visit Cuba for the purposes of tourism, President Barack Obama expanded the

categories of authorized travel to Cuba in January 2015. U.S. citizens can legally travel to Cuba if they are engaging in 12 categories of activities such as professional research, participating in an athletic event, performing in a concert, working on a humanitarian project, or taking part in educational activities.

percentage point, in Paraguay by 0.6 percentage point, in Ecuador and Peru by 0.3 percentage point, and in Chile and Colombia by 0.2 percentage point. The República Bolivariana de Venezuela's Petrocaribe program, which provides subsidized oil to certain countries, is one possible channel of negative spillovers to its LAC neighbors. The economic downturn in the country has led to a scaling-down of the program, but the impact has been limited by the sharp fall in oil prices.

A downturn in major trading partners and protracted slump in commodity prices. The baseline forecast assumes commodity prices will stabilize at around current levels. A further drop in demand from major emerging markets and continued over-supply of commodities on world markets could lead to further declines in commodity prices, which may lower government revenues, reduce export receipts, and widen current account deficits commodity exporters. Investment, especially in mining industries, could continue to decline. Countries with higher shares of commodity exports are more vulnerable to commodity price declines. On the other hand, lower oil prices in the medium term will again represent an upside risk to the forecast for oil-importing economies in the region.

Adverse effects from El Niño. Recent weather forecasts suggests that the current El Niño episode could be one of the strongest on record (World Bank 2015o). The experience of the 1997-98 episode, which inflicted widespread damage in LAC, suggests that the current El Niño weather pattern is likely to have significant adverse effects on the region's agricultural sector, as well as potentially crippling infrastructure. With growth already negative in 2015, a severe El Niño season could result in a second year of contraction for the region. A number of countries have already experienced volatile and damaging climatic effects. For example, Argentina, Chile, Colombia, Peru,

Paraguay, and Uruguay have experienced exceptionally heavy rains and flooding. Drought afflicted Brazil and the north of Uruguay, and led to emergency water restrictions (EIU 2015). Drought has also damaged crops, including coffee, over a wide swathe of Central America. As the El Niño season unfolds, worse effects might yet be in store.

Policy challenges

With commodity prices expected to stabilize around the current low prices through the medium term, economies in LAC, especially commodity exporters, will no longer benefit from commodity-driven global tailwinds to boost economic growth. Regional economies will therefore need to transition to new engines of growth, while using a combination of monetary and fiscal policies to smooth the trajectory, tailored to available policy space at the country level.

Monetary policy trade-offs. In response to tighter monetary policy in the United States (and, at a later stage, in other developed economies), central banks in LAC may need to raise interest rates for a while to stave off currency depreciation and inflationary pressure. However, in countries already grappling with weak growth, some decline in the external value of the currency would be a normal part of the adjustment process. Where expectations of low inflation are firmly anchored, depreciation causes a small, temporary, increase in the inflation rate. In countries where the nominal anchor is weak, however, a drop in the exchange rate risks setting off an inflation spiral, and the central bank may have to tighten its monetary policy stance. Moreover, the effectiveness of an interest rate hike in stemming depreciation pressures depends on the credibility of the monetary policy framework (Arteta, Kose, Ohnsorge and Stocker 2015; Eichengreen and Rose 2003).

Regaining fiscal space. The room for fiscal maneuver has deteriorated across LAC since 2008. The expansionary, countercyclical policies implemented in response to the 2008 global

---

[12]Uruguay is also expected to be adversely affected by the recession in Brazil as Brazil is the second largest destination for Uruguayan merchandise exports. In addition, the Uruguayan peso has appreciated significantly in real terms against the Brazilian real, further weighing on Uruguayan merchandise exports to Brazil.

financial crisis led to a build-up of debt and a reduction of fiscal space (World Bank 2015n, IDB 2015). The protracted decline in commodity prices and slowdown of economic growth reduced tax revenues and further eroded fiscal positions in several countries. Consequently, most were compelled to embark on new rounds of pro-cyclical fiscal tightening in 2015, deepening the negative output impact of the external shock. Economies that resisted – or were unable to implement required fiscal adjustments – have seen severe declines in fiscal balances and increases in public debt ratios. Only a handful of countries, such as Chile and Peru, have managed to undertake fiscal stimulus measures to support growth in 2015, and even in those cases, spending has been curtailed on account of lower commodity revenues. With commodity prices across the board projected to stabilize around current low levels, regional commodity exporters need to diversify away from commodity-based activities, and over time reestablish fiscal buffers before the next downturn.

Greater investment in infrastructure will be essential to boost competitiveness. The region needs to modernize its transportation infrastructure or risk impeding advances in productivity and development. Physical infrastructure will play a key role, and its modernization will require sizable financial resources. Fiscal reforms are needed to generate the needed revenues, together with strong institutions to monitor public spending. Innovative public-private investment models may help to fund projects. Policy makers undertaking fiscal consolidation, however, often include measures that reduce or postpone capital expenditures (such as Ecuador). This reduces fiscal pressures in the short term, but delays much-needed infrastructure investment, and has detrimental medium- and longer-term consequences to productivity and economic growth. The need for stable infrastructure investment again underlines the urgency of consolidating government consumption outlays when possible, and reducing dependence on commodity-based fiscal revenues.

Economic diversification. Commodities exports represented more than 50 percent of the region's exports for the years 2012-14. The current slowdown could help garner private and public sector support for renewed regional efforts to promote economic diversification. These could promote specialization based on comparative advantage, and encourage participation in cross-border value chains. The associated transfers of know-how can facilitate diversification towards other engines of growth.[13] To this end, initiatives that promote business-friendly environments, enhance workforce skills, and boost physical and telecommunication infrastructure will be crucial for private sector development.

---

[13]IMF 2015h found that LAC economies could enhance long-term growth if they shift their economies toward producing a wider scope of products that are more knowledge- or technology-intensive. For example, Ecuador would grow approximately 0.4 percentage point faster every year for the next decade if its level of economic modernization was at the LAC average.

TABLE 2.3.1 Latin America and the Caribbean forecast summary
(Annual percent change unless indicated otherwise)

(Percentage point difference from June 2015 projections)

	2013	2014	2015e	2016f	2017f	2018f	2015e	2016f	2017f
Developing LAC, GDP[a]	3.0	1.5	-0.7	0.1	2.3	2.5	-1.5	-2.3	-0.6
(Average including countries with full national accounts and balance of payments data only)[b]									
Developing LAC, GDP[b]	3.0	1.5	-0.7	0.1	2.3	2.5	-1.5	-2.3	-0.6
GDP per capita (U.S. dollars)	1.8	0.3	-1.8	-1.0	1.2	1.4	-1.5	-2.3	-0.7
PPP GDP	3.1	1.7	-0.2	0.5	2.5	2.6	-1.4	-2.1	-0.6
Private consumption	3.3	2.0	-0.8	-0.1	1.9	2.1	-1.9	-2.2	-0.4
Public consumption	2.3	2.2	0.1	-0.6	-0.5	0.9	0.1	-0.7	-2.2
Fixed investment	4.2	-0.5	-7.7	-2.2	2.9	3.5	-6.2	-5.0	-0.9
Exports, GNFS[c]	2.7	3.5	4.7	5.0	5.0	5.0	-0.8	-0.6	-0.9
Imports, GNFS[c]	4.3	2.9	-2.1	1.7	2.9	3.9	-5.4	-2.2	-1.3
Net exports, contribution to growth	-0.4	0.0	1.4	0.7	0.5	0.2	1.0	0.4	0.2
Memo items: GDP									
Broader geographic region[d]	2.9	1.0	-0.9	0.0	2.1	2.4	-1.4	-2.1	-0.7
South America[e]	3.3	0.4	-2.1	-1.1	1.7	2.0	-1.8	-2.8	-0.8
Developing Central and North America[f]	1.8	2.5	2.7	3.0	3.2	3.4	-0.1	-0.4	-0.4
Caribbean[g]	3.0	4.2	3.3	3.1	2.9	3.1	-0.2	-0.4	0.0
Brazil	3.0	0.1	-3.7	-2.5	1.4	1.5	-2.4	-3.6	-0.6
Mexico	1.4	2.3	2.5	2.8	3.0	3.2	-0.1	-0.4	-0.5
Colombia	4.9	4.6	3.1	3.0	3.3	3.5	-0.4	-0.9	-0.9

Source: World Bank.

World Bank forecasts are frequently updated based on new information and changing (global) circumstances. Consequently, projections presented here may differ from those contained in other Bank documents, even if basic assessments of countries' prospects do not differ at any given moment in time.
a. GDP at market prices and expenditure components are measured in constant 2010 U.S. dollars. Excludes Cuba, Granada, and Suriname.
b. Sub-region aggregate excludes Cuba, Dominica, Granada, Guyana, St. Lucia, St. Vincent and the Grenadines, and Suriname, for which data limitations prevent the forecasting of GDP components.
c. Exports and imports of goods and non-factor services (GNFS).
d. Includes the following high-income countries: Antigua and Barbuda, Argentina, The Bahamas, Barbados, Chile, Trinidad and Tobago, Uruguay, and Venezuela, RB.
e. Includes Argentina, Bolivia, Brazil, Chile, Colombia, Ecuador, Guyana, Paraguay, Peru, Uruguay, and Venezuela, RB.
f. Includes Costa Rica, Guatemala, Honduras, Mexico, Nicaragua, Panama, and El Salvador.
g. Includes Antigua and Barbuda, The Bahamas, Barbados, Belize, Dominica, Dominican Republic, Haiti, Jamaica, St. Lucia, St. Vincent and the Grenadines, and Trinidad and Tobago.

TABLE 2.3.2 Latin America and the Caribbean country forecasts[a]
(Real GDP growth at market prices in percent, unless indicated otherwise)

(Percentage point difference from June 2015 projections)

	2013	2014	2015e	2016f	2017f	2018f	2015e	2016f	2017f
Belize	1.5	3.6	3.0	2.5	2.6	2.8	0.5	-0.1	-0.1
Bolivia	6.8	5.5	4.0	3.5	3.4	3.4	-0.8	-0.7	-0.7
Brazil	3.0	0.1	-3.7	-2.5	1.4	1.5	-2.4	-3.6	-0.6
Colombia	4.9	4.6	3.1	3.0	3.3	3.5	-0.4	-0.9	-0.9
Costa Rica	3.4	3.5	2.8	4.0	4.2	4.4	-0.6	-0.2	-0.2
Dominica	1.7	3.4	-3.0	4.0	2.0	2.0	-4.3	2.5	0.4
Dominican Republic	4.8	7.3	5.6	4.6	3.8	3.9	0.4	-0.2	0.4
Ecuador	4.6	3.7	-0.6	-2.0	0.0	0.5	-2.5	-5.0	-4.2
El Salvador	1.8	2.0	2.4	2.5	2.6	2.8	0.2	0.0	0.0
Guatemala	3.7	4.2	3.7	3.6	3.5	3.6	-0.3	-0.3	-0.4
Guyana	5.2	3.9	3.5	3.8	4.0	4.0	-0.2	0.0	0.0
Haiti[b]	4.2	2.7	1.7	2.5	2.8	3.0	0.0	-0.7	-0.3
Honduras	2.8	3.1	3.4	3.4	3.5	3.6	0.5	0.1	0.0
Jamaica	0.5	0.7	1.3	2.1	2.4	2.6	-0.2	-0.1	-0.1
Mexico	1.4	2.3	2.5	2.8	3.0	3.2	-0.1	-0.4	-0.5
Nicaragua	4.6	4.7	3.9	4.2	4.1	4.0	-0.3	-0.1	-0.1
Panama	8.4	6.2	5.9	6.2	6.4	6.6	-0.3	-0.2	-0.1
Paraguay	14.0	4.7	2.8	3.6	4.0	4.2	-1.4	-0.5	-0.1
Peru	5.8	2.4	2.7	3.3	4.5	4.6	-1.2	-1.7	-0.5
St. Lucia	-1.9	-0.7	1.7	1.6	1.9	2.1	2.3	0.8	0.5
St. Vincent and the Grenadines	2.3	-0.2	2.1	2.7	3.0	3.4	-0.5	-0.2	-0.4

	2013	2014	2015e	2016f	2017f	2018f	2015e	2016f	2017f
Recently transitioned to high income countries[c]									
Argentina	2.9	0.5	1.7	0.7	1.9	3.0	0.6	-1.1	-1.1
Chile	4.2	1.9	2.1	2.4	2.9	3.1	-0.8	-0.9	-0.6
Trinidad and Tobago	1.7	1.0	0.0	0.5	1.2	1.5	-1.8	-1.5	-1.0
Uruguay	5.1	3.3	1.5	1.9	2.8	3.0	-1.1	-1.2	-0.4
Venezuela, RB	1.3	-4.0	-8.2	-4.8	-1.1	0.0	-3.1	-3.8	-2.2

Source: World Bank.
World Bank forecasts are frequently updated based on new information and changing (global) circumstances. Consequently, projections presented here may differ from those contained in other Bank documents, even if basic assessments of countries' prospects do not significantly differ at any given moment in time.
a. Cuba, Grenada, and Suriname are not forecast due to data limitations.
b. GDP is based on fiscal year, which runs from October to September of next year.
c. Based on the World Bank's country reclassification from 2004 to 2015.

BOX 2.3.1 Regional integration and spillovers: Latin America and the Caribbean

The Latin America and Caribbean region (LAC) is less open than other emerging and developing regions to global trade and finance. Despite a multitude of regional trade agreements, economic linkages within the region tend to be limited and largely confined to sub-regions. Estimated spillovers from growth slowdowns in Brazil are modest for its South American neighbors (Argentina, Chile, Colombia, Ecuador, Paraguay and Peru), while those from Mexico are negligible.

Introduction

Although there is considerable heterogeneity among countries, the LAC region is one of the least open regions to trade, despite a large presence in global commodity markets. Commodity discoveries, and the prospect of large domestic markets, have attracted considerable FDI and portfolio flows into the region. Among the three sub-regions, South America is most dependent on global commodity markets, while its trade and financial partners are broadly diversified. In contrast, the main economic partner of developing Central and North America, and the Caribbean is the United States. Regional trade and finance flows are limited. However, the three sub regions have forged somewhat closer sub-regional ties, especially in South America.

This box addresses the following questions:

- How open is the LAC region to global and regional trade and financial flows?

- How significant are the potential intra-regional spillovers from the region's two largest economies, Brazil and Mexico?

Brazil and Mexico are the two largest economies in the region. Brazil has slipped into recession due to a combination of global and domestic challenges. While still positive, Mexico's growth has been tepid recently, compared to the pre-crisis and immediate post-crisis years. While the low growth of the region's largest economies may weigh on the outlook of trading partners and financial counterparts elsewhere in the region, limited intra-regional ties reduce the potential drag. Growth slowdowns in Brazil are estimated to have measurable spillovers to South American neighbors (Argentina, Chile, Colombia, Ecuador, Paraguay and Peru), whereas growth decelerations in Mexico have negligible spillovers to other countries in the region.

How open is the LAC region to global and regional trade and financial flows?

Of the six World Bank developing country regions, LAC is the least open to trade, and the region's role in global trade is considerably less than its contribution to global activity (Figure 2.3.1.1). The region is not well integrated into international supply chains, in contrast to East Asia, for example (Estevadeordal 2012; De la Torre, Dider, Ize, Lederman and Schmukler 2015). The region's heavy reliance on primary commodity exports, the associated lack of economic diversification, and the narrow product base are additional contributing factors for being relatively closed. However, the region has absorbed a large share of global FDI, which has been attracted by rapidly growing domestic markets, and by commodity discoveries. Portfolio inflows into LAC have been quite high, but the stock of liabilities relative to GDP has declined (Figure 2.3.1.2). Post-crisis, LAC trade has grown broadly in line with the global economy, while remittance flows have lagged behind those of other developing regions. The anemic recovery and weak labor market in Spain, which hosts about 5 percent of South American migrants, has held back remittance flows to the sub-region (Figure 2.3.1.3). Similarly, in the United States, modest growth in the sectors employing a large share of immigrants (construction and agriculture) and stricter enforcement of immigration laws have discouraged migrant inflows from Central America, constraining remittance flows (Chishti and Hipsman 2015).

The United States and Europe continue to be the most important economic partners for the region, accounting for 40-80 percent of LAC's trade and financial flows (Figure 2.3.1.4). The United States remains the largest importer from the region (exceeding 7 percent of regional GDP in 2011-14). That said, for South and Central America as well as the Caribbean, the share of exports to the United States has steadily declined since 2000, as exports to other major destinations and other LAC economies have gained ground (Cesa-Bianchi et al. 2012).

The LAC region does have a large global presence in commodity markets. On average, primary commodities constitute more than 50 percent of regional goods exports

Note: This box was prepared by Derek H. C. Chen with contributions from Raju Huidrom, Duygu Guven, Jesper Hanson and Mai Anh Bui.

BOX 2.3.1 **Regional integration and spillovers: Latin America and the Caribbean** *(continued)*

and 9 percent of GDP (Figure 2.3.1.5). South America is, by far, the most commodity-intensive sub-region, with commodities making up more than 70 percent of merchandise exports, and nearly 10 percent of GDP. Although developing Central and North America is considerably less commodity dependent than South America, commodities still account for about one quarter of exports, and 7.5 percent of GDP. Reliance on commodity exports tends to be associated with a high correlation between commodity prices and GDP, implying a higher susceptibility to commodity price fluctuations and increased volatility in activity (Camacho and Perez-Quiros 2013).

There are important differences in regional and global integration across the three sub-regions within LAC. Regional economic links are generally modest, and mostly within sub-regions. Examples are trade among Central American countries (excluding Mexico), and trade and remittances within South America (World Bank 2005, ECLAC 2014, Villarreal 2012). Even within regional trade agreements, trade remains modest, partly reflecting low road and rail density (Scholvin and Malamud 2014). Argentina, Bolivia, Paraguay and Uruguay, which are Mercosur members, ship only 20 to 30 percent of their exports to Brazil—compared with 40-60 percent of within-region trade for member countries of the North American Free Trade Agreement (NAFTA) and the European Union (EU) (Chapter 4.1).[1] FDI flows from Brazil and Mexico are largely confined to their respective sub-regions as well (Figure 2.3.1.6).

South America's trade links are well-diversified, but its financial flows predominantly originate from Europe, and its remittances inflows originate about equally from the United States and Europe.

Central America's trade, remittances and, to a lesser extent, portfolio flows, rely heavily on the United States. Other financial flows predominantly originate from Europe. With its economic linkages enhanced by NAFTA, around 80 percent of Mexican exports are shipped to the United States. Mexico's trade with Central America is modest (with the exception of Nicaragua, which ships about 20 percent of its exports to Mexico, IMF 2012a).

FIGURE 2.3.1.1 **International linkages: Cross-region comparison**

The Latin America and Caribbean (LAC) region is the least open to trade among the six World Bank developing regions. But it absorbs a large share of global FDI. Portfolio inflows are small on a global scale, but the stock of portfolio liabilities relative to GDP is similar to the average for the other developing regions.

A. LAC share of global activity, trade and finance, 2014

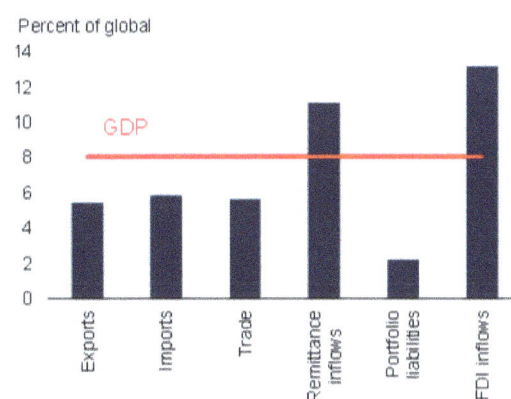

B. LAC trade and finance in regional comparison, 2014

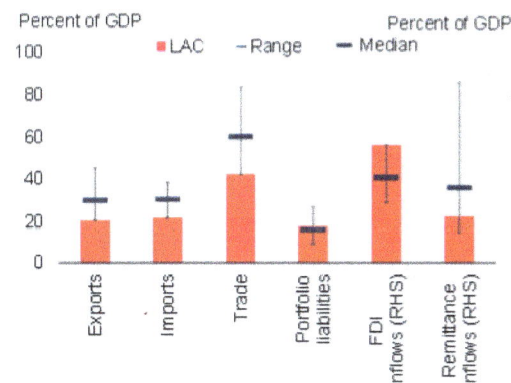

Sources: IMF October 2015 World Economic Outlook, IMF International Financial Statistics, IMF Direction of Trade Statistics, UNCTAD FDI/TNC database, World Bank Remittance and Migration Database, World Bank World Development Indicators.
B. The red bar denotes exports, imports, trade, remittance inflows, portfolio liabilities and FDI inflows in percent of GDP on average across LAC countries. The vertical line denotes the range of averages for all six developing country regions.

---

[1]Bolivia is an associate state and in the final stages of the accession to become a full and the sixth member of Mercosur.

BOX 2.3.1 Regional integration and spillovers: Latin America and the Caribbean *(continued)*

FIGURE 2.3.1.2 Evolution of openness

External ties—other than remittances—have grown broadly in line with the global economy. However, they have shrunk relative to regional GDP as a result of rapid growth led by domestic demand that was supported by policy in the wake of the crisis. Slow growth in Europe and a fragile recovery in the United States have set back remittances.

A. LAC's share of global GDP, population, trade and financial flows

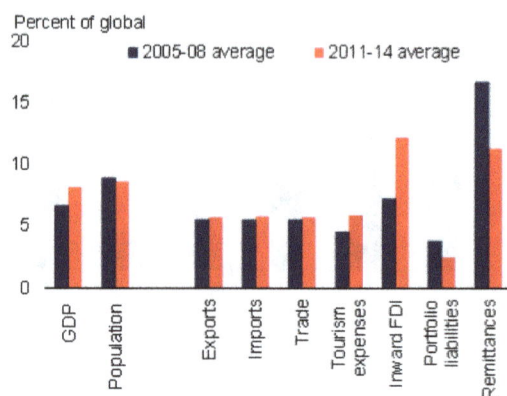

B. Trade and financial flows in percent of regional GDP

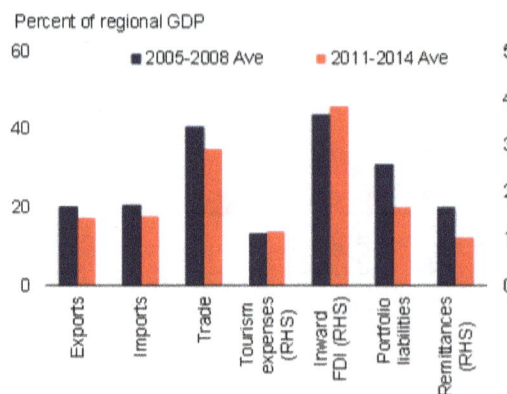

Sources: IMF April 2015 World Economic Outlook, IMF International Financial Statistics, IMF Direction of Trade Statistics, UNCTAD FDI/TNC database, World Bank Remittance and Migration Database, World Bank World Development Indicators.
Note: Tourist arrivals and tourism expenditures data are average 2011-2013.

The Caribbean is deeply tied to the United States and to Japan, via foreign claims on Caribbean banks. Similar to Central America, sub-regional trade is modest (around 16 percent of total sub-regional total merchandise exports in 2014). This may partly reflect countries having similar economic structures and a prevalence of services trade.

Major trade agreements such as NAFTA and CAFTA-DR deepened ties between LAC and North America (World Bank 2014a). The 1994 NAFTA between Canada, Mexico, and the United States, was aimed at eliminating tariffs and substantially reducing nontariff barriers in a broad range of sectors by 2008. NAFTA has greatly boosted trade and FDI flows, and at the same time increased business cycle co-movement among the three North American economies (Lederman, Maloney and Servén. 2005). For example, NAFTA is estimated to have increased Mexican exports to the United States by 5-8 percent per year. Other estimates attribute to NAFTA as much as half of the post-1993 increase in exports from Mexico to the United States.[2]

The Dominican Republic-Central America FTA (CAFTA-DR) is a free trade agreement between the United States and Central American economies (Costa Rica, El Salvador, Guatemala, Honduras, Nicaragua, the Dominican Republic), which came partially into effect in 2005 and fully in 2009. Total goods trade between the U.S. and the six CAFTA-DR partners increased from $35 billion in 2005 to $60 billion in 2013 (USTR 2015). The trade and growth benefits of the agreements would be considerably enhanced by domestic reforms and infrastructure investment (Lopez and Shankar 2011).

Regional integration has been promoted through various regional agreements within the sub-regions (Figure 2.3.1.4):

- The Mercosur (Common Market of the South) customs union came into force in 1991, and comprises five member countries—Argentina, Brazil, Paraguay, Uruguay, and the República Bolivariana de Venezuela—and Bolivia, which is in the final stages of the accession to become the sixth member. While

---

[2]See Romalis (2007); CBO (2003); Easterly, Fiess and Lederman (2003); Cuevas, Messmacher, and Werner (2002); Torres and Vela (2003); Kose, Meredith, and Towe (2005). Lederman, Maloney, and Serven (2005) estimate that Mexico's exports would have been 50 percent lower and its FDI 40 percent less without NAFTA and the agreement may have lifted GDP per capita by some 4 percent during 1994-2002.

BOX 2.3.1 Regional integration and spillovers: Latin America and the Caribbean (continued)

FIGURE 2.3.1.3 Sources of trade and financial flows

LAC has a diversified set of export markets. Remittances are predominantly from the United States, and financial inflows are mostly from Europe. However, there are considerable differences between sub-regions. Central America, Mexico and the Caribbean are most closely tied to the United States. South America is most closely tied to Europe and other countries within the region.

A. Latin America and the Caribbean

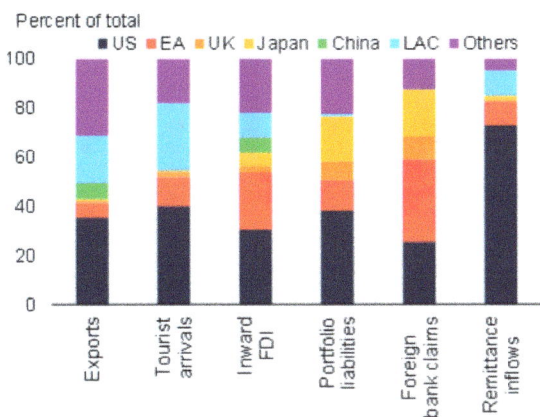

B. South America

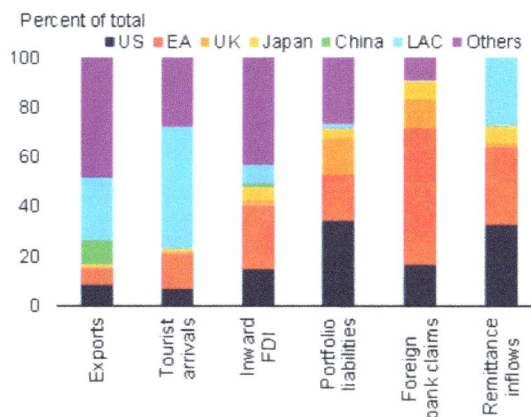

C. Central America and Mexico

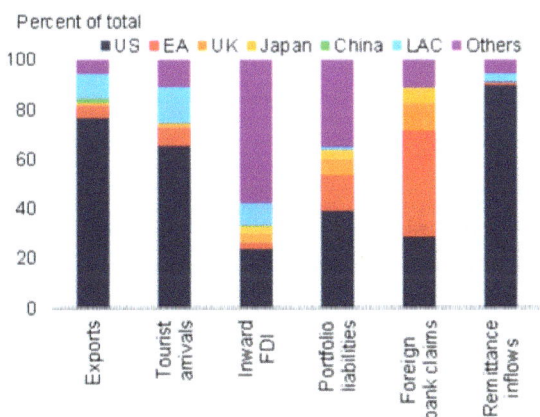

D. Caribbean

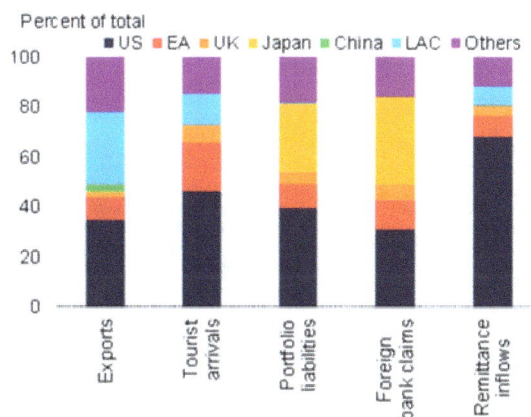

Sources: IMF April 2015 World Economic Outlook, IMF International Financial Statistics, IMF Direction of Trade Statistics, UNCTAD FDI/TNC database, World Bank Remittance and Migration Database, World Bank World Development Indicators, UNWTO, Bank for International Settlements.
Note: Exports and remittance inflows are average 2011-14. Portfolio liabilities and tourist arrivals are average 2011-13. FDI inflows are average 2010-12. Foreign banking claims are for 2014.

there has been some controversy about the net impact of Mercosur, the share of exports to other members has increased from 7.6 percent in 1990 to 13.3 percent in 2014 (Connolly and Gunther 1999).

- CACM (Central American Common Market) is an association of five Central American nations

(Guatemala, Honduras, El Salvador, Nicaragua, Costa Rica) that was formed in 1960 to facilitate regional economic development through free trade and economic integration. Exports among members have steadily increased from about 15 percent in 1990 to around 22 percent of total exports in 2014. Since its inception, CACM is estimated to have tripled

BOX 2.3.1 Regional integration and spillovers: Latin America and the Caribbean (continued)

FIGURE 2.3.1.4 LAC exports

LAC exports to the United States have grown less rapidly than those to China (especially for South America) and to other LAC countries (especially in the Caribbean).

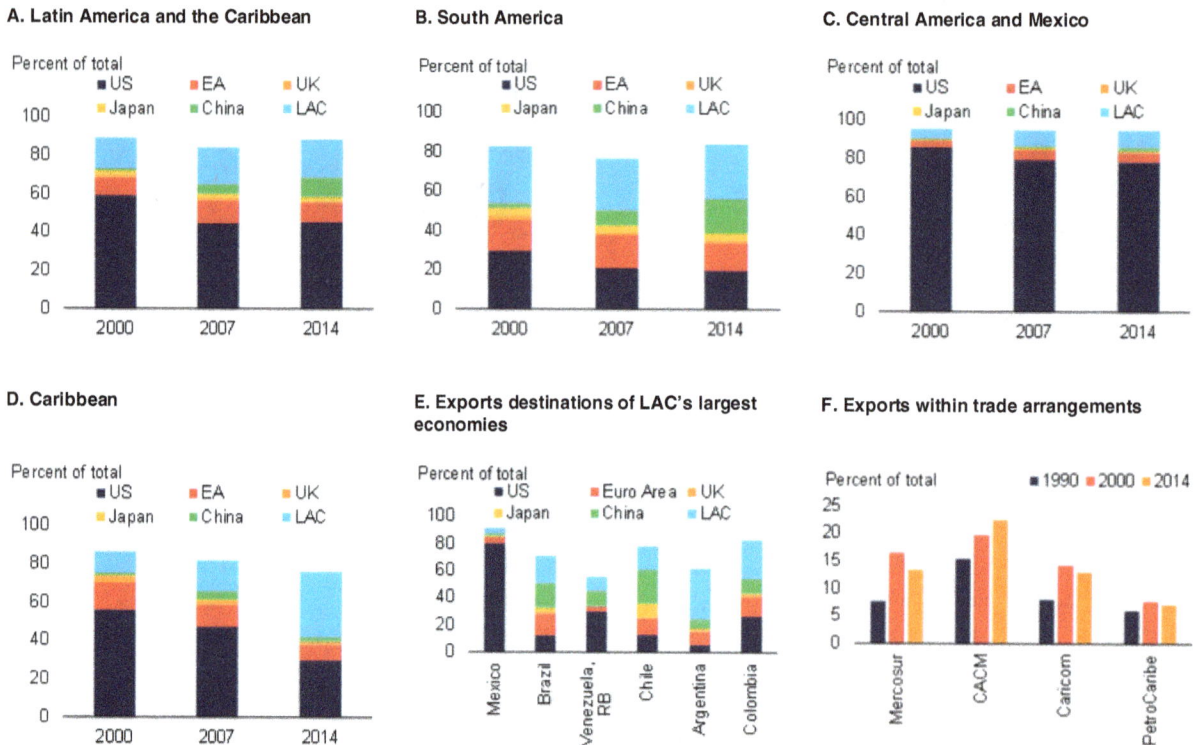

A. Latin America and the Caribbean

B. South America

C. Central America and Mexico

D. Caribbean

E. Exports destinations of LAC's largest economies

F. Exports within trade arrangements

Source: IMF Direction of Trade Statistics.
E. Data is for 2014.
F. Mercosur members: Argentina, Brazil, Paraguay, Uruguay, and República Bolivariana de Venezuela (established 1991). CACM members: Guatemala, Honduras, El Salvador, Nicaragua, Costa Rica (established 1960). Caricom members: Antigua and Barbuda, the Bahamas, Barbados, Belize, Dominica, Grenada, Guyana, Haiti, Jamaica, Montserrat, St. Lucia, St. Kitts and Nevis, St. Vincent and the Grenadines, Suriname, and Trinidad and Tobago (established in 1973). PetroCaribe members: Antigua and Barbuda, the Bahamas, Belize, Cuba, Dominica, Dominican Republic, Grenada, Guatemala, Guyana, Haiti, Honduras, Jamaica, Nicaragua, Saint Kitts and Nevis, St. Lucia, St. Vincent and the Grenadines, Suriname, and República Bolivariana de Venezuela (established in 2005). Chart shows República Bolivariana de Venezuelan exports to PetroCaribe members as a share of total exports.

member country exports compared to a baseline without such an agreement (Baier and Bergstrand 2009).

- Caricom (The Caribbean Community) is a common market established in 1973. Members consist of Antigua and Barbuda, the Bahamas, Barbados, Belize, Dominica, Grenada, Guyana, Haiti, Jamaica, Montserrat, St. Lucia, St. Kitts and Nevis, St. Vincent and the Grenadines, Suriname, Trinidad and Tobago. Empirical estimates have found that the agreement has had a modest impact on trade among members

(Moreira and Mendoza 2007). Within-agreement exports constituted 13 percent of total exports in 2014.

- PetroCaribe is an energy initiative launched in 2005 to supply Venezuelan crude oil to countries in the Caribbean region on discounted terms. Current members of PetroCaribe include Antigua and Barbuda, the Bahamas, Belize, Cuba, Dominica, Dominican Republic, Grenada, Guatemala, Guyana, Haiti, Honduras, Jamaica, Nicaragua, Saint Kitts and Nevis, St. Lucia, St. Vincent and the Grenadines,

BOX 2.3.1 Regional integration and spillovers: Latin America and the Caribbean (continued)

Suriname, and República Bolivariana de Venezuela.[3] The share of Venezuelan exports to PetroCaribe members has remained broadly unchanged since the inception of the initiative.

How large are the potential regional spillovers from Brazil and Mexico?

Brazil and Mexico are the largest economies in LAC. Together, these two countries account for 60 percent of regional GDP and trade, 50 percent of population, 75 percent of portfolio and 50 percent of FDI flows and 30-40 percent of tourism expenditures and remittance flows (Figure 2.3.1.7).

Business cycle co-movements can be indicative of intraregional spillovers. Correlations of quarterly growth suggest that business cycles of a number of LAC economies are positively correlated with those of Brazil and Mexico (Figure 2.3.1.8). South American economies tend to exhibit higher business cycle correlations with Brazil, and Central American economies have higher business cycle correlations with Mexico. These correlations appear to be driven mainly by relative trade shares, but they could also be indicative of economies responding together to a common external shock.

To examine the magnitude of spillovers from Brazil and Mexico to their Latin American neighbors, while accounting for common external factors, a series of country-specific Bayesian structural vector autoregressions (VARs) models are estimated. The VARs include G-7 growth, EMBI as a proxy for external financing conditions, growth in China (a major non-G7 trading partner for the region), growth in Brazil and Mexico as source countries of shocks, trade-weighted commodity prices, growth in each spillover destination country, and real effective exchange rates (see Annex 3.2 for details). The analysis includes 13 spillover destination countries in

FIGURE 2.3.1.5 LAC commodity exports

The LAC region's exports are heavily concentrated in primary commodities.

A. Primary commodity exports

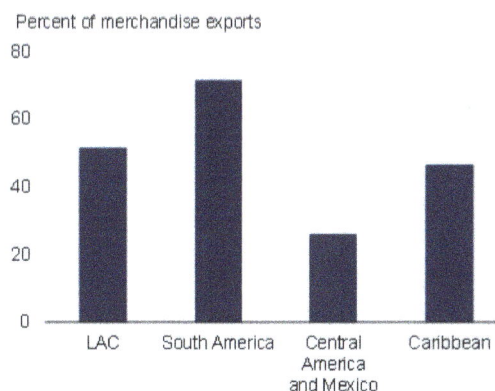

B. Primary commodity exports

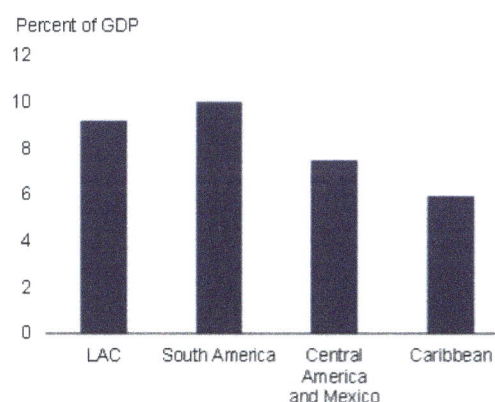

Source: UN Comtrade Database 2015.
A. and B. GDP-weighted averages for 2013-14.

LAC.[4] The data coverage is for 1998 Q1 - 2015 Q2, except for Colombia and Honduras where the data runs from 2000 Q2 – 2015 Q2, and Jamaica, where it 2002 Q2 – 2015 Q2. A dummy variable is included for the global financial crisis.

The results suggest that spillovers from Brazil to neighboring countries are moderate, while those from Mexico are negligible.

---

[3]Under the PetroCaribe program, the member countries that purchase oil from República Bolivariana de Venezuela pay for a certain percentage of the oil (depending on world oil prices) within 90 days, and the remainder is paid over a period of 25 years with an interest rate of one percent annually. Part of the cost may be offset by the provision of goods or services. Recently, to secure external funds, the government of República Bolivariana de Venezuela has renegotiated repayment, at deep discounts, of commercial credits to the Dominican Republic, Jamaica and Uruguay.

---

[4]Southern Cone countries include Argentina, Chile, Paraguay and Uruguay. Andean Community countries include Bolivia, Colombia, Ecuador and Peru. Central America and Caribbean economies include Belize, Guatemala, El Salvador, Honduras and Jamaica.

BOX 2.3.1 Regional integration and spillovers: Latin America and the Caribbean *(continued)*

FIGURE 2.3.1.6 Within-region trade and FDI

Brazil accounts for a significant share of trade and FDIs to other South American countries, while Mexico only has significant FDI links. Remittances come predominantly from outside the region.

A. South America: Export destinations

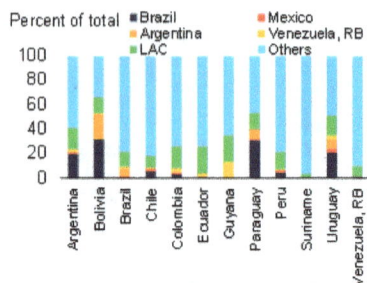

B. Central America and Mexico: Export destinations

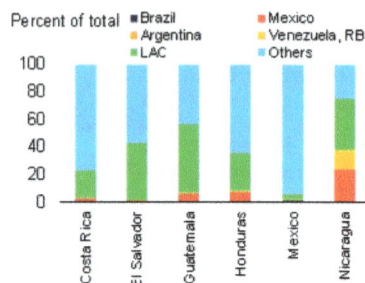

C. Caribbean: Export destinations

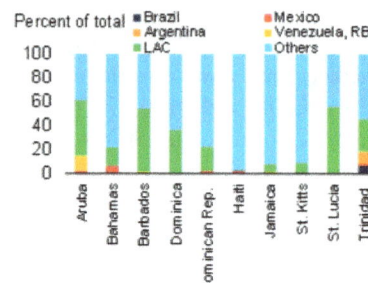

D. South America: FDI inflows

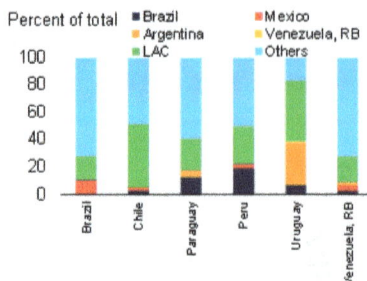

E. Central America and Mexico: FDI inflows

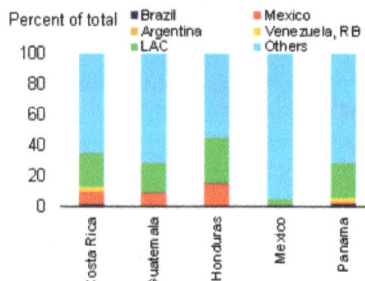

F. Remittances inflows

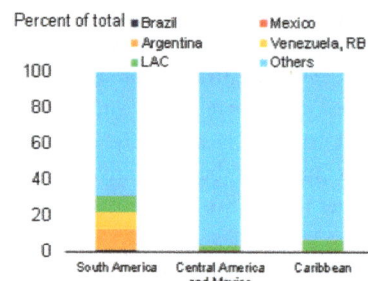

Source: IMF Direction of Trade Statistics, UNCTAD FDI/TNC database, World Bank Bilateral Remittance Matrix 2014.
Notes: A-C. Data for 2014.
D-E. Data for average of 2010-12.
F. Data is for 2014.

- *Spillovers from Brazil.* In the estimation results, growth declines in Brazil tend to have measurable or statistically significant spillovers to its South American neighbors. A one percentage point decline in Brazil's growth tends to reduce growth in Argentina, after 2 years, by 0.7 percentage point, in Paraguay by 0.6 percentage point, in Ecuador and Peru by 0.3 percentage point, and in Chile and Colombia by 0.2 percentage point (Figure 2.3.1.9).[5,6]

- Spillovers from Mexico. In contrast, spillovers from Mexico to Central America are negligible or not statistically significant (Figure 2.3.8). This result is in line with findings in other studies (Adler and Sosa 2014; Kose, Rebucci and Schipke 2005; Swiston 2010).

While there are measurable regional spillovers, particularly in South America, they are modest compared to those from the region's main external trade and financial partners. Over the two years following the growth decline, a one percentage point decrease in G7 growth lowers

---

[5]Brazil is Argentina's largest trading partner. In some sectors, such as automobiles, Brazil accounts for about 80 percent total exports. Spillovers from Brazil to Argentina play a big role in these sectors, and contracting economic activity in Brazil has adversely affected the auto industry in Argentina, spurring waves of production stoppages in major auto plants in 2015.

[6]The estimates from Adler and Sosa (2014) differ somewhat, partly because their sample time period includes the Tequila crisis of 1994.

Their results show that spillovers from Brazil are significant for Argentina, Bolivia, Paraguay, Peru, Uruguay, and the República Bolivariana de Venezuela, but less so for Ecuador.

BOX 2.3.1 Regional integration and spillovers: Latin America and the Caribbean (continued)

growth by more than 1 percentage point in Brazil, Chile, Mexico, Honduras and Ecuador. This is broadly in line with Österholm and Zettelmeyer (2008) who find a roughly one-for-one response to a change in growth in the United States. Similarly, Izquierdo, Romero, and Talvi (2008) also find a pass through of 0.6 percentage point to LAC GDP growth in response in 1 percentage point increase in G7 industrial production.

As a result of deep trade and financial links, spillovers from the United States to the region are particularly strong. Peaks and troughs of industrial production in some of the largest LAC countries—especially Mexico—tend to coincide with those in the United States (Cuevas, Messmacher and Werner 2003; Mejía-Reyes 2004). U.S. growth and U.S. industrial production are significantly correlated with growth in Mexico and Central America (IMF 2007; Fiess 2007; Roache 2008).

In addition, these estimates also show sizable linkages with China. A one percentage point growth deceleration in China reduces growth in Argentina by about 1.9 percentage points, in Brazil, Peru, Paraguay and Uruguay by 0.5 percentage point, and in Ecuador, Chile, Bolivia, Honduras, Guatemala, Colombia, El Salvador, and Mexico by 0.2 percentage point.[7] While larger than the estimated regional spillovers from Brazil and Mexico, the estimated spillovers from G7 economies to the LAC region are smallest among six World Bank regions of developing economies (see Box 3.4 and Figure 3.4.3), largely because the LAC region is more closed to the global economy than other regions. Overall, these findings are broadly in agreement with Boschi and Girardi (2011) and Caporale and Girardi (2012), who find that global factors are somewhat more important sources of output growth variability in LAC than regional factors.[8]

Conclusion

Despite a number of regional agreements, regional trade remains limited, partly reflecting the lack of an extensive

---

[7]Similar findings were reported in World Bank (2015n) and Cesa-Bianchi et al. (2012).

[8]A number of previous authors who have found that country-specific factors explain the majority of cyclical variation and output variability in LAC growth (Kose, Otrok and Whiteman 2003; IMF 2007; Loayza, Lopez and Ubide 2001; Boschi and Girardi 2011). On the other hand, other studies have also documented that external factors nevertheless do account for a significant share of growth variance of LAC economies (Izquierdo, Romero and Talvi 2008; Österholm and Zettelmeyer 2008; Aiolfi, Catão and Timmermann 2011).

FIGURE 2.3.1.7 The role of the largest economies in LAC

Brazil and Mexico are, by far, the largest economies in the region. In 2011-2014, these two countries accounted for 60 percent of regional GDP and trade, 50 percent of its population, 75 percent of portfolio and 50 percent of FDI flows, and 30-40 of tourism expenditures and remittance flows.

A. Share of regional total, 2011-14.

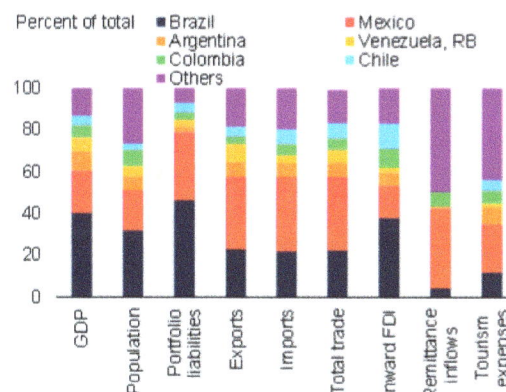

Source: IMF April 2015 World Economic Outlook, IMF International Financial Statistics, IMF Direction of Trade Statistics, UNCTAD FDI/TNC database, World Bank Remittance and Migration Database, World Bank World Development Indicators.
Note: GDP, Exports, FDI inflows and Remittance inflows are average for 2011-14. Portfolio liabilities are average 2011-13.

FIGURE 2.3.1.8 Correlations with Brazil and Mexico

Business cycles of a number of LAC economies are positively correlated with cycles in Brazil and Mexico. Correlations tend to be larger for countries in close proximity.

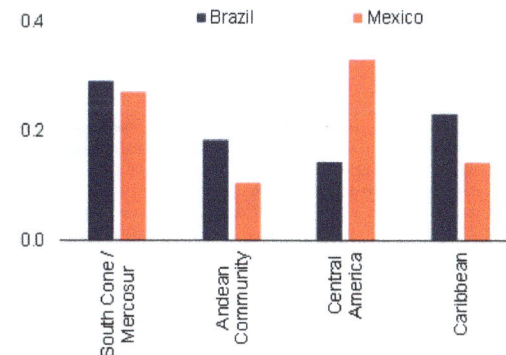

Source: Haver Analytics and World Bank staff estimates.
Note: Cross-country average of contemporaneous correlations in each country's quarterly growth with that of Brazil or Mexico.

BOX 2.3.1 Regional integration and spillovers: Latin America and the Caribbean *(continued)*

FIGURE 2.3.1.9 Spillovers from Brazil, Mexico, G7 and China

Growth shocks in Brazil have measurable spillovers to its South American neighbors - Argentina, Chile, Colombia, Ecuador, Paraguay and Peru. Estimated spillovers from growth shocks in Mexico are not statistically significant. Within-region spillovers are considerably smaller than spillovers from growth shocks in G7 countries or China.

A. Impact on growth of a 1 percentage point decline in Brazil's growth

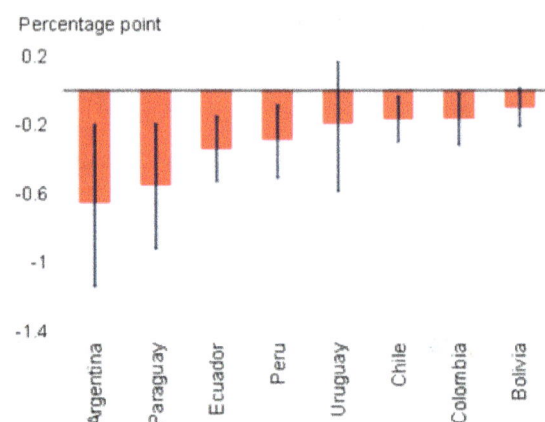

B. Impact on growth of a 1 percentage point decline in Mexico's growth

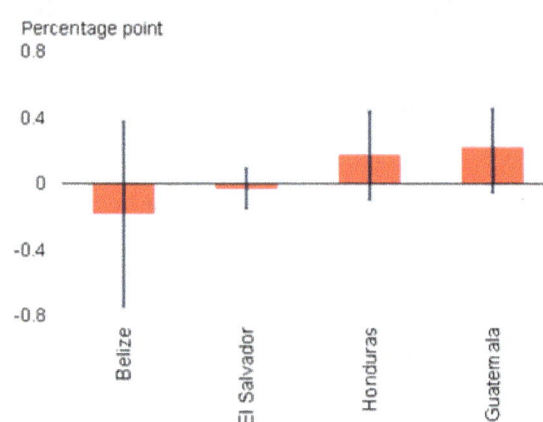

C. Impact on growth of a 1 percentage point decline in G7 growth

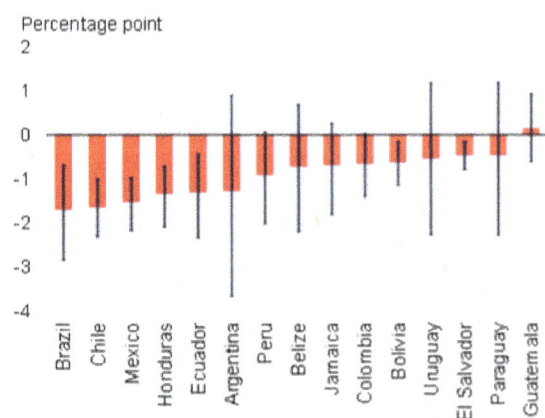

D. Impact on growth of a 1 percentage point decline in China's growth

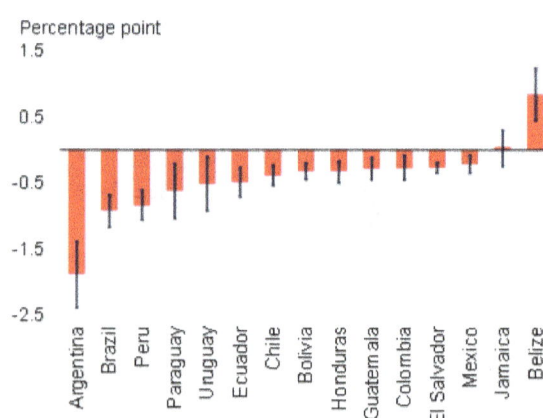

Source: World Bank staff estimates.
Note: Spillover estimates derived from impulse responses after two years from a Bayesian structural vector autoregression estimated using quarterly seasonally adjusted GDP data. The maximum data coverage is 1998Q1-2015Q2; while coverage for some countries is shorter (from 2000Q2 for Colombia and Honduras and from 2002Q2 for Jamaica). The model is estimated for each spillover destination country and the variables include, in this Cholesky ordering: G-7 growth, EMBI, China growth, Brazil and Mexico growth, the country's trade-weighted commodity price growth, the country's real GDP growth, and the country's real effective exchange rate appreciation. Quarterly GDP data was downloaded from Haver Analytics on November 18, 2015. Bars represent medians, and error bars 33-66 percent confidence bands.

international value chain network and heavy reliance on commodity exports to external markets. The lack of economic diversification and narrow product base could be another contributing factor to the generally closed nature of the region (IMF 2015h). Poor quality of regional transport networks and associated infrastructure further hinder within-region trade (World Bank 2012a; Figure 2.3.1.10). Intraregional trade linkages and FDI

BOX 2.3.1 Regional integration and spillovers: Latin America and the Caribbean *(continued)*

flows within Latin America are largely confined within sub-regions (De la Torre, Lederman and Pienknagura 2015). These linkages are stronger in South America than in Central America.

Reflecting these modest within-region ties, spillovers from growth decelerations in Brazil to some of its South American neighbors are estimated to be modest, while spillovers from Mexico are negligible. Spillovers from the region's main trading partners, however, tend to be considerably larger than within-region spillovers, albeit less than in other emerging and developing country regions.

Regional trade could strengthen in the medium term. With commodity prices expected to stabilize around current low levels, export baskets could shift towards a more diversified export product mix among regional commodity exporters, facilitating regional trade. Moreover, the sharp depreciations of regional currencies against the U.S. dollar may favor imports from intra-regional partners at the expense of those from the United States.

FIGURE 2.3.1.10 **Ease of trading across borders**

LAC economies are ranked low in terms of ease of trading across borders.

A. Rankings in Ease of Trading Across Borders, 2015

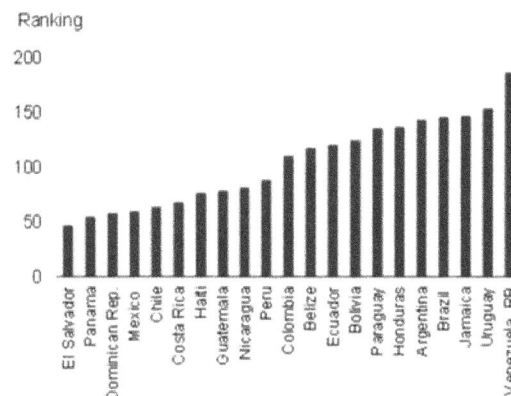

Source: World Bank 2015f.

MIDDLE EAST and NORTH AFRICA

Growth in the Middle East and North Africa was stable in 2015, at 2.5 percent. Accelerating activity in most oil-importing countries more than offset a slowing in oil exporters. Growth is expected to jump to more than 5 percent in 2016 and 2017. This reflects an expected rapid growth pickup in the Islamic Republic of Iran, the largest developing economy in the region, as sanctions are suspended or removed under the Joint Comprehensive Plan of Action. The forecast also depends on a stabilization of oil prices, and measured improvement in security in some countries. The outlook remains subject to significant downside risks stemming from possible escalation of conflict, a further decline in oil prices, and social unrest. Key policy challenges are to reduce unsustainable fiscal deficits, particularly in oil-exporting countries, and to harness the potential of the working-age population.

Recent developments

Growth in developing countries in the Middle East and North Africa was unchanged in 2015, at 2.5 percent (Table 2.4.1). In most oil-exporting countries (Algeria, the Islamic Republic of Iran, and Libya), growth slowed, as oil production and investment fell with the steep decline in oil prices since mid-2014. The situation was worsened in Libya by ongoing conflict.[1] In Iraq, however, despite protracted conflict, expansion in the oil sector was sufficient to reverse an economic contraction in 2014.

In most oil-importing countries, growth strengthened in 2015, as lower oil prices provided support to demand and allowed reductions in fuel subsidies. Activity in Egypt and Morocco rebounded significantly, reflecting rising domestic consumption (Egypt) and a strong rebound in the agricultural sector (Morocco). Reconstruction

following the 2014 war supported growth in the West Bank and Gaza, while strong investment growth boosted activity in Djibouti. However, growth in Tunisia was held back by security concerns, and in Jordan and Lebanon by spillovers from the conflict in Syria. Subdued activity in Tunisia also reflected weak credit growth linked to a delay in recapitalization of ailing publicly-owned banks.

A potentially pivotal development was the international agreement, signed in July 2015, of the Joint Comprehensive Plan of Action for limitations on Iranian nuclear development. For their part, the five permanent members of the United Nations Security Council, plus Germany and the European Union, agreed to remove and, in the case of the United States, suspend, trade and finance sanctions on the Islamic Republic of Iran. The agreement opens the door for re-integration of the country into the global economy and the reinvigoration of its oil, natural gas, and automotive sectors. Sanctions could begin to be lifted in early 2016 if the International Atomic Energy Agency (IAEA) indicates the Iranian government has fulfilled its commitments under the pact. Renewed optimism about the potential of the Iranian economy has already generated a flurry of investment interest by foreign companies.

The toll of conflict in several countries in the region showed little sign of abating in 2015. The

---

Note: The author of this section is Dana Vorisek. Research assistance was provided by Qian Li.

[1]This report covers low- and middle-income countries in the Middle East and North Africa region; Gulf Cooperation Council (GCC) countries are excluded. The developing countries are further divided into two groups, oil importers and oil exporters. Oil importers are Djibouti, the Arab Republic of Egypt, Jordan, Lebanon, Morocco, the Syrian Arab Republic, Tunisia, and West Bank and Gaza. Oil exporters are Algeria, the Islamic Republic of Iran, Iraq, Libya, and the Republic of Yemen. Syria and the Republic of Yemen are excluded from regional growth forecasts due to data limitations.

number of people in the region who are internally displaced or who have left their home countries as a result of conflict is unprecedented. In Iraq, 3.6 million people were internally displaced as of December 2014. An estimated 4.8 million people have left Syria as migrants or refugees, while 7.6 million are internally displaced. The rising outflow of migrants from Syria, and to a lesser extent Iraq, moved to the forefront of the European Union's policy agenda in 2015. The average monthly number of first-time asylum seekers to the European Union more than doubled between 2013 and the first eight months of 2015, to more than 66,000 people. Nearly one-third of asylum seekers in July and August 2015 were from Syria, up from less than one-quarter during the same months in 2014 and roughly 10 percent in 2013. Separately, high-profile terrorist attacks aimed at tourists in Egypt and Tunisia in 2015 negatively affected tourism in those countries.

The economic impact of Syrians seeking to escape war has been very heavy for Lebanon and Jordan, which the United Nations High Commissioner indicates host 1.1 million and more than 630,000 Syrian refugees, respectively, as of November. The number of Syrian refugees in Lebanon and Jordan is equivalent to a respective 25 percent and 9 percent of the populations, putting severe strain on public service delivery and infrastructure. Another 1.9 million refugees from Syria are in Turkey.

For most oil-producing countries where conflict is entrenched, oil production has dropped. In Syria and the Republic of Yemen, oil production has all but collapsed. For Syria, the decline reflects disruptions from conflict as well as trade sanctions imposed by the European Union and the United States. In Libya, production has dropped by nearly 75 percent since 2010, from an average of 1.6 million barrels per day (mbd) to 0.4 mbd in 2015. In contrast, oil production in Iraq has steadily increased, despite the conflict (Figure 2.4.1), as the important oil fields are not in the immediate geographical vicinity of the territory now controlled or contested by the Islamic State of Iraq and the Levant (ISIL). Average oil production in Iraq, at approximately 4 mbd in 2015, is more than 65 percent higher than in 2010.

Oil prices are now below fiscal break-even levels (i.e., the levels that balance the government budget) in all oil-exporting countries in the Middle East and North Africa (IMF 2015g). Violent conflict, which has reduced oil revenues while necessitating increased spending on security, is further straining government budgets of oil exporters across the region. In Algeria and Iraq, fiscal deficits deteriorated by more than 10 percentage points of GDP between 2013 and 2015, and in Libya by 50 percentage points. In Iraq and Libya, budget deficits were financed in 2015 predominantly by borrowing from state-owned banks, the Development Fund for Iraq having been exhausted by 2014. The bank borrowing is putting liquidity under strain. Algeria continues to draw on a sovereign wealth fund.

For oil-importing countries, declining oil prices, together with falling food prices, have been generally beneficial, as they have reduced the cost of imports and, in Morocco and Lebanon, contributed to higher consumption growth. Declining oil and food prices have also kept inflation subdued (Figure 2.4.2). For some countries (Jordan and Morocco), the period of low oil prices has helped stabilize government debt. Nevertheless, fiscal deficits were 10 percent or more of GDP in Egypt and Djibouti in 2015, and above 7 percent in Lebanon.

In Egypt, Jordan, and Lebanon, real effective exchange rates (REERs) appreciated during 2015, weighing on export competitiveness. In Egypt, the appreciating REER reflects high inflation, which averaged 10.3 percent in the first ten months of 2015. The central bank carried out several nominal devaluations, and restricted access to foreign currency, in attempt to resolve a deepening foreign currency shortage. In Jordan and, in particular, Lebanon, whose currencies are pegged to the U.S. dollar, real appreciation mostly reflected the rise of the U.S. dollar against the euro, as inflation was negative through most of 2015. Among oil exporters, the currencies of Algeria, the Islamic Republic of Iran, and Libya have depreciated, partially offsetting the local-currency revenue loss from lower U.S.-dollar prices of oil exports (IMF 2015g). Although international sanctions on the Islamic Republic of

Iran contributed to an episode of extremely high inflation in 2012 and 2013, inflation has moderated more recently, despite a depreciating rial.

Low oil prices are also contributing to adjustments in external balances. Whereas all oil exporters in the Middle East and North Africa had current account surpluses in 2013, balances in all of these countries except the Islamic Republic of Iran had swung into deficit by 2015, particularly in Libya, Algeria, and Iraq. Algeria and Libya have been able to rely on official reserves, but these have been depleted rapidly since mid-2014. Although Lebanon's large current account deficit (21 percent of GDP in 2015) is a vulnerability, the country has been able to finance it in recent years, mainly through portfolio investment. Capital flows to Lebanon declined sharply in the first half of 2015, however, by 33 percent year over year. Inflows to other oil-importing countries (Egypt, Morocco) were up in 2015, mostly as a result of strengthening foreign direct investment (FDI). However, the pickup in FDI to Egypt has not been as strong as expected given pledges at an international economic development conference in March 2015.

Remittance flows to developing countries in the region are estimated to have expanded by 1.6 percent in 2015, a slower pace than in 2014 (World Bank 2015l). Flows to Egypt, Jordan, and the Republic of Yemen rose, as inflows from GCC countries remained strong. Flows to Algeria, Morocco, and Tunisia, however, declined in U.S. dollar terms due to the depreciation of the euro, the currency in which 90 percent of remittance inflows are received. Remittances have represented a major source of foreign earnings for Lebanon and Jordan in recent years (16 percent and 10 percent of GDP in 2014, respectively, according to World Bank data). The inflows may have helped to smooth consumption in the weak growth environment (World Bank 2015n).

FIGURE 2.4.1 Oil production and fiscal balance

Crude oil production has declined in countries where conflict is entrenched except Iraq. Low oil prices and the direct and indirect costs of conflict are straining government budgets in oil-exporting countries in the Middle East and North Africa. Falling oil prices have helped improve fiscal balances in oil-importing countries.

A. Crude oil production

B. Fiscal balance

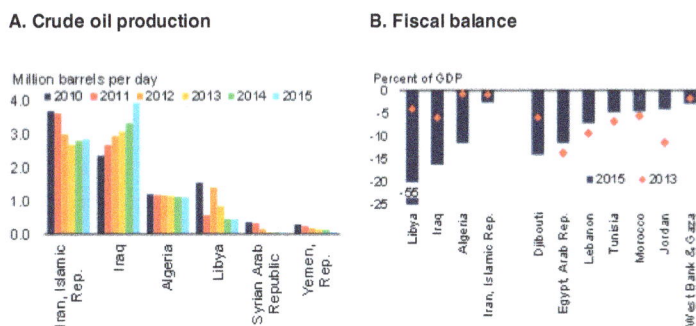

Source: World Bank, International Energy Agency.
A. Figure reflects average monthly production for each year; value for 2015 is the average for January to November.

FIGURE 2.4.2 Exchange rates, inflation, and current account balances

Low commodity prices have helped keep inflation subdued in oil-importing countries except Egypt, where rising prices are reflected in an appreciating real exchange rate. Low oil prices are contributing to adjustments in external balances, worsening deficits in oil-exporting countries and narrowing them in oil importers.

A. Inflation in oil-importing countries

B. Inflation in oil-exporting countries

C. Egypt: real effective exchange rate and foreign reserves

D. Current account balances

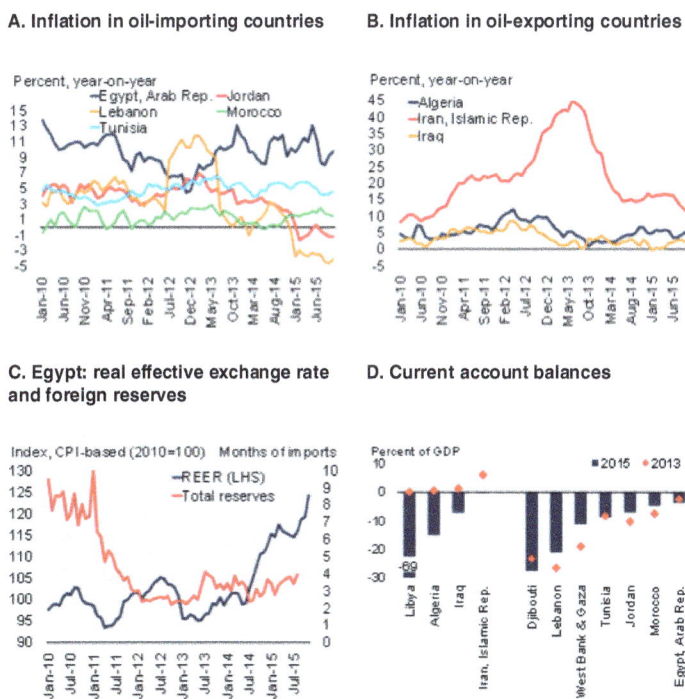

Source: World Bank, Haver Analytics.
C. Foreign reserves include gold. On left axis, an increase denotes real appreciation.

Outlook

Despite low oil prices—assumed to be $49 per barrel in 2016, broadly at 2015 levels—and several major conflicts, growth in developing countries in the Middle East and North Africa as a group is expected to rebound to 5.1 percent in 2016, and to 5.8 percent in 2017 (Table 2.4.2). The predominant reason for the improvement is an expected growth spurt in the Islamic Republic of Iran, the largest developing economy in the region, from 1.9 percent in 2015 to 5.8 in 2016 and 6.7 percent in 2017. The outlook also reflects slightly higher growth among other oil exporters, especially Iraq and Algeria, and a more modest medium-term improvement among oil importers, from 3.5 percent in 2015 to an average of 4 percent in 2016–18. The forecasts assume stabilization of oil prices and an improvement in the security situation in some countries.

Crude oil production in the Islamic Republic of Iran is expected to increase rapidly following the removal or suspension of sanctions, by an estimated 0.5–0.7 million barrels per day (mbd) in 2016 (World Bank 2015o), up from the 2015 level of 2.8 mbd. The potential increase in capital inflows in the post-sanctions environment could help expand exploitation of proven natural gas reserves, which are the largest in the world. The release of frozen Iranian assets currently overseas will also boost the economy. The ramping up of oil production over time, contingent upon significant infrastructure repair and investment, could help keep global oil supply high, and prices low, over the medium term.

A rebounding Iranian economy will affect neighboring countries within the Middle East and North Africa to varying degrees. A rapid rise in Iranian oil production would dampen growth prospects in oil-exporting countries and improve them in oil-importing countries (Ianchovichina, Devarajan, and Lakatos forthcoming). If pre-2010 -sanctions trade patterns are a guide, the export opportunities for other developing countries in the region from a rapidly growing Iranian economy may be limited, but perhaps greatest for Lebanon. Lebanese banks have already indicated that they

are interested in operating in the Islamic Republic of Iran.

Among other oil exporters, growth in Iraq and Algeria should be lifted in 2016 and 2017 by a recovery in the non-oil sector, in addition to continued oil sector growth. The baseline assumes that the impact of ISIL on Iraq's economy will slowly become more limited. In Libya, a UN-sponsored political agreement reached at the end of 2015 should allow oil production and GDP growth to recover.

Growth should also strengthen in most oil-importing countries. In Tunisia, growth should rise to 2.5 percent in 2016, predicated on a better security environment and progress on reforms. In Jordan, implementation of a new 10-year economic and social development plan is anticipated to lift confidence and push growth to 3.5 percent. The exceptions are Morocco and Egypt. In Morocco, growth is expected to revert to 2.7 percent in 2016, around the same as in 2014, as rainfall patterns reduce agricultural output from an exceptionally high level in 2015. In Egypt, growth is forecast to moderate to 3.8 percent in fiscal year 2015/16 as the tourism sector weakens following the October plane crash in the Sinai and a foreign currency shortage persists for at least part of the year. Growth in FY2016/17 should rise to 4.4 percent, driven by an uptick in investment. Rising growth in Egypt would have only a modest impact on the rest of the region, however (see Box 2.4.1).

Fiscal deficits among oil-exporting countries, although still large in some cases, will begin to narrow in 2016. The improvement reflects fiscal consolidation following the oil price drop. Iraq's 2015 budget contained spending cuts (merging of some ministries, government job cuts, and reduction in construction spending) that will help shrink the deficit in 2016. The deficit will remain wide, however. Lending from official sources will fill a large financing gap. The Algerian government intends to reduce spending by 9 percent in 2016, with cuts in utility subsidies and infrastructure projects but not in health, education, or housing. The expected budget adjustments among oil exporters are, however, unlikely to be sufficient to stabilize government debt in the absence of a significant rise in oil prices.

Fiscal deficits are expected to fall or remain broadly stable in oil-importing countries other than Djibouti. In Egypt, consolidation reflects lower energy subsidy spending and announced increases in electricity tariffs, among other things. In Lebanon, the expectation that the fiscal deficit will not fall substantially during the forecast period will contribute to a continued rise in government debt, already at approximately 145 percent of GDP at the end of 2015.

Current account deficits are expected to narrow in most countries in the region in 2016. With external financing conditions expected to tighten, however, some countries, such as Iraq, could have difficulty attracting enough foreign capital to finance their deficits. Oil-importing countries will continue to benefit from low oil prices over the medium term, while North African countries with deep trade ties with Europe (Algeria, Morocco, and Tunisia) may receive an export boost as the Euro Area economy improves (Figure 2.4.3). In the medium term, Tunisia's agricultural sector may also benefit from a deep and comprehensive free trade agreement with the European Union, on which negotiations began in October. Successfully boosting services exports, in particular through tourism, could contribute to further narrowing of current account deficits in several countries. Tourist arrivals are below pre-Arab-Spring levels across the region.

Risks

The growth outlook for the Middle East and North Africa is subject to several major and longstanding downside risks: economic spillovers from conflict; a renewed decline in oil prices; and the absence of progress in living conditions, which could reinvigorate social unrest. The Iran nuclear agreement could be an upside or a downside risk for the region: upside if economic recovery in the country is faster than in the baseline forecast following lifting of sanctions, and downside if the government's commitments are implemented more slowly than called for under the accord. Over the long term, the agreement does generate

broader risks to oil prices, depending on how fast new investment and technology can be mobilized to tap the Islamic Republic of Iran's oil and gas reserves.

The primary downside risk for the regional economy remains escalation or prolongation of conflict. In Iraq, Libya, Syria, and the Republic of Yemen, countries directly impacted by conflict, the loss of life, outward migration of skilled workers, destruction of infrastructure, and disruption of trade routes have significantly set back economic activity in recent years, and have slashed potential output. Conflict has also stalled regional trade integration that was in its infancy five years ago (Ianchovichina and Ivanic 2014). Spillovers from conflicts in the region could have ongoing impacts on neighboring countries beyond what has already occurred, through trade disruption, reduction in cross-border investment, evaporation of tourism, or an inability to manage pressure on public services from a large number of Syrian refugees. Lebanon and Jordan are particularly at risk in this regard.

Even in countries not facing large-scale conflict within their borders, security risk and political uncertainty have impacted consumer, business, and investor confidence. Egypt, for instance, had two new governments in the second half of 2015. Lebanon has been without a president since mid-2014. Terrorist attacks, such as those that targeted tourists in Egypt and Tunisia in 2015, would further damage the tourism sector. For Egypt, the contraction in foreign currency inflows that would accompany a shrinking tourism industry would not only negatively impact growth, but would exacerbate the existing foreign currency shortage.

For oil exporters, another significant risk is potential additional downward movement in oil prices should global supply stay high for an extended period of time. This could stifle growth in economies highly dependent on oil revenues and exports (Libya, Iraq, Algeria) and put further pressure on already large fiscal and external imbalances.

Across the Middle East and North Africa, lack of improvement in labor markets and living conditions increases the risk of further social

FIGURE 2.4.3 **Trade**

North African countries may experience a boost to growth through exports as Euro Area growth rises during the forecast period. Security risks weigh on the tourism industry in several countries, and tourism arrivals remain below pre-Arab-Spring levels.

A. Goods exports, 2014

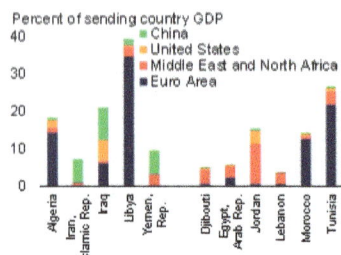

B. Average monthly tourist arrivals

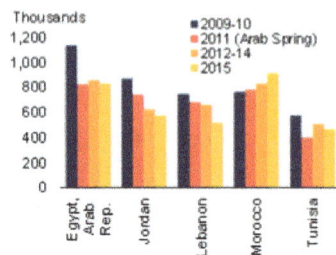

Source: IMF DOTS database, Haver Analytics, Lebanon Central Administration of Statistics, World Bank.
B. Tourist arrivals for 2015 are the average of January-August for Egypt, January-September for Jordan, and January-October for Lebanon and Tunisia.

FIGURE 2.4.4 **Labor market conditions**

Unemployment rates in the Middle East and North Africa are high relative to other developing regions and higher than before the Arab Spring in some countries. Cross-country comparisons reveal poor labor market efficiency across the region.

A. Unemployment rate

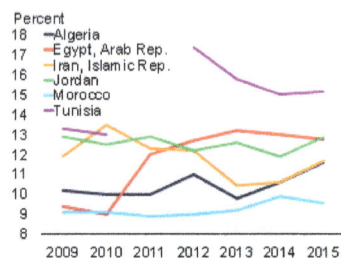

B. Labor market efficiency

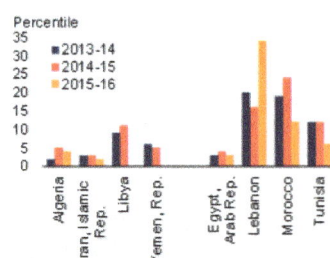

Source: World Bank, Haver Analytics, IMF, World Economic Forum Global Competitiveness Index.
A. Unemployment rates shown for 2015 are the average of Q1-Q3 rates. Data for 2011 missing for Tunisia.
B. Figure reflects percentile of individual country rankings among 135 countries ranked in 2015-16, 144 in 2014-15, and 148 in 2013-14. The labor market efficiency index includes 10 subcomponents: cooperation in labor-employer relations, hiring and firing practices, flexibility of wage determination, effect of taxation on incentives to work, redundancy costs, pay and productivity, reliance on professional management, country capacity to retain talent, country capacity to attract talent, and ratio of women to men in the labor force.

unrest. Unemployment rates, which have long been high relative to other developing regions, are above 2011 levels in Algeria, Egypt, Morocco, and Tunisia (Figure 2.4.4). Youth unemployment, at 32 percent in Jordan and 21 percent in Morocco, is more than double the overall unemployment rate. Employment growth is chronically weak or negative in countries with available data, and unemployment in the large informal sector is likely much higher than in the formal sector. A cross-country study of developing countries

including Egypt, Morocco, Tunisia, and Jordan found that the first three of these countries have significant gaps relative to other developing countries with regard not only to youth employment, but also the quantity and quality of education and skills mismatches (EBRD 2015a; Jelassi, Zeghal, and Malzy 2015).[2] Of the seven developing Middle East and North African countries assessed in the World Economic Forum's Global Competitiveness Index, five scored worst in the labor market efficiency category in the 2015-16 index, and four of these countries (Algeria, Egypt, the Islamic Republic of Iran, and Tunisia) have been in the bottom decile of rankings of labor market efficiency for the past three years.

Other indicators of living conditions are also weak. The United Nations Human Development Index, a composite measure of gross national income per capita, life expectancy, and schooling, shows less progress in Arab states in 2013 and 2014 than in any other developing region, and a decline in the index for Libya and Syria. Household surveys find that people in the Middle East were less satisfied in 2014 with their standard of living than they were in 2007, and that only 43 percent of people perceived their standard of living as improving in 2014, down from 58 percent in 2007 (Figure 2.4.5). These indicators suggest an increasing sense of disenfranchisement in the region. While the lack of progress in living conditions may be partly due to conflict, it is also self-reinforcing and has the potential to contribute to further social unrest, extremism, and violence.

Policy challenges

In view of their large budget deficits, there is a pressing need among oil exporters in the Middle East and North Africa for deeper cost-cutting and revenue-generating measures. In Algeria and Iraq, this means successful implementation of fiscal consolidation already planned. The urgency of fiscal adjustment in Iraq, Libya, and the Republic of Yemen, and to a somewhat lesser extent,

---

[2]An explanation of the variables included in these four categories and the statistical method for generating cross-country comparisons is given in EBRD (2015a).

Algeria, will become stronger in the medium term given that fiscal buffers are rapidly narrowing, financing needs are high, and borrowing capacity is weak (IMF 2015g). Furthermore, the decline in oil prices since mid-2014 is estimated to reflect a large permanent component (Husain et al. 2015), making the longstanding need for economic diversification in oil-exporting countries even more urgent.

Fiscal adjustment can also be accelerated in oil-importing countries, notwithstanding subsidy reforms already undertaken (Egypt, Jordan, and Morocco). In Egypt, introduction of a second round of energy subsidy cuts and a value-added tax has stalled. The political impasse in Lebanon is holding back the reform agenda, and impedes the functioning of public services. In Tunisia, progress on energy subsidy reductions and other fiscal adjustments has lagged. Low oil prices could be used as an opportunity to advance fiscal reforms during the forecast period.

Central banks in the region also face challenges. The new governor of the Central Bank of Egypt will need to oversee a boosting of critically low levels of foreign reserves. Additional rounds of currency devaluation are likely, which means monetary policy will have to resist pressure on an inflation rate that is already high. Iranian policymakers have said they will make it a priority to reduce inflation, which may become an easier task as sanctions are loosened.

In the medium and long term, it is critical that developing countries the Middle East and North Africa reduce inequality of opportunity and foster more inclusive growth. Working-age population growth in the region is higher than in all other developing regions except Sub-Saharan Africa and will continue to be so over the next decade. From this demographic perspective, it is imperative that labor market and other policy adjustments begin now, and that there be a special emphasis on addressing shortcomings affecting youth. Reform efforts would be well placed in two broad areas: labor market policy and public sector accountability.

FIGURE 2.4.5 Perception of standard of living

Indicators of living conditions in the Middle East have declined in recent years, suggesting an increasing sense of disenfranchisement in the region that may contribute to future social unrest.

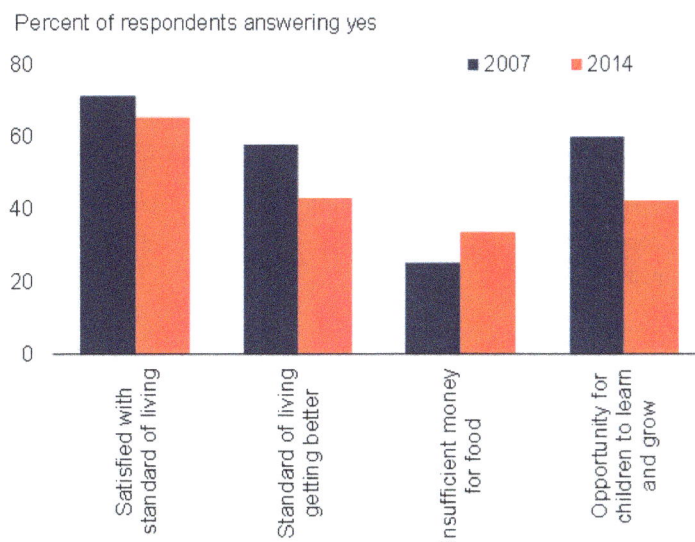

Source: Gallup World Poll 2014.
Note: Figure reflects responses to 1) "Are you satisfied or dissatisfied with your standard of living, all the things you can buy and do?", 2) "Right now, do you feel your standard of living is getting better?", 3) "Have there been times in the past 12 months when you did not have enough money to buy food that you and your family needed?", and 4) "Do most children in this country have the opportunity to learn and grow?" in nationally representative household surveys.

With respect to labor market policies, policymakers in the region should move forward with measures to remove supply-side constraints, such as improving the quality of education in some countries and implementing programs to better match labor force skills with those demanded by job markets. These efforts will need to be combined with the removal of constraints to competition and impediments to equality of opportunity among businesses, such as exclusive operating license requirements and trade barriers (Schiffbauer et al. 2015). Such measures in turn can be expected to improve labor demand. Removing rigidities in hiring, firing, and wage setting should also be a priority. To improve public sector accountability, particular effort should be made to curtail corruption, including by removing opportunities for rent-seeking among politically-connected people (World Bank 2015p).

TABLE 2.4.1 Middle East and North Africa forecast summary
(Annual percent change unless indicated otherwise)

(Percentage point difference from June 2015 projections)

	2013	2014	2015e	2016f	2017f	2018f	2015e	2016f	2017f
Developing MENA, GDP[a]	0.6	2.5	2.5	5.1	5.8	5.1	0.1	1.4	2.0
(Average including countries with full national accounts and balance of payments data only)[b]									
Developing MENA, GDP[b]	1.0	3.6	2.8	4.4	5.1	4.9	0.2	1.0	1.6
GDP per capita (U.S. dollars)	-0.9	1.7	1.0	2.8	3.5	3.5	-0.3	0.7	1.2
PPP GDP	0.9	3.6	2.8	4.5	5.2	5.0	0.1	1.1	1.6
Private consumption	2.5	2.5	2.7	3.1	3.3	3.3	-0.8	-0.5	-0.2
Public consumption	0.3	3.7	2.6	3.9	4.4	4.5	-1.2	1.0	1.5
Fixed investment	-0.1	8.3	4.9	7.3	8.8	7.9	2.0	0.6	4.8
Exports, GNFS[c]	-1.6	2.4	-0.4	7.0	7.5	8.3	-5.0	2.2	2.4
Imports, GNFS[c]	-1.2	2.0	1.3	4.5	4.9	5.1	-4.0	-1.6	-1.7
Net exports, contribution to growth	-0.1	0.0	-0.5	0.6	0.6	0.8	-0.1	1.2	1.4
Memo items: GDP									
Broader geographic region[d]	1.9	3.0	2.6	3.8	4.4	4.1	-0.5	0.2	0.6
High Income Oil Exporters[e]	3.1	3.5	2.7	2.7	3.0	3.0	-1.1	-0.8	-0.8
Developing Oil Exporters	-1.0	2.3	1.7	6.2	7.0	5.6	0.4	2.9	3.8
Developing Oil Importers	2.9	2.8	3.5	3.5	4.1	4.4	-0.4	-0.8	-0.5
Egypt, Arab Rep.	2.2	3.2	4.0	4.1	4.6	4.8	-0.3	-0.6	-0.2
Fiscal Year Basis	2.1	2.2	4.2	3.8	4.4	4.8	0.0	-0.7	-0.4
Iran, Islamic Rep.	-1.9	4.3	1.9	5.8	6.7	6.0	0.9	3.8	4.7
Algeria	2.8	3.8	2.8	3.9	4.0	3.8	0.2	0.0	0.0

Source: World Bank.
World Bank forecasts are frequently updated based on new information and changing (global) circumstances. Consequently, projections presented here may differ from those contained in other Bank documents, even if basic assessments of countries' prospects do not differ at any given moment in time.
a. GDP at market prices and expenditure components are measured in constant 2010 U.S. dollars. Excludes Syria and Republic of Yemen due to data limitations.
b. Sub-region aggregate excludes Djibouti, Iraq, Libya, Republic of Yemen, Syria, and West Bank and Gaza, for which data limitations prevent the forecasting of GDP components.
c. Exports and imports of goods and non-factor services (GNFS).
d. Includes developing MENA and the following high-income countries: Bahrain, Kuwait, Oman, Qatar, Saudi Arabia, and United Arab Emirates.
e. Includes Bahrain, Kuwait, Oman, Qatar, Saudi Arabia, and United Arab Emirates.

TABLE 2.4.2 Middle East and North Africa country forecasts[a]
(Real GDP growth at market prices in percent, unless indicated otherwise)   (Percentage point difference from June 2015 projections)

	2013	2014	2015e	2016f	2017f	2018f	2015e	2016f	2017f
Algeria	2.8	3.8	2.8	3.9	4.0	3.8	0.2	0.0	0.0
Djibouti	5.0	6.0	6.5	7.0	7.1	7.0	0.0	0.0	0.0
Egypt, Arab Rep.	2.2	3.2	4.0	4.1	4.6	4.8	-0.3	-0.6	-0.2
Fiscal Year Basis	2.1	2.2	4.2	3.8	4.4	4.8	0.0	-0.7	-0.4
Iran, Islamic Rep.	-1.9	4.3	1.9	5.8	6.7	6.0	0.9	3.8	4.7
Iraq	4.2	-0.5	0.5	3.1	7.1	6.5	1.5	-2.4	1.2
Jordan	2.8	3.1	2.5	3.5	3.8	4.0	-1.0	-0.4	-0.2
Lebanon	3.0	2.0	2.0	2.5	2.5	3.0	-0.5	0.0	0.0
Libya	-13.7	-24.0	-5.2	35.7	27.6	8.4	-5.7	20.7	16.7
Morocco	4.7	2.4	4.7	2.7	4.0	4.0	0.1	-2.1	-1.0
Tunisia	2.9	2.7	0.5	2.5	3.3	4.5	-2.1	-0.9	-1.2
West Bank and Gaza	2.2	-0.4	2.9	3.9	3.7	3.7	2.0	-0.4	-0.4

	2013	2014	2015e	2016f	2017f	2018f	2015e	2016f	2017f
Recently transitioned to high-income economies[b]									
Oman	3.9	2.9	3.7	3.2	3.0	2.5	0.0	-0.4	-0.5
Saudi Arabia	2.7	3.5	2.8	2.4	2.9	2.9	-1.8	-1.7	-1.4

Source: World Bank.
World Bank forecasts are frequently updated based on new information and changing (global) circumstances. Consequently, projections presented here may differ from those contained in other Bank documents, even if basic assessments of countries' prospects do not significantly differ at any given moment in time.
a. Syria and Republic of Yemen are not forecast due to data limitations.
b. Based on the World Bank's country reclassification from 2004 to 2015.

BOX 2.4.1 Regional integration and spillovers: Middle East and North Africa

Most of the external trade and financial ties of countries in the Middle East and North Africa (MENA) region are with countries outside the region. Trade and financial flows between MENA countries are modest. As a result, within-region growth spillovers even from the largest developing countries in the region—the Arab Republic of Egypt—are small. Spillovers from a large neighboring developing economy—Turkey——are also limited. In contrast, spillovers from G7 countries and GCC countries are considerably larger.

FIGURE 2.4.1.1 Cross-region comparison

The MENA region is one of the most open regions to global trade and remittances but receives limited financial flows by comparison with other developing regions.

A. MENA: Share of global activity, trade and finance, 2014

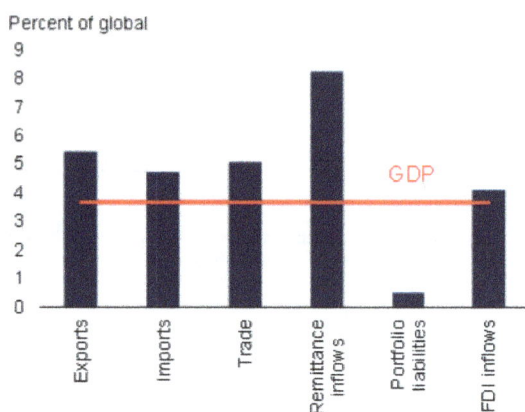

B. MENA: Trade and finance in regional comparison, 2014

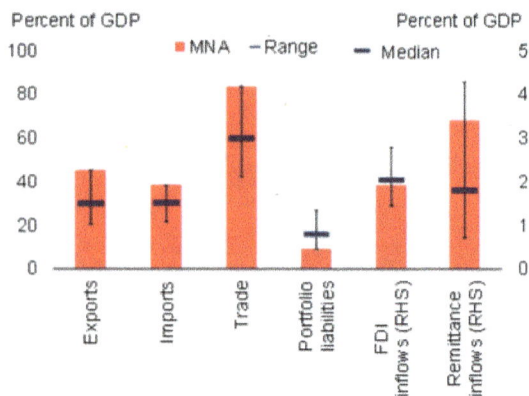

Sources: IMF October 2015 World Economic Outlook, IMF International Financial Statistics, IMF Direction of Trade Statistics, UNCTAD FDI/TNC database, World Bank Remittance and Migration Database, World Bank World Development Indicators.
B. The red bar denotes exports, imports, trade, remittance inflows, portfolio liabilities and FDI inflows in percent of GDP on average across MENA countries. The vertical line denotes the range of averages for all six developing country regions.

Introduction

The MENA region is highly open to trade and remittance flows (Figure 2.4.1.1).[1] Trade accounts for more than 60 percent of GDP for both oil exporters and oil importers in the region. There has, however, been a decline in economic integration with the rest of the world since the global financial crisis. Trade as a percentage of GDP has declined (Figure 2.4.1.2). Political uncertainty and falling commodity prices have contributed to a sharp fall in foreign direct investment (FDI) inflows to below 2 percent of GDP, about 1 percentage point below the average for other regions and considerably below the high FDI inflows pre-crisis. Remittance receipts in oil-importing countries have recovered only modestly after dropping significantly during the crisis.

With anemic growth in advanced economies, the pattern of MENA's trade and remittances links has shifted. Trade with other emerging markets, especially the BRICS (Brazil, Russia, India, China, and South Africa), has increased threefold compared to 2000 (Figure 2.4.1.3). Within-region trade and remittance flows have increased, but remain low. In addition to direct economic ties, confidence shocks, related to the recent conflicts and security issues in the region may also affect the economies of neighboring countries and are of increasing concern to policymakers.

This box addresses the following two questions:

- How open is the MENA region to global and regional trade and financial flows?

- How large are the potential intra-regional spillovers from one of the region's largest developing countries,

Note: This box was prepared by Ergys Islamaj and Jesper Hanson.
[1]Unless otherwise specified, the MENA region is defined to include oil-exporting countries (Algeria, Bahrain, the Islamic Republic of Iran, Kuwait, Oman, Qatar, Saudi Arabia, the United Arab Emirates and the Republic of Yemen) and oil-importing countries (Djibouti, Egypt, Israel, Jordan, Lebanon, Morocco, Tunisia and West Bank and Gaza). GCC stands for Gulf Cooperation Council countries. For the purposes of this box, Israel is also included as a recipient country of shocks (although it is not part of the World Bank's definition of the geographic region) since it has substantial trade ties to some other countries in the region.

BOX 2.4.1 Regional integration and spillovers: Middle East and North Africa *(continued)*

FIGURE 2.4.1.2 Trade, FDI, and remittances

The MENA region is highly open to trade and remittances despite a decrease since 2008. FDI inflows have fallen steeply in both oil exporters and importers, partly as a result of political uncertainty and falling commodity prices.

A. Trade

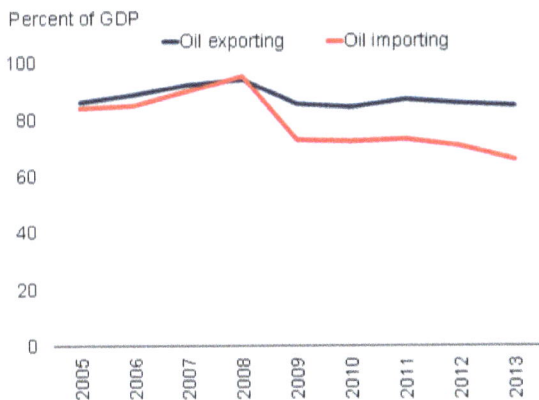

B. Foreign direct investment

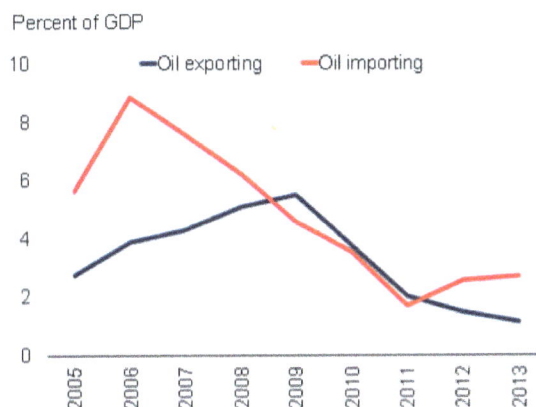

C. Remittances

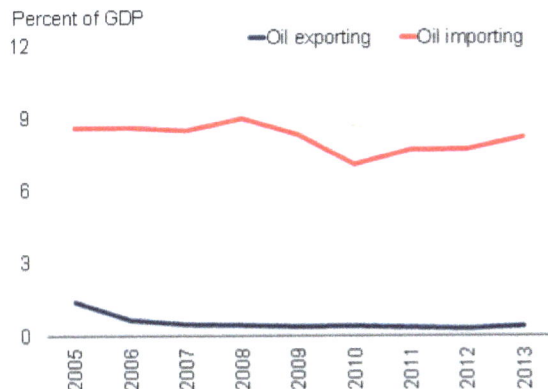

D. Exports of GCC and non-GCC MENA countries, 2011

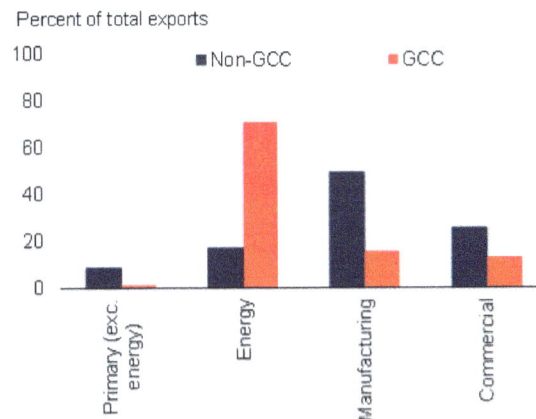

Sources: World Bank World Development Indicators; IMF Balance of Payments Statistics; World Bank Export Value Added Database.
Notes: A., B. and C. Trade is defined as the sum of exports and imports. Oil-exporting countries include Algeria, Bahrain, Iraq, Islamic Republic of Iran, Kuwait, Libya, Oman, Qatar, Saudi Arabia, United Arab Emirates and Yemen. Oil-importing countries include Djibouti, Egypt, Jordan, Lebanon, Morocco, Tunisia and West Bank and Gaza. Data unavailable for Islamic Republic of Iran, Iraq, Libya, Qatar, and the United Arab Emirates. Lines show sums of all countries in each sample.
D. GCC countries include Bahrain, Kuwait, Oman, Qatar, Saudi Arabia, the United Arab Emirates; non-GCC countries include Algeria, Djibouti, Egypt, Islamic Republic of Iran, Iraq, Jordan, Lebanon, Libya, Morocco, Tunisia, West Bank and Gaza, the Republic of Yemen. Data is unavailable for Algeria, Djibouti, Iraq, Jordan, Lebanon, Libya West Bank and Gaza, Yemen. Bars show unweighted averages.

Egypt, and from one of its largest neighboring developing countries, Turkey?

The empirical results suggest that the region is predominantly vulnerable to growth shocks originating from outside the region. Growth shocks from developing countries inside the region have negligible spillovers on other MENA countries. Potential spillovers from Gulf Cooperation Council (GCC) countries could be significantly larger, although data limitations prevent a

formal estimation. Other types of shocks—for example, of a political, security or financial nature—may also generate important spillovers that are not captured in the econometric analysis.

How open is the MENA region to global and regional trade and financial flows?

Trade and financial ties with countries outside the region far outweigh those within the region (Figure 2.4.1.3). On

BOX 2.4.1 Regional integration and spillovers: Middle East and North Africa *(continued)*

average across the MENA region during 2011-14, the United States, the Euro Area, and Japan combined accounted for 31 percent of exports, 69 percent of inward FDI, and 62 percent of banking claims on countries in the

MENA region. This average masks considerable cross-country heterogeneity, however. For many MENA countries, the Euro Area and the United States together account for more than 50 percent of export revenues and

FIGURE 2.4.1.3 Openness inside and outside the region

The main economic partners of MENA countries are outside the region, although within-region remittance and official development assistance flows are important. Since 2000, ties with the United States and the Euro Area have weakened while those within the region and the BRICS countries have strengthened.

A. Trade, investment, remittances, and official development assistance in MNA region, average 2011-14

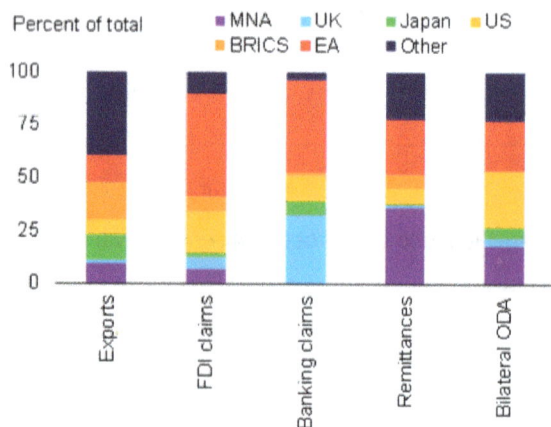

B. Trade within and outside the region, average 2011-14

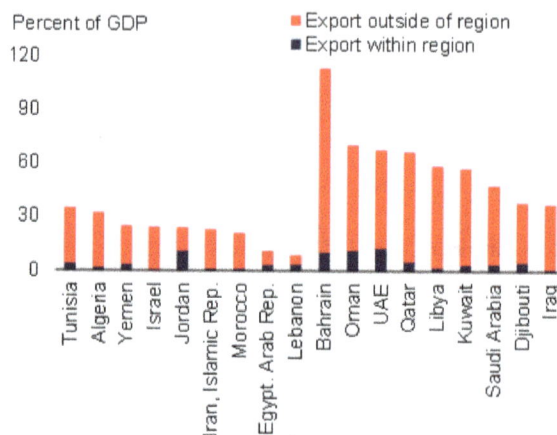

C. Evolution of trade within and outside the region

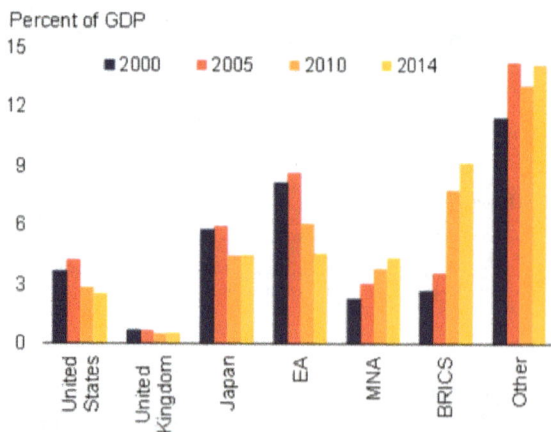

D. Remittance Inflows

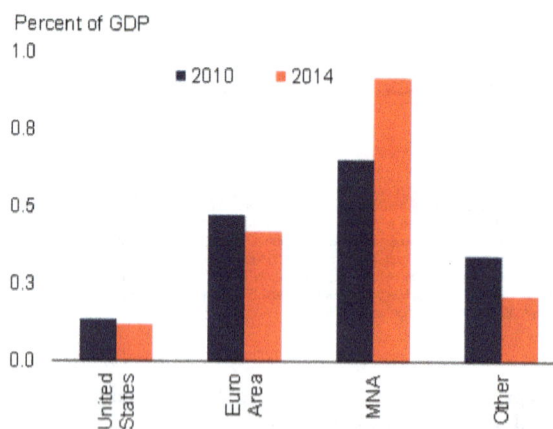

Source: IMF Direction of Trade Statistics (DOTS); IMF Coordinated Direct Investment Survey (CDIS); Bank for International Settlement (BIS) Consolidated Banking Statistics; World Bank Remittances and Migration database and WB country economists' estimates; OECD.
Notes: BRICS = Brazil, Russia, India, China, and South Africa; EA = Euro Area. Also see abbreviations above.
A. ODA = Official Development Assistance. Latest available data: 2014 for trade, remittances, BIS-reporting banks' consolidated foreign claims; 2013 for foreign direct investment and official development assistance. FDI claims from CDIS not available for China, and replaced with BBVA data. Data provided for Algeria, Bahrain, Djibouti, Egypt, Iraq, Islamic Republic of Iran, Jordan, Kuwait, Lebanon, Libya, Morocco, Oman, Qatar, Saudi Arabia, Tunisia, United Arab Emirates, West Bank and Gaza, and the Republic of Yemen. Within-region FDI reported only for Kuwait. Within-region ODA includes Kuwait, Saudi Arabia and the United Arab Emirates.
B. Includes Algeria, Bahrain, the Arab republic of Egypt, the Islamic Republic of Iran, Jordan, Kuwait, Morocco, Oman, Qatar, Tunisia, Lebanon, Saudi Arabia, the United Arab Emirates, and Yemen.

BOX 2.4.1 Regional integration and spillovers: Middle East and North Africa *(continued)*

FDI inflows. The openness of the region to global trade and finance is reflected in spillovers of global shocks to financial market activity. For example, equity returns in the MENA region move strongly with U.S. and European equity markets (Khalifa, Hammoudeh and Otranto 2013; Balli et al. 2015).[2]

Within-region remittance and official development assistance (ODA) flows remain significant and potentially constitute important channels for within-region spillovers. In contrast, within-region trade and financial links are modest by comparison with other regions. Given the proximity to the EU, one of the world's largest trading blocs, MENA countries trade predominantly with countries outside the region. Nevertheless, since they continue to face trade barriers in the EU, MENA countries trade more with each other than would be expected based on the size of their economies and transport cost (Freund and Jaud 2015). Limited within-region trade links also partly reflect close similarities in the export base of many energy-exporting countries in the MENA region.

Bilateral trade and official assistance flows from GCC to some oil importing countries have grown, but remain modest on average, with considerable heterogeneity. Since 2000, trade within the region has doubled, to an average of 4 percent of GDP. Remittances from GCC to other MENA countries have risen by one third, to 0.9 percent of GDP. Official development assistance from GCC countries to Egypt, Jordan and the Republic of Yemen increased from near-zero in 2000 to 2.7, 1.7, and 0.6 percent, respectively, of recipient government revenues during the 2011-2013 period. Since the Dubai World debt restructuring and the Arab Spring uprisings, comovement of GDP among MENA countries has increased somewhat (IMF 2013).

Two channels are particularly likely to generate within-region spillovers:

- *Remittances.* Remittance inflows ranged from 5 percent of GDP in Tunisia to close to 11 percent of GDP in Jordan during 2011-2014. More than three-fifths of these remittances were from GCC countries. While large remittances increase the risk of transmission of

negative shocks in GCC source countries to other countries in the region (IMF 2014d), remittances also help smooth consumption against unexpected variations in output in recipient countries (Balli, Basher and Louis 2013; World Bank 2015q; Abdih et al. 2012; IMF 2014d).

- *Official development assistance.* ODA from GCC to other oil-importing MENA countries was scaled up during the financial crisis of 2008 and the Arab Spring. It has remained high since then. GCC countries have provided or pledged loans and grants to Egypt, Jordan, Morocco, Tunisia and Yemen to finance infrastructure investment, balance of payments deficits, and commodity imports (Rouis 2013). ODA from Kuwait, Saudi Arabia and UAE represents more than 18 percent of total aid to the region, ranging from 4 percent of total ODA for Morocco to 72 percent of total ODA for Egypt. Historically, GCC aid to other MENA countries has varied with oil revenues (Talani 2014, Rouis et. al. 2010). The revenue losses associated with falling oil prices in GCC countries may make GCC assistance to the region less forthcoming.

Disruptions in trade and finance and displacements of large parts of the population during conflicts in parts of the region can also generate significant spillover effects to neighboring countries. These could be both positive and negative. Disruption of trade routes and trade disintegration lowers potential output. Migrants can occupy jobs previously held by low-skilled workers in the host country (Del Caprio and Wagner 2015). However, the domestic demand generated by large numbers of migrants or government expenditures related to migrants could stimulate activity. The net effect has been estimated to be positive for Lebanon—reflecting the large share of the migrant population—but negative or mixed for Turkey, Egypt and Jordan (Ianchovichina and Ivanic 2014, Cali et al. 2015, Del Caprio and Wagner 2015).

How large are the potential intra-regional spillovers from one of the region's largest economies, Egypt, and from one of its largest neighboring countries, Turkey?

Several countries in the MENA region have stronger ties with other MENA economies than others: the GCC countries and Egypt. Trade links are similarly sizeable with Turkey, one of the largest economies neighboring the MENA region.

---

[2] Khalifa et al. (2013) finds significant spillovers from U.S. equity markets to Saudi Arabia and UAE equity indices, while Balli et al. (2015) document spillovers from U.S. equity markets to all GCC countries and from European equity markets to Qatar and Oman.

BOX 2.4.1 Regional integration and spillovers: Middle East and North Africa *(continued)*

- GCC countries account for more than half of remittance inflows to Jordan and Egypt (50 and 60 respectively).

- Egypt and Turkey are sizeable export markets for Jordan, Lebanon, Morocco and Tunisia.

- Turkey remains an important trading partner for Egypt and the Islamic Republic of Iran. Anecdotal and survey data suggest sizeable informal trade between the Islamic Republic of Iran and other countries in the region.

A sufficiently long time series of quarterly data is available to estimate growth spillovers only from Egypt and Turkey to several non-GCC economies in the MENA region. A Bayesian structural vector autoregression (VAR) model is estimated, using data for 1998Q1-2015Q2. The variables are: G7 average growth; JPMorgan's Emerging Market Bond Index; growth in the shock source countries (Egypt and Turkey); trade-weighted commodity prices; and growth and real effective exchange rates of the countries subject to the external shock. Figure 2.4.1.4 shows the cumulative response after four quarters of recipient-country growth to a 1 percentage point decline in growth in Egypt or Turkey.[3]

Growth spillovers from Egypt and Turkey appear to be modest, and, in most cases, not statistically different from zero, reflecting limited within-region ties.[4] A 1 percentage point drop in Turkey's growth is associated with small or statistically insignificant growth effects across the region.[5] A 1 percentage point decline in growth in Egypt is associated with a 0.16 percentage point decline in growth in Jordan and a 0.15 percentage point decrease in growth

in Tunisia by the end of the first year. A decline in growth in Egypt does not appear to have significant effects elsewhere. The correlation between shocks to Egypt's growth and growth in Jordan and Tunisia reflect trade and remittances ties between these countries, as well as proximity in the case of Tunisia. In a similar regression using Islamic Republic of Iran as source country of the shock, estimates suggest a negligible effect of a slowdown on Israel, Jordan, Morocco and Tunisia.[6]

Growth spillovers from outside the region are larger in magnitude than those within the region, but mostly insignificant, with the exception of Morocco. A 1 percentage point decline in G7 growth is associated with an average 1 percentage point decline in growth in countries in the MENA region.[7]

These results are broadly comparable to the few available studies by other authors. Using a global VAR, Cashin, Mohaddess and Raissi (2012) show that growth shocks from Europe and the United States have a modest, but negative effect on the output growth of countries like Egypt, Jordan, Morocco and Tunisia.[8] Behar and Espinosa-Bowen (2014) suggest that non-oil trade in MENA countries would decline considerably following shocks to growth in Europe and the global economy.

Conclusion

The MENA region is highly open, but with fewer within-region ties than other regions. As a result, spillovers from the larger developing countries in the region and from neighboring Turkey are modest.

Although not estimated explicitly for lack of comparable data, spillovers from GCC countries to the rest of MENA region are likely to be significantly larger than spillovers from Egypt and Turkey, given large remittance and ODA flows from GCC to non-GCC countries in the region

---

[3]Quarterly GDP data are available from IMF's International Financial Statistics, Haver and Bloomberg for 1998Q1-2014Q4. Countries for which there were considerable differences amongst the three sources were dropped. The resulting unbalanced panel included Egypt, Islamic Republic of Iran, Jordan, Morocco and Tunisia. For Lebanon, quarterly energy production data was used as a proxy for output. For Egypt, the data starts in 2002Q2 and for Tunisia in 2000Q2.

[4]The results in Figure 2.4.4 include four lags. They are robust to alternative specifications: different Cholesky ordering, Bayesian priors, decay in the lag structure, correlation across variable lags, and number of lags.

[5]Shocks in Turkey seem to be inversely correlated with growth in Tunisia. This may reflect competition in key export sectors, especially tourism: when tourist arrivals to Tunisia declined during 2005-13, those to Turkey increased as tourists shifted their destinations during bouts of political uncertainty. Tourism has been a significant channel for the transmission of spillovers in Mediterranean countries (Canova and Dallari 2013). As expected, the estimated spillovers are smaller if the period after the Arab Spring (starting 2010Q4) is excluded.

---

[6]The response of the non-GCC MENA countries' average growth rate to a one percentage point decline in Turkey and Egypt is also near-zero. Because of the higher volatility of industrial production (IP), measured spillovers from industrial production are somewhat larger: a 1 percentage point decline in IP growth in Egypt and Turkey is associated with 0.15 and 0.2 percentage point decline in growth in the other countries.

[7]Spillovers from a decline in G7 growth to electricity production growth in Lebanon could be sizable (shown on the right axis of Figure 2.4.1.4). Those to Egypt are not statistically significantly different from zero after 4 quarters.

[8]They find that the cumulative effect after four quarters of a 1 percentage point decline in growth in Europe is not statistically significantly from zero or on the order of 0.1-0.2.

BOX 2.4.1 Regional integration and spillovers: Middle East and North Africa (continued)

FIGURE 2.4.1.4 Spillovers from Egypt and Turkey

Output spillovers between non-GCC MENA countries have been modest, reflecting the predominance of trade and financial ties of non-GCC MENA countries to economies outside the region.

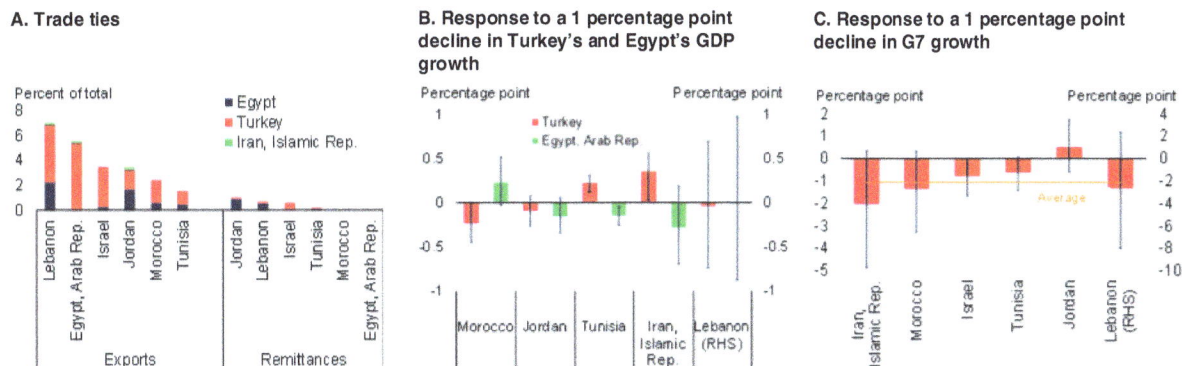

A. Trade ties

B. Response to a 1 percentage point decline in Turkey's and Egypt's GDP growth

C. Response to a 1 percentage point decline in G7 growth

Source: World Bank staff estimates.
Notes: B and C. Cumulative response of each country's growth after 1 year to a 1 percentage point decline in growth rates of Egypt, Turkey and World GDP, respectively. World GDP refers to average GDP growth in G7 countries. Energy production data used for Lebanon. Quarterly GDP data for Tunisia and Egypt are available from 2000Q2 and 2002Q2, respectively. All other series are available from 1998Q1. Bayesian VARs include Arab Spring dummies for Tunisia (2010Q4-2011Q4) and Egypt (2011Q1-Q4), financial crises dummy (2008Q2-2009Q2), a dummy for Turkey's financial crises (2001Q1), a dummy for conflict in Lebanon (2006Q1-Q4) and dummies for droughts in Morocco (2002, 2003, 2006 and 2012). Horizontal line represents MENA average response. Vertical lines show a one standard deviation confidence band. Solid bars represent medians and the error bands represent 33-66 percent confidence bands. Lebanon shown on the right axis.

(Cashin, Mohaddess and Raissi 2012, IMF 2012c). GCC economies may also have a significant effect on developing MENA countries through their investments in infrastructure, such as airlines, telecom and multi-country railway projects, as well as banking and financial ties (World Bank 2014b).

In addition, spillovers from political uncertainty, security concerns or spreading violence could also be sizeable.

Going forward, more stability in the MENA region will not only allow countries to benefit from deepening trade and finance, but will also alleviate some of the fiscal burden associated with creating infrastructure to help people displaced by conflicts. Continued turmoil will derail efforts to tackle problems of corruption, and prolong necessary reforms in the labor markets (World Bank 2015f).

SOUTH ASIA

GDP growth in South Asia rose from 6.8 percent in 2014 to 7.0 percent in 2015, the fastest rate among developing regions, as recovery took hold in India, and as the region benefited from lower oil prices and improved resilience to external shocks. A moderate further acceleration in economic activity is projected, with regional growth rising to 7.5 percent in 2018, buoyed by strengthening investment and a broadly supportive policy environment. Risks are mainly domestic. They include reform setbacks in the reform momentum in India, political tensions or conflicts in smaller economies, and, over the longer term, the commitment of governments to the necessary fiscal adjustment. South Asia may also face external headwinds from an increase in interest rates in the United States, although vulnerabilities are greatly reduced since the "taper tantrum" of 2013. Key policy challenges include the substantial non-performing bank loans in several countries, and the need for further reforms—in particular, to improve the ability of firms to do business within and outside the region, and to fully harness the ongoing demographic dividend.

Recent developments

Regional growth remained robust at an estimated 7.0 percent in 2015, helped by strengthening activity in the region's largest economies (Table 2.5.1). In India, brisk growth continued, at an estimated 7.2 percent year-on-year in the first half of the 2015/16 fiscal year compared with 7.3 percent in FY2014/15 as a whole. Monetary and fiscal restraint, the fall in global crude oil prices and a moderation in food price inflation have contributed to a steep drop in inflation and a narrowing of current account and fiscal deficits. Momentum in industrial output has slowed and both the services and manufacturing Purchasing Managers' Indices (PMIs) have softened (Figure 2.5.1). However, the investment cycle is gradually picking up, led by a government efforts to boost investment in infrastructure, particularly roads, railways and urban infrastructure. India's currency and stock markets were largely resilient over the past year, even during bouts of volatility in global financial markets.

Elsewhere in the region, macroeconomic adjustment in Pakistan under an International Monetary Fund program is progressing, while efforts to crack down on violent crime in Karachi, the country's industrial and commercial hub, are supporting investor confidence. The China Pakistan Economic Corridor (CPEC) agreement, signed in 2015, has further bolstered investor optimism, and, if implemented, has the potential to lift long-term growth. Pakistan once again tapped the international capital markets and launched a US$500 million Eurobond in September 2015, with the same maturity and coupon as its issue a year earlier.

Sri Lanka has completed a major political transition, with a national unity and reform-oriented government formed after the August 2015 parliamentary election. Growth in 2013 and 2014 was revised downward from 7.2 and 7.4 percent to 3.4 and 4.5 percent, respectively, as a result of a rebasing of the national accounts.[1] Incoming data show growth picking up mid-year, led by robust service sector growth, and supported by rising tourism inflows and strong remittances. In Bangladesh, as political tensions have abated, exports have rebounded strongly, supporting activity.

Note: The author of this section is Tehmina Khan. Research assistance was provided by Xiaodan Ding.

[1] The GDP series was rebased from 2002 to 2010. The new GDP series also captures new activities such as professional services, and better measures value added in other sectors, notably in services. In level terms, both nominal GDP and per capita GDP have increased.

FIGURE 2.5.1 **Recent developments**

Industrial activity has slowed in India and Pakistan, while external trade remains weak. Inflation has moderated sharply across most of the region, except in Bangladesh where it has contributed to an appreciation of the currency in real terms.

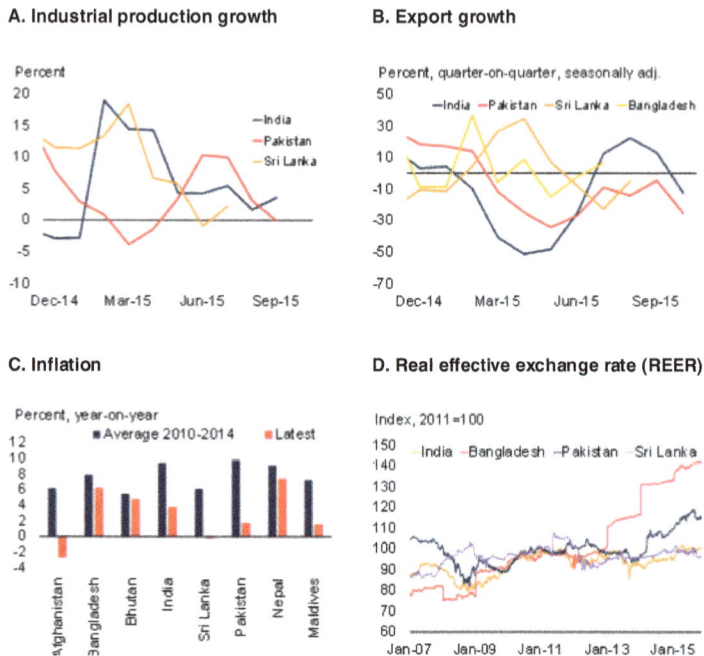

A. Industrial production growth

B. Export growth

C. Inflation

D. Real effective exchange rate (REER)

Source: World Bank, IMF, WITS, Haver Analytics.
A.B. Quarter-an-quarter, seasonally adjusted.
B. Nominal export growth.
D. An increase denotes an appreciation.

In contrast, security conditions remain unsettled in Afghanistan, as international forces reduce troop deployments. However, efforts are being made to strengthen macroeconomic stability and reduce vulnerabilities in the banking sector. Political tensions and domestic unrest have also increased in Maldives following the arrest of several politicians during 2015. In Nepal, the cost from the earthquakes in the spring of 2015 is estimated at about a third of GDP. Activity has since been further hurt by domestic protests and a closure of land trading routes through India in the second half of 2015. This has led to acute fuel and food shortages, and put a halt to reconstruction efforts. In Bhutan, tourism inflows have been affected by spillovers from the earthquake and disruption in trade in Nepal, although, overall, activity continues to be supported by the construction of major hydropower projects, notably Dagachhu, which went into production in March 2015.

Inflation, which tends to be structurally high in the region, slowed further in 2015 (Figure 2.5.1). The decline is showing signs of bottoming out, as oil prices stabilize. In India, drought for the second consecutive year in 2015 has weighed on farm output, with some indications of food price pressures starting to build toward the end of the year. However, both India and Pakistan have been on a path of fiscal consolidation over the past three years, and fiscal restraint is curbing demand-side pressures. Lower inflation has enabled central banks in India and Pakistan to cut policy rates to support activity and, in Sri Lanka, keep policy rates at record lows. In contrast, inflation in Bangladesh has remained persistently high, reflecting transport bottlenecks in early 2015, limited spare capacity, and limited pass through from low global oil prices to domestic oil prices, contributing to a significant and steady appreciation in the real exchange rate (Figure 2.5.1). The currencies of India, Pakistan and Sri Lanka, which had appreciated in real effective terms since 2013, have stabilized in recent months.

India has sharply curtailed its current account deficit, to about 1 percent of GDP in Q2 2015 (on a four-quarter rolling basis) from about 5 percent of GDP in mid-2013 when the financial markets were shaken by the "taper tantrum" financial market turmoil over U.S. Federal Reserve policy. India's central bank has rebuilt reserves while net FDI flows have remained positive. Pakistan's current account deficit has continued to narrow, reflecting lower oil import cost and strong remittance inflows.

Ongoing fiscal consolidation in India has reduced the central government's fiscal deficit to close to 4 percent of GDP (on a 12-month rolling basis), down from a peak of 7.6 percent in 2009. Pakistan has also made progress in reining in its budget deficit from 8.4 percent of GDP in FY2013 to 5.3 percent in FY2015.[2] However, debt levels remain high at 65 percent of GDP, the result of years of fiscal slippages, and interest payment costs are about 4.4 percent of GDP. Nepal is planning to substantially increase

---

[2] Including grants.

spending for reconstruction. This is expected to push the fiscal balance into a modest deficit. Fiscal discipline has weakened in Bangladesh and Sri Lanka. The deficit in Bangladesh is set to widen to 5 percent of GDP, the largest since 2008, in line with the doubling of public sector wages. In Sri Lanka, the fiscal deficit is estimated to have widened to 5.7 percent of GDP, and public debt has reached over 70 percent of GDP. Most countries in the region struggle to raise taxes, particularly from goods and services taxes (GST) or value-added taxes which are typically a lynchpin for sustainable public finances in developing countries. Persistent deficits in previous years have saddled the country with a public debt ratio amounting to 75 percent of GDP in 2014. Incomplete fiscal consolidation in 2015 and a large increase in foreign-financed capital expenditure projects budgeted for 2016 risks increasing the level of external public debt further.

Two key critical legislative reforms (GST and land acquisition) are still pending in India. Nevertheless, the government has made progress in key areas, such as energy, and in November announced major reforms to liberalize FDI in several sectors. The central bank, meanwhile, has liberalized the medium-term framework for foreign portfolio investment, in an effort to increase its role in market development and for attracting long-term investors. In Pakistan, the authority to grant tax exemptions has been transferred from the Revenue Board to parliament while efforts continue to implement an ambitious tax reform agenda. The central bank, with IMF assistance, is gradually strengthening monitoring of financial stability risks, and is in the process of instituting a modern deposit insurance scheme in line with international best practices. The new Sri Lankan government has announced governance reforms that should strengthen democratic institutions.

Outlook

Growth in the region is expected to edge up, reaching 7.5 percent by 2017, driven mainly by domestic demand. Investment growth is expected to continue strengthening in India due to

FIGURE 2.5.2 **Risks and challenges**

The region has limited trade exposure to slowing investment in China, and as a net importer of oil will continue to benefit from low global energy prices. This is particularly the case for Indian firms that are energy intensive. Insufficient jobs at home have led to large numbers of South Asians migrating overseas. Major human development and infrastructure challenges remain in India.

A. Exports by major trading partner

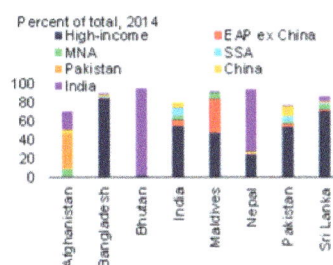

B. Energy intensity, 2007

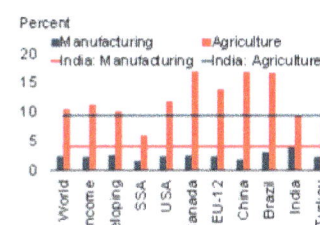

C. Stock of migrants by developing region, 2014

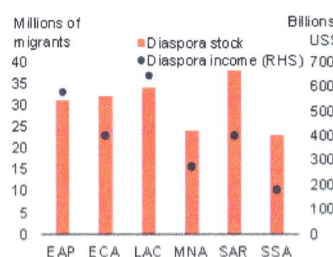

D. Human and infrastructure indicators in India

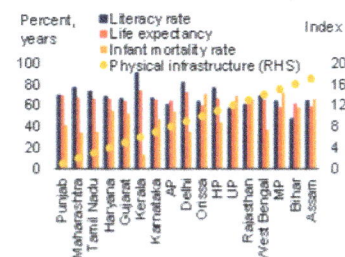

Source: World Bank; IMF Direction of Trade Statistics (DOTS); Global Trade Analysis Project (GTAP) database, Kumar (2014).
B. Energy intensity is defined as energy cost in percent of total cost per unit of output.
C. EAP stands for East Asia and Pacific; ECA stands for Europe and Central Asia; LAC stands for Latin America and the Caribbean; MNA stands for Middle East and North Africa; SAR stands for South Asia; SSA stands for Sub-Saharan Africa.
D. Data are sourced from Kumar (2014) and reflect indicators based on a variety of household, labor force and other micro-survey datasets covering the mid-late 2000s. Data for infant mortality is for 2007. Life expectancy is in years. AP stands for Andhra Pradesh, HP stands for Himachal Pradesh, MP stands for Madhya Pradesh, UP stands for Uttar Pradesh.

government efforts to accelerate infrastructure development and boost Public Private Partnerships (PPPs), and in Pakistan due to CPEC implementation. In Bangladesh and Sri Lanka, public sector wage increases and an easing of political tensions or uncertainty should bolster private consumption.

The region also has relatively limited trade exposure to slowing demand in major emerging markets (Figure 2.5.2), and as a net importer of oil will continue to benefit from low global energy prices. Generalized weakness in the global trading environment, and indirect spillovers from slower growth in major developing economies is expected to partly offset the positive impulse to exports from high-income country demand. With activity slowing in oil-rich GCC countries, growth in remittances is also expected to moderate.

Compared to most other major developing countries, India is well positioned to withstand near-term headwinds and volatility in global financial markets due to reduced external vulnerabilities, a strengthening domestic business cycle, and a supportive policy environment. Although the pace of reforms has slowed somewhat, growth is expected to strengthen to 7.9 percent in FY2017/18, from an expected 7.5 percent in FY2015/16. Progress on infrastructure improvements and government efforts to boost investment are expected to offset the impact of any tightening of borrowing conditions resulting from tighter U.S. monetary policy. Such investment will also lift potential growth over the medium term. Low international energy prices and domestic energy reforms will ease energy costs for Indian firms that tend to be energy intensive (Figure 2.5.2). Although rural incomes have suffered as a result of two successively weak monsoon seasons, urban spending has been supported by the decline in inflation, and will also benefit in the near term from public sector wage increases announced recently. India accounts for more than 90 percent of portfolio and FDI inflows to the region. Better growth prospects relative to other major developing countries should help flows remain resilient during the transition to tighter global financing conditions (although there may be volatility in the near term).

Pakistan stands to benefit from three tailwinds over the near- to medium- term, with average growth projected at 5.5 percent over the forecast period.[3] These include rising investments from China under the CPEC agreement; the anticipated return of the Islamic Republic of Iran to the international economic community; and persistently low international oil prices. CPEC will connect Western China to the Arabian Sea via the

new port of Gwadar. Estimated at around US$45 billion of investment until 2030, the initiative will finance a series of transport infrastructure projects (US$11 billion, mostly public investment) and energy projects (US$33 billion, mostly private).[4]

Increased infrastructure spending and public sector wage hikes in Bangladesh are expected to keep growth high at 6.8 percent over the medium term, but also to widen the fiscal deficit. An amendment to labor laws in September that strengthened workers' rights and workplace safety should assist export performance, particularly in light of the ongoing U.S. review of Bangladesh's trade status under its Generalized System of Preferences (GSP).

In Nepal, the devastation caused by the earthquake and the disruption of trade in 2015 have hurt investment and activity hard. Growth for FY 2015/16 has been revised down to 1.7 percent (versus an estimate of 3.7 percent prior to the trade disruption). However, there remains considerable uncertainty around the point forecast, with growth likely to range anywhere between 1-2.3 percent. Activity should gradually recover as government reconstruction spending is ramped up in the later years of the forecast period. Plans to build major hydropower projects in partnership with China and India are likely to see considerable delays in the current environment. A mild recovery is projected in Afghanistan, conditional on improvements in security and domestic reforms.

In Bhutan, growth is expected to remain strong over the forecast period, as major hydropower projects are built. Three major projects are expected to come online by 2017 that should help to boost exports and fiscal revenues. Tourism inflows are expected to support services in Bhutan and Sri Lanka. Robust service sector growth and policy efforts to improve competitiveness in the manufacturing in Sri Lanka are expected to lead to a steady pickup in growth to 6 percent in 2017, from 5.3 percent in 2015.

---

[3]For cross-country comparability, this is projected growth in real GDP "at market prices". The Government of Pakistan usually refers to growth in real GDP "at factor cost" for policy purposes. Real GDP growth at factor cost is projected at 4.5 percent in FY2015/16.

[4]The projects foreseen in the CPEC to receive funding from China's US$4 billion Silk Road Fund include partial financing for the US$1.65 billion Karot hydropower project.

Risks

Risks are mostly of domestic origin and mainly on the downside. In India, progress in reforms is not assured as the upper house of parliament, which the ruling party does not control, has the power to block the government's legislative agenda. Slow progress on land reforms could add to investment delays, and private investment growth may be unable to build further momentum. The financing of public-private partnerships also remains a challenge. A failure to pass the goods and services tax could hamper the government's ability to ramp up spending on infrastructure needs and preserve the status quo of fragmented domestic markets. In addition, although India has made good progress on reducing external vulnerabilities and strengthening the credibility of the macro policy framework, high levels of nonperforming loans in the banking sector, concentrated in construction, natural resource and infrastructure sectors, could impede a pickup in investment if left unaddressed (World Bank 2015a, IMF 2015k). There are also downside risks to growth in the near term from sub-par monsoon rainfall across most of India, and farm output growth may prove weaker than projected.

Stronger growth and investment in Pakistan is predicated on reforms to strengthen the business climate, an improvement in the security situation, implementation of the CPEC and an associated easing in energy constraints. These developments might not materialize as expected. A resumption of political tensions in Bangladesh and an escalation of existing tensions in Nepal and Afghanistan are key risks in these countries. Budget execution, particularly capital spending, has been a longstanding challenge in Nepal, and slow progress in post-earthquake reconstruction, coupled with political tensions, could dampen any post-earthquake rebound. Afghanistan, meanwhile, faces substantial fiscal risks and challenges, affecting financing of civilian and security spending.

Fiscal risks are elevated across the region. In Pakistan, with national elections due in 2018, hard won fiscal consolidation gains may be lost if spending ramps up in the pre-election period. In addition, sovereign guarantees associated with the CPEC could pose substantial fiscal risks over the medium term. Large fiscal deficits in Bangladesh and Sri Lanka increase risks that rising government borrowing will crowd out private investment. In Sri Lanka, external debt has increased since 2014, due to both private and public (mainly non-concessional) borrowing, and government contingent liabilities have also risen fast. A growth slowdown increases the risk of deteriorating public debt ratios and rising external costs of borrowing.

Although less pressing than domestic risks, external risks remain. The region will not be immune to trade and financial market headwinds if there is a slowdown in major developing countries. Other external risks include increased volatility in financial flows as U.S. monetary policy is tightened. A substantial share of South Asian migrants are also located overseas, including in GCC countries (Box 2.5), where fiscal strains are emerging and construction activity is slowing amid the slump in oil prices. With remittances a major source of support for households in several South Asian countries, any decline in inflows in the event of further oil prices declines and a sharp slowdown or fiscal retrenchment in GCC countries could hurt private consumption.

Policy challenges

South Asian countries face substantial challenges on the fiscal front. Generally, fiscal deficits and public debt levels remain high in the region including in India, Pakistan and Sri Lanka. Afghanistan has seen a sharp drop in the domestic revenue-to-GDP ratio, mainly because of the growth slowdown. The country remains dependent on high levels of donor financing to fund critical security and social spending programs. Over the longer term, anchoring fiscal sustainability will require tax reforms, given generally low tax-to-GDP ratios in the region (World Bank 2015a).

Further, as discussed in Box 2.5.1. South Asia is one of the least globally integrated regions, and

FIGURE 2.5.3 Demographic challenges

In some states, creating jobs for a rapidly growing share of young people will be a key policy challenge.

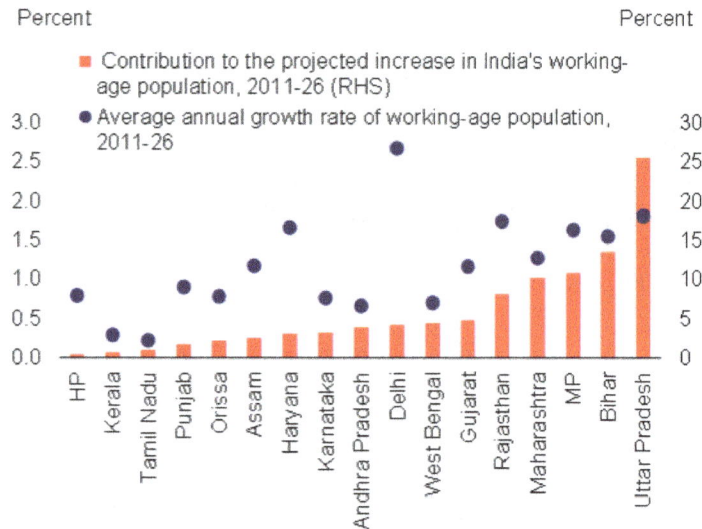

Percent   Percent

- ■ Contribution to the projected increase in India's working-age population, 2011-26 (RHS)
- ● Average annual growth rate of working-age population, 2011-26

Source: Kumar (2014).
A. HP denotes Himachal Pradesh; MP denotes Madhya Pradesh.

regional integration is even more limited. A number of factors are at work: poor connectivity within South Asia and to global markets; poor trade facilitation policies reflected in high costs of trading across borders in general; and restrictions on doing business with countries within the region that are in some cases due to strained political relations and have contributed to substantial numbers of South Asians migrating overseas in search of better employment opportunities (Figure 2.5.2c; Ahmad and Ghani, 2007; De et al. 2013; Palit and Spittel, 2013; World Bank, 2013a).

The size of private capital flows to South Asia is also much lower than to every other developing region, save the Middle East and North Africa (Box 2.5). This reflects underdeveloped capital markets, poor corporate governance, and inflow restrictions in some countries (Romero-Torres et al. 2013). Over the medium term, enhancing integration and cooperation at the national, regional, and global level will help raise levels of productivity and growth. It will also help channel domestic savings more efficiently, creating jobs, diversify growth away from a narrow set of high-income countries, and reducing poverty (Palit et al, 2013; Ahmed and Ghani, 2008, De et al. 2012).

Finally, South Asia is one of the few developing regions where the demographic dividend is expected to remain positive over the next few decades as the share of the working age population increases in size (World Bank, 2015j). For instance, in India, an estimated 300 million working age adults are expected to enter the labor force by 2040. Traditionally slow-growing and relatively under-developed Indian states of Bihar, Madhya Pradesh, Rajasthan, and Uttar Pradesh are expected to contribute more than half of the increase in country's working-age population in coming decades (Figures 2.5.2 and 2.5.3). States which perform better on various indicators of infrastructure, health, education, and investment climate seem to be the ones that best exploited the demographic dividend and in addition, also generated additional growth on top of it (Kumar 2014). Accordingly, reforms targeted at lifting these indicators—particularly in the states with the fastest growing population—will be critical to managing this transition.

TABLE 2.5.1 South Asia forecast summary
(Annual percent change unless indicated otherwise)

(Percentage point difference from June 2015 projections)

	2013	2014	2015e	2016f	2017f	2018f	2015e	2016f	2017f
South Asia, GDP[a, b]	6.2	6.8	7.0	7.3	7.5	7.5	-0.1	0.0	0.0
(Average including countries with full national accounts and balance of payments data only)[c]									
South Asia, GDP[c]	6.2	6.9	7.0	7.3	7.5	7.6	-0.1	-0.1	0.0
GDP per capita (U.S. dollars)	4.8	5.5	5.6	6.0	6.2	6.2	-0.1	0.0	0.0
PPP GDP	6.2	6.9	7.0	7.3	7.5	7.5	-0.1	0.0	0.0
Private consumption	5.5	6.0	6.5	6.6	6.3	6.2	0.0	0.3	0.1
Public consumption	6.5	7.1	8.1	7.5	6.6	6.4	-0.3	0.3	0.1
Fixed investment	2.3	4.2	4.7	9.1	11.4	11.5	-2.3	-2.2	-1.6
Exports, GNFS[d]	6.7	1.8	2.3	4.0	5.0	5.7	-0.9	-0.8	-1.9
Imports, GNFS[d]	-3.3	-1.9	1.6	4.6	5.8	6.5	-2.6	-2.2	-2.7
Net exports, contribution to growth	2.8	1.1	0.1	-0.3	-0.4	-0.5	0.5	0.5	0.4
Memo items: GDP[b]									
South Asia excluding India	5.0	5.4	5.7	5.8	6.0	6.0	0.0	0.3	0.3
India	6.9	7.3	7.3	7.8	7.9	7.9	-0.2	-0.1	-0.1
Pakistan	4.4	4.7	5.5	5.5	5.4	5.4	-0.5	1.8	0.9
Bangladesh	6.1	6.5	6.5	6.7	6.8	6.8	0.2	0.0	0.1

Source: World Bank.

World Bank forecasts are frequently updated based on new information and changing (global) circumstances. Consequently, projections presented here may differ from those contained in other Bank documents, even if basic assessments of countries' prospects do not differ at any given moment in time.

a. GDP at market prices and expenditure components are measured in constant 2010 U.S. dollars.

b. National income and product account data refer to fiscal years (FY) for the South Asian countries, while aggregates are presented in calendar year (CY) terms. The fiscal year runs from July 1 through June 30 in Bangladesh, Bhutan, and Pakistan, from July 16 through July 15 in Nepal, and April 1 through March 31 in India. 2014 data for India, Pakistan, and Bangladesh cover FY2014/15.

c. Sub-region aggregate excludes Afghanistan, Bhutan, and Maldives, for which data limitations prevent the forecasting of GDP components.

d. Exports and imports of goods and non-factor services (GNFS).

TABLE 2.5.2 South Asia country forecasts
(Real GDP growth at market prices in percent, unless indicated otherwise)

(Percentage point difference from June 2015 projections)

	2013	2014	2015e	2016f	2017f	2018f	2015e	2016f	2017f
Calendar year basisᵃ									
Afghanistan	2.0	1.3	1.9	3.1	3.9	5.0	-0.6	-1.9	-1.2
Bangladesh	6.3	6.5	6.6	6.8	6.8	6.8	0.1	0.1	0.1
Bhutan	3.9	6.3	6.8	7.2	5.6	6.0	-1.1	-1.2	-1.4
India	6.4	7.2	7.3	7.7	7.9	7.9	-0.1	-0.1	-0.1
Maldives	4.2	5.9	4.4	3.1	4.2	4.5	-0.9	-1.9	-0.8
Nepal	4.7	4.4	2.6	3.7	5.1	4.5	-1.8	-1.3	-0.4
Pakistan	4.6	5.1	5.5	5.5	5.4	5.4	0.7	1.4	0.9
Sri Lanka	3.4	4.5	5.3	5.6	6.0	6.0	-1.6	-1.0	-0.5
Fiscal year basisᵃ									
Bangladesh	6.1	6.5	6.5	6.7	6.8	6.8	0.2	0.0	0.1
India	6.9	7.3	7.3	7.8	7.9	7.9	-0.2	-0.1	-0.1
Nepal	4.1	5.4	3.4	1.7	5.8	4.5	-0.8	-2.8	0.3
Pakistan (market prices)	4.4	4.7	5.5	5.5	5.4	5.4	-0.5	1.8	0.9
Pakistan (factor cost)	3.7	4.0	4.2	4.5	4.8	4.8	..	..	..

Source: World Bank.

World Bank forecasts are frequently updated based on new information and changing (global) circumstances. Consequently, projections presented here may differ from those contained in other Bank documents, even if basic assessments of countries' prospects do not significantly differ at any given moment in time.
a. Historical data is reported on a market price basis. National income and product account data refer to fiscal years (FY) for the South Asian countries with the exception of Afghanistan, Maldives and Sri Lanka, which report in calendar year (CY). The fiscal year runs from July 1 through June 30 in Bangladesh, Bhutan, and Pakistan, from July 16 through July 15 in Nepal, and April 1 through March 31 in India. 2014 fiscal year data, as reported in the table for India, Pakistan, Bangladesh, Nepal, cover FY2014/15. GDP figures presented in calendar years (CY) terms for Bangladesh, Nepal, Bhutan, and Pakistan are calculated taking the average growth over the two fiscal year periods to provide an approximation of CY activity. Historical GDP data in CY terms for India are the sum of GDP in the four calendar quarters. Historical data from Sri Lanka has recently been revised.

BOX 2.5.1 Regional integration and spillovers: South Asia

South Asia's integration with the global economy is low and integration within the region is even more limited. The ability to do business across borders is constrained by poor business environments and policies that have weighed on competitiveness, contributed to large-scale emigration and limited the ability to do business across borders. While this has reduced exposure to global shocks in the short-term, these very factors limit the potential of South Asian firms to fully benefit from the strengthening demand in the United States and Europe over the medium term. Over the long term, enhancing regional and global integration will be critical in raising productivity and growth, providing jobs and reducing poverty.

Introduction

South Asia is one of the least globally integrated regions (Figure 2.5.1.1), both in trade and finance. However, the degree of integration at the regional level, measured by flow in goods, capital and ideas, is even lower. This is despite shared cultural ties, extensive common borders, and high population densities with large populations living close to border areas (Ahmad and Ghani 2007; Kemal 2005; Palit and Spittel 2013).

This box takes a closer look at South Asia's openness to the rest of the world, and to countries within the region itself. It discusses the following questions:

• How open is South Asia to global and regional trade and financial flows?

• How large are the potential intra-regional spillovers from the region's largest economy, India?

The box documents that spillovers from global output shocks are generally small, but large for financial shocks (for India). Regional spillovers are also small. This implies that positive spillovers to the region from the strengthening economic cycle in the US and India to other large South Asian economies will likely be modest.

How open is South Asia to global and regional trade and financial flows?

Although economic linkages between South Asia and the rest of the world have deepened in recent decades, progress has been slow and uneven (Ahmad and Ghani 2007). High-income countries and China account for the bulk of exports earnings, portfolio investments, FDI and aid (Figure 2.5.1.2). Regional integration, meanwhile, has lagged considerably (Ahmad and Ghani 2008 and Ahmad et. al. 2010). A number of factors are at work: poor transport connectivity within South Asia and to global markets; poor trade facilitation policies and trade barriers

FIGURE 2.5.1.1 Cross-region comparison

South Asia is one of the least globally integrated regions, in terms of trade and finance. However, it absorbs a large share of global remittances.

A. SAR: Share of global activity, trade and finance, 2014

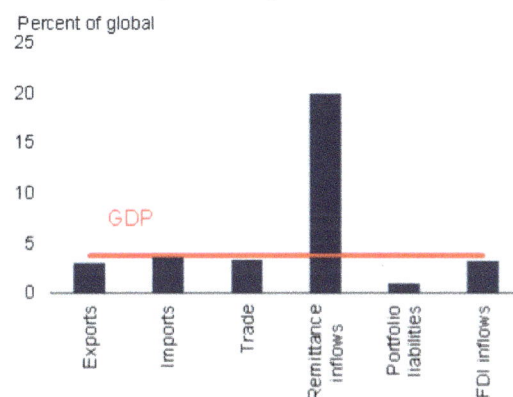

B. SAR: Trade and finance in regional comparison, 2014

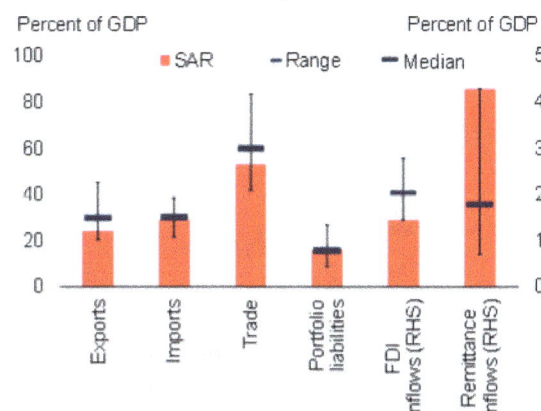

Sources: IMF October 2015 World Economic Outlook, IMF International Financial Statistics, IMF Direction of Trade Statistics, UNCTAD FDI/TNC database, World Bank Remittance and Migration Database, World Bank World Development Indicators.
B. The red bar denotes exports, imports, trade, remittance inflows, portfolio liabilities and FDI inflows in percent of GDP on average across SAR countries. The vertical line denotes the range of averages for all six developing country regions.

Note: This box was prepared by Tehmina Khan, Jesper Hanson and Raju Huidrom.

BOX 2.5.1 Regional integration and spillovers: South Asia *(continued)*

FIGURE 2.5.1.2 Regional and global integration in South Asian countries

Flows of goods and capital across borders are low compared to other regions. Exports have increased by much less over the past two decades than in other regions, and remain concentrated by destination.

A. Regional and global integration, 2014

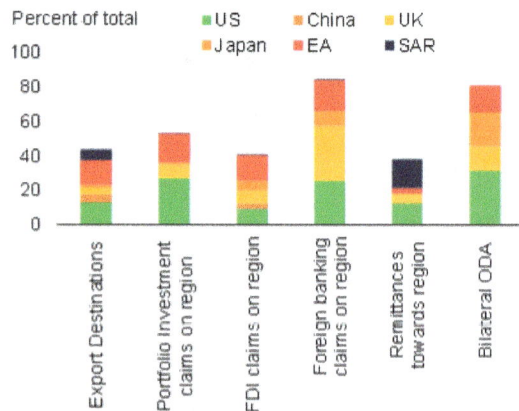

B. Increase in exports since 1990

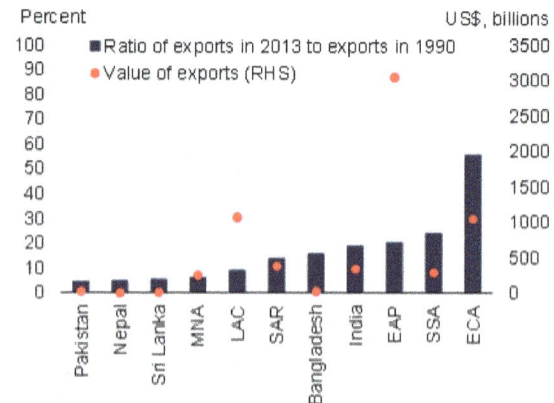

C. Trade openness, 2014

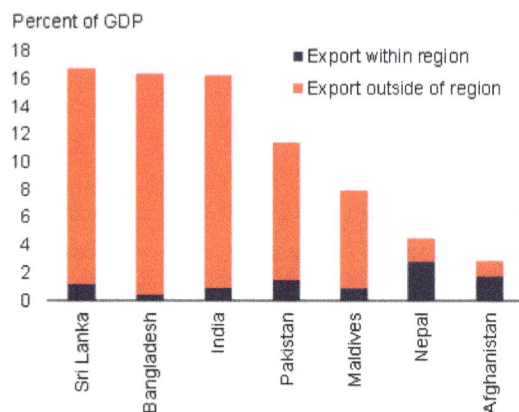

D. Exports by major trading partners, 2014

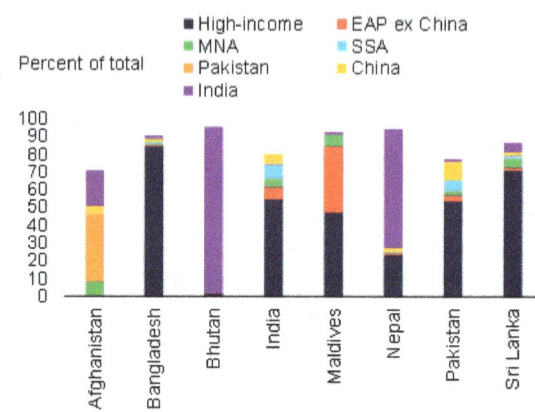

Source: World Bank, BIS, IMF, OECD.
Notes: Weighted averages.
B. EAP stands for East Asia and Pacific. ECA stands for Europe and Central Asia. LAC stands for Latin America and the Caribbean. MNA stands for Middle East and North Africa. SAR stands for South Asia Region. SSA stands for Sub-Saharan Africa.

that have resulted in high costs of trading; and restrictions on doing business with countries within the region (De et al. 2013; Palit and Spittel 2013; Romero-Torres 2014; World Bank 2013b). The exception are within-region remittances: the Bangladesh-India migrant corridor, for instance, is the third largest in the world.

Trade: Unilateral trade liberalization measures introduced in the late 1980s and 1990s have led to rising trade flows between South Asia and the rest of the world (Ahmad and Ghani 2007). Still, the degree of integration remains much lower in South Asia than in other major developing regions, with exports amounting to a fifth, or

less, of GDP in most countries. Moreover, export flows tend to be highly concentrated, with the European Union and United States as major trading partners notwithstanding a recent shift of India and Pakistan toward East Asia and Sub-Saharan Africa.

As a share of GDP, intra-regional exports are smaller than anywhere else in the world (Palit and Spittel 2013). On average, India, Pakistan, Sri Lanka and Bangladesh's exports to each other amount to less than 2 percent of total exports. Average trade costs between country pairs in South Asia are 85 percent higher than between country pairs in East Asia (Kathuria et al. 2015) reflecting border

BOX 2.5.1 Regional integration and spillovers: South Asia *(continued)*

barriers, poor infrastructure and transport connectivity, and generally poor business environments. However, unofficial trade (in narcotics, but also illegal food trade in the Punjab) is reported to be significant (Fagan 2011). Estimates of the size of unofficial trade vary between countries (Taneja 2004), with recent studies placing the value of Indian exports to Pakistan at about $1.8 bn (or nearly 1 percent of GDP, Ahmed et. al. 2014). While the larger countries in the region predominantly trade outside the region, India is the dominant trading partner for the smallest countries in the region: Bhutan (mainly hydro-electricity), Nepal (textiles, agriculture, tourism) and Afghanistan (for which, Pakistan too is a major trading partner).[1]

Capital flows: Relative to GDP, capital flows to South Asia are lower than those to East Asia and the Pacific and Europe and Central Asia regions (Figure 2.5.1.3), reflecting underdeveloped capital markets as well as inflow restrictions in some countries (Romero-Torres et. al. 2013). They are dominated by banking sector flows, mainly from the United Kingdom. Financial integration is limited by restrictive domestic policies. For instance, in India, notwithstanding some gradual liberalization over the years, and in Sri Lanka non-resident holdings of government debt remain capped.

India receives over 90 percent of the region's FDI and portfolio inflows, a substantial share of which originates from Mauritius and Singapore (low-tax countries with which India has double taxation treaties).[2] In recent years FDI has tended to head into services rather than mining or industry (World Bank 2013a). China has made substantial investments into the region in recent years, in extractives in Afghanistan, renewable energy in Nepal, port construction in Sri Lanka, and manufacturing and infrastructure in Pakistan.

Within-region FDI accounts for only a small share of all FDI inflows. Bhutan, Nepal, Maldives and Sri Lanka do, however, receive non-negligible amounts of FDI from India. Cross-border investments from India have flowed into energy and public sector-linked investment in Nepal;

chemicals, food processing, banking and garments production in Bangladesh, and a similarly diverse range of sectors in Sri Lanka over the past decade (World Bank 2013a).

Remittances: South Asia's diaspora stock is the largest among developing regions, and remittances exceed 6 percent of GDP in Pakistan, Sri Lanka, Nepal and Bangladesh. India is the largest recipient country in the world in terms of value of remittances (about $US 70 billion). By source, Gulf Cooperation Council (GCC) countries account for just over half of total remittances to the region, with the United States and United Kingdom also major source countries. Within-region migration flows are also substantial: the Bangladesh-India migrant corridor is the third largest in the world (after the Mexico-U.S. and Ukraine-Russia corridors), with more than 40 percent of Bangladeshi emigrants located in India. India also hosts large numbers of migrants from Bhutan, Nepal and Sri Lanka, and Pakistan from Afghanistan (World Bank 2015l).

Official development assistance: Although the bulk of aid flows to South Asia originate from OECD countries, among non-OECD countries both India and China are increasingly important sources of development finance (mixing grants, loans and project finance). The recently signed US$46 billion China Pakistan Economic Corridor (CPEC) agreement should see rising investment in energy, port and transport infrastructure in Pakistan over the next few years. India, meanwhile, allocates nearly two thirds of its foreign aid budget to Bhutan, and significant amounts to Nepal, Afghanistan, Sri Lanka and Bangladesh (Piccio 2015).

How large are the potential intra regional spillovers from the region's largest economy, India?

India's sizeable remittances and FDI flows to neighboring countries may give rise to spillovers. To analyze spillovers within the region, a Bayesian structural vector autoregression model is estimated using quarterly data to 2015Q2 from 1998Q1 (Bangladesh) 2002Q2 (Sri Lanka) or 2001Q3 (Pakistan), the only countries in the region with sufficient data. The model focuses on the short- and medium term effects of negative growth shocks in India on other countries in the region. The estimation includes G7 country growth, JP Morgan's Emerging Market Bond Index, India's growth, a trade-weighted commodity price index, and SAR country growth and real effective exchange rate. Data is available for Bangladesh, Pakistan, and Sri

---

[1]Several countries run sizable merchandise trade deficits with India, including Nepal, Bhutan, Bangladesh and Sri Lanka. Large imports from India mainly reflect capital goods (in Bhutan, related to hydropower investments), other production-side inputs and food in the smaller landlocked countries. In Bangladesh, for instance, these comprise mainly cotton for the garment sector, food and other consumer goods.

[2]FDI inflows from Mauritius and Singapore may also, indirectly, originate in India.

BOX 2.5.1 Regional integration and spillovers: South Asia *(continued)*

FIGURE 2.5.1.3 Financial flows to SAR

Relative to GDP, capital flows to South Asia are smaller than to other major developing regions, excluding MNA. They are dominated by banking sector flows, mainly from the United Kingdom. India receives over 90 percent of FDI inflows. South Asia's diaspora is the largest among developing regions, with a substantial number located in GCC countries.

A. Capital flows to developing regions, 2014

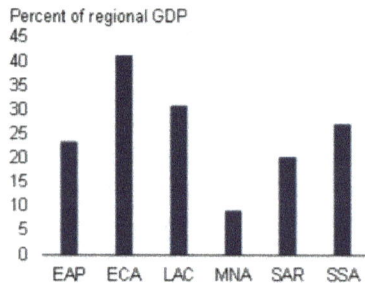

B. Composition of capital flows to South Asia

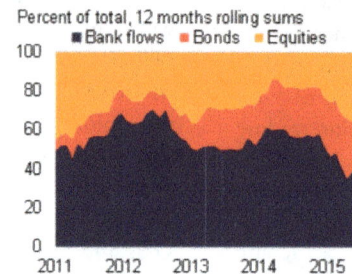

C. BIS foreign claims on SAR by source

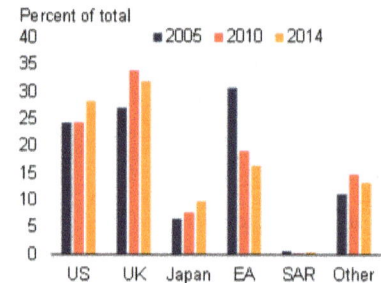

D. FDI flows by country, 2014

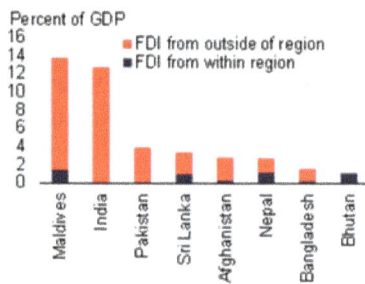

E. FDI inflows, 2003-11

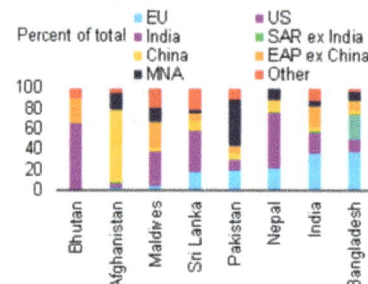

F. South Asian migrants by destination, 2013

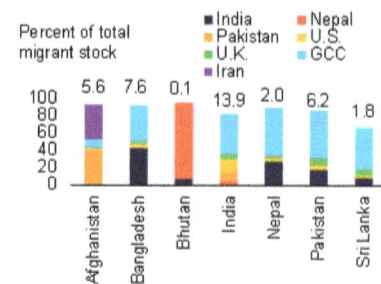

Source: IMF, World Bank, BIS, UNCTAD.
Note: Weighted averages.
A.C.E. EA stands for Euro Area. EU stands for European Union. EAP stands for East Asia and Pacific. ECA stands for Europe and Central Asia. LAC stands for Latin America and the Caribbean. MNA stands for Middle East and North Africa. SAR stands for South Asia Region. SSA stands for Sub-Saharan Africa.
F. Number above columns indicate total number of migrants in millions of people. GCC stands for Gulf Cooperation Council.

Lanka. For Bangladesh and Pakistan, industrial production growth is used to proxy real GDP growth.

The estimates suggest that spillovers from a 1 percent negative growth shock in India result in a 0.6 percentage points decline in Bangladesh, and a 0.2 percentage points fall in Sri Lanka. There are no statistically significant spillovers for Pakistan (Figure 2.5.1.4). Other studies find positive, but modest, spillovers from India to Pakistan, Sri Lanka and Bangladesh (World Bank 2013b; IMF 2014e). Using a panel regression framework covering 1961-2009, Ding and Masha (2012) find that growth in India is useful in explaining overall growth in South Asia, but only after 1995, and that a 1 percentage point increase in India's growth is associated with a 0.37 percentage point increase for South Asian countries.

Estimated within-region growth spillovers are smaller than those from the rest of the world to the region. A 1 percentage point decline in GDP growth in G-7 countries causes growth in India to fall by 1.7 percentage points. This is broadly in line with earlier findings that external spillovers to India are smaller than those in other more open economies in East Asia (Chapter 3, Box 3.5). They are, however, larger than other results in the literature that find that a 1 percentage point decline in U.S. GDP is associated with a 0.12 percent fall below baseline in India's GDP (IMF 2014e). In Bangladesh and Sri Lanka, growth falls by 1.2 and 0.5 percentage points respectively in response to a 1 percent decline in global growth, and by 2 percentage points in Pakistan (although, as before, the last result is not statistically significant). This is consistent with World Bank (2013b) that finds that a positive impulse

BOX 2.5.1 Regional integration and spillovers: South Asia (continued)

from the US or other advanced economies tends to be associated with a one- to two- quarter initial increase in cyclical real GDP in India and the rest of South Asia. Financial shocks and rising global financial volatility reduce output and depreciate the exchange rate in India (IMF 2014e, 2015j).[3]

Conclusion

Limited global and regional economic integration in South Asia partly reflects business environments that have constrained the ability to do business across borders and policies that have weighed on competitiveness, growth and job creation (Palit and Spittel 2013, De et al. 2012). For instance, an improvement in South Asia's infrastructure to around 50 percent of East Asia's could improve intra-regional trade by about 60 percent (Wilson and Ostuki 2005). Although India is major source of spillovers for some economies, poor trade and transport connectivity in South Asia also implies fewer benefits to smaller economies in the region (relative to potential) from stronger growth in India.

While the closed nature of the region (compared with other emerging market regions) has reduced exposure to large global shocks, it also limits the potential of South Asian firms to benefit from the strengthening of demand in the United States and Europe over the medium term. At the same time, the scope for negative spillovers from global financial market volatility may be rising as India increasingly integrates into global capital markets. This was evident during the "taper tantrum" of 2013, although vulnerabilities have since receded.

FIGURE 2.5.1.4 Global and regional growth spillovers

Spillovers from a growth shock in India are sizeable for Bangladesh, modest for Sri Lanka and statistically uninformative for Pakistan. Spillovers from large advanced countries are larger, reflecting greater integration with trading partners outside the region.

A. Impact of a 1 percentage point decline in India's growth

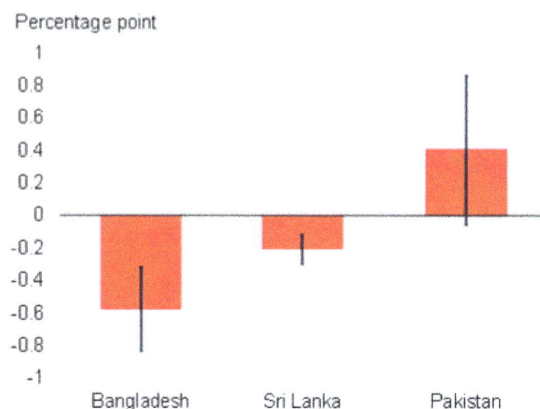

B. Impact of a 1 percentage point decline in G7 growth on growth

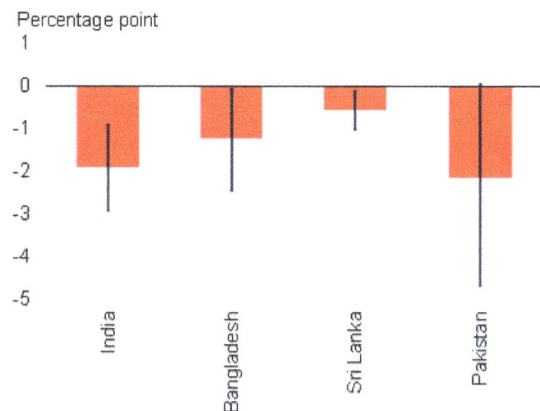

Source: World Bank.
Notes: Based on country-specific structural vector autoregressions (VARs) using the earliest possible data from 1998:1 to 2015:2 for India, Pakistan, Bangladesh and Sri Lanka; time series coverage for some countries is shorter. The country-specific VARs include G7 growth, the EMBI, a trade-weighted commodity price index, India's growth and country-specific growth of spillover source and recipients. For instance, when Pakistan is the spillover destination country, the variables include, in this Cholesky ordering: G-7 growth, EMBI, India's growth, Pakistan's trade-weighted commodity prices, Pakistan's growth, and Pakistan's real effective exchange rates. The model includes a dummy that captures the global financial crisis of 2008-09. Further details of the model, including the construction of the trade weighted commodity prices, are provided in Annex 3.2. Solid bars indicate medians and error bars indicate the 33-66 percent confidence bands.

---

[3]Although India's capital account remains relatively closed, an active offshore derivatives market in the Indian Rupee may be a conduit for volatility in global markets to currency markets.

SUB-SAHARAN AFRICA

Economic activity in Sub-Saharan Africa slowed to 3.4 percent in 2015 from 4.6 percent the previous year. A combination of external and domestic factors was responsible for the slowdown. External factors included lower commodity prices, a slowdown in major trading partners, and tightening borrowing conditions. Domestic factors included political instability and conflict, and electricity shortages. In 2016, GDP growth is projected to pick up to 4.2 percent, as commodity prices stabilize and supply constraints ease. Nonetheless, risks remain tilted to the downside. Domestic risks include political uncertainty associated with upcoming elections and the Boko Haram insurgency. In addition, power shortages might not ease as the forecast assumes. External risks include the possibilities of a further drop in commodity prices, a faster than expected slowdown in China, and a decline in capital flows as the United States normalizes monetary policy. Rising fiscal and external vulnerabilities, and domestic constraints to growth, pose challenges for policy, particularly among commodity exporters, where extreme poverty rates remain very high.

Recent developments

Economic activity in Sub-Saharan Africa (SSA) decelerated from 4.6 percent in 2014 to 3.4 percent in 2015, the weakest performance since 2009, due to a combination of external shocks and domestic constraints (Table 2.6.1). The slowdown was most pronounced among oil exporters. In Nigeria, the region's largest economy and oil exporter, growth slowed to 3.3 percent, down from 6.3 percent in 2014. Growth moderated in several mineral and metal exporters – including Mauritania, South Africa, and Zambia (Table 2.6.2). In South Africa, the economy expanded by 1.3 percent, compared with 1.5 percent in 2014. With the Ebola crisis receding, activity rebounded somewhat in Liberia, but remained weak in the other affected countries (Guinea, Sierra Leone) with GDP falling sharply in Sierra Leone as mining production contracted. Activity weakened substantially in Burundi and South Sudan amid political instability and civil strife. However, in other countries, including low-income ones and some fragile states—Côte d'Ivoire, Rwanda, and Tanzania—growth remained robust,

reflecting lower exposure to the commodity slowdown, and tailwinds from large-scale infrastructure investment.

Following their sharp decline in 2014, commodity prices weakened further in 2015 (Figure 2.6.1A). The prices of oil and metals, such as iron ore, copper, and platinum, declined substantially. Those of some agricultural commodities, such as coffee, fell moderately, although the prices of cocoa and tea showed small gains. The region's pattern of exports makes it particularly vulnerable to commodity price shocks. Fuels, ores, and metals accounted for more than 60 percent of the region's total exports in 2010-14 compared with 16 percent for manufactured goods (Figure 2.6.1B).

Lower commodity prices obliged a fiscal tightening in several commodity exporters, which caused a sharp slowdown. Angola and Nigeria are heavily dependent on oil for fiscal revenues and reserves—oil accounts for more than 60 percent of their fiscal revenues and more than 80 percent of exports. Governments in the two countries reduced expenditures sharply, which adversely impacted other areas of their economies. The decline in metal prices hit Mauritania and Zambia

Note: The author of this section is Gerard Kambou. Research assistance was provided by Xinghao Gong.

FIGURE 2.6.1 **Commodity market developments**

Following sharp declines in 2014, commodity prices weakened further in 2015. Expectations of slower global growth and abundant supplies led to a renewed plunge in the price of oil. The prices of ores and metals, such as iron ore, copper, and platinum, also declined substantially. With fuels, ores, and metals accounting for more than 60 percent of its exports, the region is particularly vulnerable to commodity price shocks.

A. Commodity prices

B. Share of commodities in SSA exports

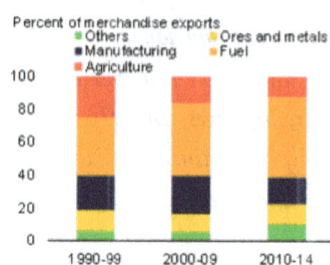

Source: World Bank, World Integrated Trade Solutions database, 2015.

hard, as low prices of copper and iron ore prompted mining companies to reduce production and to delay planned investments; exports, employment, and domestic spending fell. Exporters of agricultural commodities, which include many of the region's low-income countries, experienced a less pronounced slowdown in activity as a result of the relatively moderate decline in the price of their exports.

Low commodity prices reflected weak global demand for raw materials, including from large developing countries where growth has continued to slow. Most importantly, the region has had to deal with a pronounced slowdown in major trading partners. SSA's external trade has undergone a shift in direction towards China and away from traditional advanced country trading partners, driven by China's demand for primary commodities (Box 2.6.1). As SSA's largest national trading partner, China's rebalancing away from raw material-intensive sectors has direct implications for the region. In addition, foreign direct investment flows from China have grown rapidly in recent years and are important for several countries (e.g., Zambia and South Africa), although the United States and the Euro Area still remain the largest sources of FDI in the region. Spillovers from China's slowdown are likely to be transmitted to countries in SSA through trade and financial channels. World Bank estimates suggest

that these effects could be sizeable and have likely contributed to the ongoing slowdown in the region.[1]

Capital flows to the region slowed in 2015, as cross-border bank lending declined (Figure 2.6.2A). Many countries tapped the international bond market to finance their investment programs, taking advantage of the global low-interest-rate environment, and investors' search for yield. Côte d'Ivoire's sovereign bond issuance in February was followed by five other countries – Gabon, Zambia, Ghana, Angola, and Cameroon – with Angola and Cameroon issuing maiden 10-year bonds. Yields were higher than in previous issuances, however. They exceeded 9 percent in several countries and 10 percent in Ghana. Sovereign spreads rose across the region (Figure 2.6.2B). This indicates a re-assessment of risk among sovereign-debt investors as global headwinds, and the expectation of a rate hike by the U.S. Federal Reserve that materialized in December, weigh on the region. Increased foreign exchange liabilities, which leave many countries vulnerable to the risk that future currency depreciation could pressure debt servicing costs, would be a factor in this re-assessment.

The external headwinds of low commodity prices, of a slowdown in major emerging markets, and rising borrowing costs were compounded by domestic problems. These included severe infrastructure constraints, especially power supply, in several countries. The slowdown in Nigeria was accounted for by non-oil sectors (Figure 2.6.3A). A large part of the slowdown in manufacturing was oil-related as oil refining recorded a steep decline. However, the pronounced contraction of manufacturing in the first half of 2015 also reflected Nigeria's huge infrastructure and electricity deficits, which are impairing factory operations. In South Africa, power supply bottlenecks, compounded by a severe drought and difficult labor relations, weighed heavily on growth (Figure 2.6.3B). Insufficient power supply

---

[1]A recent World Bank study (Lakatos et al. 2015) finds that a slowdown in China's GDP growth to an average of 6 percent per year over 2016-30 and to 4.6 percent in 2030 could result in a GDP loss in Sub-Saharan Africa of 1.1 percent compared with the baseline by 2030.

emerged as a leading constraint to activity in a number of frontier markets, including Botswana, Ghana, and Zambia. In some countries (Botswana, Zambia), shortages of hydroelectric power were due to drought; in others, they were driven by underinvestment in new capacity (South Africa), and lack of reforms to encourage private investment (Ghana, Nigeria).

The growth slowdown was associated with mounting fiscal vulnerabilities in a number of countries. Fiscal deficits widened in oil exporters (Republic of Congo, Gabon, Nigeria) due to falling revenues. In other countries, the widening deficits reflected increased government spending, including on arrears (Zambia), infrastructure projects (Kenya), and subsidies (Malawi). Some countries (Angola, Ghana) implemented expenditure measures – including removing fuel subsidies and freezing public sector hiring – that reduced the deficits. In many countries, fiscal deficits are larger relative to GDP than they were at the onset of the global financial crisis (Figure 2.6.4A). As a result, government debt ratios have continued to rise (Figure 2.6.4B). While debt-to-GDP ratios remain manageable in most low-income countries, they rose rapidly in several frontier markets, led by non-concessional borrowing. By contrast, Nigeria's sovereign debt has remained low, at less than 15 percent of GDP.

External imbalances widened across the region. Current account balances turned sharply negative in Angola and Nigeria due to lower oil prices. Deficits remained large among oil importers because of low commodity prices and rising non-oil imports. In Kenya, the current account deficit remained high as security concerns weighed on tourism earnings. In South Africa, in contrast, the current account deficit narrowed on the back of export growth. In addition, the depreciation of the rand partly offset the decline in commodity prices. In Ghana, Kenya, and Namibia, the twin fiscal and current account deficits have remained large.

High fiscal and current account deficits, combined with strong demand for the U.S. dollar, kept currencies under pressure. Currencies of commodity exporters and frontier-market economies saw sharp depreciations against the U.S. dollar. However, because of inflation, the

FIGURE 2.6.2 Capital market developments

Capital flows to the region slowed in 2015, led by reduced cross-border bank lending. Several countries tapped the international bond market, taking advantage of the global low-interest rate environment and investors' search for yield. However, yields were higher, as sovereign spreads rose, reflecting a re-assessment of risk by investors as headwinds, and expectations of interest rate increases in the U.S., weighed on the region.

A. Capital flows

B. Sovereign bond spreads

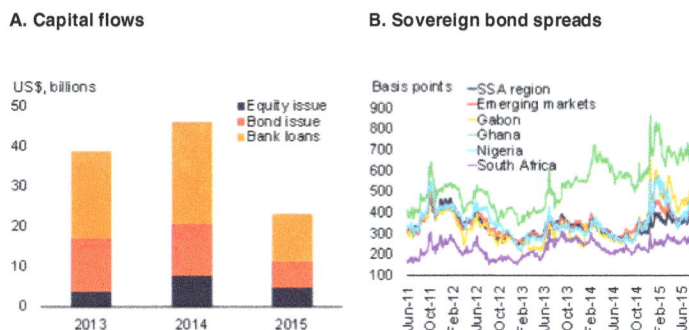

Source: Dealogic, Bloomberg.
A. Data for 2015 are from January to September.

average movement in real effective exchange rates across the entire region was relatively small (Figure 2.6.5A). The Ghanaian cedi weakened the most, by more than 30 percent, in large part because of loose monetary and fiscal policies, followed by the South African rand. The Nigerian naira was about 5 percent stronger than its 2014 average. Early in 2015, the Central Bank of Nigeria introduced a range of administrative measures to stem the demand for foreign currencies. These measures have hampered private sector activities. A severe liquidity squeeze emerged in the interbank market in the second half of 2015, prompting the central bank to reduce the cash reserve ratio.

Consumer price inflation remained moderate across the region, except in Ghana, Angola, and Zambia, where it was in the double digits (Figure 2.6.5B). Low fuel prices helped keep inflation down. However, currency weaknesses contributed to higher inflation in many countries. In Angola and Nigeria, inflation exceeded the central bank's target. Concerns about inflation led central banks in several countries to hike interest rates (Angola, Ghana, Kenya, Mozambique, South Africa, Uganda, Zambia). The Central Bank of Nigeria, in contrast, cut the benchmark interest rate in an attempt to stimulate growth. In CFA franc countries, the peg to the euro kept inflation low, and underpinned greater economic stability.

FIGURE 2.6.3 Domestic constraints

The headwinds of low commodity prices and higher borrowing costs were compounded by severe infrastructure constraints in many countries. In Nigeria, the pronounced contraction of the manufacturing sector reflected huge electricity deficits. In South Africa, power supply bottlenecks, compounded by difficult labor relations, weighed heavily on growth.

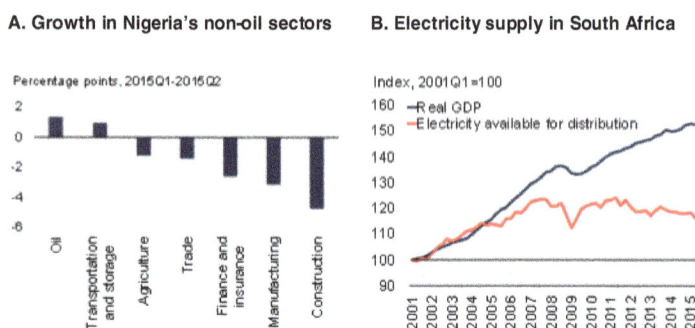

A. Growth in Nigeria's non-oil sectors

B. Electricity supply in South Africa

Source: Nigeria National Bureau of Statistics, Statistics South Africa.

Outlook

Sub-Saharan Africa faces a challenging near-term outlook. Commodity prices are expected to stabilize but remain low through 2017 (Figure 2.6.6A). The normalization of U.S. monetary policy is expected to tighten global financial conditions. Although governments are taking steps to resolve power issues, electricity supply bottlenecks are expected to persist. These factors point to a somewhat weaker recovery in 2016 than previously anticipated. After slowing to 3.4 percent in 2015, activity is expected to pick up to 4.2 percent in 2016 and to 4.7 percent in 2017-18 (Figure 2.6.6B). This projection assumes that commodity prices stabilize and electricity constraints ease (Table 2.6.1). There are, however, considerable variations within the region.

Consumption dynamics will continue to differ for oil exporters and importers. Private consumption growth is expected to remain weak in oil exporters as the removal of subsidies to alleviate pressure on budgets results in higher fuel costs, and as currency depreciation weigh on consumers' purchasing power. By contrast, lower inflation in oil importers, owing in part to lower fuel prices, should help boost consumer spending. The price level impact of currency depreciation combined with interest rate increases could, however, moderate these effects.

Investment dynamics will also differ among SSA commodity exporters. The slowdown in major emerging markets, low commodity prices, and deteriorating growth prospects in many commodity exporters, are expected to result in lower FDI flows. Exploration and development activity is expected to be curtailed in oil and gas. Continuing fiscal consolidation in oil-exporting countries is expected to result in further capital expenditure cuts, as governments seek to limit cuts in public-sector wages and protect social spending. However, in a number of low-income, non-oil commodity exporters, governments are expected to continue to invest heavily in energy and transport infrastructure in a bid to improve the operational environment for growth, drawing in part on the proceeds from previous bond issuances (Ethiopia), public-private partnerships (Mozambique, Rwanda, Tanzania), donor aid (Rwanda) and, in some cases, financing from Chinese entities (Ethiopia, Tanzania). Although debt levels may rise, they remain manageable in most low-income countries as growth has been robust.

The fiscal policy stance in commodity exporters is expected to ease gradually as commodity prices stabilize. In Nigeria, ongoing efforts to rationalize the management and operation of the Nigeria National Petroleum Corporation should also help enhance revenue mobilization. However, with oil prices projected to remain below their recent peaks, fiscal revenues are expected to remain low in Angola and Nigeria. As a result, fiscal deficits are likely to increase in these countries, despite efforts to restrain spending. Fiscal deficits are also expected to remain elevated in oil importers, as spending on goods and services, wages, and physical infrastructure continues to expand.

Net exports are expected to make a negative contribution to real GDP growth in the near term, despite currency depreciations. Still-low commodity prices will depress export receipts, especially among oil exporters, even as export volumes rise. The pull from advanced economies is expected to stay modest, given their moderate prospects for medium-term growth. Among oil importers, current account balances are expected to deteriorate in many countries on account of strong import growth, driven by capital goods imports for infrastructure projects.

In this context:

- Activity is expected to remain subdued in the region's three largest economies (Table 2.6.2). In Nigeria, power and fuel shortages, and fiscal consolidation, which weighed on activity in 2015, are expected to diminish gradually. Growth is expected to remain weak in South Africa, as inadequate power supply, weak business confidence, difficult labor relations, and policy tightening slow activity. In Angola, government spending remains constrained, and elevated inflation has weakened consumer spending.

- Among the region's frontier markets, rising oil production and diminishing fiscal and current account imbalances are expected to help lift growth in Ghana. However, in Zambia, low copper prices, compounded by regulatory uncertainty and electricity shortages, will curtail copper production, export, and investment. Meanwhile, despite pressure on the shilling, Kenya is expected to grow at a robust pace, supported by large-scale infrastructure projects, including the expansion of the railway system, which should help boost domestic trade, and a new port.

- The region's low-income countries are expected to continue to sustain high GDP growth. Many of these countries have limited exposure to the commodities that are experiencing the most severe decline in prices. Meanwhile, large-scale investment projects in energy and transport are ongoing, consumer spending remains robust, boosted by lower fuel prices, and despite low minerals prices, mining output is set to rise in several countries. Public investment, consumer spending, and mining production will help Côte d'Ivoire, Ethiopia, Mozambique, Rwanda, and Tanzania sustain rapid growth in 2016 and beyond. Several low-income countries in the West African Economic and Monetary Union (WAEMU)[2] region are

[2]WAEMU countries are Benin, Burkina Faso, Côte d'Ivoire, Guinea Bissau, Mali Niger, Senegal, and Togo. They share the same currency, the CFA franc, which is pegged to the euro.

FIGURE 2.6.4 Fiscal deficits and government debt

Fiscal deficits widened across the region. In oil exporters, it was due to falling oil revenues. In other countries, the widening deficits reflected higher government spending, including on wages, infrastructure projects, and subsidies and transfers. In a few countries, measures were implemented that reduced the deficits. In many countries, fiscal deficits are now larger than at the onset of the financial crisis. As a result, government debt has continued to rise, especially in frontier markets.

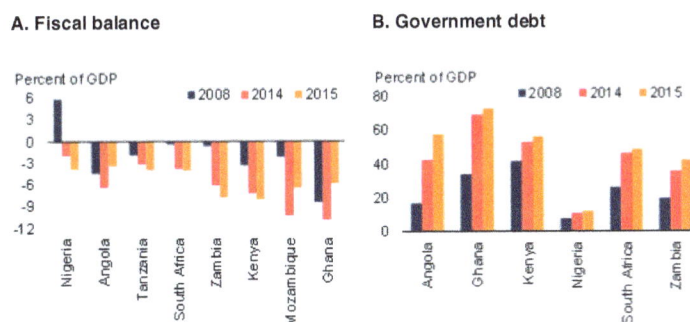

A. Fiscal balance

B. Government debt

Source: IMF Fiscal Monitor, IMF World Economic Outlook.

expected to see steady growth, helped in part by the stable currency peg to the euro.

Risks

The balance of risks to the outlook remains tilted to the downside. On the domestic front, political upheavals and conflicts in Burundi, Burkina Faso, and South Sudan suggest that political risks associated with the electoral process will remain a key issue for the region in 2016. Security risks tied to Boko Haram insurgencies are significant for Cameroon, Chad, Niger, and Nigeria; while terrorist threats remain a concern for Kenya and Mali. These events could generate greater political instability for the region if they were to escalate, hurting growth. The assumption that electric power constraints will ease might prove too optimistic. The power supply crisis may worsen, as a result of a lack of reforms, which would hold economic activity back in many countries.

Many countries of the region have domestic macroeconomic weaknesses that leave them vulnerable to shocks. In these countries, fiscal and current account deficits are sizeable and debt levels are rising. If these conditions were to deteriorate significantly, shocks could manifest themselves in substantial currency pressures, higher inflation, and lower business confidence.

FIGURE 2.6.5 Exchange rates and inflation

High fiscal and current account deficits kept currencies under pressure, particularly against the U.S. dollar. However, in real effective terms, the average exchange rate movement for SSA as a whole has been relatively small. Inflation remained moderate for the most part in the region, helped by low commodity prices, although currency weaknesses contributed to higher inflation in many countries, including Angola, Ghana, and Zambia.

A. Real effective exchange rates

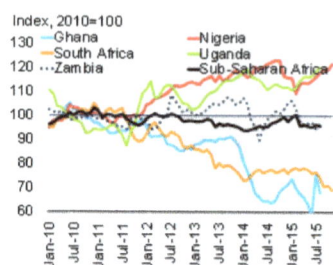

B. Consumer price inflation

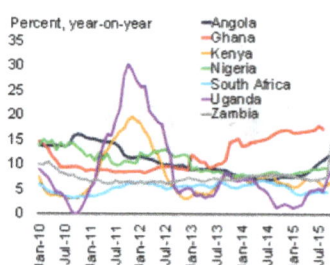

Source: Haver Analytics, World Bank.
A. An increase denotes real appreciation.

On the external front, there are a number of major risks to the forecast. A further decline in oil prices would sharply reduce government spending in oil-producing countries. A sharper-than-expected slowdown in China could result in a renewed across-the-board weakening in commodity prices, which would delay further or lead to a cancelation of planned investments in resource sectors. A sudden deterioration in global liquidity conditions could push up financing costs and result in cut-offs of capital flows.

Policy challenges

The global economic environment will be less conducive to growth in Sub-Saharan Africa over the next several years than in the recent past. Lower commodity prices and tightening global financial conditions will hinder activity. In most commodity exporters, thin buffers limit the scope for counter-cyclical policies to support economic activity without exacerbating existing fiscal and external vulnerabilities. Policies are needed to respond to growing vulnerabilities, address domestic constraints to activity, and promote non-commodity sources of growth.

Oil, mineral, and metal exporters are the most exposed to the decline in commodity prices. In these countries, exchange rate flexibility could help an adjustment to a low commodity-price environment. However, they may need to tighten their macroeconomic policy stances, and strengthen their monetary policy frameworks, to prevent inflation induced by currency depreciation from becoming a constant threat. It will also be critical for these countries to carefully manage sovereign borrowing on international capital markets.

In many countries, measures to strengthen domestic resource mobilization to reduce overdependence on revenue from the resource sector, and to raise the efficiency of public expenditures, are needed to rebuild fiscal space and resilience to shocks. Funding much-needed social programs and public infrastructure could help reduce the inequality of opportunity that is contributing to high poverty rates in the region (World Bank 2015r).

Resource-rich countries would benefit from improving their non-resource tax systems. Tax revenues in SSA, as a share of GDP, have increased since the 1980s. However, much of the improvement was driven by the growth in revenues from oil producers. Excluding resource-based revenues, there has been limited improvement in the domestic mobilization of tax revenues in the region. A number of studies (AfDB and OECD 2010) have identified broad areas in which tax systems in SSA could usefully strengthened. In the short run, policy makers need to concentrate on ways to broaden the tax base. Policy options include removing tax preferences, streamlining transfer pricing by multinational companies, and doing a better job of taxing extractive industries fairly and transparently. In the medium term, policy makers need to design strategies to bring small enterprises into the tax net and boost administrative capacity. Over the long run, instruments such as urban property taxes could help generate revenues from a more balanced tax mix.

The decline in commodity prices makes it important for resource-rich countries to improve their public investment management (PIM) system, which could help boost growth (Rajaram et al. 2014). SSA's oil-exporters, on average, have lower PIM scores than others, especially at the project appraisal and evaluation stages of the PIM process (Dabla-Norris et al. 2011), reflecting weak administrative capacity and low transparency in the use of public resources. Upgrading the quality of infrastructure investment spending in these countries would require enhancing the planning, bidding, contracting, and evaluation process of quality projects, and improving the selection and implementation of these projects (Keefer and Knack 2007).

Structural reforms are needed to alleviate domestic impediments to growth and to accelerate economic diversification. Creating the conditions for a more competitive manufacturing sector would require, in particular, a major improvement in providing electricity. Addressing power sector problems should therefore be a priority. Investments in new energy capacity (South Africa), attention to drought and its effects on hydropower (Botswana, Zambia), and a new focus on encouraging private investment (Ghana, Nigeria) would help build resilience in the power sector.

An increasing share of the world's poor resides in Sub-Saharan Africa (World Bank 2015j). Reviving growth and reducing vulnerabilities will be important for progress toward eradicating extreme poverty, and achieving the recently adopted Sustainable Development Goals. Policies to enhance domestic revenue mobilization, increase the efficiency of public spending, and boost growth and economic diversification will play a critical role in these efforts.

FIGURE 2.6.6 Outlook

Prices of SSA's commodity exports are expected to stabilize but remain low throughout 2017, China is in the midst of rebalancing growth away from raw-material-intensive sectors, and the normalization of U.S. monetary policy is expected to tighten global financial conditions. Electricity supply bottlenecks are also expected to persist in many countries. These factors point to a weaker recovery in 2016 than previously anticipated.

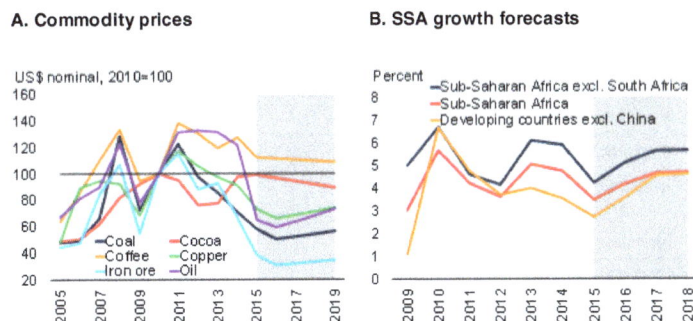

A. Commodity prices

B. SSA growth forecasts

Source: World Bank.
Note: Shaded area denotes an estimated or forecast value.

TABLE 2.6.1 Sub-Saharan Africa forecast summary
(Annual percent change unless indicated otherwise)

(Percentage point difference from June 2015 projections)

	2013	2014	2015e	2016f	2017f	2018f	2015e	2016f	2017f
Developing SSA, GDP[a]	4.9	4.6	3.4	4.2	4.7	4.7	-0.8	-0.3	-0.3
(Average including countries with full national accounts and balance of payments data only)[b]									
Developing SSA, GDP[b]	4.8	4.6	3.5	4.2	4.7	4.7	-0.7	-0.4	-0.3
GDP per capita (U.S. dollars)	2.0	1.9	0.8	1.5	2.0	2.0	-0.9	-0.6	-0.5
PPP GDP	5.0	4.9	3.7	4.4	4.9	5.0	-0.7	-0.4	-0.3
Private consumption[c]	9.9	3.2	3.1	3.7	4.0	4.1	-0.9	-0.5	-0.5
Public consumption	1.9	3.9	3.2	3.5	3.7	3.8	-0.4	-0.2	-0.1
Fixed investment	9.6	8.7	6.2	6.6	7.1	7.2	-0.5	-0.7	-0.7
Exports, GNFS[d]	-2.2	5.0	2.1	2.6	2.9	2.9	-0.7	-0.5	-0.4
Imports, GNFS[d]	6.8	3.0	3.0	3.1	3.2	3.2	0.0	0.0	0.0
Net exports, contribution to growth	-2.8	0.5	-0.3	-0.2	-0.2	-0.2	-0.2	-0.1	-0.2
Memo items: GDP									
Broader geographic region[e]	4.8	4.5	3.3	4.2	4.6	4.7	-0.7	-0.3	-0.4
SSA excluding South Africa	5.8	5.7	4.1	5.1	5.7	5.7	-0.8	-0.3	-0.2
Oil exporters[f]	5.5	5.4	3.3	4.5	5.2	5.2	-0.8	-0.3	-0.3
CFA countries[g]	4.6	5.5	4.4	5.7	6.0	5.9	0.3	0.2	0.0
South Africa	2.2	1.5	1.3	1.4	1.6	1.6	-0.7	-0.7	-0.8
Nigeria	5.4	6.3	3.3	4.6	5.3	5.3	-1.2	-0.4	-0.2
Angola	6.8	3.9	3.0	3.3	3.8	3.8	-1.5	-0.6	-1.3

Source: World Bank.
World Bank forecasts are frequently updated based on new information and changing (global) circumstances. Consequently, projections presented here may differ from those contained in other Bank documents, even if basic assessments of countries' prospects do not differ at any given moment in time.
a. GDP at market prices and expenditure components are measured in constant 2010 U.S. dollars. Excludes Somalia, Central African Republic, and São Tomé and Principe.
b. Sub-region aggregate excludes Liberia, Somalia, Central African Republic, São Tomé and Principe, and South Sudan, for which data limitations prevent the forecasting of GDP components.
c. The sudden surge in private consumption in the region in 2013 is driven by the revised and rebased NIA data of Nigeria in 2014.
d. Exports and imports of goods and non-factor services (GNFS).
e. Includes developing SSA and the following high-income countries: Equatorial Guinea and Seychelles.
f. Includes Angola; Côte d'Ivoire; Cameroon; Congo, Rep.; Gabon; Nigeria; Sudan; Chad; and Congo, Dem. Rep.
g. Includes Benin; Burkina Faso; Central African Republic; Côte d'Ivoire; Cameroon, Congo, Rep.; Gabon; Equatorial Guinea; Mali; Niger; Senegal; Chad; and Togo.

TABLE 2.6.2 Sub-Saharan Africa country forecasts[a]
(Real GDP growth at market prices in percent, unless indicated otherwise)

	2013	2014	2015e	2016f	2017f	2018f	(Percentage point difference from June 2015 projections)		
							2015e	2016f	2017f
Angola	6.8	3.9	3.0	3.3	3.8	3.8	-1.5	-0.6	-1.3
Benin	5.6	5.4	5.7	5.3	5.1	5.1	1.1	0.7	0.4
Botswana[b]	9.3	4.4	3.0	4.0	4.2	4.2	-1.3	-0.2	0.0
Burkina Faso	6.7	4.0	4.4	6.0	7.0	7.0	-0.6	-0.2	0.5
Burundi	4.6	4.7	-2.3	3.5	4.8	4.8	-7.1	-1.5	-0.4
Cabo Verde	1.0	1.8	2.9	3.5	4.1	4.1	-0.1	0.1	0.6
Cameroon	5.6	5.9	6.3	6.5	6.5	6.4	2.3	1.9	1.5
Chad	5.7	7.3	4.1	4.9	6.1	6.5	-4.9	0.2	0.5
Comoros	3.5	3.0	2.3	2.5	3.1	3.1	-1.1	-1.2	-0.7
Congo, Dem. Rep.	8.5	9.0	8.0	8.6	9.0	9.0	0.0	0.1	0.0
Côte d'Ivoire	9.2	8.5	8.4	8.3	8.0	8.0	0.4	0.6	0.5
Eritrea	1.3	1.7	0.9	2.0	2.2	2.2	-0.6	0.0	0.0
Ethiopia[b]	10.5	9.9	10.2	10.2	9.0	9.0	0.7	-0.3	0.5
Gabon	4.3	4.3	4.1	5.1	5.3	5.3	0.1	-0.1	-0.2
Gambia, The	4.8	-0.2	4.0	4.5	5.3	5.3	1.0	-0.6	-0.8
Ghana	7.3	4.0	3.4	5.9	8.2	8.2	-0.1	0.0	0.4
Guinea	2.3	-0.3	0.4	3.5	4.0	4.2	0.7	1.2	1.5
Guinea-Bissau	0.3	2.5	4.4	4.9	5.3	5.3	0.2	1.0	1.3
Kenya	5.7	5.3	5.4	5.7	6.1	6.1	-0.6	-0.9	-0.4
Lesotho	4.6	2.0	2.6	2.8	4.5	4.5	-1.4	-1.7	0.0
Liberia	8.7	1.0	3.0	5.7	6.8	6.8	..	..	..
Madagascar	2.4	3.0	3.2	3.4	3.6	3.6	-1.4	-1.4	-1.4
Malawi	5.2	5.7	2.8	5.0	5.8	5.8	-2.3	-0.6	-0.1
Mali	1.7	7.2	5.0	5.0	5.0	5.0	-0.6	-0.1	-0.2
Mauritania	5.5	6.9	3.2	4.0	4.0	4.0	-2.3	-1.7	-1.6
Mauritius	3.3	3.6	3.5	3.7	3.7	3.7	0.0	0.0	0.0
Mozambique	7.3	7.4	6.3	6.5	7.2	7.2	-0.9	-0.8	-0.1
Namibia	5.7	6.4	5.0	5.5	5.9	5.9	-0.5	0.2	0.8
Niger	4.6	6.9	4.4	5.3	9.3	5.7	-0.1	-0.2	1.6
Nigeria	5.4	6.3	3.3	4.6	5.3	5.3	-1.2	-0.4	-0.2
Rwanda	4.7	7.0	7.4	7.6	7.6	7.6	0.4	0.6	0.1
Senegal	3.5	3.9	5.0	5.3	5.3	5.3	0.2	0.3	0.1
Sierra Leone	20.1	7.0	-20.0	6.6	5.3	5.3	-7.2	-1.8	-3.6
South Africa	2.2	1.5	1.3	1.4	1.6	1.6	-0.7	-0.7	-0.8
South Sudan	13.1	3.4	-5.3	3.5	7.0	7.0	..	..	..
Sudan	3.3	3.1	3.5	3.4	3.9	3.9	0.9	-0.1	0.0
Swaziland	2.8	2.5	1.3	0.8	0.8	0.8	-0.7	-1.0	-0.8
Tanzania	7.3	7.0	7.2	7.2	7.1	7.1	0.0	0.1	0.0
Togo	5.1	5.7	5.1	4.9	4.7	4.7	0.0	0.0	0.0
Uganda[b]	3.6	4.0	5.0	5.0	5.8	5.8	-0.5	-0.7	0.0
Zambia	6.7	5.6	3.5	3.8	5.4	6.0	-2.1	-2.4	-1.5
Zimbabwe	4.5	3.2	1.0	2.8	3.0	3.0	0.0	0.3	-0.5
Recently transitioned to high-income countries[c]									
Equatorial Guinea	-4.8	-3.1	-9.3	2.3	-0.4	-0.2	6.1	-1.3	-4.1
Seychelles	6.6	2.8	3.5	3.7	3.6	3.6	0.0	0.0	-0.1

Source: World Bank.

World Bank forecasts are frequently updated based on new information and changing (global) circumstances. Consequently, projections presented here may differ from those contained in other Bank documents, even if basic assessments of countries' prospects do not significantly differ at any given moment in time.

a. Central African Republic, São Tomé and Principe, and Somalia are not forecast due to data limitations.

b. Fiscal-year based numbers.

c. Based on the World Bank's reclassification from 2004 to 2015.

BOX 2.6.1 Regional integration and spillovers: Sub-Saharan Africa

Over the past decade, regional integration in Sub-Saharan Africa (SSA) has expanded. Though still low, intraregional trade represents a growing share of the region's trade. Cross-border financing flows within Sub-Saharan Africa have increased rapidly. Nevertheless, shocks to growth in the two largest economies – Nigeria and South Africa – appear to have no measurable effects on other countries in the region.

Introduction

SSA is an open region, with diversified trade partners and sources of finance (Figure 2.6.1.1). Much of Sub-Saharan African trade takes place with countries outside the region. Advanced economies remain the largest destinations of Sub-Saharan Africa's exports. However, China and other developing countries in Asia are increasingly prominent. Intraregional trade and financial linkages within the region have expanded in recent years and look set to expand faster in the years ahead.

This box examines the extent of regional integration. In particular, it takes a closer look at linkages between SSA's two largest economies—Nigeria and South Africa—and the rest of the region to assess the potential significance of intra-regional growth spillovers. The box addresses the following questions:

- How open is Sub-Saharan Africa to global and regional trade and financial flows?

- How large are the potential intra-regional spillovers from the region's two largest economies, Nigeria and South Africa?

The region is highly open to the world economy, with a diverse group of trade and financial partners, and intra-regional ties have grown rapidly since the mid-2000s. Nevertheless, estimated growth spillovers from South Africa and Nigeria to the rest of SSA are statistically insignificant. This may reflect the globally diversified nature of SSA's global trade and financial partners. It may also reflect inadequate data for countries most closely integrated with South Africa and Nigeria.

How open is Sub-Saharan Africa to global and regional trade and financial flows?

SSA's integration into global trade networks has increased remarkably over the past three decades (UNCTAD 2013). Advanced economies remain the main trading partners for SSA. However, recent years have seen a fundamental shift in the direction of SSA trade towards China and away

from the traditional advanced country markets. The export exposure of SSA countries to advanced-economies has halved over the decade ending 2014. The fall in the share of the region's exports to the United States, to about 1 percent of GDP in 2014 from its peak of 8 percent in 2005, was particularly pronounced (Figure 2.6.1.2). This reflected in part a sharp decline in Nigeria's oil exports as U.S. oil shale production expanded. More broadly, the anemic recovery in Euro Area countries and other advanced economies following the global financial crisis underpinned the decline in the share of SSA's exports to advanced economies.

China's trade with Sub-Saharan Africa has been driven by China's fast growth of investment in capital goods that require intensive inputs of primary commodities, notably oil and metals (Drummond and Liu 2013). By 2012, China had become SSA's single largest national trading partner. Angola, Democratic Republic of Congo, Equatorial Guinea, Republic of Congo, and South Africa account for about 75 percent of SSA's exports to China (oil, metals, and mineral fuels). Similarly, Angola, Benin, Ghana, Liberia, Nigeria, and South Africa account for more than 80 percent of SSA's total imports from China (mainly machinery, chemicals, and manufactured goods).

Financial linkages between SSA and the rest of the world have grown considerably in the last decade, with some shift in composition towards flows into regional capital markets and direct investment.

- The stock of private external claims on SSA represented 40 percent of the region's GDP in 2013, slightly lower than its peak of 45 percent of GDP in 2010. Although most SSA countries have limited or no access to international capital markets, portfolio investment claims on the region—originating mostly from the U.S. and Euro Area—more than doubled between 2001 and 2010. South Africa, with its highly developed financial markets, has been the main recipient of portfolio investments. Cross-border banking claims on SSA, which before the global financial crisis had risen above portfolio claims, have since moderated. European banks have deleveraged and oriented their activities toward developing countries in Asia. Cross-border bank lending flows originate mainly from U.K. and Euro Area lenders,

Note: This box was prepared by Gerard Kambou and Jesper Hanson, with contributions from Raju Huidrom.

BOX 2.6.1 Regional integration and spillovers: Sub-Saharan Africa *(continued)*

with Angola, Botswana, Mozambique, Tanzania, and Zambia among the largest recipients. Foreign direct investments are the largest capital inflows to the region. FDI liabilities represented more than 15 percent of SSA's GDP in 2013. While the Euro Area remains an important source of FDI in the region, FDI flows from China have grown rapidly in recent years, and are mostly allocated to the natural resource and infrastructure sectors (World Bank 2015a).

- Remittances and official development assistance amounted to 2 percent and 1.5 percent of GDP in 2014 and 2013, respectively, lower than their levels in 2010. Official development assistance and remittances from advanced economies have been on a declining trend in recent years, reflecting weak growth and austerity budgets in these economies.

While most economic ties of SSA are to non-SSA countries, intraregional trade, foreign direct investment, cross-border banking flows, and remittances have risen in recent years (Figure 2.6.1.3). The number of Pan-African banking groups has increased rapidly across the region, partly influenced by rising trade flows (IMF 2015l). Furthermore, trade linkages between the region's largest economies (Nigeria and South Africa) and the rest of the region have been growing and look set to deepen.

Linkages between South Africa and the rest of the region

Trade linkages: South Africa, the region's second largest economy, accounting for 21 percent of its GDP, is an important export market for its immediate neighbors (Figure 2.6.1.4). In 2011, exports to South Africa accounted for over 80 percent of trade within the South African Customs Union, or SACU (Canales-Kriljenko, Gwenhamo and Thomas et al. 2013).[1] Exports to South Africa are particularly large for Swaziland (25 percent of GDP) and Lesotho (10 percent of GDP). Exports from SACU countries consist mostly of agricultural goods; they also include some manufacturing products, chemicals and metals. South Africa is also an important export market for countries in the 15-member Southern African Development Community (SADC) region, especially Mozambique (10 percent of GDP) and Zimbabwe (5 percent of GDP). Fuels dominate Mozambique's exports to South Africa, while Zimbabwe's exports consist mainly of agricultural goods and metals. By contrast, exports to

---

[1]SACU member countries are Botswana, Lesotho, Namibia, South Africa, and Swaziland.

FIGURE 2.6.1.1 Cross-region comparison

The region is open to global trade and finance. It accounts for about 2 percent of global GDP and trade. In relation to GDP, the levels of external trade, investment, and remittances for the average SSA economy are similar to other developing regions.

A. SSA: Share of global activity, trade, and finance, 2014

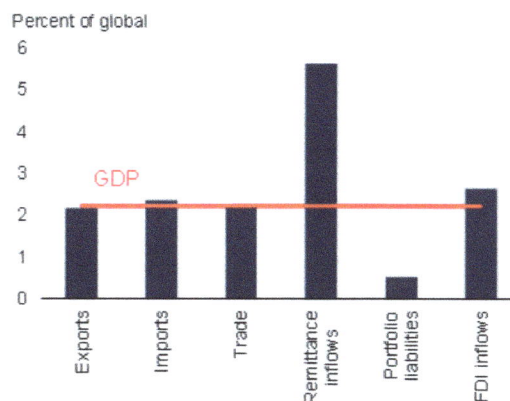

B. SSA: Trade and finance in regional comparison, 2014

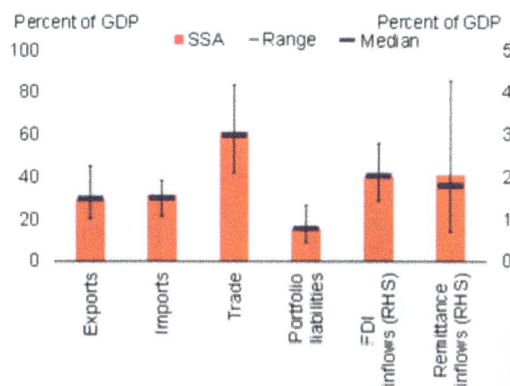

Sources: IMF October 2015 World Economic Outlook, IMF International Financial Statistics, IMF Direction of Trade Statistics, UNCTAD FDI/TNC database, World Bank Remittance and Migration Database, World Bank World Development Indicators.
B. The red bar denotes exports, imports, trade, remittance inflows, portfolio liabilities, and FDI inflows in percent of GDP on average across SSA countries. The vertical line denotes the range of averages for all six developing country regions.

South Africa account for less than 5 percent of GDP in West African countries such as Ghana and Nigeria.

Financial linkages: South Africa is the largest source of foreign direct investment for Botswana, Lesotho, Namibia, and Swaziland (BLNS) (Figure 2.6.1.4), accounting for up to 80 percent of total inward FDI in these countries. South African firms (e.g. Massmart, Nampak, MTN Group) also have a strong presence in the SADC region

BOX 2.6.1 Regional integration and spillovers: Sub-Saharan Africa *(continued)*

FIGURE 2.6.1.2 Linkages between Sub-Saharan Africa and the rest of the world

Countries in Sub-Saharan Africa increasingly participate in international trade. The region's trade has undergone a shift in direction towards China and away from traditional advanced country trading partners. Foreign direct investment liabilities have increased considerably, while remittances and official development assistance from advanced countries have declined. Relative to GDP, bilateral development assistance has halved over the last ten years to 1.5 percent of regional GDP.

A. Exports

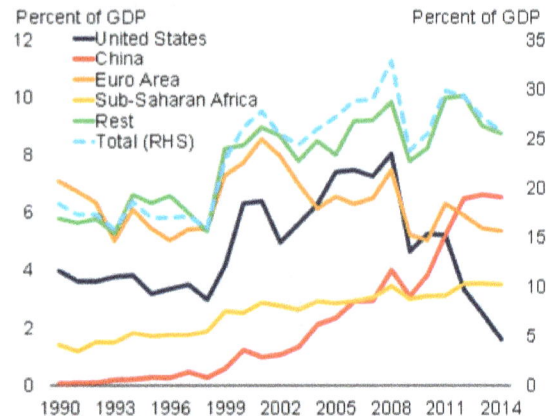

B. Financial liabilities

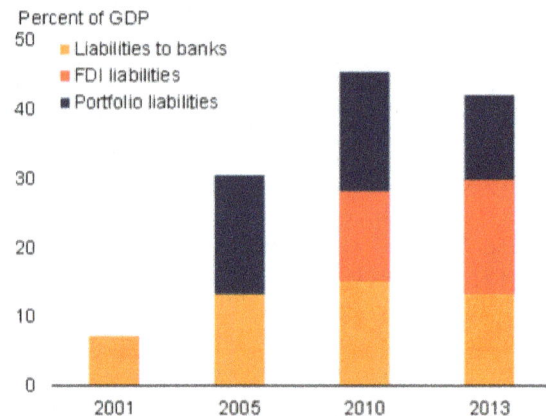

C. Remittances by source country

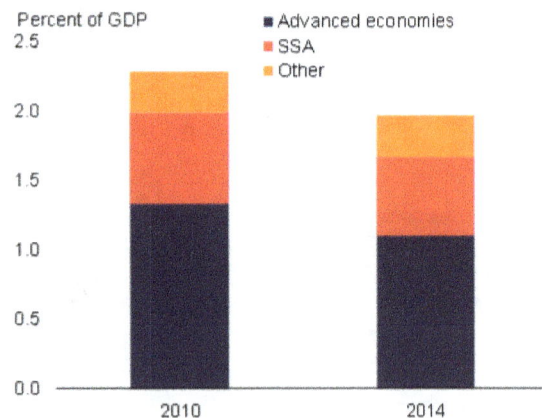

D. Bilateral official development assistance

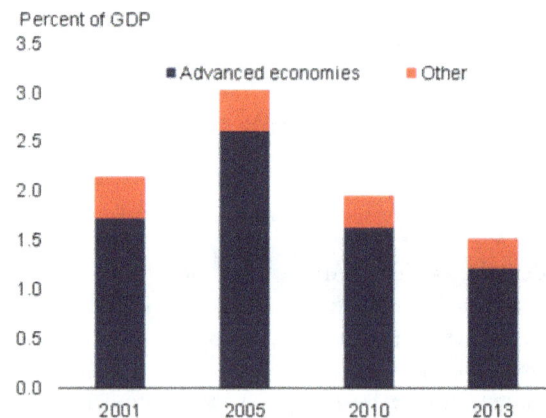

Source: IMF Direction of Trade Statistics, Coordinated Portfolio Investment Survey, Coordinated Direct Investment Survey; Bank for International Settlements Consolidated Banking Statistics; World Bank Remittances and Migration database, OECD.
B: Coordinated Direct Investment Survey (CDIS) is not available for 2001 and 2005; Coordinated Portfolio Investment Survey (CPIS) is not available for 2001. Liabilities to banks stand for claims of BIS-reporting banks on SSA countries. BIS stands for Bank for International Settlements.

(Mozambique, Zimbabwe), East African Community (Kenya, Uganda, and Tanzania) and countries in West Africa (Nigeria, Ghana). South Africa-based banks (Standard Bank, First Rand Bank, Nedbank) and other financial institutions are active across the continent, and are systemically important in neighboring countries, as gauged by deposit shares.[2] Remittances from South Africa to neighboring countries are also significant—for Lesotho,

they average more than 20 percent of GDP (2011-2014), reflecting the large number of migrant workers employed in South African mines.[3]

Institutional linkages: South Africa's monetary and exchange rate policies and the revenue sharing arrangements under SACU are significant sources of linkages.

[2]Operations are deemed systematically important if the share of their deposits in total banking system deposits exceeds 10 percent; or if their asset share exceeds 7 percent of GDP (IMF 2015l).

[3]Though still sizeable, remittances to Lesotho have steadily declined in line with the long-term decline in South Africa's gold production.

BOX 2.6.1 Regional integration and spillovers: Sub-Saharan Africa *(continued)*

- South Africa's currency, the rand, circulates freely in the Common Monetary Area (CMA) formed by South Africa, Lesotho, Namibia, and Swaziland whose currencies are pegged to the rand. Through interest rate and exchange rate movements, policy actions in South Africa immediately affect economic conditions in the CMA.

- The revenue sharing mechanism in SACU has created strong linkages between South African imports and budget revenue in BLNS. South African imports account for more than 90 percent of total SACU imports, the taxes on which are a major source of SACU customs revenue. Customs revenues across SACU are pooled and allocated to members. About 85 percent of forecast excise revenues are distributed based on the share of each country in total SACU GDP, and the remaining is distributed according to a formula that favors countries with lower per capita GDP, typically with a lag of two years. Since imports tend to be more volatile than overall economic activity, the revenue sharing mechanism contributes to significant volatility in budgetary revenue in BLNS.

Linkages between Nigeria and the rest of the region

Trade linkages: Following the data revision of 2013, Nigeria has become SSA's largest economy, accounting for 31 percent of its GDP. It is also the region's largest oil exporter. Official data suggest that trade links exist between Nigeria and a number of West African countries, but are modest (Figure 2.6.1.5). Nigeria's share in exports to the Economic Community of West African States (ECOWAS)[4] fell from an average of 7 percent in 2001-06 to 2.3 percent in 2010, but has been recovering (Chete and Adewuyi 2012). Nigeria is an important export market for agricultural or manufacturing goods from neighboring Guinea-Bissau (6 percent of exports), Côte d'Ivoire (3 percent of exports), and Niger (2.8 percent of exports). Implementation of the ECOWAS common external tariff, which became effective in January 2015, is expected to further boost sub-regional trade, including between Nigeria and the West African Economic and Monetary Union (WAEMU) member countries.[5]

---

[4]The ECOWAS member states are Benin, Burkina Faso, Cape Verde, Côte d'Ivoire, Gambia, Ghana, Guinea, Guinea Bissau, Liberia, Mali, Nigeria, Senegal, Sierra Leone and Togo.

[5]WAEMU countries are Benin, Burkina Faso, Côte d'Ivoire, Guinea Bissau, Mali Niger, Senegal, and Togo. They share the same currency, the CFA franc, which is pegged to the euro.

FIGURE 2.6.1.3 Intra-regional linkages

Most of the region's economic ties continue to be with non-SSA countries. The region's largest economies are among its leading sources of intraregional trade.

A. Exports, FDI inflows, remittance inflows

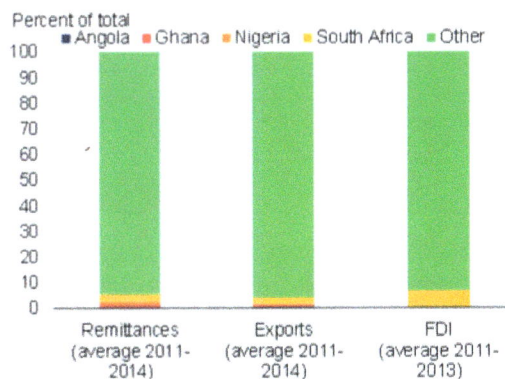

B. Leading sources of intra-regional trade, 2014 (millions of US$)

Exports to the Rest of Africa		Imports from the Rest of Africa	
Country	Value	Country	Value
South Africa	27,041	South Africa	12,504
Côte d'Ivoire	3,978	Botswana	5,985
Zimbabwe	2,782	Zambia	5,833
Zambia	2,170	Zimbabwe	3,388
Tanzania	2,161	Mozambique	3,121
Botswana	1,691	Côte d'Ivoire	2,954
Senegal	1,309	Cameroon	2,054
Congo, Rep.	1,247	Burkina Faso	1,873
Mozambique	1,190	Tanzania	1,490
Uganda	789	Malawi	1,153

Source: World Bank (remittances), IMF DOTS (exports), IMF CDIS (FDI), WITS.
A. Data on FDI liabilities is not available for Angola, Ghana and Nigeria.

Financial sector linkages: Cross-border activity of Nigerian-based banks in SSA has expanded substantially, in part as Nigerian banks follow up on opportunities to finance trade between Nigeria and countries across SSA. The number of subsidiaries of Nigerian banks licensed in foreign jurisdictions increased from two in 2002 to 64 in 2013, operating in more than 20 countries across SSA. The United Bank for Africa, the largest pan-African bank from Nigeria, has a widespread presence in SSA, and is systematically important in several countries, with 19

BOX 2.6.1 Regional integration and spillovers: Sub-Saharan Africa *(continued)*

FIGURE 2.6.1.4 Linkages between South Africa and the rest of Sub-Saharan Africa

South Africa is an important market destination for immediate neighboring countries, as well as for countries in the broader Southern African Development Community region. South Africa is the largest source of FDI for Botswana, Namibia, Lesotho, and Swaziland. It remains an important source of remittances for many countries in the Southern Africa region. South Africa-based banks are active across SSA and systematically important in neighboring countries.

A. Exports to South Africa, 2011-14

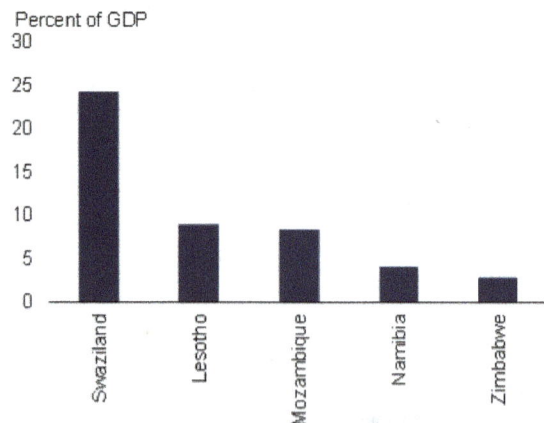

B. FDI inflows and remittances from South Africa, 2011-13

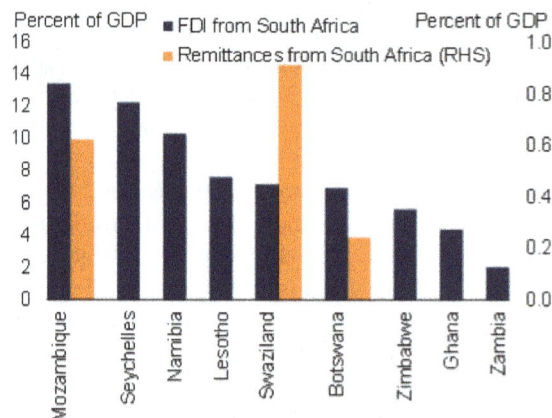

C. Selected South Africa banks: share of deposits by country, 2013

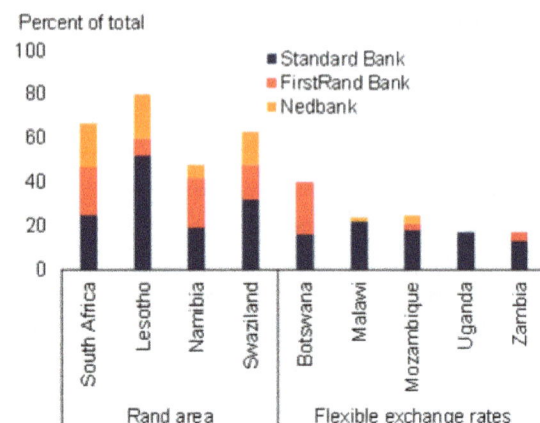

D. Selected South Africa banks: assets by country, 2013

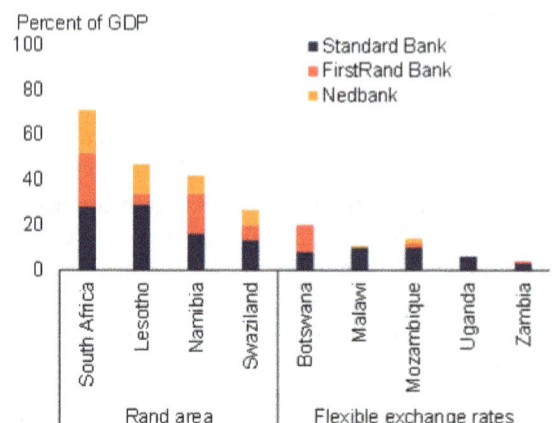

Source: IMF Direction of Trade Statistics, Coordinated Direct Investment Survey, World Bank Migration and Remittances Database, IMF staff reports.
Note: BNLS denotes Botswana, Namibia, Lesotho, and Swaziland.
A: Chart shows countries with exports to South Africa higher than 2 percent of GDP.
B: Chart shows countries with FDI from South Africa higher than 2 percent of GDP.

subsidiaries contributing 15 percent to total assets[6]. This rapid cross-border expansion increases the potential for financial sector shocks in Nigeria to be transmitted across the region. Other potential spillover channels appear limited. In particular, remittances from Nigeria to neighboring countries are small relative to GDP; and foreign direct investment from Nigeria in the region, outside the financial sector, is negligible.

Informal sector linkages: Strong informal cross-border trade links exist between Nigeria and neighboring countries that are only partially captured in official statistics. Estimates of informal cross-border trade in West Africa show that it could represent 20 percent of GDP in

---

[6]Ecobank, a full service bank based in Togo, is one of the region's largest pan-Africa Banks with operations in 36 African countries.

BOX 2.6.1 Regional integration and spillovers: Sub-Saharan Africa *(continued)*

FIGURE 2.6.1.5 Linkages between Nigeria and the rest of Sub-Saharan Africa

Trade links between Nigeria and neighboring countries remain modest. Strong informal cross-border trade links exist between Nigeria and its neighbors that are only partially reflected in official trade statistics. Cross-border activity of Nigeria-based banks has expanded in recent years. United Bank for Africa and Guaranty Trust Bank, two Pan-African banks from Nigeria, have widespread presence in Sub-Saharan Africa. United Bank for Africa is systematically important in several countries.

A. Exports to Nigeria, 2011-14

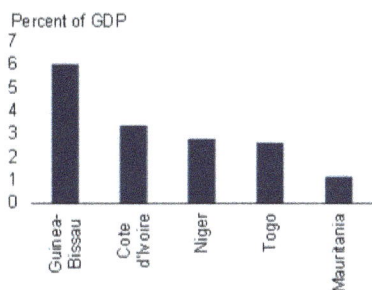

B. Selected Nigerian banks: Share of deposits by country, 2013

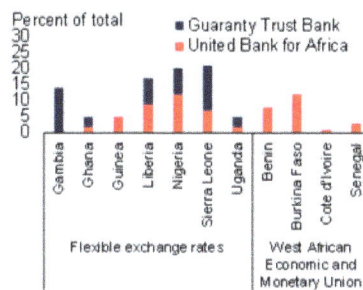

C. Selected Nigerian banks: Assets by country, 2013

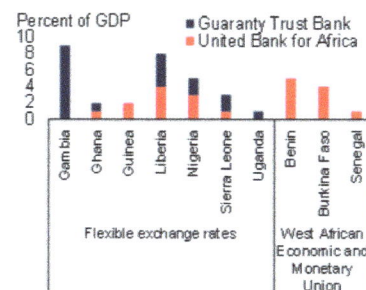

Source: IMF Direction of Trade Statistics (DOTS) database; IMF staff reports.

Nigeria (Afrika and Ajumbo 2012). In particular, a significant share of trade in agriculture goods and petroleum products is unrecorded.

- Cross-border trade in grain and livestock has helped improve food availability in Benin, Cameroon, Chad, Ghana, Mali, and Niger.[7]

- Nigerian subsidies have kept fuel prices much lower than in neighboring countries, generating strong informal trade in fuel. It is estimated that three-quarters of the fuel consumed in Benin is imported through informal channels from Nigeria (World Bank 2014c). Changes in Nigeria's pricing policies for fuel products could have significant spillovers for neighboring countries.

How large are the potential intra-regional spillovers from the region's two largest economies, Nigeria and South Africa?

A Bayesian vector autoregression model is used to estimate growth spillovers from Nigeria, South Africa, and the rest of the world. Sufficient data exists for Botswana, Ghana, and Uganda, but only from 2007 Q2 to 2015 Q2. For each of these countries, the variables in the model include own growth, South African growth, Nigerian growth, the real effective exchange rate, growth in the rest of the world (as exogenous variable), and a dummy that captures the global financial crisis of 2008-09.[8] Figure 2.6.1.6 shows the estimated response of each destination country's output growth to a 1 percentage point decline in real GDP growth in Nigeria, South Africa, and the rest of the world.

The impulse responses suggest that global growth has a significant influence on growth in Sub-Saharan Africa. Growth in Nigeria or South Africa, in contrast, does not appear to have significant spillover effects on neighboring as well as geographically more distant countries. The two largest economies in SSA have insignificant spillovers to each other.[9]

These results are broadly in line with, and complement, those found by a number of previous authors. For example, using a global vector autoregression (GVAR) model, Gurara and Ncube (2013) found a significant growth spillover effect to African economies from both the Eurozone economies and BRICS. Kinfack and Bonga-Bonga (2015) employ a GVAR model and find that Africa's real GDP has a positive response to increases in GDP in the Euro Area and in China. Spillovers of growth shocks from Nigeria and South Africa to the rest of Sub-Saharan Africa were the focus of the studies by IMF

---

[7]Nigeria supplies about 60-70 percent of Niger's grain imports (mostly maize, millet, and sorghum), thereby contributing to food security in Niger.

[8]Further details on the model, including the construction of the rest of the world growth variable, are provided in Annex 3.2.

[9]For a comparison of within-region spillovers across regions, see Box 3.4.

BOX 2.6.1 Regional integration and spillovers: Sub-Saharan Africa *(continued)*

FIGURE 2.6.1.6 Regional spillovers in SSA

Events that affect world growth spill over into SSA. Growth shocks in Nigeria and South Africa do not appear to have significant spillovers to neighboring countries.

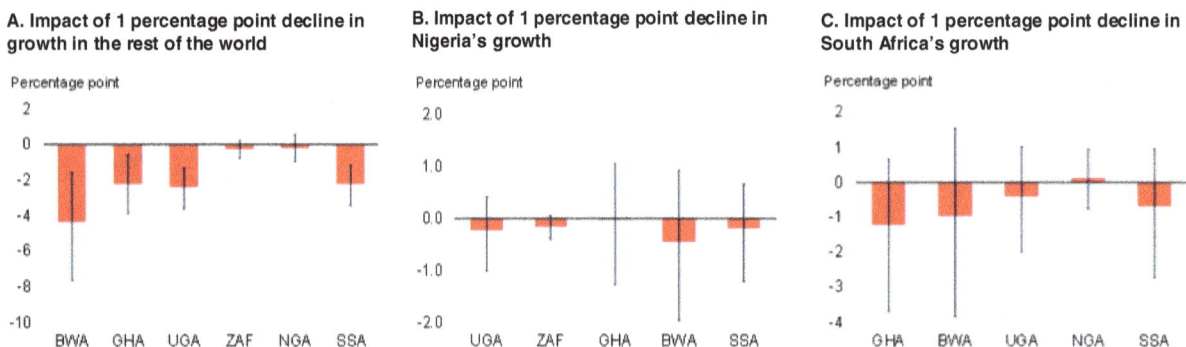

A. Impact of 1 percentage point decline in growth in the rest of the world

B. Impact of 1 percentage point decline in Nigeria's growth

C. Impact of 1 percentage point decline in South Africa's growth

Source: World Bank.

Note: The results show the cumulative change in growth after two years in response to 1 percentage point change in the rest of the world, Nigerian and South African growth based on Bayesian vector autoregression, using data for 2007Q2-2015Q2. Bars are the median estimates and the error bands represent the 33-66 percent confidence bands. SSA refers to the cross sectional median estimates across BWA, GHA, NGA, UGA, and ZAF. BWA = Botswana; GHA = Ghana; NGA = Nigeria; UGA = Uganda; ZAF = South Africa; SSA = Sub-Saharan Africa.

(2012b) and Canales-Kriljenko et al.(2013), with the latter focusing on the BLNS countries. Both studies used vector autoregression models. They find that shocks to South Africa's growth have no significant spillover effects on the BNLS countries, or the rest of the continent. Similarly, spillovers from Nigerian growth to neighboring countries were found to be insignificant, suggesting that Nigeria still has weak links with the rest of the region.

The finding that developments in Nigeria and South Africa have limited effects on growth in other countries in the region could be due to a number of factors. The first is the possibility that the economies of South Africa and those of the rest of SSA may have decoupled in the 1990s following the removal of international sanctions as apartheid ended and South Africa re-integrated into the world economy (Basdevant et al. 2014). As SSA countries integrated rapidly with the rest of the world during the 2000s, external shocks became the predominant cause of fluctuations in SSA activity (Kabundi and Loots 2007). Second, those countries that are most deeply integrated with Nigeria and South Africa—for example, Benin, Ghana, Lesotho, Namibia, Swaziland—do not have sufficiently long time series of data to estimate spillovers.

Conclusion and policy implications

While the region's main economic partners are outside the region, intraregional trade and financial links in Sub-Saharan Africa have expanded in recent years. Trade, financial, and institutional linkages between Nigeria and

South Africa, the region's two largest economies, and the rest of the region have been growing. Notwithstanding this development, the quantitative analysis suggests that growth in Nigeria and South Africa has negligible spillover effects on their neighbors as well as more distant countries.

While intra-African trade has increased in recent years, it remains low. Formal barriers to trade, including tariff and quotas, inefficient customs procedures, and the inadequate state of transport infrastructure within the region are among the major reasons for low trade flows between SSA countries (World Bank 2012b). These are several areas in which policy can make a difference. Reductions in tariff, streamlining customs procedures, and investments in infrastructure—especially for landlocked countries— would raise the prospects for mutually beneficial growth spillovers.

Policy actions are also needed to stem the rise of informality in the region by facilitating the transition of firms from the informal to the formal economy. This would require intensifying ongoing efforts to improve the business climate across the region, including simplified procedures for obtaining permits for business registration, simplified tax systems, and reduced compliance costs for laws and regulations. A strengthened capacity of government agencies to administer laws and to improve the quality and efficiency of regulations would help in making such reforms effective (World Bank 2015f).

References

Abdih Y., A. Barajas, R. Chami, and C. Ebeke. 2012. "Remittances Channel and Fiscal Impact in the Middle East, North Africa and Central Asia." IMF Working Papers 12/104, International Monetary Fund, Washington, DC.

Acharya, V., S. Cecchetti, J. De Gregorio, S. Kalemli-Özcan, P. Lane, and U. Panizza. 2015. "Corporate Debt in Emerging Economies: A Threat to Financial Stability?" Brookings Institution, Washington, DC.

Adler, G., and S. Sosa. 2014. "Intraregional Spillovers in South America: Is Brazil Systemic After All?" *The World Economy* 37 (3): 456-80.

African Development Bank and Organization for Economic Cooperation and Development. 2010. "Public Resource Mobilization and Aid in Africa." In African Economic Outlook. Paris: Organization for Economic Cooperation and Development; Tunis: African Development Bank.

Afrika, J-G., and G. Ajumbo. 2012. "Informal Cross Border Trade in Africa: Implications and Policy Recommendations." Africa Economic Brief 3 (10), African Development Bank, Abidjan, Côte d'Ivoire.

Ahmed, S., and E. Ghani, eds. 2007. *South Asia: Growth and Regional Integration.* New Delhi: Macmillan.

———. 2008. "Making Regional Cooperation Work for South Asia's Poor." Policy Research Working Paper 4736, World Bank, Washington, DC.

Ahmed, S., S. Kelegama, and E. Ghani. 2010. *Promoting Economic Cooperation in South Asia: Beyond SAFTA.* New Delhi: Sage Publications.

Ahuja, A., and M. Nabar. 2012. "Investment-Led Growth in China: Global Spillovers." IMF Working Paper 12/267, International Monetary Fund, Washington, DC.

Aiolfi, M., L. A. V. Catão, and A. Timmermann. 2011. "Common Factors in Latin America's Business Cycles." *Journal of Development Economics* 95 (2): 212-28.

Arteta, C., M. A. Kose, F. Ohnsorge, and M. Stocker. 2015. "The Coming U.S. Interest Rate Tightening Cycle: Smooth Sailing or Stormy Waters?" Policy Research Note 15/02, World Bank, Washington, DC.

Asian Development Bank. 2015. *Asian Development Outlook 2015 Update – Enabling Women, Energizing Asia.* Manila, Philippines: Asian Development Bank.

Baffes, J., M. A. Kose, F. Ohnsorge, and M. Stocker. 2015. "The Great Plunge in Oil Prices: Causes, Consequences, and Policy Responses." Policy Research Note 15/01, World Bank, Washington, DC.

Baier, S. L., and J. H. Bergstrand. 2009. "Estimating the Effects of Free Trade Agreements on International Trade Flows using Matching Econometrics." *Journal of International Economics* 77(1):63-76.

Basdevant, O., M. A. W. Jonelis, M. B. Mircheva, and M. S. T. Slavov. 2014. "The Mystery of Missing Real Spillovers in Southern Africa: Some Facts and Possible Explanations." African Department Working Paper 14/03, International Monetary Fund, Washington, DC.

Bayoumi, T., and F. Ohnsorge. 2013. "Do Inflows or Outflows Dominate? Global Implications of Capital Account Liberalization in China." IMF Working Paper 13/189, International Monetary Fund, Washington. DC.

Balli, F., S. A. Basher, and R. J. Louis. 2013. "Risk Sharing in the Middle East and North Africa." *Economics of Transition* 21 (1): 135-55.

Balli, F., H. R. Hajhoj, S. A. Basher, and H. B. Ghassan. 2015. "An Analysis of Returns and Volatility Spillovers and their Determinants in Emerging Asian and Middle Eastern Countries." *International Review of Economics & Finance* 39 (September): 311-25.

Behar, A., and J. Espinosa-Bowen. 2014. "Export Spillovers from Global Shocks for the Middle East and Central Asia." IMF Working Paper 14/80, International Monetary Fund, Washington, DC.

Blanchard, O. 2014. "Where Danger Lurks." *Finance & Development* 51 (3): 28-31.

Boschi M., and A. Girardi. 2011. "The Contribution of Domestic, Regional and International Factors to Latin America's Business Cycle." *Economic Modelling* 28: 1235–46.

Camacho, M. and G. Perez-Quiros. 2013. "Commodity Prices and the Business Cycle in Latin America: Living and Dying by Commodities?" Working Paper 1304, Bank of Spain, Madrid.

Calì, M., W. Harake, F. Hassan, and C. Struck. 2015. "The Impact of the Syrian Conflict on Lebanese Trade." Working Paper 96087, World Bank, Washington, DC.

Canales Kriljenko, J., F. Gwenhamo, and S. Thomas. 2013. "Inward and Outward Spillovers in the SACU Area." IMF Working Paper 13/31, International Monetary Fund, Washington, DC.

Canales Kriljenko, J., M. Hosseinkouchack, and A. M. Cirkel. 2014. "Global Financial Transmission into Sub-Saharan Africa—A Global Vector Autoregression." IMF Working Paper 14/241, International Monetary Fund, Washington, DC.

Canova F., and P. Dallari. 2013. "How Important is Tourism for the International Transmission of Cyclical Fluctuations? Evidence from the Mediterranean." European Central Bank Working Paper 1553, European Central Bank, Frankfurt.

Caporale, G. M., and A. Girardi. 2012. "Business Cycles, International Trade and Capital Flows: Evidence from Latin America." *Empirical Economics* (February): 1-22.d

Cashin, P., K. Mohaddes, and M. Raissi. 2012. "The Global Impact of the Systemic Economies and MENA Business Cycles." IMF Working Paper 12/255, International Monetary Fund, Washington, DC.

CBO (Congressional Budget Office). 2003. "The Effects of NAFTA on U.S.-Mexican Trade and GDP." A CBO Paper, Congressional Budget Office, Washington, DC.

Cesa-Bianchi, A., M. H. Pesaran, A. Rebucci, T. Xu, and R. Chang. 2012. "China's Emergence in the World Economy and Business Cycles in Latin America." *Economía* 12 (2): 1-75.

Chishti, M., and F. Hipsman. 2015. "In Historic Shift, New Migration Flows from Mexico Fall Below Those From China and India." Migration Policy Institute Policy Beat. May 21, 2015.

Chete, N. L., and A. O. Adewuyi. 2012. "Dynamics of Trade between Nigeria and other ECOWAS Countries." In *Accelerating Growth Through Improved Intra-African Trade*. Washington, DC: Brookings Institution.

China Outbound Tourism Research Institute. 2015. *Chinese Outbound Tourism 2.0*. Hamburg: China Outbound Tourism Research Institute.

Chinn, M. and H. Ito. 2006. "What Matters for Financial Development? Capital Controls, Institutions, and Interactions." *Journal of Development Economics* 81(1): 163–92.

Clinton, K., M. Johnson, J. Benes, D. Laxton, and T. Matheson. 2010. "Structural Models in Real Time." IMF Working Papers 10/56, International Monetary Fund, Washington, DC.

Connolly, M. P., and J. Gunther. 1999. "Mercosur: Implications for Growth in Member Countries." *Current Issues in Economics and Finance* 5(7).

Cuevas, A., M. Messmacher, and A. Werner. 2002. "Changes in the Patterns of External Financing in Mexico Since the Approval of NAFTA." Working Paper, Central Bank of Mexico, Mexico City.

———. 2003 "Macroeconomic Synchronization Between Mexico and its NAFTA Partners." Working Paper 2003-01, Banco de México, Mexico City.

Dabla-Norris, E., J. Brumby, A. Kyobe, Z. Mills, and C. Papageorgiou. 2011. "Investing in Public Investment: An Index of Public Investment Efficiency." IMF Working Paper 11/37, International Monetary Fund, Washington, DC.

De la Torre, A., T. Dider, A. Ize, D. Lederman, and S. L. Schmukler. 2015. *Latin America and the Rising South: Changing World, Changing Priorities*. Washington, DC: World Bank.

De la Torre, A., D. Lederman, and S. Pienknagura. 2015. "Doing it Right." *Finance and Development* (September): 28-30.

De, P., S. Raihan, and E. Ghani. 2013. "What Does MFN Trade Mean for India and Pakistan? Can MFN be a Panacea?" Policy Research Working Paper 6483, World Bank, Washington, DC.

De, P., Raihan, S., and S. Kathuria. 2012. "Unlocking Bangladesh-India Trade: Emerging Potential and the Way Forward." Policy Research Working Paper 6155, World Bank, Washington, DC.

Del Caprio, X. V., and M. Wagner. 2015. "The Impact of Syrian Refugees on the Turkish Labor Market." Policy Research Working Paper 7402, World Bank, Washington, DC.

Ding, D. and I. Masha. 2012. "India's Growth Spillovers to South Asia." IMF Working Paper No. 12/56, International Monetary Fund, Washington, DC.

Dobbs, R., S. Lund, J. Woetzel, and M. Mutafchieva. 2015. "Debt and (Not Much) Deleveraging." McKinsey Global Institute.

Dollar, D., and A. Kraay. 2003. "Institutions, Trade, and Growth." *Journal of Monetary Economics* 50 (1): 133–62.

Drummond, P. F. N., and G. Ramirez. 2009. "Spillovers from the Rest of the World into Sub-Saharan African Countries." IMF Working Paper 09/155, International Monetary Fund, Washington, DC.

Duval, R. A., M. K. C. Cheng, K. H. Oh, R. Saraf, and M. D. Seneviratne. 2014. "Trade Integration and Business Cycle Synchronization: A Reappraisal with Focus on Asia." IMF Working Paper 14/52, International Monetary Fund, Washington, DC.

Easterly, W., N. Fiess, and D. Lederman. 2003. "NAFTA and Convergence in North America: High Expectations, Big Events, Little Time." *Economia* 4(1): 1-53.

ECLAC. 2014. *Regional Integration: Towards an Inclusive Value Chain Strategy*. Santiago, Chile:

Economic Commission for Latin America and the Caribbean.

Eichengreen, B., and A. Rose. 2003. "Does It Pay to Defend against a Speculative Attack?" In *Managing Currency Crises in Emerging Markets*, edited by M. Dooley and J. Frankel. Chicago, IL: University of Chicago Press.

EIU (Economist Intelligence Unit). 2015. "Americas Economy: A Looming El Niño Poses Severe Risks to Latin America." October. London.

Estevadeordal, A. 2012. "Economic Integration in the Americas: An Unfinished Agenda." In *The Road to Hemispheric Cooperation: Beyond the Cartagena Summit of the Americas*. Washington, DC: The Brookings Institution.

EBRD (European Bank for Reconstruction and Development). 2015a. *Transition Report 2015-2016: Rebalancing Finance*. London: European Bank for Reconstruction and Development.

_____. 2015b. "Regional Economic Prospects in EBRD Countries of Operations: May 2015; In the Cross-currents of Diverging Monetary Policies and Russia's Recession." European Bank for Reconstruction and Development, London.

European Commission (EC). 2015. "European Economic Forecast." Institutional Paper 011, European Commission, Brussels.

Fagan, C. 2011. "Evidence of Illegal Cross-Border Flows of Funds, Goods and Services in South Asia and their Impact on Corruption." U4 Anti-Corruption Resource Centre, CMI, Bergen, Norway.

Fajnzylber, P., and J. H. López. 2008. *Remittances and Development: Lessons from Latin America*. Washington, DC: World Bank.

Fiess, N. 2007. "Business Cycle Synchronization and Regional Integration: A Case Study for Central America." *World Bank Economic Review* 21 (1): 49–72.

Fracasso, A. 2015. "Economic Rebalancing and Growth: The Japanese Experience and China's Prospects." Discussion Papers, Department of Economics and Management, University of Trento, Italy.

Freund, C., and M. Jaud. 2015. *Champions Wanted: Promoting Exports in the Middle East and North Africa*. Washington, DC: World Bank.

Gill, I. S., I. Izvorski, W. Van Eeghen, and D. De Rosa. 2014. *Diversified Development: Making the Most of Natural Resources in Eurasia*. Washington, DC: World Bank.

Gurara, D. Z., and M. Ncube. 2013. "Global Economic Spillovers to Africa: A GVAR Approach." Working Paper Series 183, African Development Bank, Tunis.

Husabø, E. 2014. "Spillovers to Europe from the Crisis in Russia and Ukraine." Economic Commentaries Series 6, Norges Bank.

Hooley, J. 2013. "Bringing Down the Great Wall? Global Implications of Capital Account Liberalisation in China." Quarterly Bulletin 2013, Q4. Bank of England, London.

Husain, A., R. Arezki, P. Breuer, V. Haksar, T. Helbling, P. Medas, and M. Sommer. 2015. "Global Implications of Lower Oil Prices." IMF Staff Discussion Note 15/15, International Monetary Fund, Washington, DC.

Ianchovichina, E., S. Devarajan, and C. Lakatos. Forthcoming. "The Lifting of Sanctions on Iran: Global Effects and Strategic Responses." Working Paper, World Bank, Washington, DC.

Ianchovichina, E., and M. Ivanic. 2014. "Economic Effects of the Syrian War and the Spread of the Islamic State on the Levant." Policy Research Working Paper 7135, World Bank, Washington, DC.

Ilahi, N., F. M. Alturki, and J. Espinosa-Bowen. 2009. "How Russia Affects the Neighborhood: Trade, Financial, and Remittance Channels." IMF Working Paper 09/277, International Monetary Fund, Washington, DC.

IDB (Inter-American Development Bank). 2015. *The Labyrinth: How Can Latin America and the Caribbean Navigate the Global Economy*. Washington, DC: Inter-American Development Bank.

International Monetary Fund. 2007. "Decoupling the Train? Spillovers and Cycles in the Global Economy." In World Economic Outlook (Chapter 4). Washington, DC: International Monetary Fund.

_____. 2011a. "Japan: Spillover Report for the 2011 Article IV Consultation and Selected Issues." International Monetary Fund, Washington, DC.

_____. 2012a. *Regional Economic Outlook: Western Hemisphere; Rebuilding Strength and Flexibility*. Washington, DC: International Monetary Fund.

_____. 2012b. "Nigeria and South Africa: Spillovers to the Rest of Sub-Saharan Africa." In *Regional Economic Outlook: Sub-Saharan Africa*. Washington, DC: International Monetary Fund.

_____. 2012c. "Saudi Arabia: Selected Issues." IMF Country Report No 12/272, International Monetary Fund, Washington, DC.

_____. 2013. "Output Synchronicity in the Middle East, North Africa, Afghanistan, and Pakistan and in the Caucasus and Central Asia." In *World Economic Outlook* (Box 3.1). Washington, DC: International Monetary Fund.

_____. 2014a. *World Economic Outlook: Recovery Strengthens, Remains Uneven*. Washington, DC: International Monetary Fund.

_____. 2014b. "IMF Multilateral Policy Issues Report; Spillover Report." IMF Policy Paper, International Monetary Fund, Washington, DC.

_____. 2014c. *Regional Economic Outlook Update: Middle East and Central Asia* (May). International Monetary Fund, Washington, DC.

_____. 2014d. "Potential Spillovers from Remittances from the Cooperation Council for the Arab States of the Gulf (GCC) and Russia." In *Spillover Report* (Box 8). Washington, DC: International Monetary Fund.

_____. 2014e. "India – Selected Issues." IMF Country Report No 14/58. International Monetary Fund, Washington, DC.

_____. 2014f. "Nigeria 2013 Article IV Consultation—Staff Report." International Monetary Fund, Washington, DC.

_____. 2015a. *Regional Economic Outlook:*

Asia and Pacific. Washington, DC: International Monetary Fund.

_____. 2015b. "2015 Spillover Report." International Monetary Fund, Washington, DC.

_____. 2015c. "People's Republic of China: Staff Report for the 2015 Article IV Consultation." International Monetary Fund, Washington, DC.

_____. 2015d. "Malaysia 2015 Article IV Consultation—Staff Report." International Monetary Fund, Washington, DC.

_____. 2015e. "Thailand Article IV Consultations—Staff Report." International Monetary Fund, Washington, DC.

_____. 2015f. "Central, Eastern, and Southeastern Europe: Reconciling Fiscal Consolidation and Growth." Regional Economic Issues series. November. International Monetary Fund, Washington, DC.

_____. 2015g. *Regional Economic Outlook: Middle East and Central Asia.* (October). Washington, DC: International Monetary Fund.

_____. 2015h. *Regional Economic Outlook: Western Hemisphere; Northern Spring, Southern Chills.* April. Washington, DC: International Monetary Fund.

_____. 2015i. *World Economic Outlook: Adjusting to Lower Commodity Prices* Washington, DC: World IMF.

_____. 2015j. *Global Financial Stability Report: Vulnerabilities, Legacies, and Policy Challenges.* Washington, DC: International Monetary Fund.

_____. 2015k. "Spillovers from Surges in Global Financial Market Volatility: India." IMF Country Report 15/62, International Monetary Fund, Washington, DC.

_____. 2015l. *Pan-African Banks: Opportunities and Challenges for Cross-Border Oversight.* Washington, DC: International Monetary Fund.

Inoue, T., D. Kay, and H. Ohshige. 2015. "The Impact of China's Slowdown on the Asia Pacific Region: An Application of the GVAR Model." Policy Research Working Paper 7442, World Bank, Washington, DC.

Izquierdo, A., R. Romero, and E. Talvi. 2008. "Booms and Busts in Latin America: The Role of External Factors." Working Paper 631, Inter-American Development Bank, Washington, DC.

Jelassi, T., A. B. Zeghal, and T. Malzy. 2015. "Fundamentally Changing the Way We Educate Students in the Middle East and North Africa (MENA) Region." Working Paper, North Africa Policy Series, African Development Bank, Abidjan.

Kabundi, A., and E. Loots. 2007. "Co-movement Between South Africa and the Southern African Development Community: An Empirical Analysis." *Economic Modelling* 24 (5): 737-48.

Kathuria, S., S. Sohaib, and M. J. Ferrantino. 2015. "How has Regional Integration Taken Place in Other Regions? Lessons for South Asia." SARConnect Issue 2. World Bank, Washington, DC.

Keefer, P., and S. Knack. 2007. "Boondoggles, Rent-Seeking, and Political Checks and Balances: Public Investment under Unaccountable Governments." *Review of Economics and Statistics* 89 (3): 566-72.

Kemal, A. R., 2005, "SAFTA and Economic Cooperation." http://www.southasianmedia.net/conference/Regional_Conference/safta.htm

Khalifa, A., S. Hammoudeh, and E. Otranto. 2013. "Patterns of Volatility Transmission Within Regime Switching Across GCC and Global Markets." *International Review of Economics and Finance* 29: 512-24.

Kim, M., Le Lesle, V., F. Ohnsorge, and S. Seshadri. 2014. "Why Complementarity Matters for Stability—Hong Kong SAR, China and Singapore as Asian Financial Centers." IMF Working Paper 14/119, International Monetary Fund, Washington, DC.

Kinfack, C. E., and L. Bonga-Bonga. 2015. "Trade Linkages and Business Cycle Co-movement: An Empirical Analysis of Africa and its Main Trading Partners using Global VAR." Economic Research Southern Africa (ESRA) Working Paper 512, Johannesburg.

Kose, M. A., C. Otrok, and C. H. Whiteman. 2003. "International Business Cycles: World, Region, and Country-Specific Factors." *American Economic Review* 93(4): 1216–39.

Kose, M. A., A. Rebucci, and A. Schipke. 2005. "Macroeconomic Implications of CAFTA-DR". In *Central America: Global Integration and Regional Cooperation*, edited by M. Rodlauer and A. Schipke. Washington, DC: International Monetary Fund.

Kose, M. A., G. M. Meredith, and C. M. Towe. 2005. "How Has NAFTA Affected the Mexican Economy? Review and Evidence." In *Monetary Policy and Macroeconomic Stabilization in Latin America*. Berlin: Springer.

Kumar, U. 2014. "India's Demographic Transition: Boon or Bane?" *Asia & the Pacific Policy Studies* 1 (1): 186–203.

Lakatos, C., M. Maliszewska, and I. Osorio-Rodarte. 2015. "China's Slowdown and Rebalancing: Potential Growth and Poverty Impacts on Sub-Saharan Africa." Unpublished Paper, World Bank, Washington, DC.

Lam, R., X. Liu, and A. Schipke. "China's Labor Market in the "New Normal." IMF Working Paper 15/151, International Monetary Fund, Washington, DC.

Lederman, D., W. F. Maloney, and L. Servén. 2005. Lessons from NAFTA for Latin America and the Caribbean. The World Bank and Stanford University Press.

Loayza, N., H. Lopez, A. Ubide. 2001. "Comovements and Sectoral Interdependence: Evidence for Latin America, East Asia, and Europe." *IMF Staff Papers* 48 (2): 367–96.

Lopez, J. H., and R. Shankar. 2011. *Getting the Most Out of Free Trade Agreements in Central America*. Washington, DC: World Bank.

Mejía-Reyes, P. 2004. "Classical Business Cycles in America: Are National Business Cycle Synchronised?" *International Journal of Applied Econometrics and Quantitative Studies* 1 (3): 75–102.

Moreira, M. M., and E. Mendoza. 2007. "Regional Integration: What in It for CARICOM?" BID-INTAL Working Paper 29.

Obiora, K. 2009. "Decoupling from the East Toward the West? Analyses of Spillovers to the Baltic Countries." IMF Working Paper, 09/125, International Monetary Fund, Washington, DC.

OECD. 2009, "Participation in Global Value Chains (GVC)." http://www.oecd-ilibrary.org/trade/interconnected-economies/gvc-participation-index-2009_9789264189560-graph5-en.

———. 2015. "Participation in Global Value Chains (GVC)." https://data.oecd.org/trade/participation-in-global-value-chains-gvc.htm. Accessed on November 1, 2015.

Österholm, P., and J. Zettelmeyer. 2008. "The Effect of External Conditions on Growth in Latin America." *IMF Staff Papers* 55 (4): 595-623.

Park, D., and K. Shin. 2015. "Financial Integration in Asset and Liability Holdings in East Asia." ADB Economic Working Paper 444, Asian Development Bank, Manila, Philippines.

Palit, A., and G. Spittel, eds. 2013. *South Asia in the New Decade: Challenges and Prospects*. Singapore: World Scientific Singapore.

Piccio, L. 2015. "India's 2015-16 Foreign Aid Budget: Where the Money is Going?" DEVEX (blog). https://www.devex.com/news/india-s-2015-16-foreign-aid-budget-where-the-money-is-going-85666.

Rajaram, A., T. Minh Le, K. Kaiser, J-H. Kim, and J. Frank. 2014. *The Power of Public Investment Management: Transforming Resources into Assets for Growth*. Washington, DC: World Bank.

Roache, S. K. 2008. "Central America's Regional Trends and U.S. Cycles." IMF Working Paper 08/50, International Monetary Fund, Washington, DC.

Romalis, J. 2007. "NAFTA's and CUSFTA's Impact on International Trade." *The Review of Economics and Statistics* 89 (3): 416–35.

Romero-Torres, J., S. Wells, and S. Selwyn-Khan. 2013. *Development of Capital Markets in Member Countries of the South Asian Association for Regional*

Cooperation. Mandaluyong City, Philippines: Asian Development Bank.

Rouis, M., S. Tabor, S. Migliorisi, E. Neumayer, and K. R. Kounetsron. 2010. *Arab Development Assistance: Four Decades of Cooperation.* Washington, DC: World Bank.

Rouis, M. 2013. "Response of the Arab Donors to the Global Financial Crisis and the Arab Spring." MENA Quick Note Series 112, World Bank, Washington, DC.

Scholvin, S., and A. Malamud. 2014. "Is There a Geoeconomic Node in South America? Geography, politics and Brazil's Role in Regional Economic Integration." Working Paper 2014/2, Instituto de Ciências Sociais da Universidade de Lisboa, Spain.

Schiffbauer, M., A. Sy, S. Hussain, H. Sahnoun, and P. Keefer. 2015. *Jobs or Privileges: Unleashing the Employment Potential of the Middle East and North Africa.* Washington, DC: World Bank.

Shiells, C. R., M. Pani, and E. Jafarov. 2005. "Is Russia Still Driving Regional Economic Growth?" IMF Working Paper 05/192, International Monetary Fund, Washington, DC.

Stepanyan, A., A. Roitman, G. Manasyan, D. Ostojic, and N. Epstein. 2015. "The Spillover Effects of Russia's Economic Slowdown on Neighboring Countries." Departmental Paper, International Monetary Fund, Washington, DC.

Swiston, A. 2010. "Spillovers to Central America in Light of the Crisis: What a Difference a Year Makes." IMF Working Paper 10/35, International Monetary Fund, Washington, DC.

Talani, L. S. 2014. *The Arab Spring in the Global Political Economy.* Basingstoke, UK: Palgrave Macmillan.

Taneja, N., and S. Pohit. 2005. "Informal Trade in India, Nepal, and Sri Lanka." In *Economic Development in South Asia,* edited by Mohsin Khan. Noida, India: Tata McGraw-Hill.

Torres, A., and O. Vela. 2003. "Trade Integration and Synchronization Between the Business Cycles of Mexico and the United States." *North*

American Journal of Economics and Finance 14 (3): 319–342.

UNCTAD. 2015. *World Investment Report 2015: Reforming International Investment Governance.* United Nations Conference on Trade and Development. Geneva: United Nations Publications.

United Nations Conference on Trade and Development (UNCTAD). 2013. *Economic Development in Africa—Intra-African Trade: Unlocking Private Sector Dynamism.* New York: United Nations.

USTR (United States Trade Representative). 2015. USTR website. https://ustr.gov/trade-agreements/free-trade-agreements/cafta-dr-dominican-republic-central-america-fta.

Villarreal, M. A. 2012. "Mexico's Free Trade Agreements." CRS Report for Congress 7-5700, Congressional Research Service, Washington, DC.

Vivek, A., and A. Vamvakidis. 2010. "China's Economic Growth: International Spillovers." IMF Working Paper 10/165, International Monetary Fund, Washington, DC.

Wilson, J. S., and T. Ostuki. 2005. "Trade Facilitation and Regional Integration in South Asia: Accelerating the Gains to Trade with Capacity Building." South Asia Region, World Bank, Washington DC.

World Bank. 2005. *Global Economic Prospects: Trade, Regionalism, and Development.* Washington, DC: World Bank.

———. 2012a. "Road Freight in Central America: Five Explanations to High Costs of Service Provision." Background Paper, World Bank, Washington, DC.

———. 2012b. "Africa Can Help Feed Africa: Removing Barriers to Regional Trade in Food Staples." World Bank, Washington, DC.

———. 2013a. "Trends and Determinants of Foreign Direct Investment in South Asia." World Bank, Washington, DC.

———. 2013b. "South Asia Economic Focus, Fall 2013: A Wake Up Call." World Bank, Washington, DC.

_____. 2014a. "Costa Rica: Five Years After CAFTA-DR Assessing Early Results for the Costa Rican Economy." World Bank, Washington, DC.

_____. 2014b. *Over the Horizon: A New Levant.* Washington, DC: World Bank.

_____. 2014c. "The Republic of Benin Diagnostic Trade Integration Study (DTIS) Update: From Rents to Competitiveness." World Bank, Washington, DC.

_____. 2015a. *Global Economic Prospects: The Global Economy in Transition.* Washington, DC: World Bank.

_____. 2015b. "China Economic Update, June 2015." World Bank, Washington, DC.

_____. 2015c. "East Asia and Pacific Economic Update, October 2015: Staying the Course." World Bank, Washington, DC.

_____. 2015d. "Malaysia Economic Monitor, June 2015: Transforming Urban Transport." World Bank. Washington, DC.

_____. 2015e. "Indonesia Economic Quarterly, October 2015: In Times of Global Volatility." World Bank, Washington, DC.

_____. 2015f. *Doing Business 2016: Measuring Regulatory Quality and Efficiency.* Washington, DC: World Bank.

_____. 2015g. "Mongolia Economic Update, November 2015." World Bank, Washington, DC.

_____. 2015h. "Taking Stock, July 2015: An Update on Vietnam's Recent Economic Developments." World Bank, Washington, DC.

_____. 2015i. "Philippines Economic Update, January 2015: Making Growth Work for the Poor." World Bank, Washington, DC.

_____. 2015j. *Global Monitoring Report 2015/2016: Development Goals in an Era of Demographic Change.* Washington, DC: World Bank.

_____. 2015k. "Europe and Central Asia Economic Update, October 2015: Low Commodity Prices and Weak Currencies." World Bank, Washington, DC.

_____. 2015l. "Migration and Development Brief 25." World Bank, Washington, DC.

_____. 2015m. "Sustaining Recovery, Improving Living Standards." EU Regular Economic Report (2), Fall 2015, World Bank, Washington, DC.

_____. 2015n. *Global Economic Prospects: Having Fiscal Space and Using It.* Washington, DC: World Bank.

_____. 2015o. "Commodity Markets Outlook, October 2015: Understanding El Niño." World Bank, Washington, DC.

_____. 2015p. "MENA Economic Monitor, October 2015: Inequality, Uprisings, and Conflict in the Arab World." World Bank, Washington, DC.

_____. 2015q. "MENA Economic Monitor, April 2015: Towards a New Social Contract." World Bank, Washington, DC.

_____. 2015r. "Africa's Pulse. Volume 12." World Bank, Washington, DC.

_____. 2016. *Global Economic Prospects: Spillovers amid Weak Growth.* Washington, DC: World Bank.

World Economic Forum. 2015. World Travel and Tourism Competitiveness Index 2015. World Economic Forum.

World Tourism Organization (UNWTO). 2015. "UNWTO Tourism Highlights, 2015 Edition." World Tourism Organization, Madrid.

CHAPTER 3

WHO CATCHES A COLD WHEN EMERGING MARKETS SNEEZE?

Since 2010, a synchronous growth slowdown has been underway in emerging markets, especially in some of the largest ones. Given the size and integration with the global economy of the largest emerging markets—the BRICS (Brazil, the Russian Federation, India, China, South Africa)— a synchronous slowdown in these economies could have significant spillovers to the rest of the world through trade and finance. Specifically, a 1 percentage point decline in BRICS growth is associated with lower growth in other emerging markets by 0.8 percentage point, in frontier markets by 1.5 percentage points, and in the global economy by 0.4 percentage point over the following two years. Spillovers could be considerably larger if the BRICS growth slowdown were combined with financial market stress. Adverse growth spillovers present challenges that need to be addressed with both fiscal and monetary policies as well as structural reforms.

Introduction

Growth in emerging markets (EM) has been slowing, from 7.6 percent in 2010, to 3.7 percent in 2015 and is now below its long-run average (Figure 3.1). This slowdown has been highly synchronized across emerging markets, with significant declines in growth in most emerging market regions.[1] In the largest emerging markets—the heterogeneous group of BRICS (Brazil, Russia, India, China, and South Africa)— growth has slowed from almost 9 percent in 2010 to about 4 percent in 2015, on average, with India being a notable exception. This slowdown reflects both easing growth in China, persistent weakness in South Africa, and steep recessions in Russia since 2014 and in Brazil since 2015.

Both external and domestic as well as cyclical and structural factors have contributed to the slowdown in emerging markets (Didier et al. 2015).

- *External versus domestic factors.* On average, external factors have been the main cause of the slowdown between 2010-13. Such factors have included weak global trade after the global financial crisis, falling commodity

prices (which have dampened prospects in the half of emerging markets that are commodity exporters), and bouts of financial market turbulence. Since 2014, however, a series of country-specific, domestic shocks have become the main source of the slowdown (Didier et al. 2015). Such country-specific challenges have included a steady slowdown in productivity growth, bouts of policy uncertainty, and shrinking fiscal and monetary policy buffers that have constrained the use of policy stimulus (Box 3.1). Total factor productivity growth, especially, has almost halved in emerging markets to just over 1 percent, on average, in 2010-14 from about 2 percent in 2000-07, on average. This has been only partially offset by higher capital accumulation, including as a result of crisis-related investment stimulus in several large emerging markets.

- *Structural versus cyclical factors.* One-off, cyclical and structural factors have driven the slowdown to varying degrees across countries. On average across emerging markets, longer-term structural factors may have accounted for about one-third of the growth slowdown during 2010-14. In individual countries, however, the contribution of structural factors has ranged from one-tenth to virtually all of the slowdown since 2010.

The slowdown follows a decade during which record-high emerging market growth transformed the global economic landscape. Emerging markets accounted for 46 percent of global growth during 2000-08 and 60 percent during 2010-14. By 2014, emerging markets constituted 34 percent of

---

Note: This chapter was prepared by Raju Huidrom, Ayhan Kose and Franziska Ohnsorge with contributions from Jose Luis Diaz Sanchez, Lei Sandy Ye, Jaime de Jesus Filho, Xiaodan Ding, Sergio Kurlat, and Qian Li.

[1]Emerging markets (EM) generally include countries with a record of significant access to international financial markets. Frontier markets (FM) include countries that are usually smaller and less financially developed than emerging market economies. Therefore, the emerging and frontier market group excludes low-income countries with minimal or no access to international capital markets. The country sample is provided in Annex 3.1.

FIGURE 3.1 Emerging market growth slowdown

Emerging market growth has slowed steadily since 2010, coinciding with a gradual recovery in advanced market economies. The slowdown is broad-based, reaching across regions and affecting an unusually large number of emerging markets for several years, comparable only to previous crisis periods. Unprecedented since the 1980s, the majority of BRICS (Brazil, Russia, India, China, and South Africa) economies are slowing simultaneously.

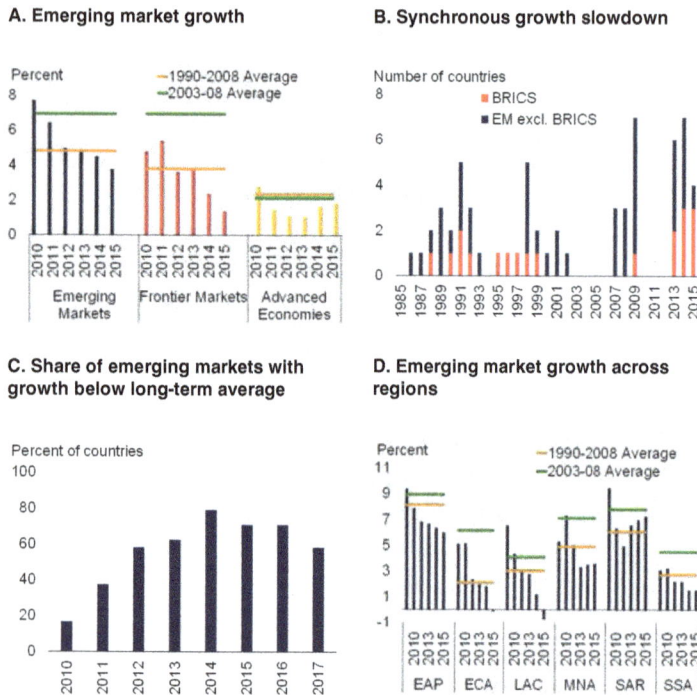

A. Emerging market growth

B. Synchronous growth slowdown

C. Share of emerging markets with growth below long-term average

D. Emerging market growth across regions

Source: World Bank Global Economic Prospects and IMF World Economic Outlook.
Note: Due to data availability, FM long-run average for 1990-2008 starts in 1993. GDP data for Czech Rep. are only available from 1990. EM, FM, and AM are defined in Annex 3.1.
A. Weighted average growth.
B. Number of emerging market countries (EM) in which growth slowed for three consecutive years.
C. Long-term averages are country-specific for 1990-2008. Long-term average for the Czech Rep. starts in 1991.
D. EAP = East Asia and Pacific; ECA = Europe and Central Asia; LAC = Latin America and Caribbean; MNA = Middle East and North Africa; SAR = South Asia; SSA = Sub-Saharan Africa.

global GDP (in current market prices), more than one-and-a-half as much as they did in 1980 (Figure 3.2). The rising share of the emerging world in the global economy was also reflected in their increased integration into international trade and finance. Emerging markets have become major export destinations for the rest of the world and important sources of remittances, commodity supply and demand, foreign direct investment, and official development assistance.

China is by far the largest emerging market, two-thirds the size of all the other emerging markets combined and twice as large as the other BRICS economies combined. Notwithstanding China's

larger size, the broader group of BRICS plays a special role. The BRICS are the largest and most regionally integrated emerging markets in their respective regions and they have been the main source of emerging market growth and integration into the global economy. During 2010-14, the BRICS contributed about 40 percent to global growth, up from about 10 percent during the 1990s. They now account for two-thirds of emerging market activity and more than one-fifth of global activity—as much as the United States and more than the Euro Area—compared with less than one-tenth in 2000.[2]

This chapter studies the following four questions:

- What are the key channels of spillovers from the major emerging markets?

- Do business cycles in BRICS move in tandem with those in other emerging markets and frontier markets?

- How large are spillovers from the major emerging markets?

- What are the policy implications?

Previous studies have typically focused on global growth spillovers from individual BRICS (Box 3.2). The chapter adds to the existing literature on spillovers in four dimensions. First, it extends the analysis to spillovers from a synchronous BRICS slowdown. Second, it includes an explicit comparison of global, regional, and local spillovers from individual BRICS. Third, it systematically differentiates the cross-border spillovers by country groups, including by region and by commodity exporter/importer status. Fourth, in a transparent framework, it examines how turbulence in financial markets can interact with the slowdown in BRICS to generate cross-border growth spillovers.[3]

---

[2]The economic size of BRICS is much larger in terms of PPP adjusted GDP. BRICS constitute about 30 percent of global activity while the United States constitutes only about 16 percent.

[3]The magnitude of spillovers may depend on the nature of the shock originating in BRICS. Given data limitations, a detailed examination of the sources of the growth shock and its implications goes beyond the scope of this chapter.

The findings are as follows:

- *Channels.* Cross-border economic linkages among emerging markets, and with BRICS specifically, have grown significantly since 2000. Reduced import demand from BRICS would weaken trading partner exports. In particular, reduced commodity demand would dampen growth in commodity exporters. Lower remittances from Russia would reduce household incomes and consumption in neighboring countries. In addition, although not estimated econometrically here, confidence spillovers could be sizeable and affect a larger group of countries (Levchenko and Pandalai-Nayar 2015).

- *Impact.* A 1 percentage point decline in BRICS growth would reduce growth in other emerging markets by 0.8 percentage point and in FM by 1.5 percentage points at the end of two years. The estimated impacts on advanced markets are modest, on average. On balance, a 1 percentage point decline in BRICS growth is estimated to reduce global growth by 0.4 percentage point at the end of two years. Notwithstanding sizeable impacts of growth fluctuations in BRICS on other emerging markets and frontier markets, those from major advanced economies remain larger still.

- *Global versus regional effects.* A growth impulse in China would affect growth in other emerging markets in East Asia by about as much as growth in other emerging markets around the world. In contrast, the repercussions of a slowdown in Russia would be mostly confined to Europe and Central Asia. Slowdowns in Brazil, India, and South Africa would mainly affect smaller, neighboring countries.

- *Interacting effects.* Slower-than-expected growth in BRICS could coincide with other strains on the global economy such as bouts of global financial market volatility. If, in 2016, BRICS growth slows further, by as much as the average growth disappointment over 2010-14, instead of picking up as forecast, growth

FIGURE 3.2 Rising economic significance of emerging markets

Emerging markets have increasingly contributed to global growth since the 1980s. Their rising economic significance is also reflected in other dimensions: trade, financial flows, and remittances.

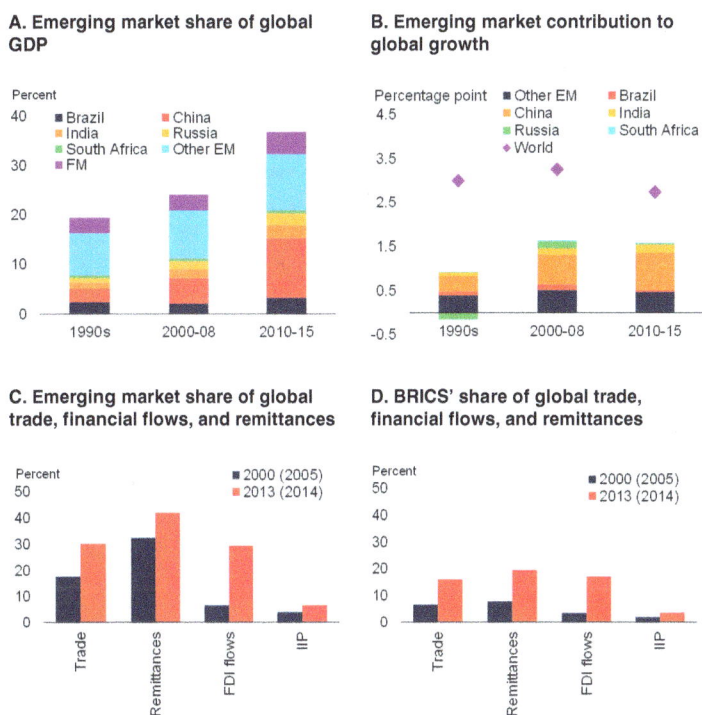

A. Emerging market share of global GDP

B. Emerging market contribution to global growth

C. Emerging market share of global trade, financial flows, and remittances

D. BRICS' share of global trade, financial flows, and remittances

Sources: World Development Indicators; UNCTAD; Bank for International Settlements; World Economic Outlook.
A. B. EM stands for emerging markets, FM for frontier markets.
C. D. Due to data constraints, global trade (exports plus imports) from 2000 and 2013; remittances (inflows plus outflows) data from 2000 and 2013; foreign direct investment (FDI) flows (inflows plus outflows) from 2000 and 2014; and international investment position (IIP, including direct investment, portfolio investment, financial derivatives, and other investment assets and liabilities) from 2005 and 2013.

in other emerging markets could fall short of expectations by about 1 percentage point and global growth by 0.7 percentage point. If such a BRICS growth decline scenario were to be combined with financial sector turbulence, e.g. similar to the 2013 "Taper Tantrum," emerging market growth could slow by an additional 0.5 percentage point and global growth by an additional 0.4 percentage point.

- *Policy responses.* The growth slowdown in BRICS has been part cyclical decline from the immediate post-crisis rebound in 2010, part structural slowdown. Hence, a mix of counter-cyclical fiscal or monetary policy stimulus and structural reforms could be used to support activity. A renewed structural reform

BOX 3.1 Sources of the growth slowdown in BRICS

BRICS growth has been slowing since 2010, increasingly because of moderating potential growth. Until 2013, the slowdown was predominantly driven by external factors, but the role of domestic factors has increased since 2014. Deceleration in productivity growth suggests that a return to pre-global crisis rates of BRICS growth is unlikely.

The so-called BRICS (Brazil, Russia, India, China, and South Africa) are the largest emerging markets, accounting for about two-thirds of emerging market GDP. BRICS growth has slowed from almost 9 percent in 2010 to about 4 percent in 2015. By 2015, three of the BRICS (China, Russia, South Africa) had been slowing for three or more consecutive years and Brazil was in a steep recession. Long-term growth expectations in these economies have been repeatedly downgraded since 2010.[1]

A country-specific Bayesian Vector Autoregression (BVAR) model helps quantify some of the sources of this slowdown (Didier et al. 2015).[2] The model explains BRICS growth as a function of domestic factors (domestic inflation, short-term interest rates, and the real exchange rate), and external factors (U.S. growth, 10-year bond yields, China's growth, the EMBI spread, and terms of trade).[3]

An unfavorable external environment—including a terms-of-trade deterioration and U.S. growth setbacks in 2013 and early 2014—appears to have been the main source of the slowdown between 2010 and the first quarter of 2014. However, since then, domestic factors—including rising short-term interest rates and, in China, real appreciations—have been the predominant cause (Figure 3.1.1). Underlying these short-term movements has been a steady decline in productivity growth. Although difficult to measure on a high-frequency and comparable cross-country basis, bouts of political uncertainty have dented investor sentiment in some BRICS.

This box addresses the following questions:

- What have been the external factors driving the BRICS slowdown?

- What have been the domestic factors driving the BRICS slowdown?

External factors

Among the most important external factors are weak global trade, a steady decline in commodity prices since 2011, and tightening global financial conditions. The model indicates that such factors were predominant 2010Q1-2014Q1 (Figure 3.1.1).

Weak trade. During 2000-07, global trade grew at an average annual rate of about 7 percent. Since 2010, however, global trade growth has slowed. By 2014, global trade had fallen 20 percent short of its pre-crisis trend (World Bank 2015a). An outright contraction in the first half of 2015—the first since 2009—reflected falling import demand from emerging markets, including from Asia and Central and Eastern Europe. Five factors have contributed to the weakness in global trade.

- Advanced markets, which constitute about 60 percent of world import demand, have been growing at a rate of less than 2 percent. By 2014, real GDP in the United States and the Euro Area was 8-13 percent below the pre-crisis trend level, and import demand was 22-23 percent below the pre-crisis trend.

- Investment demand in advanced markets has been particularly weak. Since capital goods are typically the most import-intensive component of aggregate demand, the switch in composition has reduced the income elasticity of trade.

- The maturation of global value chains has further reduced the elasticity of trade flows to activity and exchange rates (Ahmed, Appendino, and Ruta 2015).

- Higher capital requirements and tightened financial regulations have reduced banks' willingness to extend trade finance (World Bank 2015a).

- The pace of trade liberalization has slowed since the crisis.

Easing commodity prices. A steady decline in commodity prices has set back growth in commodity-exporting BRICS (Russia, Brazil, and South Africa). Prices of oil and metals have declined by 50-60 percent from their 2011 peaks and are expected to remain low for the next decade (World Bank 2015b, Baffes et al. 2015). Agricultural prices are

---

Note: This Box was prepared by Lei Sandy Ye.

[1] The average five-year ahead consensus growth forecast of Brazil, China, India, and Russia has decreased from 6.5 percent in 2010 to 4.7 percent in 2015.

[2] The Bayesian methodology follows Litterman (1986). The sample includes quarterly data for 1998Q1 to 2015Q2 for all BRICS economies.

[3] Estimates for China do not separately include its growth as an external factor.

BOX 3.1 Sources of the growth slowdown in BRICS *(continued)*

FIGURE 3.1.1 Sources of the growth slowdown in BRICS

Since 2010, the drivers of the BRICS growth slowdown have pivoted from external to domestic factors. External drivers included weak global trade and commodity prices and bouts of financial market turmoil. Domestic factors included slowing productivity growth, rising domestic policy uncertainty and eroding buffers that have constrained the use of accommodative policies. TFP growth and potential growth in BRICS have slipped to below pre-global crisis averages.

A. Contribution to BRICS growth

B. Contribution of domestic factors to BRICS growth

C. Contribution to BRICS growth

D. TFP growth in BRICS

E. Potential growth in BRICS

F. Contribution to potential growth in BRICS

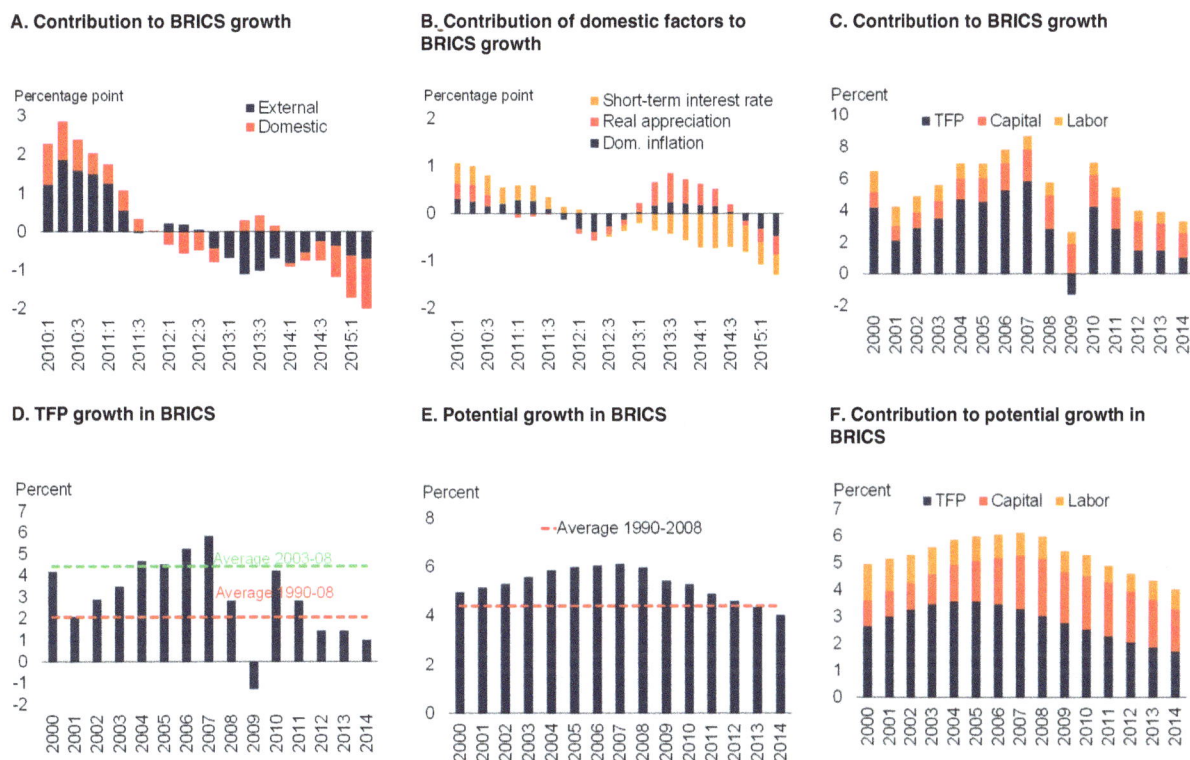

Source: Didier et al. (2015).
A. B. Each bar shows the percentage point deviation of growth from the sample mean. External factors include U.S. growth and 10-year bond yields, Chinese growth, EMBI spreads, and terms of trade. Domestic factors include domestic inflation, the real exchange rate, and short-term interest rates. Unweighted average contribution to BRICS growth, including China. Based on Bayesian VAR (Didier et al. 2015). The last observation is 2015:2.
C.D.E.F. Unweighted averages.

about 30 percent below their 2011 peaks. This has sharply worsened the terms of trade of Brazil, Russia, and South Africa. Slowing growth in commodity-importing BRICS (China, India) itself contributes to softening commodity prices (World Bank 2015b).

Tighter financing conditions. Net capital flows to BRICS have undergone bouts of volatility, culminating in sharp and sustained capital outflows in the first half of 2015. The decline in net capital flows largely reflected developments in China: in the first half of 2015, portfolio outflows from China rose ten-fold and net other investment inflows fell by four-fifths from the second half of 2014. Remittance inflows to BRICS have also slowed sharply, from a rate of increase of 15.4 percent in 2010 to under 3 percent in 2015.

The volatility of capital flows to BRICS has weighed on investment. Since 2010, investment growth in BRICS has slowed from 16 percent in 2010 to 5 percent in 2014. A series of country-specific factors have contributed to this, including political and geopolitical uncertainty, structural bottlenecks and uncertainty about major reform initiatives. The slowdown in remittances may directly impact consumption in these economies (World Bank 2015a).

Domestic factors

Domestic factors include a sustained productivity slowdown and bouts of policy uncertainty. The BVAR results suggest that since 2014Q1 these have overtaken external factors as the main contributors to decelerating BRICS output (Figure 3.1.1).

BOX 3.1 Sources of the growth slowdown in BRICS *(continued)*

Productivity growth slowdown. Domestic factors accounted for a sizable share of the slowdown in BRICS, especially since early 2014. These included a productivity slowdown. Using a production function approach, GDP growth may be decomposed into the contributions of total factor productivity (TFP), and the individual factors of production (Didier et al. 2015). Based on this decomposition, slowing BRICS growth has mostly reflected slowing TFP growth (Figure 3.1.1). Since 2012, TFP growth in BRICS has been below its historical average during 1990-2008. Slowing TFP growth has also been reflected in declining potential growth.

Uncertainty. Bouts of uncertainty in BRICS have weighed on investment. This was associated with periods of stock market and currency volatility. Looking ahead, if heightened policy, and especially political, uncertainty persists, it may constrain policymakers' ability to support growth. Counter-cyclical fiscal and monetary policies may be harder to implement when investors focus on rising uncertainty or widening vulnerabilities or both. Capital outflows and depreciations amidst weakening confidence may limit the effectiveness of counter-cyclical policies in lifting activity. Structural reforms also often stall amidst political uncertainty.

Eroding policy buffers. Since the crisis, the fiscal positions of BRICS have deteriorated considerably. On average, their fiscal balance has weakened from near-balance in 2007 to -4 percent of GDP in 2014. In South Africa, debt has increased by about 19 percentage points of GDP since

2007, and Brazil and India's debt levels are in excess of 60 percent of GDP. Monetary policy space has diverged between commodity exporters and importers. In Brazil and Russia, monetary policy is constrained by above-target inflation, partly as a result of depreciation. In contrast, low oil prices have reduced inflation and increased room for rate cuts in China and India. However, this room may diminish if inflation rebounds once oil prices stabilize.

Conclusion

The factors driving the growth slowdown in BRICS are likely to remain in place, although sharp recessions in Brazil and Russia are expected to begin to ease in 2016. The external environment is likely to remain challenging for emerging markets. As global supply chains mature, the advanced market recovery remains fragile, and emerging market growth remains reliant on government support, trade is likely to remain weak. Large investments world-wide in commodity production over the past decades are likely to keep downward pressure on commodity prices.

Domestic policy environments may become increasingly constrained as weak growth erodes the resilience of private and public balance sheets. Aging populations may dampen potential growth. Weak growth prospects are likely to continue to weigh on investment, which may, in turn, slow the technological progress required to sustain high productivity growth. A combination of countercyclical policies and structural reforms are needed to reinvigorate growth.

---

push could help lift growth prospects and, to the extent it encourages investment, support domestic demand, as well as help improve investor sentiment and capital flows. This would be especially useful for countries that have limited room for expansionary fiscal and monetary policies.

What are the key channels of spillovers from the major emerging markets?

A growth slowdown in emerging markets, in particular in one or several of the BRICS, could have significant spillover effects given their share

of global output and growth. They have become important export markets and significant sources of remittances. Some of them also supply foreign direct investment (FDI) and official development assistance (ODA) to other emerging markets, frontier markets, and low-income countries (LIC) as well as advanced markets.

Global output and growth. Since 2000, emerging markets have accounted for much of world growth. During the pre-crisis years of 2003-08, emerging market growth averaged 7.1 percent, well above its long-term average of about 5 percent. During the crisis, global activity was shored up by emerging markets, despite a sharp slowdown in 2008. Partly as a result of large-scale stimulus in the largest emerging markets, they continued to grow in 2009, when the rest of the world contracted, and they expanded strongly in 2010. Frontier markets have grown almost as rapidly as emerging markets since 2000, though from a smaller base, to 4.6 percent of global GDP in 2014.

Global trade. Emerging markets now account for 32 percent of global trade (compared with 16 percent in 1994). This has partly reflected their deepening integration into global supply chains. For example, the value added from emerging markets embedded in U.S. or Euro Area exports nearly doubled to about 7 percent in 2011 from 3 percent in 2000. Among emerging markets, the BRICS have accounted for most of the increase in trade flows to emerging markets and frontier markets between 2000 and 2014 (Figure 3.3). Most of the emerging markets' value-added trade with other emerging markets and frontier markets is with the BRICS. As the largest economies in their respective developing country regions, the BRICS also account for a sizeable share of regional exports.

Global commodity markets. BRICS have played a significant role in global commodity markets (World Bank 2015c). Rapid growth in China's industrial production through the 2000s was accompanied by a sharp increase in demand for metals and energy. Virtually all of the increase in global metals demand and more than half of the increase in global primary energy demand between 2000 and 2014 originated in China (Figure 3.4).[4] India's demand for primary energy and metals has also grown rapidly but less than China's, partly as a result of more services-based growth (World Bank 2015b). Large emerging market and frontier market commodity producers have benefited from this increased demand for their products. For several commodities, a few individual emerging markets and frontier markets accounted for 20 percent or more of global exports (e.g. Indonesia

---

[4]Chinese demand for agricultural commodities has grown in line with global demand. In general, demand for metals and primary energy tends to be highly income elastic whereas demand for agricultural commodities tends to have low income elasticities but grows in line with population (World Bank 2015b).

FIGURE 3.3 BRICS in EM and FM trade

Among emerging markets, trade linkages with BRICS, especially China, have increased in the last two decades. Advanced markets continue to be important trading partners for emerging markets.

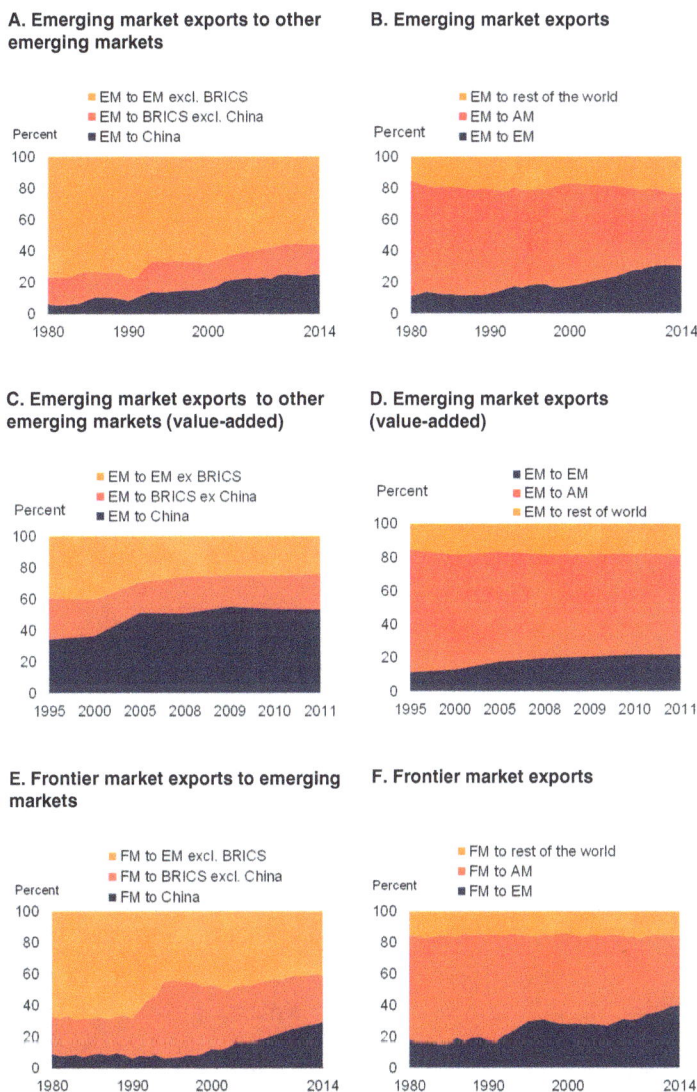

A. Emerging market exports to other emerging markets

B. Emerging market exports

C. Emerging market exports to other emerging markets (value-added)

D. Emerging market exports (value-added)

E. Frontier market exports to emerging markets

F. Frontier market exports

Sources: Direction of Trade Statistics (DOTS); OECD Trade in Value Added (TiVA) database; World Bank.
Note: EM stands for emerging markets, FM stands for frontier markets, AM stands for advanced markets.
C. D. Data only available for 1995, 2000, 2005, and 2008-11.

for nickel, aluminum and coal; Chile for copper; Russia for oil; and Brazil for iron ore and soybeans; World Bank 2015c).

During the 2000s, high prices and improved technology encouraged the development of new capacity, including U.S. shale oil production, new copper mines in Eritrea and new oil fields in

FIGURE 3.4 Commodity demand and supply

China, and to a lesser extent, India, are major sources of demand for key commodities. In addition, China is a major source of global coal production, and Russia, of oil and gas.

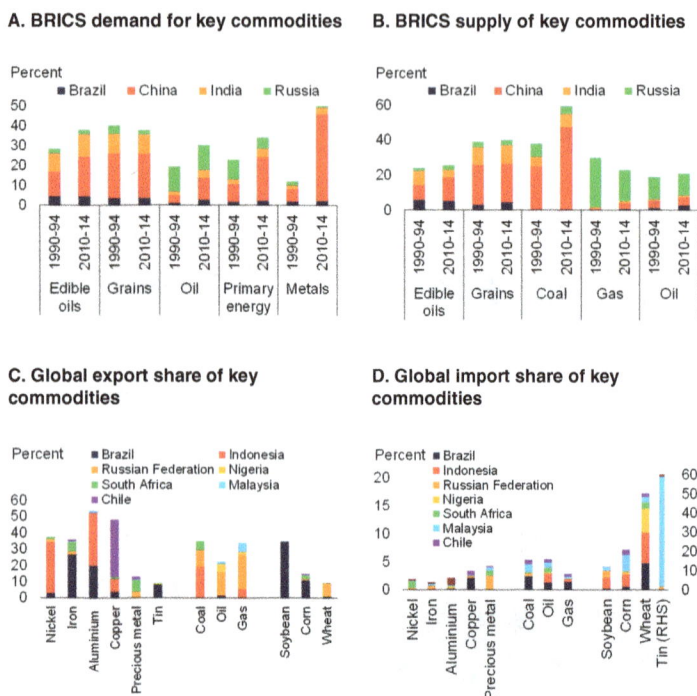

A. BRICS demand for key commodities

B. BRICS supply of key commodities

C. Global export share of key commodities

D. Global import share of key commodities

Sources: BP Statistics Review; U.S. Department of Agriculture.
C. D. Share of each emerging market in total global exports and imports of each commodity, average 2008-13. Includes exports and imports of ores (e.g. bauxite) and oil products.

Myanmar (Baffes et al. 2015, World Bank 2015c). The commodity super-cycle, however, began to unwind in early 2011 when most commodity prices began to slide as new capacity came onstream at the same time as growth in major emerging markets increasingly tilted away from commodity-intensive industrial production. Oil prices were initially kept high by OPEC production cuts but, in the second half of 2014, halved with OPEC's policy shift towards targeting market share.

Global finance. Emerging markets have started playing a major role in a wide range of global financial flows, including foreign direct investment, banking and portfolio investment, remittances and official development assistance.

- *Foreign direct investment* (FDI). Since emerging market growth prospects remain better than those in many advanced markets, emerging markets have attracted a large amount of FDI (30 percent of global FDI inflows, on average during 2000-14). Most of this amount, about two-thirds, has been received by the BRICS. Among BRICS, China is not only the single largest recipient country of FDI inflows, it has also become an important source country for FDI, especially in Sub-Saharan Africa and other natural resource-producing countries (World Bank 2015c).

- *Banking and portfolio investment.* Although from a low starting point, bank claims and portfolio investment to emerging markets have doubled since the early 2000s to about 6 percent and 5 percent of global GDP, respectively. As with FDI, BRICS account for a sizeable portion of these flows. From a much smaller base, global banking flows to frontier markets have also risen, to 1 percent of global GDP in mid-2015.

- *Remittances.* Emerging markets are now among the largest source and destination countries for remittances, accounting for 40 percent of global remittance in- and outflows. Five emerging market and frontier market source countries (Kuwait, Qatar, Russia, Saudi Arabia, and United Arab Emirates) account for 20 percent of global remittance outflows. Emerging market and frontier market recipient countries such as Egypt, India, Nigeria, Philippines, Pakistan, and Vietnam account for 28 percent of global remittance receipts. Remittances from the BRICS are significant, particularly for the ECA and SAR regions (Figure 3.5).

- *Official development assistance* (ODA). The GCC countries, especially Saudi Arabia, Kuwait and the United Arab Emirates, provided significant ODA to Egypt in 2010-14 (on the order of 7 percent of GDP in Fiscal Year 2013/14). China has become an important source for Sub-Saharan Africa while India is providing ODA to Bhutan amounting to 37 percent of GDP in Fiscal Year 2015/16 (World Bank 2015c).

Do business cycles in BRICS move in tandem with those in other emerging markets and frontier markets?

The rising role of BRICS in the world economy suggests that growth fluctuations in their economies could lead to sizeable spillovers to other emerging markets and frontier markets. As the group of emerging and frontier markets has established stronger intra-group trade and financial linkages, common movements in their business cycles have become more pronounced. Growth fluctuations in major emerging markets tend to lead growth in other emerging markets and frontier markets. In addition, growth slowdowns in major emerging markets have been associated with lower growth in other emerging markets and frontier markets and, to a much lesser extent, in advanced markets.

FIGURE 3.5 BRICS in regional trade and remittances

Exports to BRICS are particularly high in EAP, MNA, and SSA regions. BRICS constitute a major source of remittance flows to other emerging markets, especially in ECA and SAR.

A. Destinations of exports by regions **B. Remittance inflows from BRICS**

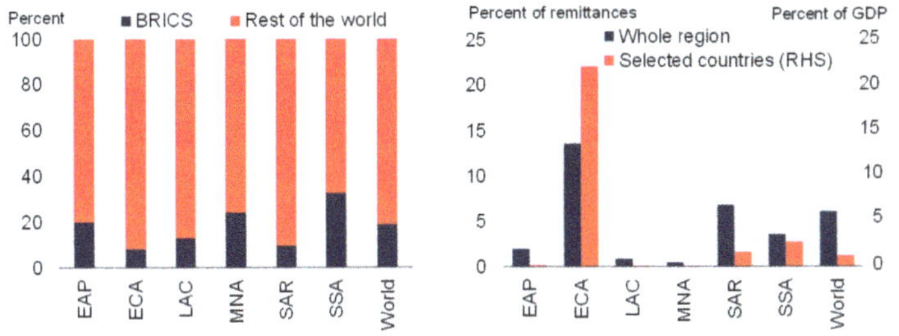

Sources: Direction of Trade Statistics (DOTS); World Bank.

Notes: EAP = East Asia and Pacific, ECA = Europe and Central Asia, LAC = Latin America and Caribbean, MNA = Middle East and North Africa, SAR = South Asia, and SSA = Sub Saharan Africa. Graphs use 2014 data for countries of all income categories.

B. Blue bars "Region" show remittance inflows from BRICS into each region. Red bars "Countries (RHS)" show remittance inflow to the three countries with the largest remittance inflows from BRICS (in percent of GDP). The three countries are Kiribati, Mongolia, and Philippines in the EAP region; Armenia, Kyrgyz Republic, and Tajikistan in the ECA region; Bolivia, Guyana, and Paraguay in the LAC region; Egypt, Jordan, and Lebanon in the MNA region; Bangladesh, Nepal, and Pakistan in the SAR region; and Lesotho, Mozambique, and Swaziland in the SSA region.

Emergence of an emerging-frontier market business cycle. The drivers of business cycles can be decomposed into global, group, and country-specific factors. This decomposition exercise is conducted for a sample 106 countries (advanced markets, emerging markets and frontier markets, and other developing countries, Annex 3.1). The global factor represents business cycle fluctuations that are common to all countries and to output, investment and consumption. The group-specific factor captures fluctuations that are common to a particular group of countries, in this case to the group of emerging and frontier markets, and the group of advanced markets and the group of other developing countries.

The degree of business cycle synchronization among emerging and frontier markets is captured by the contribution of the factor specific to emerging-frontier markets (EM-FM-specific factor) to variations in their growth. The EM-FM factor explained a small part of growth fluctuations before the 1980s, when emerging and frontier markets were little integrated with each other (and with the global economy). Since then, a common EM-FM-specific factor has emerged that now accounts for about a quarter of the variation in growth in emerging and frontier markets—almost as much as the global cycle (Figure 3.6).[5] These results suggest that a more pronounced EM -FM business cycle has emerged over time. Hence, the risk has increased that adverse developments in BRICS could be a source of a broader synchronous downturn across the EM-FM group.

Higher synchronization of growth fluctuations. Since the global financial crisis, BRICS growth has become increasingly correlated with growth in other emerging markets and frontier markets, but also with growth in advanced markets. Lead correlations—correlations between BRICS growth and other emerging market, frontier market, and advanced market growth *in the subsequent quarter*—are sizeable, suggesting the possibility of spillovers from BRICS growth to these countries (Figure 3.7). In contrast, lag correlations with BRICS growth and other countries are generally small.

[5]Business cycle synchronization here is analyzed in terms of output comovement. The results generally extend to consumption and investment as well. Business cycle co-movement could reflect both the greater trade and financial linkages between emerging and frontier markets that are discussed in the previous section and greater co-movement with common external factors.

BOX 3.2 Understanding cross-border growth spillovers

Growth spillovers can operate via trade and financial linkages. The confidence channel—consumer and business sentiment—can also be an important mechanism for cross-border spillovers of growth. The empirical literature finds sizeable spillovers from China for countries with close trade ties, e.g. countries in the EAP region, Japan and Germany among the advanced markets, and commodity exporters. Growth in Russia and Brazil tends to affect growth of their neighbors and those with whom they have strong trade and remittance linkages.

This box discusses cross-border transmission of shocks to growth and examines empirical estimates of the size of these spillovers.

Transmission channels

Trade channel. A growth slowdown can reduce growth in trading partner countries directly by lowering import demand and, indirectly, by lowering growth in third countries or by slowing technological advances and productivity growth intrinsic to imports (Kose, Prasad, and Terrones 2009; Jansen and Stockman 2004).

While this suggests greater spillovers between countries with closer trade ties, in principle, the opposite can arise when mutual trade generates particularly strong specialization. For example, close trade ties can result in heavy specialization in goods in which countries have a comparative advantage. As countries become heavily reliant on individual industries, they may become more sensitive to industry-specific shocks, with less correlation in broader growth between trading partners (Frankel and Rose 1998).[1]

Financial channel. A growth slowdown can reduce portfolio investment and foreign direct investment outflows to other countries. Arbitrage between different global financial systems could quickly propagate shocks from one country to another (Kose, Otrok, and Whiteman 2003; Doyle and Faust 2002). Rising banking sector cross-border exposures also raise the potential for growth spillovers (IMF 2014). Reduced financial flows could set back investment growth and longer-term growth potential in destination countries. International remittances may also transmit spillovers, as they tend to vary with incomes in sending countries. Some low- and lower-middle-income countries that rely heavily on remittance inflows are particularly vulnerable to disruptions in foreign labor markets that reduce remittances (Dabla-Norris, Espinoza, and Jahan 2015).

While this suggests greater spillovers between countries with larger mutual financial flows, the opposite is, in principle, also possible if incentives to diversify risk internationally are sufficiently strong. For example, if investors are concerned about growth setbacks in one country, they may choose to increase their investments in others with better growth prospects. As a result, capital could flow out of countries with negative growth shocks and into less-affected countries where it would lift activity (Canova and Marrinan 1998; Kalemli-Ozcan, Sørensen, and Yosha 2003; Imbs 2004; Heathcote and Perri 2004).

Commodity channel. A growth slowdown in a major commodity-importing country could reduce global commodity demand and reduce global commodity prices. This would set back investment and growth in commodity exporting countries around the world, even those without direct trade relations with the source country of the shock (Kose and Riezman 2001; Eicher, Schubert, and Turnovsky 2008; Broda and Tille 2002; World Bank 2015a).

Confidence channel. Trade, financial, and commodity channels do not appear to explain the unprecedented severity and cross-country synchronization of contractions and slowdowns in the global financial crisis of 2007-09 (Kalemli-Ozcan, Papaioannou, and Perri 2013; Bacchetta and van Wincoop 2014). In addition to direct economic ties, consumer and business sentiment (over and above developments in underlying fundamentals)—i.e., the confidence channel—can be an important transmission mechanism for cross-border spillovers (Levchenko and Pandalai-Nayar 2015).

Identifying the individual effects of each of these transmission channels is empirically challenging, and the literature has mostly focused on aggregate effects. The importance of each transmission channel likely depends on the nature of the underlying shock although the debate on the relative importance of different shocks is not yet settled.[2] This box focuses on the aggregate effects of growth spillovers without dwelling on their fundamental drivers.

Note: This Box was prepared by Raju Huidrom.

[1] For a detailed discussion, see Kose and Terrones (2015).

---

[2] For instance, Mendoza (1995) and Kose (2002) attribute a sizable portion of output fluctuations to international shocks through the terms of trade, while a part of the real-business-cycle literature focuses on the effects of technology shocks.

BOX 3.2 Understanding cross-border growth spillovers *(continued)*

Empirical estimates of spillovers

Advanced economies. Monfort et al. (2003) find sizeable co-movement in output among the G-7 economies during 1972-2002. Before 1985, a large part of this co-movement can be explained by common shocks (e.g., oil price swings), while in the period after 1985 spillovers, especially from North America to Europe, have become more dominant. Stock and Watson (2005) find sizeable spillovers among G7, accounting for 5-15 percent of the variance of growth depending on the country and the period examined. They, however, find that both overall co-movement and spillovers have declined since 1985, possibly reflecting lower volatility of shocks in the later period (the pre-global crisis "great moderation"). Yilmaz (2009) finds sizeable spillovers from the United States to other advanced economies, especially during the global financial crisis. Financial shocks from the United States appear to be transmitted particularly rapidly to the Euro Area (Dees et al. 2007).

Emerging markets. The literature has focused on spillovers from large EM, often with a regional perspective (Annex 3.3). For the EAP region, spillovers from China are significant, especially for EAP countries integrated into Chinese supply chains (Japan, Singapore, Malaysia and Thailand), and for commodity exporters that are less diversified, e.g. Indonesia (Duval et al. 2014; Inoue, Kaya, and Ohshige 2015; Ahuja and Nabar 2012). Beyond EAP, growth spillovers from China are also significant for Latin American countries, especially for commodity exporters (World Bank 2015a). The spillover implications of China for advanced markets and global growth are generally found to be modest (Ahuja and Nabar 2012; IMF 2014b). Among the advanced economies, Germany and Japan are most affected (Ahuja and Nabar 2012).

In the ECA region, Russia seems to influence regional growth mainly through the remittance and—albeit decreasingly—through the trade channel and somewhat less through the financial channel. Russian growth shocks are associated with sizable effects on Belarus, Kazakhstan, Kyrgyz Republic, Tajikistan, and, to some extent, Georgia (Alturki, Espinosa-Bowen, and Ilahi 2009). That said, growth spillovers from the rest of the world to ECA

countries tend to be larger than those from Russia, reflecting declining trade and financial integration with Russia and increased ties to the European Union (Andrle, Garcia-Saltos, and G. Ho 2013; Ayvazyan and Dabán 2015; Obiora 2009).

South African growth has a substantial positive impact on *long-run* growth in the rest of Africa (Arora and Vamvakidis 2005). *Short-run* spillovers from South Africa, however, are not significant, even to neighboring countries (IMF 2012a). South Africa's trade with the rest of the continent has been limited despite some increase since 1994, in part reflecting trade patterns that prevailed under the apartheid regime that ruled South Africa until 1994. There are significant growth spillovers effect to African economies from both the Euro Area and the BRICS (Gurara and Ncube 2013), with spillovers from the Euro Area exceeding those from the BRICS.

Latin America is characterized by the presence of two large countries (Brazil and Mexico) that may affect smaller neighboring economies significantly (IMF 2012b). Spillovers from Brazil to some of its neighbors can be considerable, both by transmitting Brazil-specific shocks and by amplifying global shocks. Southern Cone countries (Argentina, Bolivia, Chile, Paraguay, and Uruguay), given their sizeable export linkages, are particularly vulnerable to spillovers from Brazil. In the Andean region, however, trade linkages with Brazil are generally weak. Likewise, reflecting Central America's modest trade linkages with Mexico, growth spillovers from Mexico are modest (Adler and Sosa 2014).

Low income countries (LIC) have become increasingly integrated with emerging markets, through stronger trade links, rising cross-border financial asset holdings and capital flows, and higher remittance flows (Dabla-Norris, Espinoza, and Jahan 2015).[3] In particular, emerging markets are an important source of remittances for LIC, especially within their own region – e.g. India for LIC in Asia, Russia for LIC in ECA, and Saudi Arabia for LIC in MNA. This was most evident in the aftermath of the global financial crisis, when recovery in many LIC mirrored the economic rebound in emerging market trading partners (IMF 2010).

---

[3]Informal sector trading links are also important for LIC as a channel of transmission (IMF 2012a).

Lower growth during slowdowns in BRICS. An event study suggests that slowdowns in BRICS have been accompanied by lower growth in other emerging markets and frontier markets and, to a much lesser extent, in advanced markets. There were seven slowdown episodes which are defined as troughs in BRICS growth over five-quarter rolling windows from 1997Q2-2015Q1.[6] During these episodes, BRICS growth was, on average, about 2 percent, compared with the long-run average of 5 percent. Although there is wide variation, median emerging-frontier market growth fell by almost a percentage point during these BRICS slowdowns, and median advanced market growth eased by about one-quarter percentage point (Figure 3.8). BRICS growth shocks appear to have been at least partly transmitted through declining imports. Commodity prices—especially energy prices—decelerated sharply, and emerging-frontier market export growth slowed during these episodes.

These findings together point to the possibility of significant growth spillovers from the BRICS to other emerging and frontier markets. However, the growth slowdowns in other emerging markets and frontier markets during episodes of lower growth in BRICS may have been pure coincidence, or the result of a common external adverse shock. The next section presents a formal econometric analysis of growth spillovers from BRICS that addresses these concerns.

How large are the spillovers from the major emerging markets?

In order to quantify growth spillovers from BRICS to the global economy and to other emerging markets and frontier markets, a structural vector autoregression (VAR) model, with a recursive identification scheme, is estimated for 1998Q1–2015Q2. The model includes growth in G7 countries as a measure of activity in

advanced markets; proxies for global financial conditions (U.S. 10-year sovereign bond yield and EM Bond Index EMBI); growth in BRICS; oil prices; growth in emerging markets excluding BRICS; and growth in frontier markets.[7] Spillovers are inferred by tracing out the responses to a one-off exogenous shock to BRICS growth that reduces it by 1 percentage point on impact.[8]

Spillovers from BRICS. A growth slowdown in BRICS could reduce global growth and, especially, growth in other emerging markets and in frontier markets. On average, a 1 percentage point decline in BRICS growth could, over the following two years, reduce global growth by 0.4 percentage point, growth in other emerging markets by 0.8 percentage point and growth in frontier markets by 1.5 percentage points (Figure 3.9).[9] The stronger response of frontier markets to BRICS growth fluctuations may reflect the smaller size and greater openness of most frontier markets than emerging markets.[10]

In contrast, the estimated impact on G7 growth is, on average, modest and statistically insignificant in the structural VAR model. This may reflect both pro-active countercyclical policy in G7 countries and their net oil-importing status. G7 central banks tend to respond to external shocks, including those from BRICS, with accommodative monetary policy. To the extent that this is not fully controlled for, measured spillovers are small (Bodenstein, Erceg, and Guerrieri 2009). Furthermore, as net oil importers, G7 economies tend to benefit from the

---

[6]The seven episodes identified are 1998Q1, 2000Q4, 2003Q1, 2004Q4, 2006Q2, 2008Q4, and 2011Q3. For instance, the 1998 episode corresponds to the Russian crisis; 2008 to the global financial crisis; and 2011 to the recent growth slowdown episode.

[7]The VAR methodology follows World Bank (2015a, 2015b). Technical details of the VAR model are provided in Annex 3.2. The recursive identification scheme requires quarterly data and hence spillover analysis in this chapter is limited to those countries for which quarterly data is available. The list of countries and their categorization is provided in Annex 3.1. As is usual in standard (linear) VARs, these estimates do not capture highly disruptive shocks that trigger confidence effects, financial market swings, or policy responses to amplify growth impacts.

[8]The shock is quite persistent. BRICS growth declines by about 2.5 percentage points in cumulative terms at the end of two years due to the impact of the shock.

[9]Using a panel regression framework, Akin and Kose (2008) also find intensive intra-group growth spillovers among emerging markets.

[10]The group of frontier markets in this sample is dominated by one commodity importer (Romania) which accounts for about 45 percent of frontier market GDP.

lower oil prices induced by a BRICS slowdown. That said, slowdowns in BRICS can weigh on growth in individual advanced markets that have strong trade links with the BRICS, notably Germany and Japan. Confidence effects— although not explicitly captured econometrically here—could also amplify spillovers as discussed in detail later.

While rapid growth in BRICS has buttressed global growth, its synchronous deceleration since 2010 (India recently being the exception) has contributed to the slowdown in other emerging markets and frontier markets. In China, policies have helped rein in growth in excess capacity sectors. Geopolitical tensions, sanctions, and falling oil prices in Russia and falling commodity prices and political tensions in Brazil have weakened investor sentiment. In South Africa, energy bottlenecks and labor unrest have weighed on growth. The associated slowdowns (China, South Africa) and recessions (Brazil, Russia) have dampened imports (including commodity imports) from trading partners, remittances to Central Asia, and FDI flows from major emerging markets. In a decomposition of historical contributions to growth, the BRICS slowdown since 2010 appear to have accounted for the bulk of the growth slowdown in other emerging markets and frontier markets between 2010 and 2015.[11]

Spillovers from G7. Spillovers from BRICS remain smaller than those from advanced markets (Figure 3.10). After two years, a decline in G7 growth reduces emerging market growth by one-

[11]Because of lack of sufficiently long time series of quarterly data for low-income countries, the estimations here are restricted to emerging and frontier markets. Other studies have estimated spillovers based on annual data—in which shocks are less clearly defined—and found that growth shocks in major emerging markets can have a similarly large impact on low- and lower-middle-income country growth. During 1980-2010, a 1 percentage point decline in growth in BRICS, Mexico, Saudi Arabia and Turkey may have reduced growth in low- and lower-middle-income countries in Sub-Saharan Africa, the Middle East and North Africa, and in Europe and Central Asia by 0.5-1 percentage point in the same year (Dabla-Norris, Espinoza and Jahan 2015). During 1970-2008, a 1 percentage point decline in BRIC growth may have reduced growth in oil-exporting low- and lower-middle-income countries by about 0.7-1.4 percentage points over the following two years and in oil-importing ones by about 0.2-0.6 percentage point (Samake and Yang 2014).

FIGURE 3.6 Emergence of emerging and frontier market business cycle

Business cycles among emerging and frontier markets have become increasingly synchronous, reflecting the increased integration of these economies into global and regional trade and financial flows. A significant portion of this synchronicity is explained by an emerging and frontier market (EM-FM) specific factor.

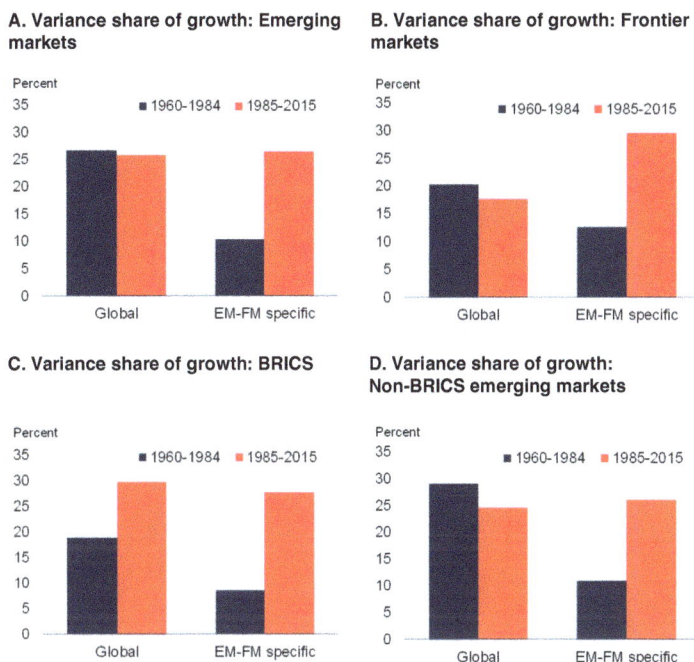

A. Variance share of growth: Emerging markets

B. Variance share of growth: Frontier markets

C. Variance share of growth: BRICS

D. Variance share of growth: Non-BRICS emerging markets

Source: World Bank staff estimates.
Note: A dynamic factor model is separately estimated over the two periods, 1960-1984 and 1985-2015, using a sample of 106 countries grouped into three regions: advanced markets (AM), emerging and frontier markets (EM-FM), and other developing countries. Variance decompositions are computed for each country and, within each country, for output in each of these two periods. Each bar then represents the cross-sectional mean of the variance share attributable to the global factor and the EM-FM-specific factor among the emerging markets (EM) and frontier markets (FM).

FIGURE 3.7 Role of BRICS in business cycle synchronization

BRICS growth tends to lead growth in other emerging and frontier markets, suggesting the possibility of spillovers from BRICS to these countries.

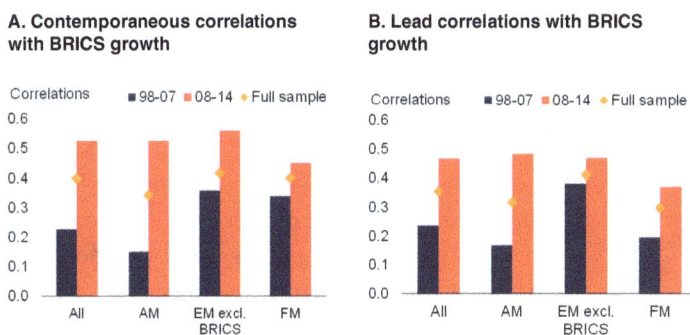

A. Contemporaneous correlations with BRICS growth

B. Lead correlations with BRICS growth

Sources: Haver Analytics; World Bank staff estimates.
Note: EM stands for emerging markets, FM stands for frontier markets, AM stands for advanced markets. For each group, the figures refer to the cross-sectional average correlation coefficient between BRICS growth and individual countries in that group. Lead correlations refer to correlations with BRICS growth and growth in the rest of the countries in the subsequent quarter. Estimates are based on quarterly data for 1997Q2-2015Q1 for 56 countries.

FIGURE 3.8 Growth slowdown in BRICS

Growth slowdowns in BRICS are associated with slowdowns in the other EM, FM, and to a lesser extent, AM. Such slowdowns are also associated with falling exports and commodity prices.

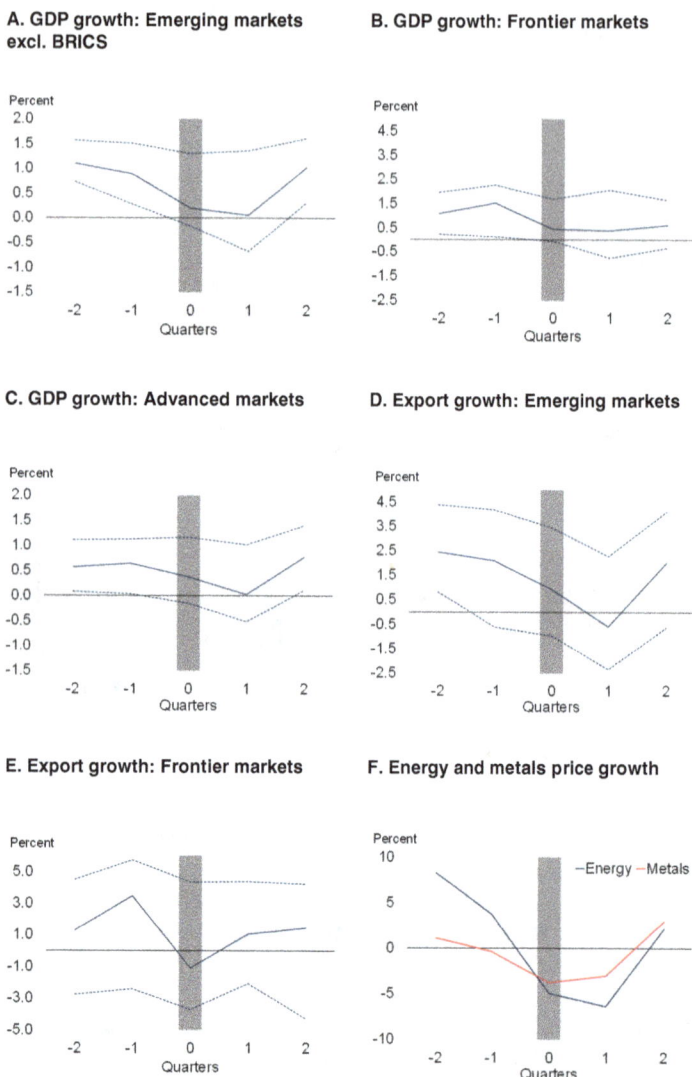

A. GDP growth: Emerging markets excl. BRICS

B. GDP growth: Frontier markets

C. GDP growth: Advanced markets

D. Export growth: Emerging markets

E. Export growth: Frontier markets

F. Energy and metals price growth

Sources: Haver Analytics; World Bank staff estimates.
Note: The graphs show GDP, export, and commodity prices growth in the quarters around a growth slowdown event in BRICS (t=0) indicated by the solid bar. Slowdown events are defined as troughs in BRICS growth over a 5-quarter rolling window. There are seven GDP slowdown events during 1997Q2-2015Q1. They are 1998Q1, 2000Q4, 2003Q1, 2004Q4, 2006Q2, 2008Q4, 2011Q3. The solid line refers to cross-sectional mean growth and the dotted lines refer to the 25th and 75th percentiles. There is one slowdown event during the global financial crisis of 2008-09; results are generally robust when that event is excluded.

market growth (excluding BRICS) and frontier market growth as well as for growth in most individual emerging and frontier markets in the sample used here.

Stronger spillovers from G7 countries reflect their larger economic size. While the BRICS account for one-fifth of global GDP, G7 countries account for almost half of global GDP. In addition, G7 countries account for a larger share of global trade and play a central role in global finance.[12] Financial flows can quickly transmit shocks originating in G7 economies around the world.

Spillovers from individual BRICS. In order to analyze spillovers from individual BRICS, the VAR model is re-estimated by replacing aggregate BRICS growth with growth in each BRICS economy, one at a time. The magnitude of spillovers varies across the BRICS (Figure 3.11).[13] A 1 percentage point decline in China's growth could reduce growth in non-BRICS emerging markets by 0.5 percentage point and in frontier markets by 1 percentage point over two years whereas a similar shock in Russia would reduce growth in other emerging markets by 0.3 percentage point. Spillovers from a growth shock in Brazil to other emerging markets would be much smaller and to frontier markets, statistically insignificant. In general, spillovers from India and South Africa to other emerging markets and frontier markets would be much smaller and/or statistically insignificant.[14]

The magnitude and reach of spillovers from major emerging markets reflect their size and integration. In current dollar terms, China's economy is more than four times the size of the next-largest BRICS economy (Brazil); its imports are six times the size of those of Russia; and its demand for primary energy and metals is four to ten times the size of that of India.

third more and frontier market growth by one-half more than a similarly sized growth slowdown in BRICS. Over the sample period, G7 growth shocks explain about 30 percent of the variation in emerging and frontier market growth at the two-year horizon, compared with 10 percent and 7 percent, respectively, explained by BRICS growth shocks. This is true for both aggregate emerging

[12]At end-2014, more than half of global banking assets and liabilities were on G7 country banks' balance sheets. The G7 accounted for one-third of global foreign direct investment flows and almost half of global portfolio investment. The IMF (2011) argues that the largest spillovers arise from U.S. growth shocks although the U.S. economy is similarly sized to the Euro Area's which has been attributed to the predominance of the United States in global finance.
[13]Details of this version of the model are presented in Annex 3.2.
[14]These estimates are generally in line with the literature (Box 3.2).

In order to analyze the regional implications of spillovers from individual BRICS, country-specific VAR models are estimated for each spillover destination country (Annex 3.2). Whereas growth fluctuations in China would have global repercussions, those in other BRICS tend to radiate more narrowly. A growth impulse in China changes growth in other emerging markets in East Asia by about as much as growth in other emerging markets around the world. On the other hand, a 1 percentage point growth slowdown in Russia reduces growth in other emerging markets in Europe by 0.4 percentage point over two years but its impact on growth outside the region is negligible. Brazil has a small impact even on its own region.[15] A sufficiently long time series of quarterly GDP data for a strict comparison is unavailable for other emerging markets in South Asia and Sub-Saharan Africa, but there are indications that spillovers from South Africa and India to their respective regions are modest (Box 3.3).

Transmission channels of spillovers. Commodity markets are a key transmission channel of spillovers (Box 3.2). China accounts for 30 percent or more of global demand for copper, iron ore, nickel, aluminum and soybeans and 10 percent of global demand for coal. Among the largest producers of these commodities are Brazil, Chile, Colombia, Indonesia, Peru, Philippines, and Poland (World Bank 2015d). This is reflected in country-specific VAR model estimates (Figure 3.12).[16] As a result of these commodity price declines, growth in commodity exporters could slow by somewhat more than growth in commodity importers.[17]

Another important channel of spillover transmission is trade. China's rapid trade

---

[15]This weaker result than found by other authors (e.g. IMF 2014b) partly reflects that the sample here excludes the Tequila crisis.

[16]These are based on country-specific VAR models. Commodity prices here refer to trade-weighted commodity prices. To provide some perspective on the size of the response of commodity prices due to a growth shock, the standard deviation of commodity prices in the sample is about 9 percent. The magnitude of the response of commodity prices is generally in line with the literature (e.g. IMF 2014b).

[17]These findings are broadly in line with the literature (World Bank 2015c; Inoue, Kaya, and Ohshige, 2015; Ludovic and Cyril 2013). For commodity importers, the commodity channel would mitigate the adverse spillover effects from a slowdown in major emerging markets.

FIGURE 3.9 Spillovers from BRICS

A growth slowdown in BRICS can have a significant adverse effect on global growth, especially in other emerging and frontier markets. The effect on advanced markets is estimated to be modest. The slowdowns in BRICS since 2010 has weighed on growth in other emerging and frontier market.

A. Impact of 1 percentage point decline in BRICS growth on growth in emerging markets excluding BRICS and frontier markets

B. Impact of 1 percentage point decline in BRICS growth on G7 and global growth

C. Contributions of BRICS shocks to growth: Emerging markets excluding BRICS

D. Contributions of BRICS shocks to growth: Frontier markets

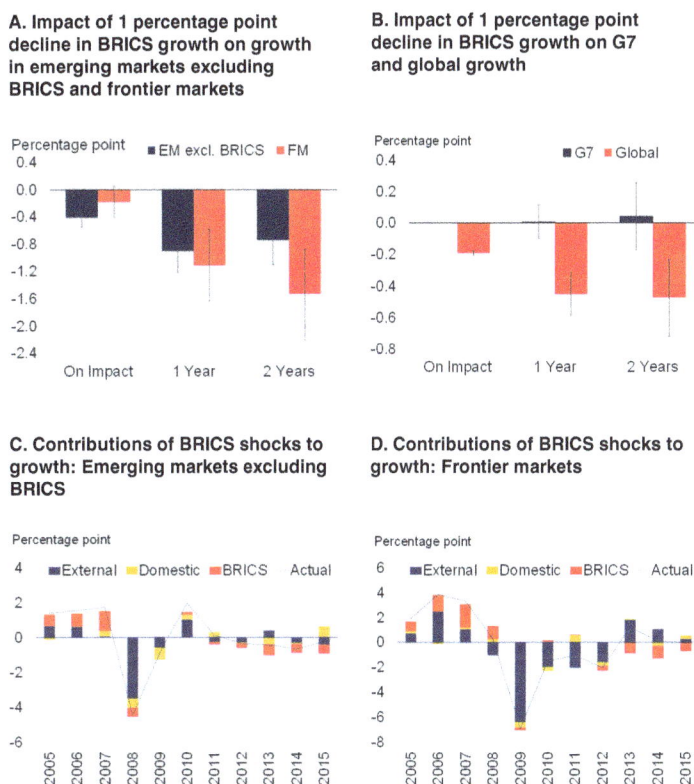

Source: World Bank staff estimates.
A. B. Cumulated impulse responses for different horizons due to a 1 percentage point decline in BRICS growth on impact. Global is GDP-weighted average of BRICS, emerging and frontier markets, and G7 responses. Bars represent medians, and error bars 16-84 percent confidence bands.
C. D. Historical decomposition of demeaned emerging market (C) and frontier market (D) growth. Domestic shock in Figure C (D) refers to the shock to emerging market (frontier market) growth. External shock refers to the combined contributions from shocks to G7 growth, U.S. interest rates, EMBI, frontier market (emerging market) growth, and the oil price. Annual figures are obtained by summing across quarters in a given year.

integration since its WTO accession in 2001 has increased the potential for global spillovers from growth shocks. In addition to emerging and frontier markets, several advanced markets are also among China's closest trading partners, including Germany and Japan. A Global Vector Autoregressive (GVAR) model is employed to estimate spillovers to a large number of advanced, emerging, and frontier markets from a growth slowdown in China, specifically through the trade channel.

To examine the implications of the growing trade presence of China, two sets of estimates are

FIGURE 3.10 Spillovers from BRICS and advanced markets

Spillovers from advanced market growth slowdown to emerging and frontier market growth are typically larger than those originating from BRICS.

A. Impact of 1 percentage point decline in G7 and BRICS growth on growth in emerging markets excluding BRICS

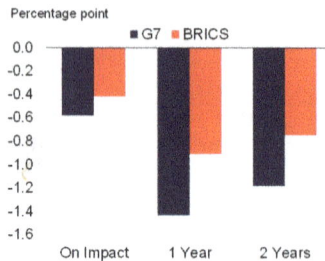

B. Variance share of growth explained by G7 and BRICS growth shocks: Emerging markets excluding BRICS

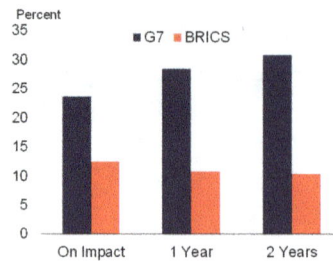

C. Impact of 1 percentage point decline in G7 and BRICS growth on growth in frontier markets

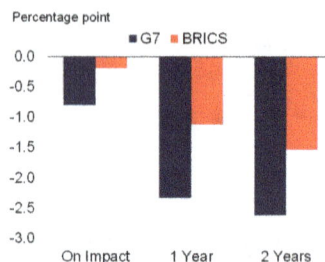

D. Variance share of growth explained by G7 and BRICS growth shocks: Frontier markets

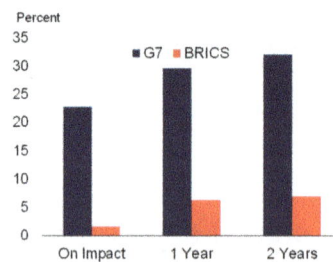

Source: World Bank staff estimates.
A. C. Cumulated impulse responses of emerging (A) and frontier market (C) growth, at different horizons, due to a 1 percentage point decline in G7 and BRICS growth.
B. D. Variance share of emerging (B) and frontier market (D) growth explained by G7 and BRICS growth shocks.

derived. The first assumes bilateral trade links as in 1998-2000 (when China accounted for 3 percent of global trade). The second assumes trade links as in 2010-12 (when China accounted for over 8 percent of global trade).[18] For the majority of countries, and especially Brazil among emerging markets and the United States, Japan, and Canada among advanced markets, stronger trade linkages have raised the estimated spillovers.[19]

[18]In addition to these direct trade links, commodity exporters are also affected by the impact of growth fluctuations in China on global commodity markets.

[19]Among the advanced economies, other studies have also found that spillovers from China to Japan can be quite significant (IMF 2014b; Inoue, Kaya, and Ohshige 2015).

The magnitude of spillovers from BRICS could be more pronounced if shocks are amplified via the confidence channel (Box 3.2). A sharp slowdown in a large BRICS economy could lead to general reassessment of investor risk sentiment. This could trigger a plunge in prices of emerging market assets, currency depreciations, equity market drops, and bond yield spikes across emerging markets. In the analysis here, such spillovers are only partially captured through the impact of a BRICS shock on the EMBI which then feeds into growth elsewhere. In the event of a severe adverse shock to BRICS, however, the EMBI could spike more sharply and the distress spread through a greater range of financial markets than suggested by these, essentially linear, response estimates.

Synchronous slowdown in BRICS. A synchronous slowdown in BRICS would have considerable global growth effects (Figure 3.13).[20] A synchronous BRICS slowdown is defined as one in which BRICS growth declines by the same amount as an isolated decline in growth in China. Activity in China's trading partners that are also closely linked to their regional BRICS would be doubly hit. As a result, emerging market, frontier market, and global growth could decline by around 0.1-0.2 of a percentage point more, over two years, in a synchronous BRICS slowdown than in an isolated slowdown in China.

With every year of slowing BRICS growth, the probability increases that the slowdown turns into an outright recession, as household, corporate, and government buffers erode and expectations of future growth prospects shift downwards (Didier et al. 2015). A synchronous, steepening BRICS growth slowdown could considerably depress emerging and frontier market growth and weigh on advanced market and global growth as well (Figure 3.14). If, for example, BRICS growth persisted at its current weak levels (3.2 percent annualized) through 2017 instead of the currently projected pickup, the rest of emerging market growth could slow by about 0.4 percentage point from the baseline forecast in 2016 and about 1

[20]This compares the results of two different regressions: one in which BRICS as a whole are included; and another in which China is included.

percentage point in 2017.[21] The impact would be considerably larger if BRICS growth were to slide below current levels. For instance, if BRICS growth slowed by as much as the average forecast downgrade during 2010-14 (0.2 percent), growth in the rest of emerging markets and in frontier markets could fall 1-1.3 and 0.5-1.5 percentage points below the baseline forecasts in 2016-17, respectively. Growth in G7 countries would fall considerably less, by about 0.3-0.6 percentage point during 2016-17. Overall, global growth would decline by about 0.7-1.1 percentage points below the baseline forecasts in 2016-17.

A perfect storm: BRICS weakness combined with financial turmoil. The current BRICS growth slowdown coincides with tightening global financial conditions. In December 2015, the U.S. Federal Reserve increased monetary policy rates for the first time since the global financial crisis and is expected to continue to gradually raise policy rates. In all likelihood, this tightening cycle will proceed smoothly as it has long been anticipated, and would have only a modest impact on emerging and frontier markets.

However, the tightening cycle carries significant risks of financial market turmoil. This could be accompanied by a broad-based repricing of emerging and frontier market assets and sizeable declines in capital inflows to emerging and frontier markets (Arteta et al. 2015). Investor sentiment could deteriorate sharply on weakening emerging and frontier market growth prospects. As a result, risk spreads for emerging and frontier market assets could widen steeply and raise overall financing costs for emerging and frontier markets, further dampening growth. An increase in financing costs can also reduce policy space, in particular fiscal space, limiting the firepower that countries need to respond to slowing growth (World Bank 2015c).

A synchronous BRICS slowdown could have much more pronounced spillover effects if it is

---

FIGURE 3.11 Spillovers from individual BRICS

The magnitude and reach of spillovers from individual BRICS differ. Spillovers from China are significant for countries in the EAP and ECA regions as well as some commodity exporters in Latin America. While spillovers from the rest of BRICS countries generally tend to be small, spillovers from Russia within the ECA region can be sizeable.

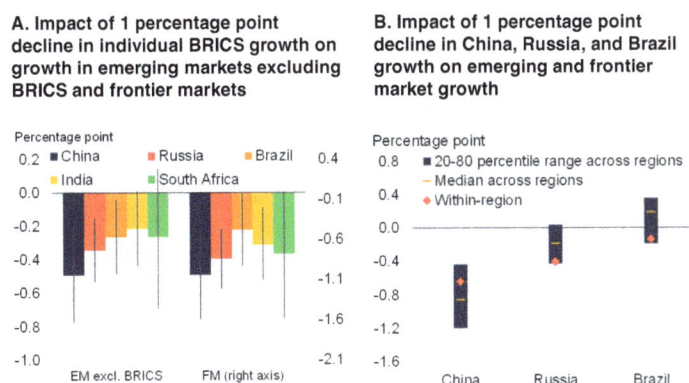

A. Impact of 1 percentage point decline in individual BRICS growth on growth in emerging markets excluding BRICS and frontier markets

B. Impact of 1 percentage point decline in China, Russia, and Brazil growth on emerging and frontier market growth

Source: World Bank staff estimates.
A. Cumulated impulse responses at the end of two years. Shocks are scaled such that China's growth declines by 1 percentage point on impact. Shock sizes for the rest of BRICS countries are calibrated such that their growth declines by exactly the same amount as China at the end of two years. These results are from the aggregate VAR model. Bars represent the median and the error bands denote the 16-84 percent confidence bands.
B. Cumulated impulse responses at the end of two years due to a 1 percentage point decline on impact in China, Russia, and Brazil growth. For each spillover source country, the bar denotes the 20-80 percentile range of the responses of all countries in all regions (excluding the spillover source country) and the orange dash denotes the respective cross-sectional median response. The red diamond denotes the cross-sectional average response across countries in the specific region as the spillover source country (excluding itself). These results are from country-specific VAR models. ECA results exclude Turkey, for which estimated spillovers are negligible. Positive estimates for shocks from Brazil are statistically insignificant.

---

combined with a tightening of risk spreads. When combined with tightening financial conditions, e.g. EMBI increasing by 100 basis points from the current level in 2015 (an increase comparable to the taper tantrum), the BRICS slowdown could cut growth in other emerging markets by about 1.3-1.5 percentage points and in frontier markets by 1-1.8 from the baseline forecasts in 2016-17 (Figure 3.14). Global growth would decline about 0.9-1.2 percentage points in 2016-17 below the baseline forecast. Financial tightening could reduce growth particularly sharply in frontier markets, with their less liquid, more volatile and fragile financial markets.

What are the policy implications?

Emerging and frontier market policies can play an important role in mitigating the persistence and depth of spillovers from slowing BRICS growth. The appropriate policy response depends on the nature of the shock and the spillovers:

---

[21]The baseline forecasts for emerging markets, frontier markets, and the G7 are constructed by aggregating the country level forecasts presented in Chapter 1 across countries in each group. Global in this exercise refers to the combined set of BRICS, emerging markets excluding BRICS, frontier markets, and the G7 used in the VAR estimation.

FIGURE 3.12 **Channels of spillovers**

Among emerging markets, spillovers from China to commodity exporters are larger than to commodity importers, suggesting a role of the commodity channel in the transmission of shocks from BRICS.

A. Impact of 1 percentage point decline in China's growth on commodity price growth

B. Impact of 1 percentage point decline in China's growth on growth in emerging and frontier market commodity exporters and importers

C. Impact of 1 percentage point decline in China's growth on growth in other countries

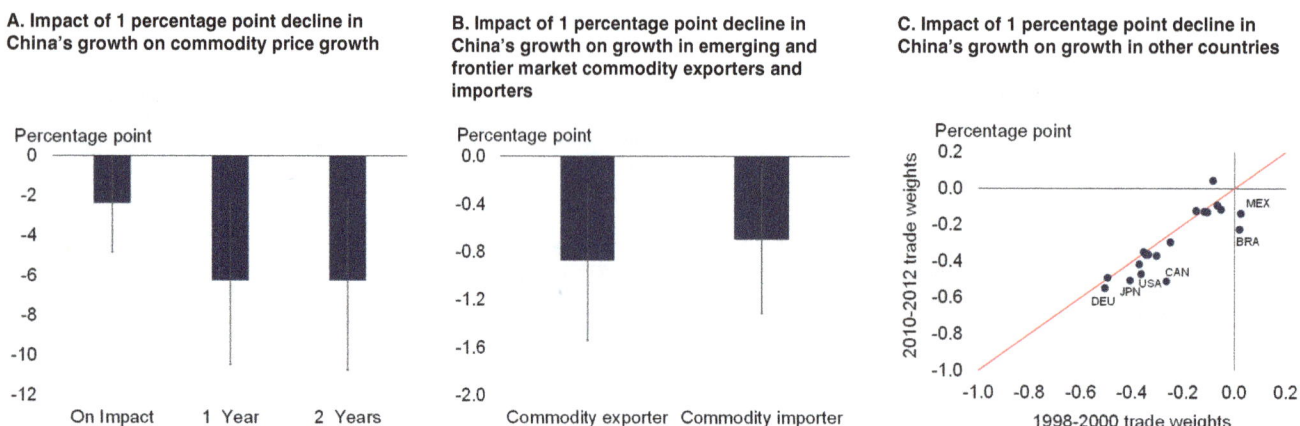

Source: World Bank staff estimates.
A. Cumulated impulse responses of trade-weighted commodity prices of commodity exporters, for different horizons, due to a 1 percentage point decline in China growth. Solid bars denote the median and the error bars denote the 16-84 percent confidence bands. The average quarterly growth rate of commodity prices is about 0.9 percent in the sample. Commodity exporters include Chile, Malaysia, Paraguay, and Peru.
B. Cumulated impulse responses of GDP growth, at the two year horizon, due to a 1 percentage point decline in China's growth. For each group, the figures refer to the cross-sectional average response across all the countries in that group. Commodity exporters include Chile, Malaysia, Paraguay, and Peru. Commodity importers include Bulgaria, Croatia, Hong Kong SAR, China, Hungary, Jordan, Mexico, Poland, Republic of Korea, Romania, Singapore, Thailand, and Turkey.
C. Based on the GVAR model described in Annex 3.2. This excludes Chile, India, Republic of Korea, Malaysia, and Turkey. Model is estimated twice, using average trade weights for 2010-12 and average trade weights for 1998-2000.

FIGURE 3.13 **Spillovers from a synchronous slowdown in BRICS**

A synchronous slowdown in BRICS would have larger adverse spillover effects on other emerging and frontier markets than just a slowdown in China.

Impact of a decline in China's and BRICS growth on global growth, growth in emerging markets excluding BRICS and in frontier markets

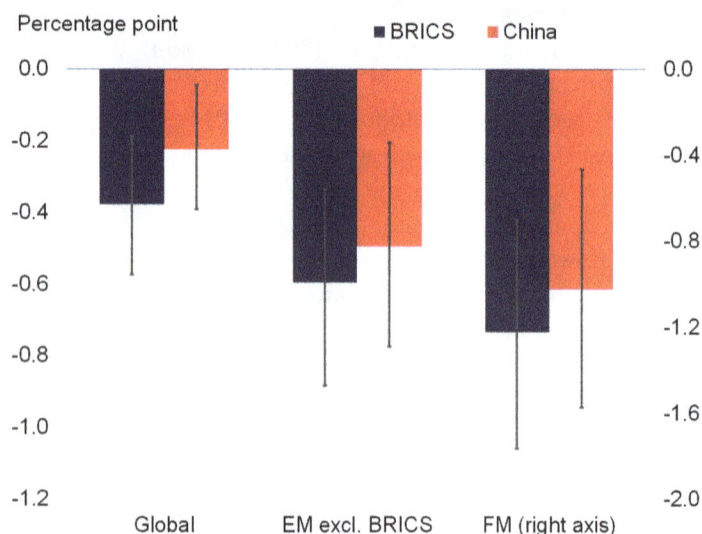

Source: World Bank staff estimates.
Note: Cumulated impulse responses of EM and global growth at the two-year horizon. The shock size is such that China's growth declines by 1 percentage point on impact. The shock size for BRICS is calibrated such that its growth declines by exactly the same amount as that of China at the end of two years. Solid bars denote the median and the error bars denote the 16-84 percent confidence bands.

- A cyclical downturn in BRICS would generate temporary adverse spillovers that could be mitigated by counter-cyclical fiscal and monetary policies;

- A structural downturn in potential growth in BRICS would require structural reforms in other emerging markets to adjust to a "new normal" of lower growth in core trading partners and sources of remittances.

About one-third of the growth slowdown in emerging markets, including BRICS, is structural and the remainder is a cyclical downturn from the immediate post-crisis rebound of 2010 (Didier et al. 2015). However, this assessment of the relative strength of cyclical and structural factors is subject to considerable uncertainty. Hence, the optimal policy mix, even in countries where spillovers from external shocks are considered temporary, includes structural policies to improve medium- and long-term growth prospects.

In addition, counter-cyclical fiscal and monetary policies can be used effectively when there is sufficient policy space (see discussion below). Many emerging and frontier markets used up much of their policy space during the global stimulus of 2009 and have yet to rebuild it (World Bank 2015a). They may therefore not be in a position to implement effective counter-cyclical stimulus. Faced with this predicament, structural reforms to lift long-term growth could help, bolster investor sentiment in the short run, help lift domestic demand to the extent they encourage investment, and support capital flows even amidst financial market tightening.

The appropriate policy response also depends on the source of the external shock. A growth shock may be more appropriately addressed with fiscal policy and structural reforms whereas a financial shock may be more effectively mitigated by monetary, exchange rate, or financial policies. The boundaries between these shocks and policies, however, may at times be blurred. This argues, again, for a policy mix of fiscal, monetary, and exchange rate policy coupled with structural reforms.

Fiscal policy. Fiscal stimulus could help stabilize a cyclical slowdown in activity. Fiscal multipliers—the change in real GDP generated by a 1 dollar increase in fiscal spending—for emerging markets are up to 0.6 in the short-term and up to 0.9 in the medium-term (World Bank 2015a). Fiscal multipliers tend to be larger during recessions than expansions, in countries with ample fiscal space, in less open economies, and for stimulus conducted through expenditure increases, especially public investment, rather than tax cuts (World Bank 2015a; Ilzetzki, Mendoza, and Vegh 2013).

A spillover-induced, cyclical slowdown in activity may be an opportunity to address sizeable infrastructure needs in emerging markets, since infrastructure investment can be a particularly effective form of fiscal stimulus.[22] While some of

FIGURE 3.14 Growth slowdown in BRICS combined with financial stress

A combination of continued weak BRICS growth and rising emerging market risk premia could considerably reduce growth in other countries.

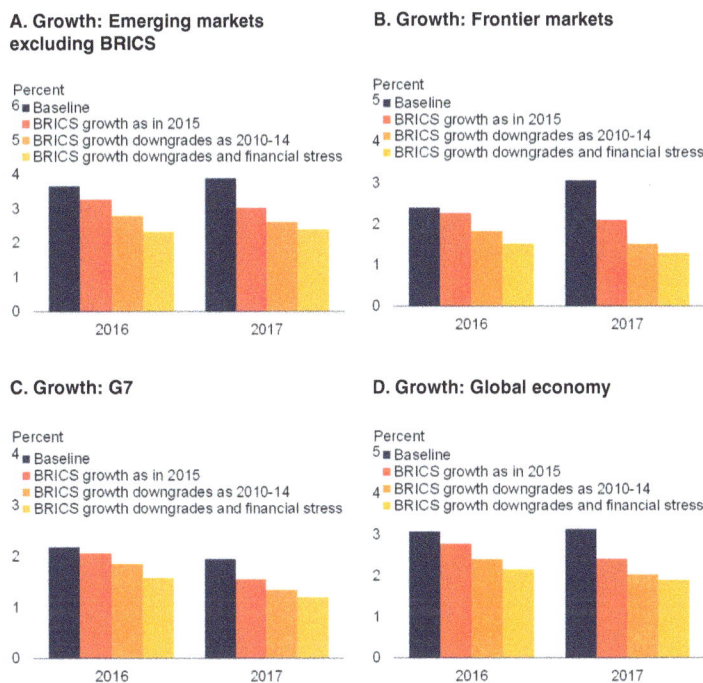

Source: World Bank staff estimates.
Note: EMBI = Emerging Markets Bond Index. Conditional forecasts of emerging markets excluding BRICS, frontier markets, G7, and global growth, with conditions imposed on future BRICS growth and EMBI. The conditions are: (i) BRICS growing at the curent rate in 2015: BRICS continue to grow at its current 2015 level (annualized rate of 3.2 percent) during the forecast horizon; (ii) BRICS growth with forecast downgrades as during 2010-14: BRICS continue to grow during the forecast horizon at its current 2015 level minus the average forecast downgrades it saw during 2010-14. The forecast downgrades are based on the World Bank forecasts. In these two scenarios, EMBI is restricted to equal the unconditional forecasts from the aggregate VAR model during the forecast horizon; (iii) BRICS growth with forecast downgrades and financial stress: The second scenario is combined with EMBI rising by 100bp during the forecast horizon. Global growth is the GDP-weighted average of BRICS, emerging markets excl. BRICS, frontier markets, and G7 growth. The baseline forecasts are a GDP-weighted average of growth forecasts presented in Chapter 1 for the sample of countries used here. Conditional forecasts are based on the aggregate VAR model.

the largest infrastructure deficits have been identified for low-income countries and frontier markets, emerging markets also lag by global comparison.

However, most emerging markets do not have the policy room to sustain fiscal stimulus over anything other than the briefest period.

---

[22]Multipliers from public investment have been estimated to range from 0.25 to 1 in emerging markets over the medium-term (IMF 2014c). Multipliers from increases in economy-wide physical capital stock have been estimated to range from 1 to 2 in Sub-Saharan Africa and Latin America and the Caribbean (Calderón and Servén 2008, 2010). Estimates of longer-term output effects of public investment vary widely but are generally positive (Bom and Ligthart 2014). In addition to raising overall growth in the country investing in public infrastructure, infrastructure investment may also foster trade (and

thus growth of partner countries), reduce income inequality, and boost employment. Infrastructure investment needs, however, have to be assessed against financing cost and implementation capacity (Kraay and Servén 2013). Because of less economic slack and lower efficiency of investment in emerging and frontier markets than advanced markets, growth benefits in the former are smaller, subject to significant uncertainty, and raise public debt (IMF 2014a; Gupta et al. 2014).

BOX 3.3 Within-region spillovers

Most countries are predominantly linked to major advanced markets in close proximity. Within-region ties are closest in Europe and Central Asia (ECA) and East Asia and Pacific (EAP), and particularly pronounced in trade and remittance flows. The largest within-region spillovers originate from China, Russia, and Brazil while those from other large emerging markets are limited.

While spillovers from BRICS are often large, those from other large emerging markets (EM) and frontier markets (FM) may also be strong within regions and especially to neighboring countries.

This box adds granularity, and expands the coverage of Chapter 3, in the following directions.

- How do within-region and global linkages compare across regions?

- How do within-region spillovers compare across regions?

How do within-region and global linkages compare across regions?

Global integration. Several developing country regions are highly open to global trade (Figure 3.3.1). Exposures to global financial investment, however, tend to be lower— indeed, for several regions, remittances have been as large a source of inflows as foreign direct, portfolio, or bank investment flows. The relative importance of these links differs across regions.

- EAP and ECA consist of countries that are highly open to trade and receive sizeable amounts of foreign direct investment (FDI) and portfolio investment but limited remittance inflows from outside the region.

- Large oil exporters in the Middle East and North Africa (MNA) are deeply integrated into global trade, and some are a large source of remittances. Following a sharp slowdown since 2005, the region now receives modest FDI inflows and little portfolio investment.

Latin America and the Caribbean (LAC) and South Asia (SAR) are generally less open to trade than other regions.[1] However, LAC has received sizeable FDI. SAR receives large remittance inflows from outside the region but limited FDI and portfolio investment (World Bank 2015e).

FIGURE 3.3.1 Openness

Most regions are highly open to global trade. Remittances inflows are of similar or greater magnitude to FDI for several regions. Over time, portfolio inflows have led to the accumulation of some sizable liability positions, especially in LAC.

A. Trade and remittance inflows, 2014

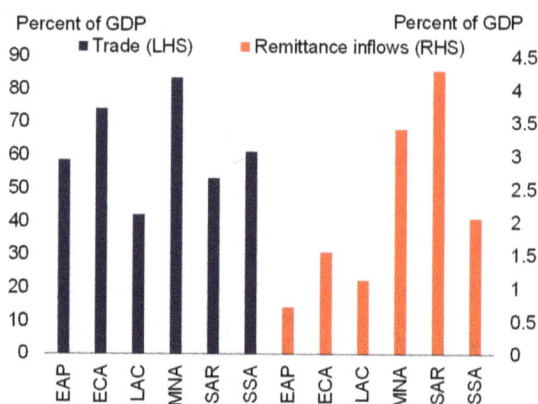

B. FDI inflows and stock of portfolio investment liabilities, 2014

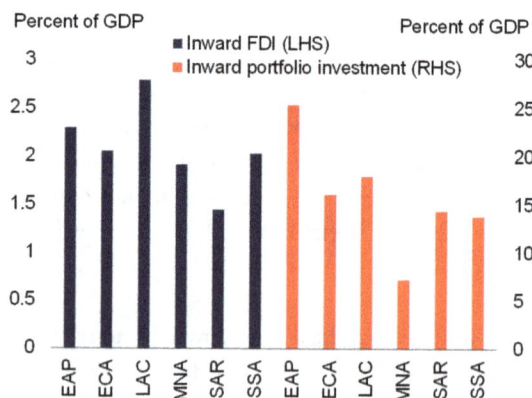

Sources: WDI; World Bank; UNCTAD; CPIS database.
Note: In percent of each region's GDP. Regions are defined as all non-advanced market countries in each region. EAP = East Asia and Pacific; ECA = Europe and Central Asia; LAC = Latin America and the Caribbean; MNA = Middle East and North Africa; SAR = South Asia; SSA = Sub-Saharan Africa.

Emerging and frontier markets in SSA are, on average, well integrated into global trade and receive considerable FDI and remittance inflows.

Integration with large advanced markets. Most regions tend to be closely linked to a neighboring major economy. For LAC, the United States is the single largest trading

---

Note: This Box was prepared by Jesper Hanson, Raju Huidrom, and Franziska Ohnsorge.

[1]LAC is generally less open to trade than other regions, although there is considerable heterogeneity across the region.

BOX 3.3 Within-region spillovers *(continued)*

FIGURE 3.3.2 Within-region integration

Within-region trade links are strongest in EAP, ECA, and LAC. Remittances from inside the region are sizeable, except for the LAC region. Except in EAP, internal FDI flows are generally quite low compared to those from the rest of the world. MNA has considerable within-region ODA flows.

A. Trade

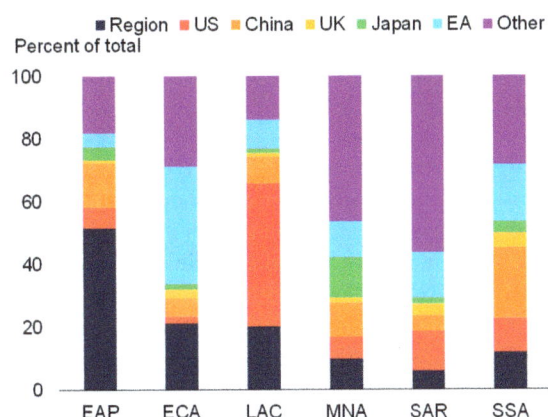

B. Remittance inflows

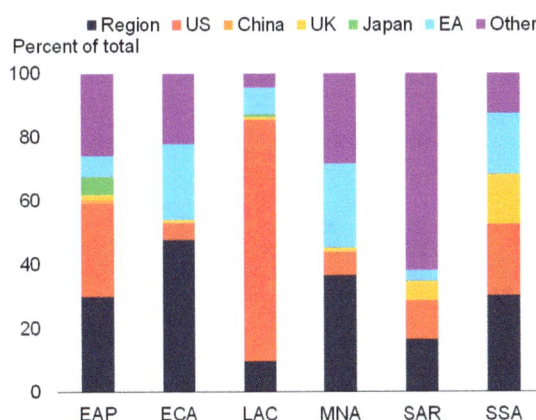

C. FDI inflows

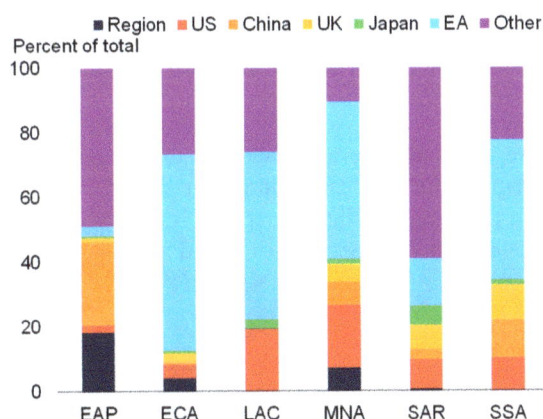

D. Official development assistance

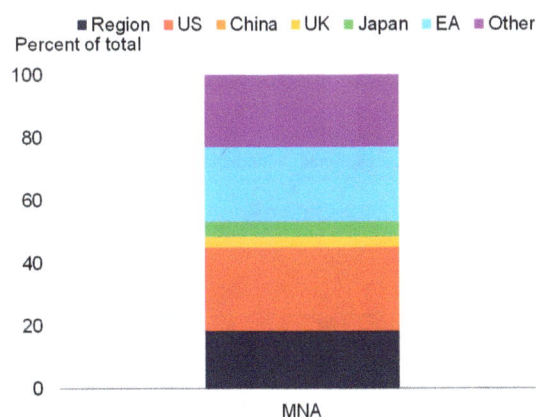

Sources: WITS; Bilateral Remittances Database; CDIS database; CPIS database.
Note: In percent of each region's total. Regions include countries of all income categories, except for United States, Canada, Euro Area, and Japan. EA = Euro Area.
A. 2011-14 average. B. 2014 C. 2011-13 average.

partner and source of remittances and other financial flows. The Euro Area and China play similar roles for ECA and EAP, respectively. Partly reflecting greater geographical distance to the world's largest economies, MNA, SAR, and SSA are more diversified in their trade and financial ties.

Within-region integration. Several regions have strong within-region trade and remittance links (Figure 3.3.2). In EAP, ECA, and LAC, within-region trade accounts for 20 percent or more of the total. In MNA, limited within-region trade reflects similar export specialization, especially of oil-exporting countries. Remittance inflows from

countries within the region represent more than 30 percent of the total for EAP, ECA, MNA, and SSA. Intra-region FDI, in contrast, is low, with the exception of EAP where both Japan and China are important sources for FDI to support supply chain integration. Likewise for official development assistance, with the exception of MNA.

How do within-region spillovers compare across regions?

The differences in within-region economic links are reflected in spillovers from shocks in large emerging and

BOX 3.3 Within-region spillovers *(continued)*

FIGURE 3.3.3 Spillovers from large emerging markets in each region

Strong within-region trade and remittance links are reflected in sizeable spillovers in ECA to a growth decline in Russia and, in EAP, to a growth decline in China. Other within-region spillovers tend to be modest.

A. Impact on growth of 1 percentage point decline in growth in large emerging markets within the region

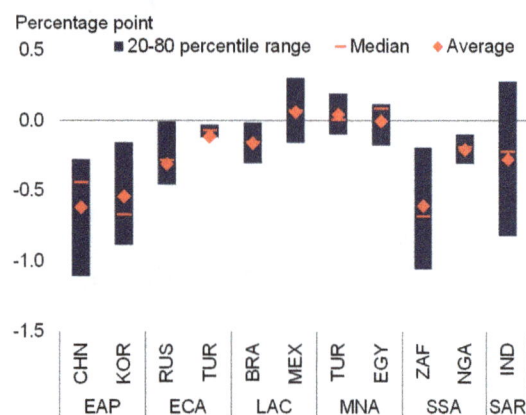

B. Impact on growth of 1 percentage point decline in G7 growth

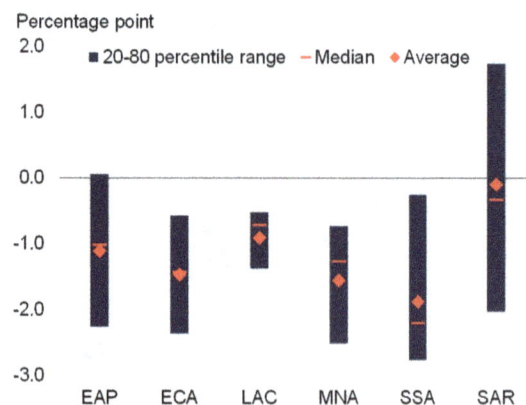

Source: World Bank staff estimates.
Note. Based on country-specific structural vector autoregressions (VARs) using the earliest possible data from 1998Q1 to 2015Q2 for 7 countries in EAP, 20 countries in ECA, 15 countries in LAC, 8 countries in MNA, 3 countries in SAR, and 4 countries in SSA. Estimation sample for the SSA region starts in 2007 and within-region spillovers in SSA are statistically insignificant. Details of the model are provided in Boxes 2.1-2.6.
B. For EAP, the shock refers to growth in G7 excluding Japan; and for SSA and ECA, the shock refers to growth in the rest of the world.

frontier markets (Figure 3.3.3). These large emerging and frontier markets include BRICS, along with Egypt, Korea, Mexico, Nigeria, and Turkey. Similar to the estimation of spillovers from BRICS, spillovers are estimated in country-specific structural vector autoregressions, including the second large emerging

market source country of shocks in each region.[2] Since the BRICS are typically the largest countries in their regions, shocks in these economies have the strongest spillovers inside their respective region.

- Strong within-region trade and remittance links are reflected in sizeable and often statistically significant spillovers – for example, in ECA to a growth decline in Russia and in EAP to a growth decline in China (Boxes 2.1, 2.2).[3]

- In other regions, spillovers are typically statistically insignificant. In SAR, a growth shock in India would have a marginal impact on growth in Pakistan and Sri Lanka, which have limited trade links with India (Box 2.5). In SSA, spillovers from growth shocks in South Africa and Nigeria are generally insignificant. In MNA, growth spillovers from Egypt and Turkey are negligible, despite the size of these two economies, because of their limited ties to other countries in the region (Box 2.3).[4] Similarly, growth spillovers in Mexico and Brazil on countries in LAC are, on average, modest although they can be sizeable for a few neighboring countries of Brazil with strong trade ties (Box 2.4).[5]

All regions are more vulnerable to growth shocks originating outside their region than shocks originating within their regions. The discrepancy is most pronounced for the highly open regions such as EAP, ECA, MNA, and SSA.

Conclusion

The emerging market and developing economy regions are generally much more vulnerable to external growth shocks than to shocks originating within each region. The within-region spillovers are limited in scope, and tend to be concentrated among neighboring countries, reflecting modest within-region trade and financial links. However, a few countries in EAP and ECA are vulnerable to a growth slowdown in large neighboring emerging and frontier markets.

[2]For the SAR region, only spillovers from India are considered.

[3]Other studies have also found significant spillovers from Russia to ECA (e.g., Alturki, Espinosa-Bowen, and Ilahi 2009; Ratha et al. 2015) and from China to EAP (e.g., Ahuja and Nabar 2012; Inoue, Kaya, and Ohshige 2015).

[4]For lack of a sufficiently long quarterly data series, Gulf Cooperation Council countries could not be included in the analysis.

[5]For instance, Southern Cone countries (Argentina, Bolivia, Chile, Paraguay, and Uruguay), given their sizeable export linkages, are subject to spillovers from Brazil (Adler and Sosa 2014).

- Oil exporters that have entered the oil price slump of 2014 with large surpluses and low debt (Oman, Qatar, Saudi Arabia, and United Arab Emirates) can still smooth the adjustment to external shocks. However, in most oil-exporting emerging markets, surpluses have already turned into sizeable deficits and rising debt.

- In several non-oil commodity-exporting emerging markets, deficits have widened by more than a percentage point from a less favorable starting position (Brazil, Chile, Peru) and debt has risen above 50 percent of GDP in 2015 (Brazil, Colombia). Further deterioration in fiscal sustainability could weaken investor sentiment.

- Similarly, several commodity-importing economies entered the emerging market growth slowdown in 2010 with deficits above 4 percent of GDP and debt above 50 percent of GDP (Egypt, Hungary, India, and Poland), and deficits remain elevated despite consolidation efforts (Figure 3.15).

Monetary policy. Like fiscal policy, monetary policy could boost growth amidst a temporary slowdown in activity.[23] Effective monetary policy stimulus, however, relies on well-functioning financial markets (Lane 2003; Chinn 2014); limited balance sheet exposures to exchange rate and interest rate risk; well-anchored inflation expectations; and policy credibility in the eyes of investors.

However, room for monetary policy stimulus has narrowed in many emerging markets. To contain inflation and financial stability risks resulting from sharp depreciations, several commodity-*exporting* emerging markets have been forced to tighten monetary policy despite faltering growth (Figure 3.16). Most have limited monetary policy room to support activity in the event of further external

---

[23]Monetary easing works through a number of channels: by reducing interest rates on government securities, interbank borrowing and bank lending; by depreciating the exchange rate; by increasing asset prices (especially equity and house prices) and thus by inflating the value of collateral for borrowing.

FIGURE 3.15 Fiscal policy and fiscal space

Fiscal space is necessary to ensure that fiscal policy is effective. Among emerging and frontier markets, fiscal space has shrunk significantly since the financial crisis as government debt and fiscal deficits have increased—and sharply in some countries. This has also been reflected in deteriorating credit ratings.

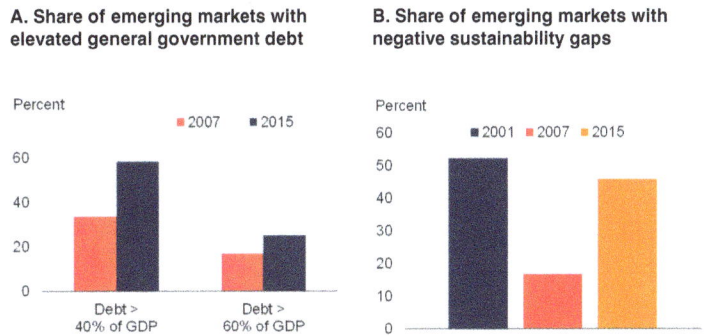

A. Share of emerging markets with elevated general government debt

B. Share of emerging markets with negative sustainability gaps

Sources: World Bank (2015a); Haver Analytics.
B. Sustainability gap is defined as the difference between the actual overall balance and the debt-stabilizing overall balance at current growth rates. A negative sustainability gap indicates an unsustainable stock of debt and deficit.

shocks. Some commodity-*importing* emerging markets with low inflation, in contrast, may have some room to dampen external shocks with further interest rate cuts. However, once oil prices stabilize and inflation begins to rise, this room may diminish.

Structural policies. The BRICS slowdown may turn out to be a sustained, structural decline in growth potential rather than a temporary cyclical downturn. This would generate spillovers that force other emerging markets to face an era of lower growth in key trading partners and sources of finance. The potential for spillovers will increase as BRICS integrate further into the global economy and as BRICS growth continues to outpace advanced market growth (notwithstanding the recent slowdown). While at times politically challenging to implement, structural reform measures can help emerging markets adjust to this new era.

Structural reforms have collateral benefits of buttressing investor confidence and lifting domestic demand—whether in the event of cyclical or structural external shocks. By lifting investor confidence in growth prospects, they can support capital inflows amidst financial market

FIGURE 3.16 Monetary policy room

Among oil-importers, the oil price drop has reduced inflation below target levels and created policy options. Among oil exporters, currency depreciation has raised inflation and added to pressures on central banks to raise policy rates. In contrast, central banks in oil importers have been able to reduce policy rates.

A. Inflation in emerging markets

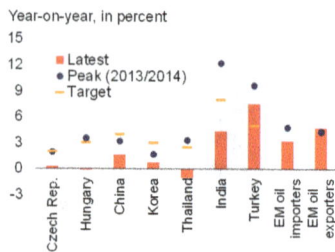

B. Monetary policy rate hikes in emerging markets

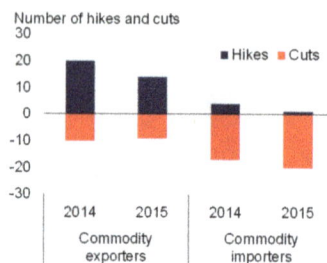

Sources: Hammond (2012); World Bank; Haver Analytics; Didier et al. (2015).
A. Latest observation is October 2015. Includes both formal and informal inflation targets.
B. Latest data for December 2015. Hikes and cuts refer to central bank rate decisions, including base rate, policy rate, repo rate, Selic rate, discount rate, reference rate, lending rate, refinancing rate and benchmark rate. The number of countries implementing rate cuts is shown with a negative sign. There are 11 commodity exporters and 13 commodity importers.

FIGURE 3.17 Growth slowdown and structural reforms

Significant reforms in governance are positively associated with growth performance. During the most recent slowdown (2010-14), economies that demonstrated the highest rise in governance quality experienced milder slowdowns.

A. Growth differential during episodes of reform spurts and setbacks since 1996

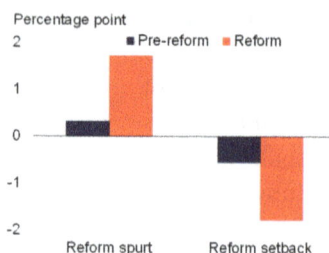

B. Growth slowdown in 2010-14 and change in governance quality in 2010-14

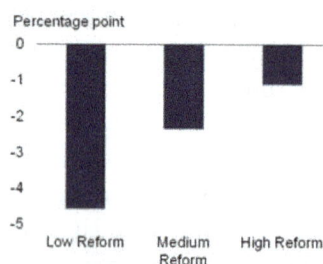

Sources: World Bank's World Governance Indicators (WGI); Didier et al. (2015).
A. The columns show the cumulative growth differential of economies during and prior to a reform spurt or setback episode, relative to those that experienced neither spurts nor setbacks. Spurt (setback) is defined by a two-year increase (decrease) by two standard deviations in one or more of the following four measures of the WGI index: regulatory quality, government effectiveness, rule of law, and control of corruption. Differentials are based on estimates from a panel data regression with time and country fixed effects. The sample spans 64 EM and FM over 1996-2014. Annex 3.2 provides additional details about the empirical exercise.

turmoil. To the extent structural reforms are associated with investment—especially in the presence of economic slack—or with increased labor force participation, they can also increase domestic demand (World Bank 2015a).

Gains in long-term growth from structural reforms could be particularly large in emerging and frontier markets because they tend to display elevated inter-sectoral dispersion in productivity and because some struggle with pervasive misallocation of capital and labor.[24] A growing literature has documented the long-term benefits from structural reforms in emerging and frontier markets, especially of reforms that improve governance and business environments. These include growth spurts triggered by reforms (Figure 3.17, Didier et al. 2015), amplification of the growth dividend from public investment, greater job creation and formal sector activity. For example, the growth slowdown in 2010-14 was least pronounced in the quartile of countries with the strongest governance environment reforms and most pronounced in those with the weakest governance environment reforms (Figure 3.17).

Conclusion

Over the next few years, growth in BRICS is likely to face persistent headwinds from low commodity prices, weak trade, and higher borrowing costs. Meanwhile, productivity growth is likely to remain weak as populations age in large emerging markets, and investment weakness slows the adoption of new technologies. A weaker external environment, and slowing growth, may further erode policy buffers and constrain the use of counter-cyclical stimulus to support activity. The strengthening recovery in advanced markets is expected to only partially offset these risks.

The results presented in this chapter suggest that continued weakness or a further slowdown in BRICS growth could add to the challenges faced by emerging and frontier markets from a deteriorating external environment. It would

[24]Dabla-Norris et al. (2013); Hsieh and Klenow (2009); IADB (2013).

weigh on growth in other emerging markets—as it has done already since 2010—and frontier markets. Activity in close trading partners of BRICS and in commodity exporters would be particularly susceptible to a setback.

In response to a 1 percentage point decline in BRICS growth, growth in other emerging markets and in frontier markets could slow by 0.8 and 1.5 percentage points, respectively, over two years. This would set back global growth by 0.4 percentage point, over two years.

There is a risk that growth weakness in BRICS will be accompanied by bouts of financial market volatility through the U.S. monetary policy tightening cycle, or in some cases domestic factors.

If, instead of the projected pickup, BRICS growth slows further—by as much as the average growth disappointment over 2010-14—and if financial conditions tightened moderately—such as during the financial market turmoil of the summer of 2015—global growth could be cut by one-third in 2016.

Policy makers in emerging markets may need to support activity with fiscal and policy stimulus, at least where policy buffers are sufficient. In all cases, countries could derive substantial gains from well-designed, credible structural reforms that retain investor confidence and capital flows in the short-run, and that lift growth prospects for the long-run.

Annex 3.1 Data

Country classification

Emerging markets (EM) generally include (non-advanced) high-income and middle-income countries with a record of significant access to international financial markets. Frontier markets (FM) include, generally middle-income, countries that are usually smaller and less financially developed than emerging markets, and have more limited access to international capital markets.

For this Chapter, emerging markets are countries that are classified as such in at least two of the three following stock indexes: S&P, FTSE, and MSCI. Frontier markets are countries that are classified as such by at least two of the same three indexes. For countries not covered by all of these three indexes, we also include those that are classified as emerging/frontier markets by Bloomberg, Citi, and JP Morgan bond indexes, even though these latter lists do not have a break down between emerging markets and frontier markets.

Data used in modelling

The structural vector autoregressions, the correlation analysis, and the event study use quarterly real GDP data from Haver, OECD, and IMF World Economic Outlook with a maximum coverage from 1997Q2 to 2015Q2. The sample includes 24 advanced markets (Australia; Austria; Belgium; Canada; Denmark; Finland; France; Germany; Greece; Hong Kong SAR, China; Iceland; Ireland;

Italy; Japan; Netherlands; New Zealand; Norway; Portugal; Singapore; Spain; Sweden; Switzerland; United Kingdom; United States), 16 emerging markets (Brazil; Chile; China; Czech Republic; Hungary; India; Indonesia; Malaysia; Mexico; Peru; Philippines; Poland; Russian Federation; South Africa; Thailand; Turkey), six frontier markets (Bulgaria; Costa Rica; Croatia; Jordan; Paraguay; Romania), and eight other economies (Cyprus; Estonia; Israel; Latvia; Lithuania; Slovak Republic; Slovenia; Taiwan, China).

The dynamic factor model uses annual growth in GDP, private consumption, and private investment for 106 countries from IMF World Economic Outlook database during 1960-2015. The sample includes 23 advanced markets (Australia, Austria, Belgium, Canada, Denmark, Finland, France, Germany, Greece, Iceland, Ireland, Italy, Japan, Luxembourg, Netherlands, New Zealand, Norway, Portugal, Spain, Sweden, Switzerland, United Kingdom, United States), 17 emerging markets (Brazil, Chile, China, Colombia, Arab Republic of Egypt, India, Indonesia, Malaysia, Mexico, Morocco, Pakistan, Peru, Philippines, Republic of Korea, South Africa, Thailand, Turkey), 25 frontier markets (Argentina, Bangladesh, Bolivia, Botswana, Costa Rica, Cote d'Ivoire, Ecuador, El Salvador, Gabon, Ghana, Guatemala, Honduras, Jamaica, Jordan, Kenya, Mauritius, Nigeria, Panama, Paraguay, Senegal, Sri Lanka, Tunisia, Uruguay, República Bolivariana de Venezuela, Zambia) and 41 other developing countries.

Emerging markets		Frontier markets			Advanced markets	
Brazil	Morocco	Argentina	Ghana	Panama	Australia	Ireland
Chile	Pakistan	Azerbaijan	Guatemala	Paraguay	Austria	Iceland
China	Peru	Bahrain	Honduras	Romania	Belgium	Italy
Colombia	Philippines	Bangladesh	Jamaica	Senegal	Canada	Japan
Czech Republic	Poland	Bolivia	Jordan	Serbia	Switzerland	Luxembourg
Egypt, Arab Rep.	Qatar	Botswana	Kazakhstan	Sri Lanka	Germany	Malta
Hungary	Russia	Bulgaria	Kenya	Tunisia	Denmark	Netherlands
India	Saudi Arabia	Costa Rica	Kuwait	Ukraine	Spain	Norway
Indonesia	South Africa	Côte d'Ivoire	Lebanon	Uruguay	Finland	New Zealand
Korea, Rep.	Thailand	Croatia	Mauritius	Venezuela, RB	France	Portugal
Malaysia	Turkey	Ecuador	Mongolia	Vietnam	United Kingdom	Singapore
Mexico	United Arab Emirates	El Salvador	Namibia	Zambia	Greece	Sweden
		Gabon	Nigeria		Hong Kong SAR, China	United States
		Georgia	Oman			

Annex 3.2 Methodology

A. VAR models

The chapter uses a structural vector autoregression model to quantify growth spillovers from BRICS to other countries, in particular emerging markets (EM) excluding BRICS and frontier markets (FM). Exogenous shocks to BRICS growth are identified using a recursive scheme, and then the spillover effects of those shocks are traced out. The recursive identification scheme requires quarterly data, and hence spillover analysis in this chapter is limited to those countries for which quarterly data is available.[1] In the baseline (aggregate) model, the variables included are, in this order: G7 growth, the U.S. interest rate, Emerging Market Bond Index (EMBI), BRICS growth, oil price, emerging market (excluding BRICS) growth, and frontier market growth.[2] The ordering is based on the presumed exogeneity, or predetermination, of variables where more exogenous variables are ordered first. For instance, it assumes that G7 growth is exogenous to emerging market growth: G7 growth shocks affect emerging market growth within a quarter, whereas shocks to emerging market growth can affect G7 growth only with a lag of at least one quarter. By ordering oil price after BRICS growth, the chapter implicitly assumes that oil prices are relatively endogenous to BRICS growth.

G7 growth, taken to be the proxy for growth in the advanced economies, is constructed as the weighted average of the growth of individual G7 economies, the weights being their respective average GDP shares during the estimation period, 1998Q1-2015Q2. BRICS growth is similarly constructed as the weighted average of growth of individual BRICS countries. Emerging market and frontier market growth are constructed as the weighted average of growth of individual emerging markets minus BRICS and frontier markets respectively.[3] The U.S. interest rate (the yield on 10-year U.S. treasury bills) and the EMBI serve as proxies for global financial conditions. The model is estimated using Bayesian techniques and inferences are made using 2000 Monte Carlo draws. A lag length of four quarters is used, which is standard for VAR models estimated with quarterly data.

To evaluate growth spillovers from each of the individual BRICS countries, the model above is re-estimated by replacing aggregate BRICS with the individual BRICS country in question as the spillover source. For instance, to obtain growth spillovers from Brazil, the model is re-estimated by including Brazil's growth instead of aggregate BRICS growth. Positive or negative correlations between growth of individual BRICS could bias the estimates upwards or downwards.

While the baseline model is used to infer spillover implications for aggregate global, emerging market, and frontier market growth, an alternative (country) specification is deployed to evaluate spillover effects for each emerging market and frontier market. This specification is used in the chapter to understand the intra- and inter-regional spillover effects from a growth slowdown in BRICS countries. Among the BRICS countries, Brazil, Russia, and China matter empirically for spillovers (Figure 3.11). To preserve model parsimony, the alternative specification considers spillovers only from these three countries. The model is estimated for each emerging market and frontier market (as spillover destination country) one at a time with the following variables: G7 growth, EMBI, China's growth, Brazil's growth, Russia's growth, commodity prices, emerging market/frontier market growth, and emerging market/frontier market real effective exchange rate. Simultaneously including all three spillover source countries (China, Brazil, and Russia) in the model allows estimating spillovers from one source

---

[1] Alternatively, a local projections model could have been used. However, this would have first required identifying exogenous BRICS growth shocks often proxied in the literature by growth forecast errors. A consistent measure of the latter is not available. Simply assuming BRICS growth as exogenous shocks is less plausible for several countries in the sample.

[2] The ordering closely follows World Bank (2015a, 2015b) and IMF (2014b). The main results in the chapter are robust to including VIX instead of EMBI in the model. The list of countries classified as emerging markets and frontier markets are provided in Annex 3.1.

---

[3] The results are robust when emerging market growth includes growth in Brazil, India, Russia, and South Africa.

country (e.g., Brazil) while explicitly controlling for the rest of the spillover source countries (China and Russia).

Commodity prices are weighted by the average share of exports of each commodity in the commodity export basket of the spillover destination country in question. With respect to the baseline model, including trade-weighted commodity prices (instead of oil prices) and the real effective exchange rate in the model results in a better empirical description of the small open economies in the sample. Finally, again in the interests of parsimony, U.S. interest rates are excluded in the alternative specification. The results are, however, robust to inclusion or exclusion of U.S. interest rates.

The estimation uses a balanced panel of quarterly observations for 57 countries between 1998Q1 and 2015Q2. Real GDP for 29 of these countries is based on the quarterly database in Ilzetzki, Mendoza, and Vegh (2013) which is extended to 2015Q2 by splicing real GDP series from the OECD Quarterly National Accounts and Haver Analytics. Real GDP data for the remainder of the 28 countries are sourced from the OECD Quarterly National Accounts and Haver Analytics. Real effective exchange rates are the narrow (wherever available) and the broad indices from the Bank for International Settlements (BIS) supplemented with the Bruegel database. The EMBI spread series is taken from J.P. Morgan. The U.S. long-term interest rate is the 10-year generic government yields from Bloomberg. Nominal oil prices are obtained from the World Bank Pink Sheet and deflated using seasonally adjusted U.S. CPI series from Haver Analytics.[4]

The trade-weighted commodity prices for each emerging market/frontier market are constructed as follows: nominal monthly prices of 35 commodities are obtained from the World Bank pink sheet.[5] As in the case of oil prices, these nominal commodity prices are deflated by the

U.S. CPI. The resulting real prices are converted into indices by setting January 2010 as 100. Then, the monthly indices are converted into quarterly indices by taking averages across the months in a given quarter. Country-specific trade weights are then applied to these real quarterly commodity price indices to yield a trade-weighted real commodity price index for each country. For a given country, the trade weights are the average share of exports of each commodity in the total commodity export basket during the period 2007-2014. Commodity exports are defined in terms of SITC 4th revision at 4 digits from the World Integrated Trade Solution (WITS) database.

While estimating the model, some of the data are transformed to yield stationary series. Thus, real GDP, oil and commodity prices, and real effective exchange rate, originally in levels, are converted into quarter-on-quarter growth rates. Any residual linear trends in those growth rates are removed. The U.S. interest rate and the EMBI are first differenced. The baseline (aggregate) VAR model uses aggregate GDP growth rates for various geographic regions and/or market groups. Those are calculated as the GDP weighted growth rates of all the countries in a given region/group. The GDP weights are calculated using the annual constant GDP (2005 US$) series from the World Bank's World Development Indicators.

B. Dynamic factor model

Dynamic factor models are widely used for identifying common elements in national business cycles (for an extensive discussion see, for instance, Kose, Otrok, and Prasad 2012). This chapter estimates a dynamic factor model that captures common factors in the fluctuations of real output, private consumption, and private investment over the 1960–2015 period in 106 countries using annual data obtained from the World Economic Outlook database. Specifically, the model decomposes fluctuations in these variables into four factors:

- A global factor captures the broad common elements in the fluctuations across countries.

- Group factors capture the common elements

---

[4]Available at http://www.worldbank.org/commodities.

[5]Commodity prices include aluminum, banana, barley, beef, chicken, coal, cocoa, coconut oil, coffee, copper, copra, cotton, crude oil, gold, ground nut oil, iron ore, lead, maize, natural gas, nickel, orange, palm oil, platinum, rice, rubber, silver, sorghum, soybean oil, soybeans, sugar, tea, tin, tobacco, wheat, and zinc.

in the cyclical fluctuations in the countries in a particular group. In this paper, the world is divided into three regions: advanced markets, emerging and frontier markets, and other developing countries.[6]

- Country-specific factors capture factors common to all variables in a particular country.

- Residual ("idiosyncratic") factors capture elements in the fluctuations of an individual variable that cannot be attributed to the other factors.

Dynamic factor models are designed to extract a small number of unobservable common elements from the covariance or co-movement between (observable) macroeconomic time series across countries. Thus, the model allows for a more parsimonious representation of the data in terms of the unobservable common elements – typically referred to as factors. From a theoretical standpoint, dynamic factor models are appealing because they can be framed as reduced-form solutions to a standard Dynamic Stochastic General Equilibrium (DSGE) model.

The dynamic factor model used in this paper has 106 blocks of equations, one for each country. For instance, the block of equations for an emerging market economy, say Mexico, takes on the following form:

$$Y_t^{MEX} = \beta_{global}^{Y,MEX} f_t^{global} + \beta_{EM}^{Y,MEX} f_t^{EMFM} + \beta_{MEX}^{Y} f_t^{MEX} + \varepsilon_t^{Y,MEX}$$

$$C_t^{MEX} = \beta_{global}^{C,MEX} f_t^{global} + \beta_{EM}^{C,MEX} f_t^{EMFM} + \beta_{MEX}^{C} f_t^{MEX} + \varepsilon_t^{C,MEX}$$

$$I_t^{MEX} = \beta_{global}^{I,MEX} f_t^{global} + \beta_{EM}^{I,MEX} f_t^{EMFM} + \beta_{MEX}^{I} f_t^{MEX} + \varepsilon_t^{I,MEX}$$

where Y, C, and I denote growth in output, consumption, and investment respectively. The global, EMFM (group), and country factors are represented by f_t^{global}, f_t^{EMFM} and $f_t^{country}$ respectively; and the coefficients before them, typically referred to as factor loadings, capture the sensitivities of the macroeconomic series to these factors. The error terms $\varepsilon_t^{i,j,k}$ are assumed to be uncorrelated at all lead

and lags and follow an autoregressive process. The same block of equations is repeated for each country in the three regions in the system. The model is estimated using Bayesian techniques as described in Kose, Otrok, and Whiteman (2003).

To measure the importance of each factor, we compute variance decompositions that decompose the total volatility of output growth into volatility components due to each factor. This is achieved by applying the variance operator to each equation in the system. For the case of output in the example above,

$$\begin{aligned}&Var(Y^{MEX})\\ &= \left(\beta_{global}^{Y,MEX}\right)^2 Var(f_t^{global}) + \left(\beta_{EM}^{Y,MEX}\right)^2 Var(f_t^{EMFM})\\ &+ (\beta^{Y,MEX})^2 Var(f_t^{MEX}) + Var(\varepsilon^{Y,MEX})\end{aligned}$$

Since there are no cross-product terms between the factors because they are orthogonal to each other, the variance in output attributable to the global factor is:

$$\frac{(\beta_{global}^{Y,MEX})^2 Var(f_t^{global})}{Var(Y^{MEX})}$$

The variance share due to the regional and country factors and the idiosyncratic term are calculated using a similar approach.

C. GVAR model

Originally proposed in a seminal paper by Pesaran, Schuermann and Weiner (2004), the GVAR methodology presents a simple and practical alternative to overcome the dimensionality problem ("curse of dimensionality") on the macro-econometric study of global macro-linkages.

The GVAR approach can be briefly described in two steps. In the first step, country-specific small-dimensional VAR models are estimated, which include domestic variables and cross-sectional averages of foreign variables. In the second step, the estimated coefficients from the country-specific models are stacked and solved in one large system, which is used in this report for impulse-responses analysis.

---

[6]For the list of countries included in each region, see Annex 3.1.

The model

Consider a panel of N countries, each featuring $k_i \times 1$ of endogenous variables observed during the time periods $t = 1, 2, \ldots, T$. Let x_{it} denote a vector of $k_i \times 1$ of endogenous variables specific to country i in time period t, and let $x_{it} = (x'_1, x'_2, \ldots x'_N)'$ denote a $k_i \times 1$ vector of all the variables in the panel, where $k = \sum_{i=0}^{N} k_i$.

A set of small-scale, country-specific conditional models can then be estimated separately. The individual models explain the domestic variables of a given economy, x_{it}, conditional on country-specific cross-section weighted averages of foreign variables, x_{it}^*. The foreign variables' expression is as follows:

$$x_{it}^* = \sum_{i=1}^{N} \omega_{ij} x_{jt}; \text{ where } \omega_{ii} = 0, \forall \ i = 1,2,\ldots,N.$$

These weights ω_{ij} are constructed using data on bilateral foreign trade. x_{it} is modelled as a VARX* model, namely a VAR model augmented by the vector of the foreign variables x_{it}^* and their lagged values:

$$x_{it} = \sum_{l=1}^{p_i} \Phi_{il} x_{t-l} + \Lambda_{i0} x_{it}^* + \sum_{l=1}^{q_i} \Lambda_{il} x_{i,t-l}^* + \varepsilon_{it} \quad (1)$$

for $i = 1,2,\ldots N$, where Φ_{il}, $l = 1,2,\ldots, p_i$, Λ_{il}, for $l = 1,2,\ldots, q_i$, are $k_i \times k_i$ and $k_i \times k^*$ matrices of unknown parameters, respectively, and ε_{it} are $k_i \times 1$ vectors of errors. Foreign variables x_{it}^* in country-specific models are treated as weakly exogenous for the purpose of estimation of unknown coefficients of the conditional country models.

The assumption of weak exogeneity can be easily tested and is often not rejected when the economy under consideration is small relative to the rest of the world and the weights used in the construction of the foreign variables are granular $(\sum_{j=1}^{N} \omega_{ij}^2 \to 0, \text{ as } N \to \infty)$.

Common variables in the country models are introduced as dominant variables as defined in Chudik and Pesaran (2013). Thus, (1) becomes:

$$\begin{aligned} x_{it} = &\sum_{l=1}^{p_i} \Phi_{il} x_{t-l} + \Lambda_{i0} x_{it}^* \\ &+ \sum_{l=1}^{q_i} \Lambda_{il} x_{i,t-l}^* + \theta_{i0} d_{it} + \sum_{l=1}^{s_i} \theta_{il} d_{i,t-l}^* + \varepsilon_{it} \quad (2) \end{aligned}$$

For the estimation of the marginal model for the dominant variables, d, feedback effects from x_t are allowed. Thus, we have the following expression for the marginal model:

$$d_{it} = \sum_{l=1}^{p_d} \Phi_{dl} d_{i,t-l} + \sum_{l=1}^{q_d} \Lambda_{il} x_{i,t-l}^* + \eta_{dt} \quad (3)$$

Following Pesaran et al. (2004) the chapter proceeds to estimate the individual VARX* in equation (2) on a country-by-country basis. The marginal model (3) is also estimated by least squares. Once the estimations have been carried on, we stack together the N models of equation (2) and the models in equation (3) and solve it all as one global system, explicitly taking into account that $x_{it}^* = \sum_{i=1}^{N} \omega_{ij} x_{jt}$.

Empirical exercise

The GVAR model is estimated for 32 countries: Australia, Austria, Belgium, Brazil, Canada, Chile, Finland, France, Germany, India, Indonesia, Italy, Japan, Malaysia, Mexico, Netherlands, Norway, New Zealand, Peru, Philippines, Republic of Korea, South Africa, Saudi Arabia, Singapore, Spain, Sweden, Switzerland, Thailand, Turkey, United Kingdom, and the United States. The estimation period is 1998Q1-2014Q4.

Three endogenous variables are considered: real output, the rate of inflation, and the real effective exchange rate. Due to the limited degrees of freedom, only one country-specific foreign variable is considered and constructed from real output. The fixed trade weights are defined as the average trade flows computed over a given period of time. These weights are used for the estimation of the individual models but also later on for the solution of the GVAR.

Finally, price indices for oil and metals are included in the model as dominant variables.

Generalized impulse-responses

In a single-country VAR, exact identification of shocks is commonly achieved by imposing a few restrictions derived from economic theory. However, in the case of a GVAR, exact identification of shocks would require an astonishing 192 (based on the number of countries considered in this chapter) restrictions derived from economic theory, $(\sum_{i=1}^{N} k_i (k_i - 1))$. Consequently, the generalized impulse responses proposed by Pesaran and Shin (1998) are used, which produce one unique set of responses. Nevertheless, it is important to note that this approach does not attempt to recover any structural shocks. Instead, this methodology describes how the system reacts after a specific historical/observable shock, taking into account the correlation among shocks.

D. The benefits of reform

Values in columns of Figure 3.17A are based on a panel data regression in which the dependent variable is real GDP growth. A reform spurt (setback) is defined as a two-year increase (decrease) by two standard deviations in one or more of the following four measures of the WGI index: regulatory quality, government effectiveness, rule of law, and control of corruption. The WGI indicators are principal components of a wide range of survey-based and other indicators. For each index, the standard deviation is measured as the average of the standard errors of the WGI index in the beginning and at the end of each two-year interval. Episodes

in which there were improvements in one measure and simultaneous setbacks in another are excluded. The sample spans 64 EM and FM over 1996-2014. This approach yields 50 episodes of significant reform spurts and 47 episodes of reform setbacks (Didier et al. 2015).

Let t denote the end of a two-year spurt or setback. The coefficients are dummy variables for spurts and setbacks over the [t-3, t+2] window around these episodes. In Figure 3.17A, "Reform" denotes the t=[-1,0] window (i.e. during the two years of improvement/deterioration). "Pre-reform" denotes the t=[-3,-2] window. For each window, each column shows the sum of coefficients. All coefficients show the growth differential of economies during an episode compared to those that experienced neither improvements nor setbacks. All estimates include time fixed effects to control for global common shocks and country fixed effects to control for time-invariant heterogeneity at the country-level. Under robust standard errors, estimates during the reform spurt window are jointly significant at the 10 percent level, and likewise for the reform setback window. The growth differentials during reform spurts associated with IMF programs are jointly significant at the 1 percent level.

Annex 3.3 Empirical estimates of spillovers from emerging markets

Author	Country/data	Methodology	Results
Ahuja and Nabar (2012) Ahuja and Myrvoda (2012)	G20/monthly, 2000-11	Factor Augmented Vector autoregression (FAVAR)	A one percentage point slowdown in investment in China is associated with a reduction of global growth of just under one-tenth of a percentage point. Regional supply chain economies and commodity exporters with relatively less diversified economies, such as Indonesia, are most vulnerable. Economies that lie within the Asian regional supply chain—Korea; Taiwan, China; and Malaysia—would also be adversely affected. Among the advanced economies, spillover effects most significant for Japan and Germany. Commodity prices, especially metal prices, could fall by as much as 0.8–2.2 percent below baseline one year after the shock.
Duval et al. (2014)	63 advanced and emerging markets/ quarterly, 1995-2012	Panel regression	A 1 percentage point decline in China's growth may lower GDP growth in the median Asian economy by about 0.3 percentage point after a year.
Inoue, Kaya, and Ohshige (2015)	26 advanced and emerging markets/ quarterly, 1979-2013	Global VAR (GVAR) with time-varying trade weights	A decline in China's real GDP has a significant impact on neighboring economies, especially on commodity exporters (e.g. Indonesia). Export-dependent countries in the EAP production cycle (Singapore, Malaysia and Thailand) and commodity exporters like Australia are also severely affected. Commodity prices (metals, crude oil and agriculture products) are also affected.
IMF (2014b)	21 advanced and emerging markets/ quarterly, 1979-2009	GVAR with value-added trade	Spillovers to advanced economies are larger than to emerging economies. A one percentage point reduction in China's growth can reduce growth in advanced economies by 0.15 percentage point at the end of one year, with effects most significant for Japan and the Euro Area. The effects on emerging economies is smallest, around 0.06 percentage point.
World Bank (2015a)	LAC region/quarterly, 1992-2014	Bayesian SVAR with Cholesky identification	A 1 percentage point reduction in Chinese growth can reduce growth in the LAC region by 0.6 percentage point at the end of two years, with effects most significant for Peru and Argentina (around one percentage point). Effects on Brazil are around 0.8 percentage point.
World Bank (2015b)	South Africa/quarterly, 2000-2014	Bayesian SVAR with Cholesky identification	A 1 percentage point reduction in Chinese growth can reduce growth in South Africa by 0.4 percentage point at the end of two years.
IMF (2014a)	Emerging markets/ quarterly, 1998-2013	Bayesian SVAR with Cholesky identification	A 1 percentage point rise in China's growth increases other emerging market economies' growth by about 0.1 percentage point on impact. The impact elasticity is high for some economies in Asia, such as Thailand, but also for commodity exporters such as Russia. Growth fluctuations in China also feed back into the global economy. A 1 percentage point growth increase in China boosts U.S. growth with a lag, the cumulative effect rising to 0.4 percentage point for a cumulative rise in China's growth to 4.6 percent after two years.
Arora and Vamvakidis (2011)	Unbalanced panel of 172 economies / annual data, 1960–2007	VARs and error-correction models for short run effects. Panel regressions for long run effects	Spillover effects of China's growth have increased in recent decades. A 1 percentage point impulse to China's GDP growth is followed by a cumulative response in other countries' GDP growth of 0.4 percentage point over five years. The trade channel is significant: about 60 percent of the impact seems to be transmitted through trade channels. Moreover, while China's spillovers initially only mattered for neighboring countries, the importance of distance has diminished over time. Long-term spillover effects are also significant and have extended in recent decades beyond Asia.
Alturki, Espinosa-Bowen, and Ilahi (2009)	Russia and 11 Commonwealth of Independent States (CIS) countries / annual and quarterly, 1997-2008.	Panel regression; Vector autoregression (VAR)	Russia appears to influence regional growth mainly through the remittance channel and somewhat less through the financial channel. There is a shrinking role of the trade (exports to Russia) channel. Russian growth shocks are associated with sizable effects on Belarus, Kazakhstan, Kyrgyz Republic, Tajikistan, and, to some extent, Georgia.

Author	Country/data	Methodology	Results
Obiora (2009)	Baltic countries and Russia / quarterly, 2000-07	VAR model	There are significant cross-country spillovers to the Baltics with those from the European Union outweighing spillovers from Russia. This reflects increasing trade and financial integration of the Baltics with EU and a declining role of Russia as an export destination for the Baltics.
Norges Bank (2014)	European countries and Russia / quarterly, 2003-13	VAR model	Spillovers from Russian GDP growth are largest for Latvia, Lithuania, Slovakia, Slovenia and Finland (i.e. countries with the largest export exposures to Russia). For Europe as a whole, spillover effects from Russia seem limited.
Arora and Vamvakidis (2005)	47 African countries and South Africa/ five-year growth, 1960-99	Growth regressions based on a panel of countries' average growth rates during five-year subperiods	South African growth has a substantial positive impact on growth in the rest of Africa: a 1 percentage point increase in South Africa five-year growth is associated with a 0.5 – 0.75 percentage point increase in five-year growth in rest of Africa.
Dabla-Norris, Espinoza, and Jahan (2015)	Low income countries (LIC) and emerging markets (EM) / annual, 1980/90 - 2008	VAR model and growth regressions	Growth in LIC depends increasingly on external factors with bulk of this attributable to economic ties developed with EM leaders (eight EM that are the largest destination of LIC exports in each region). LIC in SSA and MNA regions are particularly exposed to spillovers from the EM leaders via the trade channel. A 1 percentage point increase in GDP growth in EM leaders raises activity by between 0.5 and one percentage point in SSA LIC.
IMF (2012a)	African countries / annual, 1980/89-2010/11 for growth analysis; quarterly for inflation analysis	Pooled regression and VAR	Growth spillovers from Nigeria to neighboring countries are negligible. Given closely linked food markets, inflation spillovers are significant. There is no clear evidence that growth in South Africa's main partners in sub-Saharan Africa is affected by South African developments or policies. Global developments are, however, an important determinant of growth.
Canales-Kriljenko, Gwenhamo, and Thomas (2013)	BLNS countries (Botswana, Lesotho, Namibia, and Swaziland) and South Africa / annual, 1986-2010	VAR	South Africa's real GDP growth does not seem to contribute much to GDP growth in BLNS countries. However, spillovers from global growth are significant.
Gurara and Ncube (2013)	46 African countries and 30 developed and emerging markets/ quarterly data (GDP interpolated from annual data), 1980-2011	GVAR	There is a significant growth spillover effect to African economies from both the Euro zone economies and BRICS. In terms of the magnitudes, a percentage decline in Euro zone growth rate could lead to 0.34 to 0.6 percentage point drop in African countries' growth rates while an equivalent shock in BRICS growth could dent African growth rates by 0.09 to 0.23 percentage point. In both cases, spillover effects on fragile and resource-dependent economies are stronger than those on more diversified African countries.
Cashin, Mohaddes, and Raissi (2013)	38 countries that include advanced, emerging, MNA and GCC countries / quarterly, 1979-2011	GVAR	MNA countries are more sensitive to developments in China than to shocks in the Euro Area or the United States, in line with the direction of evolving trade patterns. Outward spillovers from the GCC region and MNA oil exporters are likely to be stronger in their immediate geographical proximity, but also have global implications.

Note: MNA = Middle East and North Africa; GCC = Gulf Cooperation Council; LIC = Low-Income Countries; LAC = Latin America and the Caribbean.

References

Adler, G., and S. Sosa. 2014. "Intraregional Spillovers in South America: Is Brazil Systemic After All?" *The World Economy* 37 (3): 456–80.

Ahmed, S., M. A. Appendino, and M. Ruta. 2015. "Depreciations without Exports? Global Value Chains and the Exchange Rate Elasticity of Exports." Policy Research Working Paper 7390, World Bank, Washington, DC.

Ahuja, A., and A. Myrvoda. 2012. "The Spillover Effects of a Downturn in China's Real Estate Investment." Working Paper 12/226, International Monetary Fund, Washington, DC.

Ahuja, A., and M. Nabar. 2012. "Investment-Led Growth in China: Global Spillovers." Working Paper 12/267, International Monetary Fund, Washington, DC.

Akin, C., and A. Kose. 2008. "Changing Nature of North–South Linkages: Stylized Facts and Explanations." *Journal of Asian Economics* 19 (1): 1-28.

Alturki, F., J. Espinosa-Bowen, and N. Ilahi. 2009. "How Russia Affects the Neighbourhood: Trade, Finance, and Remittance Channels." Working Paper 09/277, International Monetary Fund, Washington, DC.

Andrle, M., R. Garcia-Saltos, and G. Ho. 2013. "The Role of Domestic and External Shocks in Poland: Results from an Agnostic Estimation Procedure." Working Paper 13/220, International Monetary Fund, Washington, DC.

Arora, V., and A. Vamvakidis. 2005. "The Implications of South African Economic Growth for the Rest of Africa." Working Paper 05/58, International Monetary Fund, Washington, DC.

_____. 2011. "China's Economic Growth: International Spillovers." *China and the World Economy* 19(5): 31-46.

Arteta, C., A. Kose, F. Ohnsorge, and M. Stocker. 2015. "The Coming U.S. Interest Rate Tightening Cycle: Smooth Sailing or Stormy Waters?" Policy Research Note 2, World Bank, Washington, DC.

Ayvazyan, K., and T. Dabán. 2015. "Spillovers from Global and Regional Shocks to Armenia." Working Paper 15/241, International Monetary Fund, Washington, DC.

Bacchetta, P., and E. van Wincoop. 2014. "The Great Recession: A Self-Fulfilling Global Panic." Working paper, University of Virginia, Charlottesville, VA.

Baffes, J., A. Kose, F. Ohnsorge, and M. Stocker. 2015. "The Great Plunge in Oil Prices: Causes, Consequences and Policy Responses." Policy Research Note 1, World Bank, Washington, DC.

Bodenstein, M., C. J. Erceg, and L. Guerrieri. 2009. "The Effects of Foreign Shocks when Interest Rates are Zero." Discussion Paper 8006, Center for Economic Policy Research, London.

Bom, P. R. D., and J. E. Ligthart. 2014. "What Have We Learned From Three Decades of Research on the Productivity of Public Capital?" *Journal of Economic Surveys* 28 (5): 889-916.

Broda, C.M. and C. Tille. 2003. "Coping with Terms-of-Trade Shocks in Developing Countries." Current Issues in Economics and Finance. Federal Reserve Bank of New York (November).

Calderón, C., and L. Servén. 2008. "Infrastructure and Economic Development in Sub-Saharan Africa." Policy Research Working Paper 4172, World Bank, Washington, DC.

_____. 2010. "Infrastructure in Latin America" Policy Research Working Paper 5317, World Bank, Washington, DC.

Canales-Kriljenko, J., F. Gwenhamo, and S. Thomas. 2013. "Inward and Outward Spillovers in the SACU Area." Working Paper 13/31, International Monetary Fund, Washington, DC.

Canova, F., and J. Marrinan. 1998. "Sources and

Propagation of International Output Cycles: Common Shocks or Transmission?" *Journal of International Economics* 46 (1): 133–166.

Cashin, P., K. Mohaddes, and M. Raissi. 2013. "The Global Impact of the Systemic Economies and MENA Business Cycles." Working Paper 13/31, International Monetary Fund, Washington, DC.

Chinn, M. 2014. "Central Banking: Perspectives from Emerging Economies." La Follette School of Public Affairs Working Paper Series, 2014-006, University of Wisconsin-Madison, Madison, WI.

Chudik, A., and M. H. Pesaran. 2013. "Econometric Analysis of High Dimensional VARs Featuring a Dominant Unit." *Econometric Reviews* 32 (5-6): 592-649.

Dabla-Norris, E., A. Thomas, R. Garcia-Verdu, and Y. Chen. 2013. "Benchmarking Structural Transformation across the World." Working Paper 13/176, International Monetary Fund, Washington, DC.

Dabla-Norris, E., R. Espinoza, and S. Jahan. 2015. "Spillovers to Low-Income Countries: Importance of Systemic Emerging Markets." Applied Economics 47(53): 5707-5725.

Dees, S., F. Dimauro, H. Pesaran, and V. Smith. 2007. "Exploring the International Linkages of the Euro Area: A Global VAR Analysis." *Journal of Applied Econometrics* 22: 1-38.

Didier, T., A. Kose, F. Ohnsorge, and L. Ye. 2015. "Slowdown in Emerging Markets: Rough Patch or Prolonged Weakness?" Policy Research Note 4, World Bank, Washington, DC.

Doyle, B., and J. Faust. 2002. "An Investigation of Comovements Among the Growth Rates of the G-7 Countries." Federal Reserve Bulletin 427-437, Board of Governors of the Federal Reserve System, Washington, DC.

Duval, R.K. Cheng, K. H. Oh, R. Saraf, and D. Seneviratne. 2014. "Trade Integration and Business Cycle Synchronization: A Reappraisal

with Focus on Asia." Working Paper 14/52, International Monetary Fund, Washington, DC.

Eicher, T., S. Schubert, and S. Turnovsky. 2008. "Dynamic Effects of Terms of Trade Shocks: The impact on Debt and Growth." *Journal of International Money and Finance* 27 (6): 876-96.

Frankel, J., and A. Rose. 1998. "The Endogeneity of the Optimum Currency Area Criteria." *The Economic Journal* 108: 1009–1025.

Gupta, S., A. Kangur, C. Papageorgiou, and A. Wane. 2014. "Efficiency-Adjusted Public Capital and Growth." *World Development* 57 (C): 164-78.

Gurara, D. Z., and M. Ncube. 2013. "Global Economic Spillovers to Africa: A GVAR Approach." Working Paper 183, African Development Bank, Abidjan.

Hammond, G. 2012. "State of the Art of Inflation Targeting." Handbook No. 29, Centre for Central Banking Studies, Bank of England, London.

Heathcote, J., and F. Perri. 2004. "Financial Globalization and Real Regionalization." *Journal of Economic Theory* 119 (1): 207-243.

Hsieh, C.T., and P. Klenow. 2009. "Misallocation and Manufacturing TFP in China and India." *Quarterly Journal of Economics* 124 (4): 1403-1448.

Ilzetzki, E., E. G. Mendoza, and C. A. Vegh. 2013. "How Big (Small?) are Fiscal Multipliers?" *Journal of Monetary Economics* 60 (2): 239-254.

Imbs, J. 2004. "Trade, Finance, Specialization and Synchronization." *Review of Economics and Statistics* 86 (3): 723–734.

Inoue, T., D. Kaya, and H. Ohshige. 2015. "The Impact of China's Slowdown on the Asia Pacific Region: An Application of the GVAR Model." Policy Research Working Paper 7442, World Bank, Washington, DC.

Inter-American Development Bank. 2013.

Rethinking Reforms: How Latin America and the Caribbean can Escape Suppressed World Growth. Latin American and Caribbean Macroeconomic Report. Washington, DC: Inter-American Development Bank.

International Monetary Fund. 2010. *Emerging from the Global Crisis: Macroeconomic Challenges Facing Low-Income Countries.* Washington, DC: International Monetary Fund.

_____. 2011. "Article IV Consultation, the United States: 2011 Spillover Report." IMF Country Report No. 11/203, International Monetary Fund, Washington, DC.

_____. 2012a. *Regional Economic Outlook Sub-Saharan Africa October 2012: Maintaining Growth in an Uncertain World.* Washington, DC: International Monetary Fund.

_____. 2012b. *Regional Economic Outlook Western Hemisphere April 2012: Rebuilding Strength and Flexibility.* Washington, DC: International Monetary Fund.

_____. 2014a. *World Economic Outlook: Recovery Strengthens, Remains Uneven.* Washington, DC: International Monetary Fund.

_____. 2014b. "IMF Multilateral Policy Issues Report: 2014 Spillover Report." IMF Policy Paper, International Monetary Fund, Washington, DC.

_____. 2014c. "Is it Time for an Infrastructure Push? The Macroeconomic Effects of Public Investment." In *World Economic Outlook: Legacies, Clouds, Uncertainties.* Washington, DC: International Monetary Fund.

Jansen, W., and A. Stokman. 2004. "Foreign Direct Investment and International Business Cycle Comovement." ECB Working Paper 401, European Central Bank, Frankfurt.

Kalemli-Ozcan, S., E. Papaioannou, and F. Perri. 2013. "Global Banks and Crisis Transmission." *Journal of International Economics* 89(2): 495-510.

Kalemli-Ozcan, S., B. Sørensen, and O. Yosha. 2003. "Risk Sharing and Industrial Specialization: Regional and International Evidence." *American Economic Review* 93 (3): 903–918.

Kose, A. 2002. "Explaining Business Cycles in Small Open Economies: How much do World Prices Matter?" *Journal of International Economics* 56(2): 299–327.

Kose, A., C. Otrok, and E. Prasad. 2012. "Global Business Cycles: Convergence or Decoupling?" *International Economic Review* 53 (2): 511-538.

Kose, A., C. Otrok, and C. Whiteman. 2003. "International Business Cycles: World, Region, and Country Specific Factors." *American Economic Review* 93 (4): 1216-1239.

Kose, A., E. Prasad, and M. Terrones. 2009. "Does Financial Globalization Promote Risk Sharing?" *Journal of Development Economics* 89: 258–270.

Kose, A. and M. Terrones. 2015. Collapse and Revival: Understanding Global Recessions and Recoveries. Washington, DC: International Monetary Fund.

Kose, A., and R. Riezman. 2001. "Trade Shocks and Macroeconomic Fluctuations in Africa." *Journal of Development Economics* 65(1): 55–80.

Kraay, A., and L. Servén. 2013. "Fiscal Policy as a Tool for Stabilization in Developing Countries." Background Note for *World Development Report 2014: Risk and Opportunity –Managing Risk for Development*, Washington, DC: World Bank.

Lane, P. 2003. "Business Cycles and Macroeconomic Policy in Emerging Economies." *International Finance* 6 (1): 89-108.

Levchenko A., and N. Pandalai-Nayar. 2015. "TFP, News, and "Sentiments": The International Transmission of Business Cycles." NBER Working Paper 21010, National Bureau of Economic Research, Cambridge, MA.

Litterman, R. 1986. "Forecasting with Bayesian

Vector Autoregression – Five Years of Experience." *Journal of Business Economic Statistics* 4 (1): 25–38.

Ludovic, G., and R. Cyril. 2013. "Towards Recoupling? Assessing the Impact of a Chinese Hard Landing on Commodity Exporters: Results from Conditional Forecast in a GVAR Model." MPRA Paper 65457, University Library of Munich, Munich.

Mendoza, E. 1995. "The Terms of Trade, the Real Exchange Rate, and Economic Fluctuations." *International Economic Review* 36 (1): 101-37

Monfort, A., J. Renne, R. Rüffer, and G. Vitale. 2003. "Is Economic Activity in the G-7 Synchronized? Common Shocks versus Spillover Effects." Discussion Paper 4119, Center for Economic Policy Research, Washington, DC.

Norges Bank. 2014. "Spillovers to Europe from the Crisis in Russia and Ukraine." Economic Commentaries No. 6, Norges Bank, Oslo.

Obiora, K. 2009. "Decoupling from the East toward the West? Analyses of Spillovers to the Baltic countries." IMF Working Paper 09/129. International Monetary Fund, Washington, DC.

Pesaran, M. H., T. Schuermann, and S. M. Weiner. 2004. "Modelling Regional Inter-dependencies Using a Global Error-correcting Macroeconometric Model." *Journal of Business Economics and Statistics* 2: 126-162.

Pesaran, M., and Y. Shin. 1998. "Generalized Impulse Response Analysis in Linear Multivariate Models." *Economics Letters* 58 (1): 17-29.

Ratha, D., S. De, S. Plaza, K. Schuettler, W. Shaw, H. Wyss, S. Yi, and S. Yousefi. 2015. Migration and Development Brief 25, World Bank, Washington, DC.

Samake, I. and Y. Yang. 2014. "Low-income Countries' Linkages to BRICS: Are There Growth Spillovers?" *Journal of Asian Economics* 30: 1–14.

Stock, J., and M. Watson. 2005. "Understanding Changes in International Business Cycle Dynamics," *Journal of the European Economic Association* 3 (5): 968-1006.

World Bank. 2015a. *Global Economic Prospects, January 2015: Having Fiscal Space and Using It.* Washington, DC: World Bank.

_____. 2015b. *Global Economic Prospects, June 2015: The Global Economy in Transition.* Washington, DC: World Bank.

_____. 2015c. *Commodity Markets Outlook July 2015.* Washington, DC: World Bank.

_____. 2015d. *Commodity Markets Outlook October 2015.* Washington, DC: World Bank.

_____. 2015e. *Migration and Development Brief 25.* Washington, DC: World Bank.

Yilmaz, K. 2009. "International Business Cycle Spillovers." Tusiad-Koc University Economic Research ForumWorking Paper 0903, Koc University, Istanbul.

CHAPTER 4

TWO TOPICAL ISSUES:

Potential Macroeconomic Implications
of the Trans-Pacific Partnership

Peg and Control? The Links between Exchange
Rate Regimes and Capital Account Policies

Potential Macroeconomic Implications
of the Trans-Pacific Partnership

On October 4, 2015, 12 Pacific Rim countries concluded negotiations on the Trans-Pacific Partnership. If ratified by all, the agreement could raise GDP in member countries by an average of 1.1 percent by 2030. It could also increase member countries' trade by 11 percent by 2030, and represent a boost to regional trade growth, which had slowed to about 5 percent, on average, during 2010-14 from about 10 percent during 1990 -07. To the extent that the benefits of reforms have positive spillovers for the rest of the world, the detrimental effects of the agreement due to trade diversion and preference erosion on non-members, would be limited. The global significance of the agreement depends on whether it gains broader international traction.

Introduction

Over the last quarter century, trade flows of goods and services have increased rapidly (Figure 4.1.1). The value of world trade has more than quintupled, from $8.7 trillion in 1990, to more than $46 trillion in 2014. The relative importance of trade has increased too, from 39 percent of world GDP in 1990, to 60 percent in 2014. That said, global trade growth has slowed to about 4 percent per year since the crisis from about 7 percent, on average, during 1990-07. This slowdown in world trade reflects weak global investment growth, maturing global supply chains, and slowing momentum in trade liberalization (World Bank 2015).

On October 4, 2015, 12 Pacific Rim countries concluded negotiations on the Trans-Pacific Partnership (TPP), the largest, most diverse and potentially most comprehensive regional trade agreement yet. The 12 member countries are Australia, Brunei, Canada, Chile, Japan, Malaysia, Mexico, New Zealand, Peru, Singapore, United States, and Vietnam. While a detailed assessment will take time, this analysis and the assumptions used in its modelling exercise are based on a preliminary assessment of the agreement published in early November 2015.

The TPP is one of several Mega-Regional Trade Agreements (MRTAs) that have emerged since the mid-1990s. As a deep and comprehensive "new-generation" trade agreement, the TPP covers traditional barriers to trade in goods and services (e.g. tariffs, restrictions on the movement of professionals), investment activities, and other trade-related areas. Such areas include formal restrictions on some trade and investment activities, burdensome and inconsistent regulations, varying treatment of intellectual property, differing labor and environmental standards, issues specific to small and medium-size enterprises, and new challenges arising from rapidly growing digital technologies. China, the largest trading partner for most member countries of the agreement, is not included, nor is the Republic of Korea. The TPP, however, is designed as a "living agreement" to allow for membership expansion as well as broadening of coverage.

This analysis aims to address the following questions:

- How do new-generation trade agreements (such as the TPP) differ from traditional free trade agreements (FTAs)?

- What are the main features of the Trans-Pacific Partnership?

- What are the potential macroeconomic implications of the TPP?

Note: This analysis was prepared by Csilla Lakatos, Maryla Maliszewska, Franziska Ohnsorge, Peter Petri, and Michael Plummer. It partly draws from a background paper by Petri and Plummer (forthcoming).

FIGURE 4.1.1 Growth in world trade

International trade flows of goods and services have increased rapidly until the global financial crisis but then slowed.

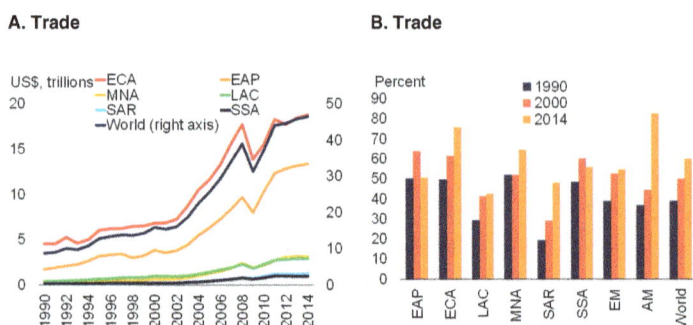

A. Trade

B. Trade

Source: World Development Indicators 2015.
A. EAP = East Asia and Pacific, ECA = Europe and Central Asia, LAC = Latin America and the Caribbean, MNA = Middle East and North Africa, SAR = South Asia, SSA = Sub-Saharan Africa. Regional aggregates include high-income and advanced countries, including the European Union.

How do new generation trade agreements differ from traditional FTAs?

Rule-making in the world trading system has shifted from global to bilateral, regional, and sectoral agreements. The Uruguay Round of multilateral trade negotiations, which culminated in the establishment of the World Trade Organization (WTO) in 1994, produced a comprehensive agreement to reduce tariffs on manufactured goods. It also expanded into areas such as agriculture, trade in services, and intellectual property. However, complex trade policy issues, including regulatory barriers, modern services trade and cross-border investment (covered in the General Agreement on Trade in Services, GATS) and the knowledge economy (key aspects covered under the Trade-Related Aspects of Intellectual Property Rights Agreement (TRIPS) have been challenging to address at a multilateral level. Hence, cooperation on these issues has recently taken place through bilateral and/or regional agreements. While there were only a few of these before 2000, their number ballooned to 266 by 2014 (Figure 4.1.2).

At the same time, the concept of deep and comprehensive FTAs has taken hold. These FTAs offer expanded market access, even for products that have previously aroused domestic sensitivities.

Provisions can go well beyond WTO standards. Specific measures include the following:

- a negative-list approach for liberalizing trade in services, which covers all sectors except those explicitly listed (as opposed to the positive list of sectors under GATS);

- new rules for internet and digital commerce;

- across-the-board national treatment for foreign investors, both pre- and post-establishment;

- streamlined regulations through standardized principles;

- enhanced intellectual property protection, with more comprehensive rules and greater enforcement obligations than in the TRIPS agreement;

- government procurement commitments (covered under the plurilateral Government Procurement Agreement in the WTO);

- competitive neutrality for state-owned enterprises;

- labor and environment codes; and

- improved dispute resolution for many issues covered in the agreement.

Regional and mega-regional trade agreements

In the 1990s, before the surge in bilateral and smaller regional agreements of the 2000s, two large Regional Trade Agreements (RTAs) emerged: the European Union (EU) Single Market (established 1993) and the North American Free Trade Agreement between Canada, Mexico, and the United States (NAFTA, established 1994). These agreements had evolved from two earlier agreements—the European Economic Community, established in 1957 with six member countries, and the Canada-US Free Trade Agreement in 1987.

Several other RTAs were established in the 1990s.

- *Mercosur*: Established in 1991, the agreement has six member states in Latin America, including Argentina, Bolivia, Brazil, Paraguay, Uruguay and the Republica Bolivariana de Venezuela.

- *South Asian Preferential Trading Arrangement (SAPTA)*: Originally signed in 1993, the agreement deepened into the South Asian Free Trade Area (SAFTA) in 2004 and now covers eight South Asian countries, including India and Pakistan.

- *Association of South East Asian Nations Free Trade Area (ASEAN)*: Signed in 1992, the agreement now includes ten East Asian countries, including Indonesia, Malaysia, and Thailand.

By 2015, the number of RTAs reached 274. The EU Single Market—now covering 28 members—and NAFTA are by far the largest RTAs in terms of GDP and trade. Together, their member countries account for 50 percent of global GDP and 37 percent of global trade (more than two times as much as the members of the smaller three RTAs combined). The EU Single Market and NAFTA are also the agreements with the largest intra-regional trade. Intra-EU trade accounts for 60 percent of total member trade, while intra-NAFTA trade accounts for 41 percent of total member trade. This compares with less than 20 percent among members of the other three RTAs (Figure 4.1.2).

Mega-regional trade agreements (MRTAs), as defined here, are regional agreements that have systemic, global impact. In other words, they are sufficiently large and ambitious to influence trade rules and trade flows beyond their areas of application.

Earlier RTAs began as initiatives to reduce tariffs. Over time they grew to reduce non-tariff barriers. More recent regional negotiations have, from the outset, focused on more ambitious, deep, and comprehensive agreements. In addition to the TPP, major new negotiations include the Regional

FIGURE 4.1.2 Importance of regional trade agreements

The number of regional trade agreements (RTAs) has grown rapidly.

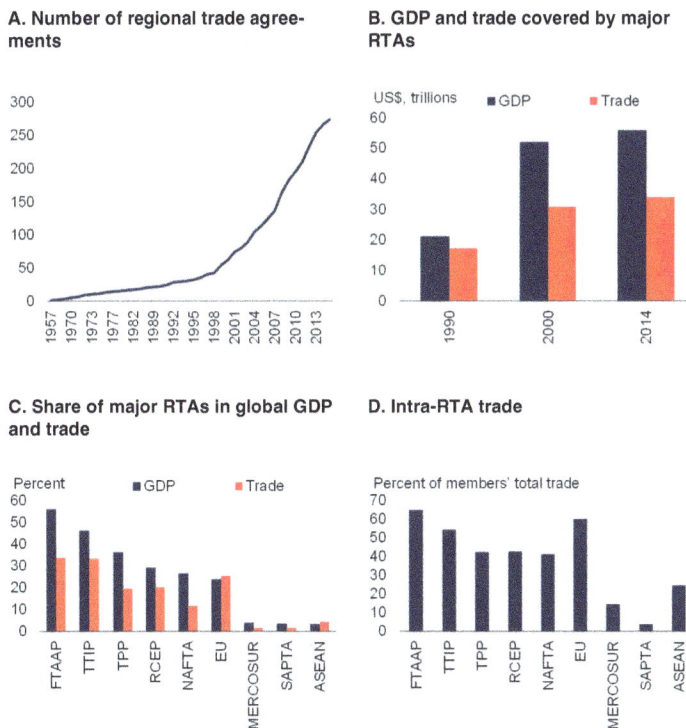

A. Number of regional trade agreements

B. GDP and trade covered by major RTAs

C. Share of major RTAs in global GDP and trade

D. Intra-RTA trade

Sources: World Trade Organization's Regional Trade Agreement database; World Development Indicators; World Integrated Trade Solution (WITS) database.
B. RTAs are reciprocal trade agreements between two or more partners and include both free trade agreements and customs unions.
C. D. SAPTA = South Asian Preferential Trading Arrangement; ASEAN = Association of South East Asian Nations Free Trade Area; EU = European Union; NAFTA = North American Free Trade Agreement; RCEP = Regional Comprehensive Economic Partnership; FTAAP = Free Trade Area of the Asia-Pacific; TPP = Trans-Pacific Partnership; TTIP = Transatlantic Trade and Investment Partnership.

FIGURE 4.1.3 RTAs: Tariffs and membership

While earlier RTAs predominantly aimed at reducing tariffs, the new generation of trade agreements focuses more on reducing the restrictiveness of non-tariff measures. There is considerable overlap in the membership of the three agreements currently under discussion in Asia.

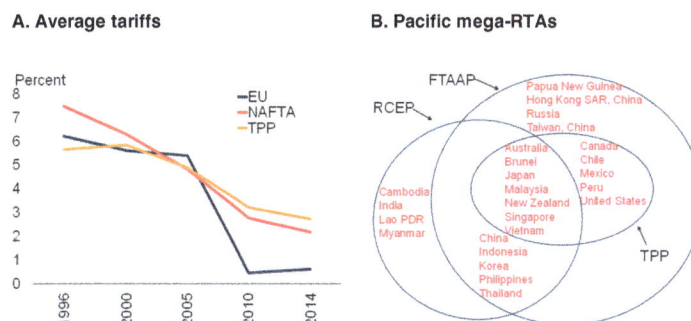

A. Average tariffs

B. Pacific mega-RTAs

Sources: World Integrated Trade Solution (WITS) database; Petri and Raheem (2014).

Comprehensive Economic Partnership (RCEP) among 16 Asian economies, and the Trans-Atlantic Trade and Investment Partnership between the European Union and the United States. An even larger Free Trade Area of the Asia-Pacific (FTAAP) among 21 Asia-Pacific Economic Cooperation (APEC) economies is also in early stages of discussion. There is substantial overlap in membership of these groups (Figure 4.1.3).

Benefits offered and challenges posed by RTAs

The rise of regional agreements has rekindled debate on whether they support or impede global efficiency and activity in member and non-member countries (WTO 2011; Freund and Ornelas 2010; World Bank 2005, Maggi 2014).

Benefits for members. RTAs open markets between partners, leading to a more efficient division of labor, technology spillovers and related productivity growth ("trade creation"; Hoekman and Javorcik 2006, Blyde 2004). A growing literature suggests that trade agreements foster domestic reforms in developing countries (Baccini and Urpelainen, 2014a,b). For example, a range of regulatory reforms have followed EU enlargement (Schönfelder and Wagner 2015; Staehr 2011; Mattli and Plümper 2004; Milner and Kubota 2005). RTAs are also often a step toward larger agreements through the process of competitive liberalization (Baldwin and Jaimovich 2010). For example, the European integration project has expanded from six to 28 members so far. NAFTA grew out of an agreement between Canada and the United States, and while it did not itself expand further, it did spawn a network of agreements between its members and third partners. The Asia-Pacific integration process appears to be following this path.

Studies of the internal political economy of trading blocs point to other positive impacts of RTAs. The domino theory of regionalism argues that as a bloc grows, potential partners likely benefit more from joining, and therefore offer better deals to secure admission (Baldwin 1993). This tilts the political calculus within blocs toward admitting new members (McCulloch and Petri

1997). Blocs that gain critical mass—for example, the European Union—will therefore likely attract a growing membership. Outside the bloc, the bloc's policies could become an external anchor for institutional reforms in potential future member countries (IMF 2003). In addition, internal political constituencies change as blocs grow.

Drawbacks for members and non-members. While RTAs may significantly benefit members, they can set back economic activity for non-members (Baldwin and Wyplosz, 2006; Krueger 1999). The competitiveness gains developed in these new blocs could potentially divert trade away from more efficient non-member exporters towards less efficient member ones (Viner 1950; Balassa 1967; Baldwin 2006), a phenomenon called the "trade diversion" effect. In addition, RTAs can result in the erosion in the value of preferences given to Least Developed Countries (LDCs) under existing duty-free, quota-free, preferential schemes, such as the "Everything but Arms Initiative" of the European Union and the "African Growth and Opportunities Act" of the U.S. This phenomenon (which applies to both regional and multilateral agreements) is sometimes called the "preference erosion" effect.

RTAs within natural trading blocs—among countries that already trade intensively with each other—tend to have modest diversion effects (Eicher et al. 2012). As a percentage of their total trade, trade among the prospective member states of TPP, FTAAP, and RCEP (35-60 percent) already exceeds that within NAFTA (Figure 4.1.2).

What are the main features of the Trans-Pacific Partnership?

The TPP will expand mutual market access among member countries by lowering tariffs and easing the restrictiveness of non-tariff measures. Non-tariff measures (NTMs) cover a wide range of measures that can be obstacles to trade, including import licensing requirements, rules for customs valuations, discriminatory standards, pre-shipment inspections, rules of origin to qualify for lower tariffs, investment measures (e.g. local content requirements), and local sourcing for government procurement. In addition, the TPP will facilitate supply chain integration by encouraging greater regional coherence in standards and regulations.

Tariff and non-tariff measures

Although both tariffs and restrictions caused by non-tariff measures between many TPP members are already low by historical and international comparison, the currently negotiated TPP, would over time eliminate nearly all of tariffs among its members, including very high ones such as the 350 percent tariff on US tobacco imports (Oliver 2015). Also, it would lower trade barriers associated with sizeable non-tariff measures in many member countries (Figure 4.1.4).

Partly due to the general decline in worldwide tariffs, but also because of the proliferation of free trade agreements among TPP countries, average intra-TPP tariffs have more than halved since 1996, to 2.7 percent in 2014 from 5.6 percent in 1996. Much of TPP trade is already covered by trade agreements, including NAFTA; the ASEAN Free Trade Area; the free trade agreement between ASEAN, Australia, and New Zealand; the free trade agreement between ASEAN and Japan; and the P4 Agreement.[1]

These averages, however, hide some high tariff barriers on individual goods. Product lines with average tariffs exceeding 15 percent—sometimes dubbed "international peaks"—often protect key domestic interests or industries (UNCTAD, 2000). In the United States and Canada, peaks comprise 3-5 percent of tariff lines. Some advanced countries still apply very high tariff rates on imports of certain items. Peru and Chile, in contrast, have zero peak tariffs.

Restrictions caused by NTMs, measured as ad-valorem equivalents, appear to be less prevalent among TPP member countries than elsewhere. TPP member countries have a higher incidence of

FIGURE 4.1.4 **The main features of the TPP**

The TPP is primarily focused on reducing the restrictiveness of non-tariff measures (NTMs), but also incorporates provisions to cut tariffs. The use of restrictive NTMs is more prevalent in TPP advanced market economies, with a higher incidence of restrictive NTMs and lower incidence of less restrictive NTMs.

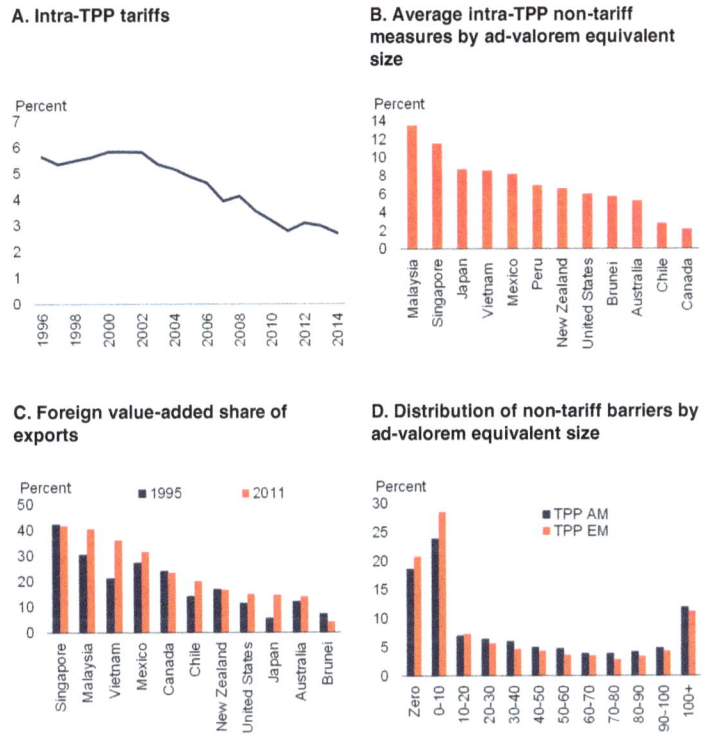

Sources: International Trade Center MACMAP database; Kee et al. (2009)
D. AM = TPP advanced market economies (Australia, Canada, Japan, New Zealand, Singapore, United States), EM = TPP emerging and frontier market economies (Brunei, Chile, Malaysia, Mexico, Peru, Vietnam).

only moderately restrictive NTMs (from zero to 10 percent) and a lower incidence of highly restrictive NTMs (greater than 100 percent) than other countries. Within the TPP group, NTMs are more restrictive in Asia than in North America and Latin America. Studies have noted that more restrictive NTMs have partially offset lower tariffs in advanced economies (Kee, Nicita and Olarreaga 2008). That said, assessing NTMs and their impact is particularly fraught with uncertainty since data on the *existence* of restrictive NTMs are highly uneven. Unlike tariffs, data on the *intensity* of NTMs is typically only inferred from bilateral trade flows.

Development of production and supply chains

In addition to promoting comprehensive market access by reducing tariffs and the restrictiveness of NTMs, the TPP seeks to facilitate the development of supply chains among its members. Supply chain integration has deepened rapidly since 1995, raising the share of foreign value added in TPP member countries' exports. TPP member countries' share of foreign value added in exports ranges from 15 percent in advanced countries such as the United States, Australia, and Japan, to 40 percent in Singapore and Malaysia (Figure 4.1.4). The upper end of this range is high by international comparison, and broadly in line with foreign content shares in Eastern Europe, which is deeply integrated into Western European supply chains (OECD 2015).[2] The expertise of advanced country firms—at either the marketing end of the chain, or in providing crucial production technologies at the upstream end of the chain—could contribute to the development of more complex value chains (Humphrey and Schmitz 2002; Kowalski et al. 2015). Conversely, supply chains also create interdependencies that can accelerate the transmission of shocks.

Supply chains involve the close coordination of production decisions among different locations. They depend on rapid and reliable ways for shipping goods, making investments, and transferring information. Attracting supply chains to an economy requires good physical connectivity through ports, roads and telecommunications—along with policies that facilitate trade in intermediate products and services, as well as foreign investment. Research suggests that liberal service sector rules are especially important, since high-quality logistics, transportation, financial and consulting services help to support supply chain connections (World Economic Forum, 2012).

The TPP also includes social and environmental provisions that may impact trade and production chains:[3]

- *Labor and environment.* Standards for labor and environmental sustainability are politically contentious. What some interpret as civil rights and sustainability concerns are seen by others as hidden protectionism and restrictions on competition (Lukauskas et al. 2013). The TPP seeks to incorporate International Labor Organization (ILO) obligations, require domestic laws to be consistent with international standards, and provides for enforcement. Environmental standards introduced in the agreement address illegal wildlife trafficking, logging and fishing. They also include provisions on conservation, biodiversity, protecting the ozone layer and environmental goods and services.

- *Intellectual property rights.* The TPP goes somewhat beyond the WTO's TRIPS agreement. It requires penalties for the unlawful commercial exploitation of copyrighted work, and prescribes measures to reduce the illegal online distribution of copyrighted material and strengthen copyright terms.[4] Some of the IP-related TPP provisions are highly controversial, including those for biologics and trademarks.[5] Proponents argue that strong rules and enforcement are necessary in order to support investments in innovation, whereas critics maintain that current levels of IP protection already stifle innovation and generate monopoly rents.[6] There is also a concern that greater IP protection will raise the cost of necessary medicines (Hersh and Stiglitz 2015; Stiglitz 2008; Gosselin 2015).

---

[2]Foreign value added accounts for 45-49 percent of exports in Hungary, Czech Republic, and Slovak Republic (OECD 2015).

[3]In addition, for the first time in the context of a free trade agreement, countries have adopted a Declaration (The Joint Declaration of the Macroeconomic Policy Authorities of Trans-Pacific Partnership Countries) that addresses unfair currency practices by promoting transparency and accountability.

[4]IP provisions lengthen copyright terms, protect clinical data developed by pharmaceutical firms from being used by competitors for a certain period of time, and set transparency standards for choosing medicines for reimbursement by national health plans.

[5]The debate around biologics (drugs and vaccines created from living organisms) centers on data developed by the innovator to demonstrate the safety and effectiveness of a product. The US was reportedly seeking 12 years of data protection while the agreement settled on five years plus additional commitments by some members.

[6]See Pugatch (2006) for a review of legal and political economy issues associated with this debate; and Boldrin and Levine (2013) for a critical view of the economic benefits of patent protection.

Although not explicitly modelled in this study, the harmonization of labor and environmental standards within the TPP could have important implications for participating developing countries, such as Malaysia, Mexico, Peru, and Vietnam. While such harmonization, which goes beyond product standards to encompass production process standards, has social and environmental benefits, it may also affect competitiveness of firms in countries that currently do not meet such standards. Trade-related product standards typically apply only to products destined for specific destinations, and a firm can choose whether to meet them. However, labor and environmental standards apply across the board to all production, including that destined for consumption at home and in non-TPP countries, and compliance is mandatory (and subject to dispute settlement).[7]

Some of these broader provisions, including labor, environmental, pharmaceutical and state-owned enterprise regulation, may require deep reforms and a difficult adjustment process in member countries. They are not modelled in the approach taken here, but could affect aggregate gains if fully implemented. For example, state-owned enterprise reform could generate significant productivity gains; tightened labor and environmental regulation could reduce competitiveness and GDP gains but achieve other regulatory objectives (Box 4.1.1). Similarly, free trade agreements are often followed by tariff reductions for non-members, which are not modelled here (Estevadeordal, Freund and Ornelas 2008; Freund and Ornelas 2010). Policy changes in non-members could enhance the benefits of TPP to them (Ciuriak and Singh 2015).

What are the potential macroeconomic implications of the TPP?

The estimations are based on a computable general equilibrium model as originally described in Zhai (2008). Annex 4.1.1 provides details of the analytical approach. The model is particularly well suited to analyzing trade policies and trade links because it allows the emergence of trade in products which were not previously traded between pairs of countries. While the model has some dynamic features (through savings and investment), it lacks positive dynamic feedback loops in member countries such as the accumulation of knowledge and the absorption of foreign technology through TPP-facilitated FDI. As a result, the benefits derived here could underestimate the eventual impact on member countries. Conversely, TPP-triggered productivity increases in member countries could undermine the competitiveness of non-member countries and exacerbate the detrimental effects on non-members.

The results rest on planned tariff cuts in accordance with the provisions of TPP and on several key assumptions about the theoretically desirable and politically feasible non-tariff barrier cuts, dubbed "actionable," and the actual cuts implemented in the TPP. The macroeconomic implications of the TPP are evaluated relative to a baseline scenario that includes pre-existing trade agreements among member countries (e.g. NAFTA, AFTA, the ASEAN-Australia-New Zealand FTA, the ASEAN-Japan FTA and the P4 Agreement).

Three assumptions are of particular importance to the results: the restrictiveness of new rules of origin, cuts in barriers to services, and spillovers from regulatory harmonization.[8]

- *"Cumulative" rules of origin* could encourage regional production networks but may require

---

[7]See Mattoo (2001). A review of the literature finds no clear empirical evidence that adherence to stronger labor standards has a significant impact on trade performance (Salem and Rozental 2012). However, there is some evidence that certain types of environmental regulation can adversely affect productivity (e.g., Greenstone, List and Syverson 2012).

[8]A further assumption is that the agreement will be implemented in 2017. However, the agreement has yet to be ratified by all its members.

FIGURE 4.1.5 Aggregate impact of TPP: GDP and trade by 2030

TPP is expected to increase member country GDP and exports. The estimated impact on non-member country GDP is negligible, on average, although some East Asian countries could face declining exports.

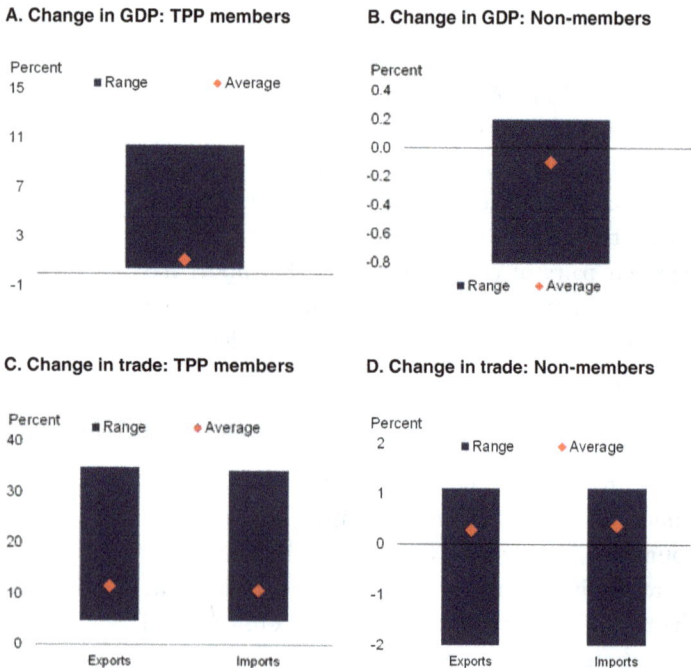

A. Change in GDP: TPP members

B. Change in GDP: Non-members

C. Change in trade: TPP members

D. Change in trade: Non-members

Source: Authors' simulations.

some producers to replace more inputs with higher-cost inputs from TPP members to qualify for low TPP tariffs. The rules of origin affect the share of exports that benefit from tariff preferences. These shares are assumed to rise from 30 percent to 69 percent over a decade in the case of apparel, but more quickly for other products. The model assumes that rules of origin lead to the replacement of 40 percent of imported inputs with higher-cost regionally originating ones, on average.

- *Existing services barriers* are estimated indirectly from bilateral trade flows (Fontagne, Guillin and Mitaritonna 2011). Only half of these estimated barriers are assumed to be actionable through policy changes, and only a part of those are assumed to be eliminated by the TPP. While this fraction will depend on actual implementation, a preliminary assessment of the TPP suggests that the provisions are broadly in line with those in the existing agreement between Korea and the

United States (e.g. provisions pertaining to greater transparency and enforceable negative lists). Therefore, the fraction of actual reductions in actionable services barriers is assumed to be similar to that observed in the agreement between Korea and the United States.

- *Non-discriminatory trade liberalization* (positive spillovers) will be a byproduct of the TPP, to some extent, as common and more transparent regulatory approaches also facilitate trade of non-members with TPP members (Box 4.1.1). Many TPP provisions that are designed to reduce the restrictiveness of NTMs focus on increasing the transparency and predictability of regulations, and still others require policies (such as rules for government procurement or electronic commerce) that are not easily restricted to members. Provided these provisions are fully implemented in a non-discriminatory manner, they will benefit members and non-members alike. At an aggregate level, 20 percent of NTM liberalization adopted in the TPP is assumed to consist of such non-discriminatory provisions. Although the debate on the precise number is not yet settled, this is at the low end of assumptions used in other studies based on business surveys (European Commission 2013).[9]

Overall member country impact. The model simulations suggest that, by 2030, the TPP will raise member country GDP by 0.4-10 percent, and by 1.1 percent, on a GDP-weighted average basis (Figure 4.1.5). The benefits are likely to materialize slowly but should accelerate towards the end of the projection period. The slow start results from the gradual implementation of the agreement and the lag required for benefits to materialize utilization rises. The benefits of the TPP would mostly derive from reductions in non-tariff-based measures and measures that benefit

---

[9]European Commission (2012) in the study of the EU-Japan FTA assumed that 65 per cent of NTM reductions yield benefits for third countries, while 35 per cent of any reductions deliver a strictly bilateral benefit, an assumption based on the examination of barriers identified with a business survey in Copenhagen Economics, 2009. European Commission (2013) in the analysis of TTIP applies the assumption of 20 per cent spillovers to non-members.

services.[10] For TPP members, only 15 percent of the GDP increase would be due to tariff cuts, whereas cuts in NTMs, in goods and services, would account for 53 percent and 31 percent of the total increase in GDP, respectively.[11]

Individual member country impact. The largest gains in GDP are expected in smaller, open member economies, such as Vietnam and Malaysia (10 percent and 8 percent, respectively).[12] Both countries would benefit from lower tariffs and NTMs in large export markets and at home and from stronger positions in regional supply chains through deeper integration (World Bank 2015b). The impact on NAFTA members (all also members of TPP) would be small, on the order of 0.6 percent of GDP, because trade represents a modest share of GDP and because existing barriers to their trade (which is already mostly among them) are already low for the most traded commodities.

Non-member impacts. Since almost half of trade is among TPP member countries, trade diversion effects could be limited (Figure 4.1.4). Non-discriminatory liberalization effects (positive spillovers) account for 21 percent of the gains of members and 42 percent of estimated global gains, reflecting improved regulatory processes and the streamlining and harmonization of NTMs and investment barriers among TPP members. As a result, aggregate GDP losses to non-members could be of limited size (0.1 percent by 2030). Only in Korea, Thailand and some other Asian countries, the estimated GDP losses would exceed 0.3 percent of GDP since they would lose competitiveness in TPP members, which are currently among their most important export

FIGURE 4.1.6 Country specific impact of TPP: GDP and trade by 2030

Vietnam and Malaysia would be among the TPP member countries benefiting most. As a result of shrinking market access and greater competition in export markets, activity in Korea and Thailand could be set back. Non-member countries like Russia could benefit from greater harmonization of standards in export markets.

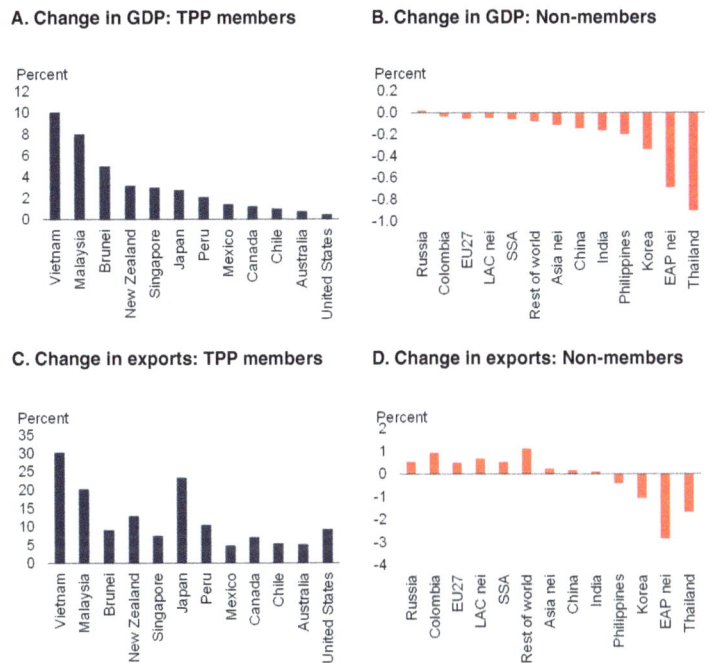

A. Change in GDP: TPP members

B. Change in GDP: Non-members

C. Change in exports: TPP members

D. Change in exports: Non-members

Source: Authors' simulations.
Note: "LAC nei" includes Argentina, Bolivia, Brazil, Costa Rica, Ecuador, Guatemala, Honduras, Rest of the Caribbean, Nicaragua, Panama, Rest of Central America, Paraguay, El Salvador, Uruguay, Venezuela RB, Rest of North America, Rest of South America. "Asia nei" includes Bangladesh, Kazakhstan, Kyrgyz Republic, Mongolia, Nepal, Pakistan, Rest of South Asia, Rest of Former Soviet Union, Rest of Western Asia, Sri Lanka. "EAP nei" covers: Cambodia, Lao PDR, and Rest of Southeast Asia. "SSA" indicates Sub-Saharan Africa.

markets (Figure 4.1.6).[13] While the adverse effects of TPP on Korea could be attributed mostly to preference erosion (due to its existing FTA with the United States), losses for Thailand and other Asian countries could be mainly due to trade diversion. This supports similar concerns raised for Asian LDCs not individually considered here, such as Bangladesh, Laos, Cambodia and Nepal (Lehmann 2015). These countries with strong comparative advantage in sectors such as apparel, textiles and footwear could face greater competition by Vietnam in TPP markets. For Russia, positive spillovers could slightly outweigh trade diversion effects. While aggregate output effects among non-members would likely be limited, the TPP could

---

[10]Some agricultural NTMs are grouped with tariff cuts in these calculations.

[11]Despite overall long-term gains, member countries could experience sizeable adjustment costs and transitional losses in the short run (Trefler 2001). In principle, factor reallocation triggered by trade liberalization can be disruptive. However, in the TPP agreement reductions in nontariff measures and implementation of common regulatory practices are back-loaded and so will be any transition effects and gains from TPP.

[12]Vietnam's textile and garment exports are expected to expand 28 percent by 2030, following the reduction of tariffs of up to 8.7 percentage points in export markets such as the United States The impact on Malaysia is slightly higher than estimated in Petri, Plummer and Zhai (2012) due to several updates to data and assumptions as explained in more detail in Annex 4.1.1.

[13]EAP nie (not elsewhere included) covers Lao PDR, Cambodia, Myanmar and Timor Leste.

FIGURE 4.1.7 Impact of TPP on sectoral output by 2030

Skilled labor intensive sectors (such as chemicals, vehicles and machinery) are likely to expand faster in some advanced economies, while unskilled labor intensive (such as textiles, apparel and metal products) sectors are likely to expand faster in some emerging and frontier market member countries.

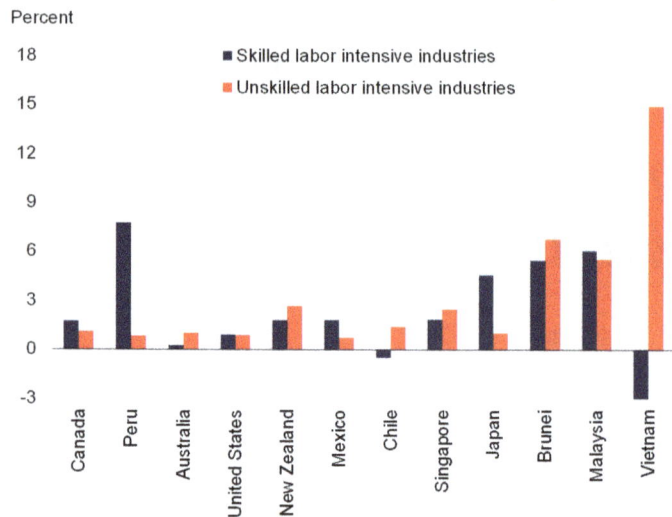

Source: Authors' simulations.
Note: Skilled or unskilled labor-intensive industries are defined depending on whether they are above or below the average skill intensity across the sample, respectively.

FIGURE 4.1.8 Comparing TPP to other trade agreements

The estimated impact of TPP on member country GDP—broadly in line with earlier studies—could be similar to impacts of other large regional trade agreements.

A. Long-term impact of major RTAs on member country GDP

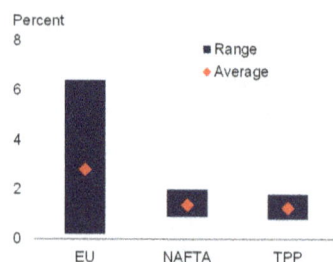

B. Estimated impact of TPP on member country GDP

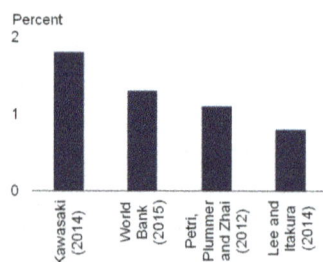

Sources: Cecchini (1988), Campos et al. (2014), Harrison et al. (1994), Baldwin (1989), Marinello et al. (2015), Vetter and Bottcher (2013); Brown et al. (1992), Cox and Harris (1992), Hufbauer and Schott (1993), Peterson Institute (2014); Kawasaki (2014), Lee and Itakura (2014), World Bank (2015), Petri et al. (2014).
A. Red dots denotes the average estimate among a number of studies; blue bars denote range. Studies include for EU: Cecchini (1988), Harrison et al. (1994), Baldwin (1989), Marinello et al. (2015, excluding their highest estimate), Vetter and Bottcher (2013); for NAFTA: Brown et al. (1992), Cox and Harris (1992), Hufbauer and Schott (1993), Peterson Institute (2014); for TPP: Kawasaki (2014), Lee and Itakura (2014), World Bank (forthcoming), Petri et al. (2014). Studies differ in methodologies. Depending on the study, the period of coverage considers either comparative static effects or long run (15-20 years) effects.

induce significant sectoral shifts. In particular, competition from TPP member countries may shift resources away from the manufacturing

sectors of non-member economies towards services sectors.

Sectoral shifts within TPP area. Although the TPP is unlikely to affect overall employment in the long run, it may accelerate structural shifts between industries based on comparative advantage and scale economies.[14] In advanced economies, these mechanisms favor traded services, advanced manufacturing, and, for some resource-rich countries, primary products and investments. In developing countries, they benefit manufacturing, especially in unskilled labor-intensive industries, and some primary production. As a result, participating advanced economy members are likely to experience a slight increase in skill premia while others benefit from a higher increase in the wages of unskilled workers (Figure 4.1.7). In the United States, for example, changes in real wages are expected to be small as unskilled and skilled wages increase by 0.4 and 0.6 percent, respectively, by 2030. In contrast, in Vietnam, TPP could increase the real wages of unskilled workers by more than 14 percent by 2030, as production intensive in unskilled labor (e.g. textiles) shifts to Vietnam.

Comparison with other studies. Results reported here are broadly consistent with those of other studies, although estimating the impact of deep and comprehensive trade agreements is still very much a work in progress. The few studies that assess the economic impact of TPP find overall impacts for members on the order of 0.8-1.8 percent of GDP. This would be similar to those estimated for existing RTAs: in the long run (15-20 years), NAFTA has been estimated to have raised member country GDP by 1-2 percent, and the European Single Market has been estimated to have lifted member country GDP by 2-3 percent (Figure 4.1.8).[15]

---

[14]Trade agreements may lead to small increases in employment if they raise wages and the supply of labor responds positively to wage increases. However, theory does not argue for strong (or even positive) labor supply effects, and empirical estimates of labor supply elasticities are generally low (OECD, ITO, World Bank 2010).

[15]Figure 4.1.8 also include estimates for the European Single Market of outlier studies such as that of Campos et al. (2014) that estimates that EU GDP per capita would be 12 percent lower on average in the absence of EU integration. A more selective recent review identifies the 2-3 percent range as most persuasive (Vetter and Böttcher 2013).

Conclusion

This analysis discussed the features of new-generation free-trade agreements and TPP, specifically, and traced out potential macroeconomic implications for member and non-member countries. As a new-generation, deep and comprehensive trade agreement, TPP addresses a wide range of complex trade policy issues that go beyond the scope of traditional trade agreements. The agreement will reduce tariffs and restrictiveness of non-tariff measures as well as harmonize a range of regulations to encourage the integration of supply chains and cross-border investment.

TPP could be an important complement to other policies to lift medium-term growth:

- By shifting resources towards the most productive firms and sectors and expanding export markets, TPP has the potential to lift overall GDP of member countries by 1.1 percent by 2030. The impact could be considerably more in countries facing currently elevated barriers to trade (as much as 10 percent in Vietnam and 8 percent in Malaysia). In countries that export labor-intensive products, incomes of low-income and low-skilled households could expand strongly.

- To the extent that the TPP produces positive spillover benefits for other countries, detrimental effects on non-member countries may be limited. Such positive spillovers could arise from harmonized regulatory regimes in TPP export markets.

- TPP could also lift member countries' trade by 11 percent by 2030. This would be an important counterweight to the trade slowdown underway since 2011. At current 2011-14 trends, member countries' trade would fall 25 percent below pre-crisis trend by 2030.

Policy reforms are needed to enhance the benefits of TPP—like other RTAs—in developing countries. Governments in several member countries see the liberalization required by the TPP as a driver for difficult policy changes. However, implementation of MRTAs, including the TPP, requires institutional capacity not available to some developing countries (Michalopoulos 1999; Hoekman et al. 2003). As the TPP is implemented over time, emphasis on the following issues would be important to mitigate unfavorable effects on developing countries:

- *Capacity building.* Capacity building and technical assistance for developing country members are an important building block of the TPP.

- *Liberal rules of origin.* TPP members and non-members will benefit if rules of origin mandating higher-cost inputs from TPP members are implemented in a permissive rather than restrictive manner.

- *Liberalize labor- and resource-intensive industries.* Low- and middle-income economies often have a comparative advantage in labor- and natural-resource intensive industries. By cutting tariffs for labor-intensive garments, the TPP thus benefits countries like Vietnam.

- *Multilateral framework.* Bringing MRTAs into a global framework would broaden the gains to a wider set of countries and reduce detrimental diversion effects for non-members. Implementation of the "living agreement" clause that keeps TPP membership open is particularly important.

Against the background of slowing trade growth, rising non-tariff impediments to trade, and insufficient progress in global negotiations, the TPP represents an important milestone. The TPP stands out among FTAs for its size, diversity and rulemaking. Its ultimate implications, however, remain unclear. Much will depend on whether the TPP is quickly adopted and effectively implemented, and whether it triggers productive reforms in developing and developed countries. Broader systemic effects, in turn, will require expanding such reforms to global trade, whether through TPP enlargement, competitive effects on other trade agreements, or new global rules.

BOX 4.1.1 Regulatory convergence in mega-regional trade agreements

TPP aims to promote a common regulatory approach, either through mutual recognition agreements or outright harmonization. Benefits for members and non-members tend to be higher when members choose mutual recognition and rules of origin are not restrictive.

Introduction

Trade policy makers like to think of standards as the seabed rocks that are revealed as the tide of tariffs ebbs. Not surprisingly, the European Union and the United States, with their relatively low tariffs, have decided to address the trade impact of mandatory standards—referred to formally as Technical Barriers to Trade (TBT) and, when they concern food safety and animal and plant health standards, as Sanitary and Phytosanitary (SPS) measures—in the context of the prospective Transatlantic Trade and Investment Partnership (T-TIP). To a more limited extent, the diverse group of countries that has just concluded the Transpacific Partnership (TPP) have also decided to adopt a "common regulatory approach" in certain respects. For the most part, the TPP initiates a cooperative process rather than an obligation of early implementation. Would all countries, within and outside the TPP, benefit from these developments?

Whereas the T-TIP has an ambitious agenda on regulatory convergence, parties to the TPP have settled on a dual approach. First, they have agreed on "transparent, non-discriminatory rules for developing regulations, standards and conformity assessment procedures, while preserving TPP Parties' ability to fulfill legitimate objectives." In this respect, the TPP rules broadly reflect, and in fact, directly incorporate some of the main rules already contained in the WTO, TBT, and SPS agreements. In specific sectors, the Parties have also agreed to promote a more streamlined regulatory approach across the TPP region. The sectors selected for such an approach include cosmetics, medical devices, pharmaceuticals, information and communications technology products, wine and distilled spirits, proprietary formulas for prepackaged foods and food additives, and organic agricultural products. The provisions of the agreement cover labelling requirements for wine, marketing authorizations for pharmaceuticals, medical devices and cosmetics, and encourage mutual recognition of standards for organic products as well as mutual recognition of conformity assessment of telecommunications equipment.

What does regulatory convergence as envisaged in the T-TIP and TPP imply? The voluminous research on preferential trade agreements, with its almost exclusive focus on tariffs and (sometimes) quotas, provides only limited illumination on the implications of agreements on standards. Baldwin (2000) presented a useful analytical framework for the analysis of mutual recognition agreements (MRAs), but assumed identical countries with identical costs of complying with standards. Few previous studies have empirically explored the impact of shared standards on trade (e.g., Swann et al. 1996, Moenius 2004, Shepherd 2007, Reyes 2011, and Orefice et al. 2012).

This box draws on one of the few papers to analyze the implications of preferential agreements on standards (Chen and Mattoo, 2008). It addresses the following questions pertaining to a common regulatory approach:

- How could it be implemented?

- What are its implications?

- What policy choices would ensure that it produces wider gains?

How could a common regulatory approach be implemented?

Based on earlier experience, notably in the European Union, three broad types of agreements are available to deal with technical barriers to trade. The TPP seems to place emphasis primarily on the third type of agreement listed below.

Mutual recognition of existing standards. The simplest, and potentially most powerful, is the mutual recognition of existing standards, whereby a country grants unrestricted access to its market to products that meet any participating country's standards. This was the approach taken in principle by the European Union following the Cassis de Dijon judgment of the European Court of Justice. Mutual Recognition Agreements (MRAs) are, however, not likely to be an option if there is a significant difference in the initial standards of the countries, as became evident in the context of the European Union.

Harmonization of standards. In such cases, a certain degree of harmonization is a precondition for countries to

Note: This box was prepared by Aaditya Mattoo.

BOX 4.1.1 Regulatory convergence in mega-regional trade agreements *(continued)*

allow products of other countries to access their markets. The most important example of such harmonization is the current approach of the European Union where directives from the European Commission set out essential health and safety requirements for most regulated products.

Mutual recognition of conformity assessments of requirements. In many other cases, neither mutual recognition nor harmonization of substantive standards are deemed feasible or desirable. Instead, countries may choose to mutually recognize each other's conformity assessment requirements (e.g., Country A trusts Country B to certify that the products made by Country B conform to Country A's standards). Examples of such initiatives are the intra-EU MRAs on some unharmonized industries and the EU's agreements with a number of other countries. A key element of these agreements is the rule of origin. Previous MRAs between the EU and US and the EU and Canada specify that conformity assessments done in one of the MRA countries, in which products are manufactured or through which they are imported, is accepted throughout the entire agreement region. Other agreements, such as the MRAs the EU has concluded with Australia and New Zealand, impose restrictive rules of origin that require third country products to meet the conformity assessment of each country in the region.

What are the implications of a common regulatory approach?

The implications of a common regulatory approach depend on the chosen approach. A significant upward harmonization of standards can be more detrimental to exporters in non-member countries than mutual recognition of standards that avoids restrictive rules of origin.

Harmonization of standards. Harmonization of product standards implies that firms do not need to create different products for different markets. In the resulting integrated market, firms can reap economies of scale. These benefits accrue not just to firms of participating countries but also to firms in third countries. However, the economic impact of standards harmonization also depends on the level at which the harmonized standard is set. The impact on the firms of a specific country depends on how the costs of meeting the new harmonized level of the standard compare with the benefits from economies of scale in integrated markets. If firms from some countries incur a higher cost in meeting the harmonized standard and reap fewer scale economy benefits in integrated markets than

firms from other countries, then the former can suffer a decline in exports to the integrated market when harmonization raises some destination countries' standards.

Available evidence suggests that harmonization within the EU tended toward the high range of initial standards due to pressure from the EU's richer members (see Vogel 1995). For example, in the late 1990s, when the EU decided to harmonize standards for aflatoxins (a group of toxic compounds produced by certain molds), eight member states—including Italy, the Netherlands, and Spain—raised their national standards substantially. This likely caused African exports of cereals, dried fruits, and nuts to Europe to decline by as much as $670 million (Otsuki et al. 2001). Recent research using firm-level data for 42 developing countries also suggests that an increase in the distance between source and destination country standards can have an adverse effect on both firm entry into exporting and export volumes (Fernandes et al. 2015).

Mutual recognition of standards. The economic impact of an MRA depends critically on the choice of rules of origin.

- *Member countries.* An MRA of standards is in effect a downward harmonization of standards since firms are now free to meet the least costly of the initial standards: trade is stimulated not only by market integration but also by the reduced stringency of the standard.

- *Non-member countries.* The implications for imports from third countries differ dramatically with rules of origin. If the firms of non-participating countries are also entitled to access the entire region by conforming to the least costly standard, then they too reap benefits.[16] In contrast, if firms of third countries are denied the benefits of the MRA and must continue to meet the original standard in each market, they will face unchanged absolute conditions but suffer a decline in relative competitiveness—and hence a decline in exports to the region.[17]

---

[16]The best example of liberal rules of origin is the EU's regime for goods: thanks to the Cassis de Dijon judgment, even the products of a third country, say a Korean medical device, admitted for sale in one EU country are free to circulate in all EU countries.

[17]Restrictive rules of origin have proved problematic for some of the EU's previous recognition agreements, such as those governing professional-services standards. For example, while a Brazilian orange admitted for sale in Portugal can be sold throughout the EU, a Brazilian engineer or accountant licensed in Portugal must fulfill separate licensing requirements to work elsewhere in the EU, forcing non-European services providers to endure costly and inefficient bureaucratic procedures.

BOX 4.1.1 Regulatory convergence in mega-regional trade agreements *(continued)*

Mutual recognition of conformity assessments falls short of an MRA of standards in that it does not lead to full market integration. Nevertheless, the MRA of conformity agreements does remove duplicated testing and certification procedures and lowers the excess costs that firms face in demonstrating compliance of their goods to the standards in each country. Whether the benefits are restricted to member countries or also accrue to non-member countries again depends on the rules of origin. If firms of third countries are denied the benefits of the MRA, they must continue to fulfil conformity assessment requirements in each market and are likely to suffer a decline in competitiveness relative to firms of member countries.

Empirical analysis. In order to test the empirical validity of these propositions, Chen and Mattoo (2008) constructed a dataset that directly identified policy initiatives of different types on standards for manufacturing industries in 42 countries over the period of 1986-2001. These include all OECD countries and 14 developing countries that are the largest exporters of manufactured goods outside the OECD and account for over 80 percent of non-OECD manufactured exports. The policy measures include each harmonization directive and MRA concluded between the countries in the set. They then estimate the significance of the impacts of these measures on bilateral trade across countries and over time, controlling for other influences.

The limited available evidence broadly confirms the intuitive results spelled out above. A common regulatory approach—whether achieved through harmonization or mutual recognition—significantly increases intra-regional trade in affected industries. For trade with non-members, however, the implications of harmonization depend on existing standards in non-member countries and of mutual recognition agreements on the rules of origin.

- *Standards in non-member countries.* With harmonization, exports of excluded *developed* countries to the region also increase, but exports of excluded *developing* countries decline. These asymmetric effects may arise because developing country firms are hurt more by an increase in the stringency of standards in some markets (as a result of

harmonization) and benefit less from economies of scale in integrated markets.

- *Restrictive rules of origin.* Mutual recognition with restrictive rules of origin reduces the probability of the relevant good being imported from non-members (even more than in harmonization agreements) and reduces trade volumes. In contrast, mutual recognition with permissive rules of origin boosts the likelihood of trade with non-members and enhances trade volumes (Figure 4.1.1.1).

What policy options could ensure gains from a common regulatory approach?

Multilateral rules on trade have taken a permissive approach to regional agreements on standards. While it is neither feasible nor desirable to restrict the freedom of countries to harmonize or mutually recognize their standards, more could be done to strike a better balance between the interests of integrated and excluded countries.

Even in the absence of international rules, two steps could be taken to avert any adverse consequences for third countries.

- *Favor MRAs, with permissive rules of origin.* T-TIP and TPP members could generally favor mutual recognition over harmonization, as long as regulatory objectives are met, and agree not to impose restrictive rules of origin. Just as producers in the member countries would be able to supply the entire market by fulfilling requirements of any member country, so would producers in third countries.

- *Balance non-trade objectives with trade losses from more restrictive standards.* Where members do consider harmonization, they could favor the less stringent of the original standards unless there is credible evidence that these would not meet regulatory objectives. This is akin to a WTO test for departures from established international standards. However, such an approach may be more feasible in the T-TIP context than in the TPP context because of much greater divergence between the standards of TPP member countries.

BOX 4.1.1 Regulatory convergence in mega-regional trade agreements (*continued*)

FIGURE 4.1.1.1 **Implications of a common regulatory approach**

Mutual recognition without restrictive rules of origin promises the greatest benefits to third countries.

A. Impact on the probability of trading with non-members

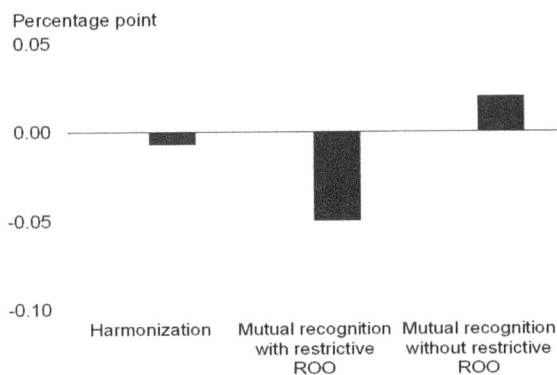

B. Impact on trade volumes with non-members

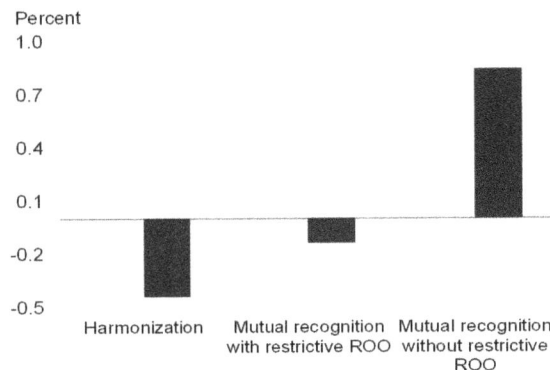

Source: Chen and Mattoo (2008).
Notes: ROO = Rules of origin.
A. Bars indicate the percentage point increase in the probability that a good is traded as a result of a common regulatory approach (Chen and Mattoo 2008).
B. Bars indicate the percent increase in average annual trade volume as a result of a common regulatory approach (Chen and Mattoo 2008).

Annex 4.1 Methodology

Modelling strategy

Results are based on a 19-sector, 29-region, dynamic computable general equilibrium (CGE) model. CGE models account simultaneously for interactions among firms, households, and governments in multiple product markets—and across several countries and regions of the world economy. Firms are assumed to maximize profits and consumers to maximize utility. After transfers among firms, households, and governments, incomes are spent on goods, or are saved and invested, both at home and abroad. The model finds an equilibrium solution by calculating prices that equate supply to demand for each product and factor of production (labor, capital, and land) in every region. The effects of FTAs are simulated by introducing changes in tariffs and other parameters, finding a new equilibrium, and comparing new prices, output, trade, income, and demand to pre-change levels.

Several innovative features of the model are based on a specification as in Zhai (2008). This relies on the theoretical work of Melitz (2003) and others that recognizes heterogeneity in firms' productivity levels, even within narrowly defined sectors. The model assumes that exports in any given sector involve special fixed costs, which only the most productive firms in the sector can cover. In this setting, FTAs affect not only inter-sectoral specialization, but also the range of products traded, and the distribution of firms within industries. Liberalization causes more varieties to be exported and imported, the expansion of the most productive firms, and the contraction of the least productive firms. This specification predicts more trade and greater benefits than conventional approaches based on inter-sectoral specialization effects alone.

The model is dynamic in the sense that simulations track changes in the volume of savings, which affects capital accumulation over time. However, the model does not include other dynamic factors proposed in the literature, such as

productivity increases from the accumulation of knowledge and other endogenous growth effects, TPP-induced inflows of foreign technology and capital, and follow-up trade liberalization that may result from an agreement. Introducing such effects can dramatically change the results, as demonstrated by experiments reported in Todo (2013).

Retrospective studies have shown that estimates based on conventional CGE models have under-predicted actual increases in trade (Kehoe, 2005). The likely reason is that traditional models projected trade increases only for products already exported (the intensive margin of trade), but had no mechanisms for anticipating new trading activities (the extensive margin of trade) (see Kehoe 2005, Zhai 2008, Hammouda and Osakewe 2008, Costinot and Rodriguez-Clare 2013). This confirms the need for modeling the extensive margin of trade in assessing trade agreements as implemented in this study. In addition, several previous CGE applications were based on comparative static models with constant returns to scale, not incorporating the potential of FTAs for stimulating investment, capital stock growth, and productivity gains (Nielsen 2003, Hammouda and Osakewe 2008, Costinot and Rodriguez-Clare 2013, Kose, Meredith and Towe 2005, Kouparitsas 1998). The present study allows for the dynamic accumulation of capital stock via investment and increases in productivity following entry and exit of firms in increasing returns to scale sectors. It does not however capture the dynamic growth effects via technological spillovers and "learning by doing" (Arrow 1962).

Compared to Petri et al. (2012), the modeling framework used here introduces numerous updates to the underlying data and modeling specifications. First, the underlying database has been updated to 2011 (compared to 2007 in the previous study) to incorporate not only macroeconomic changes but also updated tariff information. Baseline projections are updated (World Bank 2014; World Bank, forthcoming). The estimates also incorporate new trade balance projections (IMF 2015). Second, based on the latest news about the TPP, the published TPP agreement, tariffs and the scoring of NTM provisions have been updated. Finally, the updated results include, as explained below, revised non-tariff barriers and limited non-discriminatory liberalization effects (positive spillovers).

Assumptions

The results rest on a number of key assumptions, which are elaborated in more depth below. Tariff and non-tariff cuts are benchmarked against existing trade agreements. Since cross-country data is scarce, assumptions about utilization of preferential tariffs are based on eclectic survey information.

Tariff cuts. The results incorporate the full, published schedule of tariff cuts under the TPP agreement. These commit the eventual elimination of nearly all tariffs, including on major imports into the United States (such as textiles and apparel) and developing countries (such as motor vehicles). Sixty percent of these tariff cuts will enter into force immediately, but a few, like those on trucks imported by the United States, are very back-loaded. These potential tariff cuts are, however, de facto mitigated by (i) less than full utilization rate of preferential tariffs and (ii) additional costs to meet rules of origin requirements.

- *Utilization rate of preferential tariffs.* As demonstrated by prior bilateral agreements, preferential tariff rates are seldom fully utilized due to either restrictive rules of origin, the high cost of compliance compared to benefits from preferential rates, or low initial tariffs. The exercise here assumes that less than full utilization of preferences will reduce the effective tariff cuts from TPP membership. A formula is constructed to estimate utilization rates based on the preferential tariff margin and the size of the TPP relative to other agreements for which some survey data is available (Petri et al. 2012). As a result, the effect of tariff cuts introduced by TPP are reduced by 31 percent in the long run, and by

more than that for some commodities and in early stages of the agreement. For large tariffs cuts, for which the preference margin changes by more than 5 percentage points, the effect of tariffs cuts is reduced by only 10 percent (rather than 31 percent) in the long run.

- *Rules of origin.* To qualify for preferential intra-TPP tariffs, TPP member countries need to comply with sector-specific rules of origin, which require a minimum share of inputs from inside the TPP.[1] On the surface, rules of origin are particularly stringent for garments and apparel ("yarn forward"); however, a number of exceptions soften the impact. Rules of origin in automotives, in contrast, appear less restrictive than in the agreement between the United States and Korea (45 percent within-TPP content compared with 55 percent in the Korea-U.S. agreement). Again, the impact is mitigated by a revised definition of domestic and foreign content. As a result of rules of origin, where the tariff reduction is high, some inputs may now be sourced from within the TPP membership, replacing lower-cost inputs used earlier. The fraction of inputs thus replaced is estimated to depend on the tariff preference margin and the economic size (GDP) of the membership of the agreement, since larger agreements are more likely to include more efficient input suppliers (Petri and Plummer forthcoming). Specifically, for 40 percent of inputs, costs are assumed to rise by 10 percent of the tariff reductions offered by the agreement.

Actionable non-tariff measures. NTMs for goods and services sectors are constructed from the estimates of Kee, Nicita, and Olarreaga (2009), updated to 2012 for goods, and from estimates by Fontagne, Guillin, and Mitaritonna (2011), for services. Three-quarters of these measured barriers—which include regulations that increase consumer welfare—are assumed to be impediments to trade and subject to reduction

---

[1]For example, the "yarn forward" rule of origin requires a TPP member to use a TPP member produced yarn in textiles in order to qualify for duty-free access. These "yarn forward" rules in apparel seem restrictive, while rules of origin in automobiles are more liberal according to the text of the TPP agreement.

FIGURE A.4.1.1 Modeling assumptions

Key modeling assumptions relate to cuts to tariffs and NTBs. On average, the liberalization of tariffs is assumed to be more front-loaded, and that of NTBs more back-loaded. Sectors such as apparel are relatively more protected by tariff measures, processed food more by NTBs.

A. Intra-TPP average tariffs

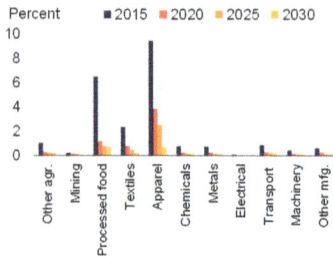

B. Restrictiveness of intra-TPP non-tariff measures on goods

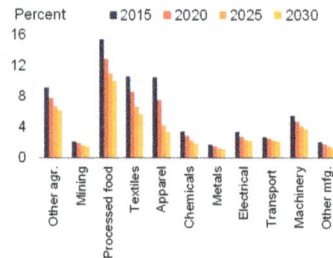

C. Restrictiveness of intra-TPP non-tariff measures on services

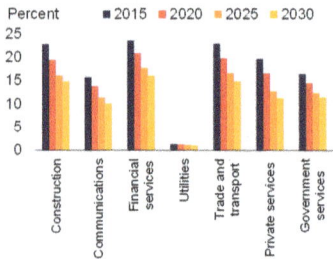

D. Scoring provisions: where agreements have greatest impact

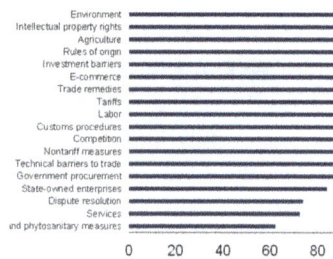

Source: Petri and Plummer (forthcoming).
A. B."Other agr." = other agricultural products, "Electrical" = electrical equipment, "Transport" = transport equipment, and "Other mfg." = other manufacturing. Restrictiveness of non-tariff measures is defined as tariff equivalent.
D. Scores range from 0 to 100, with 100 indicating full elimination of actionable barriers and 0 indicating none.

through trade policy, with the rest representing quality-increasing regulations. Further, only three-quarters of the remaining NTMs in the case of goods, and only one-half in the case of services, are assumed to be politically feasible in a trade agreement (i.e., "actionable").

Actual NTM reductions. The rationales laid out above derive the theoretically desirable and politically feasible reductions in the restrictiveness of NTM. However, trade negotiations do not necessarily achieve full liberalization of actionable barriers. A preliminary assessment suggests that the provisions in TPP resemble those in the agreement between Korea and the United States. While the actual impact depends on the degree to which these are implemented, the assumption is that the fraction of actionable NTM reductions is

similar to that in the Korea-US agreement, with some modifications based on analysis of the TPP text. This fraction is derived—for 21 separate issues areas—based on a score from 0-100, with a higher score indicating larger reductions in trade barriers by TPP compared with existing FTAs (Figure 4.1.1). The issues areas range widely from government procurement, dispute settlement, and environment to tariffs and customs procedures.

Non-discriminatory liberalization (positive spillovers). As noted above, some of the bilateral reductions in the restrictiveness of NTMs and investment barriers that countries make under an agreement are assumed to reduce barriers also against countries not participating in the agreement. These include especially efforts to improve the transparency and predictability of regulations and mechanisms to bring together regulators to encourage streamlining of regulations. Estimates of this "spillover" ratio range from 20 to 65 percent in the literature (Francois et al. 2013, Kawasaki 2014); the exercise here uses the low end of this range, or 20 percent.

Largest cuts.[2] These assumptions yield the highest tariff cuts in sectors such as apparel, where on average intra-TPP trade weighted tariffs decline by 8.8 percentage points. With respect to reductions in the restrictiveness of NTMs, the largest are in goods such as apparel, textiles and processed food (cuts by 7.2, 5.0 and 5.4 percentage points, respectively), and construction and private services (cut by 8.0 and 8.5 percentage points, respectively). In contrast, reductions would be marginal in mining. On average, the liberalization of tariffs is assumed to be more front-loaded, and that of the restrictiveness of NTMs more back-loaded. These reductions in the restrictiveness of NTMs are based on the assumption of the degree of implementation consistent with Korea-US FTA. In the event actual implementation is incomplete, the likely gains from TPP could be significantly diminished.

---
[2]These cuts are shown in effective terms, i.e. adjusting for expected use of the tariff cuts by exporters.

Peg and Control? The Links between Exchange Rate Regimes and Capital Account Policies

In a context of rising risks, choices with respect to exchange rate regimes and capital account policies are of key importance for emerging and developing countries. This essay explores the empirical links between a country's choice of currency regimes and of capital flow measures. The results suggest that developing countries appear to be more likely to have capital flow restrictions if they also have fixed exchange rates. This effect is particularly pronounced for lower-income countries, suggesting complex policy choices with respect to exchange rate regimes and capital flow measures.

Introduction

The outlook for emerging and developing countries is clouded by various downside risks, including a deterioration in global financial conditions, sudden reappraisal by market participants of lingering domestic vulnerabilities, and adverse spillovers from weaker growth (Chapter 1). Should one or more of these risks materialize, they could have significant effects on economic conditions in many emerging and developing countries. These effects may include large currency depreciations in some countries with flexible exchange regimes, reserve losses in some countries aiming to preserve exchange rate pegs, and restrictions on capital mobility in some countries facing capital flight. More generally, how countries fare and how policymakers respond to the realization of these risks will depend on a wide range of factors, but two macroeconomic policy choices play fundamental roles: the exchange rate regime (ERR) and the stance towards capital flows (i.e., the use of capital flow measures, CFMs).

A flexible exchange rate regime can provide greater room for monetary policy to stabilize output fluctuations in countries with open capital accounts, as well as encourage a more proper assessment of currency risk. However, it can sometimes be associated with volatility in currency markets, which can raise financial stability risks in countries with significant currency mismatches on balance sheets. It can also restrict monetary policy

options in countries where exchange rate fluctuations have a rapid impact on inflation or where inter-sectoral factor mobility is limited (Ostry, Ghosh, and Chamon 2012). Conversely, a fixed exchange rate regime can serve as a stabilizing nominal anchor in the presence of financial volatility. It can also boost trade, which may offset weakness in external demand (Rose 2000; Rose and van Wincoop 2001; Frankel and Rose 2002; Klein and Shambaugh 2006). However, in the presence of high capital mobility, a fixed regime may require the central bank to direct monetary policy towards the maintenance of the peg rather than towards the promotion of economic activity (Frankel, Schmukler, and Serven 2004; Shambaugh 2004; Obstfeld, Shambaugh, and Taylor 2010; Klein and Shambaugh 2015).

A country's choice of capital flow measures can affect the performance of asset markets, the cost of capital, and technological progress embodied in foreign direct investment (Henry 2007). More broadly, capital account policies can affect the pace of economic growth (Kose, Prasad, Rogoff, and Wei 2009). Accordingly, there have been extensive discussions about the appropriate role of capital flow measures. In the wake of the global financial crisis, a case has been made for the use of CFMs, recognizing that capital flows can affect the incidence of boom-and-bust cycles in financial markets. The effectiveness of these policies, however, has been the subject of debate.[1]

Note: This essay was prepared by Carlos Arteta, Michael Klein, and Jay Shambaugh. It is based on materials compiled from its background paper (Arteta, Klein, and Shambaugh forthcoming).

[1]Korinek (2011); Ostry, Ghosh, Chamon, and Qureshi (2011); Jeanne and Korinek (2010); and Jeanne, Subramanian, and Williamson (2012) argue for the use of capital controls. A more skeptical view of the use of capital controls is presented by Klein (2012) and Forbes and Klein (2015).

The joint choice of exchange rate regimes and capital account policies therefore has important implications for macroeconomic outcomes. While some studies have explored the choice of the ERR and others have examined the use of CFMs, there has been little empirical analysis on the links between ERR and CFM choices.[2] This essay documents the association between the choices of exchange rate regime and capital account policies in emerging markets, frontier markets, and other middle- and low-income countries. While this analysis focuses on emerging and developing countries, it provides some context by including data on advanced high-income economies as well. Specifically, the essay asks three questions:

- What does economic theory say about the choice of ERRs and CFMs?

- What do the data say about ERRs and CFMs?

- What are the main empirical linkages between the choices of ERR and CFM?

For this essay, emerging and developing countries are divided into three groups. The first category is *Emerging Market Economies*—in general, (non-advanced) high-income and middle-income countries with a record of significant access to international capital markets. The second category is *Frontier Market Economies*—generally middle income countries that are usually smaller and less financially developed than emerging market economies and have more limited access to international capital markets. The third category comprises other middle-income countries that are neither emerging nor frontier markets (and therefore have little to no access to international capital markets) along with low-income countries.

What does economic theory say about the choice of ERRs and CFMs?

The choice of a country's exchange rate regime can be based on a variety of theoretical considerations, including the following:[3]

- *Optimal currency area factors.* Policymakers in some countries may weigh the advantages of pegging—such as more stable trade and investment flows, particularly vis-à-vis a large trading partner—against the disadvantages of forgoing exchange rate flexibility as a stabilizer for external shocks.

- *Sources of macroeconomic shocks.* A small open economy may choose to peg if it is often subject to highly volatile shocks to its asset markets or prices. In the face of such "nominal" shocks, a fixed exchange rate could provide a nominal anchor that stabilizes prices and activity (provided that the shock is temporary). A country may also choose to peg if it faces similar economic shocks to those of the base country. In contrast, a floating exchange rate can provide greater stability if an economy is often facing "real" shocks—that is, disturbances to factors that affect its aggregate demand or supply.

- *Monetary policy independence.* The choice of currency regime may reflect an emphasis on the importance of either monetary autonomy, when the central bank is not obliged to direct its efforts towards the maintenance of a pegged regime, or of importing the monetary-policy credibility of the base country in order to better manage inflationary expectations.

The decision of whether, and how, to control capital flows weighs the benefits of a liberal regime with no capital controls against those of an environment in which the flow of capital is managed:

[2]Research on the choice of ERR includes Leblang (1999); Carmignani, Colombo, and Tirelli (2008); Klein and Shambaugh (2010); and Berdiev, Kim, and Chang (2012). Research on the use of CFMs includes Grilli and Milesi-Ferretti (1995); Quinn (1997); Chinn and Ito (2008); Schindler (2009); and Fernández, Rebucci, and Uribe (2014). Von Hagen and Zhou (2007) is one of very few studies that explore the interaction between exchange rate regimes and capital flow restrictions, finding some influences in both directions between *de facto* exchange rate regimes and capital account policies.

[3]The choice of currency regime is, of course, time variant, as there have been numerous instances of countries shifting between peg and float (Klein and Shambaugh 2008; Ghosh, Ostry, and Qureshi 2015).

- *Benefits of freely flowing international capital.* These include the scope for an efficient allocation of capital, risk diversification, and consumption smoothing. Countries with insufficient savings can draw on world savings to finance the expansion of their capital stock. The world capital market can also help countries diversify risk and, in so doing, undertake projects that would otherwise not be financed. Also, borrowing during slowdowns and paying back during expansions can help the residents of a country avoid wide swings in their consumption. Free capital flows may also be welfare-enhancing, as capital controls can generate distortions in real and financial activity if they are not properly designed.

- *Potential downsides of open capital markets.* Open capital markets could allow global financial cycles to adversely affect an economy. In this way, a country could lose control over its macroeconomic outcomes. Capital inflows could contribute to an unsustainable asset price boom and exchange rate overvaluation. Capital outflows, and especially a sudden stop, could be a source of a currency collapse, financial disruption, and a sharp decline in real activity.[4]

There may be links across the joint choice of ERRs and CFMs. The importance and extent of these links may depend upon other factors, such as financial development, openness to trade, and sectoral diversification (and, therefore, the sensitivity of domestic activity to exchange rate movements). The nature of the interaction between ERR and CFM is shaped by a number of factors, including the following:

- *The trilemma.* Countries can choose only two of the following three objectives: open capital account, independent monetary policy, and exchange rate stability. Thus, countries with fixed exchange rates would have to give up free capital mobility in order to have an independent monetary policy. In other words,

FIGURE 4.2.1 Exchange rate regime categories by country grouping

In emerging markets, floating exchange rates are more common than soft pegs or pegs. In frontier markets, pegged exchange rates are the most common regime. Other middle- and low-income countries have a relatively even distribution across the three regime categories. Advanced economies, excluding euro area countries, have a relatively even distribution of floats and soft pegs, and a lower incidence of pegs.

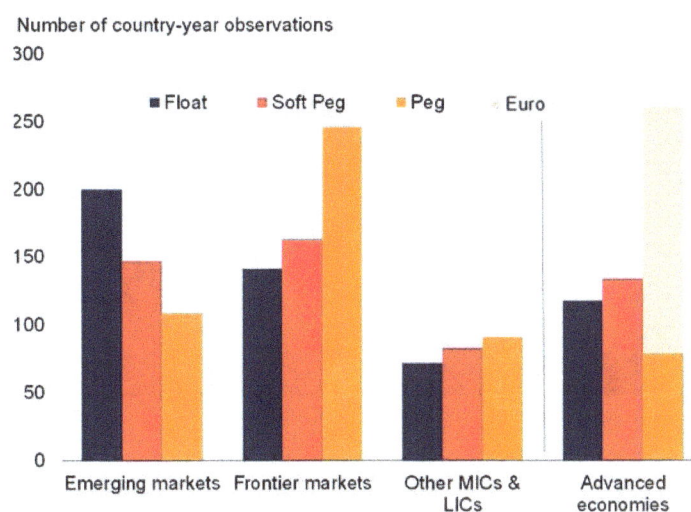

Sources: Obstfeld, Shambaugh, and Taylor (2010); authors' calculations.
Notes: MICs = middle-income countries. LICs = low-income countries. This ERR classification uses exchange rate behavior to see if a country stays within a +/- 2 percent band over the course of a year against a relevant base currency. If so, it is classified as a "peg." Otherwise, it is a non-peg. To insure the stability is deliberate and not a random lack of volatility, countries that peg for only one year are not coded as pegs. To handle one-off realignments, a country that has zero volatility in 11 out of 12 months is also considered a peg (again, as long as it is also pegged the year before or after). Soft pegs are identified as countries that do not maintain the strict boundary, but stay within 5 percent bands or stay within moving 2 percent bands in every month (that is, the change in any given month is never greater than 2 percent).

they may choose to use CFMs to stabilize the exchange rate, allowing monetary policy to focus on domestic macroeconomic goals (Shambaugh 2004; Obstfeld, Shambaugh, and Taylor 2010; Klein and Shambaugh 2015).

- *The preservation of a pegged regime.* Capital flows may also make the preservation of a fixed exchange rate more difficult since, under certain circumstances, capital flight could cause a peg to break.[5] This suggests another

---

[4]An early theory of sudden stops is presented in Calvo (1998). More recently, Rey (2013) has emphasized the spillover effects of U.S. monetary policy and volatility in U.S. asset markets.

[5]There is a large body of literature investigating why pegged exchange rates collapse (Berg, Borensztein, and Pattillo 2005). Fixed exchange rates should probably be easier to maintain if CFMs dissuade speculative attacks. However, the effectiveness of these policies depends on their credibility. If a pegged regime is perceived to be unsustainable and the exchange rate out of line with fundamentals, capital controls may be of limited effectiveness to ward off financial turmoil.

FIGURE 4.2.2 Capital control categories by country grouping

Most emerging, frontier, and other developing countries have Partially Open capital accounts, with occasional use of capital controls. Advanced economies are far less likely to use capital controls, and none do so in a persistent and systematic way.

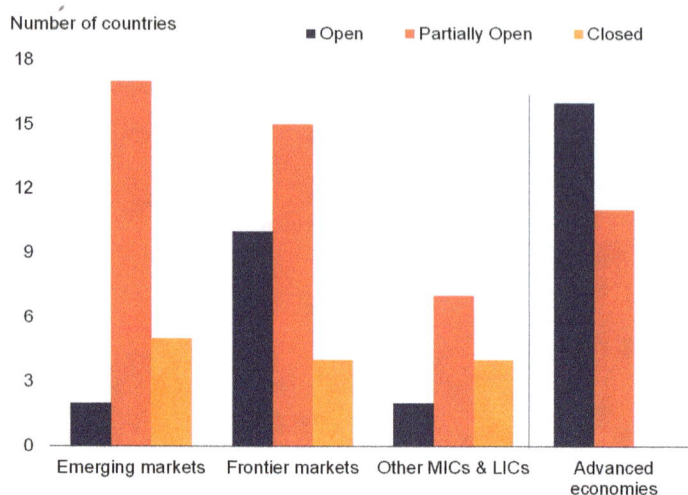

Sources: Fernández, Klein, Schindler, Rebucci, and Uribe (2015), authors' calculations.
Notes: MICs = middle-income countries. LICs = low-income countries. This CFM classification divides countries into three groups: "Open," for countries that almost never use capital controls (the average value of the capital control index over the sample period is less than 0.15, the maximum value in any one year is less than 0.25, and the standard deviation of the index across time is less than 0.10); "Closed," for countries that have capital controls in the vast majority of asset categories and for the vast majority of years (the average value of capital controls across the sample period is greater than 0.70, the minimum value is greater than 0.60, and the standard deviation is less than 0.10); and "Partially Open," for countries that make use of capital controls occasionally (i.e., countries that are neither Open nor Closed are classified as Partially Open).

link between ERR and CFM, especially for controls on outflows relative to inflows if there is a greater concern about a devaluation than a revaluation. Controls on inflows could also be important if they drive currency appreciation (with flexible exchange rates) or an asset price boom (with pegged rates).

- *The type of pegged regime.* Some of these issues are conditional on the form of the peg. For example, if the regime is a credible hard peg (e.g., a currency union), monetary autonomy is fully surrendered, and the peg's preservation is generally not a concern. In this case, capital controls may not be as prevalent as in other types of fixed exchange rate regimes.

What do the data say about ERRs and CFMs?

Combining two extensive databases on exchange rate regimes and capital flow measures, this analysis uses data on 93 countries over the period 1995 to 2013. Both the country list and the time period are determined by data availability. The set of emerging and developing countries is divided into three categories: 24 emerging market economies, 29 frontier market economies, and 13 other middle-income and low-income countries. For comparison purposes, a fourth category comprising 27 advanced high-income economies is included. (A listing of the countries in each of these four categories is provided in Annex Table 4.1.)

Exchange rate regimes

The exchange rate regime classification is based on the *de facto* regime classification from Shambaugh (2004) and updated in Obstfeld, Shambaugh, and Taylor (2010) to include a soft peg variable (see Annex 4.2 for details on the classification methodology). These studies use actual exchange rate movements to classify regimes into pegs, non-pegs, and soft pegs. Among emerging market economies, floating exchange rate regimes are more common than soft pegs or tightly pegged exchange rates (Figure 4.2.1). These observations span emerging market economies that have had floating regimes during all or almost all of the 1995-2013 period (e.g., Turkey, South Africa) and those that have had tight pegs during all the period (e.g., Qatar, Saudi Arabia, United Arab Emirates).

The exchange rate regime choice of frontier market economies is the mirror image of emerging market economies, with the highest number of observations being pegs and the fewest number of observations being floats. In this group, relatively few frontier markets have had floating regimes for most of the period (e.g., Paraguay, Zambia), while several countries have had tight pegs for all 19 years of the period (e.g., Bahrain, Cote d'Ivoire, Lebanon, Oman, Panama). Other middle- and low-income countries have an even distribution across the three exchange rate regime categories, with a few countries exhibiting floating regimes for most of the period (e.g., Algeria, Uganda) and some countries with tight pegs for all 19 years (e.g., Burkina Faso, Swaziland, Togo). For comparison, advanced economies, excluding Euro Area countries, have a relatively even distribution of floats and soft pegs and a lower incidence of pegs.

Capital flow measures

This analysis uses the Fernández et al. (2015) *de jure* capital control data. These data are used to construct an aggregate capital control indicator as the average of nine categories for both inflows and outflows (see Annex 4.2 for details on the classification methodology). For each country and for each year, the average of inflow controls and outflow controls for the nine categories of assets is computed. This aggregate indicator takes a value between 0 and 1, with 0 indicating no controls on any category of assets and 1 indicating controls on both inflows and outflows of all nine categories of assets.

These data can be used to place countries in one of three categories with respect to their use of CFMs (as in Klein 2012). The first category is "Open," for countries that almost never use capital controls. The second category is "Closed," for countries that have capital controls in the vast majority of asset categories and for the vast majority of years. The third category is "Partially Open," for countries that make occasional use of capital controls.

Among emerging and developing countries, the most common classification is Partially Open (Figure 4.2.2). These include 17 out of 24 emerging markets (including Arab Republic of Egypt, Brazil, Chile, Indonesia, Thailand, and Turkey), 15 out of 29 frontier markets (including Argentina, Bahrain, Kazakhstan, Kenya, República Bolivariana de Venezuela, and Vietnam), and 7 out of 13 other middle-income and low-income countries (including Algeria, Burkina Faso, Ethiopia, Kyrgyz Republic, and Uganda). In comparison, advanced countries are far less likely to use capital controls than countries in the other

FIGURE 4.2.3 Trade and exchange rate regimes: Frequency distributions

Pegged exchange rate regimes appear to be associated with greater trade openness than flexible regimes. The frequency distributions of trade-to-GDP ratios for economies with mostly pegged currencies lie to the right of those for more flexible currencies.

A. Trade by proportion of years with pegged exchange rates, full sample

B. Trade by proportion of years with pegged exchange rates, emerging and developing country sample

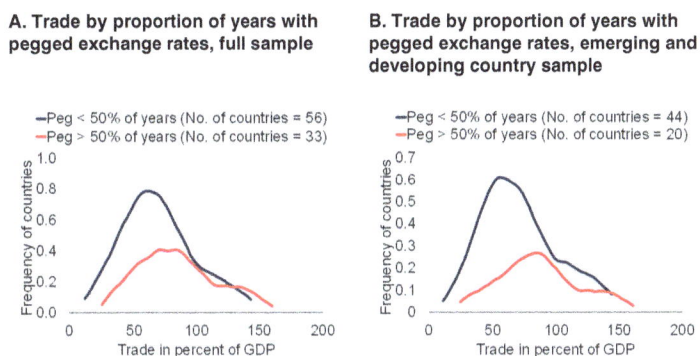

Source: Authors' calculations.
Note: These figures present kernel frequency distributions of trade relative to GDP for countries that have pegged exchange rates for less than half the years in the sample (blue lines) and for those that have pegged exchange rates for more than half the years in the sample (red lines).

FIGURE 4.2.4 Trade and capital controls: Frequency distributions

Countries that use capital controls occasionally appear to trade somewhat less than countries that have either no capital controls or those that have pervasive capital controls. The frequency distributions of trade-to-GDP ratios for the Partially Open group lie to the left of those for the other groups.

A. Trade by capital control category, full sample

B. Trade by capital control category, emerging and developing country sample

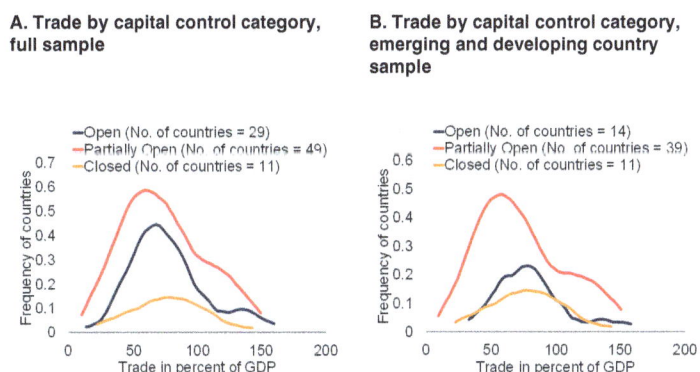

Source: Authors' calculations.
Note: These figures present kernel frequency distributions of trade relative to GDP for Closed countries (yellow line), Partially Open countries (red line) and Open countries (blue lines).

groups, and none do so in a persistent and systematic way (that is, none are classified as Closed).

FIGURE 4.2.5 Financial development and capital controls: Frequency distributions

Open countries appear more likely to be financially developed (have larger financial sectors as a share of GDP) than Partially Open and Closed countries. The distribution for the Open group of credit-to-GDP ratios is more skewed to the right than those for the Partially Open and Closed groups for the full sample—but not for the emerging/developing country sample.

A. Credit by capital control category, full sample

B. Credit by capital control category, emerging and developing country sample

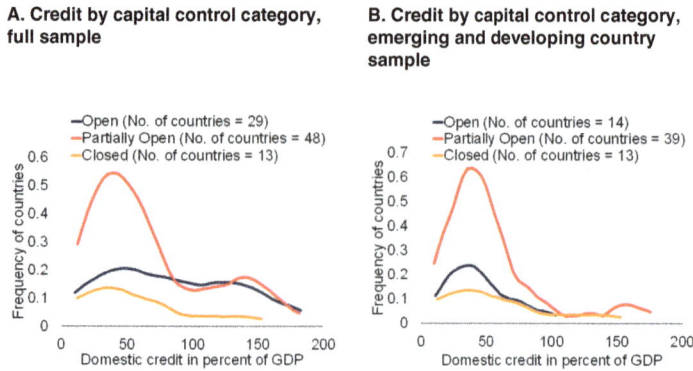

Source: Authors' calculations.
Note: These figures present kernel frequency distributions of domestic credit relative to GDP for Closed countries (yellow line), Partially Open countries (red line) and Open countries (blue lines).

FIGURE 4.2.6 Pegged regimes and capital controls

There is a statistically significant partial correlation between pegged regimes and capital controls among emerging and developing countries.

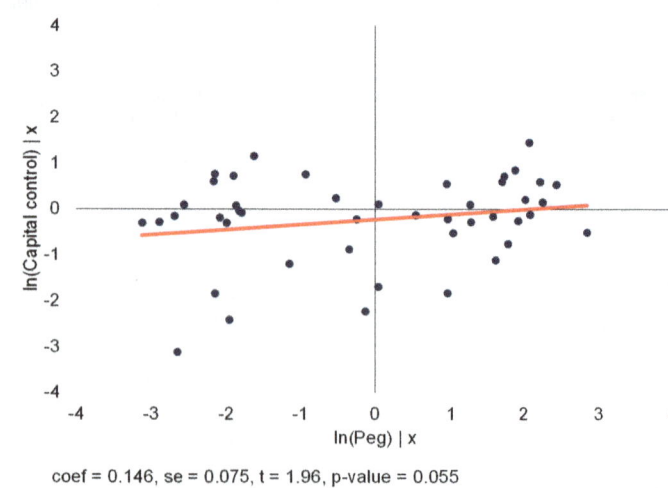

coef = 0.146, se = 0.075, t = 1.96, p-value = 0.055

Source: Authors' calculations.
Note: Using the emerging and developing country sample, this figure presents the estimate of the partial correlation between the logarithmic transformation of the capital control index and of the peg index, controlling for GDP per capita, GDP, trade share, size of the financial sector, (all of which are expressed as logarithms), and a currency union control. This is the graphical depiction of Column I of Annex Table 4.2.

Trade openness and financial development across ERRs and CFMs

Pegged exchange rate regimes appear to be associated with greater trade openness than flexible regimes, in both the full sample as well as in the sample comprised of emerging and developing countries. That is, the frequency distributions of trade-to-GDP ratios for economies with mostly pegged currencies (red lines in Figure 4.2.3) lie to the right of those for more flexible currencies (blue lines in Figure 4.2.3). In addition, countries that use capital controls from time to time appear to trade somewhat less than countries that have either no capital controls or those that have pervasive capital controls. That is, the frequency distributions of trade-to-GDP ratios for the Partially Open group (red lines in Figure 4.2.4) lie to the left of those for the other groups.

Open countries appear more likely to be financially developed (have larger financial sectors as a share of GDP) than Partially Open and Closed countries. That is, for the full sample, the distribution for the Open group of credit-to-GDP ratios (blue line in the upper panel of Figure 4.2.5) is more skewed to the right than those for the Partially Open and Closed groups. That said, a large literature on financial development and growth suggests that richer countries are more financially developed (King and Levine 1992, Sahay et al. 2015). Since emerging and developing economies tend to have more capital controls than advanced economies, the greater financial development for Open countries may largely reflect the role of advanced economies. Confining the sample to emerging and developing economies, there is indeed no apparent evidence of higher levels of financial development in Open countries—that is, frequency distributions show no discernible difference in the skewness of the Open group (blue line in the lower panel of Figure 4.2.5) relative to the others.

What are the main empirical linkages between the choices of ERR and CFM?

The discussion above suggests that the choice of ERR may predetermine the extent of CFMs. A multivariate regression model, focusing on the sample of emerging and developing countries, is used to estimate the partial correlation between capital controls and pegged exchange rates, while controlling GDP per capita, GDP, trade share, size of the financial sector, and currency union membership (Column I of Annex Table 4.2). The regression estimate shows a positive, statistically significant partial correlation between the extent of capital controls and the propensity to peg (Figure 4.2.6).[6] It also shows a statistically significant negative correlation between capital controls and income per capita, and a statistically significant positive correlation between capital controls and both income and trade.

The negative relationship between income per capita and the CFM variable is further explored by estimating a regression that allows the association of the pegged exchange rate on capital controls to vary with the level of income per capita. This is done by including an interaction term between the GDP per capita variable and the peg variable (Column II of Annex Table 4.2). These results also show the effects for the average levels of income per capita for each of the three categories of emerging and developing countries (bottom of Column II). For comparison, the fourth category of advanced economies is also included. This effect is statistically significant for the average income per capita of frontier markets and other middle- and low-income countries, but not for emerging market economies.[7] It is also insignificant for

FIGURE 4.2.7 Pegged regimes and capital controls across per capita income levels

The association between pegged exchange rates on capital controls varies with the level of income per capita for frontier markets and other middle- and low-income countries. However, there is no significant association of this kind for emerging markets or advanced economies.

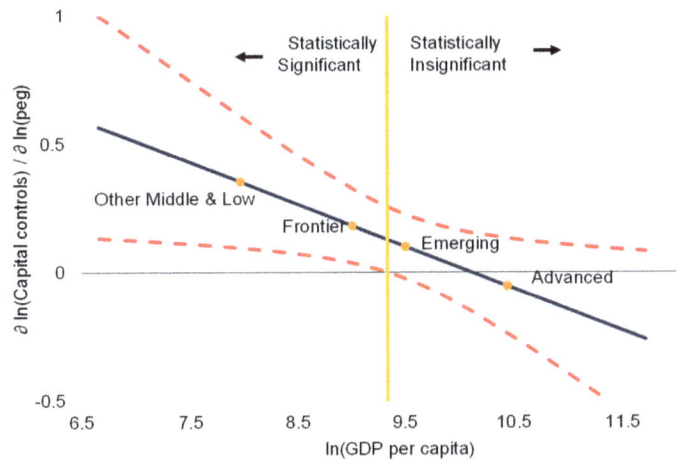

Source: Authors' calculations.
Note: This figure shows the total impact of pegging on the likelihood of capital controls at different income levels using the cross country regression reported in Column II of Table 2, by including an interaction between the logarithm of income per capita and the logarithmic transformation of the peg exchange rate variable. The bottom panel of that table shows the partial derivative ∂ ln(kci)/ ∂ ln(pegi) for the average levels of income per capita for each of the four categories of countries. In this figure, the thick solid black line shows the estimated value of ∂ ln(kci)/ ∂ ln(pegi) for each level of income per capita, and the dashed lines show the 95 percent confidence interval of this estimate. The vertical yellow line at 9.34 shows the point after which this partial derivative is no longer significant at the 95 percent level of confidence. The points on the solid line show the average values of income per capita for the four country categories.

advanced economies, providing additional evidence that the effect of peg regimes on CFMs are contingent on income per capita.[8]

Figure 4.2.7 presents the effect of pegged regimes on capital controls as a function of income per capita. The thick solid black line shows the estimated value of the effect of peg regimes on capital controls for each level of income per capita, and the dashed red lines show the 95 percent confidence interval of this estimate. The vertical

---

[6]These results do not imply causality. And while there are reasons to believe that the ERR may predetermine CFMs, joint determination or reverse causality cannot be ruled out. It may be that countries that peg prefer to have capital controls to make it easier to maintain the peg or to allow for greater monetary autonomy, or it may be that the costs of pegging are lower for countries with capital controls. Alternatively, the positive correlation may reflect ideological views of the acceptability of market intervention in both the price of foreign exchange and the flow of capital.

[7]This association should be interpreted with some care. The results primarily come from the cross section: countries that peg for long

periods also seem to have long standing capital controls. There is weak evidence of a link among countries that switch their ERR or CFM within the sample period (Arteta, Klein, and Shambaugh forthcoming). Thus, it is not clear what one should expect if a country frees up its exchange rate peg or dismantles its CFM. In addition, these results might be highlighting heterogeneity across developing regions.

[8]Additional robustness analysis using panel data methods suggests that factors associated with the nexus between ERR and CFM seem to be country-specific and relatively time-invariant (Arteta, Klein, and Shambaugh forthcoming).

line shows the level of per capita income after which this effect is no longer statistically significant. The points on the solid line show the average values of income per capita for the four country categories. The solid line is downward sloping, suggesting that the association between the capital control and peg indices decreases with an increase in income per capita. Moreover, in emerging market economies (as well as in advanced economies), there appears to be no statistically significant association between the choice of exchange rate regime and the choice of capital account policies.

Conclusion

As emerging and developing countries prepare against various risks besetting the global economy, they need to consider policy responses to adjust to external shocks. Among these policy responses, some countries might rely on exchange rate flexibility as a buffer, some might aim to minimize currency fluctuations, and some might consider capital flow measures as they seek to keep some degree of monetary policy control.

Policies concerning the choice of the exchange rate regime and the use of capital flow measures are central to macroeconomic management, especially in emerging and developing countries. An empirical exploration using a comprehensive database of exchange rate regimes and capital flow measures suggests that capital controls are more likely to be present when a country has a fixed exchange rate. Moreover, this correlation is mainly present in countries at lower levels of income per capita. These findings raise a number of policy-related issues:

- At lower levels of economic and financial development—proxied by lower levels of income per capita—policymakers may be constrained to jointly and tightly control both the exchange rate and the capital account. Accordingly, policy choices in developing countries should not be seen in isolation, and policy recommendations need to recognize

that policy choices are not independent from each other.

- Higher levels of development may allow greater discretion to implement some variant of these two policies. Alternatively, countries that are more financially developed might find it harder to control the capital account regardless of currency regime given their high level of international financial integration. In this context, attempts to control capital flows would be more likely to fail due to circumventions by market participants.

- In principle, emerging and developing countries that choose to control both the exchange rate and the capital account may still exercise monetary policy autonomy to stabilize economic conditions (Cordella and Gupta 2015). This is only possible, however, if they have the necessary monetary policy space—which has generally been narrowing recently, amid inflation and foreign reserve pressures (Chapter 1).

- These choices could also reflect preferences among policymakers. Those who have a preference for intervening in the market may see both CFM and a fixed exchange rate as desirable, whereas those who prefer to let market forces reign may prefer a floating exchange rate and unfettered capital flows. A preference for greater intervention may be more prevalent at lower levels of development, perhaps reflecting actual or perceived constraints faced by policymakers at such levels.

- Finally, it remains to be established empirically whether the joint choice to control both the exchange rate and the capital account implies welfare gains or losses—for example, in terms of output growth or financial stability—for lower-income countries.

Annex 4.2 Data and Methodology

ERR Data

The exchange regime classification is based on Shambaugh (2004) and updated in Obstfeld, Shambaugh, and Taylor (2010). It uses actual exchange rate movements to see if a country stays within a +/- 2 percent band over the course of a year against a relevant base currency. If so, the country is classified as having a "peg." Otherwise, it is classified as a non-peg. To insure the stability is deliberate and not a random lack of volatility, countries that peg for only one year are not coded as pegs. To handle one-off realignments, a country that has zero volatility in 11 out of 12 months is also considered a peg (again, as long as it is also pegged the year before or after). Soft pegs are identified as countries that do not maintain the strict boundary, but stay within 5 percent bands or stay within moving 2 percent bands in every month (that is, the change in any given month is never greater than 2 percent). Given the interest in the correlation of ERR and CFM, it is preferable to use a classification that uses only official market exchange rate behavior, not interest rates or black market exchange rates whose behavior may be a function of capital controls.

There are 1765 available observations with ERR data in the sample for 93 countries over 19 years. There are 707 pegs, 527 soft pegs, and 531 non-pegged country-year observations in the data set.

- In emerging markets, there are 109 observations of pegged exchange rates, 147 observations of soft pegs, and 200 observations of floats.

- Among frontier markets, there are 246 peg observations, 163 soft peg observations, and 141 float observations.

- In the other middle-income and low-income group, there are 91 peg observations, 83 soft pegs observations, and 72 floats observations.

- In the advanced economies group, 182 of the

261 country-year observations with a pegged exchange rate are countries in the Euro Area. After excluding Euro Area members, there is a relatively even distribution of observations among floats (118) and soft pegs (134), and a lower incidence of pegs (79).

Note the persistence of these choices across countries. There is a considerable amount of "flipping" behavior by countries (Klein and Shambaugh 2008). Exchange rate pegs frequently break, but they also frequently re-form, such that some countries flip back and forth from a peg to a float and back. That said, in shorter samples—such as this 19-year period—it is more common to find a country with just one regime (especially if limiting the categorization to the binary peg or non-peg).

In this sample of 93 countries, 30 countries never peg and 16 always do, leaving the remaining 37 countries having some pegged years and some non-peg years. Adding the 9 countries that peg in only 1 or 2 years and 6 countries that float in only 1 or 2 years, one is left with 39 countries that nearly always float and 22 that nearly always peg. The remaining 32 countries flip between floating and pegging, with 8 of these transitioning from one ERR to another only once, but the 14 flipping two or three times, and 10 flipping four or more times.

CFM Data

The capital flow measures classification is based on Fernández, Klein, Schindler, Rebucci, and Uribe (2015). This classification scheme is based on controls and requirements reported in the IMF's *Annual Report on Exchange Arrangements and Exchange Restrictions* (AREAER). This data set includes separate indicators for inflows and outflows for ten categories of assets. For this essay, as explained in the text, an aggregate indicator is constructed as the average of nine of these categories for both inflows and outflows, omitting controls on direct investment because these controls often reflect non-economic concerns, such as national security. For each country and for each year, the average of inflow controls and outflow controls for the nine categories of assets is used. This aggregate indicator takes a value between 0 and 1, with 0 indicating no controls on any category of assets and 1 indicating controls on both inflows and outflows of all nine categories of assets.

- The "Open" category is for countries that almost never use capital controls. For this category, the average value of the capital control index over the sample period is less than 0.15, the maximum value in any one year is less than 0.25, and the standard deviation of the index across time is less than 0.10.

- The "Closed" category is for countries that have capital controls for almost all (or all) categories of assets for almost all (or all) years. For this category, the average value of capital controls across the sample period is greater than 0.70, the minimum value is greater than 0.60, and the standard deviation is less than 0.10.

- The "Partially Open" category is for countries that make occasional use of capital controls. Countries that are neither Open nor Closed are classified as Partially Open.

In the data set of 93 countries, 30 are classified as Open, 13 as Closed, and 50 as Partially Open. In the emerging market group, 17 countries are classified as Partially Open, 5 as Closed, and only 2 as Open. In the frontier market group, 15 are classified as Partially Open, 10 as Open, and 4 as Closed. The other middle- and low-income group includes 7 Partially Open countries, 4 Closed countries and 2 Open countries. In advanced economies, 16 countries are classified as Open, and 11 as using CFM in an occasional fashion.

Regression Analysis in Annex Table 4.2

Annex Table 4.2 presents results of regressions where the dependent variable is a logarithmic transformation of the above-mentioned CFM measure—$\ln((100 \times kc)+1)$ where kc is capital control index (average value over sample period), in any one year $1 \geq kc \geq 0$, with larger values representing more controls in place. The main independent variables is a logarithmic transformation of the above-mention pegged regime indicator — $\ln((100 \times peg)+1)$, where peg is proportion of years country had a pegged exchange rate, $1 \geq peg \geq 0$. The other controls are the logarithms of GDP per capita, GDP, trade share, and size of the financial sector, as well as a currency union control dummy. (The regressions in Columns I and II use 64 rather than 66 observations because there are missing values for GDP variables for Argentina and Jamaica.) The plot shown in Figure 4.2.6 suggests that the results in Annex Table 4.2 are not driven by a small set of outliers.

Figure 4.2.7 shows the effect of peg regimes on capital controls as a function of income per capita. The thick solid black line shows the estimated value of the effect of peg regimes on capital controls for each level of income per capita, and the dashed red lines show the 95 percent confidence interval of this estimate (again, all expressed in logarithms). The vertical line at 9.34 means that the partial correlation is significant at the 95 percent level of confidence only for countries with the logarithm of income per capita below 9.34. The four richest countries with a value of the logarithm of income per capita below this cutoff are Algeria, Costa Rica, South Africa, and Thailand. The solid line is downward sloping, suggesting that the association between the capital control and peg indices decreases with an increase in income per capita.

A number of robustness tests using additional panel regressions were conducted and reported in the accompanying background paper (Arteta, Klein, and Shambaugh forthcoming). Those results support the central result above, and also justify the focus on using a cross-country sample rather than a panel consisting of country-year observations.

ANNEX TABLE 4.1 Listing of countries by category

Emerging Market Economies (EMEs) generally include countries with a long-established record of significant access to international financial markets. Frontier Market Economies (FMEs) include countries that are usually smaller and less financially developed than EMEs, and with more limited access to international capital markets. For this essay, EMEs are countries that are classified as such in at least two of the three following stock indexes: S&P, FTSE, and MSCI. FMEs are countries that are classified as such by at least two of the same three indexes. For countries not covered by all of these three indexes, we also include those that are classified as EME/FME by Bloomberg, Citi, and JP Morgan bond indexes, even though these latter lists do not have a break down between EMEs and FMEs. Source of classification: World Bank, IMF, Standard & Poor's, Financial Times Stock Exchange, Morgan Stanley Capital International, JPMorgan, Bloomberg, and Citigroup.

Categories	Countries
Emerging Market Economies (24)	Brazil, Chile, China, Colombia, Czech Republic, Arab Republic of Egypt, Hungary, India, Indonesia, Republic of Korea, Malaysia, Mexico, Morocco, Pakistan, Peru, Philippines, Poland, Qatar, Russian Federation, Saudi Arabia, South Africa, Thailand, Turkey, United Arab Emirates.
Frontier Market Economies (29)	Argentina, Bahrain, Bangladesh, Bolivia, Bulgaria, Costa Rica, Cote d'Ivoire, Georgia, Ghana, Guatemala, Jamaica, Kazakhstan, Kenya, Kuwait, Lebanon, Mauritius, Nigeria, Oman, Panama, Paraguay, Romania, El Salvador, Sri Lanka, Tunisia, Ukraine, Uruguay, Venezuela, RB, Vietnam, Zambia.
Other Middle and Low Income Countries (13)	Algeria, Angola, Dominican Republic, Kyrgyz Republic, Moldova, Nicaragua, Swaziland, Republic of Yemen (all middle income), as well as Burkina Faso, Ethiopia, Tanzania, Togo, Uganda (all low income).
Advanced Economies (27)	Australia, Austria, Belgium, Canada, Cyprus, Denmark, Finland, France, Germany, Greece, Iceland, Ireland, Israel, Italy, Japan, Latvia, Malta, Netherlands, New Zealand, Norway, Portugal, Slovenia, Spain, Sweden, Switzerland, United Kingdom, United States.

ANNEX TABLE 4.2 Partial correlation of capital control index with pegged exchange rate and other variables

	Cross country regressions for emerging and developing countries Dependent variable: ln (capital control indicator)	
	I	II
ln(peg)	0.15*	1.66**
(s.e.)	(0.075)	(0.69)
ln(peg)×ln(GDP/Cap)		-0.16**
(s.e.)		(0.073)
ln(GDP/Cap)	-0.52***	0.075
(s.e.)	(0.16)	(0.32)
ln(GDP)	0.52***	0.48***
(s.e.)	(0.11)	(0.10)
ln(Dom.Credit)	-0.096	-0.16
(s.e.)	(0.22)	(0.23)
ln(Trade)	0.95**	0.89***
(s.e.)	(0.39)	(0.34)
Currency Union	-1.25*	-1.40
(s.e.)	(0.72)	(1.43)
	Elasticity of ln(capital control) to ln(peg) for average values of ln(GDP/Cap) of different country groups [a]	
Other middle and low income		0.35***
(s.e.)		(0.13)
Frontier		0.18**
(s.e.)		(0.072)
Emerging		0.10
(s.e.)		(0.062)
Advanced		-0.054
(s.e.)		(0.092)
R²	0.36	0.41
No. of Obs.	64	64

[a] The values shown are $\beta_{\ln(peg)} + \ln(\text{GDP/Cap}) \times \beta_{\ln(peg) \times \ln(\text{GDP/Cap})}$ for average $\ln(\text{GDP/Cap})$ for each of the four country groups.

Sample based on values in 1995–2013.

Dependent variable: ln(capital control) is $\ln((100 \times kc)+1)$ where kc is capital control index (average value over sample period); $1 \geq kc \geq 0$ in any one year, with larger values representing more controls in place.

Key independent variable: ln(peg) is $\ln((100 \times peg)+1)$, where peg is proportion of years country had a pegged exchange rate; $1 \geq peg \geq 0$.

Other controls: Currency Union is proportion of years a country has been in currency union. GDP/capita and GDP are average values of real GDP/capita and real GDP over sample period. Dom. Credit is average of credit-to-GDP over sample period. Trade is average of (exports + imports)/GDP over sample period.

Significance Indicators: *** ≥ 99 percent, ** is ≥ 95 percent but < 99 percent, * is ≥ 90 percent but less than 95 percent.

References

Arrow, K. 1962. "The Economic Implications of Learning-by-Doing." *Review of Economic Studies* 29 (3): 155-173.

Arteta, C., M. Klein, and J. Shambaugh. Forthcoming. "Determinants of Exchange Rate and Capital Account Policies." World Bank Working Paper, Washington, DC: World Bank.

Baccini, L., and J. Urpelainen. 2014a. "Before Ratification: Understanding the Timing of International Treaty Effects on Domestic Policies." *International Studies Quarterly* 58 (1): 29-43.

_____. 2014b. International Institutions and Domestic Politics: Can Preferential Trading Agreements Help Leaders Promote Economic Reform?" *The Journal of Politics* 76 (01): 195-214.

Balassa, B. 1967. "Trade Creation and Trade Diversion in the European Common Market." *The Economic Journal* 77 (305): 1-21.

Baldwin, R. E. 1989. "On the Growth Effects of 1992." NBER Working Paper 3119, National Bureau of Economic Research, Cambridge, Massachusetts.

Baldwin, R. E., and C. Wyplosz. 2006. *The Economics of European Integration. Vol. 2.* London: McGraw-Hill.

Baldwin, R., and D. Jaimovich. 1993. "A Domino Theory of Regionalism." NBER Working Paper 4465, National Bureau of Economic Research, Cambridge, Massachusetts..

_____. 2000. "Regulatory Protectionism, Developing Nations and a Two-tier World Trade System." Center for Economic and Policy Research Discussion Paper 2574, Washington, DC.

_____. 2006. "Multilateralising Regionalism: Spaghetti Bowls as Building Blocs on the Path to Global Free Trade." *The World Economy* 29 (11): 1451-1518.

_____. 2010. "Are Free Trade Agreements Contagious?" NBER Working Paper No. 16084. Cambridge, Massachusetts.

Beck, T., A. Demirgüç-Kunt, and R. Levine. 2007. "Finance, Inequality, and the Poor." *Journal of Economic Growth* 12 (1): 27-49.

Berdiev, A., Y. Kim, and C.P. Chang. 2012. "The Political Economy of Exchange Rate Regimes in Developed and Developing Countries." *European Journal of Political Economy* 28 (1): 38-53.

Berg, A., E. Borensztein, and C. Pattillo. 2005. "Assessing Early Warning Systems: How Have They Worked in Practice?" *IMF Sta⁻ Papers* 52 (3): 462-502.

Blyde, J. 2004. "Trade and Technology Diffusion in Latin America." *The International Trade Journal* 18 (3): 177-197.

Boldrin, M., and D. Levine. 2013. "The Case Against Patents." *Journal of Economic Perspectives* 27 (1): 3–22.

Brown, D. K., A. V. Deardorff, and R. M. Stern. 1992. "A North American Free Trade Agreement: Analytical Issues and a Computational Assessment." *The World Economy* 15 (1): 11–30.

Calvo, G. 1998. "Capital Flows and Capital-Market Crises: The Simple Economics of Sudden Stops." *Journal of Applied Economics* 1 (1): 35-54.

Campos, N., F. Coricelli, and L. Moretti. 2014. "Economic Growth and Political Integration: Estimating the Benefits from Membership in the European Union Using the Synthetic Counterfactuals Method". IZA Discussion Paper Series No. 8162.

Carmignani, F., E. Colombo, and P. Tirelli. 2008. "Exploring Different View of Exchange Rate Regime Choice." *Journal of International Money and Finance* 27 (7): 1177-1197.

Cecchini, P. 1988. *The European Challenge 1992: The Benefits of a Single Market.* Aldershot, U.K.:

Wildwood House.

Chen, M. X., and A. Mattoo. 2008. "Regionalism in Standards: Good or Bad for Trade?" *Canadian Journal of Economics* 41 (3): 838–863.

Chinn, M., and H. Ito. 2008. "A New Measure of Financial Openness." *Journal of Comparative Policy Analysis,* 10 (3): 307-320.

Ciuriak, D. and H. V. Singh. 2015. *Mega Regional Trade Agreements: How Excluded Countries Can Meet the Challenge.* Available at SSRN 2680215.

Copenhagen Economics. 2009. *Assessment of Barriers to Trade and Investment Between the EU and Japan.* http://trade.ec.europa.eu/doclib/docs/2012/july/tradoc_149809.pdf.

Cordella, T., and P. Gupta. 2015. "What Makes a Currency Procyclical? An Empirical Investigation." *Journal of International Money and Finance* 55 (July): 240-259

Costinot, A., and A. Rodriguez-Clare. 2014. "*Trade Theory with Numbers: Quantifying the Consequences of Globalization.*" NBER Working Paper 18896, National Bureau of Economic Research, Cambridge, Massachusetts.

Cox, D. J., and R. G. Harris. 1992. "North American Free Trade Area and Its Implications for Canada: Results from a CGE Model of North American Trade." *The World Economy* 15: 31–4.

Economics and Statistics Administration and U.S. Patent Office. 2012. "Intellectual Property and the U.S. Economy: Industries in Focus." Washington, DC.

Eicher, T.S., C. Henn, and C. Papageorgiou. 2012. "Trade Creation and Diversion Revisited: Accounting for Model Uncertainty and Natural Trading Partner Effects." *Journal of Applied Econometrics* 27 (2): 296-321.

Estevadeordal A., C. Freund, and E. Ornelas. 2008. "Does Regionalism Affect Trade Liberalization Toward Nonmembers?" *The Quarterly Journal of Economics* 123 (4): 1531-1575.

European Commission. 2012. *Impact Assessment Report on EU-Japan Trade Relations.* Brussels. http://trade.ec.europa.eu/doclib/docs/2012/july/tradoc_149809.pdf.

———. 2013. Reducing Transatlantic Barriers to Trade and Investment: An Economic Assessment. http://trade.ec.europa.eu/doclib/docs/2013/march/tradoc_150737.pdf.

Fernandes, A., E. Ferro, and J. Wilson. 2015. "Product Standards and Firms' Export Decisions?" Working Paper 7315, World Bank, Washington, DC.

Fernández, A., A. Rebucci, and M. Uribe. 2014. "Are Capital Controls Countercyclical?" Mimeo, Columbia University.

Fernández, A., M. Klein, A. Rebucci, M. Schindler, and M. Uribe. 2015. "Capital Control Measures: A New Dataset." NBER Working Paper 20970, National Bureau of Economic Research, Cambridge, Massachusetts.

Fontagne, L., A. Guillin, and C. Mitaritonna. 2011. "Estimations of Tariff Equivalents for the Services Sector." CEPII Working Papers. 2011-24. Paris.

Forbes, K., and M. Klein. 2015. "Pick Your Poison: The Choices and Consequences of Policy Responses to Crises." *International Monetary Fund Economic Review* 63 (1): 197-237.

Francois, J., M. Manchin, H. Norberg, O. Pindyuk, and P. Tomberger. 2013. "Reducing Transatlantic Barriers to Trade and Investment: an Economic Assessment." Center for Economic Policy Research, London.

Frankel, J., and A. Rose. 2002. "An Estimate of the Effect of Common Currencies on Trade and Income." *Quarterly Journal of Economics* 117 (2): 437-466.

Frankel, J., S. Schmukler, and L. Serven. 2004. "Global Transmission of Interest Rates: Monetary Independence and Currency Regime." *Journal of International Money and Finance* 23 (5): 701-733.

Freund, C. L., and E. Ornelas. "Regional Trade Agreements." Policy Research Working Paper 5314, Washington, D.C.: World Bank.

Ghosh, A. R., J. D. Ostry, and M. S. Qureshi. 2015. "Exchange Rate Management and Crisis Susceptibility: A Reassessment." *IMF Economic Review* 63 (1): 238-276.

Gosselin, P. 2015. "Obama Is in a Bind on Drugs That Could Cost Consumers Billions of Dollars - Bloomberg Business." *Bloomberg Business*.

Greenstone, M., J. A. List, and C. Syverson. 2012. "The Effects of Environmental Regulation on the Competitiveness of U.S. Manufacturing." NBER Working Paper 18392, National Bureau of Economic Research, Cambridge, Massachusetts.

Grilli, V., and G. Milesi-Ferretti. 1995. "Economic Effects and Structural Determinants of Capital Controls." *IMF Staff Papers* 42 (3): 517-551.

Hammouda, H., and P. N. Osakwe. 2008. "Global Trade Models and Economic Policy Analyses: Relevance, Risks and Repercussions for Africa." *Development Policy Review* 26 (2): 151-170.

Harrison, G. W., T. F. Rutherford, and D. G. Tarr. 1994. "Product Standards, Imperfect Competition and Completion of the Market in the European Union." Policy Research Working Paper 1293, World Bank, Washington, DC.

Henry, P. 2007. "Capital Account Liberalization: Theory, Evidence and Speculation." *Journal of Economic Literature* 45 (4): 887-935.

Hoekman, B. M., and B. K. S. Javorcik, eds. 2006. *Global Integration and Technology Transfer.* Washington, DC: World Bank.

Hoekman, B. M., C. Michalopoulos, and L. A. Winters. 2003. "More Favorable and Differential Treatment of Developing Countries: Toward a New Approach in the World Trade Organization". Policy Research Working Paper 3107, World Bank, Washington, DC.

Hufbauer, G. C., and J. Schott. 2005. *NAFTA Revisited: Achievements and Challenges.* Washington, DC: Peterson Institute for International Economics.

Humphrey, J., and H. Schmitz. 2002. "How Does Insertion in Global Value Chains Affect Upgrading in Industrial Clusters?" *Regional Studies* 36 (9): 1017-1027.

International Monetary Fund (IMF). 2003. *World Economic Outlook; Growth and Institutions.* Washington, DC: International Monetary Fund.

International Monetary Fund (IMF). 2015. *World Economic Outlook: Uneven Growth, Short and Long-Term Factors.* Washington, DC: International Monetary Fund.

Jeanne, O., and A. Korinek. 2010. "Managing Capital Flows: A Pigouvian Taxation Approach." *American Economic Review Papers and Proceedings* (May): 403 – 407.

Jeanne, O., A. Subramanian, and J. Williamson. 2012. *Who Needs to Open the Capital Account.* Washington, DC: Peterson Institute for International Economics.

Kawasaki, K. 2014. "The Relative Significance of EPAs in Asia-Pacific." RIETI Discussion Paper Series 14-E-000.

Kee, H. L., A. Nicita, and M. Olarreaga. 2008. "Import Demand Elasticities and Trade Distortions." *The Review of Economics and Statistics* 90 (4): 666-682

_____. 2009. "Estimating Trade Restrictiveness Indices." *The Economic Journal* 119 (1): 172–99.

Kehoe, T. J. 2005. "An Evaluation of the Performance of Applied General Equilibrium Models on the Impact of NAFTA." In *Frontiers in Applied General Equilibrium Modeling: In Honor of Herbert Scarf,* edited by T. J. Kehoe, T. N. Srinivasan, and J. Whalley. Cambridge, UK: Cambridge University Press.

Kharas, H. 2010. "The Emerging Middle Class in Developing Countries." Working Paper 285, Organization for Economic Co-operation and Development, Paris, France.

King, R., and R. Levine. 1993. "Finance and Growth: Schumpeter Might be Right." *Quarterly Journal of Economics* 108 (3): 717-737.

Klein, M. 2012. "Capital Controls: Gates versus Walls." Brookings Papers on Economic Activity, Washington, DC.

Klein, M., and G. Olivei. 2008. "Capital Account Liberalization, Financial Deepness and Economic Growth." *Journal of International Money and Finance* 27 (6): 861-875.

Klein, M., and J. Shambaugh. 2006. "Fixed Exchange Rates and Trade." *Journal of International Economics* 70 (2): 359-383.

———————. 2008. "The Dynamics of Exchange Rate Regimes: Fixes, Floats and Flips." *Journal of International Economics* 75 (1): 70-92.

———————. 2010. *Exchange Rate Regimes in the Modern Era.* Cambridge, MA: MIT Press.

———————. 2015. "Rounding the Corners of the Policy Trilemma: Sources of Monetary Autonomy." *American Economic Journal: Macroeconomics* 7 (4): 33-66.

Kose, A., E. Prasad, K. Rogoff, and S. Wei, 2009. "Financial Globalization: A Reappraisal." *International Monetary Fund Staff Papers* 56 (1): 8-62.

Kose, M. A., G. M. Meredith, and C. M. Towe. 2005. "How has NAFTA Affected the Mexican Economy? Review and Evidence." In *Monetary Policy and Macroeconomic Stabilization in Latin America,* edited by R. J. Langhammer and L. V. de Souza. Heidelberg, Germany: Springer.

Kowalski, P., J. Gonzales, A. Ragoussis, and C. Ugarte. 2015. "Participation of Developing Countries in Global Value Chains: Implications for Trade and Trade-Related Policies." OECD Trade Policy Paper 179, OECD Publishing, Paris.

Krueger, A. O. 1999. "Trade Creation and Trade Diversion under NAFTA". NBER Working Paper 7429, National Bureau of Economic Research, Cambridge, Massachusetts.

Kydland, F., and E. Prescott. 1977. "Rules Rather than Discretion: The Inconsistence of Optimal Plans." *The Journal of Political Economy* 85 (3): 473-492.

Leblang, D. 1999. "Domestic Political Institutions and Exchange Rate Commitments in the Developing World." *International Studies Quarterly* 43 (4): 599-620.

Lee, H., and K. Itakura. 2014. "TPP, RCEP, and Japan's Agricultural Policy Reforms." OSIPP Discussion Paper 14E003, Osaka, Japan.

Lehmann, J. P. 2015. "The TPP, the WTO, the 21st Century Global Trade Mess and the Poverty of Nations." *Forbes,* August 3, 2015.

Lukauskas, A., R. M. Stern, and G. Zanini. 2013. *Handbook of Trade Policy for Development.* Oxford, U.K.: Oxford University Press.

Maggi, G., 2014, International Trade Agreements, Chapter 6 in Handbook of International Economics 4: 317-390. In *Handbook of International Economics,* edited by G. Gopinath, E. Helpman, and K. Rogoff. Oxford, U.K.: Elsevier.

Mariniello, M., A. Sapir, and A. Terzi. 2015. "The Long Road Towards the European Single Market." Bruegel Working Paper 11, Brussels, Belgium.

Mattli, W., and T. Plümper. 2004. "The Internal Value of External Options How the EU Shapes the Scope of Regulatory Reforms in Transition Countries." *European Union Politics* 5 (3): 307-330.

Mattoo, A. 2001. "Discriminatory Consequences of Non-discriminatory Standards." *Journal of Economic Integration* 16 (1): 78-105.

McCulloch, R., and P.A. Petri. 1997. "Alternative Paths Toward Open Global Markets." In *Quiet*

Pioneering: Robert M. Stern and His International Economic Legacy, edited by K. E. Maskus and J. D. Richardson. Ann Arbor: University of Michigan Press.

Melitz, M. J. 2003. "The Impact of Trade on Intra-Industry Reallocations and Aggregate Industry Productivity." *Econometrica* 71 (6): 1695–1725.

Michalopoulos, C. 1999. "Trade Policy and Market Access Issues for Developing Countries: Implications for the Millennium Round." Policy Research Working Paper 2214, World Bank, Washington, DC.

Milner, H. V., and K. Kubota. 2005. "Why the Move to Free Trade? Democracy and Trade Policy in the Developing Countries." *International organization 59* (01): 107-143.

Moenius, J. 2005. "Information Versus Product Adaptation: the Role of Standards in Trade" Mimeo, University of Redlands.

Mundell, R. 1961. "A Theory of Optimum Currency Areas." *American Economic Review* 51 (3): 657-665.

Nielsen, C. 2003. "Regional and Preferential Trade Agreements: A Literature Review and Identification of Future Steps." Fødevareøkonomisk Institut Report 155, Copenhagen, Denmark.

Obstfeld, M., J. Shambaugh, and A. Taylor. 2010. "Financial Stability, the Trilemma, and International Reserves." *American Economic Association Journal – Macroeconomics* 2 (2): 57-94.

OECD and WTO. 2015. "Measuring Trade in Value Added: An OECD-WTO Joint Initiative." Paris, France.

Oliver, S.. 2015. "How Quickly Are Tariffs Eliminated in the TPP?" PIIE Trade and Investment Policy Watch Blog. December 2, 2015. Washington, D.C.: Peterson Institute for International Economics.

Orefice, G., R. Piermartini, and N. Rocha. 2012. "Harmonization and Mutual Recognition: What are the Effects on Trade?" Mimeo. World Trade Organization.

Ostry, J., A. Ghosh, and M. Chamon. 2012. "Two Targets, Two Instruments: Monetary and Exchange Rate Policies in Emerging Market Economies." IMF Staff Discussion Note SDN/12/01, International Monetary Fund, Washington, DC.

Ostry, J., A. Ghosh, M. Chamon, and M Qureshi. 2011. "Capital Controls: When and Why?" *IMF Economic Review* 59 (3): 562-580.

Otsuki, T., J. S. Wilson, and M. Sewadeh. 2001. "Saving Two in a Billion: Quantifying the Trade Effect of European Food Safety Standards on African Exports." *Food Policy* 26 (5): 495–514.

Peterson Institute for International Economics. 2014. "NAFTA 20 Years Later." PIIE Briefing. Washington, DC.: Peterson Institute for International Economics.

Petri, P., and A. A. Raheem. 2014. "Can RCEP and the TPP Be Pathways to FTAAP?" In *State of the Region, 2014-2015.* Singapore: Pacific Economic Cooperation Council.

Petri, P., M. Plummer, and F. Zhai. 2012. "The Trans-Pacific Partnership and Asia-Pacific Integration: A Quantitative Assessment." East-West Center Working Papers 119, Peterson Institute for International Economics, Washington, DC.

Petri, P., and M. Plummer, forthcoming. "Mega-Regional Trade Agreements and Developing Economies." Mimeo. World Bank, Washington, DC.

Poole, W. 1970. "Optimal Choice of Monetary Policy Instrument in a Simple Stochastic Macro Model." *Quarterly Journal of Economics* 84 (2): 197-216.

Pugatch, M. P., ed. 2006. *The Intellectual Property Debate: Perspectives from Law, Economics and Political Economy.* London: Edward Elgar.

Quinn, D. 1997. "The Correlates of Change in International Financial Regulation." *American*

Political Science Review 91 (3): 531-51.

Rey, H. 2013. "Dilemma not Trilemma: The Global Financial Cycle and Monetary Independence." In *Global Dimensions of Unconventional Monetary Policy*, Federal Reserve Bank of Kansas City Jackson Hole Conference.

Reyes, J. D. 2011. "International Harmonization of Product Standards and Firm Heterogeneity in International Trade." Policy Research Working Paper 5677, World Bank, Washington DC.

Rose, A. 2000. "One Money, One Market: The Effect of Common Currencies on Trade." *Economic Policy* 15 (30): 7-33.

Rose, A., and E. van Wincoop, 2001. "National Money as a Barrier to International Trade: The Real Case for Currency Union." *American Economic Review* 91 (2): 386-390.

Sahay, R., M. Cihak, P. N'Diaye, A. Barajas, D. Ayala Pena, R. Bi, Y. Gao, et al. 2015. "Rethinking Financial Deepening: Stability and Growth in Emerging Markets." IMF Staff Discussion Note SDN/15/08, International Monetary Fund, Washington, DC.

Salem, S., and F. Rozental. 2012. "Labor Standards and Trade: A Review of the Recent Empirical Evidence." *Journal of International Commerce and Economics* 4 (2): 63-98.

Schönfelder, N., and H. Wagner. 2015. "The Impact of European Integration on Institutional Development." MPRA Paper 63392, Munich, Germany.

Shambaugh, J. 2004. "The Effect of Fixed Exchange Rates on Monetary Policy." *Quarterly Journal of Economics* 119 (1): 300-351.

Shepherd, B. 2007. "Product Standards, Harmonization, and Trade: Evidence from the Extensive Margin." Policy Research Working Paper 4390, World Bank, Washington, DC.

Staehr, K. 2011. "Democratic and Market-Economic Reforms in the Postcommunist Countries: The Impact of Enlargement of the European Union." *Eastern European Economics* 49 (5): 5-28.

Stiglitz, J. E. 2008. "Economic Foundations of Intellectual Property Rights." *Duke Law Journal* 57: 1693-1724.

Stiglitz, J. E., and A. S. Hersh. 2015. "The Trans-Pacific Trade Charade." *Project Syndicate* website. October 2, 2015.

Todo, Y. 2013. "Estimating the TPP's Expected Growth Effects." RIETI Report 153, Tokyo, Japan.

Trefler, D. 2001. "*The Long and Short of the Canada-US Free Trade Agreement.*" National Bureau of Economic Research Working Paper 8293.

UNCTAD (United Nations Conference on Trade and Development). 2000. "The Post-Uruguay Round Tariff Environment for Developing Country Exports: Tariff Peaks and Tariff Escalation." Geneva, Switzerland.

Venables, A. J. 1999. "Regional Integration Agreements: a Force for Convergence or Divergence?" Policy Research Working Paper 2260, World Bank, Washington, DC.

Vetter, S., and B Böttcher. 2013. "The Single European Market 20 Years on." DB Research, Deutsche Bank, Frankfurt, Germany.

Viner, J. 1950. *The Customs Union Issue.* New York: Carnegie.

Vogel, D. 1995. "Trading Up: Consumer and Environmental Regulation in a Global Economy" Cambridge, MA: Harvard University Press.

von Hagen, J., and J. Zhou. 2007. "The Choice of Exchange Rate Regimes in Developing Countries: A Multinomial Panel Analysis." *Journal of International Money and Finance* 26 (7): 1071-1094.

World Bank. 2005. "Regional Trade and Preferential Trading Agreements: A Global Perspective". In *Global Economic Prospects 2005: Trade, Re-*

gionalism, and Development. Washington, DC: World Bank.

_____. 2014. *Urban China: Toward Efficient, Inclusive, and Sustainable Urbanization.* Washington DC: World Bank.

_____. 2015. *Global Economic Prospects: Having Fiscal Space and Using It.* Washington DC: World Bank.

_____. Forthcoming. "Vietnam 2035: A Prosperous Country, Creative People, and Just Society." World Bank, Washington, DC.

World Economic Forum. 2012. *The Shifting Geography of Global Value Chains: Implications for Developing Countries and Trade Policy.* Cologny, Switzerland: World Economic Forum.

WTO (World Trade Organization). 2011. *World Trade Report 2011: The WTO and Preferential Trade Agreements: from Co-existence to Coherence."* Geneva, Switzerland: World Trade Organization.

Wylie, P. J. 1995. "Partial Equilibrium Estimates of Manufacturing Trade Creation and Diversion due to NAFTA." *The North American Journal of Economics and Finance* 6 (1): 65-84.

Zhai, F. 2008. "Armington Meets Melitz: Introducing Firm Heterogeneity in a Global CGE Model of Trade." *Journal of Economic Integration* 23 (3): 575–604.

STATISTICAL APPENDIX

TABLE 1: GDP Growth
(Percent)

	2013	2014	2015e	2016f	2017f	2018f	Q1	Q2	Q3	Q4	Q1	Q2	Q3
			Annual [a]				**2014**				**2015**		
World	2.4	2.6	2.4	2.9	3.1	3.1	2.1	2.2	3.0	2.5	2.2	2.4	2.8
High-Income Countries	1.2	1.7	1.6	2.1	2.1	2.1	1.0	1.4	2.0	1.9	1.5	1.7	1.9
Euro Area	-0.2	0.9	1.5	1.7	1.7	1.6	0.8	0.3	1.0	1.6	2.1	1.4	1.2
Recently transitioned high income countries [c]													
Argentina	2.9	0.5	1.7	0.7	1.9	3.0	-3.4	3.1	1.2	1.5	2.8	2.0	..
Hungary	1.9	3.7	2.8	2.5	2.7	3.0	2.8	4.7	2.7	2.9	2.2	1.9	2.3
Seychelles	6.6	2.8	3.5	3.7	3.6	3.6	..	..	..	..	..	..	..
Venezuela, RB	1.3	-4.0	-8.2	-4.8	-1.1	0.0	..	..	..	..	..	..	..
Developing Countries	5.3	4.9	4.3	4.8	5.3	5.3	5.0	4.4	5.5	4.1	3.9	4.0	5.3
East Asia and the Pacific	7.1	6.8	6.4	6.3	6.2	6.2	5.9	7.1	7.0	7.0	5.2	6.8	6.6
Cambodia	7.4	7.0	6.9	6.9	6.8	6.8	..	..	..	..	..	..	..
China	7.7	7.3	6.9	6.7	6.5	6.5	..	..	..	..	..	..	..
Fiji	4.6	4.3	4.0	3.5	3.1	3.0	..	..	..	..	..	..	..
Indonesia	5.6	5.0	4.7	5.3	5.5	5.5	..	..	..	..	..	..	..
Lao PDR	8.5	7.5	6.4	7.0	6.9	6.9	..	..	..	..	..	..	..
Malaysia	4.7	6.0	4.7	4.5	4.5	5.0	5.5	6.7	3.3	7.3	4.7	4.5	2.6
Mongolia	11.7	7.8	2.3	0.8	3.0	6.4	..	..	..	..	..	..	..
Myanmar	8.5	8.5	6.5	7.8	8.5	8.5	..	..	..	..	..	..	..
Papua New Guinea	5.5	8.5	8.7	3.3	4.0	3.8	..	..	..	..	..	..	..
Philippines	7.1	6.1	5.8	6.4	6.2	6.2	..	..	..	..	..	..	..
Solomon Islands	3.0	1.5	3.3	3.0	3.5	3.4	..	..	..	..	..	..	..
Thailand	2.8	0.9	2.5	2.0	2.4	2.7	-2.9	2.6	3.7	4.7	1.4	1.4	4.0
Timor-Leste	2.8	7.0	6.8	6.9	7.0	7.0	..	..	..	..	..	..	..
Vietnam	5.4	6.0	6.5	6.6	6.3	6.0	..	..	..	..	..	..	..
Europe and Central Asia	3.9	2.3	2.1	3.0	3.5	3.5	2.8	-1.8	0.5	1.0	2.6	3.3	..
Albania	1.4	2.0	2.7	3.4	3.5	3.5	..	..	..	..	..	..	..
Armenia	3.3	3.5	2.5	2.2	2.8	3.0	..	..	..	..	..	..	..
Azerbaijan	5.8	2.8	2.0	0.8	1.2	2.7	..	..	..	..	..	..	..
Belarus	1.1	1.6	-3.5	-0.5	1.0	1.0	..	..	..	..	..	..	..
Bosnia and Herzegovina	2.5	0.8	1.9	2.3	3.1	3.5	..	..	..	..	..	..	..
Bulgaria	1.3	1.5	2.9	2.2	2.7	2.7	0.4	2.5	1.7	2.6	3.5	2.6	2.9
Georgia	3.3	4.8	2.5	3.0	4.5	5.0	..	..	..	..	..	..	..
Kazakhstan	6.0	4.4	0.9	1.1	3.3	3.4	..	..	..	..	..	..	..
Kosovo	3.4	1.2	3.0	3.5	3.7	4.0	..	..	..	..	..	..	..
Kyrgyz Republic	10.9	3.6	2.0	4.2	3.4	4.3	..	..	..	..	..	..	..
Macedonia, FYR	2.7	3.5	3.2	3.4	3.7	3.7	..	..	..	..	..	..	..
Moldova	9.4	4.6	-2.0	0.5	4.0	4.0	..	..	..	..	..	..	..
Montenegro	3.5	1.8	3.4	2.9	3.0	2.9	..	..	..	..	..	..	..
Romania	3.5	2.8	3.6	3.9	4.1	4.0	0.5	0.4	6.3	3.1	5.7	0.2	5.7
Serbia	2.6	-1.8	0.8	1.8	2.2	3.5	..	..	..	..	..	..	..
Tajikistan	7.4	6.7	4.2	4.8	5.5	5.5	..	..	..	..	..	..	..
Turkey	4.2	2.9	4.2	3.5	3.5	3.4	5.9	-0.9	1.5	4.0	6.0	5.5	..
Turkmenistan	10.2	10.3	8.5	8.9	8.9	8.9	..	..	..	..	..	..	..
Ukraine	0.0	-6.8	-12.0	1.0	2.0	2.0	..	..	..	..	..	..	..
Uzbekistan	8.0	8.1	7.0	7.5	7.7	7.7	..	..	..	..	..	..	..

TABLE 1: GDP Growth (continued)
(Percent)

| | Annual [a] | | | | | | Quarterly [b] | | | | | | |
| | | | | | | | 2014 | | | | 2015 | | |
	2013	2014	2015e	2016f	2017f	2018f	Q1	Q2	Q3	Q4	Q1	Q2	Q3
Latin America and the Caribbean	3.0	1.5	-0.7	0.1	2.3	2.5	2.6	-1.7	1.1	1.4	-0.8	-3.4	-3.0
Belize	1.5	3.6	3.0	2.5	2.6	2.8	..	..	..	..	..	..	..
Bolivia	6.8	5.5	4.0	3.5	3.4	3.4	..	..	..	..	..	..	..
Brazil	3.0	0.1	-3.7	-2.5	1.4	1.5	2.5	-5.1	-0.4	0.3	-3.3	-8.0	-6.7
Colombia	4.9	4.6	3.1	3.0	3.3	3.5	6.2	1.2	4.3	2.0	3.5	2.1	5.1
Costa Rica	3.4	3.5	2.8	4.0	4.2	4.4	..	..	..	..	..	..	..
Dominica	1.7	3.4	-3.0	4.0	2.0	2.0	..	..	..	..	..	..	..
Dominican Republic	4.8	7.3	5.6	4.6	3.8	3.9	..	..	..	..	..	..	..
Ecuador	4.6	3.7	-0.6	-2.0	0.0	0.5	-3.0	7.9	4.4	1.3	-0.4	-1.0	..
El Salvador	1.8	2.0	2.4	2.5	2.6	2.8	..	..	..	..	..	..	..
Guatemala	3.7	4.2	3.7	3.6	3.5	3.6	..	..	..	..	..	..	..
Guyana	5.2	3.9	3.5	3.8	4.0	4.0	..	..	..	..	..	..	..
Haiti[d]	4.2	2.7	1.7	2.5	2.8	3.0	..	..	..	..	..	..	..
Honduras	2.8	3.1	3.4	3.4	3.5	3.6	..	..	..	..	..	..	..
Jamaica	0.5	0.7	1.3	2.1	2.4	2.6	..	..	..	..	..	..	..
Mexico	1.4	2.3	2.5	2.8	3.0	3.2	2.4	3.0	2.3	2.8	2.1	2.5	3.0
Nicaragua	4.6	4.7	3.9	4.2	4.1	4.0	..	..	..	..	..	..	..
Panama	8.4	6.2	5.9	6.2	6.4	6.6	..	..	..	..	..	..	..
Paraguay	14.0	4.7	2.8	3.6	4.0	4.2	..	..	..	..	..	..	..
Peru	5.8	2.4	2.7	3.3	4.5	4.6	..	..	..	..	..	..	..
St. Lucia	-1.9	-0.7	1.7	1.6	1.9	2.1	..	..	..	..	..	..	..
St. Vincent and the Grenadines	2.3	-0.2	2.1	2.7	3.0	3.4	..	..	..	..	..	..	..
Middle East and North Africa	0.6	2.5	2.5	5.1	5.8	5.1	8.0	4.3	3.8	2.2	4.3	..	..
Algeria	2.8	3.8	2.8	3.9	4.0	3.8	..	..	..	..	..	..	..
Djibouti	5.0	6.0	6.5	7.0	7.1	7.0	..	..	..	..	..	..	..
Egypt, Arab Rep.[d]	2.1	2.2	4.2	3.8	4.4	4.8	..	..	..	..	..	..	..
Iran, Islamic Rep.	-1.9	4.3	1.9	5.8	6.7	6.0	9.3	2.0	6.8	5.0	0.1	..	..
Iraq	4.2	-0.5	0.5	3.1	7.1	6.5	..	..	..	..	..	..	..
Jordan	2.8	3.1	2.5	3.5	3.8	4.0	..	..	..	..	..	..	..
Lebanon	3.0	2.0	2.0	2.5	2.5	3.0	..	..	..	..	..	..	..
Libya	-13.7	-24.0	-5.2	35.7	27.6	8.4	..	..	..	..	..	..	..
Morocco	4.7	2.4	4.7	2.7	4.0	4.0	..	..	..	..	..	..	..
Tunisia	2.9	2.7	0.5	2.5	3.3	4.5	1.7	2.0	3.2	3.3	-1.1	-2.1	1.0
West Bank and Gaza	2.2	-0.4	2.9	3.9	3.7	3.7	..	..	..	..	..	..	..
South Asia	6.2	6.8	7.0	7.3	7.5	7.5	7.3	9.2	12.6	-1.6	10.3	7.4	13.8
Afghanistan	2.0	1.3	1.9	3.1	3.9	5.0	..	..	..	..	..	..	..
Bangladesh[d]	6.1	6.5	6.5	6.7	6.8	6.8	..	..	..	..	..	..	..
India[d]	6.9	7.3	7.3	7.8	7.9	7.9	..	..	..	..	..	..	..
Maldives	4.2	5.9	4.4	3.1	4.2	4.5	..	..	..	..	..	..	..
Nepal[d]	4.1	5.4	3.4	1.7	5.8	4.5	..	..	..	..	..	..	..
Pakistan[d e]	4.4	4.7	5.5	5.5	5.4	5.4	..	..	..	..	..	..	..
Sri Lanka	3.4	4.5	5.3	5.6	6.0	6.0	..	..	..	..	..	..	..

TABLE 1: GDP Growth (continued)

(Percent)

	Annual [a]						Quarterly [b]						
							2014				**2015**		
	2013	2014	2015e	2016f	2017f	2018f	Q1	Q2	Q3	Q4	Q1	Q2	Q3
Sub-Saharan Africa	4.9	4.6	3.4	4.2	4.7	4.7	2.0	4.8	3.7	5.4	-1.6	0.5	4.0
Angola	6.8	3.9	3.0	3.3	3.8	3.8	..	..	..	..	..	..	..
Benin	5.6	5.4	5.7	5.3	5.1	5.1	..	..	..	..	..	..	..
Botswana[d]	9.3	4.4	3.0	4.0	4.2	4.2	..	..	..	..	..	..	..
Burkina Faso	6.7	4.0	4.4	6.0	7.0	7.0	..	..	..	..	..	..	..
Burundi	4.6	4.7	-2.3	3.5	4.8	4.8	..	..	..	..	..	..	..
Cabo Verde	1.0	1.8	2.9	3.5	4.1	4.1	..	..	..	..	..	..	..
Cameroon	5.6	5.9	6.3	6.5	6.5	6.4	..	..	..	..	..	..	..
Chad	5.7	7.3	4.1	4.9	6.1	6.5	..	..	..	..	..	..	..
Comoros	3.5	3.0	2.3	2.5	3.1	3.1	..	..	..	..	..	..	..
Congo, Dem. Rep.	8.5	9.0	8.0	8.6	9.0	9.0	..	..	..	..	..	..	..
Côte d'Ivoire	9.2	8.5	8.4	8.3	8.0	8.0	..	..	..	..	..	..	..
Eritrea	1.3	1.7	0.9	2.0	2.2	2.2	..	..	..	..	..	..	..
Ethiopia[d]	10.5	9.9	10.2	10.2	9.0	9.0	..	..	..	..	..	..	..
Gabon	4.3	4.3	4.1	5.1	5.3	5.3	..	..	..	..	..	..	..
Gambia, The	4.8	-0.2	4.0	4.5	5.3	5.3	..	..	..	..	..	..	..
Ghana	7.3	4.0	3.4	5.9	8.2	8.2	..	..	..	..	..	..	..
Guinea	2.3	-0.3	0.4	3.5	4.0	4.2	..	..	..	..	..	..	..
Guinea-Bissau	0.3	2.5	4.4	4.9	5.3	5.3	..	..	..	..	..	..	..
Kenya	5.7	5.3	5.4	5.7	6.1	6.1	..	..	..	..	..	..	..
Lesotho	4.6	2.0	2.6	2.8	4.5	4.5	..	..	..	..	..	..	..
Liberia	8.7	1.0	3.0	5.7	6.8	6.8	..	..	..	..	..	..	..
Madagascar	2.4	3.0	3.2	3.4	3.6	3.6	..	..	..	..	..	..	..
Malawi	5.2	5.7	2.8	5.0	5.8	5.8	..	..	..	..	..	..	..
Mali	1.7	7.2	5.0	5.0	5.0	5.0	..	..	..	..	..	..	..
Mauritania	5.5	6.9	3.2	4.0	4.0	4.0	..	..	..	..	..	..	..
Mauritius	3.3	3.6	3.5	3.7	3.7	3.7	..	..	..	..	..	..	..
Mozambique	7.3	7.4	6.3	6.5	7.2	7.2	..	..	..	..	..	..	..
Namibia	5.7	6.4	5.0	5.5	5.9	5.9	..	..	..	..	..	..	..
Niger	4.6	6.9	4.4	5.3	9.3	5.7	..	..	..	..	..	..	..
Nigeria	5.4	6.3	3.3	4.6	5.3	5.3	..	..	..	..	..	..	..
Rwanda	4.7	7.0	7.4	7.6	7.6	7.6	..	..	..	..	..	..	..
Senegal	3.5	3.9	5.0	5.3	5.3	5.3	..	..	..	..	..	..	..
Sierra Leone	20.1	7.0	-20.0	6.6	5.3	5.3	..	..	..	..	..	..	..
South Africa	2.2	1.5	1.3	1.4	1.6	1.6	-1.5	0.5	2.1	4.2	1.4	-1.3	0.7
South Sudan	13.1	3.4	-5.3	3.5	7.0	7.0	..	..	..	..	..	..	..
Sudan	3.3	3.1	3.5	3.4	3.9	3.9	..	..	..	..	..	..	..
Swaziland	2.8	2.5	1.3	0.8	0.8	0.8	..	..	..	..	..	..	..
Tanzania	7.3	7.0	7.2	7.2	7.1	7.1	..	..	..	..	..	..	..
Togo	5.1	5.7	5.1	4.9	4.7	4.7	..	..	..	..	..	..	..
Uganda[d]	3.6	4.0	5.0	5.0	5.8	5.8	..	..	..	..	..	..	..
Zambia	6.7	5.6	3.5	3.8	5.4	6.0	..	..	..	..	..	..	..
Zimbabwe	4.5	3.2	1.0	2.8	3.0	3.0	..	..	..	..	..	..	..

Source: World Bank, WDI, Haver Analytics, WEO
Note: e = estimates; f = forecast. Aggregates based on constant 2010 dollar GDP.
a. Annual percentage change
b. Quarter-over-quarter growth, seasonally adjusted and annualized
c. Based on the 2015 World Bank's reclassification.
d. Annual GDP is on fiscal year basis, as per reporting practice in the country
e. GDP data for Pakistan are based on market prices.